The Land Divided

The Land Divided

A History of

THE PANAMA CANAL

and Other Isthmian Canal Projects

GERSTLE MACK

OCTAGON BOOKS

A DIVISION OF FARRAR, STRAUS AND GIROUX

New York   1974

Reprinted 1974
by special arrangement with Alfred A. Knopf, Inc.

OCTAGON BOOKS
A DIVISION OF FARRAR, STRAUS & GIROUX, INC.
19 Union Square West
New York, N. Y. 10003

Library of Congress Cataloging in Publication Data

Mack, Gerstle, 1894-
    The land divided; a history of the Panama Canal and other
isthmian canal projects.

    Reprint of the ed. published by Knopf, New York.

    Bibliography: p.
    1. Canals, Interoceanic. 2. Panama Canal. I. Title.
TC773.M25   1974   386'.444'09   73-20044
ISBN 0-374-95242-6

Printed in USA by
Thomson-Shore,Inc.
Dexter, Michigan

Preface

JAMES BRYCE once called the Panama canal "the greatest liberty Man has ever taken with Nature." [1] Nature did not permit that liberty to be taken without a desperate struggle. For four centuries men worked and schemed, fought and died to cut a passage through the American isthmus. The story of that long conflict is the theme of this book.

A history of the isthmian canal might appropriately be subtitled *A Record of Controversy*. From its inception to its completion the canal idea furnished abundant material for endless disputes. Only at rare intervals and in exceptional circumstances was it ever discussed rationally, scientifically, and dispassionately. Generally the mere mention of the project was sufficient to produce violence, to strike sparks which immediately burst into flames of bitterness and hatred. Although the magnificently equipped and smoothly operated Panama canal of today is a triumph of man's intelligence and skill, the history of its planning reveals much more ineptitude than competence, more stupidity than wisdom, more chicanery than probity, more greed than unselfish devotion. To us who, gifted with hindsight, are no longer agitated by the pros and cons of these combats, the chief interest of the story lies in its fantastic confusion of baseness and nobility, ignorance and knowledge, failure and achievement.

Controversy over canal projects assumed various forms. The most fruitful source of disagreement was the question of location. From Tehuantepec to Buenaventura, a span of more than 1200 miles, almost every bay and inlet and river and mountain pass that appeared to offer the faintest promise of a feasible canal site became at one time or another the scene of wordy battles between its enthusiastic partisans and its equally vociferous opponents. Often the advocates of a canal — any canal — found themselves at odds with those who preferred a highway or a railway to connect the oceans. If a canal was to be built, how wide should it be? How deep? Should it be constructed at sea level or with locks? If with locks, how many and of what dimensions? Were tunnels necessary? If so, could they be bored? What would each of the rival schemes cost? How could any of them be financed? What tolls should be charged? What technical methods should be employed to dig the canal? How was construction to be organized? What labor policy should be adopted? Should the canal be owned by a government or a private company? What international relations were involved? By what treaties and concessions could conflicting interests be reconciled? All such questions and hundreds more were highly controversial, and all were fought over bitterly. The bitterness was intensified by innumerable personal quarrels due to temperamental incompatibility (and plain cantankerousness) aggravated by hardship, illness, and the enervating effects of a tropical climate.

Since the problem of location was of vital importance it is necessary to include a great many routes and schemes, some of them far removed from the site finally chosen at Panama. This book therefore is a history not only of the Panama canal but of all interoceanic canal projects throughout the length of the American continent from the Arctic Ocean to Cape Horn. Many of these were ill conceived, even frivolous, and may be dismissed briefly. Others demand much more careful consideration, and one group — the long series of projects for a canal through Nicaragua — was for years so formidable a rival of the Panama route that almost as much space must be given to it as to Panama itself.

Hundreds of books and thousands of articles have been published about the canal and canal projects, but with a few exceptions all are devoted to the discussion of a single phase of the subject or of a particular period. There are books about the political, economic, strategic, hygienic, and engineering aspects of the canal problem, about special events and episodes, individual schemes and adventures. This volume represents an endeavor to combine all of these elements, which in truth are closely related, into one general history covering the entire field in considerable detail and extending without a break from the discovery of the New World to the present day.

When I started work on this book five years ago I intended to include a chapter on the fortification and defense of the Panama canal. The war has eliminated that chapter: in wartime no up-to-date information concerning such matters can be published, and an obsolete description derived from pre-war sources would be both misleading and without interest.

All direct quotations are reproduced *verbatim et literatim,* and consequently there are numerous inconsistencies in spelling, capitalization, punctuation, accents on foreign words, etc. The only liberties I have taken with quotations are condensation (deletions being indicated by points of omission) and disregard of paragraph subdivisions in order to save space. In my own text I have accented all Spanish place names except a very few which are so familiar to American and English readers without the accents that their introduction would appear affected, as Panama, Mexico, Peru.

Many people have generously contributed to the preparation of this book. In particular I am indebted to Major General Glen E. Edgerton, governor of The Panama Canal, and to other army officers in the Canal Zone, for all the information and help they could properly give under present emergency conditions. Most of the photographs used as illustrations were obtained with the kind assistance of Mrs. M. W. Gillman in the office of The Panama Canal in Washington, of Dr. Vernon D. Tate, Miss Josephine Cobb, and Mrs. Hermine Baumhofer in the Division of Photographic Archives and Research of The National Archives, and of Miss Alice Lee Parker and Mr. Carl Stange in the Division of Fine Arts of The Library of Congress. My sincere thanks are due to Mr. Sylvester L. Vigilante, Mr. F. Ivor D. Avellino, and Miss Dorothy P. Miller of the Reference Department of the New York Public Library, and to Mr. Lindley W. Hubbell of the same library's Map Division, for much help and many courtesies; to the American Geographical Society of New York for permission to utilize their maps as source material in the preparation of many of my own maps; to Mr. Richard E. Harrison for technical advice in connection with the drawing of those maps; to Mr. Ralph F. Warren for a letter of introduction; to Mr. Oliver Cook for a photograph and several introductions; and to Lieutenant John Foster White, Jr., who accompanied me to Panama and Nicaragua in 1941 and ably assisted me to gather information in those countries. I also wish to express my appreciation of the courtesy of the various publishers who have given me permission to quote from their copyrighted works. All such quotations are specifically acknowledged in the reference notes.

G. M.

Contents

Illustrations

Maps and Diagrams

PART I

The Spanish Era

Chapter 1. The Doubtful Strait

I N A letter to Charles V dated April 1525 the governor of Castilla del Oro, Pedro Arias de Ávila, referred to the natural
waterway then supposed to connect the Atlantic and Pacific
Oceans through the Central American isthmus as *el estrecho du-
doso:* "the doubtful strait." [1] Doubtful, even at that early date, because no such channel had been discovered in spite of diligent exploration, and its existence, once taken for granted, was beginning
to be questioned. The search for that mythical strait was the chief
concern of Spanish voyagers during the first three decades of the
sixteenth century.

Columbus had believed in it firmly. He died convinced that the
Caribbean islands lay off the coast of rich Cathay and that somewhere an easy water passage led between those islands to the Indian Ocean. Assuming the world to be much smaller than it is, he
did not dream that an unknown continent thousands of miles long
and an unsuspected ocean thousands of miles wide still separated
his weatherbeaten ships from the true orient.

On August 1, 1498, during his third voyage, Columbus had first
sighted the mainland of South America near the island of Trinidad. Coasting westward along the shores of Venezuela he found
the land so fair, the natives so friendly and — not least important
— so rich in pearls and gold that he fancied himself in the neigh-
borhood of the Garden of Eden itself. The admiral's reports inspired other navigators to sail in quest of similar paradises. The
first of these expeditions was headed by Alonso de Ojeda and Juan
de la Cosa, transatlantic veterans who had accompanied Columbus
on his second voyage. With them was Amerigo Vespucci, whose relatively minor exploits have been undeservedly immortalized in the
name of the new continent. On May 20, 1499 they sailed from
Puerto Santa María with four ships and reached the northern coast
of South America in June. Their first approach to the mainland
was probably somewhere in what is now Dutch Guiana. Sailing
northwest they overlapped Columbus's route and continued as far
as Cabo de la Vela in Colombia before they turned north to Española.

The triple lure of gold, pearls, and Indian slaves enticed several other voyagers across the ocean within the year, and by the end of 1500 much of the Atlantic coast of South America was known at least superficially to Europeans. Probably the first explorer to behold the Central American isthmus was the notary Rodrigo de Bastidas of Triana, a suburb of Seville, who sailed with two vessels from Cádiz in October 1500, four months after Ojeda's return, taking with him Ojeda's pilot Juan de la Cosa and, as an obscure member of his crew, a young man whose name was to go down in history as the discoverer of the Pacific Ocean: Vasco Núñez de Balboa. Bastidas followed the course traced by Ojeda along the coast of Venezuela but instead of turning north at Cabo de la Vela continued southwest into the Gulf of Urabá. Then steering northwest he skirted the coast of Panama for more than 200 miles as far as Punta Manzanilla and the future site of Nombre de Dios — possibly even farther. Here his profitable trading enterprise was brought to an abrupt and almost fatal conclusion by the ravages of the teredos, which had eaten greedily through the wooden hulls. Bastidas made a dash for Española in his leaky vessels and barely succeeded in reaching the island before they sank. In 1504 he sailed again to the north coast of South America — which Columbus, realizing from its extent and its great rivers that it was not merely an island, had named Tierra Firme in 1498 — and brought back to Española 600 Indians to be sold as slaves.

Although the waterway supposedly leading to the Indian Ocean remained as much of a mystery after Bastidas's exploration as before, a vast expanse of unknown land and sea to the north and west still held out hopes of its discovery. The pursuit of the elusive strait in this area constituted the objective of Columbus's fourth and last voyage. With four dilapidated caravels and a crew of 135 Columbus set sail from Cádiz on May 9, 1502. He had been forbidden to land on the island of Española, the one part of the New World which already had acquired some faint semblance of European civilization; but one of his caravels proved so unmanageable that he decided to risk his sovereigns' displeasure in order to replace it with a better vessel. The governor, Nicolás de Ovando, curtly refused to make the needed exchange or even to permit the admiral's fleet to enter Santo Domingo harbor. Recognizing the signs of an approaching hurricane, Columbus had advised the governor to delay the sailing of a large fleet about to depart for Spain, but Ovando ignored the admonition. When the predicted storm broke with terrific violence Columbus's caravels took refuge in an indifferent haven some miles to the west, whence three of his four

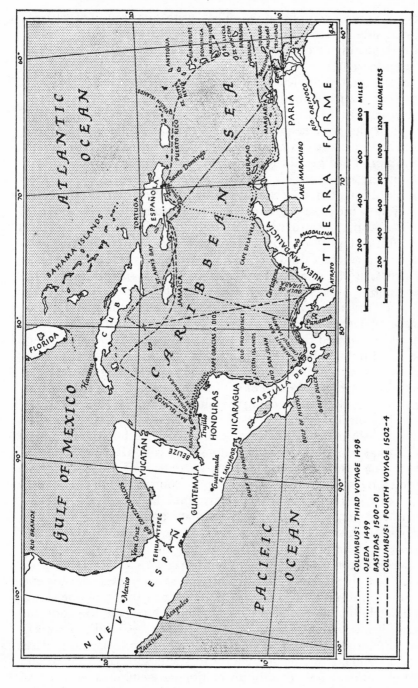

1. EARLY VOYAGES

vessels were blown out to sea. They were soon reunited without
having suffered serious damage. Ovando's great fleet which, in spite
of the warning, had already put to sea was not so fortunate. More
than a score of the ships sank beneath the enormous waves; three
or four, battered and leaky, staggered back to Santo Domingo. Only
one vessel remained in fit condition to continue its journey to
Spain; and that ironically was the one that bore Columbus's own
share of the gold taken from the Española natives. Among the
drowned were two of Columbus's most bitter enemies. At Española
the admiral had heard rumors, if not a full report, of Bastidas's explorations and resolved, since no strait had been found east of
Punta Manzanilla, to seek it farther to the northwest and if necessary follow the coast until he came upon traces of Bastidas's visit.

The hurricane proved an ill wind that blew some good. The
crumbling loyalty of Columbus's crew was revived by the seem-
ingly miraculous fulfillment of his weather forecast, the summary
destruction of his persecutors, and their own survival under his
leadership. After some delay occasioned by another storm and a
stop for urgent repairs the four ships arrived at the island of Bonacca off Honduras on July 30, 1502. Here the Indians appeared
far more civilized than any yet seen; their canoes, garments, weapons, and household gear all indicated a superior culture. Columbus took them for inhabitants of Tartary, whose magnificence had
been described by Marco Polo. Though sorely tempted to explore
their obviously wealthy country Columbus was too completely ob-
sessed by his determination to discover the strait to engage in irrelevant adventures. Accordingly he sailed first south to the mainland
near Cape Honduras, then east along the coast. Here more storms,
persistent head winds, and contrary currents impeded his progress.
For 28 days "did this fearful tempest continue, during which I
. . . saw neither sun nor stars; my ships lay exposed, with sails
torn, and anchors, rigging, cables, boats, and a great quantity of
provisions lost; my people were very weak and humbled in spirit,
many of them promising to lead a religious life, and all making
vows and promising to perform pilgrimages. . . ." [2]

At last on September 12 the battered ships rounded a cape and
turned southward into a region of calm waters and favorable winds.
To celebrate the welcome change Columbus gave the cape the
name it still bears: Gracias á Dios, or Thanks to God. For six weeks
he sailed south and east along the coasts of Nicaragua, Costa Rica,
and Panama, stopping frequently to trade with the Indians and
gather information (or misinformation, as we now know much of
it to have been) concerning the mines that supplied the natives

with their rich golden ornaments. At one settlement the natives told of a mighty river called the Ganges some ten days' journey farther on and of a "narrow place" leading to the Indian Ocean. Or so at least Columbus, eager to seize upon the slightest confirmation of his own wishful thoughts, believed. The reference to the "Ganges" was certainly no more than a chance similarity to some other name metamorphosed by the admiral's too receptive ear; the "narrow place" was genuine enough, but the Indians must have meant either a small bay or an isthmus separating two seas, not a waterway connecting them.

After exploring Almirante Bay and Chiriquí Lagoon the four caravels sailed into the harbor of Puerto Bello on November 2. Stormy weather held them there a week; and when they set out again during a brief lull another gale drove them to shelter at or very near the site of Nombre de Dios, which Columbus christened Puerto de Bastimentos — Port of Provisions — because maize grew there abundantly. There he rode out the storm for a fortnight and "again set sail, but not with favourable weather. After I had made fifteen leagues with great exertions, the wind and the current drove me back again with great fury, but . . . I found . . . another port, which I named Retrete. . . . I remained there fifteen days, kept in by stress of weather, and when I fancied my troubles were at an end, I found them only begun." [3] The harbor was probably that now called Puerto Escribanos, or Scriveners' Port. On December 5 the caravels headed back towards Veragua, the western section of the present republic of Panama, to find more gold, but again ran into storms which buffeted them unmercifully for a month. Columbus's own account of this journey was a harrowing record of hell and high water, of endless wind and rain and storm-tossed ocean: "Never was the sea seen so high, so terrific, and so covered with foam; not only did the wind oppose our proceeding onward, but it also rendered it highly dangerous to run in for any headland, and kept me in that sea which seemed to me as a sea of blood, seething like a cauldron on a mighty fire. Never did the sky look more fearful; during one day and one night it burned like a furnace, and emitted flashes in such fashion that each time I looked to see if my masts and my sails were not destroyed. . . . All this time the waters from heaven never ceased, not to say that it rained, for it was like a repetition of the deluge. The men were at this time so crushed in spirit, that they longed for death as a deliverance from so many martyrdoms." [4]

They struggled doggedly westward through this inferno, taking shelter from time to time in harbors they had passed a month or two before. From December 17, 1502 to January 3, 1503 the storm held them in what appears from the descriptions to have been either Limón Bay, the Atlantic terminus of the present canal, or the smaller Manzanillo Bay just round the corner. On January 6, the feast of the Epiphany, they anchored in the mouth of a river on the coast of Veragua and established a primitive settlement called Belén (Bethlehem) in honor of the day. Although this was theoretically the beginning of the dry season rain fell in torrents, and the forlorn Spaniards huddled in sodden misery. On February 6 Columbus sent a party into the interior to search for gold: "The Indians . . . conducted them to a very lofty mountain, and thence showing them the country all round . . . told them there was gold in every part, and that, towards the west, the mines extended twenty days' journey. . . . I afterwards learned that the *cacique* [chieftain] Quibian . . . had ordered them to show the distant mines, and which belonged to an enemy of his." [5] This proved to be a favorite trick which the Indians employed repeatedly and often successfully in their dealings with the Spaniards. By diverting the attention of their rapacious despoilers to remoter riches, preferably those belonging to unfriendly tribes, they hoped to protect their own property.

The admiral won the *cacique's* temporary friendship with gifts but "plainly saw that harmony would not last long, for the natives are of a very rough disposition and the Spaniards very encroaching; and, moreover, I had taken possession of land belonging to Quibian." [6] On March 30, while the Indians were preparing to burn the settlement and kill all the inhabitants, a Spanish force captured the chief, his family, and his servants and imprisoned them on the ships; but Quibian with his sons and some of the other Indians broke away and returned to their village, while many of those left on the vessels committed suicide by hanging. When the downpour ceased in mid-February the river level dropped suddenly, trapping the caravels inside the bar until the stream, again swollen by heavy rains early in April, scoured a channel through the choked harbor and enabled Columbus to move three of his ships into the open sea. He had intended to leave one caravel at Belén with a detachment of sailors in charge of his brother Bartolomé and was about to take leave of the colony when Indians attacked the settlement and killed a number of the garrison. By that time the shifting sands had closed the harbor mouth once more and prevented Columbus from returning to Bartolomé's assistance. Eventually the natives were beaten off and the surviving Spaniards on shore rescued, but the fourth caravel, unable to cross the bar, had to be dismantled and

left behind. On Easter Sunday — April 16, 1503 — the little settlement was finally abandoned after an existence of only three months,
and Columbus left the American mainland forever. His ships were
now so rotten from the borings of the teredo that he discarded a
second vessel at Puerto Bello. With the two remaining caravels
"pierced with worm-holes, like a bee-hive," [7] the admiral sailed
along the coast as far as Punta Mosquito, the easternmost limit of
his explorations on this voyage. He had overlapped Bastidas's path
for some distance and from Puerto Bello onward had found indications of his predecessor's passage. Although the will-o'-the-wisp
strait to the Indian Ocean still eluded him the dilapidation of his
ships made an immediate return to Española imperative. On May 1
he turned north away from the coast, but wind and tide were still
against him, and on June 25 the leaky ships, their decks barely
above water, were beached in St. Ann's Bay on the northern coast
of Jamaica.

There, in a desolate cove, with meager supplies extorted from
unfriendly natives, Columbus was marooned for a full year. Soon
after his arrival he sent two officers and several men in canoes to
Española where after a long delay occasioned by Ovando's opposition they succeeded in chartering a vessel. Meanwhile half of the
crew left with Columbus mutinied and were subdued only after
a fierce battle in which several were killed on each side. When the
rescue ship finally arrived the stranded sailors were in a sad plight.
Columbus and his men left Jamaica on June 29, 1504, but the relentless head winds still held them back, and six more weary weeks
elapsed before they dropped anchor at Santo Domingo. On September 12 they sailed for Spain and reached Sanlúcar after a storm-
tossed crossing on November 7. This was the admiral's last and
most perilous voyage. A year and a half later, on May 20, 1506, he
died at Valladolid.

During the decade following Columbus's death the search for
the strait continued, but the most significant events were connected
with projects for colonization rather than exploration. Although
Ferdinand had promised Columbus that he and his heirs forever
should be governors and viceroys of the lands he discovered, the
pledge was quickly broken. The king saw in the establishment of
a hereditary dynasty ruling over such potentially rich territories a
threat to his own supremacy. When Diego Colón, the admiral's
eldest son, brought suit in 1508 for restoration of his rights Ferdinand threw him the sop of the governorship of Española but retained control over all the conquered regions as personal posses-

sions of the Crown. Among these dominions the most important yet discovered was Tierra Firme, the South and Central American mainland.

Two claimants appeared for the post of governor of this area: Ojeda, hot-blooded, rough-mannered, and impoverished by a law-suit from which he had emerged victorious but penniless; and Diego de Nicuesa, an experienced courtier and wealthy Española planter. The wily monarch, seeing in the rivalry a splendid opportunity to apply the principle of "divide and rule," decided to appoint both men and then stir up jealous antagonism between them. He cut Tierra Firme into two provinces separated by the Gulf of Urabá and the Atrato River, named the eastern half — from the Atrato to Cabo de la Vela, now entirely within the republic of Colombia — Nueva Andalucía, and granted it to Ojeda; while he bestowed on Nicuesa the western part extending from the Atrato to Cape Gracias á Dios and including all of the present republics of Panama, Costa Rica, and Nicaragua as well as a corner of Colombia. This province was christened Castilla del Oro. Of course nobody knew the actual extent of either colony at the time; only the Atlantic coast had been explored, the hinterland was *terra incognita,* and the very existence of the Pacific Ocean was unsuspected.

Ojeda's expedition, the first to start, was accompanied and partly financed by the pilot Juan de la Cosa. With four vessels and 300 men they sailed from Española on November 10, 1509. Among Ojeda's adventurers was Francisco Pizarro, then unknown but later to become famous (or infamous) as the brutal conqueror of Peru. A more prominent ally was the pompous, pig-headed lawyer or *bachiller* Martín Fernández de Enciso, who remained in Española to round up additional colonists and provisions, with the understanding that he was to follow in another ship. Ojeda landed his men on the shores of a bay near the site of Cartagena and raided a large Indian village called Turbaco. The natives retaliated with showers of poisoned arrows and killed 70 Spaniards, including Cosa, whose warnings had been rashly ignored by the impetuous commander. Ojeda himself escaped — miraculously, in the opinion of his superstitious sailors — without a scratch.

Ten days after Ojeda's departure Nicuesa sailed from Española with seven ships and 800 recruits and reached Cartagena Bay shortly after Ojeda's disastrous battle with the Indians. Although the two governors, deliberately thrown into the cockpit by Ferdinand, had already quarreled violently over the boundaries of their respective grants they now joined forces and reopened the attack upon Turbaco, burned the village, slew or captured many of the

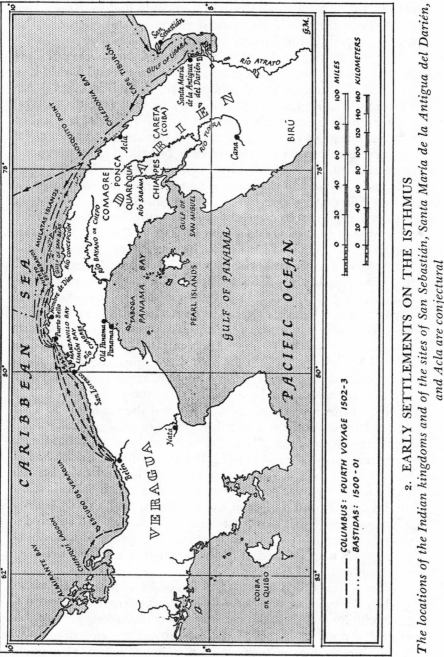

2. EARLY SETTLEMENTS ON THE ISTHMUS

The locations of the Indian kingdoms and of the sites of San Sebastián, Santa María de la Antigua del Darién, and Acla are conjectural

natives, and carried off all the gold they could find in the smoking ruins. Then the two leaders parted amicably, and Nicuesa sailed with his expedition to Castilla del Oro.

Ojeda now proceeded to the Gulf of Urabá, on the eastern shore of which he built a primitive stockaded settlement and named it — with the painful memory of poisoned arrows fresh in mind — San Sebastián. Hostile Indians, ferocious beasts, and venomous snakes kept the little colony penned within its frail palisade; tropical fevers decimated its ranks, and starvation threatened to account for the survivors. Enciso was expected daily but failed to appear. Some temporary relief was afforded by the providential arrival of a vessel laden with bacon and cassava bread and manned by 70 ruffians led by one Talavera, who extorted huge quantities of gold from the wretched colonists in payment for his scanty provisions. When these were consumed Ojeda set out for Española in Talavera's ship to spur on the long overdue Enciso, leaving Pizarro in command of San Sebastián with authority to abandon the settlement and either bring the survivors back to Española or establish a new colony elsewhere if he, Ojeda, did not return within 50 days. As soon as Ojeda boarded Talavera's vessel he quarreled with her captain and was promptly put in irons by the cutthroat crew, but when a storm threatened to wreck the ship he was released to serve as pilot. In spite of Ojeda's seamanship the high winds drove the vessel ashore on the south coast of Cuba. After a long and arduous overland journey through swamp and jungle, in the course of which half of Talavera's precious rascals died, Ojeda led the survivors to a village of friendly Indians who helped them to cross to Jamaica and eventually to Española. There Talavera and his chief subordinates were tried for piracy and hanged. Ojeda found that Enciso had already left for Nueva Andalucía with supplies and colonists. He then tried to organize yet another expedition to San Sebastián; but the insalubrity and danger of the settlement had already become notorious, and Ojeda's own reputation as a leader had suffered so severely that all his efforts to rejoin his colony came to nothing. A few years later he died at Santo Domingo, friendless, destitute, and humbled.

When Ojeda failed to reach San Sebastián within the stipulated 50 days the starving remnant of the colony prepared to return to Española. By this time the garrison had dwindled to 70 men, but even this number exceeded the capacity of the two diminutive brigantines at their disposal. With a callousness born of necessity the Spaniards waited grimly until hunger, disease, wild animals, and poisoned arrows further reduced their ranks. The emaciated survivors then crowded onto the tiny vessels and set sail, but one brigantine suddenly capsized and all on board were drowned. The crew of the other ship, commanded by Pizarro, reached the harbor of Cartagena in safety and found there the long-awaited Enciso with fresh recruits, a well-equipped vessel, and ample supplies. In spite of much sullen grumbling Enciso insisted that Pizarro and his enfeebled men should accompany him to San Sebastián and re-establish the colony. Near the mouth of the Gulf of Urabá the lawyer's ship struck a rock and foundered, carrying down with it all the stores and livestock. The settlers scrambled ashore and walked to San Sebastián, where they found the stockade and huts burnt by the natives. The desolation was too much even for Enciso, and once more — this time forever — the Spaniards deserted San Sebastián. In Pizarro's little brigantine, the only vessel left, they sailed across the gulf and founded a new colony on the western shore.

The suggestion for this fortunate move came from a member of the expedition who now for the first time emerged as a leader: Vasco Núñez de Balboa. Heretofore Balboa's status had been the anomalous and somewhat precarious one of uninvited guest. After his voyage with Bastidas he had returned to Española in 1501 and settled there as a planter; not apparently a conspicuously successful planter, for at the end of eight years he had accumulated nothing but debts. Although debtors were forbidden by law to leave the island Balboa managed to elude his creditors and join Enciso's party. The story of his escape is picturesque but probably apocryphal: he is said to have concealed himself in a large cask which was trundled to the harbor and hoisted on board the ship just before it sailed. When the vessel was safely at sea Balboa popped out of his barrel like a jack-in-the-box and confronted Enciso who, outraged by the stowaway's flippant disregard of the legal forms he himself held sacred, threatened to put him ashore on an uninhabited island. Luckily for the colonists the fuming lawyer soon calmed down and grudgingly accepted Balboa as an additional recruit. Balboa's previous exploration of the coast of Tierra Firme now proved invaluable to the stranded Spaniards. While Enciso and his lieutenants disconsolately surveyed the ruins of San Sebastián and hesitated to decide upon their next step Balboa quietly took charge. He declared that in the region called Darién, just across the Gulf of Urabá, the land was fertile, food was plentiful, and the natives, though aggressive, used no poisoned arrows. Without great difficulty he persuaded Enciso to transfer the destitute colony to this new land of promise.

If Darién did not quite fulfill Balboa's description it was .certainly a vast improvement over San Sebastián. The Indians attacked in force but were decisively defeated and put to flight. The colonists established their "capital" in the principal native village and christened it Santa María de la Antigua del Darién, an unwieldy name generally shortened to Antigua. The exact site of the town is unknown, but it was almost certainly near the westernmost mouth of the Atrato. The surrounding country was fairly fertile and had been to some extent cultivated by the natives. Prosperity seemed assured; but the turbulent settlers, no longer held together by imminent danger of starvation, at once split into factions. Enciso, indulging his passion for red tape and legal formalities, concocted an elaborate miscellany of arbitrary rules and restrictions wholly inappropriate to pioneer conditions. The straw that broke the colony's back was an edict forbidding individual settlers to barter with the Indians for gold. Unrest flared to open revolt, but Balboa neatly settled the controversy by pointing out that Antigua lay on the western side of the Gulf of Urabá and was therefore within the jurisdiction of Nicuesa; Enciso was Ojeda's lieutenant, not Nicuesa's; hence Enciso possessed no legal authority whatever. Armed with this simple syllogism the colonists promptly deposed the indignant bureaucrat and at the first town meeting held in the New World elected Balboa and Martín Zamudio joint *alcaldes* or mayors and Valdivia *regidor* or alderman. But the change failed to restore harmony. Balboa and Zamudio clashed over the division of their supposedly equal authority, and the colonists were aware that the new leaders had no more right than Enciso to govern in Nicuesa's territory. The Spaniards separated into two parties, one supporting the *alcaldes,* the other refusing to obey anyone not appointed by Nicuesa.

While Nicuesa's lands were thus being colonized by his rival's men Nicuesa himself was in grave danger farther along the coast. After leaving Ojeda in Cartagena Bay he had sailed westward in search of Veragua, reputedly the richest part of Castilla del Oro. In a harbor opposite the Mulatas Islands he left the greater portion of his fleet and with only two vessels and 90 men, including his captain general Lope de Olano, set his course in what he believed to be the direction of Veragua. A violent storm separated the two ships, and Nicuesa continued alone until, in the mouth of a rain-swollen river, a sudden drop in the water level tipped his caravel on its side. The vessel was a total loss, but the ship's boat and a few provisions were saved. The governor's crew then pro-

ceeded on foot along the shore, scrambling for days through mos-
quito-infested swamps and sometimes being rowed, a few men at a
time, across deep inlets. Finally, having overshot without knowing
it the limits of Veragua, they reached the entrance to the Chiriquí
Lagoon and were ferried across to what appeared to be another
point on the mainland but proved to be only a barren islet. During
the night the four oarsmen disappeared with the boat, leaving their
marooned comrades to die of hunger and exhaustion.

Meanwhile the officer left in charge of the main fleet had become uneasy when two months had passed without news of the
governor and had set out for Veragua with all his ships, but the
vessels were so wormeaten that he was obliged to anchor for repairs at the mouth of the Chagres River. Here he was joined by
Olano and his crew in the brigantine which, blown out of sight of
Nicuesa's ship, had survived the gale. Olano, somewhat too readily convinced that the other vessel had foundered, had shed few
tears over the governor's supposed fate. He now assumed command
of the entire fleet and sailed it to Belén, where the ships, now hopelessly damaged by teredos, were dismantled. With the soundest of
the rotten timbers Olano's men constructed a makeshift caravel.
At Belén floods, disease, starvation, and bitter quarrels soon crip-
pled and demoralized the expedition. Although the Spaniards had
planted maize the crops took some time to ripen, and meanwhile
food was so scarce that when a foraging party found a dead Indian
in the jungle they greedily devoured the putrescent corpse — a
loathsome meal which killed 30 men.

Some time later the little rowboat which had accompanied Nicuesa arrived at Belén. The four sailors who composed its crew had
not after all simply deserted their companions on the island; the
head boatman, Ribero, had tried repeatedly to convince Nicuesa
that he had sailed too far west to strike the coast of Veragua — as
indeed he had — and had stolen the boat in a desperate but loyal
attempt to find the rest of the fleet and send help to the castaways.
Olano, though by no means overjoyed by the news of his superior's
survival, dispatched his homemade caravel with fresh water and
a few palm nuts to the rescue.

Nicuesa failed to appreciate the chivalrous gesture. When he
reached Belén his first act was to arrest Olano on charges of treachery and desertion. The accusations may have been well founded,
but the governor certainly chose an unsuitable occasion to press
them. About 400 men, half of the entire expedition, had died; the
survivors were starving, disorganized, and in urgent need of a resourceful, cool-headed leader, not a stupid and revengeful one.

Nicuesa decided to abandon Belén and move the remnant of the settlement to a better location farther east. Leaving a detachment to harvest the ripening corn the colonists set out in their single patchwork vessel. When they reached the harbor of Bastimentos, discovered by Columbus, Nicuesa cried: "Let us stop here, in the name of God!" He rechristened the place Nombre de Dios, but although the sacred name was expected to bring good luck the settlers soon found themselves worse off than at Belén.

Relief appeared at the eleventh hour. Rodrigo Enríquez de Colmenares, one of Nicuesa's loyal lieutenants, had organized a search party and located the miserable little colony at Nombre de Dios: "Thus coursing along by al the coastes and gulfes neere thereabout . . . he found Nicuesa, of al lyuing men most infortunate, in manner dryed up with extreme hunger, filthy and horrible to behold, with only threescore men in his company, left aliue of seuen hundred. . . ." [8] Shortly before the rescue Colmenares had touched at Antigua, where he had tried to pave the way for the governor's eventual arrival by strengthening the Nicuesa faction. With tact, courtesy, and the judicious distribution of badly needed supplies he succeeded in persuading the settlers to send two envoys, Diego de Albites and Diego del Corral, to accompany the relief expedition and invite Nicuesa, if he should be found, to take his rightful place as head of the colony.

Had Nicuesa been a man of wisdom and understanding all might have gone well, but once washed and clothed and with good food in his belly the governor became absurdly arrogant and announced that he would depose the elected officials at Antigua, punish the colonists, and force them to disgorge their gold. Colmenares prudently suggested that such measures would only alienate the settlers, but the stubborn governor rejected his advice. Albites and Corral, alarmed by Nicuesa's vindictiveness and horrified by his inhuman treatment of Olano who, chained to a rock, complained bitterly of the governor's cruelty, hastily sailed back to Antigua and warned the inhabitants that Nicuesa's rule would inevitably mean tyranny. When Nicuesa, naïvely expecting to be received with open arms, reached Antigua some days later with the survivors from Nombre de Dios he was greeted with curses and refused permission to land. Balboa, anxious to prevent bloodshed, urged the outraged governor to remain quietly aboard his ship at least until the people had calmed down, but Nicuesa foolishly ignored him and in response to an invitation from a small group of settlers entered the town. When it was too late he realized that he had walked into a trap. He was seized by the very colonists who had treacherously enticed him ashore and on March 1, 1511 was herded with 17 of his men into his own leaky brigantine and set adrift on the stormy Atlantic. Nicuesa's fate was even more joyless than that of his rival Ojeda. He "entred into the Brigandine in an vnfortunate houre, for he was neuer seene after. They supposed that the Brigandine was drowned with all the men therein. And thus vnhappie Nicuesa fallyng headlong out of one misery into another, ended his life more miserably than he liued." [9]

Chapter 2. A Peak in Darién

W HILE the expulsion of Nicuesa eliminated one of the brawling Antigua factions it left three to keep dissension alive. One supported Enciso, who continued to protest loudly against his forcible demotion; another sided with Zamudio, the hot-headed co-mayor and the ringleader of the lawless men who had lured Nicuesa to his death; the third and largest remained loyal to Balboa, the most popular as well as the most competent leader in the community. Balboa now took steps to eject both of his troublesome rivals without violence. Magnanimously he permitted Enciso to return to Spain and present his case to the king, and at the same time he persuaded Zamudio to accompany the lawyer, ostensibly to counteract the effect of Enciso's misrepresentations. Balboa's generous treatment of the deposed *bachiller* proved in the end his own undoing. As soon as he reached Spain Enciso complained to the Council of the Indies that Balboa and Zamudio had usurped his authority. Zamudio, who was present, could and did defend himself; so it was upon Balboa that the full force of the Council's and the king's displeasure fell.

Meanwhile Balboa, unaware of the hornets' nest Enciso was stirring up overseas, devoted himself conscientiously to the welfare of Antigua, kept the disorderly settlers under control, and made some progress towards a permanent organization. Although he undoubtedly robbed, enslaved, killed, and even tortured many of the unfortunate natives his treatment of them was on the whole far more humane than that of most of his contemporaries. He preferred to win them over with kindness rather than antagonize them by a display of wanton cruelty; he waged war but rarely butchered. On the coast some 50 miles northwest of Antigua was an Indian "kingdom" ruled by the chieftain Careta. Balboa raided it and carried off great quantities of gold and other valuables as well as a number of prisoners, among them Careta and his family. Shortly afterwards he set Careta free, signed an alliance with him, and to seal the bargain married the chief's daughter.

Balboa also made friends with Comagre, a powerful *cacique* whose domain lay still farther up the coast. Comagre was a realist who preferred bribery to bloodshed. In his palace, the largest and most elaborate structure the Spaniards had yet seen in the New World, and attended by seven of his sons — the eldest of whom, Panciaco, had "an excellent naturall wit" [1] — the peace-loving chieftain courteously welcomed Balboa and his companions and gave them "foure thousande ounces of golde artificially wrought, and also fiftie slaues." [2] The slaves presented no problem, but the distribution of the gold created a diversion which was to affect profoundly the history of the world. One fifth of the treasure belonged by law to the king of Spain; and while Balboa's men were weighing the gold in the porch of Comagre's house to determine the royal share, a "brabbling and contention arose among our men about the diuiding. . . ." [3] Whereupon young Panciaco, disgusted by this exhibition of petty greed, "comming somewhat with an angrye countenaunce toward him which helde the ballaunces, he stroke them with his fiste, and scattered all the gold that was therein about the porche, sharpelye rebuking them with woordes in this effecte. What is the matter, you Christian men, that you so greatly esteeme so little portion of gold more then your owne quietnesse. . . . If your hunger of gold, bee so insatiable . . . I will shewe you a region flowing with gold, where you may satisfie your rauening appetites: But you must attempt the thing with a greater power, for it standeth you in hand by force of armes to ouercome kings of great puissaunce, and rigorous defendours of their dominions. . . . Furthermore, or euer you can come thither, you muste passe ouer the mountaynes inhabited of the cruell Canibales, a fierce kinde of men, deuourers of mans fleshe, lyuing without lawes, wandering and without Empire. . . . This iourney therefore must be made open by force of men, & when you are passing ouer these mountaines (poynting with his finger towarde the South Mountaines) you shall see another sea, where they sayle with shippes as bigge as yours. . . ." [4]

Thus did Balboa first hear of the Pacific Ocean. Panciaco's dramatic speech conjured up visions of new lands, new seas, new peoples; though to most of the Spaniards it meant no more than a promise of additional loot — a promise which made "our men, moued with great hope and hunger of golde . . . swallow downe their spittle." [5] Soon after Balboa's return from Comagre's kingdom internal dissension again boiled over at Antigua, but he quickly suppressed the revolt and imprisoned its leaders. One of the chief rebels was the *bachiller* Corral; and Balboa now expressed his opinion of all lawyers in a letter to the king dated January 20, 1513: "I beg your Royal Highness . . . to command that no *bachiller* of law . . . shall come to these parts of Tierra Firme . . . because . . . they all live like devils, and not only are they themselves wicked, but they make others wicked, and invent ways to bring about a thousand litigations and iniquities. . . ." [6]

By this time suspicious with good reason of the effect upon the Spanish court of Enciso's complaints, Balboa resolved to turn aside the king's wrath by some spectacular achievement. Panciaco's tale of a great ocean to the south stuck in his memory. If he could reach that unknown sea he might find the water route to Cathay and the Spice Islands which Columbus had sought in vain; he would bring glory to Spain and wealth to its treasury; he would be honored instead of punished by his sovereign. But Panciaco had warned that 1000 Spaniards would be needed to subdue the warlike tribes and "Canibales," and Balboa had only 200 soldiers at his disposal. Accordingly he begged Ferdinand to send him at least 500 men from Española, promising "to discover such great things, and places where there are so much gold and treasure, that with them you could conquer a large part of the world . . . and if this should not come to pass, I have nothing better than my head to pledge as forfeit." [7] Before this letter reached Spain Balboa received news from Zamudio confirming his worst fears. Not only did the Council of the Indies hold Balboa responsible for Nicuesa's death — which in fact he had done his best to prevent — but he was to be recalled to Spain for trial and supplanted by a new governor. Obviously there was no time to be lost if Balboa was to save himself from disgrace and perhaps death. The expedition to the South Sea had to be undertaken at once and completed before the edict of dismissal arrived from Spain. He could not wait for reinforcements (which in the circumstances would almost certainly have been denied him) but must rely on his own little band of colonists.

On September 1, 1513 Balboa set out with 190 armed Spaniards, several hundred Indians, and a pack of fierce dogs. They made the first stage of the journey by sea as far as Acla, a village in the kingdom of Careta, who contributed native guides and warriors as well as supplies and a description of the route. On September 6 the party headed inland. They came first to a region ruled over by Ponca, who fled in terror but was "entised with fayre speech and friendly profers" [8] to make a pact with Balboa, who "leauing all thinges in safetie behinde him, marched forward with his armie toward the mountaynes, by the conduct of certayne guids and labourers which Poncho had giuen him, as wel to leade him the way, as also to cary his baggages, and open the strayghtes [passes] through the desolate places and craggie rocks full of the dennes of wilde beastes." [9] On

September 24, after crossing "the horrible mountaynes, and many great riuers . . . ouer the which he made bridges, either with pyles or trunkes of trees," [10] Balboa reached the province of Quarequá, where 1000 armed Indians barred the way. The Spaniards fired their arquebuses at the natives who, terrified by their first experience with gunpowder, "beleeued that our men caryed thunder and lightning about with them. . . . Thus, sixe hundred of them, with their king, were slayne like bruite beastes." [11]

Leaving in Quarequá many soldiers "whiche by reason they were not yet accustomed to such trauailes & hunger, fell into diuers diseases," [12] Balboa advanced with 66 of the strongest men. On September 25 at ten in the morning they reached a hill from the top of which, the guides declared, they would be able to see the Pacific. Balboa "commaunded his armie to stay, and went himselfe alone to the toppe. . . . Where, falling prostrate vpon the grounde, and raysing himselfe againe vpon his knees . . . lyfting vp his eyes and handes towarde heauen, and directing his face towarde the newe founde South sea, he powred foorth his humble and deuout prayers before almightie God. . . . When he had thus made his prayers after his warlike maner, hee beckned with his hande to his companions, to come to him, shewing them the great maine sea heretofore vnknowne to the inhabitants of Europe, Aphrike, and Asia. Here agayne hee fell to his prayers as before. . . . All his companions did likewise, and praysed God with loud voyces for ioy." [13]

But Balboa was practical as well as devout. When the last echoes of prayers and *Te Deums* had died away he commanded his men to erect heaps of stones on the hilltop and to carve in the tree trunks the name of the king of Spain, in order to establish his claim to discovery "least such as might come after him shoulde argue him of lying or falshoode." [14] He then marched his soldiers towards the southern ocean, but before they reached it another Indian chieftain, Chiapes, attempted to turn back the invaders. After he had routed the natives Balboa, true to his policy of conciliation, made an ally of Chiapes. He summoned the troops left behind to rest at Quarequá and, on September 29, advanced to the shores of the Pacific. His first close view of the ocean must have been a sad disappointment: the tide was out, and a dreary expanse of mud and ooze stretched seaward from the beach. Balboa waited until the tide rose and then, in full armor and carrying a banner, waded into the water and "addicted all that mayne sea with all the landes adiacent thereunto, to the dominion and Empire of Castile." [15]

This ceremony took place on the feast day of St. Michael, in whose honor Balboa called this part of the Pacific the Gulf of San

Miguel. His exact route across the isthmus can no longer be traced, nor can the peak from which he first sighted the distant ocean be identified. Even the precise location of Acla, which the Spaniards occupied and fortified a year or two later, is unknown; all vestiges of the settlement had disappeared as early as 1575, but presumably it was at or near the mouth of the Aglaseniquá River on what is now called Caledonia Bay, opposite Golden Island.

It is difficult to understand why Balboa, fully aware that his own salvation depended on a speedy report of his great discovery, should have delayed his return to Antigua for nearly four months. He spent several weeks exploring the Gulf of San Miguel in native canoes and trading European trinkets for Indian gold. One chief told him of a rich land to the south and modeled a rough likeness of an animal which, he said, the inhabitants used as a beast of burden. The land was actually Peru, and the animal a llama; but since it looked very much like a camel the story only confirmed Balboa's conviction that he was on or near the coast of Asia. Early in November the Spaniards started homeward by a route some miles west of their outward trail. Progress was slow, partly because many of the men were tired and ill and partly because they stopped frequently to engage in profitable barter with the Indians. It was not until January 19, 1514 that Balboa and his men re-entered Antigua, where they were welcomed as heroes. The expedition had been in truth a remarkable achievement, not alone for its far-reaching consequences but for the manner in which it had been conducted. Although Balboa never hesitated to rob the natives with or without the cloak of "trading" he stole with such consummate grace that the Indians, far from resenting the pillage, naïvely regarded him as their benefactor; thus he left behind him a group of friendly chieftains into whose domains he could return at will. Moreover he took infinite pains, unlike most Spanish commanders of his day, to maintain the health and spirits of his own men. With almost no knowledge of medicine or hygiene he led a large force of Europeans through one of the most unhealthful regions in the world during the rainy season and brought them back after several months without the loss of a single man.

Balboa reported his discoveries and adventures to Ferdinand in a letter dated March 4, 1514, but it arrived too late to avert calamity; the new governor had already sailed. The delay was to spell tragedy not only for Balboa but for millions of wretched Indians. The governor appointed by Ferdinand to supersede Balboa, Pedro Arias (or Pedrarias) de Ávila, was that rare phenomenon, a scoundrel to whom not a single historian, contemporary or modern, has ever thrown a kind word. Pedrarias set sail from Sanlúcar on April 11, 1514. His company of 1500 men included many who were later to win renown as explorers, soldiers, or chroniclers: Hernando de Soto, discoverer of the Mississippi; Benalcázar, conqueror of Quito, and Diego de Almagro, Pizarro's future partner in the subjugation of Peru; Gonzalo Fernández de Oviedo, Bernal Díaz del Castillo, and Pascual de Andagoya, officials and historians. A few of the lawyers Balboa so bitterly resented — among them his old enemy Enciso — accompanied the expedition. The Church was represented by Juan de Quevedo, first bishop of Castilla del Oro, and a band of Franciscan friars. The governor also brought his wife, Isabel de Bobadilla, and a number of ladies to attend her.

On June 30 Pedrarias landed at Antigua, where Balboa received him with simple dignity. At first the shrewd old man treated his predecessor courteously, but as soon as he had extracted all the information the discoverer of the South Sea could give he arrested him and condemned him to pay damages for his alleged crimes against Enciso. Quevedo and some of the officials interceded for Balboa and ultimately secured his release. The sudden increase in the population of Antigua, which before the arrival of the newcomers had numbered only 450 Europeans, overtaxed the resources of the little colony, especially as a large part of the supplies brought by Pedrarias's fleet had been ruined by salt water. In one month 700 settlers died of disease or starvation.

When Balboa's report finally reached Spain Ferdinand ordered Pedrarias to follow up the discovery of the South Sea with the establishment of a chain of fortified outposts from ocean to ocean. Pedrarias sent his lieutenant Juan de Ayora with 400 men to carry out the order, but instead of crossing the isthmus Ayora savagely attacked the Indians on the Atlantic side, killing and torturing with ferocious cruelty, and sailed away to Spain with a cargo of gold and slaves. Bartolomé Hurtado, dispatched by Pedrarias to find the missing officer, fell upon the natives with the same relentless fury and returned to Antigua without Ayora but with a rich haul of captives and treasure. Other expeditions, each marked by a trail of blood across the isthmus, followed in rapid succession. In March 1515 Gonzalo de Badajoz raided the rich Indian town of Natá and a number of other settlements on the Pacific slope, but after a fierce battle his men were forced to leave their plunder and return empty-handed. In November of the same year Antonio Tello de Guzmán and Diego de Albites, with 100 soldiers, tried unsuccessfully to complete the task left undone by Ayora. Their journey was memorable chiefly for the incidental discovery of a primitive village on the south coast called by the Indians Panama, meaning "place of many fish." Another expedition under Gaspar de Morales and Francisco Pizarro plundered the Pearl Islands and laid waste the shores of the Gulf of San Miguel. Still another led by Gaspar de Espinosa ravaged the Pacific coast and established at Panama, early in 1517, the southernmost fort of the chain across the isthmus.

The enslaved Indians were herded to the gold mines, where they were brutally overworked and died by thousands. The natives defended themselves as best they could and in turn often inflicted heavy losses on their enemies. The fate of Spaniards captured by the Indians was unenviable: slow excruciating torture usually preceded death, and with a truly Gilbertian ambition to make the punishment fit the crime the Indians sometimes joyously poured molten gold down the throats of their living victims. In a short time Pedrarias and his subordinates had undone all of Balboa's work of conciliation. Sick at heart, Balboa protested to the king in a letter dated October 16, 1515 that "whereas the chieftains and natives used to behave like gentle ewes, they have now turned into savage lions . . . because of their ill treatment. . . . If this state of things continues only a year longer, the country will be so completely devastated that it will never be possible to restore it." [16] In the same letter he confided to Ferdinand his candid opinion of Pedrarias: "He is excessively impulsive; he was not greatly distressed by the loss of half his people at the very beginning; he has never punished his men for causing damage and death . . . nor has he called his captains to account for stealing gold and pearls. . . . He is highly pleased to see discord between one party and another; and if there is no discord, he will stir it up by speaking ill of one group to the other. . . . He is consumed by all the envy and cupidity in the world . . . he is unmethodical and wholly lacks the ability or talent to govern." [17]

Balboa was in a position to criticize since the king had rewarded him for his discoveries by appointing him *adelantado* of the South Sea and of the provinces of Coiba and Panama. Coiba was the territory formerly ruled by his father-in-law Careta. The royal favor rendered Balboa temporarily safe from persecution by Pedrarias, but their relations were still strained. Even Balboa's betrothal to Pedrarias's daughter María, arranged by Bishop Quevedo and agreed to as a matter of policy by the *adelantado* and the governor, reconciled them only on the surface. Apparently Balboa did not regard his Indian wife as a serious impediment to another marriage; in any event the betrothal could not immediately affect his domestic arrangements in Darién, since María was still a child in a Spanish convent.

Pedrarias, jealous of Balboa's popularity, carefully withheld from him any opportunity to increase his prestige by leading one of the numerous expeditions across the isthmus. Chafing at his enforced idleness, Balboa determined to leave Antigua and set up his provincial government on the Pacific coast. He went first to Acla, rebuilt the small Spanish settlement and fort which the Indians had destroyed, and established a base of operations for his journey. He intended to explore the inlets and islands of the Pacific shore, but there were no ships on that side of the isthmus. He therefore set about their construction, but for some reason which has never been satisfactorily explained he chose a singularly laborious method. Instead of felling trees and building the wooden hulls on the Pacific seaboard where they were to be launched he had enough lumber for four brigantines cut and assembled at Acla on the Atlantic and transported in sections across the isthmus on the backs of Indian porters, hundreds of whom toiled for several months to carry the enormous weights more than 50 miles through dense jungle and over mountain trails so rough and overgrown they could hardly be said to exist at all. Many died on the way; and when at last the wretched survivors dragged the unwieldy timbers to the banks of the Sabana River much of the wood was found to be already wormeaten and unfit for use. To make matters worse an unexpected flood swept away many of the fabricated sections, leaving only enough for the construction of two ships. With the odd leftover parts and some new timbers cut on the spot two more vessels were clumsily pieced together. When these were completed Balboa and his crews explored the coast and established their headquarters on one of the Pearl Islands.

Ferdinand died on January 23, 1516 and was succeeded as king of Spain by his young grandson, afterwards the emperor Charles V. Influenced by reports from Oviedo and others of misrule and dissension at Antigua, Charles decided to recall Pedrarias and appoint a new governor, Lope de Sosa. Rumors of the impending change reached the isthmus and were promptly relayed to Balboa, who was indiscreet enough to discuss the news with some of his lieutenants and speculate concerning its probable effect on his own fortunes. The conversation was overheard and misinterpreted by a garrulous sentry, through whose whisperings a garbled version eventually came to Pedrarias's ears. The old governor believed or chose to believe that Balboa was planning an immediate revolt against his authority at Antigua, and his suspicions were confirmed by one of Balboa's own officers, Andrés Garabito, who maliciously invented additional details of the supposed plot and as an extra flourish informed Pedrarias that Balboa never really intended to marry the governor's young daughter. These lies apparently sprang from a desire for revenge; according to Bartolomé de Las Casas Garabito had made an unsuccessful attempt to seduce Balboa's Indian wife and had been sharply reprimanded by her indignant husband.

Pedrarias, who had waited three years for an opportunity to destroy Balboa, eagerly seized upon the pretext offered by Garabito's treachery. With his habitual duplicity he wrote Balboa a letter dripping with honey and invited him to Acla for an important conference. Suspecting nothing, Balboa left his 300 faithful followers on their Pacific island and willingly accompanied the governor's messengers. Near Acla he was met by an armed force commanded by his former friend Pizarro. Without a protest Balboa allowed himself to be shackled and led to prison in the town. Brought before the court, Balboa and four companions were accused of treason and conspiracy to usurp the rights of the Crown. Unfortunately Bishop Quevedo, who had always befriended Balboa and whose influence might have secured an acquittal or at least a pardon, had gone to Spain. All five prisoners protested their innocence, but the court, which was wholly under Pedrarias's thumb, found them guilty on trumped-up evidence and sentenced them to death by decapitation.

The executions took place in the market square at Aclá in 1517. Late one afternoon the five doomed men, loaded with chains, were taken from their cells and escorted under heavy guard to the scaffold. At the head of the procession walked the town crier, proclaiming in ringing tones the triumph of justice. For the last time Balboa protested his loyalty to Pedrarias and to his king. The condemned men then partook of the sacrament, and Balboa walked firmly and proudly to the platform and placed his head upon the block. His comrades followed him "like sheep, one after the other. . . ." [18] Pedrarias, peering through a crack in the wall of a cane hut a few paces from the scaffold, gloated over the destruction of the man he hated and ordered Balboa's severed head to be stuck on a pole, where it remained on view for several days. Of all the crimes committed by this cruel governor none has been so universally condemned by posterity as his juridical murder of the wisest and most humane of the Spanish *conquistadores*.

Chapter 3. The South Sea

ALBOA's discovery infused new energy into the search for the
strait leading to the Spice Islands and the Indian Ocean.
The knowledge that a large body of water — its high tides
proved that the new sea was of vast extent — existed only 40-odd
miles in a straight line from the Atlantic strengthened the belief
that a natural waterway must connect the two. But where? While
the Central American isthmus seemed the most likely spot it was
possible that the strait might be found below the great bulge of
Brazil, where the coast had been only superficially explored. In
1517 Fernão de Magalhães — Ferdinand Magellan — a Portuguese by birth but a Spaniard by naturalization, presented to
Charles V an ambitious plan for a voyage to the Moluccas or Spice
Islands. Both Spain and Portugal claimed these islands under the
treaty of Tordesillas, but the Portuguese had been in possession
since 1511 and had closed the Cape of Good Hope trade route to
the Spaniards. Magellan, who had already taken part in a Portuguese expedition to the East Indies, insisted that the Moluccas
could be reached by sailing westward without trespassing on forbidden waters. On March 22, 1518 Charles granted Magellan a
commission for the journey, but it was not until September 20,
1519 that the little fleet of five ships sailed from Sanlúcar. Two
months later Magellan sighted the coast of Brazil near the present
city of Pernambuco. By the end of March 1520 he reached the little harbor of San Julián, 49° south of the equator, in a land he
called Patagonia (from the Spanish *pata*, a foot) because the natives had enormous feet. Here he spent the long Antarctic winter,
during which he suppressed an incipient mutiny and hanged the
ringleaders.

On October 21 the fleet rounded a promontory which Magellan
named the Cape of the Eleven Thousand Virgins (that being the
day consecrated to their memory) and entered what are now called
the Straits of Magellan. This difficult and tortuous passage, 360
miles long and in many places exceedingly narrow, runs southwest
from the Atlantic between the Patagonian mainland and the great
island of Tierra del Fuego — so named by Magellan because of the

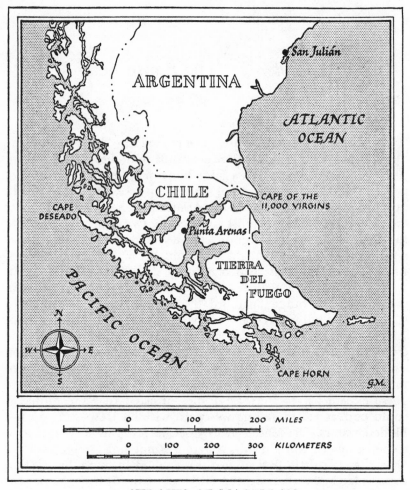

3. STRAITS OF MAGELLAN

number of native camp-fires seen on shore — then turns northwest and cuts through the southernmost spur of the Andes. Time after time his pilots were led astray by false channels which seemed to promise access to the western ocean only to end abruptly after countless twists and turns. The water was so deep and the bare forbidding cliffs on either side were so nearly vertical that the ships were obliged to anchor dangerously close to shore where a sudden squall might dash them on the rocks. The weather was stormy, the current swift and treacherous. One dark night his largest vessel, the *San Antonio*, slipped away from the rest of the fleet and disappeared into the void. Her jealous pilot, Esteban Gómez, who had persuaded her crew to desert Magellan, steered the ship back towards the Atlantic and eventually to Spain.

On November 28 the remaining vessels crept cautiously out of the strait into the open sea. Magellan called the westernmost headland Cabo Deseado — Cape Desired — because its appearance was so welcome to the frightened and weary sailors, and at the same time he gave to the gently heaving ocean the name it now bears: the Pacific. Though on this occasion the sea fortunately lived up to its not always merited reputation for placidity Magellan and his men nearly succumbed to starvation, thirst, and scurvy before they reached an island (probably Guam) 98 days after leaving Cabo Deseado. Here they obtained water and provisions from the natives, whose light-fingered habits caused Magellan to name the archipelago the Ladrones (Thieves') Islands. A few weeks later they came to the island of Cebu in the Philippines, where Magellan was killed in a fight with the natives on April 27, 1521. More than a year later one of his ships, the *Victoria,* commanded by Juan Sebastián del Cano and manned by 31 of the original crew who had started with Magellan, returned to Spain by way of the Cape of Good Hope: the first ship and the first men to complete the circumnavigation of the globe. While Magellan himself did not live to finish the voyage the importance of his accomplishment can scarcely be exaggerated. It confirmed beyond a doubt the theory, held by Columbus and many others, that the world was round; it demonstrated that the circumference of the earth was much greater than had been previously estimated; it indicated that, contrary to popular belief, more of the earth's surface was covered by water than by land; and it proved that the New World was in fact a new world and not merely part of the old.

The strait was found at last, but its discovery involved more disappointment than satisfaction. It was so far south and the Pacific was so wide that for trade between western Europe and the orient the Magellan route was longer both in distance and time than that round the Cape of Good Hope. Moreover the passage was so dangerous even during the rare spells of good weather and so nearly impossible at other times that the Good Hope course was also safer, notwithstanding its menace of capture by Portuguese warships. Curiously enough the less perilous though still difficult and stormy route via Cape Horn was not discovered until almost a century after Magellan's voyage. Two Dutch navigators, Le Maire and Van Schouten, first rounded the Horn in January 1616, and thereafter this more open passage generally supplanted the narrow strait.

Magellan's 38-day transit established a speed record that his immediate successors could not emulate. In 1526 a Spanish fleet
bound for the Moluccas and commanded by García de Loaysa took
four weary months to zigzag through the strait. A storm scattered
the ships a week after they emerged into the Pacific, Loaysa himself died at sea, and only two of the vessels were ever heard of again.
One arrived months later at the island of Tidore in the Moluccas;
the other, the 60-ton *Santiago,* sailed north and eventually reached
the Isthmus of Tehuantepec in Mexico 6000 miles from Cabo
Deseado. Alone for months on the immense uncharted ocean, the
tiny vessel carried 50 men but almost no food or water "because
the storeroom . . . was so small that her supplies were kept on
the flagship" [1] which had disappeared in the storm. The voyage
of the *Santiago,* the first ship to follow the Pacific coast of South
America from end to end, is one of the most significant milestones
in the history of exploration.

Since the new-found strait was so remote and so hazardous its discovery did nothing to discourage the quest for a more conveniently
situated natural waterway. During the next two decades Europeans
crossed and recrossed the isthmus, Mexico, and parts of the South
American continent at a dozen places, and though they found no
strait they swiftly opened up the country. In the central section of
the Americas three processes were now under way, often simultaneously: exploration, conquest, and colonization.

Balboa's death had left the isthmus without a competent leader.
Pedrarias, expecting his successor to arrive at any moment, resolved
to abandon Antigua and establish himself as a semi-independent
captain general on the Pacific slope. With such colonists as remained loyal to him and as much treasure as he could carry off he
crossed the isthmus and on August 15, 1519 founded the town of
Panama on the site of the Indian fishing village first visited by
Guzmán and Albites four years earlier. This settlement, of which
only the vine-covered ruins carefully preserved in a neat park remain today, lay some six miles northeast of the present city. At first
the town failed to prosper, largely because most of its inhabitants
were soldiers rather than settlers and preferred the slaughter and
pillage of the Indians to the more humdrum occupations appropriate to farm and civic life.

The new governor, Lope de Sosa, arrived at Antigua in May
1520, four years after the first reports of his appointment had
reached the isthmus. Pedrarias hastened across to welcome him and
remained to bury him, for Sosa fell ill on shipboard in the harbor

as he was preparing for his ceremonial entry and died before he ever set foot in his new domain. Pedrarias returned to Panama, and by 1523 most of the inhabitants of Antigua had emigrated to the Pacific coast. In September 1524 Indians attacked Antigua, massacred its remaining handful of citizens, and burned the town. It was never rebuilt. The jungle quickly swallowed up the ruins, and in a few years even the location was forgotten. Since that day no white settlement has ever been able to maintain itself permanently in the Darién section of the isthmus.

Meanwhile the search for the strait continued on the Pacific side. Early in 1522 Gil González Dávila, former paymaster of Española, led an exploring party over the mountains from the Gulf of Nicoya and discovered Lake Nicaragua. The natives informed him that a navigable river connected this great inland sea with the Atlantic, forming a waterway which extended far into though not quite through the land barrier, and Dávila was able to report to the king that "although the strait of water from one ocean to the other may not exist . . . the lake is separated from the other sea by only three leagues of land, of which two are so flat that they can be crossed by wagons, and the third, though not as level as the other two, is also passable. . . . It is narrow enough to permit the transport of spices [from the East Indies] by this road." [2] So in the very earliest days of Spanish occupation was born the rivalry between the Nicaragua and Panama trade routes, a rivalry which was to endure for centuries.

Dávila returned to Panama on June 25, 1523 with gold valued at 112,000 pesos and the announcement that he had converted 32,000 pagan souls to Christianity. Pedrarias, caring little for the souls, reached out greedily for the gold, but Dávila was on the alert and escaped with his treasure to Española. Pedrarias soon found a way to turn the discovery of Nicaragua to his own advantage. Learning that the king intended to appoint Pedro de los Ríos governor of Castilla del Oro, a post which Pedrarias had continued to occupy provisionally after Sosa's premature death, the old governor prepared to retire to Nicaragua and make himself ruler of the new territory before the arrival of Ríos. In 1524 he paved the way for his own entry by sending Francisco Hernández de Córdoba and Hernando de Soto with a body of men to establish settlements. This advance party founded two towns: Granada, on the western shore of Lake Nicaragua, and León, originally on Lake Managua but transferred to its present site between Lake Managua and the Pacific in 1610.

Before Pedrarias could follow his lieutenants Nicaragua and

Honduras were thrown into turmoil by a series of bloody conflicts. Three separate expeditions invaded the country in 1524. Dávila returned from Española in the spring and landed on the northern coast of Honduras, whence he marched overland with a small force towards the lake but, after a skirmish with a raiding party commanded by Soto, turned back to the little harbor now called Puerto Cortés. There he found a second competitor: Cristóbal de Olid, whom Cortés had dispatched from Mexico to seek a strait leading to the Pacific. But Olid had thrown off allegiance to Cortés and was preparing to seize Honduras and Nicaragua for himself. Francisco de Las Casas, sent by Cortés to overtake and punish the renegade, now landed at Puerto Cortés and joined the many-sided brawl. Olid captured both Dávila and Las Casas, but the two prisoners quickly turned the tables, overpowered Olid, and stabbed him to death. Instead of receiving the rewards they expected for Olid's assassination Las Casas and Dávila were arrested and sent to Spain for trial.

The new governor of Castilla del Oro, Ríos, landed on the isthmus in July 1526. Pedrarias defended himself so shrewdly and guilefully against the many claims and charges brought against him that he was acquitted on all counts and — apparently as a reward for his misdeeds — appointed governor of Nicaragua, the position he had already usurped. When he reached León in March 1528 he found another claimant in possession: Diego López de Salcedo, designated governor of Honduras by Charles V. Since the limits of his province were but vaguely defined Salcedo had marched as far inland as León and incorporated a large part of Nicaragua into his domain. Pedrarias, after forcing Salcedo to disgorge the annexed territory and retire to Honduras, settled down to rule and plunder Nicaragua. As in Darién he robbed the Indians, sold them into slavery, and brutally slaughtered so many that several of their larger towns were almost depopulated. To the old ruffian the slaves furnished sport as well as profit, for he organized combats between captive Indians and his fierce European dogs and watched with grim amusement the frantic struggles of the helpless natives as the powerful beasts pulled them down and tore open their throats. Fortunately Pedrarias was now approaching the end of his long life; he died at León on March 6, 1531, almost 90 years of age.

In 1527 Salcedo had commissioned Gabriel de Rojas to explore the San Juan River from the lake to the Atlantic, but before the expedition could be organized Salcedo was evicted from Nicaragua. Pedrarias then took up the project and carried it through: one of his last acts and almost the only really constructive undertaking of his career. Pedrarias placed Martín Estete in command, appointed Rojas his chief lieutenant, and assigned more than 150 men to accompany them. In 1529 the explorers crossed by boat to the eastern shore of the lake and proceeded on foot along the banks of the San Juan River to the sea — the first white men to penetrate this wild region and the first to verify the existence of a natural waterway connecting Lake Nicaragua with the Atlantic. But the river turned out to be of dubious value as a trade route, for rapids impeded its upper course and its lower reaches were shallow and choked with shifting sands. Pedrarias was not the man to finance a costly expedition merely for its scientific value; he demanded more tangible returns, so in obedience to orders Estete and Rojas combined their exploration with a slave hunt.

No more explorations of the San Juan were undertaken until 1539, when Rodrigo de Contreras, Pedrarias's successor as governor of Nicaragua (and husband of the old governor's daughter María, once betrothed to Balboa), authorized Diego Machuca and Alonso Calero to investigate the river region at their own expense. Machuca led his detachment of 200 men overland while Calero's party descended the rapids with great difficulty in two small boats. The two companies soon lost touch with each other, and both endured severe hardships. Calero had been advised to keep close to the right bank of the San Juan where numerous Indian villages could supply the Spaniards with food, but he loyally refused to abandon the search for Machuca's party stranded somewhere on the almost uninhabited left bank. Machuca could not be found, and most of Calero's men died of starvation. The survivors finally reached the coast and sailed to Nombre de Dios, where they were arrested by order of Francisco Robles, a member of the *audiencia* (supreme court) of Panama. Foreseeing that exploitation of the San Juan route might interfere with Panama's trade, Robles then sent an armed force under Gonzalo de Badajoz to seize the outlet of the river; but Contreras captured the leader and sent him to Spain in irons. The few members of Machuca's expedition who had not starved to death ultimately made their way back to the lake.

Subsequent explorations in Central America both north and south of the San Juan River failed to bring to light the long-sought strait or even another practicable site for an overland interoceanic trade route. The territories comprised in the present republics of Costa Rica, El Salvador, and Guatemala proved far too mountainous for convenient transit. The plateau of Honduras, though not much lower, held out more promise, for here the continental di-

vide was cut through by an almost level river valley running north
and south from Puerto Cortés to the Gulf of Fonseca. The distance
from ocean to ocean was about 160 miles and the maximum elevation of the valley some 2800 feet, but the grades on both sides were
easy and the terrain was fairly well adapted to road construction.
In 1539 Francisco de Montejo, conqueror of Yucatán and successor to Salcedo as governor of Honduras, proposed to Charles V the
establishment of this Honduras trade route and the diversion to it
of the traffic then flowing across the Isthmus of Panama. In 1556
Juan García de Hermosillo presented a similar plan; Felipe de
Aniñon sponsored a variation of it in 1565; and Diego García de
Palacios recommended still another in 1578. The supposed advantages of the Honduras route as set forth by its various advocates
were a healthier climate, better harbors, more docile natives, and
abundant gold in the surrounding country. All of these schemes
were vigorously opposed by the traders and governments of Panama and Nicaragua, and in the end none was carried out. Many of
the qualifications claimed for Honduras were in fact imaginary,
and even the real ones could not offset the undoubted superiorities
of its rivals to the south, where the overland transits were not only
shorter but much lower.

Next to the Isthmus of Panama and the San Juan valley in Nicaragua, the Isthmus of Tehuantepec in Mexico offered the most
hopeful prospects for the discovery of an interoceanic strait. Here
early investigations disclosed that the continent narrowed abruptly
so that the distance from sea to sea was no more than 130 miles,
while the elevation of the dividing ridge was only about 750 feet,
although the exact figures were not determined until much later.

Hernando Cortés landed at Vera Cruz on March 4, 1519 and
swiftly subdued New Spain, as Mexico was then called. Even before the completion of the bloody conquest he began to send out
expeditions in search of the strait, and for the next seven years he
persistently encouraged explorations throughout his realm. Early
in 1520 Cortés persuaded the deposed native ruler, Montezuma, to
furnish him with a map painted on cloth of a portion of the Atlantic seaboard. Equipped with this chart the first party, consisting
of ten men and including "several pilots and other persons who
were familiar with the sea," [3] sailed southeast from Vera Cruz, examining every inlet but finding none that provided satisfactory
shelter until they reached the mouth of the Coatzacoalcos River,
the Atlantic gateway to Tehuantepec. The topography of the land,
extraordinarily flat and penetrated by a broad and deep salt-water
estuary, indicated at first sight that here if anywhere was the en-

trance to the strait; but as the explorers paddled hopefully inland the increasing freshness of the water convinced them that this
was only another river after all, and after an ascent of 12 leagues
they turned back disappointed.

The next expedition sponsored by Cortés was the one commanded by Olid, who sailed from Vera Cruz on January 11, 1524
with instructions to establish a settlement near Cape Honduras
and seek for a strait in that region. This had been sent out in obedience to orders issued by the king in June 1523 and addressed not
only to Cortés but to several other provincial governors as well.
The commands varied in detail, but all stressed the importance of
the strait and urged the king's agents in the New World to search
for it diligently. At the same time Cortés prepared an expedition
to look for the strait on the Pacific side of Mexico. He sent ship-
builders to Zacatula, a small harbor northwest of Acapulco, to construct four vessels; but when they were almost completed the sails,
rigging, and pitch which had been transported with great difficulty
from the Atlantic coast were destroyed by fire. Charles V sent new
equipment but changed the orders: Cortés was now directed to
combine the quest for the strait with a search for a trade route between Mexico and the Moluccas, and incidentally to find some
trace if possible of the ships lost by the expeditions of Magellan
and Loaysa. Cortés proposed that he himself should lead the expedition, which though disguised as a voyage of exploration was actually to be an attempt to wrest the islands by force from the king
of Portugal; but events in Mexico urgently demanded his attention, and he was obliged to entrust the mission to his lieutenant
and cousin Alvaro de Saavedra de Cerón.

With three ships and 110 men Saavedra sailed about November
1, 1527. Gales dispersed the flotilla, and only the flagship reached
the Moluccas several months later. With his forces so depleted
Saavedra attempted no warlike demonstrations against the firmly
established Portuguese. Instead he traded peaceably for spices and
in June 1528 started back to Mexico with his rich cargo; but unable to proceed against the head winds alternating with dead calms
of the equatorial belt, he was forced to retrace his course to the
island of Tidore. In May 1529 he set out once more for the New
World but died at sea on October 19. With her crew reduced to
18 starving men the vessel limped back to the East Indies. Long
afterwards half a dozen survivors of Saavedra's expedition found
their way to Spain. The adverse winds encountered in this part of
the Pacific presented an almost insuperable obstacle to eastbound
traffic from the Spice Islands to the Americas until about 1565,

when Andrés de Urdañeta discovered a more practicable northerly
route favored by the prevailing west winds of the temperate zone.

North of Mexico the pursuit of the strait was carried on with as
much fervor as in the tropics, but here Spaniards were obliged to
compete with English, French, Portuguese, and Dutch mariners.
Exploration of the ice-bound seas and inhospitable shores of northern Canada proved so difficult that it proceeded with extreme slow-
ness, and the tantalizing hope of finding a water route to the East
Indies by way of the Northwest Passage was kept alive long after
it had been abandoned in lower latitudes.

In the summer of 1497 Giovanni Caboto (John Cabot), a Geno-
ese navigator in the service of Henry VII of England, explored the
coasts of Cape Breton Island and Newfoundland and discovered
the islands of Saint-Pierre and Miquelon, all of which he assumed
to be a part of the Asiatic dominions of the Grand Khan. He returned the following year, hoping to reach Cipangu (Japan), but
the Gulf Stream bore his ships northward to the eastern coast of
Greenland. Here the crew, frightened by the extreme cold and the
forbidding aspect of the ice-capped land, threatened to mutiny,
and Cabot turned back. Some doubt exists as to his subsequent
movements, but it is generally believed that he explored the shores
of Greenland, Baffin Land, and Labrador, and then followed the
coast southwest as far as the present state of Maryland, without dis-
covering the expected signs of oriental civilization.

In 1500 and 1501 Portuguese expeditions commanded by Gaspar Corte-Real and his brothers probably also reached the coasts
of Greenland and Newfoundland in an attempt to find a short water route to Asia. Far to the south Juan Ponce de León discovered
Florida on March 27, 1513 and explored much of its long coastline
but failed to find either a strait to the Indies or the fabled fountain
of youth. In 1519 Francisco de Garay, the wealthy governor of Jamaica, fitted out a strait-hunting expedition at his own expense
and two years later received permission from the king of Spain to
colonize the coast from the site of Tampico to what is now Alabama. Garay must have brought back some fantastic tales about
Florida, for the king noted that apparently "there are in one part
of this land some gigantic natives ten to eleven *palmos* in height
[the Spanish *palmo* was 8 inches], and some smaller, and others so
small that they measure but five or six *palmos*." [4] On June 12, 1523
Lucas Vásquez de Ayllón, a judge of the Española *audiencia* who
had conducted a slave raid in 1520 on the coasts of North Carolina
and Virginia, was awarded a similar commission to seek the strait

and settle new territories. Neither Garay nor Ayllón profited from these colonization projects: Garay lost his life in 1523 during a dispute with Cortés, and in 1525 Ayllón invested his entire fortune in a new expedition to the Carolinas only to see his largest ship stranded and many of his men killed by the natives.

Giovanni da Verrazzano, a Florentine, was sent in search of the strait by Francis I of France in 1524. He missed the entrance to Chesapeake Bay, landed on the eastern shore of Maryland, and marched across the peninsula to the bay, which he presumed to be part of the Indian Ocean. He failed to find the opening connecting the inlet with the Atlantic, but on his northward progress along the coast he may have been the first white man to enter the harbor of New York. In 1525 a small Spanish expedition was entrusted to Esteban Gómez, who insisted that the strait leading to the Spice Islands was to be found in the vicinity of Newfoundland. After ten months of unsuccessful search he returned to Spain with a cargo of captive North American Indians. When he entered the harbor of La Coruña "he announced that he brought slaves [*esclavos*]; a citizen of the town understood him to say cloves [*clavos*], which were one of the spices he had promised to bring back. . . . The tidings were spread throughout the court, to the great joy of all. . . . But when, soon afterwards, it was learned that the stupid messenger had mistaken *esclavos* for *clavos,* and that the boastful sailor had promised what he could not accomplish, everyone laughed heartily and lost hope of ever finding the much-desired strait; and even those who had aided Esteban Gómez in the venture were ashamed." [5] So retribution in the form of ridicule — a crushing humiliation to a proud Spaniard — overtook the cowardly pilot who had deserted his captain in the Straits of Magellan five years before.

Exploration of the Pacific coast of North America was undertaken by Juan Rodríguez Cabrillo, a Portuguese navigator in the service of Spain, who sailed past the shores of Lower California and on September 28, 1542 entered San Diego Bay. Cabrillo died in January 1543, and his Levantine pilot, Bartolomé Ferrelo, took command and continued the voyage northward along the present state of California at least as far as Cape Mendocino and possibly as far as the 42nd or 43rd parallel off the coast of Oregon. By 1552 the historian López de Gómara was able to describe with reasonable accuracy the topography of the entire Pacific coast from the Straits of Magellan to the Sierra Nevada Mountains but fell into woeful error when he tried to guess at the configuration of the unexplored lands beyond and assumed that "the coast line continues in a northerly direction until it joins Labrador or Gruntlandia [Greenland]." [6] This error persisted for more than a century and led to the waste of an enormous amount of time and effort on wild-goose chases. The separation of Asia from Alaska and the land connection of the latter peninsula with the North American continent remained in doubt until 1728, when the Danish navigator Vitus Bering explored the sea and strait which now bear his name.

Throughout the sixteenth and seventeenth centuries it was firmly believed that the Pacific and Atlantic Oceans were united by a broad waterway known as the Straits of Anian, running southwest from the North Atlantic, cutting through what we now know to be the highlands of western Canada, and possibly connecting with the Gulf of California. The precise location of this legendary strait varied considerably in contemporary maps, but few people doubted its reality. Fantastic rumors of its discovery and transit cropped up frequently and produced a good deal of international friction.

Since fame, honor, and financial reward awaited the discoverer of the fabled northern waterway many unscrupulous navigators yielded to temptation and presented false claims. One of the most picturesque of these impostors was Martin Chacke, "a Portugall of Lisbon," [7] who pretended that he had traversed the strait from west to east in 1567. Another impudent liar was Lorenzo Ferrer Maldonado, who claimed to have voyaged in 1588 from Lisbon to the orient by way of Labrador and a strait connecting with the Pacific in only three months; but his report was found to be "full of false computations, incredible adventures, and crude fabrications of all kinds. . . ." [8]

The voyage of Juan de Fuca, "named properly Apostolos Valerianos, of Nation a Greeke . . . of Profession a Mariner, and an ancient Pilot of Shippes," [9] was also of more than dubious authenticity. He announced that in 1592 he had passed from the Pacific to the Atlantic through a channel located at 47° north, and that the land was "rich of gold, Siluer, Pearle, and other things." [10] Possibly he did sail into the strait now named after him; but his description of the country certainly suggests that he saw little of it, and it is difficult to conceive that he could in good faith have mistaken the narrow island-dotted sound east of Vancouver Island for the broad and open Atlantic.

On the other hand most of the expeditions sent in search of the northern strait were serious enterprises, ably conducted and honestly reported. Such were the voyages of Frobisher, Davis, Weymouth, Champlain, Knight, Hudson, and many others. While all these added notably to the sum of geographical knowledge none succeeded in forcing a passage through the ice-filled seas to the Pacific. It was not until July 11, 1906 that Roald Amundsen, after three years of alternate freezing and thawing in the Canadian Arctic, finally completed the navigation of the Northwest Passage from ocean to ocean. Amundsen's voyage ranks high in the annals of discovery both as a scientific exploit and as an example of human fortitude; but the Northwest Passage, when found after a search lasting more than four centuries, proved to be so long, so dangerous, and ice-free for so short a season of the year as to be practically useless as an interoceanic trade route.

Chapter 4. The Dawn of the Canal

B Y 1530 the failure of countless persistent efforts to locate a natural strait had convinced most investigators that it did not exist in the tropical or temperate regions. At the same time the development of trade had created an imperative demand for some convenient transit between the seas. A few daring spirits now began to flirt with the idea of an artificial canal.

Credit for the first suggestion is generally given to Alvaro de Saavedra de Cerón, kinsman and lieutenant of Cortés and commander of that officer's ill-fated expedition to the Moluccas. Some years earlier Saavedra had served with Balboa in Darién, where he had had ample opportunity to note the extreme narrowness of the isthmus. In 1529 he is said to have proposed the construction of a canal between the Atlantic and the Pacific; but as he died that same year on the way home from the East Indies the suggestion must have been made, if at all, before his departure from Mexico in 1528. Apparently the sole authority for the existence of this project was Antonio Galvão, Portuguese historian and former governor of the Moluccas, who wrote about 1555 that Saavedra, "if he had lived, meant to have opened the land of Castillia de Oro and New Spaine from sea to sea." [1] Galvão then proceeded to discuss four possible sites for the canal, but it is uncertain whether these specific suggestions were included in Saavedra's original proposal or whether they were later additions. Still less is known about another canal project attributed to Estete and Rojas, who had explored the San Juan River in Nicaragua in 1529. It has been reported that they recommended the construction of an artificial channel to carry the river past the obstructing rapids and of a canal from Lake Nicaragua to the Pacific; but no contemporary record of this plan, if it was ever formulated, survives.

Soon after the founding of the city of Panama attention was drawn to the potentialities of the Chagres River as a link in a transisthmian trade route. In 1527 Governor Ríos ordered Hernando de la Serna, Pedro Corzo, and Miguel de la Cuesta to examine the river and the interior of the isthmus and trace a practicable location for an overland communication between the seas. They reported that the Chagres was navigable for ships for a distance of some 30 miles from its mouth and for canoes and flat-bottomed boats throughout the remainder of its course. This, later investigation proved, was an exaggeration: much of the channel was obstructed except at the height of the rainy season by sunken trees and other impediments to navigation. Serna's party also investigated a smaller stream on the Pacific slope, the Río Grande, but found it unsuitable for water-borne traffic. Charles V directed Antonio de la Gama, who succeeded Ríos as governor in 1529, to send another expedition down the Chagres in 1531. A third exploration was undertaken in 1533 in compliance with an order from the queen.

On October 10, 1533 Gaspar de Espinosa wrote to the king: "The Chagres can be made navigable at a very small cost, and will be the finest and most useful [waterway] in the world. . . . A channel for navigation could be dredged. . . ." [2] Whether Espinosa meant to suggest merely a clearing and deepening of the river halfway across the isthmus or the additional excavation of a wholly artificial canal through the divide from the great bend of the Chagres to the Pacific is uncertain. Charles evidently considered that both possibilities deserved investigation, for on February 20, 1534 he forwarded two sets of instructions to Francisco de Barrionuevo, the governor who had just replaced Gama. The first *cédula* directed Barrionuevo to have the Chagres freed from obstructions "so that it shall be navigable for the greatest possible distance in the direction of Panama" [3] and authorized him to spend up to 1000 gold pesos for that purpose. The second commanded him to organize another exploration of the hilly region between the Chagres and the Pacific by a commission of experts, who were to pay particular attention to "the ways and means to be employed to cut open the land and unite the South Sea with the river." [4] In connection with the canal project Barrionuevo was ordered to report on "what difficulties might be caused by the tides of the sea and by the elevation of the land, what it would cost in money, how many men would be required, how much time it would take, and what hills and valleys would be encountered. . . ." [5] Not least important, Charles requested the governor to ascertain what portion of the expense of construction could reasonably be assessed against the neighboring provinces, which would presumably derive the greatest benefit from a canal.

These elaborate instructions produced only scanty results. Barrionuevo delegated the investigation to his captain general Pascual de Andagoya, who obediently wrote to the king that he would un-

dertake the surveys during the ensuing dry season; but with regard to the proposed canal he ventured the opinion that "all the
gold in the world would not suffice for its execution, especially with
such help as the local workmen can furnish. The most useful thing
to be done is to clear the Chagres to the seacoast, which would
leave about five leagues to be traversed by a roadway to Panama."⁶
For the construction and maintenance of this road he estimated
that a crew of 50 Negroes would be ample. Andagoya does not appear to have carried out the promised survey, and the canal project was set aside for several years.

Between 1550 and 1555 interest in the project was revived by
the almost simultaneous publication of two books, one by the Portuguese Antonio Galvão, the other by the Spaniard Francisco López de Gómara, a chaplain in the entourage of Cortés. Galvão listed
four places where the narrowness of the land, the low elevation,
and the presence of navigable rivers — or at least of rivers which
might easily be made navigable — combined to facilitate the construction of a canal. These proposed alternatives were "from the
Gulfe of S. Michael to Vraba, which is 25 leagues, or from Panama
to Nombre de Dios, being 17 leagues distance: or through Xaqua-
tor, a river of Nicaragua, which springeth out of a lake three or
fower leagues from the South sea, and falleth into the North sea;
whereupon doe saile great barks and crayers [small trading vessels].
The other place is from Tecoantepec through a river to Verdadera
Cruz in the bay of the Honduras, which might also be opened in
a streight. Which if it were done, then they might saile from the
Canaries unto the Malucos under the climate of the zodiake [equa-
tor], in lesse time and with much lesse danger, then to saile about
the Cape de Bona Sperança [Good Hope], or by the streight of
Magelan, or by the Northwest: And yet if there might be found a
[natural] streight there to saile into the sea of China, as it hath
beene sought, it would doe much goode. . . ."⁷

Gómara, not content with mere suggestion, urged the Spanish
Crown to undertake without delay the excavation of one of these
same four sites: "The journey from Spain to the Moluccas by way
of the Straits of Magellan is so difficult and so long that, speaking
thereof many times with men acquainted with the Indies, and with
others who have studied history and have inquiring minds, we
have heard of a good, though costly, passage; which would be not
only advantageous, but a source of glory to its creator, should it be
made. This passage would have to be constructed through the solid
land . . . in one of four places: by the river of Lagartos [Chagres]
. . . or by the outlet of Lake Nicaragua, which is ascended and de-

scended by great barges, and the lake is not more than three or four leagues from the [South] sea. . . . There is also another river from Vera Cruz to Tecoantepec, by which the people of New Spain travel in boats from one sea to the other. From Nombre de Dios to Panama the distance is 17 leagues, and from the Gulf of Urabá to the Gulf of San Miguel 25; these are the other two places, and the most difficult to cut through; there are mountains, but there are also hands. Give me the man who has the will to do it, and it can be done; if courage is not lacking, there will be no lack of money, for the Indies . . . will furnish it. For the spice trade, for the wealth of the Indies, and for a king of Castile, few things are impossible. . . ." [8]

Gómara's book appears to have been first printed in 1552, Galvão's not until about 1555; and the striking parallels between the two sets of descriptions, the uniformity of estimated distances, and even certain similarities in wording suggest that the Portuguese writer probably borrowed his information from the Spaniard. Although neither had any adequate conception of the topographical difficulties of these routes the four locations upon which they agreed at this very early date — Darién between the Gulfs of Urabá and San Miguel, the valley of the Chagres, the valley of the San Juan in Nicaragua, and Tehuantepec — remained for more than 350 years the favorite potential sites for a canal. Much later the addition of two other possible transits — one from the Atrato River to the Pacific, the other across the isthmus from the Gulf of San Blas to the mouth of the Bayano River — increased the number of serious competitors to six, each subdivided into numerous variants.

Gómara's arrogant but flattering assumption that "for a king of Castile, few things are impossible" might have inspired Charles V to accept the challenge and embark on a definite program of canal construction; but the last years of his reign were fully occupied with European wars which left him little time to spare for the remote Indies. On January 16, 1556 he abdicated and retired to the monastery of Yuste, where he died in 1558. He was succeeded as king of Spain though not as emperor by his son Philip II. Although Philip inherited none of his father's enthusiasm for a canal between the oceans he appears to have at least tolerated the few proposals for the construction of such a waterway that were presented during his 42-year reign.

In 1555 or 1556 Ruy López de Valdenebro submitted to the Council of the Indies a project to eliminate the rapids in the San Juan River and make the channel navigable at all seasons from

Lake Nicaragua to the Atlantic. The Council took the suggestion seriously enough to transmit it to the *casa de contratación* (board of trade) but made no effort to carry it out. The quest for a natural strait through Central America, practically abandoned since about 1530, was revived briefly in 1565. On July 29 Philip authorized Jorge de Quintanilla, formerly a judge of the municipality of Cartagena, to search for a strait "in a certain place" [9] which Quintanilla claimed to have heard of from reliable sources. In the event of success the king promised to reward the discoverer with the governorship of the town or towns he proposed to establish as well as a trade monopoly through the new waterway. After a long delay caused by illness Quintanilla sailed from Spain to Cartagena in 1567. There he became entangled in one petty difficulty after another, and no more was heard of his project. Philip is also credited with the dispatch of two Flemish engineers to the isthmus with instructions to report on the possibility of constructing an interoceanic canal. Nothing is known of this mission except that the explorers "encountered insuperable difficulties." [10]

The canal project had vigorous opponents as well as enthusiastic supporters. The dissenters based their opposition on one or more of three wholly unrelated premises: that a canal would benefit other maritime nations more than Spain itself; that on account of the supposed difference in mean surface level of the two oceans the opening of a waterway between them would cause disastrous inundations; and that the construction of an artificial water channel where God had seen fit to place a land barrier would be an impious and sinful act. Charles V had considered the first difficulty as early as 1535, when in a royal *cédula* dated March 1 he expressed his fear lest the excavation of a canal "would open the door to the Portuguese and the French; and before such a thing could be undertaken it would be necessary to make arrangements for the defense of the waterway. . . ." [11] The presumed variation in sea level between the Atlantic and Pacific, and indeed the whole baffling phenomenon of tides, gave much concern to sixteenth-century scientists. Gómara prudently declined to guess at an explanation of the mystery: "Nobody has yet been able to solve the riddle of the rise and fall of the sea, and still less the reason why it rises in some places and not in others; therefore discussion of it is superfluous. . . ." [12]

In 1590 a book by the Jesuit priest José de Acosta dealt with both the hydrodynamic and the religious objections to the canal. Evidently the devout writer considered the former unimportant but the latter insurmountable: "Some people have proposed to cut this passage. . . . There are others who oppose this plan, claiming that it would flood the land; for they believe that one sea is lower than the other, just as in ancient times . . . it was necessary to abandon the attempt to connect the Red Sea and the Nile for the same reason, in the days of King Sesostris and later under the Ottoman empire. But for my part I hold such an enterprise to be impossible, even if this particular obstacle, about which I am not certain, should fail to prevent it; for I am convinced that no human power would suffice to demolish the very solid and impenetrable mountain range which God has set between the two seas . . . to resist the onslaughts of both oceans. And even should men find it possible, to my mind they would have good cause to fear divine punishment if they dared to alter the form which the Creator, with supreme wisdom and forethought, designed for the structure of this universe." [13]

Most historians have accepted the theory that fear of the Lord's vengeance influenced Philip II to such a degree that in the latter part of his reign he not only prohibited all attempts to build a canal but threatened with death anyone who should dare even to discuss the project. Although Philip was undoubtedly a religious fanatic, and this story fits well into familiar conceptions of his reactionary and bigoted character, there is actually very little solid foundation for the canal tradition. In fact the only authority for the tale was Antonio de Alcedo, whose geographical and historical dictionary of the Indies, published in 1787 — almost two centuries after Philip's death — contained two references to the subject. Alcedo wrote that "the Council of the Indies called the king's attention to the harmful effect it [the opening of a canal] might have on the interests of the Crown, for which reason the king commanded that thereafter nobody should propose or mention it, on pain of death." [14] The same chronicler asserted that a similar prohibition had been applied to the navigation of the Atrato River: "It is navigable for many leagues, but its passage is forbidden on pain of death, with no exception for any person whatever, to avoid the evils which ease of penetration into the interior of the country might bring to the provinces of the New World." [15] The temporary closing of the Atrato really did occur, but it was ordered by Philip V early in the eighteenth century, not by Philip II in the sixteenth. In 1886 Lucien Napoléon-Bonaparte Wyse suggested that Alcedo must have mistaken an actual prohibition by the later Philip for an imaginary one by the earlier: "In 1719 Antonio de la Pedrosa y Guerrero, president of the *audiencia* and afterwards viceroy of New Granada, in order to protect the receipts of the Cartagena custom house against losses from smuggling . . . obtained from Philip V an order for the infliction of capital punishment upon all who should undertake new explorations of the Atrato. This is the only trace I have been able to find, after an examination of the archives of Spain and New Granada, of anything even approximately related to the famous supposititious decree in which, according to Alcedo, Philip II . . . prohibited . . . discussion of a cut through the American isthmus." [16]

Prohibition or no prohibition, comparatively little time and energy were devoted to the canal project while Philip II sat on the Spanish throne. The reign of his son Philip III, who ruled from 1598 to 1621, was marked by greater activity. Samuel Champlain, who visited Panama about 1600, made a tentative suggestion for a canal to link the Chagres with the Pacific but produced no specific plan: "One may judge that, if the four leagues of land . . . from Panama to this river were cut through, one might . . . shorten the route by more than fifteen hundred leagues; and . . . the whole of America would be in two islands." [17] In 1616 Philip III instructed the governor of Castilla del Oro, Diego Fernández de Velasco, to send an exploring party to the Isthmus of Darién and report on the advantages and disadvantages as a possible canal site of the country between the Gulf of San Miguel and the Atrato River; but the exploration, if it was ever undertaken, produced no concrete result.

The portage of merchandise on muleback across the isthmus was so laborious and costly, and the little ports, especially on the Atlantic side, were so notoriously unhealthy, that Philip III asked for suggestions concerning more convenient and salubrious interoceanic trade routes. On January 23, 1620 Diego de Mercado, of Flemish birth but for many years a resident of Guatemala, submitted a report extolling with more enthusiasm than accuracy the virtues of the Nicaragua transit: "I call your Majesty's attention to two ports, one on the North Sea and the other on the South Sea, both named San Juan. . . . And the port of San Juan on the North Sea is very safe and capacious . . . it has . . . great depth of water, a good entrance and exit, no sandbar, and is well protected from the north winds. . . ." [18] Mercado's description flattered almost beyond recognition the little harbor of San Juan del Norte, later known as Greytown, at the mouth of the San Juan River. Although in 1620 it was undoubtedly in much better condition than it is today it could not even then have been considered spacious, and the sandbar which has since entirely closed the entrance was already developing into an ominous obstruction. The lower course of the river also presented a problem, for about 15 miles from the Atlantic it divided into two channels: the northern branch emptying into the harbor of San Juan del Norte carried very little water and was full of dangerous shoals, while the southern fork, called the Colorado, was partially blocked at its mouth by an almost exposed sandbar. Mercado naïvely proposed to dam the Colorado branch with palisades, by which means "it will be easy to unite all of the waters which are now divided . . . and cause them to flow together into . . . the harbor of San Juan. . . ." [19]

"The city of Granada," Mercado continued, "possesses ten or twelve vessels for the trade with . . . Puertobelo and Cartagena, which carry down fowls, corn, pitch, and other merchandise . . . and bring back to Granada wine, linen, and other articles . . . from Spain; and at present these ships ascend and descend . . . the river with the greatest trouble and difficulty. . . ." [20] The difficulty was caused by the rapids of the upper San Juan, which Mercado proposed to eliminate by removing the rocks; but he failed to suggest the means by which that operation was to be accomplished. From the lake to the Pacific he recommended the construction of an artificial canal for which he projected two alternative routes, one terminating on Papagayo (now called Salinas) Bay, the other at the port of San Juan del Sur. Here his optimism combined with his ignorance of engineering and his unfamiliarity with the country led him into the most ludicrous errors. Apparently he believed that the surface of the lake was only a few feet above the Atlantic and that the Pacific was at a still higher elevation, so that the waters of the western ocean would flow in a steady stream through the canal and lake and river to the Caribbean: "From one point on the lake . . . to the harbor of Papagayo . . . the distance is five leagues, and four of these pass through a very deep ravine . . . and from its extremity to . . . Papagayo there is only one short league . . . of rock which . . . acts as a sort of barrier. And by cutting through that one league and dredging out the . . . ravine the North and South Seas can be joined . . . and the surface of the lake will rise, because the South Sea is five or six *codos* [the Spanish *codo* measured about 18 inches] higher than the . . . lake . . . and similar conditions exist throughout . . . the four leagues between the lake and . . . San Juan del Sur, a dry flat land, easy to cut through. . . ." [21] Today we may smile at Mercado's pleasant daydreams, yet we cannot blame him too severely for an ignorance which was shared and often exceeded by his contemporaries. Many later explorers equipped with much more accurate scientific information made mistakes quite as ridiculous and far less excusable.

Chapter 5. The Fleet and the Road

AFTER Charles V renounced his claim to the Moluccas in favor of Portugal in 1529 the spice trade across the isthmus diminished rapidly, but it was soon replaced by traffic in an even richer commodity: the gold and silver bullion of Peru. The name Peru (or Birú) was at first applied only to the region just east of the Gulf of San Miguel and later extended to include the great Inca empire to the south. The original Birú territory was superficially explored and thoroughly pillaged by Gaspar de Morales and Francisco Pizarro in 1515 and again by Andagoya, then inspector general, in 1522. On this journey Andagoya fell out of his canoe and almost drowned: "What with the cold air and the quantity of water I had drunk, I was laid up next day, unable to turn. Seeing that I could not now conduct this discovery . . . I resolved to return to Panama. . . ." [1] His mishap proved not only a personal calamity but an infinitely greater catastrophe for the natives of Peru, who through this accident fell into the hands of men much less humane than the inspector general. Andagoya turned over his rights in Peru to a partnership comprising Pedrarias, Pizarro, Diego de Almagro, and Hernando de Luque. Luque, a priest, owned the revenues of Taboga Island in Panama Bay and was reputed a man of wealth, yet the conquest of the Incas seems to have been launched on the proverbial shoestring; according to Andagoya the four associates could scrape together at first no more than 60 Spanish dollars. Luque soon supplied additional funds, and on November 14, 1524 Pizarro set out from Panama on his first expedition to Peru, from which he returned almost empty-handed. A few months later Almagro bought out Pedrarias who, though his total contribution had amounted to nothing more than a single calf, owned a quarter share in the enterprise. On March 10, 1526 the three remaining partners signed their historic agreement for the conquest and partition of Peru. Since Pizarro and Almagro could not write, two of the witnesses signed for them.

The history of the military campaigns which destroyed the flourishing Inca civilization and of the subsequent quarrels and intrigues indulged in by the Spanish leaders need not be retold here.

But the conquest of Peru profoundly affected the Isthmus of Panama in one respect: for almost two centuries the thriving commerce between Peru and Spain brought prosperity to the isthmian trade route and stimulated interest in successive canal projects. Enormous quantities of gold and silver were shipped from Peru to Panama, transported overland to the Atlantic, and reshipped to Spain; while in the other direction all kinds of manufactured goods were brought from the mother country to the isthmus and distributed throughout the provinces of the New World.

The Panama transit, though the most convenient available, was far from ideal. No really satisfactory harbor existed on either side; both coasts were exceedingly unhealthy; and the transportation of merchandise across the isthmus was a prodigiously toilsome and expensive process. The harbor of the old city of Panama was an open roadstead in which the enormous tides, rising and falling 18 or 20 feet, and the very gradual slope of the sea bottom forced ships to anchor off the island of Perico, seven or eight miles away, and unload their cargoes onto flat-bottomed lighters for transfer to the shore. To make matters worse the bay was becoming shallower every year. The town possessed almost no sanitary facilities and lacked good drinking water, which had to be brought from streams a mile or more away. Fevers, dysentery, and other ailments of the tropics wrought such havoc that as early as 1531, only twelve years after its foundation, Governor Gama proposed to move the town to a less pestilential site. Andagoya opposed the transfer on the ground that the Almighty had chosen the location, and Panama remained where it was for 150 years. Although an important commercial and administrative center the city was small even at the height of its prosperity, and its buildings, public and private, exhibited few traces of metropolitan splendor. In 1607 the white population numbered about 1200: 600 men, 300 women, 300 children. In addition some 750 free Negroes, Indians, and half-breeds, and about 3700 Negro slaves of both sexes lived in the city and suburbs. The English friar Thomas Gage found the Panama Spaniards "much given to sin, looseness and venery especially, who make the blackamoors . . . the chief objects of their lust. . . ." [2]

Nombre de Dios, the Atlantic port for the Peruvian gold traffic, was a still smaller and even less agreeable town. It had been founded — if so primitive a settlement could be called a foundation — in 1510 by Nicuesa but abandoned a few months later when Colmenares rescued the stranded governor. Diego de Albites, who had been granted authority to colonize the province of Veragua farther west, resettled Nombre de Dios by accident in 1519. On the way to

Veragua one of his ships foundered near that spot; Indian canoes ferried Albites and his crew to shore, where they hastily constructed a village. Thus chance determined the selection of a site which a more deliberate choice would probably have passed by. Nombre de Dios was in fact a miserable port, exposed to the north winds; the surrounding country was swampy and unfit for cultivation, and the excessive breadth of the harbor mouth made it almost impossible to defend against hostile raiders. Yet this makeshift terminus remained the only Atlantic gateway to the isthmus for 75 years.

If the climate of Panama was unwholesome that of Nombre de Dios was deadly. Few people cared to risk their lives by residing there a day longer than necessary; and as the Spanish galleons anchored in the harbor for only a few weeks every year, the port, lively and crowded while the ships were in, was almost deserted at other seasons. French and English pirates found Nombre de Dios, without permanent fortifications and unprotected except by six bronze cannon on the beach, an easy target for repeated attacks. The feeble artillery failed to repel Drake's raid in 1572, and the municipality of Panama reported in 1577 that as a result of frequent alarms and depredations "Nombre de Dios is almost completely abandoned, and not thirty residents have remained to inhabit it." [3] In 1586 Philip II commissioned Juan Bautista Antonelli, an Italian military engineer, to examine and compare the principal ports of the Spanish Main and the Caribbean coast of Central America. In his report, submitted in 1591, Antonelli called attention to the advantages of the harbor of Puerto Bello a few miles west of Nombre de Dios and recommended the transfer of the Atlantic terminus to that site. Preliminary steps were taken to effect this change, but the actual move was delayed for several years while a branch mule track was constructed to connect Puerto Bello with the road already in use between Nombre de Dios and Panama. The removal might have been postponed indefinitely had not Drake again attacked Nombre de Dios in 1596 and this time not only sacked but burned the town. This was the final blow. The homeless remnant of its population abandoned Nombre de Dios before the ashes cooled and moved to half-built Puerto Bello. A century later Lionel Wafer painted a melancholy picture of the deserted ruins "all overgrown with a sort of Wild-Canes. . . . There is no Sign of a Town remaining. . . ." [4] Nombre de Dios has been rebuilt and exists today as a drowsy hamlet of tumbledown shacks inhabited by poverty-stricken Negroes.

The title of "city" granted to Nombre de Dios in 1537 was trans-

1. PUERTO BELLO IN 1910

2. PUERTO BELLO. SPANISH RUINS, PROBABLY OLD CUSTOM HOUSE

3. PUERTO BELLO. FORT OF SANTIAGO DEL PRÍNCIPE

ferred to the new settlement of San Felipe de Puertovelo on March 20, 1597. As a port Puerto Bello excelled its predecessor in every respect. Here the long narrow bay was well sheltered from the dreaded "northers" by projecting headlands which also furnished convenient emplacements for fortifications. As one faced the town the harbor entrance was flanked on the left by San Felipe de Todo Fierro, the famous Iron Fort, a formidable stone stronghold erected at the base of a high hill, and on the right by the only slightly less substantial citadel of Santiago del Príncipe. "The Town," wrote Wafer, "is long and narrow, having two principal Streets besides those that go across; with a small Parade [plaza] about the middle of it, surrounded with pretty fair Houses. The other Houses also and Churches are pretty handsome, after the *Spanish* make. The Town lies open to the Country without either Walls or Works; and at the East-side of it, where the Road to *Panama* goes out . . . there lies a long Stable . . . for the Mules that are imployed in the Road. . . . The East-side is low and swampy; and the Sea at low Water leaves the Shore . . . bare, a great way from the Houses; which having a black filthy Mud, it stinks very much, and breeds noisome Vapours. . . ." [5] Champlain admired the strength of the harbor defenses but pointed out a weakness which the Spaniards apparently did nothing to remedy: a short distance from the town just round the western headland a smaller cove, entirely unprotected, afforded a possible landing place for invaders.

The harbor was considered sufficiently spacious to accommodate 300 galleons and 1000 smaller vessels — an overestimation which was never put to the test — and deep enough to float large ships within a short distance of the shore except directly in front of the town, where the receding tide exposed unsavory mud flats. Though infested by teredos it was on the whole the best harbor to be found for many miles in either direction along the Atlantic coast. While never large the town contained a number of imposing public buildings of stone and brick: great warehouses, a splendid edifice for the exchange of goods at the annual fair, municipal offices, a residence for the governor, a custom house, a hospital — which though of fair size was quite inadequate to handle the vast number of fever patients when the fleet came in — as well as a cathedral and several other churches, convents, and monasteries. Most of the houses were of wood, raised above the marshy ground on masonry supports. Four suburbs of meaner aspect surrounded the town proper.

The climate, disagreeably hot and humid even in the so-called dry season from January to April and almost unbearable the rest

of the year, was no better than that of Nombre de Dios. Most of
the inhabitants gave Puerto Bello a wide berth for at least ten
months out of twelve, returning only for a few bustling weeks
while the harbor was full of ships. Even so the death rate was appalling. Champlain considered Puerto Bello in spite of its excellent
harbor "the most evil and pitiful residence in the world." [6] Gage
called it "an open grave . . . not *Porto bello,* but *Porto malo."* [7]
It was commonly believed that childbirth must result fatally for
mother and offspring, and pregnant women almost invariably traveled to Panama or to some higher, cooler village in the interior to
bear their children. It was even rumored that horses and cattle refused to breed and hens failed to lay eggs, but Humboldt skep-
tically branded such tales as exaggerations "totally destitute of
truth." [8] To make life at Puerto Bello still less pleasant, the streets
were often invaded at night by wildcats which carried off domestic
animals and sometimes attacked human beings. Venomous snakes
and poisonous insects were a constant menace, and thousands of
monkeys howled mournfully in the surrounding jungle. Most dis-
agreeable of all were the toads: "When it has rained more than
common in the night, the streets and squares in the morning are
paved with these reptiles; so that you cannot step without treading
on them. . . . They are generally about six inches in length, and
. . . nothing can be imagined more dismal than their croak-
ings. . . ." [9] Such myriads of the slimy creatures invaded the town
after a downpour that the disgusted inhabitants complained: "Every raindrop turns into a toad." [10]

Today the roofless and grass-grown but still impressive ruins of
the forts, churches, and warehouses of old Puerto Bello contrast
strangely with the flimsy huts and hovels of the modern village populated by a handful of Negroes. The present town covers only a
small part of the area of the original settlement; on the outskirts
numerous fragments of stone and rubble buildings half buried in
the encroaching jungle bear mute witness to its former extent. The
ancient road to Panama has long since become impassable, though
traces of its rough paving are yet visible under the thick matting
of grass and weeds.

Puerto Bello was not the only fortified place on this part of the
Atlantic coast. Shortly before his death Philip II commissioned Antonelli to construct the citadel of San Lorenzo, the picturesque
ruins of which still stand on top of a high cliff on the east side of
the mouth of the Chagres River. The site, commanding a wide
sweep of sea, was well chosen for the defense of the river. Unscalable precipices prevented access except from the east, where a draw-

bridge over a ditch 30 feet deep led to the single gateway. Artillery protected both land and sea approaches; storehouses and magazines inside the walls contained everything required to withstand a protracted siege. Yet the fortress sometimes suffered from neglect; in 1637 Gage reported that it "wanted great reparations, and was ready to fall down to the ground. The Governor of the castle was a notable wine-bibber. . . ." [11]

Settlement of Panama and Nombre de Dios in 1519 was followed almost immediately by preliminary work on a highway across the isthmus to connect the two ports. This transit, though it boasted the proud title of *camino real* (royal road) , scarcely deserved to be called a road at all, much less a royal one. For the greater part of its length it was only a primitive mule track, so roughly surfaced that travelers dubbed it "18 leagues of misery and curses." [12] On this uneven path the overland journey of about 50 miles usually consumed four days. By 1535 three roadside inns or *ventas* provided verminous lodging and some sort of scanty refreshment for benighted and footsore wayfarers. The original *camino real* ran almost due north from Panama and crossed the Chagres by a ford at Venta de Chagres, just above the mouth of the Pequení River.

The water route by way of the Chagres was longer but much less troublesome and for bulky commodities less expensive. In a letter to Charles V dated February 22, 1535 Tomás de Berlanga, bishop of Panama, eloquently sang the praises of the Chagres and urged the immediate construction of a good highway from Panama to the head of navigation on the river: "If this transit is improved in the manner indicated there will no longer be any need to seek a [natural] strait elsewhere, for your Majesty will become the ruler of that great world already discovered as well as of all that may be discovered in the future in the South Sea, and will be able to hold it as if under lock and key through control of this single narrow gateway. . . ." [13] Evidently the prelate had been roughly handled by the merchants of Nombre de Dios, for he also recommended the removal of that town and its inhabitants, bag and baggage: "Your Majesty would do well to command that this settlement . . . which is a nest of thieves and a tomb for travelers . . . be transferred to the mouth of the Chagres River, which is a most advantageous location." [14]

Although the king ignored Berlanga's second plea steps were promptly taken to develop the Chagres trade route. In 1536 a trading post was established at Venta de Cruces just above the great bend of the river; a wharf and warehouse were constructed, and in

a short time Cruces grew into a sizable village, the most important settlement in the interior of the isthmus. A royal decree dated
December 1, 1536 awarded the Cruces trade monopoly to the city
of Panama and forbade any individual to erect a competing warehouse in the vicinity; but private traders were allowed to construct
storehouses exclusively for their own merchandise at other points
on the river banks. Similar warehouses had already been opened
at Panama, Nombre de Dios, and Venta de Chagres. To protect
cargoes in transit Cruces was lightly fortified and garrisoned about
the end of the sixteenth century. In the rainy season the Chagres
route largely superseded the *camino real*, especially for articles of
relatively low value for their size. From January through April,
the months of shallow water, river traffic was virtually suspended,
and all merchandise was transported across the isthmus by pack
train.

From Cruces to Panama the road was fairly level, reasonably
well surfaced, and in some places broad enough to permit the passage of carts, though it is unlikely that wheeled vehicles were ever
utilized over the entire 18 miles of roadway between the two towns.
But the main road from ocean to ocean was paved with more good
intentions than stone blocks and at the height of the wet season
turned into an impassable quagmire of slippery mud. Fortunately
this occurred just when the Chagres was highest and most easily
navigable so that traffic was never completely interrupted. Although perfunctory repairs kept the trail from falling into a state
of utter dilapidation a single heavy downpour would suffice to
wash away long stretches and undo the work of months. Even the
discontinuous sections of firm pavement became through neglect a
menace rather than an aid to travel, for the broken, sharp-edged,
up-ended fragments of stone blocks cut the mules' feet and caused
painful and often fatal accidents. The high mortality rate among
the overburdened, ill-tended pack animals added greatly to the
expense of conveyance. Early in the seventeenth century transportation charges for ordinary merchandise between Panama and
Puerto Bello by the overland route amounted to about $30 for a
single mule-load of 200 pounds. Notwithstanding the exorbitant
cost the official shipments of Peruvian gold and silver were almost
invariably carried across the isthmus by land, for this very special
traffic usually took place in the spring, the season of low water in
the Chagres.

When Drake raided a pack train near Nombre de Dios in 1573
he reported that transisthmian commerce required the services of
28 separate *recuas* (droves) of animals, "the greatest . . . of seav-

entie Moyles [mules], the lesse of fiftie" [15] — which would bring the total number to about 1700. But by 1607, when trade was declining, the number of mules had been reduced to 850. 320 Negro slaves were employed to care for and load the beasts. Many of these mules were bred in distant parts of Central America and driven to Panama over what must have been an even more primitive trail than that across the isthmus. Drake also noted that the Spanish traders "are wont to take their journey from Panama to Venta Cruz [Cruces] . . . ever by night, because the Countrey is . . . by day very hot; but from Venta Cruz to Nombre de Dios . . . they travell alwayes by day . . . because all that way is full of woods, and therefore very fresh and coole. . . ." [16] Unless the climate of the isthmian jungle has deteriorated remarkably since Drake's day the freshness and coolness must be taken with a grain of salt. A more convincing reason for daylight transit was the condition of the trail, which made travel in the dark so hazardous as to be practically impossible. John Cockburn, an English sailor who crossed the isthmus about 1730, found parts of the road "not above two feet broad, having precipices on each side four or five hundred feet deep; so that by the least slip of a mule's foot, both itself and rider must be dashed in pieces. . . ." [17]

Travelers on the *camino real* often survived bruises and broken bones only to suffer graver injuries at the hands of *cimarrones* or runaway Negro slaves. By 1570 about 3000 of these outlaws were at large on the isthmus, and their numbers were constantly being augmented both by their own fecundity and by the capture of other slaves from isolated *haciendas*. The *cimarrones* banded themselves into three principal groups, of which the largest maintained headquarters at Santiago del Príncipe near Puerto Bello, the second hovered on the outskirts of Nombre de Dios and preyed on the inhabitants, and the third roamed the hills between that town and Panama, harassing the pack trains and terrorizing travelers.

About 1554 the Spanish authorities at Nombre de Dios undertook a campaign against the local *cimarrones* and after two years of guerrilla warfare defeated them and captured their "king," who was sent to Spain in irons. Although the fugitive slaves then agreed to a treaty in which they promised not to molest the Spaniards in return for their own liberation from serfdom, peace was of short duration. A few years later attacks on the overland highway were again in full swing. Thoroughly at home in the jungle, the naked *cimarrones* apparently melted into thin air when pursued, "for there is no way to catch them on account of the incredible impenetrability and ruggedness of the country, access to which is greatly impeded by thick undergrowth and thorny bushes, through which the Negroes pass unharmed, because they smear their bodies with a kind of pitch which protects them from the thorns." [18]

The first step towards organization of trade between Spain and the Indies was taken almost immediately after the return of Columbus from his first voyage. In May 1493 Ferdinand and Isabella directed Juan Rodríguez de Fonseca, archdeacon of Seville and future bishop of Burgos, to supervise preparations for the admiral's second expedition; and for the next ten years this powerful and businesslike churchman administered almost singlehanded the transatlantic commerce of Spain. On January 20, 1503 a *casa de contratación* or board of trade, the first organization for the administration of colonial affairs, was inaugurated at Seville. For two centuries the colonial trading privilege was restricted to the city of Seville and its seaport at the mouth of the Guadalquivir River, Sanlúcar de Barrameda — a monopoly which did much to retard the development of Spain's overseas empire.

At first ships were permitted to sail to the Indies singly or in small flotillas of two or three. But about 1526 the presence of English, French, and Dutch corsairs in American waters forced the Spaniards to prohibit such voyages, though rare exceptions were made for unusually swift and well-armed merchantmen. The first large treasure fleet, composed of about twenty cargo vessels and some smaller tenders, sailed in 1537, and in 1543 the *casa* issued a set of rules for the organization of regular convoys. The ordinances provided for two voyages a year, each flotilla to consist of at least ten vessels protected by a man-of-war; but in practice the legal minimum of one warship per fleet was usually exceeded. After 1553 four men-of-war were assigned to each regular fleet, but during intervals between official voyages any group of six or eight properly armed merchantmen could cross the Atlantic. These rules were not always meticulously observed. Some years the fleet was guarded by only two warships, at other times by six or even more; while in 1556 it appears to have sailed without any armada at all.

Wind and weather determined the transatlantic schedules, at least in theory. During the first years the treasure from Mexico was transported in small vessels to Havana or Santo Domingo to be picked up on the homeward voyage by the Nombre de Dios fleet, already laden with the gold and silver of Peru. A phenomenal increase in the output of the Mexican mines soon made this arrangement inadequate, and after 1564 two separate fleets were dispatched annually, one to Mexico, the other to Nombre de Dios. From Sanlúcar by way of the Canaries to the West Indian island of Dominica both fleets usually followed the same route, though occasionally ships bound for Nombre de Dios entered the Caribbean through the "Galleons' Passage" between Trinidad and Tobago. From Dominica the Mexican flotilla proceeded to Vera Cruz, the other to Cartagena and then to Nombre de Dios or (after 1596) to Puerto Bello. The voyage from Spain to Vera Cruz generally required about ten weeks, to the isthmus a week or two less.

The two fleets rarely left Spain together, for weather conditions along the Spanish Main favored navigation at one season, those prevailing in the Gulf of Mexico at another. The fleet for Vera Cruz set out in April or May in order to reach its destination before the autumn hurricanes swept across the gulf, while that bound for the isthmus sailed in August or September so as to arrive at the beginning of the dry season. Both fleets were expected to winter in the Indies and meet at Havana in March. For the homeward voyage from Havana the two groups joined forces, sailing through the dangerous Bahama Channel and between the Virginia capes and the Bermudas until they reached the zone of favorable winds at about the 38th parallel, then due east to the Azores and Spain. The returning fleets carefully avoided the Bermudas, which enjoyed a most curious and evil reputation; but the skeptic López de Gómara assured his readers that the islands were "not, as unfounded rumor alleges, peopled by satyrs." [19]

Heavy import and export tolls were imposed, and an additional charge known as the *averia* was levied on the treasure fleets to defray the cost of the armed convoys. The combined taxes became so onerous that the temptation to smuggle grew irresistible, and contraband trade flourished in spite of reiterated edicts and the infliction of increasingly severe penalties. The colonists, always short of manufactured goods, welcomed purveyors of illicit commodities with open arms and paid for these articles with gold and silver bullion which they illegally neglected to enter in the official registers. At times contraband trade greatly exceeded in value legitimate commerce; in 1624 the Spanish factor at Cruces reported that while registered merchandise passing through the *venta* amounted to 1,446,346 pesos, the probable value of smuggled goods totaled 7,597,559 pesos. In 1660 the entire system of registration, duties, and *averia* was abolished and replaced by a fixed tax of 790,000 ducats on each fleet, paid jointly by the Seville merchants, the colonial traders, and the royal treasury. Since the change eliminated only one of the many incentives to illicit trade smugglers continued to prosper. Colonial markets were so well stocked with contraband goods that when the Spanish galleons visited Puerto Bello in 1662 after an absence of two years they were obliged to return to Europe with most of their cargoes unsold.

In 1713 the treaty of Utrecht granted England the right to send one registered merchant vessel of 500 tons burden each year to Puerto Bello. Apparently the Spaniards did not expect so limited a concession to interfere seriously with their own commerce, but the English factor at Puerto Bello shrewdly outwitted the local authorities. Each time the English ship paid its annual visit it was secretly accompanied by other vessels, laden with similar merchandise, which remained just out of sight of land. As soon as the single authorized ship had unloaded its cargo in the harbor it would be restocked under cover of darkness by one of the waiting tenders and again emptied. The process was repeated until the contents of the entire fleet had been delivered on shore. The ethics of such a ruse may have been questionable, but the profits were prodigious. The Spanish port authorities who permitted the trick must have been afflicted with either remarkably poor eyesight or distressingly itchy palms.

Vessels composing the armed convoys were allowed to carry the royal revenues, amounting usually to a fifth of the total yield of precious metals, and sometimes a limited quantity of privately owned bullion as well. Transport by the armada of other freight, except emergency cargoes rescued from vessels disabled at sea, was forbidden so that the fighting ships should at all times have ample space for soldiers, guns, and military stores. But the temptation of huge profits led captains to overload their warships with prohibited merchandise, above decks as well as below, to such an extent that the usefulness of the ships in battle was often gravely impaired. Bales and boxes heaped on deck hampered the operation of the unwieldy cannon, and men-of-war were sometimes so weighted down with illicit cargoes that most of the artillery was submerged below the water line.

The arrival of the treasure fleet at Cartagena sent couriers flying in all directions. One journeyed over the Andes to Lima with instructions to the viceroy of Peru to forward at once to Panama the annual accumulation of bullion and other products: vicuña wool, olives, wine, and hides. Another toiled up the steep mountain trails to Bogotá, whence local messengers were speedily dispatched to various parts of what are now Colombia and Venezuela. A third courier traveled by water to Nombre de Dios or, later, Puerto Bello. The authorities at Panama thereupon prepared to receive and forward the shipments from Peru, and traders from all parts of the isthmus gathered at the Atlantic terminus of the *camino real*. Transport of Peruvian silver from the Potosí mines to the coast at Arica usually required about 15 days and by water from Arica to Callao another week; but as these shipments were made at frequent intervals throughout the year, a great quantity of bullion was stored at Callao ready for conveyance to Panama as soon as the announcement of the arrival of the Atlantic fleet at Cartagena reached Peru. Within a fortnight after receipt of the news the Pacific treasure fleet set sail from Callao. The voyage to Panama, in the course of which the vessels from Peru were joined by others laden with gold from the province of Quito, generally consumed about three weeks, but the return journey southward often lasted two months or more on account of persistent head winds. From Panama the precious cargoes were transported across the isthmus, the bullion and other valuables on mules, the rest by mule train to Cruces and thence, if the river had not fallen too low, by flatboat down the Chagres.

Because both Nombre de Dios and Puerto Bello were so unhealthy the Atlantic fleet remained at Cartagena until the Peruvian vessels arrived at Panama. The stopover at Cartagena was enlivened by the pageantry of the annual "little" fair, at which manufactured articles from Spain were exchanged for the gold, emeralds, pearls, indigo, cacao, and tobacco of the neighboring provinces. The "little" fair seemed bustling enough to the inhabitants of Cartagena who, except during those few weeks, had nothing to do but drowse in the sun; but it was insignificant compared with the much livelier and more important "great" fair of Nombre de Dios or Puerto Bello. At first the fleet usually anchored at the Atlantic terminus of the isthmian trade route for two months, but so many traders, soldiers, and sailors died each year of fevers and dysentery that the period of loading and unloading was soon shortened by law to 40 days. When Gage visited Puerto Bello in 1637, after Spanish colonial trade had begun to decline and the size of the fleets to dwindle, a fortnight sufficed for the exchange of commodities. Yet while the fair lasted it presented a spectacle of intense animation. The good friar "wondered . . . to see the *requas* of mules . . . from Panama, laden with wedges of silver; in one day I told [counted] two hundred mules laden with nothing else, which were unladen in the public market-place, so that there the heaps of silver wedges lay like heaps of stones in the street, without any fear or suspicion of being lost. Within ten days the fleet came. . . . It was a wonder then to see the multitude of people in those streets which the week before had been empty. Then began the price of all things to rise, a fowl to be worth twelve reals, which . . . I had often bought for one . . . and so of all other food and provision, which was so excessive dear that I knew not how to live but by fish and tortoises. . . ." [20]

After 1580 irregularities began to appear in the sailings of the treasure fleets. Often a yearly voyage would be omitted, and by the end of the seventeenth century gaps of two or even three consecutive years were not uncommon. At the same time the average number of vessels in each fleet decreased, though an increase in tonnage of the individual ships largely compensated for this reduction. The Thirty Years' War (1618–48) not only bankrupted the treasury and paralyzed the industry of Spain but also brought ruin to the Seville merchants and traders. To add to their difficulties the Guadalquivir River, the principal highway of commerce between the inland warehouses of Seville and the port of Sanlúcar, was silting up rapidly. By 1717 the river had become too shallow for use, and the monopoly of the Indies trade was transferred to Cádiz. It did not remain a monopoly much longer. The ports of northern Spain clamored for a share, and in 1728 the trading company of Guipúzcoa, one of the Basque provinces, was granted the privilege of sending registered ships from its port of San Sebastián to Caracas in Venezuela. In 1734 a similar charter authorized the Galicia company to dispatch two ships a year to the Mexican towns of Campeche and Vera Cruz. These competing enterprises, added to the illegal activities of contraband traders, left little more than the royal fifth of colonial produce to be carried by the original Andalusian fleets. In 1748 the convoy system was finally abolished after more than two centuries of operation.

Chapter 6. Drake

THE PAPAL bull of donation of 1493, amended a year later by the treaty of Tordesillas, had awarded to Spain all of the New World except the easternmost bulge of South America afterwards known as Brazil. But most of this vast territory remained sparsely settled for many years, and the governments of other maritime nations refused to recognize Spain's claim to lands over which it exercised dominion only on paper. Disregarding Spanish pretensions, English, Dutch, French, and Portuguese mariners preyed relentlessly on Spanish fleets and harried Spanish colonial ports. These alien marauders may be roughly divided into three principal groups: the corsairs of the sixteenth century, the buccaneers of the seventeenth, and the pirates of the eighteenth.

The corsairs were nothing worse than traders in contraband goods who defied the Seville monopoly but otherwise kept the peace, rarely committing either theft or murder. English corsairs appeared in the West Indies early in the sixteenth century. In 1518 an English trading vessel touched at Santo Domingo on the island of Española and was fired upon by order of the Spanish governor. Another English merchantman ventured into the Caribbean in 1527, and in 1530 William Hawkins engaged in contraband trade with the natives of Brazil. At the same time French, Dutch, and Portuguese corsairs developed an illegitimate commerce with the Spanish colonies. At first this trade was conducted on a small scale, but as the century wore on well-organized trading companies with ample capital began to compete with independent corsairs and eventually caused far greater injury to Spanish commerce. A West Indian Company, chartered by Elizabeth of England in 1564, was followed by a Dutch West India Company in 1621 and a French Compagnie des Iles de l'Amérique in 1626.

Francis Drake, the first and by far the greatest of the Elizabethan raiders, did not fit precisely into any of the three categories of corsair, buccaneer, or pirate. Drake was not merely a despoiler; his reputation rests on a more honorable foundation, for he was an eminent navigator and explorer as well as an able commander.

His first voyage to the Caribbean occurred probably in 1565, when he sailed under the command of John Lovell from Africa to the northern coast of South America with a cargo of Negro slaves. In 1567 he participated in a second expedition of the same kind, this time under John Hawkins, a son of William Hawkins and Drake's distant cousin. After Hawkins and Drake had disposed of their slaves at various ports along the Spanish Main a hurricane drove their little flotilla to take shelter in September 1568 in the harbor of Vera Cruz, a port forbidden to the English. Hawkins was able to satisfy the local authorities that his violation of the law was due to stress of weather and that his intentions were pacific, but he was less successful with the commander of a Spanish fleet which sailed into the harbor on the following day. From the ensuing naval skirmish only two of the smaller English ships — the *Minion* and the *Judith,* captained respectively by Hawkins and Drake — escaped to England.

Drake resolved to avenge his defeat by a series of attacks on Spanish colonial commerce — attacks calculated to bring in a handsome profit as well as to soothe his wounded pride. He took his time and laid his plans carefully. To familiarize himself with the coast and with the movements of the treasure fleets he made a third voyage — his first as an independent commander — to the Spanish Main in 1570, and a fourth in 1571, which netted him a modest fortune in loot and a fearsome reputation along the Caribbean shores. In a single tiny ship of 25 tons, the *Swan,* he trailed the Spanish fleet to Cartagena in February 1571 and captured the dispatch boat on its way to Nombre de Dios, so that the customary notification of the convoy's arrival failed to reach the isthmus, and no preparations were made to receive it. Drake then joined forces with a squadron of French raiding vessels which had terrorized the coast for the past two years. Together the Englishmen and Huguenots advanced up the Chagres River probably as far as Cruces, plundered barges and warehouses, and withdrew with their booty. On his way back to the *Swan* Drake attacked and robbed a flotilla of small boats carrying cargoes from Nombre de Dios to the mouth of the Chagres. This audacious raid on the vital transisthmian trade route, hitherto considered safe from alien depredations, threw the Spaniards into a panic.

Drake returned to England with his plunder and on May 24, 1572 set sail once more from Plymouth, this time with two ships, the little *Swan* and the 70-ton *Pasha,* and 73 men. Early in July they landed on the isthmus, probably at the little harbor now called Puerto Escondido — Hidden Port — where they were unexpectedly joined by another English vessel manned by 30 sailors under the command of James Rause, as well as a Spanish caravel captured by Rause only the day before. Leaving Rause in charge of the ships at the Isle of Pines, Drake's party set out for Nombre de Dios, which they reached on July 29. The single sentry on the waterfront fled at the approach of the English boats, and before the surprised garrison could be mustered Drake and his companions had landed on the beach in the early morning darkness and dismounted the six brass cannon upon which the Spaniards relied for the defense of the harbor. The Englishmen, carrying flaring torches, then marched into the town with a loud fanfare of trumpets and roll of drums, which so frightened the sleepy citizens that they dashed helter-skelter to the surrounding hills. By that time the garrison had rallied in the plaza and "presented us with a jolly hot volley of shot. . . . We . . . having discharged our first volley of shot, and feathered them with our arrowes . . . came to the push of pike. . . . For our men . . . in short time tooke such order among these Gallants . . . that . . . they, casting down their weapons, fled all out of the Towne. . . ." [1]

Drake then led his men to the governor's house, where a great quantity of Peruvian silver was stored. The Englishmen's eyes were dazzled by the sight of solid silver bars, each weighing 35 to 40 pounds, piled in a heap 12 feet high and covering a floor space 70 feet long and 10 feet wide. The value of the metal could not have been much less than $5,000,000, but the enormous weight made it impossible for the raiders to carry away more than a few ingots. The even more valuable gold and precious stones were kept in a strongly built stone warehouse on the waterfront, into which the spoilers now attempted to break. They would probably have been successful if Drake, who had been severely wounded in the thigh during the skirmish in the plaza, had not collapsed from loss of blood. Disregarding his own pain he commanded his men to seize the treasure; but when they learned that the garrison was drifting back into the town and that reinforcements from Panama were almost at the gates the Englishmen prudently retired with their wounded leader to the pinnaces, abandoning the rich booty in the warehouses but picking up on the way a few odds and ends of portable loot.

The attack on Nombre de Dios had not been a conspicuous success; the marauders had secured only an insignificant amount of plunder, several of their men besides Drake had been seriously hurt, and the Spaniards were now on guard. Soon after Drake and his crew returned to the Isle of Pines, Rause, convinced that no

more depredations could be undertaken that year, sailed away to
England. For the next few months Drake made his headquarters on
the shore of an inlet in Darién which his men called Port Plenty
because it abounded in deer, wild hogs, and fish. There the raiders
were joined by a small band of *cimarrones* whose leader, Pedro
Mandinga, informed Drake that the Spanish fleet had arrived at
Nombre de Dios on January 5, 1573 and that the treasure-laden
mules were about to start overland from Panama. This was the
opportunity for which Drake had waited six months. With only
18 Englishmen and 30 *cimarrones* he left Port Plenty on February
3 to waylay the pack train.

A week later Drake, perched in the top of a tall tree, caught his
first glimpse of the Pacific and vowed that if he lived he would sail
an English ship on that ocean. By February 14 he was in sight of
Panama and the Peruvian treasure fleet at anchor in the bay. One
of his *cimarrones* entered the town and reported that three *recuas*
of mules — one laden with provisions, one with silver, and one
with gold and gems — were to set out from Panama that night.
Drake retired to a point on the road about two leagues south of
Cruces and there set up an ambush which, but for the imprudence
of one drunken sailor, would almost certainly have resulted in a rich
haul: "We had not laine thus in ambush much above an houre,
but we heard the *Recos* comming. . . . Now though there were
. . . great charge given . . . that none of our men should show
or stirre themselves, but let all that came from *Venta Cruz* [to-
wards Panama] to passe quietly . . . because we knew that they
brought nothing but Marchandise from thence, yet one of our men
called *Robert Pike,* having drunken too much *Aqua vitæ* without
water, forgat himselfe. . . . And when a Cavalier from *Venta Cruz*
past by, unadvisedly he rose up to see what he was. . . . By this the
Gentleman had taken notice by seeing one all in white (for that we
had all put our shirts over our other apparell, that we might be sure
to know our owne men in the pell mell in the night)." [2] Nevertheless Drake waited, hoping against hope that the warning had not
reached the pack train on its way from Panama. He was soon reassured by a loud tinkle of bells, and his disappointment was all the
keener when his men, having captured the first *recua* without resistance, found the mules laden with nothing but provisions. The
Spaniards, warned by the rider from Cruces, had craftily sent ahead
the relatively valueless consignment of food to lure Drake into the
open. The Englishmen and Negroes were now in a precarious position. Unwilling to risk a retreat by the long and difficult path by
which he had come, Drake boldly struck out for Cruces, took the

town by surprise, and plundered it of its few valuables without harming the inhabitants. The raiders returned to their Atlantic base, unmolested but almost empty-handed, and resumed their sporadic aggressions against Spanish ships.

A few weeks later Drake's forces were approximately doubled by an alliance with a shipload of 70 French corsairs commanded by Captain Le Testu. This unforeseen stroke of luck encouraged Drake to attempt one more raid on the pack trains. On March 31 he concealed a party by the side of the road about a mile outside the gate of Nombre de Dios. This time the adventurers were more fortunate. They dispersed the surprised guards and captured the entire train of 190 mules bearing about 30 tons of silver, but were able to carry away only half of the booty in the small pinnaces; the rest was buried or hidden and ultimately recovered by the Spaniards. Le Testu was badly wounded "with hayle-shot in the belly" [3] and had to be left behind, but Drake and his men escaped and on August 9, 1573 returned safely to Plymouth.

For the next five years Drake, occupied with the Irish wars, left the American continent alone, but a series of raids by other English adventurers gave the Spanish colonials no rest. In the spring of 1575 Gilbert Horseley and his French colleague Sylvester ascended the San Juan River in Nicaragua and captured several frigates laden with produce from Granada, after which they plundered a settlement on the coast of Veragua and threatened the ports of Trujillo and Puerto Cortés in Honduras. A year later Andrew Barker of Bristol, who had suffered ill treatment at the hands of the Inquisition, attempted to settle his score by harrying the Atlantic coast of the isthmus. After he had captured two or three Spanish frigates he was killed in 1577 on an island off Honduras, and a few survivors of his crew made their way back to England, where they "shortly after came to miserable ends." [4]

Much more disturbing to the Spaniards were the activities of Drake's lieutenant John Oxenham, who returned to the isthmus in 1576 with his own ship. Drake's vow to sail an English vessel on the Pacific had deeply impressed Oxenham, who secretly resolved to be the first Englishman to navigate those waters and who paid for that distinction with his life. Oxenham landed on the coast of Darién, made friends with the *cimarrones,* and marched his crew to the Gulf of San Miguel. They built pinnaces and in February 1577 attacked and plundered the Pearl Islands, where they felt it their duty as good Protestants to wreck and desecrate the churches. From the islands Oxenham headed for Panama, but the garrison prevented a landing. He then turned south and after looting a treasure

ship from Guayaquil sailed back to the Gulf of San Miguel and
established a base on the Chucunaque River.

By this time the Spaniards were thoroughly alarmed. A naval
force commanded by Pedro de Ortega Valencia was sent from
Panama in pursuit of the raiders, and another under Diego de
Frias Trejo from Callao. Ortega, the first to reach the Gulf of San
Miguel, diligently searched one river after another until he came
upon signs of English occupation. Taking the camp by surprise,
Ortega killed a dozen sailors and returned to Panama with a few
prisoners, but Oxenham and most of his men remained at large.
Early in May the punitive squadron commissioned by the viceroy
of Peru sailed from Callao to Panama; but the president of the
Panama *audiencia,* jealous of his own authority, delayed it for two
months, and it was not until August that Frias entered the Gulf of
San Miguel. The raiders had split into small bands, and it took
Frias several months to round them up, but in April 1578 he returned to Panama with 18 English prisoners, including Oxenham
himself, and 40 Negroes, as well as the bulk of the stolen treasure.
The slaves were returned to their former owners, and 13 Englishmen were promptly hanged. Oxenham and four of his officers were
taken to Lima, where they were executed in November 1580.

At that time Drake had just completed the greatest adventure of
his life, the circumnavigation of the globe — the first such voyage
since that of Magellan's lieutenant Cano 60 years earlier. On December 13, 1577 he sailed from Plymouth with four ships and a
pinnace. In June 1578 the flotilla anchored in the Patagonian harbor of San Julián, where the Englishmen discovered a grim re-
minder of Magellan's sojourn: the bleached and dangling skeleton
of one of the three mutineers hanged by the Portuguese navigator.
The warning failed to deter one of Drake's own men from attempting to foment a similar rebellion, and when Drake resumed his
southward voyage Thomas Doughty's freshly decapitated corpse
was left at San Julián beside the dry bones of his predecessor.

Drake now reduced his squadron to three vessels and changed
the name of his flagship from *Pelican* to *Golden Hind.* The ships
entered the Straits of Magellan on August 20 and passed through
to the Pacific in the remarkably short time of 16 days. But Drake's
good fortune abandoned him at the western end of the channel.
One of the smaller ships foundered in a storm with all on board,
and a disloyal captain made off with the other and sailed away to
England just as Gómez had deserted Magellan. The rest of Drake's
long voyage round the world was accomplished by the *Golden
Hind* alone. The flagship touched at Valparaiso and proceeded up

the coast, plundering small Spanish vessels, until it reached Callao in February 1579. After looting 30 ships in the harbor Drake set out in pursuit of the Peruvian treasure galleon and stripped it of bullion and precious stones. More booty fell into his hands as he sailed along the coasts of Mexico and California in search of the Northwest Passage. The northern limit of his journey is uncertain, but he probably reached some point on the Oregon coast before he turned westward across the Pacific in July. On September 26, 1580, almost three years after its departure, the *Golden Hind* dropped anchor in Plymouth Harbor.

Drake returned to England to find himself a national hero. He was knighted by Elizabeth and elected mayor of Plymouth. In 1585, when long-smoldering hostilities broke out openly between Spain and England, Drake sailed in command of a fleet of 25 ships to the West Indies, captured and burned Santo Domingo in January 1586, took Cartagena, and prepared to attack Nombre de Dios and Panama; but malaria incapacitated so many of his men that he abandoned the campaign against the isthmus and, after destroying St. Augustine in Florida, returned to England. In April 1587 he "singed the king of Spain's beard" by burning 100 Spanish vessels in Cádiz harbor, where they were being fitted out for an invasion of England. The Spaniards, delayed for a year by Drake's exploit, finally set sail in July 1588. Elizabeth's navy aided by wind and weather defeated Philip's unwieldy armada, and the threatened invasion collapsed.

The amazing speed and facility with which Drake had sailed through the Straits of Magellan in 1578 dismayed the Spaniards, who had been able to negotiate the dangerous passage only with the greatest difficulty. In order to reaffirm Spain's claim to the straits Philip II ordered the viceroy of Peru to send another exploring expedition through the channel. The task was entrusted to Pedro Sarmiento, who traversed the strait from west to east and sailed to Spain, where he proposed the establishment of a fortified colony on the strait to protect the Spanish trade route and discourage the intrusion of foreign fleets. The project hung fire for three years, but in 1584 Sarmiento set out with several hundred colonists and soldiers. He erected a fort, Nombre de Jesús, near the Atlantic entrance to the passage and manned it with a garrison of 150. At the narrowest point of the strait 45 miles farther in he built his principal settlement, Ciudad del Rey Felipe, a fortified town of some 400 colonists, including 30 women. Having supplied these outposts with provisions for eight months, Sarmiento sailed for home.

But the settlers had underestimated the harshness of the climate, and disaster overwhelmed them with the onset of the Antarctic winter: "The Plants would not grow, nor the Trees bear Fruit; nor any of their Labours prosper. And besides . . . the *Indians* . . . broke in upon them in a very violent Manner . . . so that at last, they died like so many Dogs, in their Houses . . . and the Stench of the putrefying Carcases infecting those that survived, they were forc'd to quit the Town . . . and go rambling about upon the Sea-Coasts, living at a barbarous Rate upon Leaves and Roots, and Sea-Herbs, or what Animals they could . . . light on." [5] The wretched colonists had starved and frozen in vain, for the attempted fortification of the straits failed to prevent its transit by another English adventurer. In 1586 Thomas Cavendish sailed from Plymouth to the Pacific, preyed on Spanish shipping, circled the globe, and returned to Plymouth after a voyage lasting two years. Entering the Straits of Magellan on January 6, 1587, Cavendish reached deserted Rey Felipe to find hundreds of skeletons clothed in rotting garments; many had died in their beds, others were lying where they had fallen in the desolate streets.

After the defeat of the armada Drake remained in Europe for seven years. For almost the only time in his adventurous life he engaged in peaceful pursuits: he built corn mills and represented Plymouth in Parliament. But Drake was not cut out to be a sober burgher; he itched for the high seas and another chance to raid the Spanish colonies. With his old friend John Hawkins he prepared a new expedition, much more ambitious than the earlier ones. Supported by a fleet of about 25 vessels and a large land force commanded by Sir Thomas Baskerville they set sail from Plymouth on August 28, 1595.

Drake's last voyage was luckless from the start. In November Hawkins died at sea off Puerto Rico, and when Drake attempted to raid the city of San Juan he was driven off after causing a certain amount of damage. A few minor forays along the Spanish Main yielded little profit, and on or about Christmas Day the fleet anchored in the harbor of Nombre de Dios. The garrison scattered, and the raiders sacked the town but found little of value. With 700 men Baskerville started overland towards Panama, where he expected to find gold and silver in plenty; but the Spaniards defended the road with such determination that the invaders "were constrained with the loss of many of their best men, and much grief, to return to their ships. . . ." [6]

The disappointed raiders then burned Nombre de Dios, destroyed all the Spanish vessels in the harbor, and sailed west to the

island of Escudo de Veragua near the Chiriquí Lagoon. At Nombre
de Dios Drake had fallen ill with dysentery or possibly some tropical fever, and his condition grew steadily worse. Baskerville made
preparations for a raid on the San Juan River in Nicaragua, but
for some reason the project was abandoned, and the English fleet,
after a fortnight at Escudo de Veragua, turned eastward once more
and headed for the half-built new town of Puerto Bello. Not far
from the entrance to the bay, on January 28, 1596 at four o'clock in
the morning, Drake died at sea "of a Flux, and grief for his bad
successes in this Voyage. His death was exceedingly lamented by all
the Company. His Corps being put into a Coffin of Lead was let
down into the Sea, the Trumpets in a doleful manner Ecchoing
out their lamentations for so great a loss. . . ." [7] Drake's death
brought the ill-starred expedition to a close. Baskerville assumed
command and after burning one of the unfinished forts at Puerto
Bello as a final gesture of defiance sailed with the fleet home to
England.

Chapter 7. The Buccaneers

WHILE no sharp line can be drawn between the Elizabethan adventurers and their successors the buccaneers they did differ in many respects. The Elizabethans were sailors, the buccaneers usually planters or herders unable to make a living ashore because of the strict Spanish monopoly of trade. Sixteenth-century raids were generally isolated affairs each conceived and carried out by a single leader, whereas the buccaneers of the seventeenth century often organized themselves into groups and acted in concert. These associations were loose and unstable, constantly broken up and reconstructed as the popularity of individual commanders waxed and waned. Again, the Elizabethans planned their expeditions in Europe, sailed from European ports, and returned to Europe when their voyages ended; while the buccaneers were usually residents of the West Indies who raided from and took refuge in Caribbean bases.

During the seventeenth century Spain lost one colonial possession after another to rival nations. By 1610 the English, French, and Dutch had gained footholds in Guiana on the South American mainland. England took the Bermudas in 1609 and divided the island of St. Kitts with the French in 1623. English colonists settled on Barbados and Tobago in 1625, on Nevis in 1628, on some small islands off the Mosquito coast of Nicaragua in 1630, on Antigua and Montserrat in 1632. In 1638 an English colony was cutting logwood in Belize. The conquest of Jamaica followed in 1655. By 1635 France occupied the islands of Tortuga, Guadeloupe, St. Lucia, and Martinique, and by the treaty of Ryswick in 1697 gained possession of Haiti, the western end of the island of Española. Curaçao fell to the Dutch in 1634, and the Danes, after one false start, established a permanent colony on St. Thomas in 1672. Spanish neglect during the preceding century of the smaller West Indian islands and outlying portions of the mainland had made the conquest of these territories by other nations a fairly easy matter, but once they had been settled by foreigners and had begun to develop profitably the Spaniards tried desperately to regain possession of them, persistently harried the islanders, burned their towns, and destroyed their crops and ships. Many of the English, French, and Dutch settlers, ruined by these attacks, endeavored to recoup their losses and at the same time revenge themselves on their persecutors by joining the buccaneers.

The buccaneers derived their name from the Indian word *bucan,* a smokehouse for the drying and curing of meat. In the early days of the conquest the Spaniards had imported cattle into Española, where the herds multiplied and grew wild after the Indian population had been decimated by harsh treatment. The cattle were hunted by French and English smugglers who settled on out-of-the-way coves and eluded the sporadic efforts of the Spanish authorities to dislodge them. Since salt was scarce and costly, the meat was dried in the sun and preserved by smoke. The French called their smokehouses *boucans* and the men who did the curing *boucaniers,* which the English corrupted into "buccaneers."

Spain was frequently at war with one European power or another, and the buccaneers whose nationality happened to be that of Spain's enemy of the moment often received commissions from their home governments or from local colonial authorities which raised their vessels to the status of privateers. These official papers gave little protection to buccaneers unlucky enough to fall into the hands of their enemies; the Spaniards refused to recognize their captives as prisoners of war and cheerfully hanged them with their commissions tied about their necks. The French buccaneers called themselves *flibustiers,* a word of doubtful origin. It may have stemmed, like the English word "freebooter" which means much the same thing, from the Dutch *vrijbuiter,* but this derivation is uncertain. In English *flibustier* became "filibuster" and in time acquired a special meaning.

The first English raider to venture into Spanish colonial waters after Drake's death was William Parker, who sailed from Plymouth in November 1601. On February 7, 1602 he landed a small force at Puerto Bello, looted the town, burned one of the suburbs, and sailed away two days later. This was an isolated raid of the Elizabethan variety rather than a buccaneer exploit. The damage was relatively slight, but Spanish morale was profoundly shaken by the audacity with which Parker snapped his fingers at the port's elaborate defenses.

The most celebrated of all buccaneers was the Welshman Henry Morgan, born about 1635. By some historians Morgan has been damned as a merciless brute, by others praised for his humanity and forbearance. Alexandre Olivier Exquemelin, also known as John

Esquemeling, one of his followers whose account, first published in 1678, was the chief contemporary source of information about Morgan, represented his commander as a cruel and bloodthirsty yet inspiring leader "who always communicated vigour with his words, [and] infused such spirits into his men as were able to put every one of them instantly upon new designs. . . ." [1] Brutal as Morgan and some of the other English buccaneers undoubtedly were, none appears to have been guilty of the excesses attributed to the worst of the French captains, one of whom in particular, L'Olonnois, gained an unenviable reputation for ferocity even among his far from squeamish colleagues. After one raid L'Olonnois was reported to have chopped off the heads of 90 Spaniards with his own sword, and after another to have thrown the crews of four captured vessels into the sea. Some of the more improbable stories pictured him as a veritable monster who habitually tore out and devoured the hearts of his slain prisoners, washing them down with drafts of warm human blood.

Little is known of Morgan's early life. He is said to have been kidnapped at Bristol as a lad and taken to Barbados, where he was sold as a "slave" — more probably bound out as an indentured servant or apprentice — for a term of years. The date of his initiation into the ranks of the buccaneers is uncertain, but his career was well launched before his uncle, Edward Morgan, was appointed lieutenant governor of Jamaica in 1664. Edward's death after a year in office failed to retard his nephew's rapid advancement. In 1665 Henry Morgan probably participated in a daring raid on the Mexican province of Campeche, followed by the capture of Trujillo in Honduras and a foray up the San Juan River and across Lake Nicaragua to Granada. A year later he assisted Edward Mansfield (or Mansveldt) to attack Curaçao. Mansfield, one of the most capable and popular of the buccaneer leaders, organized his unruly followers into a disciplined military force and in 1664 ousted the Spaniards from the island of Santa Catarina or Old Providence about 150 miles off the coast of Nicaragua. Morgan may also have accompanied Mansfield on this earlier expedition. Mansfield's career, though active, was short. After his death in 1668 the buccaneers on Santa Catarina surrendered the island to a Spanish force.

Morgan's first venture as an independent commander was the capture and sack of Puerto Príncipe, now called Camagüey, an important inland town in Cuba, in 1668. Later in the same year he embarked on a more ambitious undertaking, an attack on Puerto Bello with nine ships and 460 men. Leaving their transports in a neighboring cove, the buccaneers rowed to a landing a few miles from the town, continued their journey on foot, and at dawn surrounded one of the smaller forts before the Spaniards suspected their presence. The buccaneers herded the garrison into one room, blew up the fort, and swarmed into the city, while the governor retired with all the soldiers and townsfolk he could rally to the strongest of the remaining fortresses and prepared to defend it vigorously. The buccaneers attacked with fire-balls, but heavy gunfire and showers of stones kept them at a distance. They finally succeeded in placing ladders and scrambled into the citadel, whereupon the garrison surrendered; but the governor defended himself with desperate courage until he was killed. The raiders placed the Spanish prisoners under guard and threw the wounded into a separate dungeon "to the intent their own complaints might be the cure of their diseases, for no other was afforded them." [2] That night the buccaneers "fell to eating and drinking . . . committing in both these things all manner of debauchery and excess. These two vices were immediately followed by . . . rape and adultery committed upon very honest women, as well married as virgins, who being threatened with the sword were constrained to submit their bodies to the violence of these lewd and wicked men." [3]

With several shiploads of booty and a ransom of 100,000 pieces-of-eight Morgan sailed back to Jamaica. His improvident followers were soon as poor as if they had never looted Puerto Bello and "ceased not to importune him for new invasions and exploits, thereby to get something to expend anew in wine and strumpets. . . . " [4] In 1669 he raided the towns of Maracaibo and Gibraltar in Venezuela, collected a huge ransom, and returned safely to Port Royal. The proceeds of this expedition were flung away as casually as before, and in a few months the men were clamoring for more worlds to conquer.

Until now Morgan's raids had all been officially "commissioned" by Governor Thomas Modyford of Jamaica, who was in turn at least tacitly supported by his home government. But on July 8, 1670 Spain and England signed at Madrid a convention known as the treaty of America, confirming England's title to the West Indian and mainland territories already conquered and forbidding the ships of either power to enter ports belonging to the other without special license. As soon as rumors of the impending treaty reached Morgan's ears he resolved to undertake at least one more expedition against the Spanish colonies, and Modyford, unwilling to lose his share of the profits, hastily issued a new commission. Morgan and his captains met on the island of Tortuga, where they

made preparations for a raid on a scale never before attempted and
drew up an elaborate code of rules. When all was ready the fleet
sailed for Cape Tiburón on the coast of Darién. On December 2,
1670 Morgan offered his captains a choice of three objectives for
the proposed raid: Cartagena, Vera Cruz, Panama. The majority
voted for Panama, the richest of the three prizes.

The buccaneers, unfamiliar with the overland routes to Panama,
decided to obtain guides from the island of Santa Catarina, which
the Spaniards had reoccupied and turned into a penal settlement.
On December 20 the English fleet anchored off the island, and
Morgan demanded the surrender of the garrison. The local governor agreed; but to save his own face he persuaded Morgan to
allow the Spanish troops to make a show of resistance. An absurd
sham battle in which much powder was wasted but no damage done
took place that night, after which the forts were solemnly handed
over to the buccaneers together with two or three Indian guides.

Although this was the beginning of the dry season, which always
made navigation on the Chagres difficult and transit over the *camino real* relatively easy, Morgan for some reason decided to advance on Panama by the water route. The project required as a preliminary step the capture of the fortress of San Lorenzo at the mouth
of the river. This task was delegated to one of the captains, Joseph
Bradley, in command of four ships and 400 men, while Morgan
himself and the rest of the crews and vessels waited at Santa Catarina. Probably the attack would have failed had not a lucky accident favored the raiders. One of the wounded buccaneers pulled
an arrow out of his torn flesh, wrapped the dart in cotton, and shot
it back into the castle from his musket. The flash ignited the cotton, and the blazing arrow falling on a thatched roof started a fire
which spread to a powder magazine and blew up a section of the
stronghold. Both sides fought desperately, and when Bradley's
men finally forced their way in "the Spaniards who remained alive
cast themselves down from the castle into the sea, choosing rather
to die precipitated by their own selves . . . than to ask any quarter for their lives." [5] When the defenders yielded at last only 30
men were found alive out of the original garrison of 314. Every
officer, including the governor, had perished. The buccaneers also
sustained heavy losses: of their 400 men 100 were dead and at least
70 badly wounded. Bradley himself was injured so severely that he
died a few days later.

When Morgan received word of the capitulation he sailed at
once with his main force to San Lorenzo, collected a great number
of small boats, and with about 1200 men started up the Chagres on

January 9, 1671. Shallow water impeded their progress, and after a day or two the buccaneers were obliged to abandon most of the boats and continue their advance partly in some of the smallest canoes and partly on shore. Morgan had expected to find abundant food in the interior, but the forewarned Spaniards had destroyed everything edible in their retreat towards Panama. After several days of starvation the raiders found in a deserted village a few empty leather bags, which they cooked and ate "as being desirous to afford something to the ferment of their stomachs, which now was grown so sharp that it did gnaw their very bowels, having nothing else to prey upon." [6] On the seventh day they reached Cruces, abandoned like all the other settlements and partly consumed by fire. The provisions had been destroyed, but the buccaneers killed and ate a few stray dogs and cats and broached some jars of wine, which after their prolonged fast made them all violently ill. Here they left the canoes and marched overland towards Panama. Nine days after their departure from San Lorenzo they sighted the city in the distance and at the same time came upon a herd of cattle, some of which they slaughtered and ate half raw. That night they camped on the plain outside the city just beyond range of the Spanish guns.

Early on the morning of January 18 the buccaneers, with drums beating and trumpets sounding, advanced on the capital. The Spanish force of 400 horsemen and 2400 foot soldiers vastly outnumbered the raiders, but the latter were better marksmen and coolly shot the oncoming riders out of their saddles as fast as they galloped within range. Without cavalry protection the Spanish troops, though they fought with great courage, were soon routed. As a last resort the defenders drove a herd of wild bulls towards the buccaneers, expecting them to gore and trample the attackers to death; but the animals, frightened by the shooting, stampeded in all directions, and only a few charged into Morgan's lines. At the end of two hours the Spaniards broke and fled, leaving 600 dead on the battlefield. The next step was the capture of the city itself. On the landward side Panama was protected by a few isolated batteries, but there were neither walls nor forts since the defenders had never expected the city to be attacked from that direction. The Spanish soldiers were forced to retreat step by step, and in three more hours Morgan was master of Panama.

What happened next remains a mystery to this day. Panama was almost completely destroyed by fire, but nobody knows who started the conflagration. Exquemelin accused Morgan of having " caused certain men privately to set fire unto several great edifices of the city," [7] while the president of Panama reported that the city was set alight by the inhabitants themselves to prevent its sack. There is good reason to believe that the city was destroyed by the Spaniards rather than by the buccaneers, unless indeed the inflammable houses caught fire by accident during the battle. Morgan's expedition was undertaken for profit, not revenge, so it is unlikely that he would have burned a rich town deliberately before stripping it of its treasure. The destruction of Panama must have pained the raiders almost as much as the residents. Although Morgan's men worked feverishly side by side with the defeated Spaniards to extinguish the flames, by midnight the entire city was reduced to a heap of smoking ashes.

The roofless walls of half a dozen churches and public buildings still stand, for Panama was never rebuilt on its old site. In 1674 a new city was founded about six miles southwest of its original location. This time the Spaniards neglected no precautions and enclosed the city in an immensely strong stone wall from 20 to 40 feet high reinforced by numerous fortified towers. So costly were the defenses that when the bills were presented the Council of the Indies inquired tartly whether the walls were constructed of silver or of gold.

Morgan and his men remained in the vicinity of the destroyed city almost a month, digging in the ruins for treasure, rounding up prisoners, capturing and looting Spanish ships in the bay, and giving free rein to their passions for food, drink, and lechery. Many of the wealthier citizens were held for ransom, and not a few were tortured cruelly. One group of buccaneers, eager to secure greater prizes for themselves, plotted to seize one of the vessels in the harbor and embark on a raid of their own, but Morgan nipped the project in the bud by ordering the masts of all ships at anchor to be chopped down and burned. On February 14, 1671 the raiders started back to San Lorenzo with 600 captives and 175 pack animals laden with plunder. At Cruces they regained their canoes and, paddling slowly down the shallow river, reached the Atlantic on February 26. Morgan sent a delegation of prisoners to Puerto Bello with a demand for a ransom for the fortress of San Lorenzo and when the demand was ignored ordered the demolition of the citadel. At San Lorenzo he doled out 200 pieces-of-eight to each of his followers, "which small sum they thought too little reward for so much labour and such huge and manifest dangers as they had so often exposed their lives unto." [8] Whether or not Morgan really did hold back a disproportionate share of loot for himself, as Exquemelin claimed, his men grew violently discontented and even threatened mutiny. Morgan prudently evaded conflict by slipping

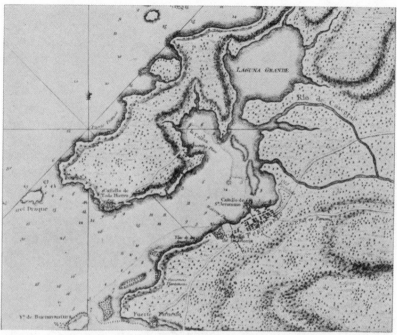

4. PUERTO BELLO HARBOR ABOUT 1760

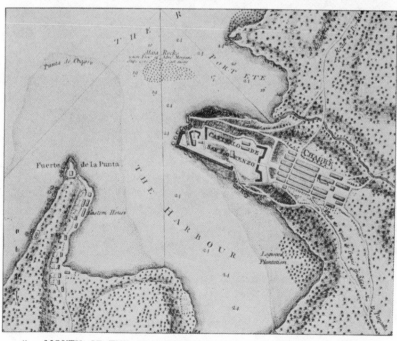

5. MOUTH OF THE CHAGRES RIVER AND FORT OF SAN LORENZO
ABOUT 1760

6. PANAMA VIEJO. RUINS OF THE CATHEDRAL

7. PANAMA VIEJO. MONASTERY OF SAN JOSÉ

away in the night with three or four ships manned by trusted Englishmen, leaving the rest to their own devices.

When Morgan reached Jamaica he found himself in difficulties. The English government piously disavowed his illegal activities. Modyford was taken to London and imprisoned in the Tower, and in April 1672 Morgan himself was sent to London in irons. But the pendulum swung rapidly from disgrace to honor. Both Modyford and Morgan soon bought their way out of prison and into the good graces of Charles II, and in 1674 Morgan was knighted and appointed lieutenant governor of Jamaica, a post he occupied until his death in 1688. As an officer of the Crown Morgan lived soberly and apparently performed his official duties in an exemplary manner. So completely did he sever all connections with his turbulent past that when any of his former followers appeared before him charged with buccaneering he virtuously inflicted on them the maximum penalties prescribed by law.

Although the treaty of America outlawed the English buccaneers it failed to put an immediate end to their activities. Raids on the Spanish colonies by bands of French and English sea rovers continued with undiminished vigor, but their character changed after Morgan abandoned his predatory career. With the exception of his overland march against Panama Morgan had confined his operations to the Caribbean, while his successors directed most of their attacks against the Pacific coast. No single leader took Morgan's place. Instead, various groups of buccaneers joined forces under several commanders of approximately equal rank, an arrangement which inevitably led to constant rivalries and kaleidoscopic changes, schisms and reshufflings.

For a few years after Morgan's retirement the Spanish colonies enjoyed peace broken only by occasional minor raids, but from 1679 to 1688 one incursion after another kept the Indies in a constant state of alarm. The first of these was an attack on Puerto Bello in 1679 led by John Coxon, Bartholomew Sharp, and three other English captains. On the way they were joined by a French vessel commanded by La Sound. The buccaneers landed some distance from Puerto Bello, marched along the coast for three nights, and sacked the town. Early in 1680 Coxon and Sharp, with Captains Peter Harris, Richard Sawkins, Edmund Cook, Mackett, and Robert Alleston, organized a much more impressive raid on Darién. Their first objective was Real de Santa María, a settlement on the Tuyra River used by the Spaniards for the storage of gold from the rich mines of Cana. With seven ships they sailed from Jamaica to

Golden Island in what later came to be known as Caledonia Bay. This expedition was distinguished by the presence of three men who afterwards wrote vivid accounts of their exploits: William Dampier, Lionel Wafer, and Basil Ringrose. The reports of Dampier and Wafer are particularly valuable, though their authors occupied only minor posts in the enterprise. Dampier was a scientist interested primarily in geography, botany, zoology, and the laws governing winds and tides rather than adventure or gain. He shared the toil as well as the profits of his associates but not their quarrels or debauches. If a man of Dampier's education and attainments seems out of place in such rough company it must be remembered that in the seventeenth century there was no way in which he could have pursued his researches in those distant regions except as a member of some buccaneering expedition. Wafer was also an educated man, a surgeon whose profession made him a valuable asset to the frequently wounded and ailing buccaneers. Wafer was blessed with a sharp eye, an excellent memory, an amiable disposition, and an unusual ability to make friends with the suspicious natives.

From Golden Island the buccaneers crossed to the mainland on April 5, 1680. Guided by Andrés, a Cuna Indian chief and self-styled "emperor" of Darién, they attacked and burned Real de Santa María on April 15, but the Spanish garrison had received warning and hidden the gold. A few days later the raiders reached the Pacific, embarked in canoes, and captured some small Spanish vessels in which they sailed into the Bay of Panama and blockaded the city, then under construction on its new site. A Spanish force in three ships challenged the English marauders but was defeated after a desperate struggle. This sea battle inaugurated a disastrous period of changing leadership and successive mass desertions which ultimately destroyed all semblance of unity among the buccaneers. In the fight Harris was killed and Coxon was accused of cowardice, while Sawkins was hailed as the hero of the day. After a bitter quarrel Coxon departed with 70 men, and Sawkins took his place as head of the expedition. Sawkins's triumph lasted but a few weeks, for on May 23 he was killed in a raid on Pueblo Nuevo (now Remedios), and Sharp succeeded to the command. The prompt withdrawal of Sawkins's friends who refused to serve under another leader, combined with the previous defection of Coxon's crew and a number of deaths from wounds and disease, left Sharp with only 146 men.

On June 6, 1680 Sharp's buccaneers sailed south in quest of plunder, captured a few Spanish ships, and raided two or three.

towns on the coasts of Peru and Chile; but profits were scanty and the men discontented. On Christmas Day they reached one of the islands of the Juan Fernández group, where after another violent disagreement Sharp was deposed, and John Watling took command. After only a month Watling was killed during an unsuccessful attack on Arica in northern Chile, and the discomfited raiders sailed northward again to Isla de Plata. There still another dispute resulted in the resumption of the leadership by Sharp and the consequent withdrawal of 44 of the remaining buccaneers. With about 70 loyal members of his crew Sharp cruised and plundered in the south Pacific. A fair amount of booty fell into their hands, but through ignorance Sharp's men threw away their richest prize, a shipload of 700 ingots of a metal which the buccaneers, supposing it to be lead or tin, contemptuously discarded only to discover when it was too late that the single bar they had kept was pure silver. After a stormy passage round Cape Horn Sharp eventually reached England, where he was tried for piracy and acquitted.

Dampier and Wafer had opposed Sharp's reinstatement and elected to join the disgruntled buccaneers who "chose rather to return in Boats to the *Isthmus,* and go back again a toilsom Journey over Land, than stay under a Captain in whom we experienc'd neither Courage nor Conduct." [9] They landed on the shores of the Gulf of San Miguel on May 1, 1681 and started across the isthmus on foot. Four days later an accidental explosion of gunpowder severely injured Wafer's leg, but he limped on until a Negro slave assigned to carry his surgical kit ran away with all his liniments. The buccaneers, leaving Wafer at an Indian village with four other white men who could no longer keep up with their companions, pushed on towards the Atlantic. At first the Indians treated their charges kindly, and Wafer's injury healed in three weeks; but when the Indian guides sent ahead with the main party failed to return within the allotted time the natives prepared to burn the helpless hostages alive. The opportune arrival of the Cuna chieftain Lacenta averted the sacrifice; Wafer and his colleagues were released, but after wandering in circles for more than a week they returned, starving and drenched, to the village. This time their reception was more cordial, since during their absence the missing guides had arrived with generous presents.

Once more the five stranded buccaneers set out across the isthmus but were stopped at another village by Lacenta, who told them they could not reach the Atlantic during the rainy season and must remain where they were for several months. The chief's watchfulness made escape impossible until Wafer won his own and his companions' freedom by a timely demonstration of surgical skill: "It so happen'd, that one of *Lacenta's* Wives being indisposed, was to be let Blood; which the *Indians* perform in this manner. The Patient is seated on a Stone in the River, and one with a small Bow shoots little Arrows into the naked Body of the Patient, up and down . . . as fast as he can, and not missing any part. . . . I . . . told *Lacenta* . . . I would shew him a better way, without putting the Patient to so much Torment. . . . I bound up her Arm with a piece of Bark, and with my Lancet breached a Vein. But this rash attempt had like to have cost me my Life. For *Lacenta* . . . swore by his Tooth, that if she did otherwise than well, he would have my Heart's Blood. . . ." [10] Luckily the operation was successful, and the grateful chieftain showered gifts and honors upon Wafer, who "was carried from Plantation to Plantation, and lived in great Splendour and Repute, administring both Physick and Phlebotomy to those that wanted. . . ." [11] Lacenta's exuberant friendliness proved as inconvenient as his former hostility, for the Indian was now unwilling to part with this surgeon who could perform miracles. After some months Wafer persuaded his host to release him and his fellow captives, promising to return and marry Lacenta's daughter, who "was not then marriageable." [12] The five Englishmen were escorted to the Atlantic coast, where they were soon picked up by the main body of buccaneers.

The happy outcome of Wafer's sojourn among the Cuna Indians must be regarded as a remarkable tribute not only to his professional skill but to his extraordinary ability to adapt himself to the customs and prejudices of the natives. The Cuna tribes were then and remain today traditionally inhospitable and independent; before Wafer's day the only European who had succeeded in winning their complete confidence was Balboa, and after Wafer no white man was ever again so fully favored with their friendship.

When Wafer and his four companions rejoined the other buccaneers their two ships, together with some vessels belonging to French *flibustiers,* cruised in the Caribbean for several months. Late in 1682 the ship in which Dampier sailed anchored in Chesapeake Bay, and the crew settled on shore for the winter. In April 1683 they were joined by the other shipload of buccaneers, including Wafer, and the united parties worked out plans for a new expedition into the Pacific. They set sail on August 23 and, after capturing two more ships, entered the Straits of Magellan on February 6, 1684. A leisurely voyage up the Pacific coast brought them to the Gulf of Nicoya in Costa Rica, where their captain, John Cook, died. Under his successor, Edward Davis, the buccaneers raided the Spanish ports in South America without substantial profit. The numerous islands off the coast were left in peace, for they were innocent of Spanish settlements — a deficiency which led Wafer to conclude that the islands must be worthless, since "to be sure if there were any Hony the Bees would be there. . . ." [13]

In October Davis was joined by Captain Swan, an English trader turned buccaneer because his legitimate commercial ventures had gone awry. In February 1685 they sailed together into Panama Bay, where they were reinforced by a contingent of *flibustiers* commanded by Grogniet, L'Escuyer, and other captains as well as by a party of Englishmen led by Captain Townley. The combined French and English forces now comprised 960 men and ten ships, with which the leaders determined to risk an attack upon the approaching treasure fleet from Peru. But the Spaniards, forewarned, had already landed the bullion at a small port far to the west and with fourteen ships and three times as many guns as the buccaneers could boast were more than a match for their enemies. On May 29 a running fight took place. The result was inconclusive; from dawn to dark the Spanish fleet chased the buccaneers round Panama Bay but withdrew the next day, and the battle caused little damage on either side. The French and English captains dared not steer their ships within range of the Spanish batteries on shore. The defenders of the new city of Panama had found it difficult to decide which side of the town needed the strongest protection: when the city was first rebuilt the vivid memory of Morgan's destructive raid on old Panama induced the Spaniards to concentrate all their artillery on the landward side of the walls, but the advent of the buccaneers under Coxon, Sawkins, and Sharp in 1680 had awakened the authorities to danger from the sea, and when the raiders returned five years later they found Panama defended by cannon on all sides.

True to buccaneer form harsh words followed the drawn battle of Panama Bay. When the English captains taunted Grogniet with cowardice the *flibustiers* retired to continue operations by themselves and sacked Remedios, Nicoya, David, and other small settlements on or near the Pacific coast. Later Townley threw in his lot with Grogniet, and together they invaded Nicaragua and burned Granada in April 1686. In September Townley died, and the *flibustiers* headed south towards Ecuador.

Meanwhile the English buccaneers under Davis and Swan had left Panama and in August 1685 attacked and plundered the city of León in Nicaragua. Swan and Davis then separated, for once without a quarrel, and the two chroniclers, Dampier and Wafer, also parted, Dampier sailing with Swan across the Pacific to the

Philippines while Wafer remained with Davis. After a long sojourn
in the East Indies Dampier made his way back to England in 1691.
For more than a year Davis cruised in the Pacific, raiding coast
towns and plundering Spanish merchantmen. In May 1687 he
entered the harbor of Guayaquil just in time to join Grogniet and
his *flibustiers* in an attack on the city, during which Grogniet was
killed. Here the raiders again separated: all of the French and many
of the English buccaneers sailed northward to the Gulf of Fonseca,
scuttled their ships, crossed Nicaragua, and in time drifted back
to the West Indies. Davis himself went south, rounded the Horn,
and after somewhat mysteriously losing his vessel and most of his
crew in the Caribbean landed in Pennsylvania with Wafer and one
other companion. Here in June 1688 they were arrested by the
English authorities, convicted of piracy, and imprisoned at James-
town for a year. After an absence of more than a decade Wafer returned to England in 1690.

The great days of the buccaneers were now over. When in 1689
a swing of the political pendulum temporarily united England and
Spain against France, French *flibustiers* and English buccaneers
parted company and never again acted in concert. The last major
exploit of the seventeenth-century raiders was the capture and
plunder of Cartagena in May 1697 by a force of French regulars
commanded by Baron de Pointis and assisted by some 1200 *flibustiers*. After the treaty of Ryswick in September 1697 English and
French colonial ports were closed to the buccaneers who, deprived
of their refuges on land, could no longer continue their activities
at sea. Some chose less adventurous careers as planters, traders, or
merchant mariners; others degenerated into common pirates whose
descendants, outlawed and hunted by all European governments,
preyed sporadically upon legitimate commerce throughout the
eighteenth century.

Some of the literary by-products of buccaneering were more important to future generations, though perhaps not to the raiders
themselves or to their victims, than the actual destruction of life
and property. The journals of Dampier and Wafer, published in
the last years of the seventeenth century, gave the world a more
complete and accurate description of tropical America and did
more to dispel erroneous conceptions of its inhabitants, fauna,
flora, and topography than any books previously written or for
that matter any published within the ensuing hundred years.
Dampier's scientific objectivity in a period of almost universal
ignorance and credulity stamps him as an observer far in advance
of his time. His healthy skepticism concerning fantastic interpre-

tations of natural phenomena is refreshingly illustrated by his comment on the belief, commonly accepted in his day, that the Atlantic and Pacific Oceans were connected by an underground channel beneath the isthmus: "The great Tides in the Gulph of *St. Michael* have doubtless been the occasion of that Opinion . . . that the Isthmus of *Darien* is like an Arched Bridge, under which the Tides make their constant Courses, as duly as they do under *London-Bridge*. And . . . some have said, that there are continual and strange Noises made by those Subterranean Fluxes and Refluxes . . . and also that Ships sailing in the Bay of *Panama* are toss'd to and fro at a prodigious rate . . . at other times they are drawn or suck'd up, as 'twere, in a Whirl-Pool and ready to be carried under Ground into the *North-Seas,* with all Sails standing. . . . But if this were so, 'tis much that I and those that I was with, should not have heard or seen something of it. . . ." [14]

Between 1699 and 1711 Dampier made two more voyages round the world and in the double rôle of privateer and official explorer undertook a cruise among the islands of the south Pacific. In September 1704 his ship dropped anchor near one of the Juan Fernández Islands off the coast of Chile, where the sailing master, Alexander Selkirk, who had quarreled with his captain, was put ashore at his own request. Before the ship sailed Selkirk regretted his imprudence but was refused permission to re-embark and remained alone on the island until February 1709, when he was rescued by another English vessel in which Dampier was again serving, this time as pilot. Thus Dampier twice participated in the famous adventure upon whch Defoe based *Robinson Crusoe*.

Chapter 8. Scots Colony

ALMOST before the ink had dried on the treaty of Ryswick a new incursion, outwardly peaceable but actually much more formidable in its implications than the violent raids of the buccaneers, threatened the Spanish empire overseas. The ostensible purpose of this project, the establishment of a Scottish colony on the Isthmus of Darién, was trade; but having once secured a firm foothold the settlers would have been in a position to extend their sovereignty over the rest of the isthmus, destroy the Spanish commercial monopoly, divert the lion's share of traffic with both the West and the East Indies to their own ships and ports, and ultimately control the Pacific and Caribbean sea lanes. The consequences were clearly foreseen by the wisest of the Scottish leaders, William Paterson, who wrote in 1701 that if English and Scottish colonists should occupy the isthmian ports, "through them will flow at least two-thirds of what both Indies yield to Christendom. . . . Thus these *doors* of the seas, and the keys of the universe, would . . . be capable of enabling their possessors to give laws to both oceans, and to become the arbiters of the commercial world. . . ." [1]

But Paterson's dream never crystallized into reality, and Spain maintained its ever-weakening hold on the isthmus for another century. The government of England not only withheld its patronage from the Scots colony but actively opposed it, and without English aid the enterprise was doomed from the start. Although England and Scotland had been joined under a single Crown since the accession of James I in 1603 the two kingdoms were still governed by separate Parliaments and remained in effect independent of each other until they achieved permanent union in 1707. Had that union occurred ten years earlier the English government would probably have made the colonization its own and, with the help of its powerful navy, carried it through to a successful conclusion.

The accession of William III in 1688 coincided with a sudden increase of wealth in which Scotland shared for the first time, and although the boom collapsed in 1696 half a dozen years of unwonted prosperity had enabled the thrifty Scots to put aside substantial savings. The Darién venture appeared to present an ideal opportunity for the profitable investment of these nest eggs. In June 1693 the Scottish Parliament passed an act authorizing the formation of stock companies to engage in trade with any nation at peace with England and Scotland and to establish trading posts or colonies in suitable locations. In conformity with the general terms of this act a "Company of Scotland Tradeing to Affrica and the Indies" was organized in 1695 by a group of wealthy London merchants, both English and Scottish, of whom the most prominent was William Paterson.

Paterson was born in Dumfriesshire in 1658. Little is known of his youth except that he lived for some years in the West Indies, where he acquired a fortune, a keen interest in the commercial problems of the Caribbean, and the conviction that the American isthmus was destined to become a vital link in the trade routes of the world. After his return to England Paterson's financial genius soon won him a position of influence among London business men. He repeatedly urged the establishment of a stable and uniform currency system and drew up a comprehensive plan, adopted in 1694, for the organization of the Bank of England. He served as a member of the bank's original board of directors but resigned in 1695 after a series of disagreements with his colleagues. On many subjects besides finance Paterson held enlightened views far in advance of his age. He advocated religious liberty, free trade, universal education, public libraries, and the abolition of imprisonment for debt. He abstained from liquor in a period and country excessively addicted to strong drink. For years he ardently sponsored union between England and Scotland and played an influential part in the negotiations that led to its consummation.

The Scots attempted to justify their invasion on the grounds that Spanish claims deserved recognition by other powers only in territories actually conquered and settled by Spaniards; that the Darién or Cuna Indians "were never subdued, nor receiv'd any *Spanish* Governour or Garrison amongst them"; [2] and that therefore the Isthmus of Darién was open to colonization by anyone. This ingenious argument failed to take into account conditions in the New World. While the fierce resistance of the natives had indeed prevented permanent Spanish settlement of a few miles of Darién coast, the adjacent areas on either side were undeniably occupied by Spaniards, and in the vast sparsely populated expanse of the Americas the existence of such scattered gaps — many of much larger extent than Darién — could not reasonably be held to invalidate Spain's claim to sovereignty over the entire region.

At first William III appeared to favor the plan, and the company founders, encouraged by hopes of official backing in England, prepared to finance their undertaking. But the vigorous protests of the Spanish ambassador combined with the no less energetic opposition of the East India Company caused William to reconsider and turned a large majority of the English Parliament against it. Most of the English subscribers, unwilling to risk official displeasure, hastily withdrew their pledges. Unable to procure financial support in London, Hamburg, or Amsterdam, Paterson now reduced the company's capital to £400,000, all of which he proposed to obtain in Scotland. Between February 26 and August 1, 1696 about 1400 Scottish investors enthusiastically subscribed the entire amount — on paper. But only a small part was paid in at once, and subsequent calls found the overoptimistic subscribers unable to meet their obligations in full. The total sum eventually collected came to £219,094.

English opposition had inflamed the national pride of the Scots and overborne their native caution to such an extent that for a time the venture took on the aspect of a holy crusade rather than of a prosaic commercial enterprise. Sober calculation would have demonstrated that £400,000 — equivalent in purchasing power to many millions of pounds today — was an excessive sum for Scotland to raise alone. Yet the venture might not have failed altogether had Paterson been permitted to retain the leadership. But at this juncture he became involved in an unfortunate financial transaction which, though his own conduct in the affair appears to have been entirely blameless, caused something of a scandal and lost him the confidence of the other directors of the Scottish company. Although he was finally allowed to accompany the expedition to Darién as a volunteer he held no official position, exercised no authority, and was therefore in no way responsible for the fatal mistakes that subsequently wrecked the colony.

Almost two years elapsed between the closing of the subscription lists in Edinburgh and the departure of the first group of settlers. During the interval ships were built and stores collected. Inexperience and poor judgment combined with graft filled the company's warehouses with a hodge-podge of ill-chosen supplies, defective in quality, often insufficient in quantity, and on the whole quite unsuitable for tropical use. Hogsheads of spirits occupied a vast amount of precious cargo space, with the result that stores of food and other necessaries were cut down far below the required minimum. For the spiritual edification of the colonists — and presumably of the illiterate Indians — 1500 Bibles were taken along. The Scots, accustomed to a cold climate, burdened themselves with a varied assortment of inappropriate wearing apparel. Walter Harris (or Herries), who accompanied the expedition and afterwards became one of its most venomous critics, asserted that the useless items included "Perewigs 4000, some long, some short, Campaigns, *Spanish* Bobs and Natural ones; and . . . being made of *Highlanders* Hair, which is Blanch'd, with the Rain and Sun, when they came to be open'd in the *West Indies,* they lookt like so many of *Samsons* Fireships that he sent amongst the *Philistines,* and could be of no use to the Collony, if it were not to mix with their Lyme when they Plaster'd the Walls of their Houses. . . ." [3]

So many applications from would-be colonists poured in that the directors were able to select those whose qualifications seemed most likely to contribute to the success of the enterprise. That they did not always choose wisely appears obvious, since so many of the settlers afterwards failed to measure up to the exacting standards of pioneer life. Yet among the 1200 who sailed with the first expedition were many admirable men and women who under proper leadership would have made excellent colonists. The spiteful Harris certainly exaggerated when he sneered that "none . . . that were Worth the hanging would list themselves, and we were oblig'd to take Tag, Rag and Bobtail. . . ." [4] He had even less justification for his scurrilous misrepresentation of Paterson and his heartless comment on the death of Paterson's wife soon after her arrival in Darién: "His former Wife being at rest . . . he wanted a Help that was meet for him, and not being very nice, went no further than the Red-fac'd Coffee-woman, a Widow in Burchin-Lane, whom he afterwards carry'd to the *Isthmus* of *Darien;* and at her first landing thrust her about Seven Foot under Ground." [5]

The three ships, with two much smaller vessels — a pink and a snow — sailed out of the Firth of Forth on July 19, 1698. On October 30 they anchored off the coast of Darién. 44 of the colonists and crew had died at sea, and many more were ill. The future looked black, but the downcast Scots were somewhat cheered by an encounter with two boatloads of convivial Indians, "very free and not at all shey. . . . They got drunk and lay on board all night. . . ." [6] A few days later the Scots discovered an excellent harbor which they named Caledonia Bay and founded their settlement of New Edinburgh on a sandspit. For defense they dug a moat across the neck of the peninsula, erected the wooden fort of St. Andrew at the tip, and mounted a battery of 16 naval guns.

Huts were rapidly constructed and the sick cared for. The Cuna chieftain Andrés, who had aided the buccaneers in 1680, visited the colony and agreed to an alliance with the newcomers, who subsequently negotiated similar pacts with other Indian leaders. Another guest who appeared only ten days after the colonists landed was less welcome. An English man-of-war commanded by Captain Richard Long arrived from Jamaica with orders to inform William III concerning the activities and intentions of the settlers. Long's report on the strength of the colony and the difficulty of dislodging it caused the English government to instruct all its colonial governors to abstain from trade with New Edinburgh and to lend no assistance whatever to the Scots.

Meanwhile the colonists organized a local government headed by seven councilors. Petty jealousies prevented the election of a long-term chief executive, so each councilor in turn served as president for one week only — a system hardly conducive to orderly and consistent administration. During his brief term of office each president seemed determined to reverse the policy of his predecessor, and the colony's affairs were soon in a state of hopeless confusion. Factional strife led to bitter personal quarrels which severe penalties did little to check: "He who shall use any provoking or upbraiding words or gestures, or shall give the ly . . . to another of equal quality . . . shall, besides giving honourable satisfaction . . . upon his knees, be . . . condemned to hard labour . . . for . . . six moneths." [7] Imprisonment awaited any colonist "who shall blaspheme . . . or use any curse or imprecation. . . ." [8]

In spite of 32 additional deaths during the first seven weeks at New Edinburgh the council wrote optimistically to Scotland and urged the prompt dispatch of a second expedition. But the colonists continued to die like flies, and Paterson himself suffered an attack of fever that almost proved fatal. A shortage of essential supplies bred discontent; sodden drunkenness unrelieved by any compensating Latin gayety only added to the gloom; interminable sermons by long-faced ministers of the kirk provided the sole entertainment. On top of all this fear of imminent attack by Spanish forces kept the colony in a constant state of alarm. Andrés sent warnings of troop concentrations at Puerto Bello and of Spanish warships at Cartagena. The threat failed to materialize at once, and the only encounter that actually took place between this first Scots expedition and the Spaniards was a minor skirmish in which two colonists were killed and several wounded. The Spaniards hesitated to attack because they could not at first bring themselves to believe the assurances of William III that he disapproved of and would not protect the settlement.

With the advent of the rainy season conditions became so intolerable that the council decided to abandon New Edinburgh and return to Scotland. Paterson, too ill to do more than protest feebly, cast the only negative vote. On June 16, 1699 the survivors set sail from Darién. The voyage home turned out to be even more disastrous than the outward journey. Of the five vessels, the snow had already fallen into the hands of the Spaniards, and the pink leaked so badly that it had to be abandoned. One of the larger ships reached Jamaica with her crew so depleted that it could proceed no farther. In August the two other ships, *Unicorn* and *Caledonia*, limped into the harbor of New York, whence Captain Robert Drummond of the *Caledonia* wrote: "In our passage . . . hither . . . I have hove overboard 105 Corps. . . . I have buried eleven since I came heire already. . . ." [9] *Unicorn* had lost approximately the same number and was in such a dilapidated condition that it could not risk the Atlantic crossing. *Caledonia*, the only ship of the first expedition to complete the homeward voyage, was patched up in New York and sailed on October 12. Of the 1200 original colonists 744 had died, many were stranded in Jamaica, and some of the survivors chose to remain in New York. Paterson, now recovered from his fever, was among the few who returned to Scotland.

While the *Caledonia* was being overhauled in New York the refugees received word that the directors in Scotland had already sent out three relief ships. The first of these, a small brigantine with a cargo of provisions, was wrecked off the coast of Scotland in February 1699. The others, *Olive Branch* and *Hopeful Binning of Bo'ness* (a contraction of Borrowstounness, a seaport on the Firth of Forth), set sail a few months later with additional supplies and 300 settlers, who reached New Edinburgh in August only to find the colony deserted. Some of the new arrivals advocated resettlement of the village, others clamored for an immediate withdrawal. Within a few days the accidental burning of the *Olive Branch* with its entire cargo put an end to the debate, and the members of the second Scottish expedition hastily crowded on board the *Hopeful Binning* and sailed to Jamaica, where they remained and where many of them soon died.

The third and last group of Scots colonists, 1300 in number, sailed from the Clyde on September 24, 1699 in four ships: *Rising Sun, Duke of Hamilton, Hope,* and *Hope of Bo'ness.* The recurrence of "hope" and "hopeful" in these names may have been considered a good omen, but this third expedition encountered no better fortune than its forerunners. Before the settlers reached New Edinburgh on November 30, 160 had died. The discovery of what was supposed to be a deposit of gold threw the colony into a frenzy of excitement, soon turned to bitter disappointment: "That which was called gold dust is indeed very thick . . . but it proves really nothing att all but shiny stuff [pyrites?], verifying the proverb, 'tis not all gold that glisters. . . ." [10]

The new colony was governed by a council of four and like its predecessor was soon torn by dissension. The Spaniards, convinced at last that William III really had no interest in the Scottish venture, threatened to attack, but their plans were frustrated by the prompt action of one of the councilors, Alexander Campbell, who led a force of colonists and Indians through the jungle, took the Spanish camp by surprise, and dispersed the soldiers. The Scots' brief triumph turned once more to alarm on February 23 when Spanish warships anchored in the bay. A series of skirmishes slowly broke down the resistance of the settlers, already weakened by fever and a scarcity of supplies. On March 18 all of the councilmen except Campbell voted to capitulate, but the haughty Spanish commander, Juan Díaz Pimienta, imposed such harsh conditions that the Scots indignantly withdrew their offer. The besiegers then surrounded the fort, depriving the colonists of access to their only water supply. When on March 30 Pimienta again proposed to negotiate, this time on unexpectedly generous terms, the Scots surrendered. Pimienta allowed them to keep their arms, ammunition, and personal property, and on April 11, 1700 they embarked with colors flying and drums beating and set sail for home. In a few years the flimsy town of New Edinburgh melted away under the tropical downpours and disappeared, but vestiges of the moat are said to be still visible, and on the maps traces of the short-lived settlement survive in the names Caledonia Bay and Puerto Escocés — Scots Harbor.

None of the four ships ever reached Scotland. *Hope of Bo'ness* leaked so profusely that her captain barely succeeded in keeping her afloat as far as Cartagena, where he sold her to the Spaniards for a small sum. *Hope* went to pieces off the rocky coast of Cuba. *Duke of Hamilton* and *Rising Sun* arrived at Charleston in South Carolina but were completely wrecked by a hurricane that destroyed most of the shipping in the harbor. The passengers and crew of the *Duke* were rescued, but almost all on board of the other ship were drowned. Among the few saved from the *Rising*

Sun was a great-great-great-great-grandfather of Theodore Roosevelt, the Reverend Archibald Stobo, who had been invited to preach that day by some Scottish residents of Charleston and had already gone ashore with his daughter Jean when the storm broke. Only a handful of the 1300 members of the third expedition eventually drifted back to Scotland. 940 had died on the voyage or in Darién, and most of the survivors either chose or were obliged by circumstances to settle in the New World.

The tragic failure of their repeated attempts to colonize the isthmus profoundly shocked the Scottish people. A wave of furious resentment against the English, whom the Scots blamed for the catastrophe, swept Scotland from end to end; although Paterson, scrupulously fair-minded, endeavored to calm his enraged compatriots by pointing out that at least some of the fault lay with themselves, whose mismanagement had certainly contributed to the ruin of the enterprise. But Paterson was too practical a business man to content himself with lectures on abstract justice. Nothing could be done to restore the dead or expatriated colonists to their families, but part of the squandered money might be recovered for the bankrupt shareholders. For several years Paterson exerted all his influence to secure indemnities from the English government. By an agreement arrived at after much heated discussion the stockholders of the Company of Scotland were finally reimbursed in full with 5% interest. This concession mollified the Scots and removed one of the chief obstacles to political union, which took place in 1707.

Paterson was keenly interested in the interoceanic transit problem, but while fully aware of the advantages of a canal he foresaw no immediate prospect of its construction and emphasized instead the importance of good roads. Two routes or "passes" seemed to him especially promising: one connecting Panama with the Chagres at Cruces, the other from Caledonia Bay to the Gulf of San Miguel by way of the Tubugantí, Chucunaque, and Tuyra Rivers. Two other sites, somewhat inferior, might be considered: from the mouth of the Río Concepción east of Point San Blas to the Pacific near Chepo, and from the Gulf of Urabá to the Gulf of San Miguel by the Atrato, Cacarica, Paya, and Tuyra valleys. At the bottom of the scale he placed Nicaragua and an overland communication between Vera Cruz and Acapulco.

Paterson's contemptuous dismissal of the Nicaragua transit and his omission of Tehuantepec betray the inadequacy of his information. Although he diligently questioned every explorer he met

and read as many books on the New World as he could find his
knowledge of American topography was actually inferior in many
respects to that displayed by Gómara and Galvão, whose descriptions of interoceanic routes antedated his own by 150 years. Assuming that Englishmen would eventually control the isthmus,
Paterson included in his treatise a warning against the establishment of another commercial monopoly on the Spanish model. England must command the seas and the strategic ports, but the privileges of trade should be free to all nations on reasonable terms. A
selfish policy, he prophesied, would invite strife and retaliation,
perhaps even the construction of a canal by an enemy power: "A
total exclusion, or exorbitant duty or difficulty, would . . . gradually eat or break through stone walls. . . . The greatness of the
prospect [of trade] might move and enable them [rival nations],
not only to encounter the difficulty and hazard of long and dangerous voyages by sea, or travels by land, but even to turn the
course of rivers, drain lakes and morasses, to dig or blow up the
very rocks and mountains, or as (it is pretended) *Hannibal* did,
invent a new way or ways to melt them. . . ."[11]

Chapter 9. The Eighteenth Century

SPAIN, weakened and impoverished by incessant warfare, slipping gradually down from her proud eminence as the first power in Europe to a position of relative insignificance, lost touch step by step with her overseas possessions. Trade between Europe and the Pacific coast passed into the hands of English, French, and Dutch merchants, who to evade the vexatious restrictions imposed by Spanish colonial authorities on the isthmus diverted most of their shipping to the longer passage through the Straits of Magellan or round Cape Horn. With the abandonment of the Spanish convoy system in 1748 the once flourishing commerce of Panama and Puerto Bello declined to almost nothing. By completely reversing the dog-in-the-manger policy of his predecessors Charles III energetically tried to re-establish commercial relations with the colonies. In 1765 he abolished the Cádiz monopoly and opened eight other Spanish ports to trade with the West Indies. Before 1780 he had granted commercial privileges to practically all the important American ports then in existence except those of Venezuela, which still remained under the exclusive control of the Guipúzcoa company. Unfortunately these wise reforms came too late to produce more than a languid revival of Spanish enterprise. Other maritime nations had already captured by force the trade that Spain had for so long refused to share.

Notwithstanding the commercial paralysis that crept year by year over Central America the eighteenth century was by no means wholly devoid of incident. Sporadic foreign raids continued to plague the colonies. During periods of official peace these depredations were conducted by stray remnants of the once powerful buccaneer groups; in time of war with Spain enemy naval squadrons harried the coasts. The incident of "Jenkins's Ear" provided England with a pretext for a vigorous naval attack on the isthmus. In 1731 an English brig commanded by Robert Jenkins was boarded in the West Indies by the crew of a Spanish *guardacostas* or coast patrol whose captain plundered the brig and cut off one of Jenkins's ears. For some years Jenkins aired his grievance in England without exciting much official sympathy, but by 1738 his complaints, reinforced by those of other traders who had suffered at Spanish hands, succeeded in kindling public indignation. Edward Vernon, a naval officer and at one time a member of Parliament, urged a declaration of war against Spain and secured permission to lead a squadron against Puerto Bello. On November 21, 1739 his fleet entered the harbor, opened fire on the fort of San Felipe, and captured it in a few hours. The other strongholds surrendered the next day, and Vernon occupied the town and demolished the forts. Early in 1740 he resumed the campaign with an unsuccessful attack on Cartagena. On March 22 his squadron anchored off the mouth of the Chagres and bombarded the fortress of San Lorenzo, which surrendered two days later.

Emboldened by his easy victories, Vernon now planned an attack on the city of Panama. On March 28, 1742 he appeared once more at Puerto Bello. The town, unable to resist because its harbor defenses were still in ruins, dispatched a delegation to Vernon, who "sent their deputies back that evening, highly pleased . . . and desired their company on the next morning to breakfast with me, where they came accordingly. . . . I sent . . . fourscore soldiers . . . to take possession of the King's custom house . . . and I had the same evening a visit from all the clergy, who seemed all in good humour. . . ."[1] While these social amenities were in progress Vernon called a council to discuss the proposed expedition to Panama. To his profound disgust his officers vetoed the project, and the fleet sailed back to Jamaica without striking a blow.

Nevertheless Vernon's appearance at Puerto Bello served a useful purpose by diverting Spanish attention from the activities of another English naval officer, Commodore George Anson, who was busily raiding ports on the Pacific coast of South America. Later that year Anson crossed the Pacific in his flagship *Centurion* — the only vessel remaining of the six he started with — and on June 20, 1743 captured the Spanish galleon *Nuestra Señora de Covadonga* bound from the Philippines to Acapulco with a cargo valued at 1,500,000 pesos. Having disposed of his rich prize at Macao, he sailed round the Cape of Good Hope back to England. Anson's seizure of the galleon enriched not only himself and his crew but indirectly the world; for among the ship's papers he discovered a number of useful maps and charts as well as a secret manual of navigation, compiled by Cabrera Bueno and printed at Manila in 1734, which made available to other nations a wealth of information concerning Pacific trade routes hitherto jealously guarded by Spain.

The unfortunate town of Puerto Bello again became the victim of English aggression in 1745, when Captain Kinhills attacked the battered port. His bombardment served only to stimulate Spanish efforts to reconstruct the Atlantic defenses, and by 1752 the Puerto Bello forts as well as San Lorenzo were rebuilt and once more strongly garrisoned.

In 1779 Spain joined France in support of the rebellious British colonies in North America, and England retaliated with a naval expedition designed to separate the northern Spanish American provinces from those south of Lake Nicaragua. Major Polson commanded the British forces while the naval operations were placed in charge of a 21-year-old post captain, Horatio Nelson. "I intend," Nelson wrote, "to possess the Lake of Nicaragua, which for the present may be looked upon as the inland Gibraltar of Spanish America. As it commands the only water pass between the two oceans . . . by our possession of it Spanish America is divided in two." [2]

The British troops, disembarking at San Juan del Norte early in April 1780, paddled up the San Juan River to Castillo Viejo, a Spanish fort located some 80 miles (by the winding river) from the Atlantic and 45 miles from the lake. After a short siege the garrison surrendered to the vastly superior enemy forces on April 29. Nelson's youthful egotism impelled him to brag a little of his first victory: "Major Polson . . . will tell you of my exertions: how I . . . carried troops in boats one hundred [*sic*] miles up a river, which none but Spaniards since the time of the buccaneers had ever ascended. . . . It will then be told how I boarded . . . an outpost of the Enemy, situated on an Island in the river; that I made batteries, and afterwards fought them, and was a principal cause of our success. . . ." [3] His triumph was brief, for with the onset of the rainy season fever ravaged the English troops. Of 200 men from Nelson's own ship only 10 survived, and Nelson himself was invalided home so ill that he never fully recovered his health. In January 1781 the invaders abandoned Castillo Viejo and withdrew to Jamaica, having accomplished nothing. Afterwards Nelson blamed the failure on the late start: "Had the expedition arrived at San Juan's harbour in . . . January, the violent torrents would have subsided, and of course the whole Army would not have had occasion, which was the case in April, to get wet three or four times a day in dragging the boats." [4]

A grandiose paper project conceived by one James Creassy in 1790 might have tempted British imperialists, but the government apparently ignored it. His plan contemplated the conquest of the isthmus by combined sea and land forces and the establishment of a transit under British control: "On this extraordinary Isthmus . . . the standard of Liberty should be erected, for all who are groaning under Spanish Slavery to flock to. . . . New Colonies would . . . soon be planted . . . and all the springs of wealth and Industry . . . flow in torrents from every part of the Globe into the Mother Country. . . . New discoveries would be opening daily to employ the ingenious, and the enterprizing spirit of this Commercial Nation, and new life and energy would be added to this Drooping Country. . . . If this Passage is once secured to Great Britain, I doubt not but she would soon . . . cut or form a canal through to the South Sea. . . ." [5]

Throughout the century misfortune haunted the gold mines at Cana in Darién, the richest on the isthmus. In August 1702 about 500 English raiders and 300 Indians marched overland from the Atlantic coast to Cana, and most of the Spaniards fled, taking their gold with them. The Englishmen attempted to operate the mines with the forced labor of Negro slaves abandoned by their owners, but the output proved disappointing, and after a week they returned to their ships. In 1725 the Spaniards were again temporarily driven from Cana by a violent uprising of the Cuna Indians, and two years later the collapse of the poorly buttressed galleries engulfed large sections of the mines and materially diminished their production. For the next 50 years attacks by isolated bands of English and French marauders, as well as savage onslaughts by the unpacified natives, frequently interrupted operations at Cana. Many Spanish owners of mines and plantations left the district, and those who remained dared not venture out of their houses except in groups of six or more. To remedy this situation the viceroy of New Granada ordered the construction of several forts on the Atlantic coast and in the interior of Darién. The work was carried out in 1785 under the supervision of the governor of Panama, Colonel Andrés de Ariza, who built and garrisoned outposts at Molineca and Real de Santa María on the Tuyra River, at Yavisa on the Chucunaque, and at El Príncipe on the Sabana, and opened a footpath from El Príncipe to the confluence of the Sucubtí and Chucunaque Rivers. In 1788 Colonel Manuel Milla de Santa Ella, adjutant of the Spanish post at Agla on Caledonia Bay — probably on or very near the lost site of ancient Acla — passed over this trail to El Príncipe, descended the Sabana, and recrossed the isthmus by way of the Chucunaque. Milla's report and map were to figure prominently in later canal projects. Like all previous measures designed to subdue the Cuna tribes by force this attempt to hem them in between fortified outposts ended in failure. By the terms of a treaty concluded with the Indians in 1790 the Spaniards agreed to remove all their garrisons in Darién except the one at Yavisa.

A few peaceable explorations alternated with the eighteenth-century invasions and threats of invasion of the Spanish colonies. In 1735 the French government sent out a scientific expedition under Charles-Marie de La Condamine to determine the circumference of the earth by measuring arcs of the meridian along the equator near Quito. On its way to Ecuador the party crossed the Isthmus of Panama in December 1735 and made a hasty examination of the terrain, which La Condamine recommended in glowing terms to the Académie des Sciences as an excellent location for a canal. Antonio de Ulloa, a young Spanish scientist who accompanied the mission, took barometric observations as he paddled up the Chagres and recorded the rise in elevation from the mouth of the river to Cruces. He also noted in passing some curious impressions of the tropical fauna and lost his appetite when offered a meal of roast monkey because of its resemblance to "an unhappy, weeping child about two years of age." [6] Ulloa was disappointed not to see one of the two-headed snakes rumored to abound near Panama, though he was skeptical about the existence of such monsters: "It is very probable that the creature has only one head, and, from its resembling a tail, has been imagined to have two." [7]

The project for a transit by road or canal across the Isthmus of Tehuantepec was revived dramatically in 1771 by the discovery of several bronze cannon, cast long before at Manila, in the fortress of San Juan de Ulúa at Vera Cruz. The find puzzled the authorities: how had these heavy and cumbersome pieces of artillery been transported from the Pacific to the Atlantic coast of Mexico? Obviously not by sea, for at that date no Manila ships had yet reached Vera Cruz by way of Cape Horn or the Straits of Magellan, and vessels from the Philippines had been using the Good Hope route for only a few years. The Mexican viceroy, Antonio Bucareli, ordered an investigation which disclosed that the cannon had been brought across the Pacific in a galleon, landed near the sandbar of San Francisco on the Tehuantepec coast, ferried across the lagoons and up the Río Chicapa in small boats, dragged over the divide, and floated on barges down the Coatzacoalcos to the Gulf of Mexico. This revelation naturally suggested the opening of a

Tehuantepec route for interoceanic trade. If artillery could be transported across the isthmus ordinary merchandise should certainly pass over without difficulty.

In 1774 Bucareli directed Colonel Agustín Cramer, governor of San Juan de Ulúa, and his assistant, Miguel del Corral, to survey the Tehuantepec region from the mouth of the Coatzacoalcos to the Pacific. The isthmus had never before been thoroughly explored, and it was generally supposed that the Coatzacoalcos was connected through some tributary with both oceans. Cramer blasted this hope but reported that an artificial cut only 18 miles long would suffice to connect the navigable streams on opposite sides of the watershed. Nothing was done to put the canal project into execution, but in 1798 a new boat landing, Embarcadero de la Cruz, was established at the confluence of the Coatzacoalcos and Sarabia Rivers, and a primitive road constructed from that point over the divide to the town of Tehuantepec. By this land-and-water route, which avoided the troublesome portage past the seven rapids or *malpasos* of the Coatzacoalcos, a small amount of interoceanic trade trickled across the isthmus.

In 1779 Charles III ordered a survey of the Nicaragua route by the Spanish engineers Muestro and Ysasi, who reported that the height of the mountain range separating the lake from the Pacific made the construction of a canal impracticable. Hodgson and Lee, the British agents on the Mosquito coast and at Belize, accompanied the expedition unofficially and brought back to England enthusiastic descriptions of the fertile lake district and its importance as a link in an interoceanic transit. Their accounts were at least indirectly responsible for the choice of Nicaragua as the objective of Nelson's invasion a few months later. In 1781, as soon as the British troops had retired, Charles III instituted another exploration of Nicaragua, this time under the command of Manuel Galisteo. Galisteo's survey was a more thorough and altogether more scientifically conducted undertaking than that of his predecessors. He took a series of levels 100 yards apart between Lake Nicaragua and the Pacific and established with reasonable accuracy for his day the elevation of the lake surface and of many points on the divide, though he missed the lowest pass. But his observations produced no tangible results. For 50 years Galisteo's report lay buried in the archives of Guatemala, whence it was unearthed and published about 1830 by Thompson, the British envoy to Central America.

With the exception of La Condamine's comments on the Isthmus of Panama the first signs of French interest in interoceanic communication — the thin edge of a wedge which in the nine-teenth century was to be driven deeper and deeper, literally as well as figuratively, into the heart of the isthmus — appeared be-tween 1785 and 1791. During those years four separate canal proj-ects were hatched by private citizens of France, none of whom had ever visited Central America. Three of them were unofficially sub-mitted to the Spanish government and promptly rejected. In 1785 La Nauerre placed before the Académie des Sciences a plan for a canal to connect the navigable waters of the Chagres with the Pacific at or near Panama. Although the author betrayed a naïve ignorance of the difficulties involved by estimating the cost at only 1,000,000 francs ($200,000) he impetuously presented his scheme to the Spanish ambassador in Paris, the Conde de Aranda, who forwarded it to Floridablanca, Prime Minister of Charles III, with the remark that La Nauerre impressed him as "a torrent of ver-bosity and conceit, but learned in scientific theory." [8] The Coun-cil of the Indies sent the documents to the viceroy of New Granada with instructions to investigate the feasibility of the project, but after the king countermanded the order in April 1787 the plan was consigned to oblivion in some dusty Spanish pigeonhole.

After the accession of Charles IV in 1788 Comte Louis-Hector de Ségur proposed to Floridablanca the construction of a canal through Nicaragua by way of the great lake and its smaller neigh-bor Lake Managua: "If . . . the king does not wish to bear the cost . . . and if he will permit foreigners to do so, we are confi-dent that we can organize a company to finance it. . . ." [9] In 1791 another Frenchman, Jean Benjamin de Laborde, also recom-mended the route through the two lakes, which he proposed to connect either by an artificial canal or by deepening the bed of the Tipitapa River. "If this project is ever completed," he rhapsodized, "how much time will be saved! How many misfortunes averted! How many men spared danger and saved from death, or at least from frightful sickness! And what incalculable benefits will accrue to commerce!" [10] Many of Laborde's suggestions so closely resem-ble those proposed by Ségur that the two men may well have been collaborators rather than rivals, and their schemes actually but a single project.

About 1790 still another French plan for a Nicaragua canal was presented to and declined by the Spanish government. Its author, Martin de La Bastide, recommended a direct artificial channel some 14 miles long from Lake Nicaragua to the Pacific instead of the circuitous route through Lake Managua. Heretofore all ad-vocates of a canal had assumed as a matter of course that the Spanish (or in a few instances the British) government would pay for and execute the project. Now for the first time in these schemes of Ségur, Laborde, and La Bastide a group of private individuals proposed to undertake the work. La Bastide's specific suggestions for the organization, financing, and privileges of his company — including extensive land grants, trading concessions, and exemption from duties and taxes — were to serve as models for many future enterprises of the kind.

La Bastide also pointed out that a strongly fortified and garrisoned commercial settlement on Lake Nicaragua would provide a centrally located military base from which Spain could defend her colonies. He warned the Spaniards that "rapacity is the dominant characteristic of the English nation," [11] but in his opinion an even greater potential menace was the infant republic of the United States, which because of its proximity could more easily send an invading army against Central America. With uncanny vision he predicted the rapid expansion of the United States and the growth of the aggressive spirit that was to culminate in the doctrine of Manifest Destiny: "The territories of this new power produce none of the valuable commodities and contain none of the rich mines of gold and silver that abound in the Spanish possessions. Such wealth cannot fail to excite its cupidity. . . ." [12] And like an eighteenth-century Cassandra the Frenchman dinned his prophecies into unbelieving ears: "Already one can peer into the future and foresee the efforts which this vigorous nation will make, sooner or later, to push its way gradually towards the south, to penetrate into the fertile lands of Louisiana, and then to spread over New Mexico, where are located the rich mines of Santa Fé. . . ." [13]

Even at this early period La Bastide's suspicions were not altogether without foundation. On January 25, 1786 Thomas Jefferson, then United States minister to France, had written to his friend Archibald Stuart: "Our confederacy must be viewed as the nest, from which all America, North and South, is to be peopled. We should take care, too, not to think it for the interest of that great Continent to press too soon on the Spaniards. Those countries cannot be in better hands. My fear is, that they are too feeble to hold them till our population can be sufficiently advanced to gain it from them, piece by piece. . . ." [14] A little later rumors of isthmian canal projects aroused Jefferson's curiosity, and on December 11, 1787 he wrote from Paris to William Carmichael, diplomatic representative of the United States at Madrid: "I have been told, that the cutting through the Isthmus of Panama . . . has at times been thought of by the government of Spain, and that they once proceeded so far, as to have a survey and examination made of the ground; but that the result was, either impracticability or too great difficulty. . . . I should be exceedingly pleased to get as minute details as possible on it, and even copies of the survey, report, &c., if they could be obtained at a moderate expense." [15] On May 27, 1788 he wrote again: "With respect to the Isthmus of Panama, I am assured . . . that a survey was made, that a canal appeared very practicable, and that the idea was suppressed for political reasons altogether. . . . This report is to me a vast desideratum, for reasons political and philosophical." [16] Actually the Spaniards had made no recent survey of the Panama region, and what Jefferson had in mind was probably Cramer's report on Tehuantepec, Galisteo's on Nicaragua, or both. In any event Carmichael does not appear to have obtained for him anything more useful than Ulloa's notes on Panama written in 1735.

Benjamin Franklin's attention had already been directed to the canal project in a curious manner. While in Paris he received a letter from a Provençal peasant named Pierre-André Gargaz, then serving a 20-year term in the galleys at Toulon for a murder which, he swore, he had never committed. The letter, dated February 14, 1779, contained a manuscript entitled *Conciliateur de toutes les nations d'Europe, ou Projet de paix perpétuelle entre tous les Souverains de l'Europe et leurs Voisins,* which the prisoner asked Franklin to publish. At first Franklin dismissed the peace project as the brain-child of a crank. But Gargaz was a persistent crusader, and after his release in March 1781 walked all the way to Paris to call on Franklin, who was so deeply impressed by the man's sincerity and good sense that he had the book printed at his own press in Passy. Gargaz believed that ease of travel and communication would help to bring about world peace and that the construction of canals at Panama and Suez would greatly facilitate such communication: "To cut these two isthmuses will be very difficult and expensive, but it will not be impossible for the Sovereigns of Europe, as soon as they shall be united by a Congress upright and perpetual; because, if they spend upon these two canals as much as they have spent upon War during the last fifty years, it is very certain that both will be completed in about fifteen years." [17] Unhappily this visionary convict's little pamphlet, like so many later well-intentioned peace proposals, failed to impress or probably even to reach the bellicose statesmen and rulers to whom it was addressed.

Chapter 10. Independence

UNTIL well into the first quarter of the nineteenth century no popular demand for separation existed in Spanish America. At the top of the social scale the powerful clergy and the landed and commercial aristocracy constituted politically conservative groups; at the lower end the ignorant, poverty-stricken peasants and laborers, largely of Indian or Negro blood, formed an inert mass almost impervious to revolutionary theories.

Nevertheless a handful of intellectual leaders found inspiration in the liberal doctrines of Rousseau, the successful rebellion of the British colonies in North America, the violent upheaval of the French revolution, and the emancipation in 1804 of Haiti, the first Latin American country to throw off allegiance to its European homeland. In South America the movement originated with Antonio Nariño of Bogotá, who printed and distributed a Spanish translation of the *Declaration of the Rights of Man and of the Citizen*, a manifesto issued in 1789 by the French Constituent Assembly. But the real father of independence was Francisco Miranda, born at Caracas in 1754. At least as early as 1784 Miranda began to plan the liberation of the Spanish colonies. Between 1790 and 1804 he traveled from one European court to another, exhausting his strength in vain efforts to obtain financial and military support. In 1797 he was joined in Paris by José del Pozo y Sucre and Manuel José de Salas, representatives of a prematurely organized revolutionary junta of deputies from the cities and provinces of Spanish America. On December 22, 1797 the three commissioners drew up an appeal to the British Prime Minister, William Pitt. In return for aid in the struggle for independence the radical leaders proposed to grant Great Britain certain privileges, including special transit rights through the projected canals to be cut at both Panama and Nicaragua. The United States was to participate in these concessions if its government chose to co-operate.

Neither the British nor the United States government took kindly to this proposal at the time. In 1804, when Spain joined Napoleon in the war against England, Pitt's Cabinet did make tentative preparations for an expeditionary force to help emancipate the Spanish colonies but soon abandoned the plan. Two years later Miranda equipped a small vessel in the United States and landed at Coro in Venezuela, expecting to find the populace ripe for rebellion, but his stirring call to arms met with no response, and he was forced to leave without having accomplished anything.

The apparently unshakable loyalty of the colonial landowners to the Spanish monarchy might have delayed separation for many years and perhaps prevented it altogether if events in Spain itself had not precipitated a crisis. In 1807 Napoleon's armies invaded Spain, in March 1808 Charles IV abdicated in favor of his son Ferdinand VII, a few weeks later Ferdinand in turn abdicated at Bayonne, and in July Napoleon's brother Joseph marched triumphantly into Madrid as king of Spain, to be driven out again almost immediately by the infuriated citizens. For the next 15 years turmoil and confusion ravaged the peninsula. Towards the end of 1808 Napoleon himself invaded Spain and restored Joseph to his throne, upon which he sat uneasily until the Spanish troops reinforced by the British under Wellington obliged him to relinquish it forever in 1813. During the French occupation a system of provisional juntas or regional committees patriotically strove to maintain at least a semblance of Spanish jurisdiction over the unconquered remnants of the country. Ousted from Seville by the French, the central junta moved in January 1810 to Cádiz, where it disbanded after having transferred its authority to a new Cortes or Parliament. This liberal Cortes designated three regents to govern Spain, abolished the Inquisition, curbed the powers of Church and aristocracy, and drew up the progressive constitution of 1812. With the restoration of Ferdinand VII after the final expulsion of Joseph Bonaparte in 1813 the pendulum swung once more towards reaction.

Inevitably these kaleidoscopic changes in the political fortunes of the mother country created profound disturbances in the colonies, which in theory belonged not to the nation but to the king in person. Hence the abdications of Charles IV and Ferdinand VII in 1808 immediately raised the question: "To whom do these Crown colonies now owe allegiance?" Certainly not to the French usurper, who was hated as cordially in Spanish America as in Spain itself. To pioneers of liberation like Miranda the removal of two legitimate monarchs in rapid succession offered a providential opportunity to insist that the single thread binding the colonies to Europe had been broken.

In a history of the isthmian canal the campaigns and battles of the Latin American wars of independence are of much less importance than the political alignments that followed the close of hostilities. The year 1825 found Latin America independent but politically unstable. Immense distances, impenetrable jungles, and unscalable mountain ranges separated one section from another; roads were few and poor, communication difficult, slow, and uncertain. Topography, fierce local patriotism, and the adoption by nearly all of the new states of a federal or decentralized form of government modeled on that of the United States combined to foster disunion. South of the equator the national entities created during the revolutionary period held together, though not without some sectional turmoil and shifting of frontiers, but the more brittle confederations in the north began to break up almost immediately.

Bolívar's republic of Gran Colombia, proclaimed in 1819, disintegrated in 1830 into three independent states. Venezuela set up its own government with the capital at Caracas; the old province of Quito became the republic of Ecuador; and the remaining third entered upon a protean career which in little more than half a century was to give the country four names: Republic of New Granada (1830–61), Confederación Granadina (1861–63), United States of Colombia (1863–86), and Republic of Colombia, its present designation. Bolívar, ill and discouraged, retired from the presidency in April 1830 and died the following December. The confederation of Central America survived precariously until 1838, when chronic unrest culminated in the dissolution of the federal Congress and separation into five states: Guatemala, El Salvador, Honduras, Nicaragua, and Costa Rica. Throughout the rest of the century frequent attempts were made to reunite the little republics into a single political unit, but all ended in failure.

The Isthmus of Panama never formed part of the Central American federation. On November 28, 1821 Panama declared itself independent of Spain and voluntarily sought inclusion in the republic of Gran Colombia. By the terms of the incorporation Panama expressly reserved the right to secede. When Gran Colombia split into three parts in 1830 a separatist faction in Panama favored the resumption of independence, but after some hesitation the isthmus attached itself to New Granada. The association was little more than nominal; the local officials in Panama, separated by weeks of tedious and dangerous travel from their superiors at Bogotá, jealously clung to their semi-autonomous pretensions and viewed with suspicion all attempts, real or fancied, of the central government to encroach upon their authority. In November 1840 an outbreak of civil war in New Granada temporarily wrecked the unstable union. The provinces of Panama and Veragua exercised their right to secede, formed the independent "State of the Isthmus," adopted a constitution, and elected Tomás Herrera President. William Radcliff, an American citizen residing at Panama, urged recognition of the isthmian republic by the United States, but on January 28, 1842 Daniel Webster, then Secretary of State, rejected his plea. Events fully justified Webster's discretion, for the seceding provinces had already rejoined New Granada on December 31, 1841, and recognition of their independence after that date would certainly have created an embarrassing situation. Intrinsically Panama's brief interval of total independence was of slight moment, but it established a precedent which was to be turned to good account by the advocates of separation in 1903.

The geographical boundaries between the independent states of Latin America followed in general the limits of the old Spanish provinces in effect at the beginning of the revolutionary period, but many of the new frontiers extended for hundreds of miles through unexplored regions in which the locations of rivers, mountain ranges, and other natural landmarks were unknown, and in the absence of accurate surveys the lines of demarcation were necessarily vague. Inevitably disputes arose over lands claimed by two or more neighboring countries. A few were settled without bloodshed, but most led to armed conflicts ranging from minor border clashes to full-dress wars. During the nineteenth century every nation in Latin America became involved at one time or another in such controversies, and several frontier areas remain in dispute today.

While the struggle for independence was still in progress the provisional governments of some of the new states took steps to secure recognition by other powers, especially Great Britain and the United States. Bound to Spain by a formal alliance, the British government hesitated to jeopardize its relations with that country by overt encouragement of the rebellious colonies, but English merchants, foreseeing great benefit from the opening of Latin American ports to English shipping, favored emancipation.

Popular opinion in the United States naturally sympathized with the independence movement in Latin America. As early as 1817 the United States government prepared for commercial recognition by sending commissioners, followed by consuls, to some of the new republics, while a strong party in Congress eloquently led by Henry Clay clamored for an exchange of diplomatic repre-

sentatives as well. But Secretary of State John Quincy Adams, unwilling to antagonize Spain during the delicate negotiations for
the cession of Florida, prudently postponed formal recognition
until Spain's ratification of the Florida treaty in 1821 removed the
last reason for delay. On March 8, 1822 President Monroe sent a
special message to Congress recommending the recognition of the
Latin American nations. Both houses passed resolutions advocat-
ing recognition and appropriated funds for diplomatic establishments. Manuel Torres, sent by Bolívar as chargé d'affaires of Gran
Colombia, was formally received by Monroe's Cabinet in June.
Recognition of Colombia was followed almost immediately by that
of Mexico, Argentina, Chile, and a little later of the other new
states. In 1823 the British Foreign Secretary, George Canning, sent
a commission to Colombia and Mexico and appointed consuls in
the principal ports of Latin America. Great Britain accorded full
diplomatic recognition to Argentina early in 1825 and to the other
republics shortly afterwards. The principal powers of continental
Europe soon followed suit. Spain, reluctant to admit the irrevocable loss of her possessions, finally recognized Mexico in 1836 and
the other countries at intervals during the next half century. Honduras, the last, was not granted recognition by Spain until 1894.

In 1823, when the independence of the Spanish American republics seemed inevitable, a new menace to their national security suddenly appeared in Europe. At the Congress of Verona in
October 1822 the chief members of the so-called Holy Alliance —
Russia, Prussia, Austria, and France — had agreed upon an invasion of Spain to overthrow the liberal government of 1820. France
was to undertake the active campaign with the moral and material
support of her allies, and at the same time vague proposals were
made for the reconquest, with the assistance of the Alliance, of
Spain's American colonies. Great Britain, represented by the Duke
of Wellington, uncompromisingly opposed the entire project, but
in spite of British protests the French armies entered Spain on
April 7, 1823 and within six months had completely overpowered
the forces of the Spanish Cortes and restored the captive despot,
Ferdinand VII, to his throne. Canning promptly informed the
French that England would tolerate no interference with the *de
facto* independence of Latin America and warned the United States
government of the threatened intervention. Canning then suggested to Richard Rush, the United States minister in London,
that the two Anglo-Saxon nations should issue a joint declaration
to the effect that they considered Spanish recovery of the colonies
hopeless, that they did not intend to seize any portion of Latin

America for themselves, and that they would oppose the transfer of Latin American territory to any other power. Monroe, Jefferson, and Madison thought well of Canning's proposal, but John Quincy Adams objected to a joint declaration and persuaded the President to make a statement on behalf of the United States alone.

On December 2, 1823 the President formulated the famous Monroe Doctrine in a message to Congress. Two sentences contained its essence: "With the existing colonies or dependencies of any European power we have not interfered, and shall not interfere. But with the governments who have declared their independence, and maintained it, and whose independence we have, on great consideration and on just principles, acknowledged, we could not view any interposition for the purpose of oppressing them, or controlling in any other manner their destiny, by any European power, in any other light than as the manifestation of an unfriendly disposition towards the United States." [1]

In 1821 Bolívar, hoping to draw the new republics closer together, somewhat prematurely invited the provisional governments of Peru, Argentina, and Chile to send delegates to an international congress to be held at Panama. Unsettled conditions prevented the meeting at that time; but in December 1824 Bolívar, alarmed by the intrigues of the Holy Alliance, revived the project and expanded it to include all of the Latin American states as well as Great Britain, Holland, and the United States. The response was disappointing. Bolivia and Paraguay ignored the invitation; Chile, Argentina, and Brazil accepted in principle but sent no delegates; the Dutch emissary arrived without credentials since the Netherlands had not yet recognized the new nations; the British envoy held informal conversations with the other representatives but attended no regular meetings. Only Gran Colombia, Peru, the Central American federation, and Mexico participated actively.

Political discord at home blocked the effective co-operation of the United States. The Latin American agenda proposed as the principal objects of the congress the formation of a league to prosecute the war against Spain and the Alliance, the drafting of an international convention of navigation and commerce, and consideration of an attempt to liberate Puerto Rico, Cuba, the Philippines, and the Canary Islands. Although most of the items on this program were of little concern to the United States President Adams felt that participation in the discussions might serve some useful purpose. Accordingly he appointed as envoys to the congress Richard Anderson and John Sergeant and on December 26, 1825 requested the approval of the Senate and an appropriation for the mission. Unfortunately his acceptance of the invitation without the previous consent of the Senate had deeply offended that body, and the President's political opponents seized the opportunity to wage a vigorous campaign against the resolution. Not until May 24, 1826 did the bill become law, and by that time it was too late. Neither of the American envoys reached the rendezvous; Anderson died at Cartagena, and Sergeant did not set sail for Panama at all.

The truncated congress convened on June 22, 1826 and held ten sessions, in the course of which the representatives of Colombia, Peru, Central America, and Mexico drafted a treaty of perpetual union, league, and confederation (whatever that might mean in practice) to which the other American republics and Brazil might subscribe within a year. Since Colombia alone ratified the treaty it was never carried into effect. After three weeks the congress adjourned, intending to resume its deliberations some months later at Tacubaya in Mexico, a healthier spot than low-lying Panama. This time the United States commissioners — Sergeant, one of the two original envoys, and Joel Poinsett, after whom the poinsettia plant is named — arrived at the meeting-place, but none of the Latin American delegates appeared, and the congress never reassembled. Bolívar commented wryly on the failure of his pet project: "The Panama congress . . . is something like the Greek madman who, seated on a rock, believed that he was directing the courses of the ships that sailed past him. Its power will be but a shadow, its decrees merely suggestions: nothing more." [2] While this first attempt to achieve unity among the new nations of the western hemisphere had in fact died stillborn it foreshadowed the sturdier and more significant Pan-American conferences of recent years.

PART II

The Battle of the Routes

Chapter 11. Humboldt

F ROM the Kingdom of *New Grenada* to the environs of the capital of Mexico," wrote Alexander von Humboldt in 1811, "there is not a single mountain, a single level, a single city, of which we know the elevation above the level of the sea. . . . Even the height of the mountains which traverse the isthmus of Panama is not yet known." [1]

Humboldt emphasized again and again the vital necessity for thorough explorations and exact measurements of *all* promising canal sites as indispensable preliminaries to the construction of a waterway at any one of them. These parallel examinations, he urged, should be made under approximately similar conditions and if possible by a single group of investigators in order that the relative advantages and disadvantages of the various routes might be measured by the same yardstick. Although the wisdom of his recommendation would appear self-evident no such examination of the rival routes by one party of engineers or even by different groups operating under a uniform set of standards was organized until 1870, when the United States Navy Department sent out some half dozen almost simultaneous expeditions whose reports were based on effectively comparable surveys. Before that time only detached exploring parties, each covering one or two or at most three of the potential canal sites, struggled through the matted jungles of Central America and the isthmus, took observations, made reports and estimates, and only too often returned with ranks depleted by fever, dysentery, and starvation. Some of these surveys, admirably conducted by able and honest engineers, brought to light information of the highest value; many more, perfunctorily and inefficiently misdirected by pseudo-scientists or by capitalists with axes to grind, equipped with instruments of doubtful precision, and served by inexpert technicians, reported incredibly fantastic observations and conclusions. Inaccurate and sometimes deliberately distorted measurements of altitudes and distances gave rise to extravagant hopes and bitter partisanship; for without uniformity of method or direction, who could determine the truth or falsity of conflicting claims?

While the advocates of various routes hurled fanciful statistics at each other international rivalries added to the confusion. With the exception of two Mexican surveys of Tehuantepec all of the important nineteenth-century explorations for a canal site were undertaken by citizens of one or another of three countries: Great Britain, France, and the United States. The British engineers were in general capable and trustworthy, but they were few in number, and their total contribution was relatively slight. Of the far more numerous French investigators none but Garella approached the problem in a strictly scientific spirit. Most of his compatriots seem to have been curiously susceptible to self-delusion and were only too eager to draw the most astonishingly optimistic conclusions from a series of hasty, incomplete, poorly equipped, and inadequately staffed expeditions. On the other hand almost all of the explorations directed by American engineers, whether employed by private companies or by the government, were carried out soberly, painstakingly, thoroughly, and with commendable detachment. Most of the really useful spadework accomplished between 1825 and 1880 must be credited to such men as Childs, Hughes, Trautwine, Lull, Menocal, Selfridge, Barnard, and Shufeldt, whose conscientious surveys established accurately and for all time those topographical measurements so insistently demanded by Humboldt. But national jealousies, euphemistically called patriotism, caused French and American explorers to regard each other's activities with jaundiced eyes. Throughout the century French engineers and promoters displayed a tendency to accept as gospel the reports of their own countrymen and to ignore or dismiss lightly the results of American surveys; and in their turn the Americans — with, it must be admitted, better reason — preferred to rely exclusively upon measurements and data furnished by prior American expeditions.

Humboldt's writings stimulated public interest in the canal idea more powerfully than all previous proposals taken together. Before his time projects for a canal had been sporadic, tentative, and ineffectual. The few surveys undertaken under Spanish auspices were hopelessly inadequate, and the inert and impoverished Spanish government consistently rejected suggestions presented by ingenious foreigners. With the achievement of independence a more progressive spirit bloomed in Latin America. At the same time the growth of maritime commerce, the invention of the steamboat, the rapid expansion and increasing wealth of the United States, and the development of new markets in the teeming countries of the

Far East created among international merchants and capitalists a vigorous demand for shorter and speedier trade routes. Between 1825 and 1904 scarcely a year passed without its quota of explorations, concessions, stock companies, and prospectuses for a canal through some section of Mexico, Central America, or the isthmus. And almost without exception the sponsors of these various projects derived at least part of their inspiration from Humboldt. His theories were quoted — and misquoted — *ad nauseam*, his authority was invoked to bolster addle-pated schemes of which he would certainly not have approved had he known of them. Yet Humboldt, though he traveled for five years in the American tropics, had never set eye or foot on any one of the canal sites he suggested, nor did he ever claim to have done so. His ideas concerning the different routes came wholly from reading and hearsay. We know now that many of those ideas were mistaken, but his principles were sound, and considering the limited and distorted information at his disposal he reached some eminently sensible conclusions.

In March 1799 Charles IV granted Humboldt and the naturalist Aimé Bonpland permission to explore some of the remoter areas of Spanish America. Sailing from La Coruña in June, they spent several months in Venezuela and traced the courses of the Orinoco River and its tributaries. After a short sojourn in Cuba Humboldt proceeded to Cartagena, thence up the Magdalena and across the mountains to Bogotá, where he remained until September 1801. He reached Quito after four months of difficult overland travel and passed the following year in Ecuador and Peru. In January 1803 he sailed from Callao to Guayaquil and thence without touching at any intermediate port to Acapulco; thus missing entirely the narrow neck of the continent, the only section suitable for the construction of a canal. He remained in Mexico nearly a year, paid brief visits to Philadelphia and Washington — then just beginning to emerge from the Potomac mud — and returned to Europe in August 1804. During his five years in America Humboldt took copious notes on every conceivable variety of natural phenomenon from meteor showers to the fertilizing properties of guano, and his experiences and observations in the New World provided him with material for no less than 30 volumes published in sections between 1805 and 1834 under the general title of *Voyage aux régions équinoxiales du Nouveau Continent.*

In his discussion of the canal problem Humboldt presented nine tentative projects, listed from north to south, all offering in his opinion "a greater or less probability either of canals or interior river communications." [2] Of these locations the first two lay so far

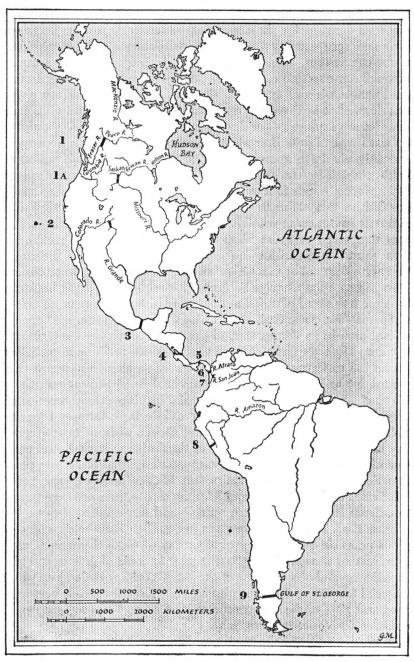

4. HUMBOLDT'S NINE ROUTES

to the north over the broadest and highest parts of the North American continent that an interoceanic canal was unthinkable; all that could be hoped for in those regions was a wagon road or at best a small artificial inland waterway connecting navigable rivers. His first suggestion called for a link across part of what is now British Columbia between the Peace River and the Tacoutche Tesse, "supposed the same with the river of *Colombia*." [3] The "Tacoutche Tesse" was not the Columbia, as Humboldt presumed, but the Fraser River, and its lower course as plotted on maps of Humboldt's time later proved wholly imaginary. Even if the Fraser and Peace Rivers had been navigable to near their respective sources — which they were not — such a communication between the Pacific and Arctic Oceans would have been of almost no commercial value. Humboldt admitted that "all that part of the west of North America is still but very imperfectly known" [4] — clearly an understatement at a period when the vast Canadian wilderness had scarcely been penetrated by white men.

As a variant of this passage Humboldt suggested the opening of a continuous waterway from the Gulf of Mexico to the Pacific by means of an artificial canal between the headwaters of "the *Nelson* river, the *Saskashawan,* and the *Missoury*. . . ." [5] Here again he was misled by inadequate knowledge of those as yet unexplored regions, for the Nelson River actually flows into Hudson Bay, not into the Pacific. "The journey of Captain Lewis," he continued, ". . . may throw considerable light on this interesting problem." [6] Although the results of the Lewis and Clark expedition, which would have demonstrated the absurdity of an interoceanic canal in the heart of the Rocky Mountains, were known as early as 1806, five years before the publication of this volume, Humboldt had apparently neglected to bring his notes up to date.

For his second project, located in the present state of Colorado, Humboldt contemplated only a wagon road to connect the sources of the Rio Grande and the Colorado River: "But . . . however easy the carriage may be across the mountains, no communication will ever result from it comparable to that opened directly from sea to sea." [7] "However easy" seems a curious phrase when applied to a transit over 10,000-foot ranges, and the idea of a steady stream of commercial traffic through the Grand Canyon appears even more fantastic. Once more it must be remembered that even Humboldt, perhaps the most erudite scientist of his day, could have had but a hazy conception of Rocky Mountain topography. Almost his only source of information concerning this route was the report of an exploration by two Spanish friars, Escalante and Domínguez, who traversed this region in 1776.

At Tehuantepec, the site of his third route, Humboldt "feared that the breadth of the isthmus . . . as well as the sinuosity of the rivers and the condition of their beds may prevent the opening of an interoceanic canal large enough to accommodate the ships engaged in trade with China and the northwest coast of America: nevertheless it will be of vast importance either to build a waterway for small vessels or to improve the highway that runs [from the town of Tehuantepec to Embarcadero de la Cruz] through Chihuitan and Petapa. This road was opened in 1798 and 1801. . . ." [8]

Humboldt placed his fourth route in Nicaragua, where "the ground appears . . . very little elevated. . . ." [9] But this route too had its drawbacks: "The coast of *Nicaragua* is almost inaccessible in . . . August, September, and October, on account of the terrible storms and rains; in January and February, on account of the furious north-east and east-north-east winds called *Papagayos*." [10] He found certain topographical resemblances between the lake region of Nicaragua and that portion of the Scottish highlands traversed by the Caledonian canal, opened to navigation in 1822, but Nicaragua appeared to present fewer obstacles.

Although Humboldt devoted more space to his fifth project, a canal across the Isthmus of Panama, than to any other it was not in the end his first or even his second choice: "This canal would have to pass through a hilly tract, of the height of which we are completely ignorant. . . ." [11] While he suspected what we now know, that the narrowest portion of the isthmus does not coincide with the lowest elevation, he demanded exact figures: "What is the height of the mountains at the point where the Isthmus is narrowest? What is the breadth . . . where the chain of mountains is least elevated? These are the two great questions which an enlightened government should endeavour to resolve. . . . No measure of elevation, and no level has ever yet been executed in the Isthmus of Panama. . . . It is unfair, therefore, to accuse the ministry of Madrid of a wish to conceal matters of which they have never had any more knowledge than the geographers of London and Paris." [12]

Humboldt also turned his inquiring mind to the problem of tides and the vexed question of the relative surface levels of the two oceans: "In every age and climate, of two neighbouring seas, the one has been considered as more elevated than the other. . . . In America, the South Sea is generally supposed to be higher at the isthmus of Panama than the Atlantic. . . . Trivial causes of a local nature, such as the configuration of the coast, currents and winds . . . may trouble the equilibrium which ought necessarily to exist between all the parts of the ocean. . . . But these trivial inequalities, far from obstructing hydraulic operations, would even be favourable for sluices [locks]. . . ." [13] We know today that the normal level of the oceans and of the seas opening directly into them is the same throughout the world, and that the small differences observed in certain coastal areas are in fact due wholly to "trivial causes of a local nature." Yet on the isthmus this fact was not definitely established until Colonel George M. Totten, chief engineer of the Panama Railroad, reported in 1855: "Although my observations make the mean level of the Pacific from 0.14 to 0.75 [feet] higher than the mean level of the Atlantic, this is probably owing to local circumstances alone. We may therefore decide that there is no difference in the *mean levels*. . . ." [14]

For some reason — probably lack of information — Humboldt omitted detailed discussion of two important canal sites east of Panama: one across the narrowest part of the isthmus near Mandinga Bay in the Gulf of San Blas, the other from Caledonia Bay or some adjacent inlet in Darién to the Gulf of San Miguel. Both were to figure prominently in mid-century projects, but Humboldt neglected them entirely in his earlier works and mentioned them only casually in a volume published in 1825.

Humboldt located the Pacific terminus of his sixth project on Cupica Bay in Colombia, which he proposed to connect artificially with the Napipí River, a tributary of the Atrato. A Basque pilot named Gogueneche had explored this region superficially about 1799 but appears to have taken no precise measurements. Humboldt admitted that this area, like all others under discussion, demanded a more careful survey, for not even the exact latitude and longitude of Cupica Bay or of the confluence of the Napipí and the Atrato had yet been determined: "All that we positively know . . . is, that between Cupica and the left bank of the Atrato, there is either a land-strait, or a total absence of the Cordillera. . . ." [15] Humboldt rarely permitted himself so dogmatic a word as "positively," and he would have done well to modify it here. The American naval expedition of 1871 proved that the ridge between Cupica Bay and the headwaters of the Napipí rises at its lowest point 612 feet above sea level — four times as high as the lowest gap in Nicaragua and more than twice as high as the summit of the Panama transit.

The Atrato again served as a link in Humboldt's seventh proposed communication: "In the interior of the [Colombian] prov-

ince of *Choco,* the small ravine . . . *de la Raspadura,* unites the
neighbouring sources of the . . . *Rio San Juan* and the small river
Quito [a tributary of the upper Atrato]. . . . A monk of great activity, *curé* of the village of *Novita,* employed his parishioners to
dig a small canal in the ravine *de la Raspadura,* by means of which,
when the rains are abundant, canoes loaded with cacao *pass from
sea to sea.* This interior communication has existed since 1788, unknown in Europe. The small canal of Raspadura unites, on the
coasts of the two oceans, two points 75 leagues distant from one another." [16] Humboldt claimed to be the first to announce the existence of this artificial waterway. Obviously the idea of a secret canal
in actual operation intrigued him, as it was to intrigue many later
investigators. Much has been written about the Raspadura canal,
but the accounts are so contradictory that few undisputed facts
emerge from the mists of legend. Such a canal may well have been
constructed for the use of light canoes during the rainy season; on
the other hand it is possible that the whole story was a figment of
somebody's exuberant imagination. In 1886 Wyse offered a plausible if not altogether convincing explanation of the origin of this
ditch: "In 1788, the *curé* of Nóvita, Antonio de Cereso, overseer of
an estate belonging to the great Mosquera family of Popayán, and
Francisco Sea, representative of the Salinas family, resolved, in order to end their interminable quarrels over boundaries, to have a
demarcation trench dug between the Perico and Raspadura Rivers. During the torrential winter rains, this trench permits light
canoes, even today, to pass from one ocean to the other without an
overland portage." [17]

Rumors of similar communications at various points on the
isthmian watershed were current during the nineteenth century.
Wherever two streams, one discharging into the Atlantic, the other
into the Pacific, flowed from sources separated only by a narrow
ridge, a tradition of a native portage or canoe-slide was almost sure
to spring up. Presumably some of these reports were well founded
as far as they went, but it was a far cry from the portage or haulage
of a small boat to the construction of a full-size interoceanic canal.

The two southernmost of Humboldt's projects, like the first two
in the extreme north, traversed stretches of the American continent so broad and mountainous as to preclude any serious consideration of a canal: they were road-and-river communications, nothing more. His eighth proposal called for a short highway over the
crest of the Peruvian Andes from the Santa or the Rimac — small
rivers on the Pacific slope — to the headwaters of one of the great
tributaries of the Amazon. The ninth and last route, from the Gulf

of St. George on the coast of Patagonia to the Estero de Aysen, an inlet of the Pacific in Chile, involved some 250 miles of extremely difficult overland travel and moreover lay so far south that its use would have saved but little distance and almost no time over the passage through the Straits of Magellan or round Cape Horn.

Humboldt expressed a tentative preference for Nicaragua as the most advantageous site for an interoceanic canal: "It seems likely enough that . . . Nicaragua . . . will be selected for the great enterprise. . . ." [18] The Cupica-Napipí route came second, Tehuantepec third, Panama fourth. While the Raspadura line might serve for domestic commerce he thought it unsuitable for a waterway of large dimensions. But he reiterated his opinion that it would be "imprudent . . . to begin construction at any one point without explorations and surveys of the others; above all it would be a mistake to undertake such a work on too small a scale; for . . . the cost does not increase in the same proportion as the canal section and the breadth of the locks. . . ." [19]

In conclusion he touched briefly and somewhat pessimistically upon the political problems raised by the canal project. He insisted that the benefits of a waterway "should accrue to every nation . . . which will contribute to its execution by the purchase of shares" [20] and warned that any attempt on the part of a single power to operate it for exclusive profit would precipitate a grim conflict: "I confess that neither my confidence in the moderation of governments, monarchic or republican, nor my trust — sometimes a little shaken — in the progress of enlightenment . . . is strong enough to overcome this fear. . . ." [21]

Among the countless Europeans inspired by Humboldt's dream of a canal was the aged Goethe, living in peaceful but still intellectually active retirement at Weimar. Eckermann recorded the poet's prophetic words spoken on February 21, 1827: "All this is reserved for the future. . . . But I should wonder if the United States were to let an opportunity escape of getting such work into their own hands. It may be foreseen that this young state, with its decided predilection to the West, will, in thirty of forty years, have occupied . . . the . . . land beyond the Rocky Mountains. It may . . . be foreseen that along the whole coast of the Pacific Ocean . . . important commercial towns will gradually arise. . . . It is absolutely indispensable for the United States to effect a passage from the Mexican Gulf to the Pacific Ocean; and I am certain that they will do it. Would that I might live to see it! — but I shall not. . . . It would be well worth the trouble to last some fifty years more for the very purpose." [22]

Chapter 12. Panama: 1820–1848

URING the years following independence a flood of projects for a Panama canal inundated the government of Gran Colombia and its successor New Granada. Bolívar approved of the enterprise in theory, but none of the earliest proposals found favor in his eyes or in those of his Congress, and indeed none deserved to be taken seriously. In 1822–3 Colonel William Duane of Philadelphia visited Bogotá and after his return attempted to form a company to excavate "the *strait of Panama,* to effect which I have made proposals to the Colombian government (sustained by capitalists). . . ." [1] A year or two later Captain Charles Stuart Cochrane of the British navy opened negotiations for a similar charter. He had just investigated the Raspadura watershed, which he accepted with reservations as a possible canal site, but found the Panama route more desirable and "formed a plan for a company to be established in England for effecting this, which will be laid before the ensuing [Colombian] Congress. . . ." [2] In 1825 Welwood Hislop, a Jamaican merchant, solicited "the exclusive privilege for uniting the . . . oceans, in that part which he may deem most expedient . . . either by means of a canal or a rail-way. . . ." [3] Having no conception of the cost or difficulties involved, Hislop requested the concession for only 21 years and allowed himself but one year's grace before the commencement of operations. In the end none of these propositions was accepted, and later that year the Bogotá government, alarmed by the threat of a rival canal in Nicaragua, took matters into its own hands. Acting on official instructions, the Colombian envoy in London appealed for financial support from Great Britain to enable Colombia to build its own canal, but he was obliged to report failure.

In 1827 Captain John Augustus Lloyd of the British army and Captain Maurice Falmarc, a Swedish officer in the Colombian military service, requested permission to survey the isthmus. Bolívar granted the petition — reluctantly, Lloyd admitted. Starting from the Pacific end they commenced the survey on May 5, 1828, but the rains had already set in, and when they reached the Chagres at the end of June they were forced to discontinue their labors for that

year. Weather was not their only enemy. The military governor of
the province, General Sarda, "a fierce and jealous Biscayan" [4] with
a personal grudge against Bolívar, maliciously hampered the engineers, who were "refused all pecuniary assistance . . . and pur-
posely exposed . . . to the murderous attacks of the brigands then
infesting the Isthmus." [5] Nevertheless they resumed their survey in
February 1829 and completed it after a fashion.

Since circumstances restricted the explorers to the few pathways
already cut through the jungle they discovered no summit elevation less than 620 feet above the sea, but Lloyd was convinced that
a much lower pass existed within a few miles of the road. The two
engineers proposed to utilize the Chagres River from its mouth to
its junction with the Trinidad, and from that point to the Pacific
to construct first a railroad and then a canal. For the railroad they
suggested two alternative routes, one leading to Panama City and
the other to a port near Chorrera, about 15 miles farther west.
This was to be but a preliminary step in the construction of the
canal, which should follow the bed of the Trinidad River. Superficial as it was, the survey by Lloyd and Falmarc was the most reliable yet undertaken on the isthmus. To them must be credited
the first serious recommendation of Limón Bay as the Atlantic
terminus of a canal, a suggestion incorporated into most subsequent projects including the one in operation today. Limón Bay
was in every respect a better terminal harbor than the mouth of the
Chagres, but the breakwaters required to make it secure were to
cost a great deal more than Lloyd imagined. His enthusiasm also
led him to claim for the interior of the isthmus certain natural
blessings later discovered to be illusory: "Its resources are immense,
and its fertility the most rapid and wonderful. It possesses the finest waters, the most varied, abundant, and precious forests in the
world, an inexhaustible supply of building materials of all kinds
. . . whilst food . . . is equally abundant and cheap." [6]

In his discussion of labor for canal construction Lloyd's insular
prejudices led him to strange conclusions. He favored the importation of convicts — not, as had been proposed, from Great Britain,
France, and the United States jointly, since "such a concentration
of vice would be highly objectionable," [7] but from the British Isles
and British India alone. In spite of the climate Lloyd considered
the isthmus eminently fitted for colonization by Englishmen, voluntary settlers as well as convicts, who would "present a human
barrier of such formidable power, as to limit . . . any attempts
of the . . . United States, towards aggrandizement and increase
of territory. . . ." [8] True to form, Lloyd had nothing but con-

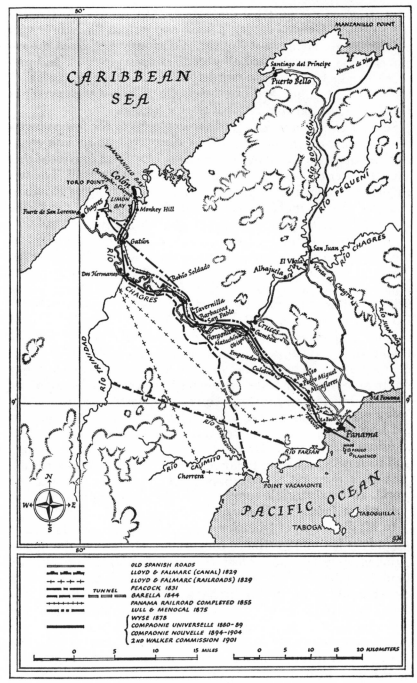

5. PANAMA PROJECTS, 1829–1904

tempt for the Panamanians, "the most superstitious, and the least freed from the shackles of their religion, of all the Columbians. . . . Billiards, cockpits, gambling, and smoking in low company, are their exclusive amusements. . . . Their best quality is great liberality to the poor, and especially to the aged and infirm." [9]

In 1833 the government of New Granada attempted to reopen negotiations with Great Britain, France, Spain, the Netherlands, and the United States for financial aid in behalf of an isthmian canal or railroad, but again the venture failed, and the disillusioned authorities, abandoning hope of official backing, resolved to appeal to private enterprise. On May 25, 1834 the Bogotá Congress authorized the President to conclude a contract with any individual or company for a road, railroad, or canal. Exactly a year later the Congress passed another act offering additional privileges to the constructors of a rail or water communication. This second decree had a definite purpose. A canal contract had been under discussion for some months, the details were almost settled, and just this extra inducement was needed to close the deal. Four days later, on May 29, 1835, the Congress issued a canal charter to Baron de Thierry.

It was typical of the perversity which ran like a twisted thread through the record of nineteenth-century canal projects that this first concession granted by New Granada should have been awarded to the most scatter-brained of all conceivable applicants. Charles, self-styled Baron de Thierry — his right to the title was never firmly established — was a fantastic character, so irresponsible, so gullible, and so steeped in delusions of grandeur that it is difficult to escape the conviction that he was actually insane. Born about 1795, probably in London, of a French *émigré* family, he entered Cambridge as a fellow commoner. In 1820 a missionary presented him to two Maori chiefs from New Zealand, then still an independent nation. The two Maoris, impressed by de Thierry's fluent chatter, invited him to establish a colony in their country and agreed to sell him 40,000 acres in North Island. In 1823 he received a deed to the property.

Two years later de Thierry assembled a group of prospective colonists and prepared to sail with them to New Zealand, but their departure was prevented by the condemnation of one vessel as unseaworthy and the abandonment of the others by the dissatisfied pioneers and crews. In 1826 de Thierry and his family went to the United States, where they existed precariously until in 1834 they set sail for the West Indies. At Pointe-à-Pitre on the French island of Guadeloupe de Thierry met a Jewish capitalist named Augustin Salomon, his business associate Sylvain Joly de Sabla, Major Fergus, the governor's aide, and three other men, Vigneti, Bertholini, and Morel. Salomon and de Sabla were highly respectable and respected merchants, but the reputations of at least one or two of the others were at best dubious. With these six partners de Thierry formed a syndicate to build an interoceanic canal and, accompanied by several of his new associates, proceeded to Panama, where he remained about six months.

De Thierry looked upon the canal project as nothing more than a means to stimulate trade between Europe and New Zealand, a mere stepping-stone to his antipodean colony. He knew nothing and cared less about engineering, and his examination of the isthmus was so superficial as to be virtually nonexistent. Nevertheless his representations convinced the uncritical Congress of New Granada, and in May 1835 he secured his concession. The allowance of only three years for construction clearly indicated the failure of both de Thierry and the Congress to appreciate the magnitude of the task. The artless baron gave additional proof of his incompetence by pointing out a number of absurdly frivolous objections to a transisthmian railroad, which he dismissed as infeasible "not only from the circumstance that the ground is very uneven, but because the primitive surface has been . . . covered to the depth of many feet with dead leaves. . . . If the Grenadian government had proposed to establish a railroad of gold, it might have been considered more practicable than one of iron; for . . . the country possesses materials for the former, and . . . would be absolutely dependent on foreign nations for those of the latter. . . . The communications will be at all times liable to be interrupted by . . . the action of a single immoral individual, in removing some rails during the night. . . ." [10] How he proposed to excavate a canal without removing the dead leaves and importing implements of foreign iron does not appear.

In June 1835 de Thierry chartered a small vessel and set out with his family for the south Pacific, leaving the canal to dig itself. By this time his pretensions had expanded, and he now claimed that the Maori chiefs had elected him "Sovereign Chief" of New Zealand. At his first stop, the island of Nukuhiva in the Marquesas, he annexed the island to his dominions and another title to his name, King of Nukuhiva. At Tahiti, where he remained for almost two years, he persuaded Queen Pomare to allow him to recruit and drill an "army" of 18 natives, but his military ambitions were thwarted by the arrival in November 1835 of the British ship *Beagle*, commanded by Captain Robert Fitz-Roy, in which Charles Darwin served as naturalist. De Thierry never returned to Panama, made no attempt to utilize his canal concession, and apparently abandoned the enterprise as lightly as he had undertaken it. In May 1837 he sailed from Tahiti to Sydney, collected about 100 white settlers — not convicts, but for the most part ne'er-do-wells and trollops — and conducted them to New Zealand, where nearly all promptly deserted. When New Zealand became a British colony in 1840 the unhappy baron lost his lands, the remnant of his colony, and his last hope of coronation by the Maoris. In 1856, nine years before his death, the New Zealand government awarded him a grant of 106 acres in settlement of his claim to 40,000.

The next project for a Panama transit, though it lacked the picaresque trimmings of the de Thierry adventure, ended in fiasco no less complete. President Jackson appointed Colonel Charles Biddle of Philadelphia his special emissary to investigate "the present state of the projects for uniting the Atlantic and Pacific oceans" [11] in both Nicaragua and the Isthmus of Panama. On May 1, 1835 Secretary of State John Forsyth instructed Biddle to proceed direct to San Juan del Norte, cross Nicaragua to the Pacific, visit in turn Guatemala, Panama, and Bogotá, procure all documents relating to the transit, and carefully examine the two routes under consideration. All this was quite specific and should have given no occasion for misunderstanding, but in a postscript Forsyth modified his orders to allow the envoy a little more latitude: "The route marked out above was prescribed to you, because it was believed that, by following it, you might gather the best information in the shortest time; but you are not to consider yourself tied down to it, and may deviate from it whenever it may be necessary. . . ." [12]

This permission to deviate proved fatal, for Biddle interpreted his instructions so liberally that he obeyed neither their letter nor their spirit. Omitting Nicaragua and Guatemala altogether, he sailed at once to Panama by way of Havana and Jamaica. Later, in a deathbed letter to Forsyth, he endeavored to justify his failure to visit Nicaragua: "I had ascertained from the most authentic sources . . . that . . . a communication . . . by the San Juan river and lake Nicaragua, was utterly impracticable. In the second place, the intercourse between the United States and the mouth of the San Juan river was such as to render it impracticable to arrive at that port without chartering a vessel for the express purpose." [13] Both excuses were pitifully lame. Biddle reached the mouth of the Chagres on November 27, 1835, paddled up the river to Cruces, and rode on to Panama. This single journey across the isthmus, which consumed at most four days, was sufficient to satisfy Biddle that a canal at that site was as impracticable as in Nicaragua: "The difficulty of accomplishing such a work, and its utter inefficiency when accomplished, were . . . apparent to all men, whether of common or uncommon sense. . . ." [14]

Without further investigation Biddle concluded that a transit across the isthmus could be made feasible only by the operation of a line of shallow-draft steamers from the mouth of the Chagres to Cruces and the construction of a railroad about 15 miles long from that point to Panama. So far Biddle had consistently lagged behind his instructions; now he began suddenly and exuberantly to exceed them. In Panama he had been sought out and made much of by a group known as the *Amigos del País,* who persuaded him to join a syndicate to build and operate a combined steamboat-and-railroad transit from the mouth of the Chagres to Panama. Although the de Thierry privilege would not expire until May 29, 1837, Biddle hastened to Bogotá to secure a concession for his own project to go into effect as soon as the other should lapse. There he was received cordially by the United States chargé d'affaires, Robert Mc-Afee, who introduced him to President Santander and to the Foreign Minister, Lino de Pombo. On June 22 the Congress granted to Biddle and his colleagues the right to operate steamboats on the Chagres and a highway or railroad from Cruces to Panama for 45 years, dating from the expiration of de Thierry's concession.

Biddle was jubilant, but not for long. Forsyth stormed at his neglect of the canal route investigation, and the unfortunate McAfee received an even sharper and not altogether merited reprimand for his participation as go-between in a private deal. Biddle returned to the United States in September 1836, but before he could be called formally to account for his failure to carry out his mission he died after a short illness. Deprived of Biddle's co-operation and unable to raise funds on their own account because of the financial panic of 1837, his associates in Panama and Bogotá soon lost their enthusiasm for the rail-and-water transit. By the time the de Thierry grant expired five months after Biddle's death the syndicate had melted away, and the new concession never became effective.

De Thierry's former partners did not give up so easily. When the baron's privilege lapsed in May 1837 two members of the Salomon group, de Sabla and Morel, hastened to Panama to investigate the transit situation for themselves. After a brief and sketchy survey Morel announced the startling discovery of two astonishingly low passes through the watershed at elevations respectively of only 34 and 37 feet above the sea. Since these gaps, if authentic, would have been hundreds of feet lower than any previously known, the figures were naturally viewed with some suspicion. When Morel, who was not an engineer and who had taken no observations with levels or other instruments, was challenged to substantiate his claim, he confessed abjectly that it was all a mistake, "the result of an error which he was totally unable to explain, all the more incomprehensible to him because it had not the slightest foundation in fact." [15]

Nevertheless the Congress of New Granada conceded to Augustin Salomon et Compagnie on March 30, 1838 the exclusive right to construct and operate a canal, railroad, highway, or a combination of all three across the Isthmus of Panama. The canal privilege was to run for 60 years from the date of its opening to traffic, the railroad and highway concession 45 years. Before actual work could be undertaken political disturbances put a temporary stop to all transit preparations. In November 1840 the provinces of Panama and Veragua seceded to form the independent State of the Isthmus and did not resume their allegiance until December 1841. By that time the Salomon concession had become unpopular in both Panama and Bogotá. The chancellor of the French consulate at Panama introduced an anti-Semitic note: "The keys of the world are here; but the name of Señor *Salomon* does not seem to me sufficiently Christian to qualify him for the rôle of their guardian St. Peter. . . ." [16] More serious opposition developed among the patriotic officials in Bogotá, many of whom still clung to the hope of a transit owned and controlled by the government of New Granada and financed by foreign loans. In November 1839, before the secession of Panama, the New Granadian minister in London, Manuel Mosquera, had endeavored to pave the way for such loans by securing a joint guarantee of the neutrality of the isthmus by the governments of Great Britain, France, and the United States, but the proposal received no more encouragement than its forerunners of 1825 and 1833. In June 1842 the Bogotá Congress declared all transit concessions *caducados* (lapsed) and in the autumn of 1843 specifically proclaimed the abrogation of the Salomon grant; but that company, although it had accomplished no work as yet, refused to accept the annulment and insisted that its concession remained in force. The company's representatives in Paris had already appealed to François Guizot, the French Foreign Minister, to support its claim, while at the same time Mosquera was again pressing the French government to participate in an international guarantee of isthmian neutrality. Guizot, although willing to have a canal constructed either by private enterprise or by the governments of France, Great Britain, and New Granada acting in concert, refused to make a definite recommendation without a new and thorough survey. Accordingly, in September 1843, he directed Napoléon Garella, an engineer distinguished for topographical work in the Pyrenees, and his assistant Jacques de Courtines, an official of the French Department of Public Works, to proceed to Panama and make an exhaustive study of the entire problem.

Garella explored and measured the isthmus for several months and submitted a voluminous report. Unceremoniously dismissing Morel's "discovery" as the fraud it was, he found the altitude of the divide at its lowest point to be about 475 feet above mean sea level. For some reason his conscientious survey failed to locate a much deeper depression a few miles farther east and approximately 200 feet lower, which remained undiscovered until 1849. Garella's plan called for a canal with its Pacific terminus on a small bay protected by the curve of Point Vacamonte, some ten miles west of Panama, which he considered superior as a port to Panama itself. The most noteworthy innovation proposed by Garella was the construction of an immense tunnel about 3.3 miles long to carry the canal through the divide. The summit level of the canal would be 167 feet above the sea, requiring 18 locks on the Atlantic slope and 17, including one tide lock, on the Pacific. Humboldt condemned the project as "altogether chimerical. . . . To diminish the number of locks he proposes to construct an enormous tunnel. . . . But its opening is placed so high that it still needs . . . 30 to 40 locks! This is an absurdity, not a canal suitable for interoceanic navigation." [17] Garella estimated the total cost of a canal 23 feet deep, including harbor improvements and tunnel, at $26,000,000.

His scheme received one endorsement, enthusiastic though of doubtful practical value, from a most unexpected source. In 1848 Marquis Claude Drigon de Magny, a member of the French religious order of Saint-Pie, recommended to Pope Pius IX the construction of canals at both Panama and Suez and the colonization of the adjacent lands under the temporal and spiritual supervision of the brotherhood: "The order of Saint-Pie . . . alone could give [to a settlement] . . . that religious and moral character which makes colonization beneficial, not only to the civilizing nation, but also to that which is being civilized. . . ." [18] Religion and hydrau-

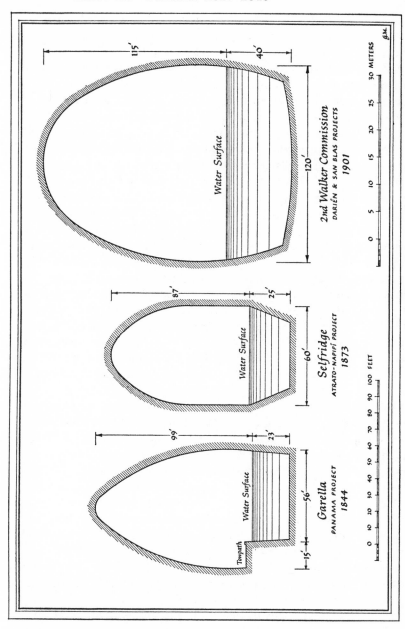

6. TYPICAL TUNNEL CROSS SECTIONS

lics made strange bedfellows, and this naïve piety did nothing to advance the canal project.

No attempt was made to carry out Garella's proposals. The French government took no steps to negotiate a treaty with New Granada, and the Salomon associates, forced at last to relinquish their concession under protest, abandoned their plans for a canal but exerted one more effort to establish a transit by railroad. In 1845 they launched a new enterprise, the Panama Company, and through their attorney and agent Mateo Klein obtained from the New Granadian Congress a charter to build and operate a railroad across the isthmus. The contract, signed at Bogotá on May 10 and approved on June 8, 1847, provided for completion of the railroad within six or at most eight years. After completion the concession was to run for 99 years, during which the government of New Granada "engages neither itself to make, nor to grant to any other Company . . . the power to establish another iron rail-road or Macadamized road . . . between the two oceans . . . [nor] to open a maritime canal across the Isthmus . . . without the consent of . . . [the] Company." [19] But the revolutionary outbreaks of 1848 in Europe upset all banking arrangements and prevented payment by the Panama Company of the 600,000 francs demanded as security, and on June 8, 1848, just one year after the approval of the contract, the Congress of New Granada declared it forfeited.

While French promoters were making and unmaking plans for an interoceanic transit England kept a close watch over the isthmus. In October 1831 the corvette *Hyacinth* anchored off the mouth of the Chagres, and the acting master, George Peacock, obtained a week's leave to visit the city of Panama. On his journey he "observed that the land near Gorgona became high in detached hills, but thought that . . . the water sheds would be found advantageous for . . . a canal, with probably not above 150 or 200 feet of deep cutting . . . at the highest point. . . . That a railroad might be made he had not the least doubt. . . ." [20] Peacock's observations were admittedly superficial, but on his map he traced a suggested canal route which followed with remarkable fidelity the line eventually adopted for the present waterway.

The earliest steamships to maintain a general commercial service in the Pacific were the *Peru* and *Chili*, 800 tons each, belonging to the Pacific Steam Navigation Company. The two vessels were brought out through the Straits of Magellan under their own steam in 1840 and for several years made regular and enormously profitable runs between Valparaiso and Panama. The line was British, but its guiding spirit was William Wheelwright of Massachusetts. He had first crossed the isthmus in 1825 and had repeated the journey a number of times. His explorations of the Pacific slope between Chiriquí and the Bayano River convinced him that the Chagres-Panama route offered "natural advantages for connecting the two oceans . . . much greater than at any other part of the isthmus" [21] and that "the level is so complete that it would only be necessary to have locks at either end of the canal, while its total length would not exceed thirty miles." [22] If Garella wanted too many locks in his canal Wheelwright was satisfied with too few; moreover he had gravely underestimated the width of the isthmus at that point.

In 1842 the Royal Mail Steam Packet Company inaugurated a passenger, mail, and cargo service between England and the West Indies. Three years later the line sent its colonial superintendent, W. B. Liot, to investigate the Panama transit problem. Liot reported that a canal could not be made to pay for at least half a century and recommended the construction of a highway between Panama and Puerto Bello, which he considered the best harbor on the Atlantic side. When he returned to England he "was deputed by several gentlemen of high commercial *status* in the City of London, to ascertain whether the British Government . . . were willing to afford such guarantees and immunities as might secure a transit company against undue risk, should the incorporation of such a body be decided upon to establish a Macadamized carriage road or a railroad from Portobélo to Panama. The Government, however, discouraged the overtures . . . and suffered the . . . project to be abandoned. . . ." [23] Nevertheless the Royal Mail inaugurated a monthly steamer service to the Atlantic port of Chagres in 1846, made some temporary repairs to the dilapidated trail, and maintained a makeshift system of canoe-and-mule transport across the isthmus until the railroad superseded it a few years later.

In 1847 the government of New Granada employed Evan Hopkins, an English mining engineer, and his New Granadian assistant Hurtado to survey the isthmus from Veragua to Darién. The vast expanse of territory to be covered made a thorough examination impossible, but Hopkins saw enough to persuade him that the Isthmus of San Blas and the region between Panama and Chagres offered the best facilities for a transit. Of the two he preferred the Panama route, though he firmly denied Lloyd's contention that the country could provide materials for canal construction and lands suitable for European settlement.

During the first half of the century dozens of surveying parties had examined the narrow portion of the continent between Tehuantepec and the Atrato, yet enormous tracts remained unknown, and even in the explored regions conflicting reports on the topography gave rise to infinite confusion. Thousands of measurements had been taken, but nobody had yet discovered the lowest gaps in the continental divide. Numerous concessions for highways, railways, and canals had been granted, extended, and annulled, yet not a spadeful of earth had been turned. No paved road between the oceans existed at any point. In 1850 transit conditions on the isthmus were little better than they had been when Balboa first crossed to the Pacific in 1513.

Nevertheless significant progress towards the eventual construction of a canal had been made — not in the field of engineering, but in that of diplomacy. In 1846 representatives of New Granada and the United States signed a treaty by which, in return for certain commercial privileges and concessions, the United States guaranteed the neutrality of the Isthmus of Panama and the sovereignty of New Granada over that territory. Neither government could foresee that little more than half a century later the treaty of 1846 would provide a juridical pretext for United States intervention in behalf of Panamanian independence and turn the scale in favor of American ownership and construction of the Panama canal.

When the treaty was drafted the governments of western Europe and the United States were more deeply concerned with the political aspects of an interoceanic canal than with the technical problems involved in its construction. Had either New Granada or Nicaragua been a powerful, wealthy, industrialized nation no international question would have arisen; one country or the other — possibly both — would have attempted to finance, build, operate, and fully control its own waterway with no more outside assistance than, for example, the British government had required for the construction of the Caledonian canal. But since both states were weak, poor, and commercially backward, the project was inevitably swept into the maelstrom of foreign politics.

New Granada had repeatedly appealed to Great Britain and France for guarantees of neutrality and sovereignty as well as financial aid for the construction of a highway, railroad, or canal, but had received only rebuffs. By 1846 relations between New Granada and Great Britain had become decidedly strained. The British government had shown an alarming disposition to interfere in Spanish American affairs by its insistence upon a protectorate over the Mosquito coast of Nicaragua and its championship of Costa Rican claims in a boundary dispute between that republic and New Granada, and British capital had enabled General Juan José Flores, the exiled dictator of Ecuador, to obtain three ships in London for a projected *coup d'état*. Although a vigorous protest by the Ecuadorian envoy caused the British Foreign Secretary, Palmerston, to prohibit the departure of the Flores expedition, rumors of the maneuver had already reached Bogotá and inflamed anti-British sentiment. Having lost faith temporarily in England, the government of New Granada turned to the United States for protection.

For two decades the United States government had endeavored to persuade New Granada to abolish certain discriminative duties on American products. Until now all overtures had been rejected, but in 1846 the New Granadian authorities abruptly shifted their position. Benjamin A. Bidlack, the new chargé d'affaires, reached Bogotá on December 1, 1845 and immediately entered into negotiations with the Foreign Minister, Manuel María Mallarino, for the settlement of the long-standing controversy. Mallarino and the President of the republic, Tomás Cipriano Mosquera, favored cancellation of the differential charges but demanded in return a guarantee of the neutrality of, and New Granadian sovereignty over, the isthmus. Although Bidlack, prodded by Mallarino, wrote repeatedly to Washington for instructions, his dispatches were ignored; and after hesitating for several months to commit his government to such a guarantee without specific authority from the State Department the envoy finally decided to act on his own responsibility.

The treaty was signed on December 12, 1846. The first 34 articles provided for reciprocal commercial arrangements in peace and war and involved no radical changes of policy on either side. In article 35 New Granada granted to United States citizens and shipping all of the commercial privileges enjoyed by its own citizens and vessels and guaranteed "that the right of way or transit across the Isthmus of Panama upon any modes of communication that now exist, or that may be hereafter constructed, shall be open and free to the Government and citizens of the United States, and for the transportation of any articles . . . of lawful commerce, belonging to the citizens of the United States. . . ." [24] In return the United States guaranteed "the perfect neutrality of the beforementioned Isthmus, with the view that the free transit from the one to the other sea may not be interrupted or embarrassed in any future time while this treaty exists; and, in consequence, the United States also guarantee, in the same manner, the rights of sovereignty and property which New Granada has and possesses over the said territory." [25]

After a short debate the New Granadian Congress ratified the treaty in May 1847, but in Washington it was subjected to a long delay. The State Department received the document with apathy colored by suspicion. After some hesitation — since Bidlack had acted without specific instructions — Polk transmitted the treaty to the Senate on February 10, 1847 with a message of recommendation: "The importance of this concession to the commercial and political interests of the United States can not easily be overrated. . . . No person can be more deeply sensible than myself of the danger of entangling alliances. . . . The ultimate object . . . is to secure to all nations the free and equal passage over the Isthmus. If the United States . . . should first become a party to this guaranty, it can not be doubted . . . that similar guaranties will be given . . . by Great Britain and France. . . . Besides, such a guaranty is almost indispensable to the construction of a railroad or canal across the territory. Neither sovereign states nor individuals would expend their capital . . . without some such security for their investments." [26]

Preoccupied by the war with Mexico, Polk exhibited little impatience for ratification, and the Senate displayed even less. Consideration of the pact did not commence until January 3, 1848. Meanwhile Mosquera, more anxious than the Americans for the treaty's confirmation, sent General Pedro Alcántara Herrán to Washington as envoy extraordinary and minister plenipotentiary. For several months Herrán campaigned unostentatiously for the treaty through conferences with administration and Senate leaders. He was rewarded by its ratification on June 3, 1848, after a single day's debate, by a vote of 29 to 7. On June 12, exactly 18 months after its signature, the treaty was proclaimed.

When the government of New Granada proposed the treaty it had not intended to hand over to the United States special privileges and exclusive responsibilities on the isthmus. Bogotá contemplated a succession of similar conventions with Great Britain (in spite of the momentary coolness) , France, and if possible Spain and the Netherlands. Nor, as Polk's message clearly indicated, did the United States government at that time demand or expect to be appointed sole protector of the transit. Until about 1870 United States policy consistently favored an international rather than an exclusively American control of the interoceanic transit, wherever it might be located, and in fact the Taylor-Fillmore administration actively opposed the assumption of such obligations by the

United States alone and emphatically disapproved of the commitments entered into by Polk. But no other nation saw fit to avail itself of the opportunity to participate in an analogous agreement, and the United States unexpectedly and unintentionally found itself possessed of unique rights over all transit routes in the territory of New Granada.

In practice application of the treaty was complicated by an irreconcilable difference in the emphasis placed by the two contracting parties upon the provisions of article 35. To New Granada the importance of the article consisted in the guarantee of sovereignty, to the United States in the right to insure uninterrupted communication across the isthmus. Thus when, as sometimes happened, an upheaval menaced New Granadian sovereignty over the isthmus but left the transit unmolested, the United States refused to interfere; while on other occasions it intervened to protect the transit even though that sovereignty was not in danger.

Chapter 13. Gold Rush

JAMES MARSHALL's discovery of gold in Sutter's mill race on January 24, 1848 brought new life to the commercially stagnant isthmus. Shipload after shipload of transients filled the Chagres with dugouts, crowded the miserable trails with footsore pack mules, and turned sleepy Panama into a roaring city of saloons, brothels, dance halls, and gambling dens. Fever-breeding mosquitoes swarmed in clouds from the hot wet jungle, and hundreds of bearded prospectors were left to rot in the cemeteries while thousands more, yellow and wasted, dragged themselves after months of waiting aboard ships bound for California.

Steamship service between the Atlantic and Pacific coasts of the United States by way of Panama had been planned and partly organized shortly before the discovery of gold. On March 3, 1847 Congress passed two separate acts designed to improve communication with the west coast. One directed the Secretary of the Navy to contract for the transportation of the mails between Panama and Oregon by steamers or sailing vessels constructed according to plans approved by the Navy Department and operated under its supervision. The second act empowered the Postmaster General to award another contract for the conveyance of mails by steamer from New York and New Orleans to Chagres, overland across the isthmus, and again by steamer from Panama to Astoria at the mouth of the Columbia River, touching at Monterey, San Francisco, and possibly other intermediate points. This bill limited the government's subsidy for the Pacific service between Panama and Astoria to $100,000 per year. Evidently the compensation was too low to attract investors, for in his annual report for 1847 the Postmaster General announced that no acceptable bid had been submitted. The Secretary of the Navy, whose appropriation under the other bill was not restricted to any specific amount, fared better. Congressional generosity to the Navy Department was inspired largely by the belief that merchant steamers could be readily converted into auxiliary warships, just as in the past sailing vessels had been refitted as privateers. Before it was discovered that paddle-wheel steamers with their vast areas of exposed, easily crippled machinery were peculiarly ill adapted to naval warfare several vessels had been designed and launched with such possible reconstruction in mind.

On April 20, 1847 Secretary of the Navy John Mason awarded a contract to Albert G. Sloo of Cincinnati for the operation of "a line of steamships, to consist of at least five vessels, for the transportation of the U. S. Mail from New York to New Orleans . . . touching at Charleston . . . Savannah and Havana, and from Havana to Chagres and back, twice a month. . . ." [1] The concession was to run ten years, and the government granted an annual mail subsidy of $290,000. On August 17, 1847 Sloo, a speculator without funds or credit of his own, turned his contract over to a group of more affluent New York capitalists, among whom were George Law, "a self-made man, having no previous experience in shipping, but with a record of successful enterprise in the construction of canals, bridges and railroads," [2] and Marshall Owen Roberts, "who had been previously interested in water transportation and who proved to be a particularly able hand at stock manipulation and the acquisition of lucrative government contracts." [3] Armed with the mail concession, Law, Roberts, and a few associates organized the United States Mail Steam Line. Very soon after the start of operations the company established a direct service between New York, New Orleans, and Chagres and reduced the number of calls at Havana.

On May 4, 1847 Mason advertised for bids for a monthly mail contract, also valid for ten years, on the Pacific side between Panama and Astoria. Here the conditions were much less tempting than in the Atlantic. The distance to be covered on each voyage was at least twice as great; Oregon was sparsely settled; the Mexican War was still in progress, and California had not yet become irrevocably part of the United States; gold was still undiscovered; the Pacific coast produced little except furs, hides, and lumber, bulky commodities which could be shipped more cheaply round Cape Horn by sailing vessel than across the isthmus, where two trans-shipments and an overland portage added enormously to the expense. Nevertheless Arnold Harris of Arkansas offered to perform the stipulated service for an annual subsidy of $199,000, and on November 16, 1847 the contract was signed. In this transaction Harris appears to have acted merely as an agent, for three days later he assigned the contract to William Henry Aspinwall of New York, a wealthy and enterprising merchant. Although he could not have foreseen the phenomenal prosperity of the Panama transit that was to follow the discovery of gold in California Aspinwall believed firmly in the future of the Pacific coast and was willing to risk a long-term investment for the sake of eventual profits. Moreover his steamship line was to be only one link in the chain of communication with the west; he had already formulated a plan for the construction of a railroad across the isthmus and proposed to combine the sea and land routes into a great unified commercial system.

With Aspinwall as president and a number of prominent directors the Pacific Mail Steamship Company was chartered on April 12, 1848 with a capital of $500,000, increased to $2,000,000 in 1850. Three new steamers, the *California, Oregon,* and *Panama,* were already nearing completion. All were wooden paddle-wheel steamers of approximately the same size, between 1000 and 1100 tons, about 200 feet long and 34 feet beam, not including the projecting paddles. Since with only three vessels it was impossible to maintain a monthly service as far north as Astoria the Secretary of the Navy permitted the company to make San Francisco its steamship terminus and deliver the mails to Oregon by sailing ship. This arrangement remained in force for about a year until additional steamers were placed in operation.

The *California* left New York on October 6, 1848. Although the discovery of gold had occurred more than eight months earlier the first reports gave no indication of the vast extent of the deposits, and the stampede to the west had not yet begun. When the *California* sailed she carried not a single passenger bound for the Pacific coast of North America and only a few for South American ports. She was equipped with cabins for 50 or 60 first-class passengers and with steerage berths to accommodate 150 to 200. Since there were no machine shops or storage warehouses on the Pacific coast she carried a complete set of spare machinery as well as enough provisions to feed the crew and the few passengers she was expected to transport for a whole year. The *California* reached Rio de Janeiro 26 days out of New York, breaking all existing records for the run, and remained there for three weeks to take on coal and undergo urgent repairs. On December 7 she entered the Straits of Magellan, where contrary winds and currents delayed her for six days and once nearly drove her upon the rocks. After touching at Valparaiso the steamer arrived at Callao on December 27. Until now the voyage had been marked by nothing more than the ordinary hazards and monotonies of the sea, but from Callao onward it became very lively indeed. Stories of the fabulous wealth of the California mines had preceded the steamer, and the town seethed with excitement. Peruvians in quest of gold and adventure boarded the almost empty vessel, and when the *California* sailed from Callao on January 10, 1849 she carried 17 cabin and about 80 steerage passengers all booked to San Francisco. When she anchored in the harbor of Panama a week later bedlam broke loose.

The United States Mail Steam Line, contractor for the Atlantic service between New York, New Orleans, and Chagres, had not yet obtained delivery of its own new steamers from the shipyards. To comply with the time clause in its contract the company chartered the small steamer *Falcon* for the first run to the isthmus, where she was to make connection with the expected arrival of the *California* at Panama. The *Falcon* sailed from New York on December 1, 1848 with only 29 passengers holding through tickets to California, and most of those were either missionaries or government employees. But by the time she left New Orleans on December 18 the gold fever had broken out in earnest all over the country, and 178 prospectors weighted down with a motley assortment of pots, pans, pickaxes, and miscellaneous equipment picked up at random — much of it utterly useless — were packed like sardines in the cabins and hold of the diminutive *Falcon*. Streaming across the isthmus from Chagres, the passengers reached Panama on January 7. Before the *California* arrived at that port ten days later three sailing vessels and three more steamers, *Crescent City, Orus,* and *Isthmus,* were on the way with additional hordes of gold-seekers. Within a few weeks more than 500 impatient emigrants had poured into the city and were clamoring for passage in the *California,* which already carried almost 100 Peruvians from Callao and was built to accommodate at the very most 150 more passengers.

The few lucky ones who held through tickets to California purchased before their departure from the United States secured berths without difficulty, but the remaining hundreds besieged the offices of the Pacific Mail's agents, Zachrisson and Nelson, with demands for accommodations which simply did not exist. To relieve the pressure the agency chartered the sailing packet *Philadelphia,* then unloading coal at Panama, for the voyage to San Francisco; but many of the restless adventurers, fearing that the best claims would all be staked out before the arrival of the slower ship, refused the substitution, and in any event the *Philadelphia* could carry only a fraction of the waiting emigrants. The Americans bitterly resented the pre-emption of half of the *California's* precious space by the Peruvian passengers and demanded their instant expulsion. General Persifor Smith, on his way to assume command of the United States military garrisons in California, went so far as to send an arrogant letter to William Nelson, United States consul at Panama as well as agent of the Pacific Mail, in which he threatened to exclude by force the Peruvians and other aliens from the gold diggings.

The Peruvians refused to surrender their passages and during the entire fortnight of the *California's* stopover at Panama remained cooped up on board, not daring to go ashore lest the irate Americans should prevent their re-embarkation. The Pacific Mail agency supported the foreigners, insisting that when they had purchased their tickets at Callao the extraordinary demand for accommodations at Panama could not have been anticipated and that the steamship line, as a common carrier, was obliged to sell transportation to the first applicants. Captain Marshall of the *California* finally pacified the Americans with the assurance that the Peruvians would sleep on deck so that the steamer would still hold its full quota of Yankees. Extra bunks were hastily installed in the dark and stuffy hold, and on January 31 the *California* left Panama with about 365 passengers — half again as many as she was designed to carry — and scarcely an inch of elbow room. Facilities for cooking and serving meals for such a crowd were pitifully inadequate, and complaints were heard on all sides. To add to the general unpleasantness the engine-room crew mutinied in protest against the punishment of a stoker who had hidden a stowaway, but at Mazatlán Captain Marshall put the ringleaders ashore and replaced them with Mexicans. When the *California* was about 300 miles short of Monterey the fuel supply gave out. Under sail the ship made little headway, and as provisions and drinking water were almost gone the situation was extremely grave. Spars, doors, bunks, and wooden fittings were chopped up to feed the engines, but when everything combustible had gone up in smoke the steamer was still far from port. Fortunately as some of the inner planking was being ripped out for fuel about 100 extra sacks of coal were found, enabling the *California* to wheeze slowly into the harbor of Monterey, where more wood was cut on shore. On February 28, 1849 the first of the gold rush steamers dropped anchor in San Francisco Bay.

Within a week the entire crew except the captain had deserted and set out for the mines, but even with her crew intact she could not have left immediately. Although the Pacific Mail had contracted with the Hudson's Bay Company for regular deliveries of coal from Vancouver Island and from England, the first shipment did not reach San Francisco until April. Meanwhile the *Panama* had started from New York on December 1, 1848, but a broken piston forced her to limp back to port under sail. A week later the third of the sister ships, the *Oregon,* put to sea and reached Panama on February 23, to be greeted by a howling mob of applicants for passage. The *Oregon* sailed from Panama on March 12 with nearly 300 passengers and arrived at San Francisco 20 days later. Taking a hint from the deserted *California,* Captain Pearson of the *Oregon* managed to hold most of his crew by increasing their pay tenfold. With 70 tons of coal remaining in her bunkers and the assistance of her sails she was able to reach the Mexican coaling port of San Blas, and on May 5, 1849 the *Oregon* completed her first southbound voyage to Panama. There she met the *Panama,* with the damaged piston repaired, about to sail for San Francisco. With two steamers in the harbor the supply of berths more nearly equaled the demand, though both vessels were still uncomfortably crowded. The *California,* coaled and manned at last, started south from San Francisco on May 1, and by June the service had settled down to a regular schedule of monthly departures from either end of the run.

The gold rush was now in full swing, and the Pacific Mail steamers reaped huge profits. Annual dividends sometimes amounted to 25% or even 30%. By 1850 eastbound traffic began to assume respectable proportions: prospectors who had already "struck it rich" returned with their nuggets and gold dust to the comforts of the civilized East; others, having lost everything but the price of a steamship ticket, straggled home to begin again at the bottom; still others, determined to settle permanently in California, went to visit their families or bring them out to the Pacific coast. During the year 1853, 15,502 passengers arrived at San Francisco via Panama while 10,533 traveled east by the same route. Heavy freight was still shipped round Cape Horn, but the Pacific Mail carried express parcels at a prodigious profit. One of the most important sources of the line's income was the steady stream of gold bullion from California, all of which was transported by way of Panama for several years.

The Pacific Mail soon had to face competition. In the spring of 1850 George Law added a Pacific service to his Atlantic concession, operating between Panama and San Francisco four small steamers which cut so deeply into the profits of the Pacific Mail that the latter purchased them in May 1851. In 1850 the Empire City Line placed three steamers on the same route, two of which were bought by the Pacific Mail a few months later. The Empire City promptly acquired another vessel, the *Union,* but it went ashore after one or two voyages, and with only one steamer left the line carried on a losing battle against the strongly entrenched Pa-

cific Mail. In September 1850 Wheelwright's Pacific Steam Navigation Company was tempted by the high passenger fares to extend
its service to San Francisco, but the first voyage proved a financial
failure, and the experiment was not repeated. In July 1851, just
when the Pacific Mail had rid itself by purchase or otherwise of all
serious competition in the Pacific, the most formidable and tena-
cious of all its rivals — the Vanderbilt line, with a transit across
Nicaragua — entered the arena. The two companies fought savagely for the California trade until 1865, when the Pacific Mail
bought out both Vanderbilt and the United States Mail Steam
Line and inaugurated a through service under one management
between New York and San Francisco.

In the first years of the gold rush, when every inch of space on
anything that would float found a ready purchaser, a most heterogeneous collection of vessels carried passengers between San Francisco and Panama: sailing ships of all shapes and sizes, flat-bottomed
river steamers, harbor tugs, and antiquated broken-down transatlantic liners. The eager gold-seekers were seldom inclined to be
finicky about their accommodations, although many did complain
of the overcrowding and resented the presence of rough-mannered,
noisy, or drunken fellow travelers. One pioneer described his companions as "the roughest, most uncouth lot of desperadoes that
ever climbed over a ship's side. . . . There were of course not
berths for more than half. . . . Anything like regularity in serving meals . . . was impossible; in fact, often-times the whole cabin
dinner as it left the galley was seized *in transitu,* and carried off in
triumph by the steerage passengers. The scenes enacted at table
were brutal beyond description, and fights and brawls were generally the accompaniments of every dinner. . . . Sea-sickness was
universal, while the Isthmus fever was making sad havoc among
our number; day after day some poor fellow . . . was unceremoniously buried over the side. . . . As we got into better weather
. . . our delectable fellow passengers emerged from their lairs and
then commenced such a saturnalia as is not often enacted on the
ocean. Drinking and gambling became the order of the day. . . .
Our long dining-tables . . . were occupied by roulette . . . faro
banks, and . . . every known game; fights of course were frequent, but fortunately none terminated fatally. . . ." [4]

Those who tired of waiting in fever-stricken Panama for the
crowded steamers and took passage in sailing vessels for San Francisco often fared even worse. In May 1849 Julius Pratt paid $200
for the privilege of embarking with 400 other travelers in the 500-

ton *Humboldt:* "The hold . . . was cleared out and bunks of boards were arranged in tiers along the sides so that each cube of space, measuring six feet high, wide, and deep respectively, should contain nine persons. This did not provide for all, but the rest were to . . . sleep on deck or in the boats hung at the davits. . . . We were three weeks drifting amid adverse currents and calms before we could get out of the Bay of Panama, and after that made but slow progress. . . . Forty-eight days were passed on this prison ship, and our rotten and wormy provisions and our intolerably nasty water were almost exhausted when we entered the . . . harbor of Acapulco. . . ." [5] By that time Pratt had had enough. He waited at Acapulco two months and finally reached San Francisco in the *California.*

The persistent calms of the equatorial Pacific, responsible for endless delays to shipping since the dawn of navigation in those waters, provided the advocates of rival routes with a powerful argument against the Panama transit until late in the nineteenth century, when steamships had so generally driven sailing vessels from the seas that the lack of wind no longer mattered. After leaving Panama sailing ships bound for California were often forced to proceed almost due south for hundreds of miles in order to strike favorable winds which would drive them north and west to their destination. At the peak of the gold rush any hulk, no matter how unseaworthy, that happened to lie at anchor in Panama Bay was pressed into service: "Schooners of from thirteen to twenty-five tons, that had been abandoned as worthless, were soon galvanized, by pen and type, into *'the new and fast sailing schooner.'* These were immediately filled up at from $200 to $300 per ticket, passengers finding themselves. . . ." [6] One can readily sympathize with the pioneer who after a long and miserable voyage under sail advised other travelers "to attempt to *swim* from Panama to San Francisco, rather than take passage in a *sailing* vessel." [7]

After the first feverish months conditions improved rapidly. The slow sailing ships and obsolete steamboats were replaced by a fleet of new steamers specially built for the Panama service, comfortable enough though not always completely up to date in construction or mechanical design. Of the 110 steamers operated on that run between 1848 and 1869 — some of them for only a single voyage — all but two had wooden hulls although iron was already in fairly general use elsewhere, and paddle wheels continued to churn Pacific waters long after the more efficient screw propellers had superseded them on other trade routes. Many of the Panama steam-

ers were unusually roomy, and some offered widely advertised lux-
uries. The 2000-ton Pacific Mail liner *Golden Gate,* placed in service in 1851, could accommodate 850 passengers without excessive
crowding; though in truth the space per passenger then considered
adequate would satisfy few modern globe-trotters. In the *Champion* a steerage area measuring approximately 30 by 50 feet contained 247 bunks, arranged in three tiers, and each bunk was intended to hold three persons. Greater comfort was provided for
cabin passengers. The *John L. Stephens,* built in 1852, boasted a
rudimentary ventilation system and even a bathroom.

Some of these early steamers with their inefficient engines and
clumsy paddles bowled along at speeds only slightly inferior to
those made by today's express liners. In good weather the *Golden
Gate* covered the 4000-odd miles between Panama and San Francisco, with one stop at Acapulco, in only 13 days, and by 1866 the
through voyage from New York to San Francisco, including two
transfers and the rail journey across the isthmus, could be made in
21 days — four days less than the overland mail coaches required
to travel from St. Louis to California. Fares were exceedingly erratic. In 1849, when they were highest, the official price of a first-
class ticket from New York to San Francisco — not including the
cost of the isthmian transit — was about $450, and of steerage pas-
sage $225; but the same ticket often changed hands several times,
and as each transaction netted the seller a handsome profit the final
purchaser sometimes paid as much as $1000 for a steerage berth
from Panama to San Francisco. Taking the gold rush period as a
whole the cost of the passage from New York to California via Panama, exclusive of the crossing of the isthmus, averaged about $200
first class, $175 second class, and $100 steerage. Although the agents
in Panama attempted to regulate the distribution of tickets as
fairly as possible on the principle of first come, first served it was
not always easy to establish the exact order of priority among so
many applicants. To avoid quarrels the agents occasionally sold a
certain number of tickets by lottery, which probably solved the
question of precedence as equitably as any other system would have
done. Cut-throat competition naturally brought about a drastic if
temporary reduction of rates, often to the point of severe loss to
the transportation companies. For a short period in 1855, just after
the completion of the Panama Railroad, cabin passages for the entire voyage from New York to San Francisco were sold for only $50
and steerage tickets for $10, *including* the transisthmian train fare
of $25. This meant of course that the rival steamship companies
were actually paying passengers to travel in their ships.

The gold rush took the isthmus by surprise, and for the first few months the scanty and haphazard transportation facilities from Chagres to Panama were completely swamped by the tidal wave of emigrants. Passengers disembarking at Chagres found themselves plunged into a hurly-burly of yelling boatmen, who quickly learned to demand exorbitant prices for seats in their leaky dugouts. In the confusion the more timid gold-seekers and those with the leanest purses were often stranded for days or weeks at Chagres, where the devil in the form of fever was more than likely to seize the hindmost. In January 1849 General Persifor Smith complained to the Secretary of War: "No preparation was made here by the steamboat company for transporting passengers across the isthmus, or affording them any information or aid in relation to it. The roads are almost impassable even for mules, and the number of boats in the river and animals on the roads are entirely insufficient." [8]

Among the pioneers were numerous sober, respectable, educated men, some of whom left picturesque and often amusing records of the hardships of the isthmian transit. Charles F. Hotchkiss left New York in September 1849 "with a great crowd of gold-seekers, a singular compound of men, and but five women — in which both ladies and gentlemen were extremely scarce. . . . Gambling, rum and oaths were the circulating medium the whole trip, morning, noon and night. Gold was the absorbing topic of conversation. . . . We . . . arrived at Chagres, a low, miserable town, of thirty thatched huts, and the passengers got on shore as best they could, in miserable shore canoes, under an old roll of the Caribbean Sea, in which several were swamped. Chagres . . . was poorly prepared for the immense emigration. . . . No eating houses or saloons. . . . Our little party of four . . . concluded a bargain with two brawny natives to pole us through to Crusus [Cruces], took them before their alcalde . . . paid the bill . . . they to feed themselves, four hours per twenty-four given for rest, and forfeit a flogging if they did not perform. A wise . . . arrangement . . . for the rascals mutinied . . . the next morning, and refused to go forward unless we gave them food. We remonstrated, took possession of the craft ourselves, shoved her off shore . . . and waited events. Four Yankees, with each a pistol . . . against two natives, stark naked, was considerable odds in our favor, and we intended to keep it. . . . They gave in, and at it they went. . . . We found Crusus quite a neat village. . . . The hotel was a horrid place . . . both in its eating and sleeping department — the latter . . . consisted of bunks, full of vermin. . . . The demand [for mules] far exceeded the supply. Current price ten dollars . . . to Pan-

ama — no reclamation on either side if he died on the journey.
. . . [The] passages through the gorges are only of sufficient width
for a pack animal, and on entering them from either end, a . . .
loud whistle or hoot of the man in charge of the train is given, and
answered by the other, and the party omitting to give this notice,
if met in the gorge, must back out. . . ." [9]

In 1850 Joseph Gregory published a little guidebook filled with
useful information and sage advice for isthmian travelers. Evidently the debarkation arrangements at Chagres had improved
within the past year: "The Steam Ship Company provide for the
landing of the passengers and their baggage, using the ship's quar-
ter-boats for the former, and the launch of the Steamer Orus for
the latter, conveying the whole to the Orus, which vessel lands the
passengers on what is called the American side of the river. . . .
Three or four taverns are kept at this landing by white men, one
or two of whom are Americans. After seeing your baggage safely
landed . . . your first object should be to secure a good canoe —
one holding four or five persons is the most preferable. . . . The
great secret . . . is to get off early in the morning, and be liberal
to the men that work the canoe. You can coax, better than drive
them. At the end of about two days you will reach Gorgona, where
it is tempting to stay, but should you go on shore there, you will
experience great difficulty . . . in getting your boatmen into their
canoe again. This is their worst fault generally. . . . At Gorgona,
interested persons will advise you to take the road to Panama from
that point. *Pay no attention* . . . for that road is totally impassable for nine months in the year. Push on without delay to Cruces,
and if you arrive there in the morning, you will hardly be able to
get on the Panama road before the next morning. Meanwhile you
can call at Funk's and Pleise's houses. They forward baggage by
mules to Panama. Ascertain their charge . . . *but let no promises
induce you to leave your baggage to be forwarded after you, but
see it start at least.*" [10] Lest his readers should find the many complications disheartening this pioneer Baedeker ended his recital
with a consoling tribute to nature: "The voyage up the Chagres
. . . has been by some persons execrated in tolerably strong terms,
not to say diabolical. As far as my own feelings were concerned, I
. . . never beheld more magnificent scenery, or luxuriant vegetation. . . ." [11]

Another emigrant painted a none too alluring picture of the
city of Panama in the early days of the gold rush: "Most of the
principal houses . . . had been converted into hotels . . . kept
by Americans. . . . There was also numbers of large American

. . . shops. . . . Although all foreigners were spoken of as 'los Americanos' by the natives, there were . . . men from every country in Europe. The Frenchmen were the most numerous, some of whom kept stores and very good restaurants. There were also several large gambling saloons . . . always crowded. . . . Life in Panama was pretty hard. . . . There was . . . a great deal of sickness, and absolute misery, among the Americans. Diarrhœa and fever were the prevalent diseases. The deaths were very numerous, but were frequently either the result of the imprudence of the patient himself, or of the total indifference . . . of his neighbours, and the consequent want of any care or attendance. . . . The heartless selfishness . . . was truly disgusting. . . . There was an hospital attended by American physicians, and supported to a great extent by Californian generosity; but it was quite incapable of accommodating all the sick. . . . The sickness was no doubt much increased by the . . . filthy state of the town. . . ." [12]

In February 1850 Cornelius K. Garrison and his partner Fretz, operators of a Panama gambling establishment, acquired a stable of native horses and 100 Kentucky mules and organized a transportation service for passengers, baggage, and merchandise across the isthmus. The undertaking was managed efficiently and honestly as well as profitably, and the partners soon expanded their activities to include a bank at Panama. This first attempt to systematize the chaotic isthmian transit relieved the harassed emigrants of responsibility for their own equipment, eliminated the necessity for individual negotiations with unreliable native boatmen and mule drivers, and assured the safe and prompt delivery of their possessions. If the new enterprise robbed the crossing of some of its earlier piquancy it certainly diminished its irritations. Until the Panama Railroad drove canoes and mules out of business in 1855 Garrison and Fretz, as well as a number of rival agencies organized on similar lines, transported passengers, personal baggage, express parcels, and tons of bullion across the isthmus with only a negligible percentage of loss or damage.

Emigrants traveling independently in small groups were by no means safe from attack and robbery. Lawless bands harried the Cruces and Gorgona trails and defied the New Granadian authorities. On his return journey to New York in the spring of 1851 the luckless Julius Pratt lost his trunk and his precious sack of gold dust at Panama, spent three days searching for them, missed the regular mule train to Gorgona, and eventually set out for Chagres with only one or two companions: "I knew nothing of the great risk in traveling alone, as the natives two years before appeared to me an exceptionally honest people. But . . . contact with American roughs had changed them to thieves and murderers, and the whole route . . . was infested with American, English, and Spanish highwaymen. . . . Near . . . Gorgona, we met five horsemen, a bad-looking lot . . . who . . . wheeled around to join us. We lost no time in starting at a run. They . . . made a rapid pursuit, but became . . . scattered. . . . We kept in advance until we came within sight of the village, when they fell back. We learned that they made their headquarters at the public house where we stopped, and were known there as desperate . . . outlaws. Robbery and murder were of frequent occurrence . . . and we were told . . . that on the day of our arrival a party of eight coming up the river were . . . robbed, and murdered by their boatmen. . . ." [13]

A curious little book entitled *The Derienni; or, Land pirates of the Isthmus,* published anonymously in 1853, purported to be "a true and graphic history of robberies, assassinations, and other horrid deeds perpetrated by those cool-blooded miscreants, who have infested for years the great highway to California. . . ." [14] According to this lurid tale five members of the vicious gang were captured by a self-appointed posse of American residents of Panama, where they were executed on July 27, 1852. The account was unquestionably graphic, but its literal truth may be doubted. The quaintly stilted style combined sticky sentiment with dime-novel blood and thunder: "On the Isthmus . . . existed . . . a desperate and rapacious set of men, combining their united strength for plunder, and even murder, if necessary to the accomplishment of their base and foul designs. . . . The Derienni comprised intellect, perseverance, daring and unanimity, worthy of a better cause. . . ." [15]

Chapter 14. Panama Railroad

O N December 28, 1848 the government of New Granada
awarded the transisthmian railroad concession, forfeited
by the French company represented by Mateo Klein, to
a triumvirate of Americans: William Henry Aspinwall, Henry
Chauncey, and John Lloyd Stephens. The new contract closely followed the pattern of the Klein agreement, with which it was linked
by specific reference, but the duration of the privilege was reduced
from 99 to 49 years. The government reserved the right to redeem
the concession and acquire the road at the expiration of 20 years
for $5,000,000, at the end of 30 years for $4,000,000, or after 40
years for $2,000,000. In April 1850 the contract was re-written as
an independent document with all references to the Klein charter
eliminated.

As directors of the Pacific Mail Aspinwall and Chauncey already
had a financial stake in the development of an isthmian transit.
Stephens, though a lawyer by profession, was better known as an
explorer and amateur archæologist. In 1839 President Van Buren
had sent him to secure the information regarding the Nicaragua
route which Biddle had neglected to obtain four years earlier. During the course of this journey and a second one made in 1841 Stephens traveled widely through all of the Central American states
and the little-known Mexican provinces of Chiapas and Yucatán,
recording his impressions of the topography, the customs of the inhabitants, and as much as was then visible of the ruined and buried
Mayan cities. So accurate were his observations, so vivid his descriptions, and so lucid his style that his two books rank high among
the great travel works of all time.

A few days before the signature of their contract Aspinwall,
Chauncey, and Stephens petitioned the United States Congress to
grant them the official recognition and support which would encourage private capitalists to invest in the railroad. Although the
House Committee on Naval Affairs recommended an annual mail
subsidy of $250,000 no appropriation was made at that time. In
April 1849 the Panama Railroad Company was incorporated under the laws of New York, and a few months later Stephens was

elected president and Colonel A. J. Center vice president. Several of the directors also occupied seats on the board of the Pacific Mail, but the two corporations were otherwise separate. While the charter authorized the company to sell stock to the amount of $5,000,-000 the first subscription, opened in June 1849, was limited to $1,000,000. Even with the gold rush well under way the public absorbed less than half the issue, and the directors were obliged to purchase the remainder.

Shortly before the contract was concluded the railroad promoters employed James L. Baldwin to undertake a preliminary survey, during the course of which he discovered a pass through the divide at an elevation of only 337 feet above mean sea level — about 140 feet lower than the minimum altitude recorded by Garella. In January 1849 a much more elaborate and thorough survey to determine the exact line of the railroad was begun by Brevet Lieutenant Colonel George W. Hughes, assisted by Baldwin, Edward W. Serrell, J. J. Williams, and other technicians. This expedition found a still lower gap, 275 feet above sea level, which subsequent explorations have proved to be the lowest summit existing anywhere along the continental divide outside of Nicaragua. Hughes anticipated no serious difficulties, but it soon became evident that he had underestimated the destructive forces indigenous to the tropics. Ties made of native timber or of imported spruce and pine decayed with such alarming rapidity that within a few years it was necessary to replace them with lignum vitæ from the province of Cartagena, a wood so hard that holes had to be bored before spikes could be driven into it, exceedingly durable but correspondingly expensive to cut and shape. The chief surveyor's confidence in the safety of Limón Bay was rudely shattered on December 31, 1854, just before the completion of the railroad, when a violent hurricane from the northeast tore into the exposed side of the harbor and wrecked every vessel anchored in the new port. Until the breakwaters which Hughes had considered superfluous were constructed some 60 years later as part of the canal works similar storms frequently wrought havoc in the bay and disrupted transisthmian communications.

Hughes also cherished illusions concerning the healthfulness of the isthmus: "On the question of *health,* I consider the adverse accounts . . . much exaggerated; such of the inhabitants as live here in the *manner of civilized beings* enjoy as good health as the people of the north, and, of the great numbers of emigrants who have passed over during the present season, but few have suffered from local diseases." [1] Since he left the isthmus early in June he escaped the long rainy season during which malaria, yellow fever, and dysentery ran riot. The construction gangs who toiled on the railroad for the next five years were not so fortunate. Hughes thought the feasibility of a canal "more than problematical, unless all consideration of cost be disregarded. . . . We shall be compelled . . . to largely increase Mr. Garella's estimate; and . . . it will not be very extravagant to place it at . . . $50,000,000. I do not wish to be understood as asserting that Mr. Garella's project is absolutely impracticable. . . ." [2] His assistant Serrell expressed himself less cautiously: "The very considerable length through the base of the water-shed . . . together with the fact that no adequate sources exist for the supply of [water to] a summit level and lock· ages . . . must for ever preclude the possibility of connecting the two oceans at this point by water communication. . . ." [3]

Immediately after the company's incorporation the directors awarded a contract for the building of the entire road to two prominent engineers, John Cresson Trautwine and George Muirson Totten (usually called "Colonel" Totten, though he held no military rank), who proceeded to the isthmus with a large staff of assistants to locate the precise line of the railroad and organize the work of construction. At first they proposed to build the section from Gorgona to the Pacific before starting on the Atlantic portion, on the theory that flat-bottomed steamers could navigate the Chagres as far as Gorgona and maintain communication with the Caribbean until the railroad should be completed. But when the contractors found their two steamboats, drawing only 18 inches, unable to proceed up river they changed their plans and determined to commence construction at the Atlantic terminus, which Trautwine had located on Manzanillo Island on the east side of Limón Bay. To secure possession of this island of 650 acres or approximately one square mile the railroad company traded back to New Granada twice that area of the lands conceded to it in another part of the country.

The gold rush was now in full spate, and while the growing tide of emigration promised eventual prosperity to the railroad it enormously increased the difficulties and expenses of construction. The demand for boatmen, muleteers, and porters made it almost impossible for the railroad contractors to hire native laborers; wages rose to unprecedented heights, and the cost of materials augmented in proportion. Totten and Trautwine, faced with ruin, petitioned the railroad company to release them from their obligations. By an amicable arrangement the contract was annulled, and the company

itself assumed the burden of construction, retaining Totten as chief
engineer and Trautwine as his principal assistant. Totten left immediately for Cartagena to engage workmen, while Trautwine and
Baldwin, accompanied by a few natives hired at exorbitant wages
on the isthmus, went to Manzanillo Island. In May 1850 they began to clear the land for the Atlantic terminus of the railroad. The
site of the future city of Colón reeked of desolation: "It was a virgin swamp. . . . The air was . . . swarming with sand-flies and
musquitoes. These last proved so annoying to the laborers that,
unless their faces were protected by gauze veils, no work could be
done, even at midday. Residence on the island was impossible. The
party had their quarters in an old brig . . . anchored in the bay.
Thus situated, with a mere handful of native assistants — most of
the original forty or fifty having previously deserted on account of
the higher wages and easier life promised them by the Transit —
Messrs. Trautwine and Baldwin struck the first blow upon this
great work. No imposing ceremony inaugurated the 'breaking
ground.' Two American citizens, leaping, axe in hand, from a native canoe upon a wild and desolate island, their retinue consisting
of half a dozen Indians, who clear the path with rude knives, strike
their glittering axes into the nearest tree; the rapid blows rever-
berate from shore to shore, and the stately cocoa crashes upon the
beach. . . ." [4]

After Totten returned with 40 laborers early in June the clearing of the marshy island progressed more rapidly, but it was still
out of the question for engineers or workmen to spend even a single night on shore. The rainy season had set in, torrents of water
deluged the island, and myriads of mosquitoes swarmed in the sop-
ping underbrush. At night the entire party crowded into the ancient brig. Inside the vessel the suffocating heat and voracious insects made sleep impossible, and nearly all preferred to lie on the
open deck under the pelting rain. The miseries of seasickness increased the general discomfort as the ship rocked ceaselessly in the
Atlantic swell. With constitutions undermined by toilsome days
and restless nights more than half of the men were soon laid low
by malaria or dysentery. Since the party had no doctor the patients
either died or recovered with only the most rudimentary attendance by their unskilled colleagues. After a few weeks the railroad
company purchased an old steamboat, the *Telegraph,* lying abandoned at Chagres, and sent her to Limón Bay as an auxiliary dormitory. This somewhat improved living conditions, but the men
were still far from comfortable.

In August 1850 actual construction work on the railroad commenced at the Atlantic terminus. Another camp was established at Gatún, 7 miles away on the banks of the Chagres, to which point steamboats brought materials, machinery, and provisions, while the roadbed was carried across the swampy lowlands on piles and rock fills. Hospitals were erected and immediately filled to the last cot. At one time illness and desertions so reduced the working force that operations came to an almost complete standstill, but the advent of the dry season in January brought a welcome abatement of the fever. Before April wooden docks had been erected on the shores of Manzanillo Island, the line located as far as Barbacoas 16 miles beyond Gatún, and work begun at several intermediate points. On October 1, 1851 the first train of construction cars rolled over the line from Limón Bay to Gatún.

Meanwhile the financial resources of the company were almost exhausted. The $1,000,000 realized from the sale of stock had been expended, the market value of the shares had declined to almost nothing, and the directors found themselves obliged to borrow on their personal credits in order to continue the work. Hope for the ultimate completion of the road had fallen to a low ebb when an accident unexpectedly reawakened public interest in the enterprise. In November 1851 two steamers filled with California-bound passengers, the *Georgia* and *Philadelphia*, arrived at Chagres during a violent storm. After unsuccessful attempts to land the passengers in small boats had caused the loss of several lives by drowning the two vessels took refuge in the slightly more sheltered haven of Limón Bay, whence the emigrants, more than 1000 strong, demanded transportation on the railroad as far as Gatún. Although the company officials demurred on the ground that no passenger cars were yet available their objection was quickly overcome, and the cheering gold-seekers were hauled on flatcars over the 7 miles of completed roadbed. The incident proved an excellent advertisement for the line; stock prices rose, and investors were inspired with renewed confidence.

By July 1852 the tracks extended to Barbacoas, about halfway across the isthmus, where the bridge across the Chagres was to be constructed. The road up to that point had cost far more than the company had anticipated, and after the premature death of Stephens in October and the installation of William C. Young as the new president of the railroad the directors decided to complete the section from Barbacoas to the Pacific by contract, hoping that this method would prove more economical. The contract was awarded to Minor C. Story, whose organization began its task with an attempt to build the bridge over the Chagres, some 300 feet wide at Barbacoas and flowing between steep banks. In April 1853, when the structure was almost completed, a sudden flood carried away the main span. This disaster combined with repeated outbreaks of fever and other ailments so delayed progress that after 14 months of work under the contract system the bridge was still unfinished, and only 8 miles of roadbed beyond Barbacoas had been graded. The bankrupt contractors retired, and Young resigned the presidency in favor of David Hoadley, who held the office until 1871. The railroad conÍpany, once more taking construction into its own hands, rebuilt the bridge more substantially. In May 1854 the line was opened as far as Gorgona, entirely eliminating the canoe trip up the Chagres and leaving only 18 miles of the old transit to be traversed by mules. The Pacific Mail celebrated with a spirited advertisement in the San Francisco papers: [5]

31 MILES BY RAILROAD!
SAFETY AND SPEED! NO SICKNESS!
NO RIVER TRAVEL!

Under the company's own supervision construction advanced simultaneously from Panama and from Gorgona to the summit of the ridge. In this region, where the hilly terrain necessitated several deep cuts, landslips frequently impeded progress — ominous precursors of the great slides that were later to obstruct the canal. On January 27, 1855, "at midnight, in darkness and rain, the last rail was laid, and on the following day a locomotive passed from ocean to ocean. . . ." [6] The railroad was open throughout its entire length, but it was far from complete. During the next four years embankments were reinforced, wooden bridges replaced by iron ones, ballasting made heavier, decaying ties replaced, grades reduced, curves straightened, intermediate stations established, and a telegraph line installed across the isthmus. An iron pier replaced the wooden one at Panama, and at the Atlantic terminus a new iron lighthouse 60 feet high superseded the antiquated wooden tower. The completed railroad measured 47.57 miles in length, with a single track supplemented by sidings at suitable points.

For two years the Atlantic terminus on Manzanillo Island remained without a name. Stephens suggested that the settlement should be called Aspinwall, and on February 2, 1852 the city was formally christened and incorporated. A section of the swampy island was filled in, streets laid out, buildings erected, and a small reservoir for the storage of fresh water constructed about two miles away on the mainland. Yet this busy port through which thousands of travelers passed each year presented a deplorably shabby and forlorn appearance: "It would be hard to find in any other part of the tropics so many wretched hovels as can be found in Aspinwall. . . . All sorts . . . of buildings have been . . . erected, huddled together without regard to ventilation; inhabited by . . . people, living more like pigs than human beings. . . . The plan . . . on paper, is quite attractive; the city is regularly laid out, and has its public square, its lots devoted to public buildings. . . . Leaving the back street, a few steps would carry you into swamp knee deep. . . . The 'public square' is now only promenaded by the alligator or water moccasin. . . ." [7] The town's name gave rise to a long-drawn-out and ludicrous dispute. The government and citizens of Colombia insisted upon calling it Colón, while the Americans clung stubbornly to their own choice. The clumsy compromise Aspinwall-Colón satisfied neither side, and the childish deadlock persisted until 1890, when the Colombian government ended the controversy by instructing its postmasters to return to the senders all mail addressed to Aspinwall. Since then Colón has been the town's official name.

During the construction period the railroad company struggled valiantly but not always successfully to maintain an adequate working force and to preserve that force's health. Laborers were recruited in New Granada, Jamaica, England, Ireland, France, Germany, Austria, India, and China, but "it was soon found that many of these . . . were little adapted to the work. . . . The Chinamen, one thousand in number, had been brought . . . by the Company, and every possible care taken which would conduce to their health and comfort — their hill-rice, their tea, and opium . . . had been imported with them — they were carefully housed and attended to — and it was expected that they would prove efficient. . . . But they had been engaged upon the work scarcely a month before almost the entire body became affected with a melancholic, suicidal tendency, and scores of them ended their unhappy existence by their own hands. Disease broke out among them, and raged so fiercely that in a few weeks scarcely two hundred remained. The . . . Irishmen and Frenchmen also suffered severely, and there was found no other resource but to reship them . . . and replenish from the neighboring provinces and Jamaica. . . ." [8]

Fantastic rumors concerning the appalling death rate among Panama Railroad workers had already spread throughout the United States, where it was commonly reported that a man had been buried for every tie laid on the roadbed. In 1884 a literal-minded defender of the transit took the trouble to point out the absurdity of this canard: "The . . . Railroad is about 47½ miles long, it requires about 74,000 ties for that distance. . . . At no time has the railroad company had more than 4,000 men altogether on the . . . works. Modern arithmetic is insufficient to solve this problem." [9] Actually the maximum number of laborers employed at one time on railroad construction was probably about 7000, but even so the death-for-every-tie rumor undoubtedly exaggerated the true figures many times over. Unfortunately the company kept no mortality statistics for its dark-skinned workmen so the total number of deaths is unknown, but the records showed that 293 white employees died from all causes during the five construction years.

Until the first transcontinental railroad was completed in 1869 the Panama Railroad reaped a golden harvest. If its cost — almost $8,000,000 or about $168,000 a mile, including the improvements made between 1855 and 1859 — was far greater than anticipated, so was its earning power. The line charged exorbitantly high rates, probably the highest of any railroad in the world: $25 or more than 50 cents a mile for each adult passenger, with half-price tickets for children under 12 and quarter-price for those under 6; 5 cents per pound for personal baggage; and $1.80 per cubic foot for express parcels. These charges, excessive as they appeared, amounted to so much less than the cost of transportation by any other route — except for bulky freight of low unit value — that travelers and shippers paid them without protest.

Long before the railroad was completed money began to pour into its treasury. In 1853, with only 23 miles in operation, the line carried 32,111 passengers; in 1854, with 31 miles finished, 30,108. When the road was opened from ocean to ocean in January 1855 it had already earned more than $1,000,000. By 1859 the total gross receipts for eight years — during the first three of which the line extended only part way across the isthmus — amounted to over $8,000,000, while the running expenses, including depreciation, for the same period came to little more than $2,000,000. With the reduction of grades, improvement of the roadbed, and purchase of more powerful locomotives service was speeded up and the capacity of the road increased. Before 1867 the time required for the journey had been cut from six hours to three or less, and the railroad possessed ample facilities for the rapid handling of enormous crowds: "Fifteen hundred passengers, with the . . . mails, and the freight of three steam-ships, have not unfrequently been transported . . . during a single half day. . . . The arrangements for the loading and unloading of cargoes are unusually perfect . . .

and . . . frequently less than two hours pass between the *arrival of the largest ships,* laden with from two to three hundred tons of merchandise, besides the baggage of from four to eight hundred passengers, and the *departure of the trains* for Panama. . . ." [10]

From 1856 to 1870 inclusive the annual dividends never fell below 12% and in 1868 reached 44%. In 1865 the capital was increased from $5,000,000 to $7,000,000. During the entire existence of the company prior to its acquisition by the United States government in 1904 it distributed in dividends a grand total of $37,-798,840. In the early days the railroad derived much of its revenue from the transportation of gold bullion from the California mines, a commerce of which the Panama transit held a virtual monopoly until the transcontinental railroad commenced operation in 1869: "The amount of specie conveyed over the road from 1855 to 1867 was over seven hundred and fifty millions of dollars, *without the loss of a single dollar;* and during the same period there were sent . . . some 300,000 bags of mail . . . not one of which was lost. And of the many thousands of tons of freight . . . the losses in transportation . . . has [*sic*] been comparatively trifling" [11] The road failed to maintain this high standard in later years. Joseph L. Bristow, special commissioner appointed by Theodore Roosevelt to investigate the Panama Railroad and submit recommendations for its improvement, reported in 1905: "Referring to the complaints that goods shipped by way of Panama are frequently damaged by careless handling and that losses occur by theft, it appears that many . . . are well founded. . . . The complaints as to the congestion of business . . . also appear to be justified. . . ." [12]

While its phenomenal prosperity made the Panama Railroad the envy of transportation companies throughout the world three ominous clouds darkened its horizon: the redemption clause in its charter, threatened competition by the new transcontinental railroad, and mismanagement by the company's own executives. In the contract of 1848 the government of New Granada had reserved the right to purchase the road for $5,000,000 after 20 years. As the end of that period approached little doubt existed that New Granada — or rather the United States of Colombia, the name assumed by the republic in 1863 — would seize the opportunity to acquire so valuable a property for much less than it was then worth. To avert such a disaster to their pocketbooks the directors sent Totten to Bogotá to secure an extension of the concession on the best possible terms, and after weeks of delicate and difficult negotiation a new contract was signed on August 16, 1867; but the conditions imposed heavy financial burdens on the company. The

franchise was prolonged for 99 years from that date, and at the end
of that time the road would revert without compensation to Colombia. In return the company agreed to pay Colombia $1,000,000
on the day the contract received the approval of the Bogotá Congress, as well as an annual rental of $250,000.

In 1848 the New Granadian government had pledged itself not
to permit the construction of a highway, a canal, or another railroad across the isthmus without the consent of the Panama Railroad. The contract of 1867 modified this exceedingly important
provision and fixed geographical limits to the area of immunity
from competition. The railroad's monopoly now applied only to
the region west of a line drawn from Cape Tiburón to Point Garachiné in Darién, and even in the monopoly area "the right which
is conceded to the company to give its consent does not extend to
its opposing the construction of a canal across the Isthmus of Panama (except on the actual route of the railroad itself), but only to
its exacting an equitable price for such privilege, and as indemnification for the damages which the railroad company may suffer by
the . . . competition of the canal. . . . The sum . . . finally designated, shall belong one-half to the railroad company, and one-
half to the Government of Colombia." [13]

Although after 1869 diversion of the lucrative California trade
to the transcontinental route was inevitable the directors of the
Panama line could have done much to maintain its prosperity by
assiduously developing new commercial connections and carefully
fostering those already in existence. Common sense called for a policy of conciliation, not of arrogance; but at the very time when the
executives, faced with the loss of their California traffic, should
have been making a supreme effort to cultivate the good will of
every shipping line that touched at the isthmian ports, they perversely antagonized many of their best customers.

For several years the Pacific Steam Navigation Company had
complained that the Panama Railroad exacted a higher percentage
of the charges on through shipments to and from the west coast of
South America than was warranted by the services rendered. In an
attempt to adjust the controversy Colonel Center went to Peru to
confer with the manager of the steamship line, George Petrie. Center and Petrie drew up an agreement whereby the receipts for the
transportation of through freight were to be divided equally between the Panama Railroad, the Pacific Steam Navigation Company, and whatever steamship company conveyed the merchandise
to or from the Atlantic side of the isthmus. When the railroad's
directors in New York contemptuously rejected this reasonable

compromise the Pacific Steam Navigation Company promptly organized an independent service between its Pacific ports and Liverpool through the Straits of Magellan, built a number of large fast steamers, transferred its repair shops and coaling station from Taboga Island to Callao, and severed all commercial connections with the Panama Railroad.

Not content with the loss of one golden-egged goose, the Panama Railroad Company now proceeded with almost incredible short-sightedness to wring the neck of another. In the summer of 1866 the Panama, New Zealand and Australian Royal Mail Company, a subsidiary of the Royal Mail Steam Packet Company, inaugurated the first steamship service between Panama and the antipodes. At the beginning traffic was light and expenses disproportionately heavy, but the prospect of future profits seemed reasonably bright. The Panama Railroad's co-operation in the form of liberal freight rates, credits, and perhaps loans — which at that time the railroad could well have afforded — might have kept the struggling steamship line alive during its lean initial years; but with fatuous disregard for their own interests the railroad executives withheld their aid, and after a few unprofitable voyages the steamship company went into liquidation in April 1869.

The Panama Railroad began to suffer almost immediately from the competition of the transcontinental line plus the ineptitude of its own board. Dividends dropped from 44% in the peak year of 1868 to 26% in 1869, 12.5% in 1870, and 3% in 1871. On April 1, 1872 the executives reported: "Although . . . the Stock of the Company has, within the past three years, undergone a severe and painful revulsion, yet the Directors . . . cannot but look back with pride and pleasure to the fact, that, since . . . 1849, $20,000,-000 have been returned in Dividends to the Stockholders. . . ." [14] The pride and pleasure of the directors in the road's former prosperity must have given cold comfort to the owners of the now depreciated shares. Within the next few years the financial position of the company slowly improved, but it never again approached its earlier record. From 1872 to 1880 annual dividends fluctuated between 9% and 16%. During this period huge blocks of stock changed hands with startling frequency: "The old régime of respectability was ended, and Panama shares became another Wall Street football." [15] Joseph F. Joy, Hoadley's successor as president of the road in 1871, was superseded in turn a year later by Alden B. Stockwell. Stockwell, a shrewd speculator who knew nothing of railroad operation and cared little for the welfare of the road, acquired a sufficient number of proxies to enable him to dictate the choice of directors and insure his own election as president. In 1874 Russell Sage cornered enough shares and proxies to swing the votes to himself, only to be replaced the following year by Trenor W. Park, who held the office of president and retained a controlling interest in the stock until the French canal company purchased it in 1880.

Although the Panama Railroad lost most of its California passenger and express business after 1869 it remained a formidable rival of the overland route as a carrier of ordinary freight. To reduce that competition the Transcontinental Railway Pool, an association embracing all of the railroads in the United States operating between the Missouri River and the Pacific seaports, entered into a contract with the Pacific Mail whereby the steamship company agreed to limit its freight shipments between New York and San Francisco by way of Panama to 1200 tons a month in each direction and to allow the pool to fix the rates. For this concession the pool paid the Pacific Mail $90,000 a month, afterwards reduced to $75,-000. The arrangement, though clearly in restraint of trade and harmful to the public interest, was not at that time actually illegal. The passage of the interstate commerce act in 1887 compelled the dissolution of the pool, but its successor, the Association of Transcontinental Railways, carried on its monopolistic practices in much the same fashion and continued the monthly bribes to the Pacific Mail. That corporation in turn had negotiated a contract with the Panama Railroad Company on February 1, 1878 which gave the Pacific Mail the exclusive right for the next 15 years to through rates on merchandise shipped between New York and San Francisco in either direction over the Panama Railroad, while all other steamship lines were obliged to pay the much higher local rates across the isthmus. The Pacific Mail paid the railroad $75,000 a month for this privilege but later reduced this sum to $55,000. The Panama Railroad thus became a party to a system of rate fixing which flourished in one form or another until shortly after the United States government acquired the road in 1904.

Chapter 15. Panama: 1855–1876

THE TIES that bound the inhabitants of the isthmus to New Granada were at best tenuous, and the Panamanians, isolated by ocean, mountains, and jungle from the rest of the country, deeply resented every attempt of the central government to interfere in isthmian affairs. Local pride found an outlet not only in chronic rebellion against Bogotá but also in fierce hatred of the swaggering Yankees who swarmed across the isthmus on their way to or from California. Undoubtedly the animosity was justified in many instances. While some — perhaps most — of the emigrants behaved in exemplary fashion the conspicuous excesses of an irresponsible minority kept the isthmus in a turmoil throughout the early years of the gold rush. Most of the pioneers carried arms, often more formidable in appearance than in action, and drunken brawls were not infrequent. The violence and bloodshed incident to such disturbances naturally intensified the antagonism already existing between Panamanians and North Americans. With the train laid for a major explosion, only a spark was needed to set it off. About a year after the completion of the railroad accumulated rancor produced the incident known as the "Watermelon War."

On the morning of April 15, 1856 about 940 passengers disembarked from the steamer *Illinois* at Colón and were transported by train to Panama, whence they were to sail the next day for San Francisco in the Pacific Mail liner *John L. Stephens*. About seven that evening the emigrants were gathered in or near the Panama railroad station, at that time located on the waterfront. Alongside the pier lay the steam tender *Taboga* in which the passengers were to be ferried out to the ship, but as the tide was out the tender was not expected to leave until eleven that night. The mails, baggage, and some of the freight had already been placed aboard the *Taboga*, as well as more than half of the passengers. Most of the others, including 50 or 60 women and children, were still waiting in the station to have their tickets stamped, while a few had wandered off to near-by refreshment stands and hotels. Suddenly shots were heard, and a mob of infuriated Negroes fell without warning upon the startled Americans.

Eye-witness descriptions of the riot were so confused and contradictory that its immediate cause could not be determined with
absolute certainty, but most accounts agreed that it was begun by
a drunken American passenger, Jack Oliver, who refused to pay for
a 10-cent slice of melon he had snatched from the stand of a Negro
huckster. The Negro drew a knife and followed Oliver with insistent demands for his dime to which the drunk paid no attention,
but his soberer companion finally tossed the fruit-seller a coin and
ordered him off. By that time the Negro had lost control of his
temper and continued to hurl abusive epithets at the two Americans. According to the official report of Amos B. Corwine, the special commissioner appointed by the United States government to
investigate the ensuing riot, Oliver drew his pistol, which a Negro
(not the melon peddler) seized and fired. The shot merely singed a
bystander, but within a short time a large crowd of blacks swarmed
out of their cabins and attacked two of the hotels.

The Pacific Mail agent, Captain McLane, sent an urgent message to the local chief of police, Colonel Garrido, while the excited
natives, having driven the Americans from the hotels, swept on to
the railroad station: "Many of the passengers ran down to the
wharf to embark . . . the rest crowding into the [ticket] office.
. . . All the arms in the office were a double barrelled gun, a pair
of pistols, a sabre, and fourteen old flint muskets . . . which . . .
were given out and loaded. . . . An old cannon belonging to the
Company was dug out of the sand and loaded . . . with rivets . . .
but . . . all who had authority, gave positive orders that it was
not to be fired unless an advance was made by the mob. . . . In the
meantime, most of the . . . persons at the Station had got inside
the Company's fence, and sheltered themselves, as well as possible,
from the bullets that now flew about fast. . . . No attempt was
made by the police to restrain the mob; but, on the contrary, they
joined the people and commenced firing on the Depot. . . . Col.
Garrido had . . . sent on board the *Taboga*, disarmed the passengers, and taken away the ship's gun. . . . In examining the
[railroad] offices afterwards, a horrid sight presented itself, many
dead and wounded, horribly mutilated, lay all about; the floor was
covered with blood, all the furniture, books, papers, etc., of the
Company were destroyed. . . . Some of the cars were injured . . .
and the Telegraph wires cut, and an attempt was made to fire the
Depot, but . . . it did not succeed. . . . Fifteen lives were known
to be lost, all passengers . . . except two. . . ." [1]

A week later the governor of Panama reported that two natives
and 15 Americans had been killed, 13 natives and 16 Americans

wounded. He emphatically denied that the police had abetted the rioters and maintained that the besieged Americans had fired the first shots, while Corwine insisted that "the dispute . . . relative to the slice of watermelon was seized on as a pretext by the colored population . . . to assault the . . . Americans . . . and plunder their property . . . but that the assault on the Railroad Station was . . . *deliberately planned* by the Police and mob. . . ." [2] Admitting that the natives had some cause for resentment, since completion of the railroad had thrown thousands out of work and the *Taboga* had replaced the rowboat ferries to and from ocean steamers in the bay, he concluded "that the Government of New Granada is unable to . . . enforce order . . . and afford adequate protection to the transit. . . . I . . . *recommend the immediate occupation of the Isthmus, from Ocean to Ocean, by the United States* . . . unless New Granada . . . can satisfy us as to her ability and inclination to afford . . . proper protection and make speedy and ample atonement. . . ." [3]

Corwine's report was dated July 18, 1856. At that time the United States had no military or naval force in the vicinity to undertake the suggested occupation, but soon after the report reached Washington two warships, the small sailing vessels *Independence* and *St. Mary's,* were sent to Panama. On September 19 a detachment of 160 men commanded by Commodore William Mervine landed and with the consent of the local authorities took possession of the railroad station. The city remained quiet, and three days later the troops withdrew to their ships without having fired a shot. This brief and bloodless occupation — the first instance of armed intervention on the isthmus — was fully justified in the opinion of official Washington by the clause in the treaty of 1846 whereby the United States guaranteed the neutrality of the isthmus "with the view that the free transit from the one to the other sea, may not be interrupted or embarrassed. . . ." [4] Since the riot had been a purely internal affair the neutrality of the isthmus had not been menaced, but freedom of transit had most certainly been embarrassed. Thus the United States established the precedent, destined to have far-reaching consequences, that it possessed the right to intervene in order to guard the transit not only against aggression by a foreign power hostile to New Granada but against interruption or damage due to the inability or unwillingness of New Granada itself to furnish adequate protection.

After intervention came insistent demands for indemnity. President Pierce appointed James B. Bowlin, United States minister to New Granada, and Isaac E. Morse plenipotentiaries to settle the details with the New Granadian commissioners, Lino de Pombo, the Foreign Minister, and Florentino González. In an atmosphere tense with mutual distrust and anger numerous conferences were held at Bogotá in February 1857. Although official affidavits by the consuls of Great Britain, France, and Ecuador at Panama supported the New Granadian claim that the Americans had been the aggressors and the local police innocent the United States delegates ignored these foreign witnesses and pressed their demands. On February 4 Bowlin and Morse submitted four proposals: that Panama and Colón should be made free self-governing cities under New Granadian sovereignty and should jointly control a belt from sea to sea 20 miles wide, with the railroad as its center line; that New Granada should cede to the United States several islands in Panama Bay for use as naval bases; that New Granada should transfer to the United States its rights in the Panama Railroad; and that New Granada should pay damages for the loss of life and destruction of property caused by the April riot. For these concessions the United States offered to pay $2,000,000 — far less than the value of New Granada's reversionary rights in the railroad alone. Bogotá indignantly rejected the propositions, and the Americans withdrew them.

The acrimonious correspondence that ensued served only to widen the breach. Both parties assumed an air of injured innocence. The American delegates, refusing to acknowledge that their compatriots had been even indirectly responsible for the disturbance, peremptorily demanded $400,000 as indemnity for the damage wrought. The deadlock was finally broken by an agreement dictated by the United States and embodied in the Cass-Herrán treaty, signed on September 10, 1857, whereby New Granada admitted liability and consented to pay the indemnity. The United States Senate ratified the convention on March 8, 1859, but the loss of the treaty draft in a Magdalena River wreck delayed ratification by New Granada for several months, so that the pact did not go into effect until November 8, 1860. It provided for a commission to apportion the damages due to the riot of 1856 as well as payments on other minor claims presented by United States citizens; but the commission failed to finish its task, and on August 19, 1865 a new treaty was proclaimed and another commission appointed to complete the awards. In the final settlement New Granada was obliged to pay $195,410 in indemnities arising from the Panama riot, $65,070 on other claims, $9277 for commission expenses, and $142,637 interest — a total of $412,394. Throughout the decade of negotiation and dispute the harsh arrogance of the

United States government had embittered relations with New Granada, deeply offended the other Latin American republics, and created widespread ill feeling out of all proportion to the paltry sums involved.

Between 1857 and 1863 an almost unbroken succession of factional disturbances agitated New Granada. Several times the safety of the Panama Railroad was threatened, though in fact it did continue to operate without interruption throughout this troubled period. In 1860 a local brawl in a Panama suburb, during which six white inhabitants were killed and three wounded by stray bullets, brought about a second intervention by the United States. On September 27 a detachment of American troops under Commander Porter landed from the *St. Mary's* and occupied strategic points in the city until October 7, when the outbreak subsided and the armed force re-embarked. Meanwhile the leader of the New Granadian Liberals, Tomás de Mosquera, conducted a vigorous campaign against the Conservative government and succeeded in 1861, after the "War of the Hundred Fights," in establishing his party in power and himself as President of the Confederación Granadina, the next in the series of names adopted by the republic; but when he took steps to have himself proclaimed military dictator the provisional government appealed to the United States for protection and intervention. Preoccupied with its own Civil War, Washington was in no position to interfere actively in Latin American affairs. Nevertheless the Secretary of State, William H. Seward, made a tentative proposal to the British and French governments for a joint occupation of the isthmus, but those governments had little sympathy for the Federal cause and refused to co-operate with the United States. Fortunately intervention proved unnecessary. Unable to obtain sufficient political support for a *coup d'état*, Mosquera renounced the dictatorship scheme and in 1863 proclaimed a new liberal constitution under which the eight provinces enjoyed a considerable degree of autonomy. The name of the republic was changed again, this time to United States of Colombia.

On March 9, 1865 another political squabble caused Captain Middleton of the *St. Mary's* to land a small detachment of American troops at Panama for a single day, but Bogotá's official request for a more prolonged and extensive intervention was rejected by Seward, who wrote to his minister to Colombia on November 9: "The purpose of the stipulation [in the treaty of 1846] was to guarantee the Isthmus against seizure or invasion by a foreign power only. It could not have been contemplated that we were to become a party to any civil war in that country." [5] Seward's position was not altogether consistent. In none of the three previous instances of armed intervention had a foreign power been involved; the transit had been menaced by factional clashes only. Actually it was impossible for the United States to protect the railroad without incidentally aiding one or the other of the opposed local parties. Before 1902 American intervention usually proved advantageous in effect though perhaps not in intention to the régime in power rather than to the revolutionary faction.

The terms of the treaty of 1846 were too general to be wholly satisfactory to either Washington or Bogotá. In 1866 demands for a new and more specific agreement were intensified by a report that Mosquera intended to sell Colombia's interest in the Panama Railroad to a group of English capitalists headed by William Henry Cotterill. Cotterill had in fact made two proposals for the purchase, but the Colombian Congress rejected both and in 1867 granted the railroad company its 99-year contract. In December of that year the government of Colombia presented to Peter I. Sullivan, Burton's successor as United States minister, the preliminary draft of a new treaty providing for the construction of a canal by the United States government, a canal zone 12 miles wide, free terminal ports, joint defense by the United States and Colombia, a neutrality guarantee modeled on that of 1846, and arbitration of possible disputes over interpretation. Sullivan recommended the draft to the Department of State as a useful basis for discussion and suggested confidentially that a little judicious bribery in Bogotá would not come amiss: "Should you prefer this mode of acquiring a foothold on the Isthmus . . . you can, I believe, succeed by spending a good deal of secret service money in engineering the treaty through the Colombian Congress. . . ." [6] At the same time he proposed an alternative — and equally dishonorable — method by which the United States might wring concessions from Colombia. On September 1, 1867 a mob had attacked four Americans at Cartagena, killing two of them, and Sullivan thought the incident might be used as a diplomatic club for the intimidation of Bogotá: "Should you choose to acquire the desirable privilege, otherwise than by treaty, you will have to push the Cartagena murders to the wall, muster up all the existing claims against this government, nurse both complaints for a reasonable time, and then make a bold and decisive demand for redress, which can not be given. In that case, you will have a good pretext for seizing upon Colombian property as indemnity for the said wrongs and injuries." [7]

Seward very properly adopted neither of these shifty suggestions. Instead he sent Caleb Cushing, Attorney General during the Pierce administration, to Bogotá with liberal instructions to negotiate a new convention, which was concluded on January 14, 1869. It provided for a canal zone 20 miles in width to be subdivided into a series of lots or sections fronting on the canal "equally distributed between the two Governments, so that neither . . . shall have two contiguous . . . lots" [8] — a clumsy arrangement which would have been exceedingly difficult to work out in practice. The concession was to remain in force for 100 years after the completion of the canal and then revert to Colombia without compensation. While the grantee named was the United States government that government had the right to devolve its privileges and obligations upon any United States citizen or company but not upon a foreign power or its citizens. President Johnson submitted the pact to the United States Senate on February 15, but a month later the Colombian Senate rejected it by a vote of 16 to 8. The inhabitants of the isthmus, who naturally favored the treaty, promptly threatened to secede, and in October the provincial legislature of Panama passed a unanimous resolution urging the Bogotá Congress to reconsider.

Meanwhile Grant had succeeded Johnson as President, and General Stephen A. Hurlbut replaced Sullivan as minister to Bogotá. In November 1869 the Colombian government, yielding to pressure from Panama, reopened negotiations and in the following January concluded another treaty granting to the United States, in addition to the privileges enumerated in the Cushing convention, free transit for American warships through the canal at all times and the right to build and maintain docks and repair yards at both terminals. On March 31, 1870 Grant transmitted the new agreement to the Senate, which would probably have approved it had not the Conservative members of the Colombian Congress seen fit to attach 17 unacceptable amendments. The result was that the Hurlbut convention, like that arranged by Cushing, failed to achieve ratification, and the original treaty of 1846 remained in force until 1903.

Notwithstanding the breakdown of negotiations with the United States Bogotá clung to the hope of a canal through Colombian territory. In February 1873 the Peruvian Foreign Minister, José de la Riva-Agüero, asked the Colombian minister at Lima, Teodoro Valenzuela, if the Colombian government was "disposed to enter into a negotiation with Peru, either to undertake the work jointly, or with the help of all the Spanish American republics . . . interested in its completion. . . ." [9] Valenzuela replied in the affirmative, but the project seems never to have progressed beyond the stage of polite conversation.

The fourth instance of United States armed intervention on the isthmus occurred on April 7, 1868, when two or three naval officers and a dozen sailors were landed at Colón from the *Penobscot* to quell an incipient riot. In May 1873 the outbreak of what actually amounted to civil war gave rise to a succession of disturbances, two sufficiently serious to necessitate the occupation of Panama City by United States forces. 200 men came ashore from the *Tuscarora* and remained in the city for 15 days. During the summer the revolutionary movement subsided, but on September 24 another clash caused the landing of a large detachment from the *Benicia* and *Pensacola*. By October 6 quiet prevailed once more, and most of the American sailors returned to their ships.

On March 19, 1866 the Senate passed a resolution introduced by Senator Conness of California requesting the Secretary of the Navy to communicate all available information concerning the various canal routes and a comparison of their relative merits. Rear Admiral Charles H. Davis prepared a brief report largely derived from the heterogeneous and often unreliable notes of Spanish, French, English, and American explorers but supplemented by a number of excellent maps. Davis's researches convinced him that "there does not exist in the libraries of the world the means of determining, even approximately, the most practicable route for a ship canal. . . . It may be thought premature to say that the time has arrived for its execution. But it will not be denied that the present opportunity is the most favorable that could possibly arise for conducting, on our part, the preliminary surveys without interruption, interference, or unwelcome participation [by foreign governments]." [10]

The suggestion was not followed up immediately, but Grant's inauguration introduced a new and more aggressive note into the canal policy of the United States. Whereas all previous administrations had contemplated some form of international protection of and control over an interoceanic waterway, Grant declared himself unequivocally in favor of exclusive ownership and supervision by the United States. This direct application or rather extension of the Monroe Doctrine to the canal issue fitted so well into the current Manifest Destiny pattern of American thought that it was almost immediately adopted as a permanent clause in the foreign policy of the country. Thenceforth every President except Cleveland stressed the desirability if not the actual necessity of American domination over any isthmian canal.

In 1869 Grant instructed Commodore Daniel Ammen, chief of the Bureau of Navigation, to organize a series of elaborate surveying expeditions under the command of the Secretary of the Navy. The task was executed with admirable efficiency. The choice of the resourceful Ammen as general supervisor of the preliminaries was fortunate; the leaders of the several expeditions were all experienced officers of the highest integrity, energetic and meticulous; the technical equipment was the best obtainable and ample in quantity, excellent discipline prevailed, the commissaries were well stocked, and such care was taken to safeguard the health of the men that considering the primitive conditions under which they lived for months and the limited knowledge of tropical hygiene at their disposal remarkably few cases of serious illness occurred. Above all the entire set of explorations from Tehuantepec to the Atrato conformed as closely as possible to the same standards, and the separate reports were compared and judged by a single body, the Interoceanic Canal Commission appointed by Grant on March 15, 1872 and composed of Admiral Ammen, Brigadier General Andrew A. Humphreys, Chief of Engineers of the army, and C. P. Patterson, superintendent of the Coast Survey. Thus for the first time Humboldt's conditions for a satisfactory survey were fulfilled. So reliable were the measurements obtained by the explorations of 1870–5 that they remain substantially unchallenged today. Unfortunately the commanders of these expeditions were in general more adept at fact-finding than at drawing conclusions from their facts: nearly all tended to underestimate the difficulties and costs of canal construction and presented specific projects far less sound than the observations and computations upon which they were based. Each leader fell more or less in love with his own pet scheme and perhaps subconsciously sought to tip the scales gently in its favor.

Although the surveys undertaken by Hughes in 1849 had been directed towards the location of a railroad, not of a canal, they had incidentally disclosed more complete information concerning the topography of the Isthmus of Panama than existed before 1870 with regard to any other proposed transit. Perhaps for this reason the naval expedition to Panama was postponed until all of the less familiar routes had been investigated. The Panama party did not leave New York until January 5, 1875, almost exactly five years after the start of the Darién expedition, the first of the series. Commander Edward P. Lull headed the group, and the post of chief engineer was occupied by Aniceto G. Menocal, member of a prominent Cuban family and an exceedingly able technician. Lull had previously accompanied the Darién party in 1870 and had commanded the Nicaragua expedition in 1872–3, while Menocal had served as chief engineer of the Nicaragua surveys. By the time they reached Panama both men appear to have already made up their minds (perhaps without fully realizing the extent of their bias) in favor of Nicaragua. Their examination of the Panama route was more superficial than that devoted to any of the other projects, and their conclusions concerning it were less fully justified by future developments. The solution actually adopted for the present canal, the construction of a dam across the Chagres to form a great artificial lake at the summit level, does not seem to have occurred to them.

Lull and Menocal began by discarding all projects for a sea level canal at Panama on account of the excessive cost. For a lock canal the only source of an adequate water supply was the Chagres, but floods made the river difficult to control. The engineers therefore proposed to keep the unruly river out of the canal bed by means of a gigantic aqueduct 1900 feet long and supported on 12 culverts, which would carry the canal across the Chagres near the village of Matachín, where the surface of the Chagres at low water was approximately 42 feet above mean sea level. Allowing 35 feet for the river's rise in flood season, 15 for the spring of the culvert arches, 6 for the thickness of masonry over the arches, and 26 for depth of water in the canal, the summit level was established at an elevation of 124 feet above the sea. This altitude would necessitate 12 locks 500 feet long and 65 wide on each side of the summit. Menocal estimated the total cost, not including buildings, administrative expenses, or interest on the investment, at $94,511,360.

By the end of 1875 the heads of all the naval expeditions had handed in their reports, and the Interoceanic Canal Commission settled down to a "long, careful, and minute study" [11] of facts and figures. On February 7, 1876 it issued a unanimous decision in favor of the Nicaragua route. Panama received only brief consideration: "The deep cut would probably be subject to land-slides, from which the Panama Railroad has suffered seriously, and the canal would be exposed to serious injury from flood. . . . The cost of the whole work . . . is estimated to exceed by nearly fifty per cent. that of the Nicaragua route. . . ." [12]

Chapter 16. Nicaragua: 1823–1850

LAKE NICARAGUA, with a maximum length of 101 miles, maximum breadth of 45 miles, and surface area of about 3000 square miles, is the largest body of fresh water between the Great Lakes of North America and Lake Titicaca in the Andes. The elevation of its surface above mean sea level averages about 107 feet, and much of it is deep enough to float the largest modern steamers. Lake Managua, about 40 miles long and covering an area of 438 square miles, shallower than Lake Nicaragua and with an average surface elevation approximately 25 feet higher, is separated from its larger neighbor by a strip of low land some 18 miles wide through which flows the small Tipitapa River, the only connection between the lakes.

From a point near the southeast corner of Lake Nicaragua the San Juan River makes its way with many twists and turns to the Atlantic. In a straight line the distance from lake to river mouth is about 70 miles, by the winding river channel 122 miles. Throughout the upper half of its course the river is navigable for large vessels or could be made so with only minor artificial improvement except where its flow is impeded by a series of rapids for about 12 miles. The lower half of the river cannot be navigated in the dry season by any craft much larger than a canoe. About 10 miles inland from the Atlantic it divides into two channels: the northern branch, the San Juan proper, with its mouth at San Juan del Norte, and the Colorado branch emptying into the ocean 12 miles farther south. About 1675 the Spanish governor of the captaincy general of Guatemala, Francisco Fernando de Escobedo, endeavored to stop the incursions of English buccaneers into Nicaragua by diverting the river water into the then shallow Colorado in order to close the main branch to the enemy. He succeeded not only in discouraging the raiders but also in permanently ruining the channel, though how much of the damage was due to Escobedo's dams and how much to natural causes is uncertain. The northern fork, deprived of most of its water, soon dwindled to a mere trickle crisscrossed by sandbars, and the harbor of San Juan del Norte gradually silted up. The Colorado, while much deeper, has even less commercial value because it is subject to floods, dangerously barred at its mouth, and wholly without a natural harbor.

On its western side Lake Nicaragua is separated from the Pacific by a ridge only 12 miles wide at its narrowest point and broken up by a number of convenient depressions. While on the Atlantic side the only possible terminus for a Nicaragua canal is at or near the port of San Juan del Norte, the Pacific coast offers at least six alternative harbors, though nearly all are small unprotected roadsteads: Salinas Bay, San Juan del Sur, Brito, Tamarindo, Realejo, and the Gulf of Fonseca. For a canal terminating at any of the first three ports an artificial channel would have to be cut through the narrow isthmus west of Lake Nicaragua; the other projects involve a much longer transit to the northern end of Lake Nicaragua, up the Tipitapa River, through Lake Managua, and across the intervening land to the Pacific. Before the discovery in 1851 of a remarkably low pass on the more direct line this circuitous route was believed by many to be the more practicable.

In July 1823, immediately following the secession of Central America from Mexico, Manuel Antonio de la Cerda, afterwards governor of Nicaragua, laid before the Constituent Assembly at Guatemala City a proposal for the construction of a canal; but the Assembly was too busy with the organization of a new federal government to pay much attention. A proposition sponsored by Barclay, Herring, Richardson & Company of London in 1824 was received with similar indifference, but a few months later a project submitted by an association of American capitalists headed by Colonel Charles Bourke and Matthew Llanos evoked a more sympathetic response from the Central American authorities. Bourke and Llanos claimed that in December 1824 they had sent to the mouth of the San Juan an armed brig "having on board engineers and other persons charged to make a survey of the proposed route. . . . Whether the . . . engineers . . . ever reached their destination is unknown. . . ." [1] On February 8, 1825 Antonio José Cañas, Central American minister at Washington, suggested to Secretary Adams the construction of a Nicaragua canal by the combined efforts of the United States and the republic of Central America.

The confusion incident to the change of administration and the inauguration of Adams as President delayed the reply of the new Secretary of State, Henry Clay, until April 18. Clay was interested but cautious: "A false step . . . might lead to the most mischievous consequences." [2] Two days later Clay instructed Colonel John Williams, the newly appointed chargé d'affaires to Central America, "to ascertain if surveys have been made of the proposed route of the canal, and if entire confidence may be placed in their accuracy. . . . It is not intended that you should inspire . . . any confident expectation that the United States will contribute, by pecuniary or other means, to the . . . work, because it is not yet known what views Congress might take of it. . . ." [3]

Congress was not yet ready and would not be ready for many years to adopt the canal project as a national enterprise, but Williams's report encouraged another group of American investors to negotiate for a concession. This scheme was initiated by Aaron Palmer, a New York merchant, who sent a confidential agent, Charles de Beneski, to Guatemala to arrange the terms. On June 24, 1826 the agent signed a contract with the Central American Foreign Minister, Francisco Gómez de Argüello, and in October Palmer transferred his concession to the Central American and United States Atlantic and Pacific Canal Company, whose directors included Governor De Witt Clinton of New York, Stephen Van Rensselaer, and Edward Livingston. No new survey was made, and the company's sole source of information concerning the canal route appears to have been Galisteo's report of 1781. Upon this dubious foundation Palmer based his estimate of the cost of the work at only $5,000,000. Unable to raise that sum in the United States, Palmer proceeded to London. But British capitalists refused to be tempted, and the concession lapsed.

For the next few years internal dissension and a temporary dissolution of the Central American union into its constituent states prevented the award of further contracts. In March 1829 General Werweer, a representative of the king of the Netherlands, reached Guatemala City in the midst of these disturbances and as soon as peace was restored concluded two treaties with Central America. The first, dated April 14, 1830, paved the way for a Dutch loan of $3,000,000; the second, signed in September, provided for the construction of a Nicaragua canal by a Dutch company. All of this was duly reported to Livingston, Jackson's new Secretary of State, who considered the treaty conditions "such as we should have no great reason to complain of. . . ." [4] "Should the grant not be completed," he wrote to the United States envoy to Central America, Jeffers, "you will endeavor to procure for the citizens of the United States, or for the government itself, if Congress should deem the measure constitutional and proper, the right of subscribing to the stock. . . ." [5] But in the summer of 1830 Belgium revolted against Holland and established itself as an independent kingdom, and the Dutch king was obliged to abandon his canal plan.

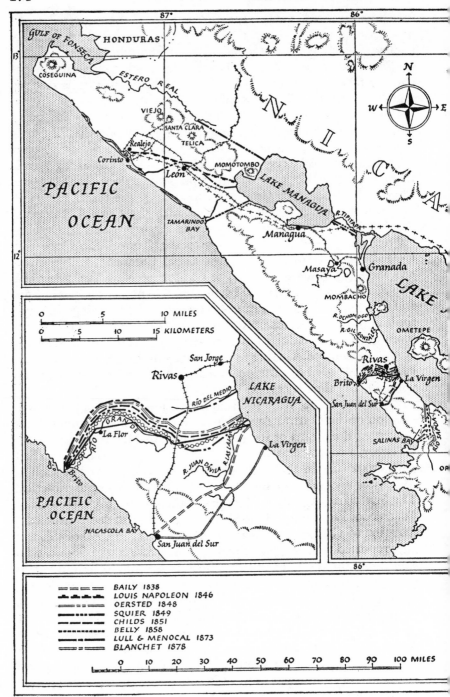

7. NICARAGUA PROJECTS

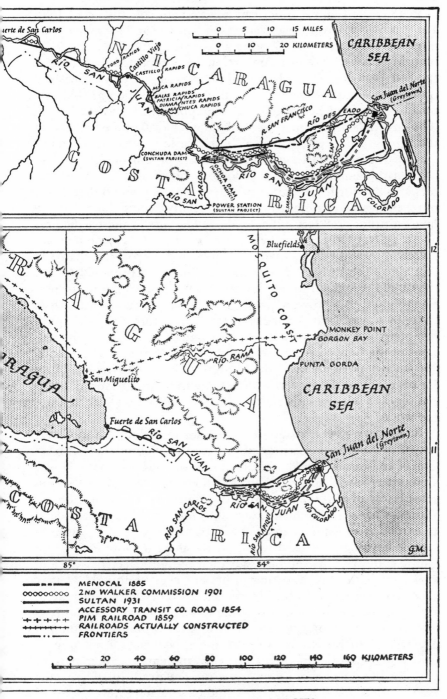

7. NICARAGUA PROJECTS

In 1837 the Central American government commissioned John Baily, a British naval officer retired on half pay and for many years a resident of Nicaragua, to locate a route for a canal. After several months of conscientious examination Baily reported that most of the San Juan River could be made navigable, though "it will require many improvements. . . . Still there are no forcible reasons to despair of being able to accomplish such a work. . . ." [6] The only difficult problem would be the removal of the rocks from the rapids, an operation which "must be left to the intelligence . . . of the many distinguished engineers of Europe. . . ." [7] He advised the damming of the Colorado and rediversion of its waters into the northern branch, which he thought would then scour out a navigable channel to its mouth. Baily's computation of the lake's altitude, 128 feet 3 inches above *low tide* in the Pacific, was about 15 feet too high. Between the lake and the Pacific he completely missed the lowest gap and could find no pass less than 487 feet above the surface of the lake. He therefore proposed to run the canal through a tunnel varying in length according to its location. Should this prove impracticable he suggested an alternative route by way of Lake Managua to Realejo. Before Baily had quite completed his investigations in 1838 one of the periodic dissolutions of the Central American republic abruptly ended his labors, and since none of the individual states would assume responsibility for his payment the surveyor was left "with no reward for his arduous services but the satisfaction of having been a pioneer in a noble work." [8]

In January 1838 a group of Americans including Aaron Clark, mayor of New York, petitioned Congress to sponsor the construction of an isthmian canal. The memorial was referred to the House Committee on Roads and Canals, whose chairman, Charles Fenton Mercer of Virginia, reported on March 2, 1839 that "the expediency has . . . been suggested, but on very incompetent data, to extend an open cut [at sea level] from sea to sea . . . and attempts have been made to trace on the maps a route for this gigantic enterprise. As yet, none such has been discovered . . . and it is confidently believed that none will ever be found." [9] After this discouraging preamble Mercer discussed briefly and in general terms the possibility of constructing a lock canal at Panama, Nicaragua, or some other site. In conclusion the committee requested President Van Buren "to consider the expediency of opening or continuing negotiations with the Governments of other nations . . . for the purpose of ascertaining the practicability of . . . the construction of a ship-canal . . . and of securing forever, by suitable treaty stipulations, the free and equal right of navigating such canal to all nations. . . ." [10]

Van Buren dispatched John Lloyd Stephens to Central America, where he found the political situation still too unsettled to permit the negotiation of any treaties. In February 1840 Stephens reached Nicaragua and after a conference with Baily at Granada estimated the cost of a canal at $20,000,000 to $25,000,000. A personal inspection of the western part of the route made a painful impression on the American explorer. Of the primitive trail from Lake Nicaragua to the Pacific he wrote pithily that "the desert of Arabia is not more desolate, and the track of the Children of Israel to the Red Sea a turnpike compared with it," [11] and of the little port of San Juan del Sur, the proposed Pacific terminus of the canal: "I had been sanguine, almost enthusiastic, in regard to this gigantic enterprise; but on the spot the scales fell from my eyes. The harbor was perfectly desolate; for years not a vessel had entered it . . . for miles there was not a habitation. . . . It seemed preposterous to consider it the focus of a great commercial enterprise; to imagine that a city was to rise up out of the forest . . . and become a great portal for the thoroughfare of nations. . . ." [12] Small wonder that after such a disillusionment Stephens should have chosen a few years later to associate himself with the Panama Railroad.

Meanwhile the scramble for concessions continued, but all were short-lived and without practical effect. In 1838, soon after the division of Central America into five states, Nicaragua and Honduras authorized one Peter or Pierre Rouchaud to organize a French company to construct a canal. Another contract for the same purpose is said to have been awarded to a Central American prelate, Jorge Viteri y Ungo, afterwards bishop of El Salvador. In the same year a third grant empowered George Holdship, representing an association of New York and New Orleans merchants, to build a canal, open a bank, and colonize the country on a large scale. All of these grandiose projects began and ended in impressive rituals involving yards of parchment and immense blobs of red wax.

Having failed to obtain the support of the United States government, the local sponsors of a Nicaragua canal now turned to France. In 1842 the future Napoleon III, then a prisoner in the fortress of Ham in northern France, received an invitation from "several influential persons of Central America . . . with a view of inducing him to ask for his liberation, and proceed to America, where, as they said, the Prince would be welcomed with enthusiasm. . . ." [13]

The closely guarded Louis Napoleon was obliged to decline this tempting offer but continued to exchange letters with his distant correspondents. Two years later Francisco Castellón, Central American minister to France, endeavored to induce the government of Louis-Philippe to co-operate in the construction of a canal. The government refused but permitted the envoy to visit Louis Napoleon at Ham, where he tried once more to persuade the prince to secure his freedom, emigrate to Nicaragua, and place himself at the head of a canal company. His importunities had no effect, and on December 2, 1844 Castellón awarded a canal concession to a Belgian corporation; but after his return to Nicaragua he found his contract not "so favourably received as I had reason to expect," [14] and the grant lapsed.

Louis Napoleon escaped from Ham in May 1846 and took refuge in England, where he endeavored "to secure the co-operation of all persons of enlarged and intellectual minds" [15] in the canal project by publishing a pamphlet extolling its advantages. Knowing nothing about either Nicaragua or engineering, he swallowed whole the information and recommendations sent him by Castellón. That gentleman, a native of the inland city of León, patriotically but illogically envisaged a canal that would serve the local interests of Nicaragua more specifically than the requirements of international commerce: a canal of immense length passing through both lakes and the town of León and terminating near Realejo. Tutored by Castellón, Louis Napoleon filled the pages of his pamphlet with extravagant nonsense: "As Constantinople is the centre of the ancient world, so is . . . Leon . . . the centre of the new. . . . In order that the Canal should become the principal element of the advancement of Central America, it must be cut through, not the narrowest part . . . but through . . . the most populous, the most healthy, and the most fertile. . . ." [16] In other words all considerations of topography, cost, and global utility should be subordinated to the presumptive welfare of a small and unimportant community.

The total length of the canal from San Juan del Norte to Realejo was to be 278 miles, of which 82 miles would be artificial excavation. The summit level between Lake Managua and Realejo was given as 212 feet above the sea — a remarkably accurate guess considering that the country had never been surveyed. Less realistic was the prince's (or rather Castellón's) estimate of $20,000,000 as the total cost. The revolutionary movement of 1848 enabled Louis Napoleon to return to France and in December to win the presidential election. Thereafter his tempestuous career, first as head of

8. RIVAS AND THE CONTINENTAL DIVIDE SEPARATING LAKE NICA-
RAGUA FROM THE PACIFIC OCEAN

9. SAN JUAN RIVER AT CASTILLO VIEJO

10. SAN JUAN DEL SUR

11. LAKE MANAGUA AND MOMOTOMBO VOLCANO

THE POSTAGE STAMP MENTIONED ON PAGE 435 WAS DESIGNED FROM A PHOTOGRAPH
TAKEN WITHIN A FEW YARDS OF THIS SPOT

the republic and later as emperor, kept him fully occupied until the debacle of 1870. He had no time to spare for the Nicaragua canal, and this project like so many others came to nothing. The ambitions of Napoleon III in the western hemisphere took a different and more sinister form in the disastrous attempt to dominate Mexico through his unfortunate puppet Maximilian.

In 1848 Andreas Oersted, a Danish naturalist, undertook a cursory examination of the divide between Lake Nicaragua and the Pacific at a point some 20 miles south of the line traversed by Baily. From the mouth of the Sapoa River on the western shore of the lake Oersted proceeded southward up the valley of that stream, then turned west across the summit of the ridge and down the Pacific slope to Salinas Bay, a much larger and more sheltered harbor than the tiny cove of San Juan del Sur. The Dane's investigations were too informal to be called a survey; he was not an engineer, he possessed no proper instruments, and the time at his disposal was exceedingly short. To do him justice he put forward no claim to scientific accuracy and merely ventured the opinion that a canal could be built on the Sapoa line. He computed the elevation of the summit to be only 270 feet above sea level — a fantastic error, for in 1872 the lowest point on the divide along this route was found to lie 1031 feet higher than the ocean. Apparently influenced by Oersted's report, the Costa Rican government, which then claimed sovereignty over that territory, awarded a contract to an English company in 1848 for the construction of a canal by way of the Sapoa, but nothing was done to carry out the project.

A few months later the commencement of the California gold rush prompted additional applications for Nicaragua canal concessions. On February 16, 1849 William Wheelwright of the Pacific Steam Navigation Company solicited such a contract, but the Nicaraguan government took no action on the proposal. On March 14 a similar offer by Dr. David Tilden Brown on behalf of a group of American capitalists resulted in the grant of a concession to the Compañía de Tránsito de Nicaragua, which was ratified by the Nicaraguan Congress but disapproved by the President.

Meanwhile a grave international controversy threatened to disturb peaceful relations between Great Britain and the United States. The dispute involved two points: the title of Costa Rica, supported by Great Britain, to the southern bank of the San Juan River and of Lake Nicaragua; and the British claim to a protectorate over the Mosquito coast, including the harbor of San Juan del Norte, the Atlantic terminus of every project for a Nicaragua canal. Nicaragua denied both claims, and the United States took the part of Nicaragua.

Costa Rica based its demands upon the provincial boundaries established in colonial days, but as the maps and descriptions in those ancient documents were extremely vague and often hopelessly contradictory various interpretations could be drawn from them. Costa Rica's title to the south bank of the lower portion of the river and to joint sovereignty with Nicaragua over that part of its course was in fact well founded; its claim to the upper half of the river and the southern shore of the lake had less justification. Nicaragua claimed exclusive sovereignty over the entire course of the river and the whole shore line of Lake Nicaragua, and consequently the sole right to award canal concessions. The question remained a subject of bitter dispute until April 15, 1858, when the two governments concluded the Cañas-Jerez treaty fixing the boundary from Punta Castilla at the mouth of the San Juan River (leaving San Juan del Norte just inside Nicaraguan territory) along the right or south bank of the river to a point three miles below Castillo Viejo, a little more than halfway to the lake; then, after swinging southwest for about four miles, parallel to the river but two miles south of it to a point two miles east of the lake; thence two miles south of and parallel to the lake shore to the Sapoa River; and finally southwest along a straight line to Salinas Bay. The treaty gave Nicaragua exclusive dominion over the San Juan River but conceded to Costa Rica perpetual navigation rights from its mouth to near Castillo Viejo. Nicaragua agreed not to conclude any future canal contracts without consulting Costa Rica.

This seemed a reasonable compromise; but in 1876 Nicaragua, rendered arrogant by the Interoceanic Canal Commission's decision in its favor, declared the treaty void, and the boundary dispute again embittered relations between the neighboring states for several years. On December 24, 1886 the two republics concluded the Esquivel-Román convention whereby they agreed to submit the controversy to the arbitration of President Cleveland. On March 22, 1888 Cleveland reaffirmed the validity of the Cañas-Jerez treaty, which "does not give . . . Costa Rica the right to be a party to grants which Nicaragua may make for interoceanic canals; though in cases where the . . . canal will involve an injury to the natural rights of Costa Rica, her opinion or advice . . . should be more than 'advisory' or 'consultative.' It would seem in such cases that her consent is necessary, and that she may thereupon demand compensation for the concession she is asked to make; but she is not entitled as a right to share in the profits that . . . Nicaragua may reserve for herself as a compensation for such favors and privileges as she, in her turn, may concede."[17]

An enormous mass of diplomatic correspondence testifies to the complexity of the disagreement over the Mosquito coast between Great Britain on the one hand and the United States and Nicaragua on the other. British hegemony over the Mosquito territory, like that over Belize (British Honduras) farther north, began about 1630 with the establishment of small settlements of buccaneers and logwood cutters on the coast. Though Great Britain never asserted actual sovereignty over the Mosquito region as it did over Belize it did maintain a loose form of protectorate over this vaguely defined strip of Central American territory. According to minimum British claims the Mosquito "kingdom" covered an area about 225 miles long from the Tuapi Lagoon on the north to Punta Gorda, midway between Bluefields and San Juan del Norte, on the south, and extending inland about 40 miles; but at one time during the heat of controversy these boundaries were unofficially expanded by British extremists to include the entire Caribbean coast from Cape Honduras to the Chiriquí Lagoon. Since the Mosquito Indians — properly Misskito, as the name had no connection with that of the insect — probably never numbered more than 1500 souls their pretensions to dominion over so vast an area were palpably absurd. These natives, a Carib people mixed with Negro and some white stock, were variously described by James Buchanan as "a miserable, degraded, and insignificant tribe" [18] and by an anonymous English writer as "a bold and independent race."[19] The British government insisted on somewhat dubious grounds that these Indians had never been conquered by the Spaniards and that consequently their lands belonged to none of the republics carved out of the old Spanish empire; while Honduras and Nicaragua, heirs to a portion of that empire, claimed sovereignty over their respective segments of the Mosquito coast as integral parts of their territories.

Actually the Mosquito Indians and the Central American states were mere pawns in a major conflict between Great Britain and the United States, the two great rivals for commercial supremacy in the western hemisphere. That rivalry did not become acute until about 1848, when the acquisition by the United States of immense areas of Mexican territory, including California, alarmed Great Britain for the safety of its own colonies and investments in Latin America.

The British government had no objection to the construction of a canal through Nicaragua, but it was determined to oppose firmly any attempt on the part of the United States to secure control of that canal or the concession to American citizens of exclusive privileges in connection with it. To prevent Nicaragua from granting such a concession the British government hastily reasserted its protectorate over the Mosquito coast — until 1840 merely a passive arrangement — and proclaimed the sovereignty of the Mosquito kingdom over the port of San Juan del Norte and the San Juan River from its mouth to the Machuca rapids, rather more than halfway to the lake. Since the river channel offered the only practicable route for a canal, and San Juan del Norte the only possible site for an Atlantic terminus, recognition of the Mosquito claim would have automatically invalidated any concession granted by Nicaragua alone. While the British move may have been justified by the fear, by no means altogether groundless, of a United States monopoly in the canal area, the American people deeply resented what they considered a jealous attempt to deprive them of a vital commercial artery. Unfortunately the controversy persisted even after it became clear that the United States did not propose to demand exclusive canal privileges. By the revival of the protectorate and the support of the Mosquito claim to a section of the canal route the British government had placed itself in a position from which it could not withdraw without serious loss of "face," and its efforts to preserve its prestige intact while conceding practically all tangible points prolonged the dispute for at least ten years.

The active phase of British intervention on the Mosquito coast was initiated by Colonel Alexander Macdonald, superintendent of Belize. Apparently without instructions from his home government but with its subsequent approval Macdonald and the Mosquito king (a native chieftain who assumed the name Robert Charles Frederick) landed at San Juan del Norte in August 1841, raised the Mosquito flag, reaffirmed the British protectorate, and claimed the port in the name of the Mosquito kingdom. The Nicaraguan commandant refused to obey Macdonald's order to evacuate the town and was carried in a British ship to Cape Gracias á Dios, where he was put ashore and left to return to civilization as best he could. After Macdonald's retirement from San Juan the Nicaraguan forces reoccupied the port and remained in undisputed possession until 1847. In 1842 the Mosquito king died and was succeeded by his young son, George William Clarence, with Macdonald as self-constituted regent. Two years later Macdonald appointed his secretary, Patrick Walker, to the post of British resident at Bluefields, the Mosquito capital.

These aggressions produced a voluminous exchange of diplomatic correspondence between Great Britain and Nicaragua, but nothing significant occurred until October 25, 1847, when George Hodgson, the English senior member of the Mosquito council of state at Bluefields, sent an ultimatum to the Nicaraguan government demanding the withdrawal of all Nicaraguan troops from San Juan del Norte before January 1, 1848. Nicaragua rejected the note, and on February 8 a small British squadron commanded by Captain Granville Loch in the *Alarm* took possession of the town. British forces pursued the retreating Nicaraguans up the river and on February 12 captured a small fort at the junction of the San Juan and Sarapiquí Rivers. On March 7 an armistice was signed, by which Nicaragua agreed not to disturb the *status quo* at San Juan del Norte but reserved the right to settle the controversy if possible by negotiation with the British government. During this crisis the Nicaraguan government had appealed to Washington three times but had received no reply. The English inhabitants of San Juan del Norte changed the name of the port to Greytown in honor of Sir Charles Edward Grey, governor of Jamaica.

When news of the seizure of San Juan del Norte reached Washington Buchanan directed Elijah Hise, recently appointed chargé d'affaires to Central America, to investigate the matter and to conclude treaties with Guatemala and El Salvador but not, for the present, with Nicaragua, Honduras, or Costa Rica. Notwithstanding this specific prohibition Hise requested the government of Nicaragua to send a commissioner to Guatemala City to negotiate a pact with the United States. On June 21, 1849 Hise and the Nicaraguan envoy, Buenaventura Selva, signed a treaty granting to the United States "or to a company of the citizens thereof, the exclusive right . . . to . . . construct . . . a canal . . . or roads, either railways or turnpikes" [20] across Nicaragua. The United States would have the right to erect fortifications along and at the ends of the transit. In return the United States undertook "to protect and defend . . . Nicaragua in the possession and exercise of the sovereignty and dominion of all the country . . . within the just and true limits and boundaries of the . . . State. . . ." [21] As an example of an entangling alliance the Hise-Selva convention went far beyond any agreement hitherto concluded by the United States government. Not only was it an *exclusive* grant with no provision for the adherence of other powers but it obliged the United States to defend by force *all* territory claimed by Nicaragua within its much-disputed boundaries. The treaty of 1846 with New Granada had not been exclusive in intent though it became so in fact through

the failure of other nations to subscribe to it; and it had committed the United States to a guarantee of the actual transit only, not
of the whole country.

But the Hise-Selva treaty was never submitted to the United
States Senate, partly because Hise had flagrantly exceeded his authority and partly because he was no longer the official representative of his government when he signed it. In March 1849 Zachary
Taylor replaced Polk as President, and two months later the new
Secretary of State, John Clayton, issued an order for Hise's recall,
though the order did not reach Guatemala until after the conclusion of the pact and the arrival of Hise's successor, Ephraim George
Squier. After his return to Washington Hise defended himself in
a rueful note to Clayton: "If I have erred . . . I at least thought
that I was doing right. . . ." [22]

Unlike Hise, Squier did have explicit authority to negotiate a
treaty with Nicaragua as well as with all other Central American
states. A few days after his arrival in Nicaragua he met David L.
White, the representative of the American Atlantic and Pacific
Ship Canal Company, a new corporation headed by "Commodore"
Cornelius Vanderbilt. So far White's efforts to secure a canal concession for his company had met with no success, but Squier's assurances of a guarantee by the United States government overcame
Nicaraguan reluctance. The contract was signed at León on August 27, 1849 and ratified by the Nicaraguan Congress on September 22. The company engaged itself to commence preliminary surveys within one year and to complete the canal within 12 years,
after which the concession was to run for 85 years. It also promised
to pay Nicaragua $10,000 upon ratification, $10,000 a year until
the canal should be put in operation, and thereafter a specified
percentage of the net profits. In addition Nicaragua would receive
10% of the net profits of any railroad or highway constructed by
the company before the completion of the canal. Since the company did build and operate a carriage road within a few years,
while the canal remained a paper project, this last provision was
the only one actually to go into effect. Later it became a source of
violent controversy between the transit company and the republic.

To satisfy Nicaragua's demand for an official guarantee of this
contract Squier immediately negotiated a treaty of commerce and
friendship between the United States and Nicaragua, which the
Nicaraguan Congress ratified on the day it confirmed the private
canal concession. By this treaty the United States and Nicaragua
jointly undertook to protect the canal company "from any acts of
invasion, forfeiture, or violence. . . . The United States distinctly

recognizes the rights of sovereignty and property which . . . Nicaragua possesses in and over the line of said canal. . . ." [23] The two governments also agreed "that none of the rights, privileges, and immunities . . . conceded to the United States and its citizens, shall accrue to any other nation, or to its citizens, except such nation shall first enter into the same treaty stipulations. . . ." [24] To Taylor and Clayton, both anxious to reduce American obligations to a minimum, this treaty seemed a vast improvement over the Hise-Selva convention since it bound the United States to protect only the canal route and proposed to share even this limited responsibility with other nations.

But the British government found the Squier treaty far from satisfactory. While it allayed British apprehensions concerning a possible American monopoly over the canal line it expressly affirmed Nicaraguan sovereignty over the entire transit. Great Britain, firmly pledged to the support of the Mosquito claims and somewhat less firmly to recognition of Costa Rica's title (which added another twist to the snarl by conflicting with the pretensions of *both* Nicaragua and the Mosquito kingdom), could not acknowledge Nicaragua's sovereignty without an ignominious reversal of policy. Therefore it was essential for Great Britain to prevent ratification of the Squier treaty by the United States Senate and at the same time to reach some understanding with the United States which would enable the American canal company to complete its project without subjecting the British government to the humiliation of a formal renunciation of its protectorate.

On the other hand the United States government, while no less anxious to settle the controversy, demanded as a *sine qua non* the abandonment of the Mosquito protectorate and the withdrawal of the Mosquito claim to the lower portion of the San Juan River. In the autumn of 1849 Clayton suggested this solution to Palmerston. While the two governments continued to observe the diplomatic amenities, popular resentment was rising ominously, and unmistakable threats of war could be heard on both sides of the Atlantic. In December Palmerston sent Sir Henry Lytton Bulwer to Washington with instructions to find some formula that would satisfy both governments. The British envoy first persuaded President Taylor to postpone transmission of the Squier treaty to the Senate, and by the time Taylor did submit it on March 19, 1850 negotiations between Bulwer and Clayton had already progressed so far that the Senate deferred its consideration until the next session. In the end the Squier convention was permitted to lapse without ratification.

On April 19, 1850 Clayton and Bulwer signed the famous treaty
between the United States and Great Britain which was to plague
the statesmen of both nations until it was superseded by the Hay-
Pauncefote treaty more than half a century later. After a stormy
debate in the Senate it was ratified by a vote of 42 to 11 and proclaimed on July 5. The Clayton-Bulwer convention was frankly a
compromise and, in the circumstances, could have been nothing
else. Yet with all its faults it did serve to avert the possibility of a
disastrous war. In article 1 the United States and Great Britain declared that neither "will ever obtain or maintain for itself any exclusive control over the said ship-canal; agreeing that neither will
ever erect . . . any fortifications commanding the same, or . . .
occupy, or fortify, or colonize, or assume or exercise any dominion
over Nicaragua, Costa Rica, the Mosquito coast, or any part of Central America. . . ." [25] The two governments also engaged to protect and guarantee the neutrality of the completed waterway. Although the Nicaragua route was the only one specifically involved
article 8 proposed to extend this protection to all other transit projects, especially those in Tehuantepec and Panama. This last provision did not go into effect automatically but required the conclusion of additional treaties with each of the states concerned. The
United States already controlled the Panama route under its pact
of 1846 with New Granada, but Great Britain had not seen fit to
negotiate a parallel agreement. In 1857 the British government belatedly proposed to give effect to article 8 by means of a joint convention between the United States, Great Britain, and France
which would guarantee the neutrality of the Panama transit. President Buchanan declined to participate, Great Britain and France
made no further moves, and the United States remained the sole
guarantor.

The ambiguous wording of article 1 left a dangerous amount of
leeway for interpretation, and it soon became apparent that the
American and British governments chose to interpret it in very different senses. Just before the final exchange of ratifications Bulwer
presented to Clayton a declaration to the effect that the British government understood that the agreement not to occupy or dominate
any part of Central America did not apply to the existing British
settlements in Belize or its "dependencies" — a vague term which
was to lead to trouble later. To this Clayton consented, though with
misgivings. A more serious difference of opinion arose over the old
apple of discord, the Mosquito protectorate. Although the British
government had given up the substance of its control over the
Mosquito coast it had not surrendered the form. Clayton believed

at first that this empty form preserved for reasons of prestige would soon be relinquished; since Great Britain had agreed not to occupy, fortify, colonize, or exercise dominion over the Mosquito kingdom it was no longer in a position to "protect" that territory effectively and might therefore as well withdraw completely. But Palmerston had no intention of yielding the point, though he displayed a willingness to conciliate the United States by proposing various compromise solutions. In October 1850 he suggested the cession of San Juan del Norte to Costa Rica in order to eliminate that port as a subject of dispute between Nicaragua and the Mosquito kingdom. The Nicaraguan minister in London indignantly rejected the proposal. Palmerston then instructed the Mosquito authorities to declare Greytown a free port at which no customs duties were to be levied, but he insisted that the mention of the Mosquito coast as a separate entity in article 1 of the Clayton-Bulwer treaty constituted an acknowledgment by the United States of that kingdom's independence under the British protectorate. Nicaragua's title to the canal route and its Atlantic terminus was therefore no clearer than before the conclusion of the treaty.

During his stay in Nicaragua Squier found time to absorb and express a few ideas concerning the canal project. He favored the long route by way of Lake Managua in the mistaken belief that a lower summit could be found between that lake and the Pacific than between Lake Nicaragua and the same ocean, and suggested three alternative lines: the first to the port of Tamarindo about 18 miles from Lake Managua, the second to Realejo, and the third — Squier's favorite — to the navigable waters of the Estero Real flowing into the Gulf of Fonseca. The Estero Real was in fact not navigable at all for even small ships, and this plan would have necessitated an artificial canal at least 75 miles long between Lake Managua and the gulf. The only sound aspect of Squier's projects was his high estimate of the expense: "Assume it to cost $100,000,000, which may be as near the truth as any other calculation; still . . . its benefits . . . will . . . compensate for the expenditure of double that amount, startling as it may at first appear." [26]

Chapter 17. Nicaragua: 1850–1860

WHEN the American Atlantic and Pacific Ship Canal Company obtained its charter in 1849 the gold rush to California was already well under way. Hence the potential value of the concession was enormous, and Vanderbilt and his associates were determined to cling to it at all costs. But the controversy between Great Britain and the United States placed the company in a very precarious position. Since the Squier treaty demanded by Nicaragua as a guarantee of the canal contract had not been ratified the validity of that contract without the supporting treaty was doubtful; and the company could not claim the joint protection of Great Britain and the United States under the Clayton-Bulwer treaty, for the canal charter had been granted by Nicaragua alone in defiance of the pretensions of the Mosquito kingdom and of Costa Rica, which Great Britain continued to defend. At first these difficulties appeared more theoretical than actual. Nicaragua, still hoping for ultimate ratification of the Squier convention, did not in fact declare the contract void, and the British government placed no obstacles in the way of the company's preliminary operations.

The company's first task was the establishment of a steamboat service on Lake Nicaragua. In the summer of 1850 it purchased the *Orus,* then serving as a tender at the port of Chagres, and attempted to send it up the San Juan River to the lake. When the *Orus* was wrecked on the rocks of Machuca rapids the canal company dispatched a smaller steamer, the *Director,* which Vanderbilt himself piloted safely through the dangerous channel and across the lake to Granada, where it arrived on January 1, 1851.

The second step was the organization of a thorough survey of the entire canal route. The task was entrusted to Orville W. Childs, a civil engineer whose discoveries furnished the topographical foundation for all subsequent practicable projects for a Nicaragua canal. Childs established his headquarters at Rivas on August 27, 1850, quickly eliminated Oersted's route by proving conclusively that the Sapoa pass lay at a much greater elevation than the Danish explorer had surmised, carefully examined three or four other depressions, rejected them all, and at last hit upon a line extending from the mouth of the Lajas River to the Pacific harbor of Brito, a small bay 9 miles northwest of San Juan del Sur. Here he made his momentous find: a summit only 46 feet above the ordinary high-water surface of the lake or 153 feet above mean sea level. He had located a gap about 120 feet lower than the minimum height of the Panama watershed — the lowest gap in the entire continental divide that stretches its immense length from the Arctic Ocean to the Straits of Magellan.

As laid out by Childs the western section of the canal from deep water in the lake to deep water in the Pacific would be 18.9 miles long. The summit level of the canal was to be the surface level of the lake, from which a series of 14 locks would descend to the sea on either side. From Lake Nicaragua to the Atlantic, 119.31 miles by the canal line, the upper portion followed the bed of the San Juan with short bypasses to avoid the rapids, but on account of the shallows and obstructions in the lower course of the river the easternmost section was to be diverted into an entirely artificial cut north of and roughly parallel to the river. The canal was to be 17 feet deep and 50 feet wide at the bottom, while the breadth at the water line varied from 78 feet in rock to 118 in soft earth. The locks measured 250 feet in length by 60 in width. These dimensions were too small to accommodate the largest steamers afloat even in 1850, and any canal constructed on such a scale would soon have become altogether obsolete. Childs estimated the total cost at $31,538,319 and the construction period at six years.

The canal company submitted its engineer's report to the Secretary of War, Charles M. Conrad, who in turn referred it to two army engineers, Colonel John James Abert and Lieutenant Colonel William Turnbull. On March 20, 1852 these officers reported that in their opinion the project was practicable and the estimate sound; but before permitting the company to proceed the United States government, anxious to comply with the spirit of the Clayton-Bulwer treaty, transmitted the Childs report to the British government, which instructed Colonel Edward Aldrich of the Royal Engineers and James Walker, an eminent civil engineer, to examine the plans. These experts also pronounced in favor of the scheme. In the autumn of 1850, before Childs had well started his surveys, Vanderbilt went to London to procure financial aid for the canal project. The response was discouraging, and the directors, apparently without great reluctance, abandoned the enterprise — temporarily, it was believed at the time, though in fact the American Atlantic and Pacific Ship Canal Company never made a serious attempt to construct or even plan an interoceanic waterway.

Nevertheless the company did not permit its concession to lapse. The charter granted two distinct privileges: the right to construct a canal, and the right to build and operate a railroad or highway to serve as a temporary transit during the period allowed for the completion of the canal. The canal would require enormous capital, and its earnings could not begin to accrue for many years, while a provisional communication sufficiently convenient to draw much of the gold rush traffic away from Panama could be placed in operation without delay and would produce immediate profits. Vanderbilt therefore induced the Nicaraguan government to permit the separation of the transit concession from the canal privilege. The latter remained under the control of the original (and now inactive) company, while the same directors organized a second corporation, the Accessory Transit Company, to handle the lucrative California trade. On August 14, 1851 the Accessory Transit Company received its independent charter and the grant of an exclusive right of way, though it had actually commenced operations some weeks earlier. Under the shrewd management of its president, Vanderbilt, the transit company soon became a powerful competitor of the Panama line. From San Juan del Norte passengers and freight were conveyed up the San Juan River in small steamboats drawing but a few feet of water to Fuerte de San Carlos, where they were transferred to larger steamers for the 55-mile trip across the lake to La Virgen — called by the Americans Virgin Bay — near the mouth of the Lajas River. The overland transit from that point to San Juan del Sur was accomplished at first on muleback over a rough trail, but after the completion of a macadamized road in 1854 the short journey from lake to ocean could be made quickly and comfortably in coaches gaily painted blue and white, the national colors of Nicaragua. 25 such vehicles each drawn by four mules and followed by a long line of wagons carrying freight and baggage made up the usual convoy.

In 1851 Vanderbilt inaugurated a through transportation system to California with steamship services between New York and San Juan del Norte on the Atlantic side and between San Juan del Sur and San Francisco on the Pacific. Although the Vanderbilt steamer lines were carelessly operated — one of his crack vessels, *North Star,* was described as "a floating pig sty," [1] and four of his other ships were wrecked within little more than a year — they provided stiff competition to the Panama route until the completion of the isthmian railroad in 1855. In 1853 10,062 emigrants reached San Francisco via Nicaragua compared with 15,502 by Panama, while the eastbound flow of passengers from San Francisco was almost evenly divided between the two routes. The Panama route provided safer and more comfortable steamers and a more rapid overland crossing, but the Vanderbilt line offered slightly lower fares, shorter sea voyages in both oceans, and a somewhat more healthful transit from sea to sea. Undoubtedly travelers across Nicaragua had less to fear from malaria and other fevers; on the other hand serious outbreaks of cholera ravaged Nicaragua more frequently than Panama.

In April 1853 Vanderbilt sold his ocean fleets to the Accessory Transit Company, which renamed the west coast line the Nicaragua Steamship Company and installed Cornelius Garrison, one of the organizers of the first transport service across the Isthmus of Panama, as its agent in San Francisco. Under his able supervision the operation of the line rapidly improved, and the disastrous shipwrecks came to an end. Then in the late summer of the same year Vanderbilt suddenly decided to re-enter the maritime competition in both the Atlantic and Pacific with a new company, the Independent Line, and fight all of the existing services: the Pacific Mail, the United States Mail, and the Nicaragua Steamship Company. As a subsidiary of the Accessory Transit Company the last-named corporation exercised exclusive control over the right of way across Nicaragua; but no such monopoly yet existed at Panama, so Vanderbilt placed his new steamers on the run to and from the isthmus. After one year of highly successful competition the Independent Line was bought out by the Pacific Mail and United States Mail. By a secret clause in the agreement Vanderbilt forced the two purchasing companies to pay him a monthly subsidy of $40,000 (later increased to $56,000) in exchange for his promise not to establish yet another steamship line. The truce lasted until 1859, when the 10-year mail contracts of the two older lines expired and their payments to Vanderbilt ceased. The Commodore immediately bought several steamers, secured the mail contract for himself, and inaugurated a new period of violent competition which ended — this time permanently — with the purchase of Vanderbilt's fleet by the Pacific Mail in 1865.

The failure of the Clayton-Bulwer treaty to settle the Mosquito controversy was soon demonstrated by an incident at San Juan del Norte. On November 21, 1851 one of Vanderbilt's steamers, *Prometheus,* lay at anchor in the harbor on the eve of her departure

for New York. Although the town had been declared a free port local officials continued to levy a small and quite legitimate charge
on shipping for the upkeep of the harbor. The *Prometheus* was
the only vessel whose captain had consistently refused to pay these
dues on the ground that his company had received its charter from
Nicaragua and did not recognize the jurisdiction of the Mosquito
kingdom. This time the exasperated port authorities boarded the
ship, presented their bills and a warrant for Captain Churchill's
arrest, and notified him that neither he nor his vessel would be allowed to leave until the debt was paid. Churchill immediately ordered the *Prometheus* to sea, but the British brig-of-war *Express*
followed her out of the harbor and forced her to return by firing
two warning shots across her bows. Vanderbilt, on board the *Prometheus*, then paid the port charges under protest, and the vessel
was allowed to proceed to New York. When the Accessory Transit
Company filed its complaint the Secretary of the Navy ordered the
commander of the United States home fleet, Commodore Foxhall
A. Parker, to San Juan del Norte, and the State Department protested vigorously to the British government. On January 10, 1852
Lord Granville, Palmerston's successor, disavowed the use of force
by Captain Fead of the *Express* and apologized for the interference
with American shipping.

Although the incident ended with mutual expressions of good
will it served as a warning that the fundamental disagreement still
persisted and might boil over again at any moment. Both governments now made serious attempts to compose their differences.
Daniel Webster, who had replaced Clayton after the death of President Taylor, had already yielded one point by admitting the possible title of Costa Rica to a portion of the canal route. At the same
time the British consul at San Juan del Norte made a conciliatory
gesture by withdrawing from active participation in the government of the town, which thus became a free port in fact as well as
in name.

Meanwhile the United States and Great Britain found themselves at odds over another ambiguity in the Clayton-Bulwer treaty.
The British government had declared, and Clayton had conceded,
that the treaty recognized British sovereignty over Belize and its
"dependencies," without specifying the dependencies. Under this
head Great Britain now claimed the islands of Roatán and Bonacca
as well as several smaller islets off the northern coast of Honduras
and on March 20, 1852 formally annexed them as the crown colony
of the Bay Islands. The United States denied the British title, and
for the next seven years this new controversy widened the breach

between the two countries. The appointment of Solon Borland as American minister to Central America in April 1853 did nothing to improve international relations. Borland not only urged abrogation of the Clayton-Bulwer treaty but acted officially as if it had already ceased to exist. Without authorization he negotiated a new treaty with Nicaragua whereby the United States again guaranteed Nicaraguan sovereignty over the entire canal route and implicitly denied Costa Rican claims. The horrified State Department hastily repudiated the pact.

A little more than a year after the *Prometheus* affair the Accessory Transit Company clashed once more with the local authorities at San Juan del Norte. The company, having obtained a concession for the establishment of a coal depot on a beach across the river, proceeded to erect an entire town of warehouses, stores, hotels, and other buildings. On February 3, 1853 the officials at San Juan del Norte ordered the unauthorized structures removed within 30 days and when the company failed to comply sent an armed force which destroyed several buildings and tore down the American flag. This incident was smoothed over, but during the next few months a series of minor squabbles increased the tension until an explosion seemed inevitable. It came with the arrival at San Juan del Norte of the company's river steamboat *Routh* on May 16, 1854. On the voyage down the river the captain had shot and killed a colored boatman, and when the *Routh* reached San Juan a band of angry Negroes led by a marshal attempted to board the steamboat and arrest the captain. Borland, a passenger on the *Routh*, denied the right of any local functionary to arrest an American citizen and ordered the Negroes to return to San Juan, which they did. When Borland went ashore that night to meet the United States resident commercial agent, Joseph W. Fabens, a shouting and cursing mob surrounded the agent's house. Borland was struck in the face by a broken bottle.

Secretary of State Marcy directed Fabens to insist upon an apology and payment of damages. The corvette *Cyane* was dispatched to San Juan, and Commander George Hollins was instructed to use force if he and Fabens considered it necessary to secure redress. Fabens and Hollins computed the damages at $24,000 and jointly presented their demands, which the local officials ignored. On the morning of July 13, 1854 Hollins, after sending a boat to take away any residents who wished to leave, trained the *Cyane's* guns on San Juan del Norte and bombarded the town. That afternoon he completed the destruction by setting fire to what was left of the flimsy settlement. When the news reached the United States Hollins was roundly condemned in the press. The British government entered an emphatic protest and demanded an immediate disavowal. Although the bombardment was in fact wholly unjustified Marcy could not disavow it, since both Fabens and Hollins had been specifically authorized to employ force if satisfaction could not be obtained without it. The United States government rejected the British protest, and in his next message to Congress President Pierce pointedly defended Hollins's cannonade. The British government, unwilling to go to war over the affair, yielded, and the unfortunate incident was closed.

So far in spite of almost incessant international quarrels, local insurrections, and occasional isolated outbreaks of violence, the situation in Nicaragua had involved very little actual combat. But in 1855 the spectacular activities of an American firebrand suddenly plunged the country into a bloody war.

Unstable political conditions in both Central America and the United States provided an ideal culture medium for the breeding of filibustering expeditions. For years Nicaragua had been torn by factional disputes in which neither of the two chief parties, the Legitimists (Conservatives) and Democrats (Liberals), had been able to gain a decisive victory. Within six years the country changed Presidents fifteen times. León became the stronghold of the northern or Democratic faction while Granada in the hands of the Legitimists dominated the southern half of the country. When the Legitimist Frutos Chamorro was elected President in 1853 his defeated opponent, Francisco Castellón, conceived the idea of enlisting foreign volunteers to help him overthrow the régime and install his own party in power. Such volunteers could be recruited in the United States, where headstrong believers in Manifest Destiny were searching eagerly for new Latin American fields to conquer. For obvious reasons this expansionist sentiment was strongest in the southern states. The rapid increase in the population of the industrial North threatened to upset the delicate balance between free and slave states, and plantation owners hoped to restore the equilibrium by the annexation of tropical regions suitable for the employment of slave labor. Although the United States government officially opposed such aggressive moves popular sentiment encouraged them openly in the South and with greater caution in other sections.

William Walker, born in Nashville in 1824, studied first medicine and then law before he became one of the editors and owners of the New Orleans *Crescent*. In 1850 he moved to San Francisco and then to Marysville in the Sacramento Valley, where he again practised law. Three years later he embarked upon a more adventurous enterprise: a rash attempt to establish an independent American state in Mexico. With 45 men he landed at La Paz in Lower California in November 1853, proclaimed the peninsula a republic with himself as President, and after obtaining additional recruits advanced into the state of Sonora. Mexican troops harried the invaders, whose ranks were quickly reduced by wounds, illness, hunger, and desertion, and with the remnant of his force Walker retreated to San Diego, where he surrendered to United States army officers and was sent back to San Francisco to stand trial for violation of the neutrality laws. After his acquittal he settled down in San Francisco as editor of a local newspaper. Through one of the proprietors of the paper, Byron Cole, Walker became interested in Nicaragua as a promising field for exploitation and conquest. In 1854 Cole went to Nicaragua and made a contract with Castellón to enlist 300 volunteers in the United States for service in the Democratic army. To circumvent the neutrality laws these filibusters were to be labeled "colonists." Cole sent the contract to Walker, who selected the first contingent of 58 men and purchased a leaky old brig, the *Vesta*. After a delay of several months due to financial difficulties the *Vesta* sailed from San Francisco on May 4, 1855 and anchored in the harbor of Realejo on June 16.

Although theoretically under Castellón's orders Walker soon found himself at odds with his commander. The Democratic leader had invited the filibusters to Nicaragua to strengthen the position of his party; the American adventurer, who cared nothing for local politics, aspired to the exploitation or even annexation of the whole country. Castellón died of cholera a few months after the arrival of the Americans, and Walker made himself commander-in-chief of the Democratic forces. Early in September he landed his small group of volunteers at San Juan del Sur, captured the transit highway, and routed a Legitimist detachment at La Virgen. Encouraged by the arrival of a few recruits and by the friendliness of the Accessory Transit Company's representative, Charles J. McDonald, Walker took possession of one of the company's two lake steamers, sailed to Granada, and captured the Legitimist capital in a surprise attack on October 13. Ten days later he negotiated a peace treaty with the Legitimist commander, General Corral, and set up a provisional government with Patricio Rivas, an elderly man of moderate political views, as President, Corral as War Minister, and Walker himself as commander-in-chief of the entire Nicaraguan army and in effect dictator. But Corral, dissatisfied, wrote some treasonable letters which fell into Walker's hands, and for this indiscretion he was tried by court-martial and shot early in November. The execution of the idol of the Legitimist army cost Walker the loyalty of thousands of Nicaraguans.

Meanwhile another and quite independent American filibustering expedition headed by Colonel Henry L. Kinney was stirring up trouble at San Juan del Norte. In 1839 the Mosquito king had granted to Stanislaus Thomas Haly, a former resident of Jamaica, and to Samuel and Peter Shepherd, natives of Georgia who claimed to be British subjects, certain large tracts of land along the Atlantic coast near the mouth of the San Juan River. Since these grants had been made without the approval of the British government Colonel Macdonald, superintendent of Belize, requested their annulment. The Mosquito chieftain, having been well paid in whisky and red calico, rejected the British demand; but after his death in 1842 Macdonald as regent declared the grants invalid. Haly and the Shepherds, who had acquired a dubious title to some 22,500,000 acres or about two thirds of the maximum area claimed for the Mosquito kingdom, refused to surrender their rights, which they sold to an American company organized by Kinney. Among Kinney's associates was Joseph Fabens, who had been forbidden by Marcy to participate in the venture and whose disobedience cost him his government post.

Kinney and Fabens, ostensibly planning to establish an American colony in their newly purchased domain, collected about 500 emigrants in New York, chartered the steamer *United States,* and prepared to sail on May 7, 1855 — three days after Walker left San Francisco in the dilapidated *Vesta.* But whereas Walker had gained the support of the powerful Accessory Transit Company that corporation opposed the Kinney expedition because Kinney had derived his title, such as it was, indirectly from the Mosquito government which the transit company had never recognized. To prevent Kinney's departure transit officials in New York warned the United States government that Kinney proposed to violate the neutrality regulations by fitting out an armed expedition against a friendly nation. A few days before the scheduled sailing date federal agents arrested Kinney and Fabens and blockaded their steamer. Fabens appeared when the trial opened on June 5, but Kinney and 13 companions escaped to San Juan del Norte, where they were joined by Fabens, whom the United States government had failed to convict. Early in September Kinney organized a provisional government at San Juan with himself as governor, which both the British authorities and the Accessory Transit Company, for once in agreement, refused to acknowledge. Discouraged and almost bankrupt, Kinney and Fabens now decided to join forces with Walker. But Walker had no use for Kinney and no desire to antagonize the transit company. Kinney soon left the country but returned in 1858 and made another attempt to install his own government at the port. When this too failed he abandoned his claim for good.

Garrison, the San Francisco agent of the Accessory Transit Company, and Charles Morgan, its New York manager and after Vanderbilt's resignation in 1853 its president, now began to take a more active interest in Walker's venture. By the terms of the original charter of 1849 the company had agreed to pay Nicaragua $10,-000 a year for 12 years if the canal was not completed before the expiration of that period, as well as 10% of any profits derived from the operation of a temporary communication. From 1849 to 1855 the corporation had paid the fixed annual indemnity but nothing whatever on the profits account from its lucrative steamboat-and-highway transit. The company claimed that it had made no such profits, while the Nicaraguan authorities alleged with good reason that this was merely a trick of bookkeeping: that the company had deliberately fixed a low rate for the overland transit in order to avoid its payment to the government but had more than made up the loss by increasing its ocean steamer fares in which Nicaragua had no share. Since the company kept all its records in the United States it was difficult for the Nicaraguans to prove their contention.

Garrison and Morgan endeavored to turn this dispute to their own advantage by inducing the Nicaraguan government to annul the company's charter on the ground of non-fulfillment of its obligations and to issue a new charter which through the elimination of Vanderbilt and the other partners would give the San Francisco and New York managers complete control of the corporation. To consummate this financial hocus-pocus Garrison and Morgan used Walker, unsophisticated in the ways of Wall Street, as a tool. They offered to transport to Nicaragua free of charge all volunteers for service in Walker's army if Walker would undertake to procure from President Rivas the revocation of the transit company's contract and the award of a new one to themselves. Walker, in desperate need of troops, agreed and was rewarded by a flood of volunteers. The promise of free transportation attracted several hundred adventurous young men, decent citizens as well as riffraff, and recruiting went on openly in New York, San Francisco, and New Orleans. At least one New York newspaper carried the company's advertisement offering employment to single men "a short distance out of the city." [2] Popular sympathy favored the filibusters, and the United States marshals could do little to stop their illegal departure since the volunteers all held steamer tickets and claimed to be ordinary passengers.

Walker promptly paid his debt to Garrison and Morgan by persuading Rivas to annul the original charter on February 18, 1856, but the aged President, unexpectedly obstinate, refused to sign the new contract until many of its excessively generous provisions had been modified or eliminated. By this move Walker gained two friends but made a much more powerful enemy: Vanderbilt. The thoroughly angry Commodore quickly turned the tables on his unscrupulous colleagues and on all who had helped to further their plot. By skillful manipulation of the stock market he ousted Morgan from the presidency of the company, then instituted suits against Morgan, Garrison, and Walker, closed the interoceanic transit, and withdrew his ocean steamers. The last move stopped the flow of recruits and supplies to Nicaragua for six weeks and placed Walker in an exceedingly difficult position until Morgan and Garrison were able to organize a temporary steamship service of their own.

That position was made more precarious by the determined hostility of Costa Rica. The President, Juan Rafael Mora, the government, and the politically conservative majority of the people sympathized strongly with the Legitimist faction in Nicaragua. Although Walker did his best to conciliate Costa Rica, Mora mobilized his troops and on March 4, 1856 led an invading army of about 4000 out of San José to meet Walker's 600 American filibusters. Walker lost 100 men in the first engagement and retired to Granada, while the Costa Ricans occupied Rivas and the transit. On April 11 Walker attacked Rivas and captured the plaza but was forced to withdraw in a few hours. What Walker and his small detachment were unable to achieve cholera accomplished for them. The disease broke out in virulent form at Rivas and spread so rapidly that Mora abandoned the town and started for home. The stricken Costa Rican army left heaps of dead along the road while the wretched survivors carried the pestilence to San José. The malady also ravaged Nicaragua and infected Walker's troops, though less severely than the natives. Before the epidemic subsided it had taken, according to unofficial estimates, from 10,000 to 12,000 lives.

A quarrel between Walker and President Rivas disrupted the provisional government, and on June 29, 1856 Walker was elected

President — probably by fraudulent manipulation of the ballots. In July Guatemala, Honduras, and El Salvador joined forces against the American dictator, and in September the allied armies invaded Nicaragua from the north. Costa Rica entered the coalition in November. Although the Central American armies overwhelmingly outnumbered Walker's troops they were disorganized and poorly led, and the filibusters were able to retire in good order from Granada to La Virgen. Walker might have been able to hold out indefinitely if Vanderbilt had not turned against him. Vanderbilt's strategy was simple and effective. He knew that if Walker's enemies could seize the San Juan River and the transit road the filibusters would be cut off from reinforcements and supplies; with the transit closed Garrison and Morgan would have to withdraw their Atlantic and Pacific steamers and would soon be driven out of the business they had usurped; and he — Vanderbilt — would probably be given back his concession by a grateful Nicaraguan government. Accordingly he sent two agents to San José in November 1856. Mora placed Costa Rican troops at their disposal, and within a month they had captured La Virgen and Fuerte de San Carlos, seized two steamers on the lake and four river steamboats at San Juan del Norte, and sealed up the transit at both ends. Hemmed in at Rivas with some 900 men, only 500 of whom were fit for service, Walker was now in a hopeless situation. Skirmishes, starvation, disease, and wholesale desertions rapidly decimated his small force. On May 1, 1857 Walker surrendered to a United States naval officer, Commander Charles H. Davis of the sloop-of-war *St. Mary's*. The women and children from besieged Rivas as well as the sick and wounded of Walker's army were taken to San Juan del Norte and thence in the *Cyane* to Colón, while Walker himself and the more robust survivors were carried from San Juan del Sur to Panama. All were eventually sent back to the United States.

It has been estimated that the total number of men enlisted under Walker was 2518 but that his effective force never exceeded 1200 at any one time. Of this total about 40% were killed in action or died of disease, 28% deserted, 10% were discharged for various reasons, 4% were captured or unaccounted for, and only 18% — 463 men — took part in the final surrender. The allied armies probably lost four or five times as many men, but no reliable figures are available.

In New Orleans and New York Walker was acclaimed as a hero by the adventure-loving public. He called on President Buchanan and with arrogance undiminished by defeat protested energetically against the interference of Commander Davis. Then he returned to New Orleans and organized a second expedition to Nicaragua. He landed at San Juan del Norte on November 24, 1857, but the prompt arrival of British and American men-of-war frustrated his plans, and he was obliged to surrender again and return to the United States. In New Orleans he was tried for violation of the neutrality laws, but after one jury disagreed the charge was not pressed.

The final chapter of Walker's turbulent career was written not in Nicaragua but in Honduras. Although the dispute between Great Britain and Honduras was settled in November 1859 by the return of the Bay Islands to Honduras local unrest still offered a promising opportunity for fishing in troubled waters. Walker now resolved to "liberate" the English settlers on Roatán, who deeply resented their transfer to Honduran sovereignty, and with that island as a base organize yet another invasion of Nicaragua. In June 1860 he landed on Roatán with a party of recruits, but the expected revolution failed to materialize. After cruising along the coast of Honduras for several weeks he suddenly attacked the fortified town of Trujillo on the mainland and captured it on August 6. Two weeks later the British warship *Icarus* reached the port, and her commander, Nowell Salmon, demanded Walker's surrender. The filibusters escaped that night but were overtaken by Commander Salmon's men on September 3 and brought back to Trujillo. Salmon sent all of his prisoners to the United States except Walker and one other officer, whom he turned over to the Honduran authorities. On September 12, 1860 Walker was executed at Trujillo by a Honduran firing squad.

After Walker's expulsion from Nicaragua in 1857 the political turmoil gradually subsided. The Legitimist and Democratic factions united against the provisional government set up by Rivas, who fled to England, and a Legitimist President, General Tomás Martínez, was elected by a constitutional convention without opposition. But the transit remained closed, and although its importance had been greatly diminished by the opening of the Panama Railroad it still possessed sufficient value to make its control profitable. Three groups now claimed the exclusive concession: the holder of the original charter, the American Atlantic and Pacific Ship Canal Company, headed by H. G. Stebbins, its president, and Joseph L. White; the Accessory Transit Company, with Vanderbilt once more at the helm; and Morgan and Garrison, who insisted upon the validity of their privilege. In June 1857 Stebbins and White won the first round by securing a new contract from the

Nicaraguan minister to the United States, Irisarri. When Vanderbilt protested Buchanan sent William Carey Jones as a special envoy to Nicaragua to investigate and report. Jones, "rarely sober and never diplomatic," [3] proved a poor emissary, and his mission accomplished nothing. Nevertheless on November 16, 1857 Irisarri and Cass signed a treaty providing for a neutral transit across Nicaragua under the military protection of the United States. In general the conditions were similar to those in the unratified Squier treaty of 1849.

Vanderbilt persuaded the government of Nicaragua to revoke the Stebbins and White concession, which was transferred to his own company on March 8, 1858. Vanderbilt, who was receiving a fat subsidy from the Pacific Mail to stay out of the shipping business, had no intention of reopening the Nicaragua transit but was determined to keep his competitors from doing so. He quickly eliminated one of the rival organizations by making peace with Garrison and Morgan, who withdrew their claims. Stebbins and White proved more stubborn adversaries. In November 1858 they sent a steamer with 320 passengers to San Juan del Norte, but when the Nicaraguan authorities refused permission to cross their territory the ship was obliged to proceed to Colón and transfer its California-bound passengers to the Pacific Mail. This one voyage ended the attempts of Stebbins and White to defy Vanderbilt. The transit was never again placed in operation, steamboat traffic on the San Juan River virtually ceased, and the dusty highway between La Virgen and San Juan del Sur almost disappeared in the tropical undergrowth. Today the road is impassable, but communication between Lake Nicaragua and the Pacific is maintained by a railroad from the lake port of San Jorge to San Juan del Sur.

When the Cass-Irisarri treaty was sent to Nicaragua for ratification President Martínez, who distrusted Yankees and wished to keep the transit closed, transmitted the document to his Congress with the expectation that it would be rejected. When to his dismay the Congress approved the pact he pretended to sign it and delivered to the agents of Stebbins and White a sealed parcel supposed to contain the legally subscribed treaty. Actually he had not affixed his signature, and the convention was never ratified. Martínez was inspired to play this trick by the opportune arrival of a new applicant for a canal concession: a French newspaper editor named Félix Belly.

Today the ludicrous adventures of Monsieur Belly are remembered chiefly as a comic interlude in the history of the isthmian canal, but to the wretched man himself his misfortunes brought infinite distress. It would have been difficult to find anyone less well qualified either by temperament or training to organize and successfully carry out such a gigantic enterprise. Without money, technical experience, executive ability, influential connections, or a glimmer of common sense he stumbled blindly into pitfalls which an intelligent child would have avoided. With a perversity that amounted to genius he approached almost every problem wrong end to. Time after time his gullibility led him to seek association with men who took advantage of him and then cast him off; apparently nobody could resist the temptation to fleece so obviously helpless a lamb.

He first applied for financial aid to an acquaintance who after promising the necessary backing promptly went bankrupt. Six months later he borrowed a few thousand francs from another sponsor and hopefully set out alone for Central America, reached San Juan del Norte in March 1858, and traveled by canoe and mule to San José, where he was received cordially by President Mora. Belly had decided to visit Costa Rica first before going on to Nicaragua because the political aspects of the enterprise seemed to him far more important than the engineering problems, of which he understood nothing. On April 15 Costa Rica and Nicaragua concluded the Cañas-Jerez treaty giving to Nicaragua the south bank of the San Juan River above Castillo Viejo and the entire southern shore of Lake Nicaragua. Belly immediately proposed the construction of a canal from the lake by way of the Sapoa River to the Pacific at Salinas Bay and suggested that the center line of the canal throughout its entire length from the Atlantic to the Pacific should become the frontier between the two countries. Characteristically he ignored the careful surveys made by Childs (though he had read the American engineer's report) and based his choice of route entirely upon Oersted's earlier and admittedly superficial exploration. He was convinced that even should the Sapoa route require twice as much excavation as the one proposed by Childs the political expediency of a settlement of the boundary dispute would more than counterbalance that disadvantage.

Belly's proposal insured him a warm welcome in Costa Rica since it would give that republic sovereignty over the right bank of the San Juan from source to mouth and over the southern shore of the lake as well as equality with Nicaragua in the control and revenues of the canal — far greater concessions than Costa Rica could claim under the Cañas-Jerez treaty. Mora, full of enthusiasm, agreed to go with Belly to Nicaragua for a consultation with Martínez. The delegation reached Rivas on April 24, and on May 1

Mora and Martínez signed a joint contract awarding Belly an exclusive canal concession for 99 years. Apparently Martínez expected that this charter plus his own surreptitious nullification of the Cass-Irisarri treaty would automatically eliminate the three rival American claimants. He was soon undeceived, for Cass hastened to notify both Nicaragua and Costa Rica that if the contract with Belly should be found to violate any rights previously granted to United States citizens, reparations would be exacted.

After a month in Nicaragua Belly proceeded to Washington, where he encountered coolness and suspicion on all sides. The French government had officially disclaimed any interest in Belly's enterprise, and he was generally regarded as an impostor. Disappointed, he sailed back to Europe as soon as he could borrow money for the passage and reached Liverpool with 18 francs in his pocket. In Paris he peddled his contract from door to door without receiving a sign of encouragement from any responsible group of capitalists. Then "to educate the public and the bankers" [4] he decided to publish a pamphlet setting forth the glowing prospects for profitable investment in his canal; but since his ignorance of the technical problems was profound he entrusted that section of the brochure to an engineer, Thomé de Gamond. The latter did not consider it necessary to visit Nicaragua himself; with nothing but the scanty and unreliable information placed at his disposal by Belly he concocted a detailed and altogether worthless scheme for a canal.

With Thomé de Gamond and a few other associates, all lavish with promises but regrettably short of cash, Belly now organized a provisional company in Paris and in February 1859 returned to Central America with surveyors and engineers. The financial stringency was acute: when he left France Belly had been able to collect only $10,000, and by the time he reached his surveying headquarters at Fuerte de San Carlos half the sum had been expended. In spite of the assurances of his French backers no more money was sent out, and Belly was left with $5000 to defray the expenses of 45 technicians for several months. On April 13 the Nicaraguan Congress ratified the concession, but only after the addition of amendments which completely destroyed any possibility of a profitable return to the canal company and the elimination of what was to Belly the vital clause in the agreement: the establishment of the canal itself as the Costa Rican frontier.

To make matters worse Belly soon found himself involved in bitter quarrels with his own engineers, who contemptuously ignored his recommendations, neglected to keep him informed of the results of their surveys, and when his inadeqate funds gave out entirely broke into open revolt. Belly returned to Paris, leaving his recalcitrant assistants to find their own way home. His associates in Paris now turned against him and attempted to force him out of the canal company. Hopelessly entangled in lawsuits and pursued by insistent creditors, he took refuge first in Algeria and then in Geneva, depositing his power of attorney in the hands of a supposed friend, J. B. Roussel. In February 1861 Roussel sold Belly's share in the enterprise to Edouard Loos for $260,000, whereupon Belly, claiming that the sale had been made without authority and that he had received none of the proceeds, instituted a new suit for the recovery of his property. Since no work had been begun in the two years that had elapsed since the ratification of the charter the concession expired in April 1861. In November 1862 Belly went back to Central America to negotiate a new contract. He found conditions sadly changed; the recent invasion of Mexico by the forces of Napoleon III had turned all of Latin America against France, and Belly was snubbed where he had once been welcomed. In May 1865 his action against Loos and other associates, which had dragged through the French courts for four years, ended with the restoration to Belly of the disputed shares — now worthless, since the concession had lapsed — and the award of damages to the amount of $10,000, which he was unable to collect. Legally vindicated but financially ruined, Belly abandoned the project. Before he finally retired from the scene he published a full account of his tribulations in a ponderous volume, a wail of anguish 900 pages long.

A year or two before Belly's first appearance in Central America Great Britain and the United States made another determined effort to reach an agreement concerning the controversial clauses of the Clayton-Bulwer treaty. On October 17, 1856 Lord Clarendon and the American minister in London, George M. Dallas, signed a treaty providing for withdrawal of the British protectorate over the Mosquito kingdom, precise delineation of the frontier between Belize and Guatemala, and return of the Bay Islands to Honduras with certain reservations to safeguard the interests of British residents. By these concessions Great Britain yielded every one of the long-disputed points; but the conditional provisions of the Bay Island settlement failed to satisfy the United States Senate, which introduced various amendments before ratifying the pact on March 12, 1857. The British government in turn found these changes unacceptable, and after the rejection of counter-proposals the treaty was dropped. In his annual message of December 8, 1857 Buchanan, weary of the interminable conflict, proposed abrogation of the Clayton-Bulwer convention.

Lord Napier, the British minister in Washington, hoping to avert abrogation, had already suggested the dispatch of a special British commissioner to Nicaragua, Honduras, and Guatemala to end the troublesome disputes by the negotiation of separate treaties with each of the three states, which would enable Great Britain to make the desired concessions without too obviously seeming to yield to the demands of the United States. By voluntarily renouncing its claims in favor of the weak Central American republics the British government could save its face and appear before the world in a benevolent light. But the commissioner, Sir William Ouseley, bungled his mission deplorably. Lord Malmesbury, Clarendon's successor, had instructed the envoy to negotiate commercial treaties with Nicaragua and Costa Rica as well as a supplementary treaty with Nicaragua for the surrender of the Mosquito protectorate. Ouseley blundered by first concluding the commercial pact with Nicaragua, which that country ardently desired, and thus threw away his power to bargain over the Mosquito settlement. Malmesbury recalled him and entrusted the negotiations to Charles Lennox Wyke, the British chargé d'affaires in Central America. The United States government, convinced at last of the sincerity of Great Britain's desire to settle the disputes, directed Alexander Dimitry, American minister to Nicaragua and Costa Rica, and Beverly Clarke, who held a similar post in Guatemala, to assist Wyke in every possible way. But the well-meant gesture hampered the British agent more than it helped him, for Dimitry completely misinterpreted his instructions while Clarke received his too late to carry them out.

Fortunately Wyke needed no support from his American colleagues. An astute and experienced diplomat, he accomplished in a few months single-handed what his predecessors had failed to effect in ten years. On April 30, 1859 he concluded a treaty with Guatemala which fixed for some time at least the boundaries of British Honduras. In 1893 this frontier was modified by a new convention, but the settlement has never satisfied Guatemala, and the boundary line is still in dispute. On November 28, 1859 Wyke signed a treaty with Honduras providing for the immediate cession of the Bay Islands to that republic and recognition of Honduran sovereignty over the northern portion of the Mosquito coast. In return Honduras agreed to pay the Indians $5000 annually for ten years. Wyke now turned to Nicaragua and on January 28, 1860 concluded the treaty of Managua, the most important of the three conventions, whereby Great Britain abandoned all claims to a protectorate over the Mosquito kingdom. San Juan del Norte was to remain a free port under Nicaraguan sovereignty. Nicaragua consented to pay the Mosquito Indians $5000 a year for ten years as compensation for the loss of their independence and to establish a reservation with definite boundaries within which the Indians should enjoy almost complete autonomy. The treaty of Managua was duly confirmed by the Nicaraguan Congress on May 28 and proclaimed by the President on June 4, 1860. Wyke was rewarded with a knighthood; Nicaragua and Honduras recovered all of the territories they claimed; the United States was satisfied; and Great Britain had made a gratifying display of generosity to smaller nations. All of these governments rejoiced that the long controversies over the interpretation of the Clayton-Bulwer treaty had come to an end. Unhappily the rejoicing was premature.

Chapter 18. Nicaragua: 1861–1899

W HILE the British government punctiliously observed Wyke's agreements one English naval officer embarked on a private enterprise of his own which if successful might have nullified many of the beneficial effects of the new treaties. In 1859 Commander Bedford Clapperton Pim, senior officer of the small British patrol fleet on the Atlantic coast of Central America, conceived a project for a railroad across Nicaragua which he believed could more than hold its own in competition with the Panama route. A fanatical chauvinist and aggressive imperialist, Pim felt nothing but contempt for what he considered the weakness of the British Liberal party in tamely relinquishing the Bay Islands and Mosquito protectorate. His hatred of the United States amounted to an obsession, and he rejoiced openly when the Civil War threatened to disrupt the Union: "No one can say to what lengths the bullying propensities of the Yankees would have been carried, and how long our Liberal Government would have borne the constant humiliations to which they were subjected, had not an end been put to the system by the division in the United States, which . . . gives the people of that country quite enough to do to mind their own affairs." [1]

Pim first investigated the San Juan River but decided that the shallow lower reaches could never be made navigable and that the harbor of San Juan del Norte, now rapidly silting up, would soon become altogether useless as a port. Since he had never believed in the practicability of a canal the impending doom of San Juan del Norte did not greatly distress him. He selected another Atlantic terminus on an inlet just south of Monkey Point, named it Gorgon Bay after his ship, H. M. S. *Gorgon,* and purchased the bay shore, the adjacent islands, and a railway concession from the Mosquito king — ignoring the fact that both the land transfer and the concession would become invalid after the restoration of Mosquito sovereignty to Nicaragua, which Wyke was then negotiating.

The railroad was to run from Realejo to León and Managua, then across the Tipitapa River and along the eastern shore of Lake Nicaragua to the village of San Miguelito, where it would turn eastward to Gorgon Bay. Although he admitted that the section between San Miguelito and Gorgon Bay had never been surveyed he anticipated no difficulties. At Gorgon Bay "a church should be erected, and schools established, then, with the blessing of the Almighty upon the undertaking, there can be no fear for the result. . . . Every mile the iron road penetrates into the country will be a positive gain to civilization; while those strong moral and religious feelings inherent in every Englishman, and which more than anything else have elevated Great Britain to her present pitch of greatness, would be fostered and encouraged. . . ." [2] But as an added inducement to hard-headed investors he confidently predicted a 25% profit.

In January 1860 Pim proceeded to Managua to enlist Wyke's aid in securing a charter from the Nicaraguan government for the section of his railroad which would run through territory over which the sovereignty of Nicaragua was undisputed. The chargé d'affaires gave him no encouragement, and the disappointed commander returned to his ship with a poor opinion of his country's diplomats and diplomacy. Pim's rebuff at Managua was soon followed by a sharp reprimand from the British Admiralty: "My Lords are unable to account for an officer in Commander Pim's position having failed to perceive that his proceedings and conduct on the occasion [of his private purchase of Gorgon Bay] were liable to be misrepresented, as the acts of an officer in her Majesty's service, authorized by her Majesty's Government. His extreme imprudence . . . is deserving of the strongest censure; he . . . has incurred the marked displeasure of their Lordships, and has proved himself to be unfit for the duties with which he has been entrusted." [3] Evidently this severe censure was considered sufficient punishment, for Pim was not dismissed from the navy. He retired from active service in 1861, returned to Central America, and in 1864 obtained a railroad charter from the government of Nicaragua. In 1866 he organized the Nicaraguan Railway Company to carry out his project, but the company failed to attract capital and was soon dissolved. For several years Pim practised as a barrister in England, specializing in admiralty cases. Eventually his superiors forgave or forgot his indiscretion in Nicaragua, and in 1885, a year before his death, he was promoted to the rank of rear admiral on the retired list.

After Félix Belly's ignominious exit the situation with regard to the ownership of the transit and canal concessions grew more confused than ever. Although the charter granted to Stebbins and

White as representatives of the original American Atlantic and Pacific Ship Canal Company had been revoked by the Nicaraguan government and transferred to Vanderbilt in 1858 Stebbins and his associates refused to admit the legality of the annulment. They organized a new corporation, the Central American Transit Company, elected William H. Webb president, and on March 20, 1861 secured another contract which presumably superseded all previous grants. The new company made no attempt to reopen the transit or undertake the construction of a canal, but it did persuade the United States government to send a commission of Coast Guard hydrographic experts under the command of Captain P. C. F. West to determine the practicability of deepening the harbor of San Juan del Norte and rendering the San Juan River navigable at all seasons for steamboats of light draft. Before West could terminate his survey the Central American Transit Company quarreled with the Nicaraguan government, which thereupon — without troubling to annul the existing charter — awarded the canal concession to Michel Chevalier, a Frenchman who appears to have been unofficially supported by Napoleon III. This contract, similar in general to that granted to Belly, was signed in Paris on October 6, 1868 and confirmed by the Nicaraguan Congress on March 15, 1869. But the Costa Rican authorities refused to concede the same privileges through the territories under their control, and since the emperor, on the brink of catastrophe at home, was in no position to exert pressure on a foreign government the scheme collapsed. The Central American Transit Company, with John E. Body as president in place of Webb, recovered its concession but contented itself with the appointment of committees and the passage of vague resolutions urging Congress to adopt the Nicaragua route.

Throughout these troubled years the lack of a formal treaty between the United States and Nicaragua hampered the diplomatic representatives of both nations at every turn. Since 1849 three conventions had been concluded but all had failed to achieve ratification. On June 21, 1867 the United States minister to Central America, Andrew B. Dickinson, and the Nicaraguan Foreign Minister, Tomás Ayón, signed a new treaty which was ratified a year later and finally proclaimed in August 1868. Like the abortive Squier and Cass-Irisarri conventions the Dickinson-Ayón treaty provided for a guarantee by the United States of the neutrality of the canal, but with due regard for the Clayton-Bulwer treaty the United States carefully avoided any assumption of exclusive transit rights. At the time such a general agreement was considered satisfactory; later, as American demands for special canal privileges grew more insistent, the treaty proved inadequate. But repeated efforts to alter it failed, and it remained in force until superseded by the Bryan-Chamorro treaty in 1916.

Meanwhile a new conflict was brewing over the Mosquito coast, which by the treaty of Managua had become an autonomous Indian reservation under Nicaraguan sovereignty. The Nicaraguan government, complaining that English settlers and traders at the Atlantic ports continued to direct the policies of the territory just as if the protectorate still existed, refused to pay the stipulated annual indemnity of $5000 to the Indians, and the controversy, supposedly ended forever by Wyke's treaty, flared up once more. The British government bided its time until it had prepared and fully documented its case, then in 1880 demanded submission of the dispute to the arbitration of the Austrian emperor. Nicaragua, technically — and for the most part morally — in the wrong, was obliged to agree, and in July 1881 Franz Josef handed down a decision almost wholly in favor of Great Britain. Nevertheless no final settlement was reached until 1894, when the Mosquito Indians voted to abolish the reservation, surrender their autonomy, and accept full rights and obligations of Nicaraguan citizenship.

In his report of 1866 Admiral Davis saw little hope for a Nicaragua canal: "It may be safely asserted that no enterprise, presenting such formidable difficulties, will ever be undertaken with even our present knowledge of the American isthmuses. Still less is it likely to be entered upon while such strong and well-founded hopes are entertained . . . of finding elsewhere a very much easier, cheaper, and more practicable route. . . ." [4] By "elsewhere" Davis meant the Isthmus of Darién, which he considered the most promising site for investigation. The Davis report was followed by the organization of United States naval expeditions to survey all of the suggested locations for a canal. The Nicaragua party headed by Commander Alexander F. Crosman reached San Juan del Norte on April 7; 1872. Five days later Crosman and five seamen were drowned while attempting to cross the bar at the mouth of the river in a small boat, and the leadership devolved upon Commander Chester Hatfield, who moved the expedition to La Virgen and commenced a preliminary survey. Half a dozen small field parties investigated the various passes between the lake and the Pacific but of course found none more advantageous than the gap discovered by Childs.

When the rainy season interrupted operations in July Hatfield and his assistants went back to the United States, leaving only a few men to execute a hydrographic survey of Lake Nicaragua. The expedition, reorganized and placed in charge of Commander Edward P. Lull, with Aniceto G. Menocal as chief civil engineer, returned to Nicaragua in December 1872. The two leaders, accompanied by Colonel Maximilian Sonnenstern, an engineer in the employ of the Nicaraguan government, inspected the route through Lake Managua to Realejo. They found that a canal by way of the smaller lake would require three additional locks on each side of the divide as well as many miles of supplementary excavation. They also noted "one other objection, which would of itself be fatal to the line: the geological formation . . . is entirely volcanic; a line of volcanoes, nine in number, and all more or less active, extends from the lake toward Realejo, nearly parallel to, and in close proximity with, the proposed line of canal. . . . The soil and the underlying rock are so extremely porous that even in the wet season . . . all the rain . . . [is] drunk up by the earth. . . . If a canal were built through this region, it would be impossible to keep it full unless it were made artificially water-tight from one end to the other, which would involve a cost equal to that of the excavation. For all of these reasons we regard the route as utterly impracticable." [5] As the rivalry between Nicaragua and Panama grew more and more bitter towards the end of the century these volcanoes became a valuable asset to sponsors of the Panama line and a correspondingly acute embarrassment to those in favor of Nicaragua.

The surveyors wasted little time on a canal route suggested by a local resident: "It is quite remarkable how few intelligent persons there are . . . in Central America, who have not some theory . . . as to the best route for a canal. These theories are generally based on information received from hunters, India-rubber men, and others, whose calling makes them acquainted with the mountain-passes. And odd as the assertion may seem, the fact that these *practicos* regard a pass as low and favorable for a canal, is almost a certain indication that it is the worst possible location . . . their judgment being based entirely upon the fact that the rise is so gradual as to be inappreciable to them. . . . A glance will show that, although the profile CDF actually has a greater, and, to

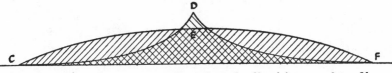

8. *Comparison between steeply and gradually rising canal profiles*

persons traveling over it, would seem to have a very much greater summit-level than the profile CEF, yet the amount of excavation would be greatly less. . . ." [6]

Exploration of the valleys of the Sapoa, Ochomogo, Gil Gonzales, and Buena Vista Rivers — all found to be much higher than the pass discovered by Childs — left the naval surveyors with but two possibilities: the route proposed by Childs from the mouth of the Lajas River to Brito, and a variant of that line substituting the valley of the Río del Medio for that of the Lajas. Lull and Menocal favored the second alternative because on the Lajas line, though the summit was 88 feet lower, the ravines were narrow, rocky, and tortuous, and the flood waters of the Río Grande and other streams would either sweep destructively into the canal or require expensive artificial channels to conduct them independently to the sea.

Early in March 1873 the party moved across the lake to the San Juan River. Where the rapids impeded its upper course Lull recommended the construction of four dams with a short section of canal at each bypass, and to avoid the shallow lower reaches he proposed to excavate an artificial canal all the way from the mouth of the San Carlos to San Juan del Norte, running more or less parallel to the San Juan as far as the San Juanillo and thence in a nearly straight line to the Atlantic. There were to be ten locks 400 feet long by 70 wide on either slope, and the depth throughout was fixed at 26 feet. The cost including an allowance of 25% for "contingencies" was estimated at $65,722,147.

Lull submitted his report with those of all the other naval expeditions to the Interoceanic Canal Commission, which unanimously decided on February 7, 1876 that "the route known as the 'Nicaragua route' . . . possesses, both for the construction and maintenance of a canal, greater advantages, and offers fewer difficulties from engineering, commercial, and economic points of view, than any one of the other routes. . . ." [7]

Although the Central American Transit Company still nominally held the canal concession it had accomplished absolutely nothing, and the Nicaraguan authorities no longer considered themselves bound by the terms of that contract. On March 16, 1877 the government granted a monopoly of steam navigation privileges on the San Juan River and Lake Nicaragua (but not the right to construct a canal) to F. A. Pellas, an Italian resident of San Juan del Norte. Pellas soon transferred his contract to a corporation known as the Nicaragua Mail Steam Navigation and Trading Company, a somewhat pretentious title for an organization engaged in small-scale inland commerce.

At the same time a French promoter, Aristide-Paul Blanchet, was negotiating with Nicaragua for a new canal concession. Blanchet's project followed closely the route selected by Lull and Menocal but differed from theirs chiefly in an extension of the summit level of the canal — the surface level of Lake Nicaragua — to a point much nearer the Atlantic. The Nicaraguan Chamber of Deputies approved a bill awarding him the contract in 1878, but the Senate rejected it by one vote. In 1880, after a second failure to persuade the Congress to grant him the canal charter, he abandoned the plan.

The decision in favor of a sea level canal at Panama rendered by the international congress summoned by de Lesseps in 1879, the organization of a French company to build such a canal, and even the commencement of actual construction on the isthmus failed to discourage the Nicaragua enthusiasts. Most American engineers were convinced that the French enterprise must soon come to grief; while public opinion in the United States, alarmed by the prospect of foreign control over a communication so vital to American trade, demanded an American canal through Nicaragua even should the Panama canal be successfully completed. Late in 1879 a group of Americans including General George B. McClellan, Rear Admiral Ammen, Captain Seth Ledyard Phelps, Levi P. Morton, and Aniceto G. Menocal organized the Provisional Interoceanic Canal Society. Ex-President Grant, then on the last lap of a world tour, was invited by cable to join the promoters and, to the gratification of all, accepted. Phelps was elected president of the society, and Menocal proceeded to Nicaragua to arrange the terms of a contract. He induced the government to reject Blanchet's proposals in favor of his own, and on May 22, 1880 the Nicaraguan Congress confirmed the award to the Provisional Interoceanic Canal Society. It provided for a 99-year concession dating from the opening of the canal; two years were allowed for surveys and the organization of a construction company, and one year more for the commencement of actual work, during which the company must spend at least $2,000,000; and the canal was to be completed within ten years after the expiration of the first two-year period. The date of final completion might be postponed if necessary, but the preliminary periods were not to be prolonged in any circumstances. At the end of 99 years the canal would revert to Nicaragua without compensation to the grantees.

In conformity with the new contract the society reorganized as
the Maritime Canal Company of Nicaragua with at least half of its
directors drawn from the group of original founders. Led by Ammen and Menocal, the company made strenuous efforts to enlist the
support of the United States Congress. The Senate called upon the
Navy Department for information concerning all the projected
routes, and on April 28, 1883 Lieutenant John T. Sullivan submitted a lengthy report. Sullivan favored the Nicaragua line, though
he conscientiously noted four defects: its relatively great length,
the necessity for locks, the lack of natural harbors, and the volcanic nature of the country. On the other hand he found that while
the actual excavation would be 8 miles longer than at Panama the
sea voyage between New York and San Francisco would be several
days shorter, there were no grave engineering difficulties, construction materials and subsistence supplies could be obtained locally,
the rainfall was relatively light, and a canal through Nicaragua
would cost less than half as much as by any other route. Practically
all of these advantages were in fact nonexistent; the Sullivan report
overemphasized the virtues and minimized the imperfections of
the Nicaragua project.

On December 15, 1881 Senator John F. Miller of California introduced a bill providing for political and financial guarantees to
the canal company by the government. The measure was referred
to the Senate Committee on Foreign Relations, discussed at length,
amended, and passed on to the House Committee on Foreign Affairs, which after several months of careful consideration and the
addition of further amendments finally reported it back in July
1882. Then the whole matter was postponed until the next session,
and when the bill again came before the House more delays ensued
so that it was not acted upon until just before Congress adjourned.
By a narrow margin it failed to receive the two-thirds vote required
for passage. Three factors contributed to the defeat of the Nicaragua canal bill: the opposition of the French Panama canal company; the equally determined opposition of Captain Eads, inventor and enthusiastic sponsor of a ship railway project across
Tehuantepec; and the restrictions imposed by the Clayton-Bulwer
treaty on exclusive neutrality guarantees by the United States
government.

The Clayton-Bulwer treaty, never popular in the United States,
had by this time come to be regarded as an insuperable obstacle to
the construction of a canal under conditions acceptable to the
American people. Official sentiment had undergone a radical

change since 1850. Whereas during the administrations of Taylor and Fillmore, Pierce, and Buchanan the government had been satisfied with mere participation in international guarantees shared with European powers and had indeed tried to encourage the collaboration of other nations in such commitments, Grant had instituted a trend towards exclusive political control of an isthmian canal. At first this tendency manifested itself only as a disposition to lend official backing to private American companies; not until the end of the century did a policy of outright government ownership and operation of the canal win many supporters in Washington.

But the Clayton-Bulwer treaty stood squarely in the way of control by the United States alone. While Buchanan had suggested its abrogation in 1857 on the ground of ambiguity Grant proposed either abrogation or radical modification in 1876 because he held that the provision for joint protection of the transit by Great Britain and the United States conflicted with vital American interests Grant's Secretary of State, Hamilton Fish, made diplomatic overtures to the British government for abrogation by mutual consent but received no encouragement and soon dropped the matter. At the same time he attempted to replace the Dickinson-Ayón treaty with Nicaragua by a new convention more favorable to the United States; but the Nicaraguan government demanded an indemnity for the bombardment of San Juan del Norte in 1854 as a preliminary step towards reconsideration of the treaty. Fish emphatically rejected the suggestion, and negotiations came to an abrupt end.

During the Hayes administration efforts to amend or abrogate the Clayton-Bulwer treaty were renewed with no better success. The negotiations then devolved upon Garfield's Secretary of State, James G. Blaine, and after Garfield's assassination upon Frederick T. Frelinghuysen. Neither was able to make the slightest impression upon the British Foreign Office, and the voluminous diplomatic correspondence only served to demonstrate the weakness of the American position. Abrogation or modification of the treaty would obviously benefit the United States at the expense of Great Britain, and the American statesmen had nothing to offer in exchange for the surrender of British rights.

Rebuffed by Great Britain, Frelinghuysen reopened negotiations with Nicaragua for a new treaty to supersede the unsatisfactory Dickinson-Ayón convention. The Nicaraguan government, chastened by the adverse decision of the Austrian emperor and now in a mood to welcome closer ties with the United States, sent a special commissioner, Joaquín Zavala, to Washington. On December 1, 1884 Frelinghuysen and Zavala concluded a treaty which for the first time clearly embodied the principle of public ownership, construction, and operation of an interoceanic canal. The convention provided that the canal "shall be built by the United States . . . and owned by them and the Republic of Nicaragua. . . . There shall be perpetual alliance between the United States . . . and . . . Nicaragua, and the former agree to protect the integrity of the territory of the latter." [8] Nicaragua was to receive one third of the net profits, the United States two thirds.

Unquestionably ratification of the Frelinghuysen-Zavala convention would have established a virtual protectorate over Nicaragua, reduced the Clayton-Bulwer treaty to a scrap of paper, and involved the United States in another bitter controversy, if not a war, with Great Britain. Nevertheless President Arthur transmitted it to the Senate on December 10, 1884 with a message of recommendation, and many of the legislators considered its ratification worth the risk of British hostility and international dishonor. Late in January 1885 the treaty received 32 affirmative votes out of a total of 55 — five votes less than the needed two thirds. A motion to reconsider was introduced, but before any further steps could be taken Cleveland's inauguration altered the political complexion of the government. In his first annual message to Congress the Democratic President indicated a return to a conciliatory and unaggressive foreign policy. He thereupon withdrew the treaty, and it was not again submitted for ratification.

While congressional committees engaged in leisurely debates on the bill to furnish government support to the Maritime Canal Company that corporation found itself unable to commence active operations within the stipulated two years, which expired in May 1882. Phelps and Lull hastened to Nicaragua and, in spite of the clause prohibiting an extension of the preliminary period for any reason whatsoever, secured a prolongation until September 30, 1884. When at last it became evident that Congress would do nothing to aid the enterprise Grant and McClellan came to the rescue and exerted their influence to organize a private syndicate to finance the project under the direction of the banking firm of Grant and Ward, in which the ex-President held a partnership. But in 1884 the bank failed to the accompaniment of a resounding scandal, and General Grant, discredited, almost penniless, and already suffering from the throat cancer which caused his death a year later, could render no further assistance to the canal company. This bankruptcy deprived the company of its only hope of financial backing, and on September 30, 1884 its concession lapsed.

The elimination of the private canal corporation spurred advocates of government ownership to renewed activity. Anticipating the early ratification of the Frelinghuysen-Zavala treaty, Secretary of the Navy William E. Chandler commissioned Menocal to lead another surveying expedition to Nicaragua to verify and possibly improve upon the route located in 1872–3. That route had already undergone one important alteration. When Menocal visited Nicaragua in 1880 to obtain the original charter for the Provisional Interoceanic Canal Society he had reinvestigated the section between the lake and the Pacific, decided to abandon the Río del Medio location approved by Lull and himself in 1873, and adopted the much lower Lajas route suggested by Childs. He proposed to overcome the chief objection to this line — the impossibility of crowding both the canal and the Río Grande into a single narrow valley — by damming the Río Grande near its source and diverting its waters eastward into Lake Nicaragua, leaving its original bed free to carry the canal to the Pacific. The Río Grande would then flow through an artificial cut to the Juan Dávila River, a tributary of the Lajas, and so to the lake.

Menocal's new expedition reached Nicaragua on January 7, 1885. He decided to locate the principal dam at Ochoa, a short distance below the mouth of the San Carlos and approximately where he and Lull had proposed to place it in their original plan; but between that point and the Atlantic he made radical changes in the earlier design. Instead of an artificial channel almost parallel to the north bank of the San Juan as far as the San Juanillo and thence in a more or less straight line to San Juan del Norte he now suggested a much shorter and straighter canal which would leave the river just above the Ochoa dam and follow the valley of the San Francisco, a small tributary, thus cutting off the great loop of the San Juan near its mouth.

Cleveland's firm stand against government ownership and his withdrawal of the unratified Frelinghuysen-Zavala convention cleared the way for a revival of private initiative. On December 3, 1886 Ammen, Menocal, and several colleagues organized a second Provisional Canal Association, and Menocal was once more dispatched to Nicaragua to secure a concession. The charter, signed on March 23, 1887 and confirmed by the Nicaraguan Senate on April 23, closely followed the terms of the grant to the first society in 1880. Nicaragua was to receive 6% of all stock, bonds, or other securities issued by the company, the minimum value of the republic's quota to be not less than $4,000,000. Although Cleveland

as arbitrator decided in March 1888 that Costa Rica was not entitled to a share in the canal profits, if any, the Provisional Canal
Association prudently avoided possible complications by voluntarily offering compensation to that country. On August 9, 1888
the Costa Rican Congress ratified a concession covering such portions of the canal route as lay within its jurisdiction, for which the
association agreed to pay 1.5% of its total issue of securities or not
less than $1,500,000.

Meanwhile the directors launched an extensive publicity campaign throughout the United States. Lectures, pamphlets, and a
flood of newspaper articles stimulated public interest in the project; resolutions passed by state legislatures, boards of trade, and
chambers of commerce poured into Congress. On January 10, 1888
a bill providing for the incorporation of the Maritime Canal Company of Nicaragua was introduced in the Senate, and on the same
day a similar measure was presented to the House. Since these bills
asked only official recognition, not financial aid, they passed without serious opposition and on February 20, 1889 were approved
by Cleveland. On May 4 the company was formally organized with
a capital of $100,000,000 in common stock and authority to issue
5% bonds to the amount of $150,000,000. The directors took
over the concession awarded to the Provisional Canal Association,
elected Hiram Hitchcock president, and appointed Menocal chief
engineer. To carry on the actual work the auxiliary Nicaragua Canal Construction Company had already been incorporated and
was now ready to commence preliminary operations.

Sponsors of the Nicaragua route apparently no longer had much
to fear from the competition of Panama. The French canal company had just been declared bankrupt, work had virtually ceased,
and prospects for the eventual completion of the Panama waterway seemed dim indeed. But no sooner had Congress approved the
incorporation of the Maritime Canal Company than opposition
developed in another quarter. A resident of Kansas, A. L. Blackman, claimed ownership of the residual rights of the long-defunct
American Atlantic and Pacific Ship Canal Company, and in behalf of this claimant and others Representative James D. Richardson of Tennessee introduced a bill on August 20, 1890 to repeal
the charter just granted to the new corporation. The measure was
referred to the House Committee on Commerce, which rejected it
on the grounds that Blackman's title rested on flimsy evidence and
that "it would seem unreasonable to expect Congress to consider
for a moment a proposition to destroy or cripple an enterprise of

such magnitude . . . except for most convincing reasons." [9]

In June 1889 an advance party commenced a final survey. So thoroughly did they examine every foot of ground that, as Menocal reported with pardonable pride, "though the axial distance of the land survey (exclusive of the lake and river) is less than fifty miles, the length of lines actually surveyed by transit and level . . . is not less than 4000 miles." [10] While the new exploration confirmed the general findings of the 1885 survey it suggested several improvements. Between the Ochoa dam and the Atlantic Menocal now proposed a series of small artificial lakes or basins surrounded by embankments, which would reduce the total length of excavated canal. West of Lake Nicaragua another dam was to be constructed at La Flor to flood part of the Río Grande valley and render unnecessary the diversion of that river into the lake.

Actual construction was begun on October 9, 1889 and prosecuted vigorously. Within a few months the engineers had constructed a breakwater to protect the harbor of San Juan del Norte; dredged out portions of the silted lagoon; built warehouses, machine shops, and a wharf equipped with steam cranes; established a headquarters settlement about two miles from San Juan and erected offices, hospitals, and living quarters; built telegraph and telephone lines from San Juan del Norte to Castillo Viejo; blasted a section of the Machuca rapids to facilitate steamboat navigation; dredged a channel inland from San Juan del Norte 1.5 miles long for the canal itself; constructed 11.5 miles of railroad parallel to the canal line; and imported locomotives and freight cars. Since no highways existed anywhere along the route the construction of a railroad for the transportation of supplies and removal of excavated material was an essential preliminary to work on the canal proper. 1600 laborers built this first section of the railroad (the only section, in fact, ever completed) in four months. Before the tracks could be laid through the coastal swamp it was found necessary to construct a corduroy foundation of solid wood 4 feet thick protected by a substantial layer of sand.

In the summer of 1890 the company purchased from the American Contracting and Dredging Company much of the equipment used by that firm in the construction of the Panama canal: 7 powerful dredges, 2 tugboats, 20 lighters, several launches, a complete machine shop, and an assortment of tools, spare parts, pumps, and stationary engines. This apparatus, which had lain idle since the collapse of the French company at the end of 1888, was transported safely from Colón to San Juan del Norte with the exception of one dredge lost at sea. Americans with a taste for symbolism professed to see retributive justice in the fate of this dredge. Its name was *Comte de Lesseps.*

The directors soon found themselves alarmingly short of money. In 1890 they had entered into negotiations with the English banking house of Baring Brothers for financial backing, but within a few months that firm failed. The company then turned to private investors in the United States, but without some financial guarantee by Congress to give the undertaking at least the appearance of a national enterprise it was obvious that many potential subscribers would hold aloof. Accordingly friends of the company now made another appeal for official support. On January 10, 1891 Senator John Sherman of Ohio introduced a bill authorizing the government to guarantee an issue of the canal company's bonds to the amount of $100,000,000 bearing interest at 4%. As security the government was to hold $70,000,000 worth of the company's common stock. Senator John T. Morgan of Alabama, the most energetic and able of the pro-Nicaragua legislators, delivered a forceful speech in favor of the measure: "Our attitude . . . is one of natural, peaceful, inevitable, and beneficent growth and expansion, in which all the world will find a rich harvest of blessings. The attitude of Great Britain . . . is selfish, obstructive, aggressive, grasping, and domineering. . . . The platitudes of the Clayton-Bulwer treaty, in which each party yielded something to the other that neither possessed . . . have become a stale demand upon the people of both nations. . . ." [11] But the Senate, still unwilling to risk an overt violation of that awkward treaty, hesitated to commit itself to a policy so perilously close to outright government ownership, and the bill was shelved before it could reach a final vote.

Public opinion, influenced and organized by agents of the canal company, protested loudly against legislative inaction. On December 15 the New York Chamber of Commerce adopted a resolution urging Congress to pass the guarantee measure. The governor of California, the state which because of its geographical location expected to benefit most from the opening of a canal, summoned a national canal convention at St. Louis early in June 1892. The governors of 30 states and territories responded by appointing about 300 delegates, who requested Congress to support the enterprise and recommended the company's securities to "the generous and patriotic people of the United States." [12] The St. Louis meeting was followed by a still larger convention at New Orleans on November 30, attended by some 600 representatives from every state and territory and resulting in the adoption of similar resolutions. Heartened by these and other evidences of public support, Sherman presented another bill for government aid on December 23, 1892. The measure differed slightly from that of 1891: instead of merely holding a large block of shares as security the government was now to own outright common stock to the value of $80,500,000. But the Senate again evaded a decision, and a similar bill introduced in the House also failed to pass.

While the American public and press generally favored official patronage of the canal enterprise there was no lack of opposition from various sources, both interested and disinterested. Friends of the Compagnie Nouvelle du Canal de Panama, successor to the bankrupt French company, engaged in an active propaganda campaign to prevent completion of the Nicaragua project. Spokesmen for the powerful transcontinental railroads attacked it savagely, claiming that canals were obsolete and that the railroads could transport freight from coast to coast cheaper than ships. One of the most persistent critics of the Nicaragua project was Joseph Nimmo, Jr., chief of the Treasury's statistical bureau, who year after year poured out pamphlets asserting that the canal could never compete with the railroads, that all sailing vessels and many steamships would continue to use the Cape Horn route, and that "the passage of war vessels would involve the construction of expensive fortifications. . . . An adequate force of naval vessels can be constructed for the perfect defense of our Pacific Coast ports at one-tenth the cost of the Nicaragua Canal. . . ." [13] The canal company, hurling itself into the battle of statistics, heatedly denied all of Nimmo's gloomy contentions.

The failure of Congress to approve the Nicaragua bills left the canal and construction companies in a worse position than before. With prestige materially impaired by the rebuff they were obliged to renew their appeals for private subscriptions. The construction company had already sold at half price 120,000 shares nominally valued at $100 each. Surveys, purchase of equipment, and the execution of preliminary work had almost exhausted the $6,000,000 thus realized, and the construction company now called for bids on an issue of $5,000,000 in gold bonds. When the response from Wall Street proved disappointing the company proposed an issue of bonds of low denomination to be sold to small investors, but before the plan could be put into effect the panic of May 1893 shook the financial foundations of the country. Unable to dispose of its securities, the construction company passed into the hands of a receiver on August 30, 1893.

After the failure of the Nicaragua Canal Construction Company the parent corporation, the Maritime Canal Company, made valiant efforts to rehabilitate the project. The construction company's affairs were wound up, its debts paid off, and in the spring of 1895 a new contracting firm, the Nicaragua Company, was chartered under the laws of Vermont. But the financial crisis persisted, and work could not be resumed. On January 22, 1894 the bill for a government guarantee of the company's securities was once more introduced in the Senate. Although Morgan eloquently urged its passage it emerged from the Committee on Foreign Relations in an emasculated form and was handed over to the House, where it was further amended and weakened. The net result was indefinite postponement of action on the bill and the appropriation on March 2 of funds for the organization of a board of engineers, known officially as the United States Nicaragua Canal Board and popularly as the Ludlow commission, to investigate and report on the technical aspects of the problem.

The board, composed of Lieutenant Colonel William Ludlow of the Engineer Corps, Mordecai T. Endicott, a naval engineer officer, and Alfred Noble, a civilian expert, inspected the Nicaragua route in May and June 1895. Their report approved the general plans of the Maritime Canal Company but recommended a number of changes in details, increased the estimate to $133,472,893, and advised a thorough re-examination of the canal line. The new surveys were duly carried out between 1897 and 1901 by the so-called first and second Walker commissions; but as those investigations took into consideration the possibility of purchase of the French canal at Panama by the United States their discussion will be postponed to a later chapter.

After the cessation of canal construction it became necessary to provide for the maintenance of inland water transport service on the San Juan River and Lake Nicaragua, for which the concession had been acquired by the Maritime Canal Company in 1889. Since the canal company could no longer afford to operate the steamboat system the former grantee, the Nicaragua Mail Steam Navigation and Trading Company, was reorganized and in November 1894 secured a 10-year extension of its charter. In 1897 the Atlas Steamship Company, Ltd., a British line, bought the transport concession and equipment, transferred them to its subsidiary the Caribbean and Pacific Transit Company, and obtained a 30-year franchise with the proviso that the contract would not be permitted to interfere with the eventual opening of a canal.

The Maritime Canal Company's own concession was due to expire on October 9, 1899, and no hope existed for the completion of the canal or even the resumption of active operations before that date. Anticipating by almost a year the date of forfeiture, the Nicaraguan government granted a "promise of contract" for a new canal concession to Edward Eyre and Edward F. Cragin on October 31, 1898. The charter was to become effective immediately upon the expiration of the Maritime Canal Company's contract, after which a period of six months was allowed for the organization of the Eyre-Cragin corporation, to be called the Interoceanic Canal Company. The contract called for the commencement of construction within two years thereafter and completion of the canal within ten more — that is before April 9, 1912. On behalf of their backers, said to include John Jacob Astor, Levi P. Morton, and William R. Grace, Eyre and Cragin deposited $100,000 in the Nicaraguan treasury immediately after the ratification of their charter and agreed to add $400,000 to this sum on or before August 9, 1900. But they failed to make this second payment, and their contract was forthwith declared null and void.

Thus by the end of the century the two great rival canal projects had come to grief. In Nicaragua work had stopped altogether; in Panama excavation continued under French direction but at a slow pace and on a small scale. At both locations private enterprise had proved inadequate to the gigantic task. The only remaining hope for ultimate completion of either canal lay in its ownership, construction, and operation by the United States government.

Chapter 19. Tehuantepec

AT the Isthmus of Tehuantepec Mexico tapers to a slender waist only 130 miles wide from sea to sea, while the continental divide here sinks to a mere range of hills approximately 750 feet high at the point of greatest depression. The isthmus is thus both narrower and very much lower than any part of the land barrier north of Nicaragua. In the Tehuantepec region the axis of the continent swings almost due east and west, so that the transverse valley of the Coatzacoalcos River runs in a general north-south direction. These peculiarities of the isthmian topography attracted the attention of Cortés in his futile search for an interoceanic strait; Gómara and Galvão included Tehuantepec among the four most promising canal sites as early as 1555; and it maintained its position as a rival of Panama, Nicaragua, and the other transit routes farther south until almost the end of the nineteenth century.

Spurred by the publication of Humboldt's works, the liberal Spanish Cortes resolved on April 28, 1814 to grant permission for the construction of a Tehuantepec canal. But by 1814 the independence movement in Mexico was already well advanced, and it was too late for any Spanish government to either give or withhold permission for such a project. In 1824 the federal government of Mexico appointed a commission headed by Colonel Juan de Orbegozo, an officer of the Mexican General Staff, to survey the isthmus, and in the same year the local government of the state of Vera Cruz assigned a similar task to another group of explorers under the command of Tadeo Ortiz. Both surveys were superficial, and their reports offered little encouragement to champions of a canal. Ortiz omitted all discussion of a waterway and recommended construction of a carriage road from the confluence of the Coatzacoalcos and Malatengo to the Pacific, while Orbegozo found a canal impracticable and suggested either a highway or railroad.

On March 1, 1842 the federal government granted to José de Garay a concession for a canal or railroad across the isthmus. Garay placed his preliminary survey in the hands of an engineer of Italian descent, Gaetano Moro, whose party reached the town of Te-

huantepec on May 28 and explored the route diligently for nine
months under difficult conditions. Jolting over rough roads had
injured the instruments, rainy weather hampered progress, the
incessant wind blew down landmarks, flickering vapors and disturbing mirages confused the observations. Nevertheless Moro
considered his survey sufficiently accurate and thorough to prove
beyond question the feasibility of a canal. The Coatzacoalcos was
to be made navigable by dredging as far as the Malatengo, whence
a canal 50 miles long would be cut through Tarifa Pass to the navigable waters of the Chicapa on the Pacific side. From the mouth of
the Chicapa a channel would be dredged through the two salt lagoons, Laguna Superior and Laguna Inferior, to a terminal outlet
at the *barra* (sandspit) of San Francisco. The project would require no less than 161 locks — an absurd number for a busy canal.
Moro's conception of costs was no more realistic than his multiple-
lock design. He estimated the expense of construction at $17,000,-
000 but hoped to reduce that figure to $12,000,000. Unfortunately
such undervaluations were the rule rather than the exception in
isthmian canal schemes.

On February 9, 1843 the federal authorities, encouraged by
Moro's optimistic report, directed the provincial governors of
Oaxaca and Vera Cruz to turn over to Garay the vacant lands stipulated in the contract; on October 6 President Santa Anna ordered the same officials to furnish 300 convicts for labor on the
canal; and on December 28 the obliging President extended for
one year the period allowed for the commencement of excavation,
which would have expired July 1, 1844. But in 1845, before the
start of actual work, Santa Anna was removed from office and exiled. By a decree dated November 5, 1846 his successor, the temporary dictator General Mariano de Salas, granted Garay another
postponement until November 1848. Meanwhile war broke out between Mexico and the United States, local disturbances agitated
the provinces, and work on the canal became impossible. In 1847
Garay sold his concession to two Englishmen residing in Mexico,
Manning and Mackintosh, who made no effort to begin operations. By the treaty of Guadalupe Hidalgo, ratified in May 1848,
the war ended and the United States acquired immense territories
from Mexico for the sum of $15,000,000. While the treaty negotia-
tions were still in progress President Polk authorized the American
envoy, Nicholas Trist, to double the amount of compensation if
the Mexican government would give the United States exclusive
rights of transit across Tehuantepec. The Mexican commissioners
refused the offer on the ground that Mexico "had several years be-

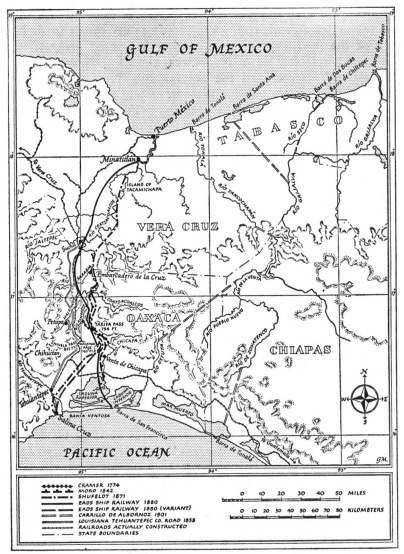

9. TEHUANTEPEC PROJECTS

fore made a grant to one of her own citizens, who had transferred
his rights . . . to English subjects, *of whose rights Mexico could
not dispose. . . ."* [1]

What the Mexican government could not dispose of the English
owners of the Garay concession could and did. In 1849 the Tehuantepec Railway Company, incorporated in New Orleans and
headed by Peter A. Hargous and his brother Louis Eugene, pur-

chased the transit privilege and in 1850 sent out two exploring parties. One of these under the leadership of Pierre E. Trastour investigated the harbors on the Pacific coast, while the larger expedition commanded by Brevet Major John Gross Barnard of the Engineer Corps examined the land route. To divert to Tehuantepec a share of the gold rush traffic a transit had to be completed at the earliest possible moment, so the surveyors located only a railroad line and made no effort to plan a canal. Barnard's party reached Minatitlán on Christmas Day, 1850. For nearly five months the survey proceeded without a hitch, but on May 22, 1851 the Mexican Congress unexpectedly and inexplicably declared the prolongation of Garay's concession, granted in November 1846 by the short-lived *de facto* government of General Salas, null and void. Therefore by implication neither the original grant nor any of its subsequent transfers was any longer valid. On June 3 the governor of Tehuantepec ordered the Americans to suspend work and leave the country. Although Barnard protested energetically against this unceremonious expulsion, pointing out that the government had hitherto adopted without question all decrees of the Salas administration, he was forced to abandon the survey and return to the United States.

In 1852 the Mexican government awarded a new Tehuantepec concession to Albert G. Sloo, the impecunious grantee of the original contract for a steamship line between New York and Chagres. Sloo formed a corporation known as the Compañía Mixta to construct a railroad, but since he lacked funds of his own he was obliged to borrow $600,000 from an Englishman named Falconnet to pay the price demanded by the government, giving Falconnet a lien on his grant as security. Peter Hargous then re-entered the fight for control of the road by purchasing Falconnet's lien and after several stormy clashes reached an agreement with the Sloo interests. Another corporation, the Louisiana Tehuantepec Company, was organized with Emile La Sère as president and Senator Judah P. Benjamin of Louisiana as legal representative. The company secured a charter from the Mexican government on September 7, 1857 and sent out a surveying party under the command of Lieutenant Colonel W. H. Sidell to determine the most advantageous route for a railroad. But the company lacked capital and temporarily contented itself with the construction of a highway extending about three fifths of the way across the isthmus from the Pacific near Salina Cruz to the village of Suchil at the confluence of the Coatzacoalcos and Jaltepec Rivers. Between Suchil and Minatitlán the company operated a light-draft steamboat and between Minatitlán and New Orleans a larger steamer, the *Quaker City*. In the Pacific another steamship line ran between Salina Cruz and San Francisco. The transit was opened in the autumn of 1858 but never developed into an important competitor of the Panama Railroad. Although on rare occasions when everything happened to go well the mails reached California more speedily than by any other route the service in general was poorly organized and irregularly maintained. The river steamboat frequently ran aground, leaving the passengers to find their way to Suchil by their own efforts; inns were primitive and dirty; the highway was no better than a rough and rutted trail; the wheeled vehicles were decrepit; and the Pacific steamer often sailed without waiting for delayed westbound travelers, who were obliged to cool their heels at their own expense until the next voyage several weeks later. In spite of extensions granted in 1859 and 1860 the company could not fulfill the conditions of its charter, and on October 15, 1866 the concession was annulled. Once more it reorganized under the name of Tehuantepec Railway Company and on October 6, 1867 obtained a new charter for a railroad, wagon road, and telegraph line, valid for 70 years. A detailed project for a wagon road and railroad was adopted by the directors and approved by the Mexican government, but again lack of funds prevented active prosecution of the work.

Although the Davis report of 1866 concluded that Tehuantepec had little to recommend it as a canal site the region was among those carefully examined by the United States naval surveys of 1870–5. The expedition, commanded by Captain Robert Wilson Shufeldt, landed on the Atlantic side on November 11, 1870. In official Mexican circles resentment against the United States due to the war of 1846–8 — the underlying cause of the abrupt expulsion of the Barnard party — had long since abated, and the federal government not only extended a cordial welcome to the naval surveyors but appointed three Mexican engineers to co-operate with them and submit an independent report. At the same time local antipathy to "gringos" still persisted in the state of Oaxaca. "President Juarez," reported Shufeldt, "detailed a battalion . . . of six hundred men . . . for the protection of the surveying party in the disturbed districts, and . . . this duty was performed . . . with alacrity and evident desire to assist us. . . ." [2] The expedition remained on the isthmus until the end of April 1871 and explored the ground minutely.

Shufeldt located the summit of the canal at Tarifa and computed the elevation of that pass — the lowest on the isthmus — to be 754.4 feet above sea level. He proposed to construct a canal 144 miles long from the island of Tacamichapa in the Coatzacoalcos to the Pacific at Salina Cruz. The worst feature of the plan was the inordinate number of locks, about 70 on each slope — almost as many as in Moro's design. Even with an average lift equal to that of the present Panama canal locks, approximately 28 feet, this project would have required 27 on either side of the summit. The delays in transit would have been endless, the canal one long and exasperating bottleneck. The Tehuantepec route had one real advantage, and one only, over all its rivals: it offered the shortest ocean passage between the Atlantic and Pacific seaboards of the United States. But this was insufficient to counterbalance its cardinal defect, the altitude of the pass, almost three times as high as the lowest gap on the Panama line and five times as high as that in Nicaragua. Shufeldt appreciated the difficulties and made no extravagant claims for his project. If Tehuantepec would not do for a full-size interoceanic waterway it might still be utilized profitably, he thought, as a passage for small vessels.

While Shufeldt's surveyors mapped and measured the isthmus the Tehuantepec Railway Company was undergoing a thorough reorganization under the presidency of Simon Stevens. On December 20, 1870 the Mexican government granted it a revised concession for a canal, a railroad, or both. Stevens urged the Interoceanic Canal Commission to choose the Tehuantepec location: "Nowhere on the globe is there a healthier or more equable climate. . . . Nowhere are there such boundless supplies of the most valuable woods. . . . It will only remain for me to show that here a surface canal can be constructed not only without encountering engineering difficulties, but that the topography of most of the route is decidedly favorable; that the supply of water is ample; that harbors adequate to the needs of the transit can be provided. . . ." [3] These were the exaggerations of a promoter, not the disinterested observations of a scientist. They failed to move the commission, which in 1876 voted unanimously in favor of a Nicaragua canal. Tehuantepec was dismissed in a few words: "Assuming a common standard of dimensions . . . and of price of materials and labor . . . the estimated cost . . . would largely exceed that of the Nicaragua route." [4]

This verdict definitely eliminated Tehuantepec as a potential canal site. Only one subsequent project for a canal through the Mexican isthmus was suggested, and that was utterly worthless. In 1901 two Mexican engineers, Colonel Ángel M. Carrillo de Albornoz and Juan Pablo del Río, proposed the construction of an interoceanic waterway some miles east of Tehuantepec. This region, they claimed, though slightly broader than the isthmus proper, possessed certain virtues which more than compensated for the additional length of the transit: rivers of greater volume and more gradual descent, and a divide far lower than that on the isthmus itself. How or where the Mexicans obtained their measurements is a mystery, for the summit of the Tehuantepec route was well known to be no more than 755 feet above sea level, while east of the isthmus the watershed is actually nowhere less than 2000 feet high. With a faith that ignored mountains where it could not move them the author of a pamphlet describing this "discovery" confidently asserted that "today no doubt whatever exists concerning the practicability of constructing a *canal without a single lock* in Mexican territory" [5] and proceeded to outline no less than six variations of the proposed route. Five of these started on the Pacific side of the *barra* of Tonalá about 75 miles east of Salina Cruz and meandered across hills and dales to five different terminals on the Gulf of Mexico: respectively the *barras* of Tonalá (not to be confused with the sandbar of the same name on the Pacific), Santa Ana, Dos Bocas, Chiltepec, and Tabasco. The sixth and preferred line ran from the *barra* of San Francisco on the Pacific coast to that of Santa Ana on the Atlantic. The authors of these plans prudently avoided all technical details and neglected to present an estimate of the cost. The scheme never received serious consideration and attracted no more attention than it deserved.

If hopes for a Tehuantepec canal received their deathblow in 1876 the railroad project remained very much alive. Since the days of the first Hargous company the concession had passed through the hands of numerous grantees, none of whom had accomplished anything tangible. On June 2, 1879 the Mexican government awarded a 99-year charter to Edward Learned of Pittsfield, Massachusetts, who actually constructed 22 miles of roadbed for which he was paid a subsidy of $12,000 per mile. In 1882 he surrendered his privilege, and after a brief interlude of construction under a Mexican contractor named Sánchez, who added a few more miles, the government transferred the franchise to an Englishman, E. McMurdo. The work advanced briskly for a time, but after McMurdo's death the concession lapsed once more. In 1894 three American engineers, Elmer L. Corthell, C. S. Stanhope, and J. H. Hampson, finally completed the railroad. The lack of adequate harbor facilities at either end rendered it almost useless, and in 1898 the government signed a new contract with an English firm, S. Pearson & Son, Ltd., for the improvement of the road and the construction of harbors at Salina Cruz on the Pacific and Puerto México at the mouth of the Coatzacoalcos. In 1902 the same company was assigned the task of operating the railroad and terminal ports for 51 years. The government and the contractors confidently expected the road to compete successfully with the Panama canal, especially for traffic between the Gulf ports of the United States and the Pacific coast. In this they were disappointed; since its formal opening on January 23, 1907 the Tehuantepec Railroad has carried local passengers and a fair amount of domestic freight, but its coast-to-coast commerce has been almost negligible. The present war has revived interest in the Tehuantepec line as a potential means of interoceanic communication in the event of damage to the Panama canal, and steps are now being taken to repair the roadbed and modernize its antiquated equipment.

In 1880 Captain James Buchanan Eads proposed to construct across the Isthmus of Tehuantepec a highly unconventional substitute for a canal: a "ship railway" by which large sea-going vessels, fully laden, could be lifted bodily from the water at one terminus, conveyed across the solid land on huge wheeled platforms or cradles, and deposited intact in the opposite harbor, thus eliminating the necessity for troublesome and costly transfers of cargo at either end. Fanciful as it sounds, the suggestion was not at that time really so preposterous. Today the idea of trundling the *Queen Mary* or *Queen Elizabeth* over the mountains on a flatcar seems absurd enough, but for ships of 6000 or 8000 tons — the ocean greyhounds of 60 years ago — the mechanical difficulties did not appear insuperable. Between 1830 and 1880 railroad construction had advanced by leaps and bounds. Each year roadbeds became more solid, rails heavier, locomotives more powerful and efficient. There seemed then to be no limits to the miraculous feats a steam engine might be expected to perform.

Some precedent already existed on a small scale for the ship railway. Since 1840 light canal boats had been successfully transported by rail for a short distance over the Allegheny Mountains. The application of a similar system, greatly magnified, to the portage of ocean liners across the American isthmus had been suggested before 1850 by a Dr. William F. Channing of Providence, who selected the Panama route for his proposed experiment; but when the project was turned down in favor of a less spectacular but much cheaper ordinary railroad he submitted his patented plans, some years later, to the British owners of a right of way across Honduras.

This time the idea was received more cordially, but a financial crisis intervened and the scheme was abandoned once more. It cropped up again in a somewhat different form and with another sponsor — Jean Koderle, the Austrian forestry commissioner at Bregenz on the Lake of Constance — at the Congrès International des Sciences Géographiques held in Paris in August 1875. The assembled savants dismissed it airily as "an ingenious and picturesque theory rather than a practical conception. . . ." [6]

These tentative suggestions were but preludes to the elaborate, carefully worked out projects of Captain Eads. Eads was neither a tyro nor a visionary but an extremely successful practical technician of wide experience, considered by many the leading civil engineer of his day. Born in Indiana in 1820, he first achieved prominence by the invention of appliances for raising sunken ships. During the Civil War he designed and built 14 ironclads for the Federal navy, "among which," he claimed, "were the first eight . . . the United States ever owned. These were built, and most of them had been in action, before the *Monitor* was launched. . . ." [7] From 1867 to 1874 he designed and supervised the construction of the great steel bridge across the Mississippi at St. Louis. A little later he acquired fresh laurels by successfully deepening and stabilizing by a system of jetties the silt-encumbered channel of the lower Mississippi.

The ship railway was to run from Minatitlán to the *barra* of San Francisco or alternatively to Salina Cruz. Its length would be about 134 miles and its maximum elevation at Tarifa, where it would cross the summit through a 17-foot cut, 738 feet. Eads estimated the cost at $50,000,000. Each terminal basin, 3000 feet long and 30 feet deep at the outer end, was to be provided with a huge sunken steel pontoon as large as the cradle. As soon as the empty cradle was hauled into position on its rails at the bottom of the dock, directly over the pontoon, the ship would be floated into place above it. Next the pontoon would be pumped out and gradually raised until the keel block of the cradle came into contact with the keel of the ship along its entire length. Hydraulic rams in the pontoon would then push up a series of hinged supports or blocks set into the floor of the cradle until they fitted snugly against the curved bottom and sides of the vessel. The upper surface of each block, faced with rubber, was to be equipped with a universal joint so that it would automatically adjust itself to the form of the hull at any point of contact. The weight of the ship would thus be distributed evenly over the whole cradle. When the supports were locked into place and the rams withdrawn into the pontoon, the ship and

12.   EADS SHIP RAILWAY. A STEAMER IN TRANSIT

13. EADS SHIP RAILWAY. A FLOATING TURNTABLE

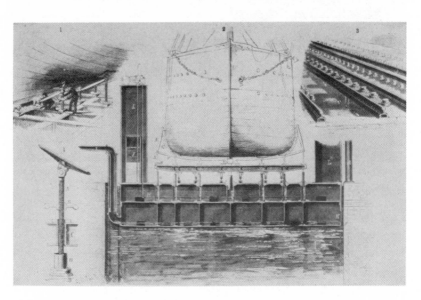

14. EADS SHIP RAILWAY. DETAILS OF PONTOON AND CRADLE

cradle would be ready to begin the overland journey. The entire
process of fitting the ship into the cradle would consume, Eads
estimated, not more than half an hour. At the opposite end of the
line the supports were to be removed by a similar operation carried out in reverse order, and the ship would float off the cradle.

For six or seven years Eads worked ceaselessly on his project,
modifying and improving the details. In his original plan of 1880
the roadbed carried twelve parallel rails spaced four or five feet
apart. The cradle, 300 feet long and between 50 and 60 feet wide
— large enough to support a vessel weighing, with its cargo, 6000
tons — would be borne on 1200 wheels, 100 on each rail. It was to
be drawn by two locomotives, each five times as powerful as the
largest freight engines then in existence. One locomotive would
run on the four outer rails on the right side of the roadbed, the
other on the four left-hand rails, while the four intermediate rails
would serve to carry a tender supplying coal and water to both engines. In a subsequent plan the cradle was lengthened to 350 feet
and given 1380 wheels, 115 to a rail. By 1885 the number of rails
had been reduced to six and the complement of locomotives increased to three, each running on only two rails and hauling its individual tender. In this new design the roadbed was to be about 50
feet wide.

For such an enormous, unwieldy, and practically rigid structure
weighing thousands of tons abrupt changes of direction were obviously out of the question. Nevertheless Eads contended at first
that there would be sufficient play in the bearings to allow the cradle with its burden to follow with perfect safety a moderate curve
of not less than one mile radius. Later, growing more cautious, he
decided that the sharpest curve must have a radius of at least 20
miles. No grade steeper than 1% could be permitted. In 1880 Eads
thought that an average speed of 10 or 12 miles per hour could be
maintained and that the overland trip could be accomplished in
13 to 16 hours, including the time required for locking the ship
into its cradle at one terminal and releasing it at the other. Five
years later his associate Elmer L. Corthell considered 8 or 10 miles
per hour a reasonable estimate. Unfortunately the rugged topography made an even approximately straight line from sea to sea
impossible; at five points the route changed direction abruptly.
Eads proposed to solve this problem by means of floating turn-
tables upon which the entire contraption could be shifted bodily
through any desired angle. While some arrangement had to be
made to enable ships to pass each other, Eads did not consider a
double system of multiple tracks necessary throughout the entire

transit but proposed instead a series of sidings or turnouts which would also serve as improvised drydocks for ships requiring emergency repairs.

In 1880 Eads persuaded the directors of the Tehuantepec Railway Company, who had as yet undertaken no work upon either a railroad or a canal, to abandon both of these projects and merge their interests with his. On May 6, 1881 the Mexican government awarded them a very liberal concession for a ship railway, granting in addition to the customary lands and privileges a guarantee of $1,250,000 a year for 15 years, dating from the opening of the line, on condition that a supplementary pledge of $2,500,000 annually should be obtained on similar terms from other sources — preferably the United States government.

The ship railway project had already been well aired in Washington. When de Lesseps visited the United States in March 1880 and presented his Panama canal plan to the Interoceanic Canal Committee of the House of Representatives, Eads was invited to appear before the same body. The ship railway, he contended, could be constructed for half the cost of a lock canal or one fourth that of a sea level waterway, could be built in much less time, would transport more vessels per day, and would cost less to maintain and operate. Although his contempt for such a feeble compromise as a ship railway was boundless de Lesseps dismissed the plan with all the urbanity for which he was famous. He informed the House committee that "he had listened to the remarks of Mr. Eads with respect, because he knew Mr. Eads to be an engineer who has done the most remarkable work of the day. . . . A ship railway had nothing to do with the canal which he [de Lesseps] proposed to construct. . . ." [8]

Less good-natured opposition soon developed among the Nicaragua partisans led by Ammen and Menocal, and for some years Ammen waged a wordy battle with Corthell culminating in the publication of a pamphlet in which the admiral ridiculed without mercy "all the various operations and advantages of taking a laden ship out of the water . . . and whisking her over a distance of 140 miles or more. . . ." [9] Corthell retorted hotly in another pamphlet, other engineers and naval officers took part in the controversy, and both sides quoted copiously from expert opinions upon the merits and demerits of the ship railway. The chief target of its adversaries was the hypothetical susceptibility to severe strain of a ship transported overland on a wheeled cradle. Eads himself scoffed at their fears and insisted that the railway would carry an ocean liner "with as much safety as a child in its mother's arms." [10]

To secure the annual guarantee of $1,250,000 promised by Mexico Eads had to persuade the United States Congress to underwrite his enterprise to the extent of an additional $2,500,000 a year. In this he was unsuccessful, though he stipulated that the subsidy should become effective only after he had proved to the satisfaction of Congress that his railway could transport a 3000-ton ship uninjured aross the isthmus. The contest for congressional support soon developed into a three-cornered fight between the Panama canal, the Nicaragua canal, and the Tehuantepec ship railway. De Lesseps found himself in the most advantageous position, for he alone of the three claimants made no material demands on Congress; he counted on private subscriptions, not on the United States government, for financial backing. While he regarded the ship railway as a less serious threat than Nicaragua he was anxious to prevent official recognition of either project. Eads in turn considered the Nicaragua promoters, who like himself were petitioners for a government appropriation, a graver menace than the independent Panama company. Eads and de Lesseps's American agent therefore joined forces in an energetic lobby against Nicaragua.

Harassed and confused by these conflicting pretensions, each sustained by volumes of statistics, charts, diagrams, technical descriptions, and endless columns of figures, the House Interoceanic Canal Committee floundered helplessly. On February 22, 1881 a majority of the committee reported in favor of a bill to incorporate the ship railway company and guarantee a 6% dividend on its $50,000,000 capital for 15 years. Five members flatly disagreed and submitted a minority report. The net result was that neither Eads nor the Nicaragua adherents secured a financial guarantee from Congress, and de Lesseps, who "had demanded nothing of the government but the confusion of his enemies," [11] emerged as the only victor. Eads continued to fight valiantly for his ship railway, but when he died in 1887 his scheme died with him. Corthell made several ineffectual attempts to revive it and as late as 1896 was still writing magazine articles in its favor, but by that time the increase in size of ships had rendered the original plans obsolete, and no new genius appeared to expand and improve them. The ship railway project remains an untried experiment, a mechanical curiosity, the almost forgotten eccentricity of a great engineer.

Chapter 20. Atrato

THE CANAL projects comprised in the southernmost or Atrato River group differed from all others in that they contemplated a cut through a portion of the main continent of South America, not some relatively narrow section of the Central American isthmus. Here at the extreme northwest corner of the continent the Pacific coast line of Colombia runs almost due north and south, while on the Atlantic side the Atrato flows north roughly parallel to the Pacific shore into the deeply indented Gulf of Urabá. Near the gulf the river divides into several mouths, forming a broad flat delta. Considering the river as a navigable extension of the Atlantic, the region between it and the Pacific becomes in effect an isthmus varying in width from 28 to 45 miles. Since the crest of the ridge lies close to the Pacific the headwaters of the Atrato's principal tributaries extend to within a few miles of the western coast and thus appear to offer — at least on the map — a number of promising alternative routes for an interoceanic waterway. Very near the source of the Atrato itself rises another large river, the San Juan, which flows south and then west into the Pacific not far from Buenaventura, the chief Colombian port on that ocean.

Humboldt had tentatively recommended two canal schemes in the Atrato area, one connecting Cupica Bay with the Napipí River, the other an enlargement of the Raspadura canal supposedly linking the Atrato and San Juan. A British naval officer, Captain Charles Stuart Cochrane, visited the Raspadura site about 1824 and estimated that the 400 yards separating the two river valleys could be cut through for $500,000 — certainly a modest estimate for any kind of interoceanic waterway, however diminutive. Other officers of the British navy explored the region back of Cupica Bay. In 1827 Captain Charles Friend is said to have walked across the divide from the headwaters of the Napipí to the bay in only 50 minutes. A French doctor, J. F. Landreau, examined the Cupica-Napipí route in 1846 and reported a depression in the ridge not more than 40 feet above the sea, but later and more accurate surveys established the elevation of the lowest gap at something over 600 feet. In December 1847 the British ships *Herald* and *Pandora*, commanded respectively by Captain Henry Kellett and Lieutenant Commander James Wood, anchored for four days in Cupica Bay while parties were sent out to make a hydrographic survey of the adjacent coastal waters. Berthold Seemann, who accompanied the expedition, recorded that Kellett and Wood set out on a brief excursion inland and "after walking several hours . . . came to a river, which they supposed or were told flowed into the Atlantic Ocean. If such was really the case, it might afford facilities for . . . a canal. . . ." [1] Wood guessed the altitude of the divide to be between 300 and 400 feet. In the voluminous report on interoceanic transits submitted to Congress by Representative John A. Rockwell in 1849 a Baltimore engineer, J. H. Alexander, expressed the opinion that of all the canal routes suggested the Raspadura project was "the most worthy of careful examination and the most likely to be attended with success" [2] and that the Cupica-Napipí line also merited attention.

On June 18, 1851 the government of New Granada awarded two Atrato canal concessions, one through the Raspadura divide and the other by the Napipí River to Cupica Bay. Except for the location there was little difference between the two documents. The grantees of the Raspadura charter, Ricardo de la Parra and Benjamín Blagge, organized the Atrato and San Juan Transportation Company and issued an alluring prospectus: "The Canal is to be . . . completed in ten years. . . . The country . . . is very healthy. . . . The . . . rich Province of Chocó . . . is . . . equal in its gold and silver mines to any part of the world. . . ." [3] The mention of precious metals suggests that the company may have been interested primarily in the exploitation of its conceded lands, to which the canal would provide access from both oceans. But no work was undertaken, and the concession lapsed.

The second of these charters granted to Manuel Cárdenas and Florentino González, in behalf of the Inter-Oceanic Canal Company, the right to construct a canal between the Napipí River and Cupica Bay. The promoters dedicated their project to Humboldt and adopted as their slogan "The Humboldt Line," implying that the illustrious German scientist had recommended that route above all others. Actually Humboldt, while he insisted that no decision could be made until all possible sites had been thoroughly investigated, had provisionally placed the Nicaragua route first. When this prospectus appeared in 1854 Humboldt was 85 years old. He probably never heard of the project and almost certainly did not authorize the attachment of his name to it. After quoting freely from the enthusiastic but unscientific descriptions of Friend, Lan-

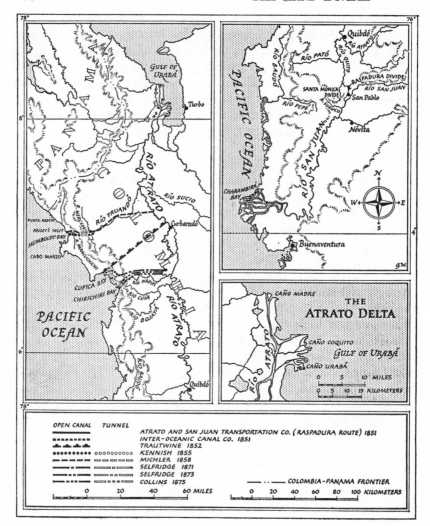

10. ATRATO PROJECTS

dreau, Kellett, Wood, and Alexander the company proceeded to
base its plans upon Landreau's report, the most optimistic and inaccurate of all. The corporation's labors began and ended with its
prospectus, and this charter too was annulled.

Both the Raspadura and Cupica concessions were in fact premature, for the country was still almost unknown, and not a single
instrumental measurement of distance or altitude had been made
at any point. The first thorough exploration of the Atrato region

was undertaken in 1852 by John C. Trautwine, one of the chief engineers of the Panama Railroad, and financed by a group of New York capitalists, among whom the leading spirit was the "mystical and imaginative" [4] Frederick M. Kelley, an indefatigable promoter of interoceanic canal projects. This was Kelley's first venture in that field. During the next 25 years he organized several other expeditions in the valley of the Atrato and in the San Blas district and devoted much time and labor to the preparation of plans, estimates, and scientific data. Undiscouraged by successive failures, he is said to have spent at least $125,000 out of his own pocket on these excellent surveys without ever receiving a penny in return.

Accompanied by his assistants Henry McCann and Dr. Mina B. Halsted, Trautwine reached the Atrato delta in June 1852. He found all of the half dozen *caños* or mouths excessively shallow but thought that one, the Caño Coquito, could be made navigable at moderate expense for vessels drawing 6 to 8 feet. As an alternative he suggested the excavation of a short artificial channel to connect another outlet, the Caño Urabá, with the gulf. For a month the explorers chugged slowly up the winding river to Quibdó, 220 miles from the mouth, in an oven-like launch "reeking with that villainous compound of smells which codfish, semi-putrid jerked beef, unearthly cheese, and other odorous abominations of the cargo exhaled day and night; sleeping in shape of a note of interrogation on a piece of thin floor-matting . . . shared . . . by roaches, whose name was legion; tormented almost into sickness and fever by insects of microscopic dimensions, but of gigantic biting powers . . . eating our meals in a cabin three and a half feet high . . . where our eyes were generally regaled with the smoke from the cook's fire, or offended by hind-shortened views of our black cook himself, perfectly naked, sitting in the entrance to our cabin, perhaps paring his toe-nails, picking his teeth with one of our forks, or vigorously scratching his well-populated head over our stereotyped dessert of boiled rice. . . ." [5]

Trautwine found the marshy overflowed banks of the Atrato completely uncultivated and uninhabited as far as its confluence with the Sucio, 61 miles from the sea. From that point to the first village, Curbaradó, 35 miles farther up the Atrato, one or two mean huts were visible. In a borrowed canoe he ascended the Napipí for 8 miles but turned back the same day profoundly disappointed: "The soil . . . is open and porous, being composed in great part of . . . dead leaves, logs, and entire trees, the accumulations of ages. No material could be more entirely unfit for forming canal

banks . . . or offer greater difficulty in the foundations of the
locks. . . . The entire region . . . is liable to overflow, from one
to three or four times a year. . . . How would embankments of
soft marsh-mud, and leaves, stand under . . . these rains? . . .
Stone and timber fit for construction are entirely wanting. . . .
Even admitting . . . that laborers *could* be set to work on these
marshes, I suspect that very few would live four months; or be able
to render efficient service for more than as many weeks." [6]

At Quibdó the Atrato is joined by the Quito, which Trautwine
ascended in a small boat to its confluence with the Pató, then westward up that stream. The sudden fluctuations in the volume of
water convinced him that no canal could be built over this route.
From the headwaters of the Pató he crossed the divide on foot to
the Baudó, flowing south and west to the Pacific. Trautwine had
been assured that the summit of this divide rose only 18 feet above
the Atrato at Quibdó, but when he had clambered to a height of
500 feet, according to his instruments, and still found himself at
least 200 feet below the pass, he put away his level and "climbed
over the remainder in unspeakable disgust." [7] On the western side
of the ridge he hired another boat and floated down the Baudó to
the Pacific, noting that the river was sufficiently broad and deep
to permit navigation by large vessels; but sandbars at its mouth and
the total lack of an adequate harbor rendered it useless for interoceanic communication. He then retraced his course for some
miles up the Baudó, followed its tributary the Pepé, and recrossed
the divide at a different point. There he descended the Suruco to
the San Juan, traversed the Santa Mónica divide to the headwaters
of the Quito, and returned to Quibdó.

The final stage of this fatiguing exploration took Trautwine up
the Quito and over the Santa Mónica ridge once more, then down
the San Juan to the Pacific. He had intended to examine the site
of the much-discussed Raspadura canal a few miles east of the
Santa Mónica divide but was dissuaded by his Indian guides, who
assured him that the water in the Raspadura creek was so low that
the boat, though it drew but 8 inches, could not pass. Having by
this time crossed several of these narrow watersheds and found
them all unsuitable for an interoceanic transit, he saw no reason
to waste time in an inspection of the unpromising Raspadura ridge.
He very sensibly pointed out that the excavation of a small ditch
connecting two shallow brooks at this or any other point was a very
different matter from the construction of a water channel for ocean
liners: "Now, it is . . . quite probable, that a Cura, interested in

the boating business, may have exercised sufficient influence over
. . . his flock . . . to induce them to cut down a few bushes, and
hollow out a short gutter . . . and such a ditch may have been
used as part of a canoe-slide across the intervening eminence, until filled up again by the rain-washes. . . . Precisely the same kind
of canal could now be made by a dozen expert laborers, in a few
days. But . . . it would be difficult to command the energy required to keep it open. A few months' rain would fill it with gravel;
the people would shrug their shoulders, and pronounce it a case
of 'Dios lo quiere'. . . . I was at San Pablo . . . but 64 years after
the date given to Humboldt as that at which the Cura's canal was
dug; yet persons living near the spot . . . told me they had never
heard of it; nor did I meet with one . . . that had. This is not . . .
proof that no ditch was dug; but merely that it was a work of such
entire insignificance as to create little or no impression even in a
region where internal improvements are entirely unknown." [8]

From Charambirá Bay, the silt-choked outlet of the San Juan,
Trautwine made his way to Buenaventura, "a mean hole," [9] and
thence to Panama. He had found no canal route sufficiently promising to warrant further investigation; but apparently feeling it his
duty to lighten his gloomy report with one faint ray of hope, he
ventured a single positive proposal. Since none of the Atrato tributaries could be utilized to advantage, the only possible line for a
canal, in his opinion, would be from the Atrato near Curbaradó
straight across country to Cupica Bay. This was merely a suggestion, not a recommendation. He calculated the cost of such a cut at
$325,000,000. Preposterous as this huge figure appeared at the time
and for many years thereafter, it turned out to be an exceedingly
shrewd guess.

Trautwine's report disappointed Kelley, but the optimistic promoter refused to concede defeat without further corroboration. In
1853 he sent two separate expeditions, one in charge of an engineer
named Porter and the other under the command of James C. Lane,
to re-examine the headwaters and western tributaries of the Atrato.
In general their reports agreed with Trautwine's. In 1854 Lane
undertook yet another exploration and ascended the Truandó
River to its source near the top of the divide. Illness prevented him
from completing the journey to the Pacific, but he estimated — or
rather underestimated — the summit elevation to be about 250
feet above sea level. In November 1854 Kelley commissioned Captain William Kennish to lead a fifth expedition in search of an
Atrato canal route. Kennish found between Punta Ardita and

Cabo Marzo a large crescent-shaped bay, 35 miles across from cape
to cape, at one side of which he "beheld with pleasure a fine and
spacious inlet" [10] near the mouth of the Paracuchichi River. From
this cove, which he named Kelley's Inlet, he crossed the divide and
descended the Truandó to the Atrato. Kennish reported that a sea
level canal was practicable but would require the construction of
a tunnel 3.25 miles long. He estimated the total cost at $145,407,-
042 and the time at 12 years.

All of this pleased Kelley much better than Trautwine's realistic pessimism. In 1856, having quite arbitrarily reduced the estimate to $75,000,000 and the construction period to 9 years, Kelley
went to London and presented his project before the Institution
of Civil Engineers; then to Paris, where he submitted it to Napoleon III; and finally to Berlin to consult the aged Humboldt,
who commended the explorations but emphatically disapproved
of the tunnel. A year later Congress authorized an official survey to
check the results of the Kennish expedition. Lieutenant Nathaniel Michler, an army topographical engineer, was detailed to carry
out the work on land, while Lieutenant T. A. Craven of the navy
undertook the hydrographic investigations. The party left New
York in October 1857 and returned the following May. The surveys, executed with great care, satisfied Michler that a sea level
canal could be constructed over that route; but he recommended
certain modifications, among them the substitution of two shorter
tunnels for one long one, and computed the cost at $134,450,154.
This was too steep a price for Kelley, who thereupon turned to the
Isthmus of San Blas in the hope of finding a less expensive route.

On April 28, 1855 the government of New Granada awarded a
99-year concession for an Atrato canal large enough to accommodate vessels of 400 tons to Joseph Gooding, an American jeweler
residing in Bogotá, and Ricardo Vanegas. No work was performed
under this contract, and on January 25, 1866 Colombia — as the
republic was now called — granted to Henry Duesbury a charter
for a canal to be cut anywhere between 4° and 8° north latitude,
which covered the entire area of the San Juan and Atrato basins.
Five months later this too was annulled, and the President of Colombia was authorized to conclude a new contract; but no more
applicants appeared.

The Davis report of 1866 held out little hope for the Atrato-
Truandó canal project and none at all for the route by way of the
upper Atrato and the San Juan River: "The examination of the
headwaters of the Atrato . . . proved that nature forbids us alto-

gether to entertain the idea of the union of the two oceans in this direction." [11]

The United States naval surveys in the Atrato region comprised three separate expeditions: one led by Commanders Thomas Oliver Selfridge and Edward P. Lull in 1871, another under Selfridge in 1873, and a third commanded by Lieutenant Frederick Collins in 1875. The first party reached the Gulf of Urabá on December 29, 1870. Here Selfridge permitted himself a flight of poetic fancy: "Ours was the first ship whose keel had ever plowed these waters, and thoughts could not but arise whether this magnificent bay was destined ever to remain grand in solitude as well as in proportions, or would it one day be covered with sails from every clime?" [12] Actually the Gulf of Urabá was one of the first bodies of water in the western hemisphere to be visited by Spanish vessels: Bastidas had sailed into it as early as 1500, Ojeda founded the ill-fated colony of San Sebastián on its eastern shore in 1510, and shortly afterwards Balboa established Antigua on the opposite coast. In 1827 Captain Friend had entered the Atrato through the gulf, and when Trautwine arrived in 1852 a more or less regular monthly steamboat service was in operation between Cartagena and Quibdó by way of the gulf and the Atrato.

Lull directed the hydrographic survey of the gulf and delta, while Selfridge led his party up the Atrato to the Napipí and then westward along that tributary and over the divide to Cupica Bay. He chose the Caño Urabá, one of the more southerly mouths of the Atrato, as the one best adapted to navigation by large vessels. At its confluence with the Napipí the Atrato was found to be 40 feet above sea level. Thence the canal would follow the valley of the Napipí, rising by means of 9 locks to a summit level of 130 feet, flow through a gigantic tunnel about 5 miles long, and descend to the Pacific through 13 locks. Selfridge enthusiastically sang the praises of his own project: "Its prominent advantages are freedom from swamps; its construction in rock which admits of a closer calculation of cost than with any other material, greater durability and less cost for repair; its shortness; the fact that the heaviest . . . work is within five miles of the Pacific . . . giving great facilities for the movement of supplies, etc., and . . . affording . . . the most healthy inhabited spot in the tropics; the excellency of its harbors; and . . . the least expensive [route]. . . ." [13] Most if not all of these claims were open to question. Excavation in solid rock was a most costly operation, as the builders of the Panama canal discovered some years later; the practicability of a tunnel so much larger than any ever before attempted was by no means assured;

and the "freedom from swamps" conflicted with Trautwine's description of the soggy banks and marshy hinterland on both side
of the Napipí's lower course.

The second Atrato naval expedition, also commanded by Selfridge, left Panama on January 23, 1873 and penetrated into the
interior from the Pacific side. Selfridge carefully examined the
course of the Bojayá River and its tributary the Cüía but found
this line inferior to the Napipí route. He then resurveyed the Napipí and discovered a better profile for the western section through
the valley of the Doguadó tributary, which would shift the Pacific
terminus a few miles south to Chirichiri Bay. He proposed to reduce the cost materially by adopting much smaller dimensions for
the canal and tunnel and submitted four different projects, varying in elevation of summit level, number of locks, and length of
tunnel. The cheapest would cost about $50,000,000, the dearest
$90,000,000.

The third and last of the naval surveys in the Atrato area began
work in February 1875 under the command of Lieutenant Frederick Collins, who suggested several minor alterations in the route,
increased the dimensions, and raised the summit level to 143 feet
above the sea. His estimate amounted to $98,194,394.

When the Interoceanic Canal Commission voted in favor of the
Nicaragua route it condemned the Selfridge and Collins projects
on all counts: "After the canal has . . . reached the Napipi River
at the point where it is proposed to cross that stream, the execution
of the remainder of the work will require the greatest skill in engineering; and its cost cannot be estimated . . . with any accuracy, though it must necessarily be extraordinarily great. The rainfall and the duration of the rainy season . . . are greater than
upon the Panama route, and . . . much greater than . . . upon
the Nicaragua route. Unlike all of the other routes . . . for this
route supplies of every kind, as well as laborers . . . would have
to be brought from considerable distances, still further swelling
the cost. Finally . . . the cost of . . . maintenance would be
greater. . . ." [14] Kennish's and Michler's proposed canals via the
Truandó River to Kelley's Inlet fared no better.

Since 1876 only one or two half-hearted attempts have been
made to revive the Atrato projects. As recently as 1929, when proposals for a Nicaragua canal to supplement the existing Panama
transit were under discussion, Rear Admiral Colby M. Chester recommended an alternative communication between the Atrato and
the Pacific which "would have the advantage of a sea-level waterway, but would require tunneling through the Andes for about

nine miles and dredging the river bed for about twenty miles each side of the Isthmus. Admiral Chester holds that the canal could be built for $200,000,000, or one-fifth of the estimated cost of . . . the canal through Nicaragua." [15] Just how Chester arrived at this estimate was not divulged. The scheme attracted few supporters, and it seems certain that most engineers of today would reject without hesitation any plan for a canal with a long tunnel, no matter how advantageous it might be in other respects.

Chapter 21. Darién

THE NAME of Darién has sometimes been applied loosely to the entire isthmus as far west as the Costa Rican frontier, but it properly belongs only to the southeastern portion or "root" nearest the South American mainland. Here the land barrier is narrowest where Darién Harbor, an extension of the Gulf of San Miguel, cuts deeply into the Pacific shore line. From Darién Harbor to Caledonia Bay the distance across the isthmus in a straight line is a little less than 40 miles. The crest of the divide lies close to the Atlantic coast, an unbroken chain 700 to 2500 feet in height, but farther south near the Gulf of Urabá the ridge sinks to an elevation of approximately 500 feet at one or two points. On the Pacific side the opening between the Gulf of San Miguel and Darién Harbor is split by the large island of San Carlos into two channels, Boca Grande and Boca Chica. Two important streams flow into Darién Harbor: the short, broad, relatively straight Sabana — more marsh than river — from the north, the longer and more winding Tuyra from the southeast. About 20 miles from the Sabana's mouth its largest tributary, the Lara, enters from the east. The principal tributary of the Tuyra, the Chucunaque, follows so tortuous a course that "it would be almost impossible to double up a stream so as to get more length in the same space. . . ." [1]

On the map this narrow isthmus appears easy to cross. In reality it is one of the most impenetrable areas in the world. On the Pacific side jungle and swamp, on the Atlantic jungle and mountain, effectively block the way to the interior. Even today there are no roads or white settlements in Darién though it lies within 150 miles of the Panama canal. The rivers and a few primitive trails provide the only means of communication between the squalid villages. Eventually the great Inter-American highway will be extended through Darién to the South American mainland, but this is admittedly one of the most difficult sections of the entire road. When Tschiffely undertook his 10,000-mile horseback ride from Buenos Aires to Washington in 1925 this was the only portion of his route he was unable to traverse by land because of physical obstacles.

In addition to its dense jungles and semi-liquid bogs Darién opposes a man-made barrier to exploration. For centuries the Cuna Indians of the Atlantic coast have firmly resisted all attempts by white men to subdue them, "civilize" them, or secure a foothold in their territory. The brutalities of Pedrarias and his contemporaries turned the Cuna people into relentless foes of all Europeans, and although they willingly guided English and French buccaneers across the isthmus, treated Wafer and his companions kindly, and befriended the wretched Scots at New Edinburgh, they did so only through hatred of the common enemy the Spaniards. Both Balboa and Wafer were offered Cuna women in marriage, but in general the Darién Indians went to extreme lengths to keep their blood pure. For a short time during the eighteenth century they relaxed their rules sufficiently to permit a colony of French Huguenots to settle on the Atlantic coast. Some of the Frenchmen married into the tribe and bred children of mixed blood, but about 1757 the Cuna rose, slaughtered the colonists and their half-breed offspring, and resumed their traditional policy of isolation which they have maintained rigidly ever since. To anthropologists the Cuna present an interesting problem, largely because of their unusually high percentage of albinos. Today, although they acknowledge the nominal sovereignty of the republic of Panama, they remain practically independent and untouched by European modes of life. White travelers and traders, while seldom actually molested, are not encouraged to remain on shore even one night. Father Gassó, a Spanish Jesuit missionary, was by exception permitted to live among the Cuna on one of the San Blas Islands from 1907 to 1915, but he was never welcomed by the more conservative natives, and his efforts to convert them met with little success. Colonel Gorgas, who as chief sanitary officer of the Panama canal came into frequent contact with the islanders during the American construction period, wrote in 1915: "In the ten years that we have been at work . . . the San Blas Indians have acquired considerable confidence in us, and have become quite friendly. They come to the hospitals very freely for treatment and surgical operations, and the men can now be seen almost any day in Colon trading. . . . While the Indians recognize the overlordship of . . . Panama, I doubt if the President, or any other white official, would be allowed to spend a night in the San Blas country, nor would they . . . allow any official of the Canal Commission to spend a night in this domain." [2]

Cuna territory comprises the Atlantic seaboard of the Darién and San Blas regions, the islands off the coast, and both sides of the watershed, extending rather less than halfway across the isthmus. The Pacific shores are inhabited partly by more docile Indian

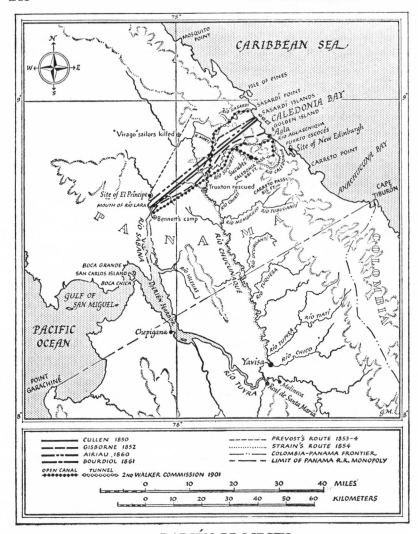

11. DARIÉN PROJECTS

Rio Sabana — Caledonia Bay Section

tribes, partly by Negroes with a thin strain of Spanish blood. There
is very little communication between the natives of the opposite
coasts; the Cuna keep themselves proudly apart, and the less aggressive people of the Pacific lowlands dare not venture uninvited
into Cuna lands. This strict exclusion of all aliens, combined with
the perverse nature of the terrain, delayed exploration of the interior for many years. From 1790, when all Spanish outposts except

Yavisa were abandoned, until about 1850 the Darién hinterland apparently remained unvisited by white men. Even Humboldt, thirsty for information concerning possible canal sites, could learn practically nothing about its topography.

In 1850 an Irish doctor, Edward Cullen, created a mild sensation in England with the announcement that he had found a short and easy canal route between Caledonia Bay and the confluence of the Lara and Sabana Rivers. He claimed the discovery of a gap in the watershed at an elevation of not more than 150 feet above sea level and insisted that in 1849 he had crossed the entire isthmus several times without the slightest difficulty, each journey taking only a few hours. There can be little doubt that Cullen was a liar of the first water. Subsequent investigations proved that the gap existed only in the doctor's exuberant imagination, and he was never able to produce any satisfactory evidence that he had traversed the isthmus even once. Yet he succeeded in convincing three distinguished and presumably hard-headed engineers, Charles Fox, John Henderson, and Thomas Brassey, who formed a syndicate to finance a preliminary survey and engaged Lionel Gisborne, an English civil engineer of excellent repute, to carry out the exploration.

Cullen set out at once for Bogotá to secure a canal concession, and about May 1, 1852 Gisborne and his assistant H. C. Forde reached Cartagena, where Cullen was to join them. Friction developed between the doctor and the engineer even before they met. Cullen was detained at Bogotá by a delay in the negotiations while Gisborne fumed with impatience until June 1, when he learned that Cullen had obtained a 99-year charter for which he had agreed to pay New Granada $120,000 within one year. Still Cullen lingered, and on June 12 the exasperated technicians hired a small schooner and sailed to Puerto Escocés near the abandoned Scottish settlement of New Edinburgh on Caledonia Bay. "Dr. Cullen is not with us," Gisborne reported sourly. "After waiting six weeks he has no reason to complain if the expedition succeeds or fails, without him. . . ." [3] On June 17 Gisborne and Forde started overland from Puerto Escocés. Unable to locate the mythical 150-foot pass in the position indicated on Cullen's map, they soon lost their way and for two days rambled uncertainly in a labyrinth of watercourses and jungle-covered hills. They assumed — mistakenly — that they had already crossed the main divide, but before they could verify this they were halted by a band of Cuna Indians who sternly ordered them back and threatened them with death should they attempt to land on that coast again. The engineers then proceeded to Colón by sea, crossed to Panama, and made a fresh start from the Pacific side.

On June 30 they reached Darién Harbor and paddled up the Sabana. A few miles above the mouth of the Lara they left the canoe, set out on foot, and soon "came to a considerable body of water flowing east, and gradually bending to the north-east. . . . The direction of the rising ground satisfied us that this river must flow into the Atlantic. . . ." [4] Unfortunately it did no such thing. Because the dense forest prevented a clear view for more than a few yards the explorers were unable to see that a high ridge of mountains still barred their way to that ocean. Believing themselves within a few miles of the northern coast and remembering their recent encounter with the Indians, Gisborne and Forde prudently returned to Panama, where on July 30 the elusive Dr. Cullen at last made his appearance. The meeting was stormy. The doctor blustered and threatened, but Gisborne, now justifiably suspicious of his good faith, refused to give him any information concerning his own investigations.

Gisborne reached England in August, having spent in all about 40 days on the isthmus, of which actual exploration had consumed but eight. Although he had seen almost nothing of the country he rashly presented an optimistic report and strongly recommended construction of a sea level canal to cost $60,000,000. Gisborne has been severely criticized for his hasty judgment, and he certainly based his project on the most superficial of investigations. Yet he was not a common impostor like Cullen; he honestly believed that he had crossed the main watershed from both sides, though in fact he had not even *seen* it from either direction. When he discovered his mistake two years later he admitted it frankly and did his best to make amends. By that time 11 men had died horribly as a result of his initial error.

The British syndicate, reorganized as the Atlantic and Pacific Junction Company, issued a prospectus inviting the public to subscribe $375,000 for the purchase of the concession and the prosecution of more detailed surveys, which were again entrusted to Gisborne and Forde. Their experience with hostile Indians had convinced them that this new exploring party would have to be large, well armed, and protected by war vessels off the Atlantic coast. At the same time the directors of the company, hoping to dispose of their securities not only in England but in other countries, wished to give the expedition at least the appearance of an international undertaking. The governments of Great Britain, France, the

United States, and New Granada agreed to participate officially, and a general plan of procedure was drawn up with Caledonia Bay as the chief base of operations. France sent one warship, the *Chimère,* commanded by Lieutenant Jaureguiberry. New Granada assigned Colonel Codazzi, head of the National Topographical Commission, and two special delegates, Castilla and Polanco, and furnished a large corps of laborers, including many convicts, to carry supplies. The United States was represented by the corvette *Cyane* under Commander Hollins and an exploring party officered by Lieutenant Isaac G. Strain, Passed Midshipmen Truxton and Latimer, and First Assistant Engineer Maury. The British contingent, more imposing than any of the others, consisted of two entirely separate units. On the Atlantic side the brig *Espiegle* in charge of Commander Hancock and the schooner *Scorpion* commanded by Parsons were ordered to join the international naval force, while a Pacific expedition under Commander J. C. Prevost in the steam sloop *Virago* was sent to the Gulf of San Miguel.

The *Virago* party was the first to start its survey and had already returned to the ship before any of the Atlantic groups reached Caledonia Bay. On December 19, 1853 the explorers ascended the Sabana in small boats and started to walk in what Prevost assumed to be the direction of Puerto Escocés. Unluckily the charts were far from accurate, and the line they followed would eventually have brought them to the Atlantic many miles west of their objective. For 15 heartbreaking days they hacked their way through the jungle and at the end had advanced but 26 miles from the river landing. On January 2 Prevost divided his party, leaving four men to guard the provisions while the remainder pushed on for two more days. By that time, though the main divide had not yet been crossed, they had reached an altitude of at least 800 feet. Obviously Cullen's gap did not lie along that route, so they returned to the spot where they had left their four companions, but found men and stores gone. Suspecting an Indian raid, they proceeded cautiously until they "suddenly came on the murdered remains of three of our former comrades, all lying obliquely across the road, and pierced with several gunshot wounds. . . . Nothing could be seen of the remaining man . . . and it is presumed he was either shot with the others and escaped farther into the bush, where he died . . . or . . . that he is . . . a miserable prisoner. . . ."[5] The party, fearing an ambush, left the corpses where they lay and hastily retreated to the *Virago.*

Meanwhile the Atlantic expeditions were getting under way. Gisborne, Forde, Cullen, and four civil engineers sailed from England on December 17, 1853. The original plan had designated Cartagena as the meeting-place of the international groups, but this was changed to Jamaica — too late to alter the destination of the American party, which reached Cartagena on January 4. There is good reason to believe that the United States government took but a half-hearted interest in the exploration and that it was Strain himself, eager for adventure, who urged the project upon his superiors. The orders issued to Hollins by Secretary of the Navy James C. Dobbin on December 12, 1853 indicated nothing more than grudging acquiescence: "You are sent on this expedition because it is within the limits of the cruising grounds of the Home Squadron and it can add but little to the ordinary expenses; the result may prove beneficial to the commerce of the world. . . ." [6] Official indifference failed to discourage Strain, who although still a young man had spent 16 years in the navy and was already a seasoned explorer. In 1843 he had conducted an expedition into the interior of Brazil and five years later had explored the peninsula of Lower California. In 1849 he crossed the Andes from Valparaiso to Buenos Aires. To so experienced a traveler the short journey across Darién seemed in anticipation only child's play.

When Hollins and Strain arrived at Cartagena Gisborne was still in Jamaica; but Forde and the other English assistants, on their way to Darién Harbor via Panama to begin surveys on the Pacific side, requested the Americans to proceed to Caledonia Bay and wait there for the British, French, and New Granadian expeditions. At Puerto Escocés Strain found two of the commissioners from New Granada, Castilla and Polanco, and accepted their offer to attach themselves to his group. The Cuna chiefs, intimidated by the guns of the *Cyane,* reluctantly agreed to allow the explorers to cross their territory without molestation as long as native lives and property were respected but refused flatly to supply guides or render any assistance whatever. Strain now saw no reason to await the arrival of the British and French ships. On January 20, 1854 he landed his party of 27 men — mostly volunteers from the crew of the *Cyane,* with Truxton second in command — and disappeared into the jungle.

Three days later the other contingents sailed into the harbor, to be greeted by Hollins with the unwelcome news that Strain's party had already left for the interior. The precipitate departure of the Americans was to stir up later a waspish controversy. Gisborne protested that "independent action on the part of any of the naval commanders was sure to frustrate the object and increase the difficulties" [7] of the entire project and complained that "although every . . . officer . . . was ordered to co-operate, there was no head to the whole expedition. . . ." [8] Hollins and Strain maintained stoutly that the American party had not been instructed to co-operate with anybody. In this they were technically correct: Dobbin's order contained no specific mention of joint action. Nevertheless the preliminary correspondence certainly indicated that the combined expeditions were intended to proceed as a unit, and both Strain and Hollins must have been well aware of the international character of the enterprise.

Strain's party ran into trouble at the very beginning, for in landing on the beach one of the boats overturned, and some of the supplies were lost in the surf. Strain considered this only a trifling mishap since he expected to complete his reconnaissance and return to the *Cyane* in less than eight days. Besides food could probably be purchased from the Indians, and almost certainly there was plenty of game in the jungle. From the shore a low ridge masked the true and much higher divide of the cordillera. The explorers climbed this first elevation and followed the course of the small Caledonia River in search of Cullen's gap. Naturally they could not find it and, advancing inland, crossed the summit at an estimated altitude of 1300 feet. On the third day two officers and three men became separated from the main party through a misunderstanding of orders and eventually made their way back to the *Cyane*. On the sixth day the rest of the men reached the Cuna village of Sucubtí, which they found abandoned and in flames. This evidence of native unfriendliness disappointed Strain, who had written to Dobbin on January 10: "We have many rumors in regard to the hostility of the Darien Indians. . . . All I believe to be exaggerated. . . ." [9] Dobbin's order to Hollins had expressly forbidden armed conflict: "You will instruct Lieut. Strain, that should unfortunately any obstacle be interposed by the Indian tribes . . . he will . . . retire from the undertaking unless it can be accomplished without unfriendly collision and . . . hazard of human life. . . ." [10]

A few miles beyond Sucubtí Strain and his crew met five Indians who offered to guide them to the Sabana and provide canoes to carry them to Darién Harbor, which they assured Strain could be reached in three days. The stroke of good fortune did not last, for the next day they encountered a large band of hostile Indians who induced the volunteer guides to desert. The Americans had eaten all their provisions but confidently expected to find thriving plantations along the trail. Just before they fled the guides had pointed out a large river which they called the Chucunaque; the

Sabana, they insisted, lay ahead. But Strain, convinced that the Indians were deliberately trying to mislead him and that the river just crossed was actually the Sabana, determined to follow its banks to the Pacific. The mistake was fatal. The Indians had not lied, and the river was in fact the immensely long and fantastically crooked Chucunaque. Had Strain taken the guides' advice and proceeded only five or six miles farther to the west he would have come to the trail cut by Prevost's party a month before and so reached Darién Harbor by way of the Sabana in a few days; but at that time he knew nothing of Prevost's journey or the existence of such a path.

Day after day Strain and his men forced their slow way down the winding Chucunaque, impeded at every step by matted undergrowth, tormented by suffocating heat and vicious insects, and in imminent danger of starvation. This was uninhabited country, and the hoped-for banana plantations failed to appear. Palm nuts grew here and there, but they had to be shot down from the trees, there was little ammunition to spare, and the nuts they did obtain proved so intensely acid that a few mouthfuls completely destroyed the enamel of the men's teeth and corroded their stomachs and intestines. During the first week they caught a few fish; then their only hook broke, and all efforts to fabricate others out of wire failed for lack of tools to improvise a barb. Occasionally they shot iguanas and once a wild hog. They brought down a few small birds which served only to whet the appetites of the famished sailors, and one day Strain shot a buzzard, but the loathsome stench of the carrion-eater's flesh made the men turn away in disgust. Soon, as they grew less fastidious, buzzards and creatures even more repulsive were devoured greedily to the last revolting sinew. Once Truxton picked up a toad, bit off and spat out the head, and gulped down the still squirming body. Maury thereupon snatched up the rejected head and swallowed it, saying: "Well, Truxton, you are getting quite particular!" [11]

Progress through the jungle became so difficult that Strain made two attempts to float the party in detachments down the river on makeshift rafts. The first time they were blocked by an impenetrable mass of driftwood, and the second raft was built of such heavy timber that it sank at once. As the men grew weaker their marches became shorter and more painful. On February 13, 16 days after the expedition had started down the Chucunaque, Strain decided to push ahead with three of the strongest men in a desperate attempt to obtain help at the nearest settlement, Yavisa, leaving the main party in charge of Truxton to follow at a slower pace.

Meanwhile the international expedition had bogged down at

Caledonia Bay. Four days after Strain's departure from Puerto Escocés 50 men from the English and French ships landed on the beach and hunted in vain for the elusive pass through the mountains. Several other parties sent out to search for Strain returned without news. Cullen, having failed to guide the explorers to the low gap whose discovery he had so airily proclaimed, was now in disgrace. "It is proved beyond all doubt," Gisborne reported, "that Dr. Cullen never was in the interior, and that his statements are a plausible net-work of fabrications." [12] To keep the doctor out of further mischief Hancock held him a virtual prisoner aboard the *Espiegle*. Cullen, sulky and defiant, escaped to the *Scorpion* and wrote Hancock an abusive letter but was promptly recaptured and forced to apologize. When the *Cyane* left on February 28 Cullen was taken along as a passenger to Colón, where he found the American residents so indignant at the disappearance of Strain's party, for which they held Cullen's misrepresentations largely responsible, that he fled in the first vessel sailing for New York. His later history is obscure. He was mentioned in connection with the Crimean War, during which he apparently served as an army surgeon. Afterwards he resumed his agitation for a Darién canal and for several years bombarded the United States government with plans and diagrams which impressed nobody except a few gullible laymen.

To Gisborne the realization that he had been duped by Cullen and misled by his own optimism was a bitter pill. His report of 1852 was now waste paper, his professional reputation in serious jeopardy. Although satisfied that Cullen's gap was a myth he resolved to settle the question by crossing the isthmus to the junction of the Lara and Sabana, where Forde had been instructed to establish his base. Threats and cajolery procured Gisborne Indian guides, and on February 7 he set out with three companions. Keeping well to the west of Strain's route they soon came to the three unburied corpses of Prevost's sailors: "Their clothes and provisions were untouched, their bones still forming connected skeletons, clean picked by vultures, presented . . . a hideous appearance. . . ." [13] Five days after he left Puerto Escocés Gisborne reached Forde's camp on the Sabana, expecting to find the surveys well advanced; but Forde was at Panama recuperating from an attack of fever, and the panic caused by the murders had scattered the native laborers. During Forde's absence another engineer, William C. Bennett, took charge of the outpost.

Early in March the *Virago*, now under Commander Marshall, returned to Darién Harbor. Marshall had been instructed to seek

redress from the Indians for the murders as well as to assist and
protect the surveying parties, but Gisborne pointed out that these
duties were incompatible and urged the naval officer to send a detachment in search of Strain's party instead of a punitive expedition against the Cuna. This was both sensible and magnanimous,
for Gisborne believed that Strain's failure to wait for his French
and British colleagues was responsible for·any disaster that might
have befallen the missing Americans. Marshall willingly agreed to
the substitution but postponed the relief expedition a few days in
order to transport Gisborne and some of his assistants to Panama.
The *Virago* then returned to Darién Harbor, and on March 17 the
rescue party commanded by Lieutenant Forsyth set out in a paddleboat up the Tuyra River towards Yavisa.

When Strain and his three companions headed down the Chucunaque on February 13 to procure assistance their progress was
discouragingly slow. Every foot of advance had to be literally
carved out of the jungle, and food became scarcer than ever, for
the guns had rusted. Only one rifle was still usable, and for that
but three cartridges remained. Twice more, with infinite labor,
they built rafts. The first proved unmanageable in the snag-filled
current, but the second stayed afloat and bore them down the last
few miles of river without mishap. On March 9 — 24 days after
they had taken leave of the main party and 49 after their departure
from Puerto Escocés on what was to have been a week's easy jaunt
— the four men, exhausted, famished, almost naked, and with bodies cruelly torn by briers, staggered into the village of Yavisa.

Starvation had reduced Strain's weight from 145 to 75 pounds,
and the others were in no better condition; but their spirits were
unbroken, and they lost no time in organizing relief for the 18 men
who, they believed, could not be far behind. Learning that the
Virago, upon which they depended for supplies and passage to Panama, was about to leave Darién Harbor, Strain decided to place
one of his men, Fred Avery, in charge of the relief party while he
himself proceeded to the coast to detain the ship. The next day
Avery started back up the river with 11 natives and a stock of provisions in canoes, and Strain and the two other Americans paddled
down to Darién Harbor. At the village of Chepigana they learned
that the *Virago* had just sailed for Panama with Gisborne's party
and would not return for five days. No provisions were obtainable
at Chepigana, but the natives informed Strain that Bennett's camp
on the Sabana was well stocked. Bennett received the Americans
warmly and supplied them with food, money, and clothing. Though
pitifully weak, Strain would allow himself no rest until his men

were safe. Two hours after his arrival at Bennett's camp, where he left his companions, he was on his way back to Yavisa alone.

A few days later Avery turned up at Yavisa with bad news. He had found a grave on the river bank 60 miles above the village and upon it a letter from Truxton, dated March 6, saying that he had determined to make an attempt to lead his men back to the Atlantic. It must have been a hard decision for the young midshipman, but he had heard nothing from Strain for 20 days, one of his men had died of starvation, and another had disappeared. This man was later picked up by Avery and brought to Yavisa, where he died. Avery's Negro boatmen had refused to proceed farther up the river when they saw the grave. Damning the natives' cowardice, Strain now made a final heroic effort to send help to his command. Once more he set out in a canoe for Darién Harbor, but 18 miles below Yavisa he met Forsyth and his boatload of British sailors who had left the *Virago* early that morning. With Strain on board the paddleboat proceeded to Yavisa, where the relief party obtained canoes and started up the Chucunaque the next morning.

On the afternoon of March 23 they saw smoke ahead, heard faint cheers, and found Truxton and his crew camped on the river shore. The rescued men greeted Strain with hysterical joy: "Upon landing, those . . . upon the bank crowded around me to express their satisfaction at our arrival, and my own safety. . . . Mr. Truxton . . . threw his arms about my neck, and sobbing from . . . concentrated emotion, said, 'My God, Captain, did I do right in coming back?' Several were enfeebled to the last degree, and at least four would never have marched from the spot; but all had made a march of several hours that day, and there was no where an evidence of despair." [14] Dr. Ross of the *Virago* reported that " a more wretched set of human beings were never beheld; so emaciated were they, that, clothed in their rags, they appeared like spectres; some had retained their arms and blankets, while others, scarcely able to drag along their own bodies, had thrown theirs away. . . . In nearly all, the intellect was in a slight degree affected, as evinced by childish and silly remarks, although their memory, and the recollection of their sufferings, were unimpaired. . . . They were literally living skeletons, covered with foul ulcers. . . ." [15]

In addition to the two deaths already noted three more men had perished of starvation before the rescue party appeared. On March 12 Castilla, one of the New Granadian commissioners, died, and the next day Polanco, too weak to proceed, was reluctantly abandoned where he lay. The relief party found his corpse stretched across Castilla's grave. The fifth to go was the oldest sailor, Lombard, who heroically refused to be a burden to the others and insisted upon being left behind. Propped against a tree, he smiled cheerfully as his comrades vanished into the jungle. Strain was especially gratified by the discipline preserved by the starving crew. Throughout the entire march Truxton kept his journal up to date, and each night separate campfires were lighted for officers and men. While the maintenance of such distinctions of rank in the very shadow of death may seem exaggerated, Strain believed that only this insistence upon naval tradition kept the party together and prevented cannibalism. One man, driven temporarily insane by hunger, did try to dig up one of the corpses but was stopped in time by Truxton's threat to blow out his brains.

On March 27 the whole party arrived at Yavisa, where another sailor died, and three days later they pitched camp on the shore of Darién Harbor within reach of the *Virago*. Even now Strain's stern sense of duty drove his wasted body to fresh activity. He proceeded to Panama in an open boat and thence, partly on muleback and partly by the uncompleted railroad, to the *Cyane* at Colón. He was greeted as one risen from the grave, for Hollins had long ago lost hope that any member of the expedition still lived. Strain collected money and supplies and, without stopping to rest, recrossed the isthmus, chartered a sloop, returned to Darién Harbor, and brought his men to Panama. There the seventh and last victim of privation succumbed. With the survivors Strain reached Colón on April 25 and sailed in the *Cyane* for the United States.

Before the rescue the Panama newspapers had heaped abuse on Gisborne's head: "From what we read, hear, and see, we believe him to be an unprincipled adventurer. . . . The presumption and impudence of the man is most wonderful, and he evinces an egotism which . . . is disgusting in the extreme. . . ." [16] It does not appear that Strain ever met either Gisborne or Cullen face to face. Apparently unaware of the sinister part played by Cullen, he blamed Gisborne alone for the misinformation that had brought so much suffering to his expedition; nor did he ever give the English engineer credit for his timely and fruitful efforts to send help to the starving Americans, though he gratefully acknowledged Bennett's assistance. All this was unjust to Gisborne, who if he had deceived Strain had also deceived himself. On the other hand Gisborne, while he criticized Strain severely for his failure to cooperate with the international forces, generously paid homage to that officer's courageous and resourceful leadership. As soon as he returned to England Gisborne submitted a frank report to the At-

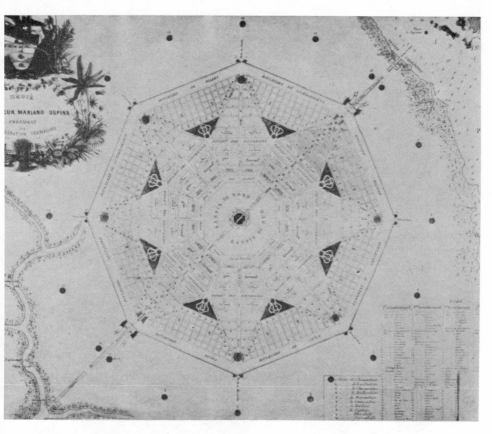

15.   AIRIAU'S PLAN FOR THE CAPITAL OF DARIÉN

16.   MEMBERS OF THE SELFRIDGE EXPEDITION IN THE DARIÉN
JUNGLE, 1870

lantic and Pacific Junction Company and manfully accepted full responsibility for his previous mistake.

Strain, although well enough to take part in a hydrographic survey for the location of a projected transatlantic submarine cable in 1856, never fully recovered his health, and when he returned to the isthmus the following year his weakened constitution broke down under the first attack of fever. He died at Colón on May 14, 1857 at the age of 36. Responsibility for the failure of the Darién expedition and for its tragic outcome appears to rest in some degree on the shoulders of all three principals. Strain certainly violated the spirit, if perhaps not the letter, of his instructions by not waiting for the other parties. Gisborne's first report was worthless, and his honorable recantation came too late to avert calamity. But the archvillain was Edward Cullen — boaster, liar, and unmitigated fraud.

The discovery in 1854 that the true minimum elevation of the cordillera between Caledonia Bay and Darién Harbor was approximately 1000 feet above sea level instead of 150 brought British investigations of that region to a full stop and suspended American explorations for 16 years, but for some strange reason it appeared actually to encourage French promoters. Half a dozen projects, all hopelessly impracticable, emanated from France within as many years.

The first and least realistic of these schemes was conceived by one A. Airiau, who in 1860 secured for himself and his associates a provisional canal concession, soon permitted to lapse. Perversely ignoring the difficulties encountered by Gisborne and Strain, Airiau concocted a grandiose plan for a sea level canal in Darién and the establishment of a large European colony. An accomplished draftsman, Airiau embellished the presentation of his project with meticulously drawn, daintily colored maps and diagrams in which mountains and swamps vanished as if by magic. He pictured Darién as a smiling open country almost as flat as Holland, dotted with prosperous farms and orchards and traversed by a broad, straight artificial waterway. His crowning absurdity, the element upon which he lavished the most loving care, was a splendid city geometrically laid out on both banks of the canal in the middle of the isthmus and destined to become "the greatest metropolis of the commercial world." [17] He designed this dream capital with every detail complete, even to the naming of streets, the location of fountains and statues, and the planting of trees. While Airiau's project was not without merit as an abstract study in city planning its realization would have seemed almost as incongruous in the Darién wilderness as on the outer ring of Saturn.

In December 1860 another French company obtained a Darién canal charter and commissioned a civil engineer, H. Bourdiol, to undertake preliminary surveys. The party started from the mouth of the Lara the following April and laboriously cut through the jungle to the Chucunaque. So dense was the undergrowth that the overland journey of not more than 15 miles in a straight line consumed an entire month. The rainy season had set in, the Negroes deserted, and most of the French explorers were incapacitated by fever. Only seven reached the Chucunaque, where their investigations came to an end. Although he had not crossed or even glimpsed the main divide Bourdiol did not hesitate to submit a project for a lock canal from the junction of the Sabana and Lara Rivers to the Chucunaque, then almost due north to the headwaters of the Mortí, where it turned east to its Atlantic terminus on Caledonia Bay opposite the Sasardí Islands. Since he had not personally inspected the ridge Bourdiol could not decide between a tunnel and an open cut but ventured an estimate for either project of about $34,000,000.

The first published suggestion for a canal running southeast towards the Atrato River instead of northeast to Caledonia Bay appeared in a pamphlet issued in 1864 by a French naval lieutenant, Henry Bionne, who tentatively proposed a waterway from Darién Harbor up the Tuyra to the mouth of the Paya, up that tributary to some point near the summit of the divide, across the ridge through the most convenient pass, and down the Arquia River to the Atrato. Bionne did not claim to have visited this region and admitted that much of it was unexplored; he merely pointed out that the route deserved investigation. The suggestion brought almost immediate results. In 1865 Lucien de Puydt reported the discovery of a gap only 150 feet above sea level between the headwaters of the Pucro and those of the Tanela, a small stream flowing into the Gulf of Urabá at the northern edge of the Atrato delta, and proposed a sea level canal along this line with an Atlantic terminus on the little bay of Puerto Escondido a few miles north of the Tanela's mouth. But de Puydt's figures aroused suspicion when he confessed that he had not actually reached the pass but had merely computed its elevation theoretically by measuring the velocity of the stream some distance lower down.

A more elaborate though not much more reliable survey was organized the same year by Anthoine de Gogorza, a United States citizen residing in Cartagena. In 1864 he had visited Spain and

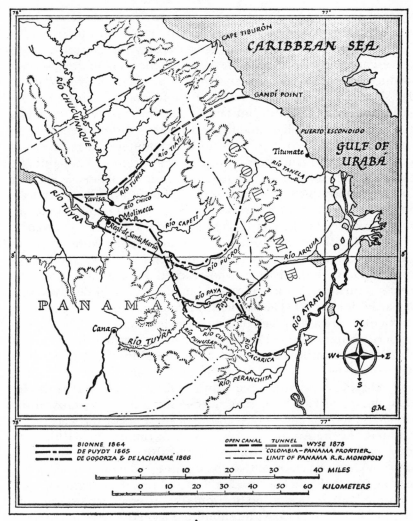

12. DARIÉN PROJECTS

Río Tuyra — Gulf of Urabá Section

copied a number of eighteenth-century maps and documents, including those prepared by Milla in 1788, which led him to believe that a low pass existed somewhere between the upper tributaries of the Tuyra and the lower tributaries of the Atrato. Armed with this information he enlisted the financial support of a group of French capitalists, including the directors of the Compagnie Générale Transatlantique, and in November 1865 arrived at Panama, where he was met by the steamship company's representative, Jules Flachat, an engineer employed on public works on the French island of Guadeloupe. Since de Gogorza's party was not yet ready to leave Panama Flachat, whose leave of absence was limited, set out at once with three companions on a preliminary tour of Darién. He sketchily explored the Tuyra and a few of its principal tributaries for about a month but lacked the time to advance as far as the main divide. What he did see discouraged him; he found no indication of a deep depression in the mountain range and held out little hope for a transit through that region: "Without the slightest fear of error . . . I maintain that a canal . . . without locks is impossible. . . ." [18] Or if possible it would cost at least $120,000,000 and take 20 years to build. A lock canal, he thought, might conceivably be constructed for $60,000,000 or $70,000,000.

The steamship line, chilled by Flachat's report, withdrew from the enterprise; but de Gogorza had already summoned another engineer, Louis de Lacharme, who reached Panama just after Flachat's return to Guadeloupe. On January 12, 1866 de Lacharme departed for Darién Harbor with instructions to investigate with particular care a supposed pass near the headwaters of the Cuë, an upper tributary of the Tuyra; but when he reached the mouth of the Paya some miles below the Cuë he found the elevation already 145 feet above sea level. Obviously the Cuë must lie even higher, so Lacharme decided to follow up the Paya instead. From the Indian village of Paya near that river's source the party crossed the divide on foot in eight hours to the headwaters of the Cacarica, a tributary of the Atrato, where the lack of canoes obliged them to turn back. De Lacharme computed the altitude of the summit at only 290 feet and claimed that the dividing ridge interposed a barrier not more than a few hundred feet in breadth — a gross miscalculation both vertically and horizontally. After an exploration consuming in all but 14 days he submitted a report recommending a lock canal to run in a straight line from a point on the Tuyra near the village of Real de Santa María to the village of Paya, where it would bend sharply towards the south and connect with the Cacarica on the Atlantic slope.

De Gogorza carried de Lacharme's report to the United States, where he succeeded in arousing sufficient interest to secure the appointment of a Coast Survey employee, R. E. Halter, to verify the results of the previous examinations. In January 1867 de Lacharme was again called to Panama to join this new expedition; but before he arrived Halter's assistant, Robinson, fell ill, the American party returned to the United States, and the exploration was abandoned.

De Gogorza then went to France and for a decade carried on an energetic campaign in behalf of his project.

In the Davis report of 1866 Darién occupied more space than any of the other potential canal sites: "It is to the isthmus of Darien that we are first to look for the solution of the great problem of an interoceanic canal." [19] When the United States naval surveys were organized in 1870 the Darién party was in fact the first to start. In anticipation of a favorable report by the naval expedition and the probable ratification of the Hurlbut treaty with Colombia, the Darién Canal Company of America was provisionally organized to build a canal between Caledonia Bay and Darién Harbor. In 1870 the company announced a little prematurely: "One great feature of this line is, that locks, artificial harbors and embankments are dispensed with. . . . It is estimated that the [cost] . . . will not exceed seventy million dollars. . . ." [20] The failure of the treaty and the naval experts' adverse findings blasted the company's hopes, and nothing was done to carry out the plan.

The naval expedition to Darién, consisting of Commanders Selfridge and Lull, 33 officers and technicians, and about 250 sailors and marines, reached Caledonia Bay on February 21, 1870 and devoted two months to careful surveys of the Atlantic watershed. Nowhere did they discover a sign of Cullen's pass or of any depression in the range less than 1000 feet above sea level, nor could they locate at any point a supply of water adequate to fill a lock canal of large dimensions. Selfridge had intended to carry his surveys all the way across the isthmus but changed his mind when he learned that the steamer *Nyack*, ordered to co-operate with him on the Pacific side, had been delayed at Callao. The hitch actually made little difference; since the practicability of the canal route depended upon the discovery of a low pass through the divide near the Atlantic, and since it was now well established that no such pass existed, further exploration would have accomplished nothing of value. When the *Nyack* finally reached Darién Harbor on April 13 Lieutenant Commander Eastman undertook an independent survey of the Sabana River as far as the mouth of the Lara; but by the time he heard of the ship's arrival Selfridge had completed his work at Caledonia Bay and shifted his own force to the next region to be surveyed, the Isthmus of San Blas.

Although the Cuna remained sullenly suspicious the formidable size of the expedition, the presence of armed marines to guard the working parties, and the rigid discipline maintained by Selfridge prevented an open clash: "The most peremptory orders were given

. . . that the property of the Indians should be perfectly respected. Fruit of no kind was to be picked without their consent; their villages were not to be entered; and any outrage of their women would be visited with the severest punishment. These orders were strictly enforced . . . and it was doubtless from this cause, and the show of force and vigilance displayed, that we never met with any unfriendly act. . . ." [21] Selfridge described the Cuna as "much lower in stature than the North American Indians, being rarely . . . over five feet six inches in height. They are a muscular race, capable of great exertion. . . . They are very peaceable in their natures, and I could learn of no conflict between the villages, but yet independent and resolute against foreigners. . . . They are exceedingly averse to labor, except the little required in the cultivation of their fields, and no assistance from this source would be obtained for the work of the canal. . . . During our stay . . . no women were ever met with, and upon our approach they were always removed from the villages. . . . Their independence . . . prevents the use of presents to any extent. . . . Individuals would refuse to receive gifts, until they had obtained the permission of their head-men, and I could never prevail upon any of the chiefs to accept anything in my official capacity. . . . As a whole, this tribe are cowardly, but treacherous. . . ." [22] Their favorite but not very effective stratagem had not changed since the days of Columbus: "The sole desire of each community was to get rid of us; and if they could succeed in directing our attention elsewhere, they were very willing to tell any stories that would take us away. This was my universal experience; each village insisting that no pass or path existed in their vicinity, but telling us of others, whose people were equally persistent in denying. . . ." [23]

In January 1870 a French company organized to execute de Gogorza's canal project requested an American army officer, Brevet Brigadier General Wilhelm Heine, military attaché at the United States legation in Paris, to inspect the Darién route. When Heine reached Caledonia Bay in March Selfridge delegated two members of his own party to accompany him to the Atrato delta and across the divide to Paya, but they were unable to procure canoes or native boatmen and returned without having set foot on shore. Notwithstanding this reverse General Heine was quite satisfied, merely from a single brief glimpse of the distant range, that the pass indicated by de Gogorza and de Lacharme really existed. In August 1871 he announced his "verification" in a lecture delivered before the Congrès des Sciences Géographiques, Cosmographiques et Commerciales at Antwerp: "On the evening of March 13 [1870]

. . . the clouds . . . dispersed and the setting sun distinctly outlined the profile [of the ridge]. We were at anchor in the Gulf of
Urabá, at a distance of 10 to 12 miles from these mountains. . . .
Towards the west-south-west the mountains disappeared completely. . . . A rise of 200 feet would have been clearly visible. . . ." [24] And on the following day Heine added pompously:
"At last the truth about the Isthmus of Darién is revealed by M. de
Gogorza's discovery. Doubt is no longer possible." [25] Deeply impressed, the erudite geographers thereupon adopted and vigorously applauded a resolution: "The congress recommends the
achievement of this savant [de Gogorza] to the attention of the great
maritime powers and of all scientific societies." [26]

In December 1870 a second naval éxpedition, again commanded
by Selfridge and Lull, sailed to the Gulf of Urabá to investigate the
Atrato routes. This time most of the marines were left at home,
since the Atrato Indians were known to be much more friendly and
hospitable than the Cuna. From the gulf Selfridge sent several detachments into the interior to survey the passes recommended by
Bionne, de Puydt, de Gogorza, and de Lacharme. One party followed de Puydt's route up the Tanela in search of his mythical 150-
foot gap. At a point 33 miles above the Tanela's mouth the appearance of a band of Cuna Indians plus a shortage of provisions forced
the Americans to turn back, but they had already reached an altitude of 638 feet, and the crest still lay several miles ahead. "This
survey," Selfridge reported, "completely explodes Mr. De Puydt's
story. I never believed it, but ordered the survey . . . that there
might be no lingering doubts. . . ." [27] Other groups explored the
valleys of the Cacarica and Peranchita on the Atlantic side and
of the Paya, Cuë, and Tuyra on the Pacific slope. They conclusively
disproved the existence of any gap as low as the 290 feet announced
by de Lacharme, but near the headwaters of the Cacarica they did
locate one pass only 410 feet above the sea. This might have seemed
promising had not an examination of the Pacific side of the ridge
and the Tuyra basin convinced Selfridge that excavation of a canal
through the broken terrain would be preposterously expensive.

The Interoceanic Canal Commission gave scant consideration
to any of the Darién routes, dismissing them all briefly as impracticable; but that did not immediately exclude them from further
competition. The Darién explorations undertaken in 1876 and
1878 by Lieutenant Wyse will be described later, as they form part
of the history of the French era. In 1898 the transit cropped up
again in a petition addressed to Congress by Thomas Wright Hurst
of Chicago. Supporting his argument with copious quotations from

Cullen, Airiau, and "other high authorities," [28] Hurst recommended the formation of a Darién Ship Canal Company to dig a canal between Darién Harbor and Caledonia Bay, but the project received no encouragement.

Although the second Walker commission organized in 1899 devoted most of its attention to Panama and Nicaragua it assigned six surveying parties to an investigation of the San Blas and Darién regions. The elevation of the lowest point of the ridge, Caledonia Gap, was found to be 681 feet. The commission formulated tentative plans for a sea level canal from the junction of the Sabana and Lara Rivers to Caledonia Bay and selected three alternative routes. The total cost of a canal on the Caledonia River line with a tunnel 4 miles long was computed at $320,040,000; on the Aglaseniquá, tunnel 3.6 miles, $283,440,000; on the Sasardí, tunnel 1.6 miles, $263,340,000. Since all these estimates were very much higher than those for either Panama or Nicaragua the commission advised the elimination of the Darién projects. No attempt to revive them has since been made.

Chapter 22. San Blas

THE SLIMMEST portion of the entire isthmus connecting North and South America is the San Blas region between Panama and Darién. From the mouth of the Bayano (also called Chepo) River on the Pacific coast to Mandinga Bay on the Atlantic the breadth of the land barrier is not more than 30 miles. Here the crest of the divide lies near the Atlantic, though it does not hug the shore quite as closely as in Darién. Here too the Indians of the Atlantic coast hindered exploration during the nineteenth century and even today maintain their isolation, but the Pacific slope, dotted with white settlements and plantations, is much less primitive than the corresponding area of Darién. As a canal site the Isthmus of San Blas possesses one outstanding advantage, the extreme shortness of the overland transit, and one paramount drawback, the altitude of the cordillera, 1000 to 1500 feet in height. The most prominent feature of every project for a San Blas canal is a long tunnel through this ridge.

The earliest record of an attempted exploration of this territory was made by William Wheelwright, who sailed into Mandinga Bay about 1837 with the intention of crossing "the *terra incognita* of the Isthmus" [1] to the Pacific. Although the Indians turned him back at the very start a glance at the unbroken range convinced him that the country was unsuitable for a canal. That opinion was not shared by the English engineer Evan Hopkins and his New Granadian colleague Hurtado, commissioned by the government of New Granada to explore and roughly survey the isthmus in 1847. Starting from the mouth of the Bayano they examined a large area on the Pacific slope but were refused permission by the Indians to continue their journey to the Atlantic. From what he had seen, however, Hopkins concluded that San Blas was second only to Panama as a canal route. A little later another Englishman, Laurence Oliphant, spent a few days at the town of Chepo but proceeded no farther inland. There he heard tales of a regular system of interoceanic canoe portages similar to those rumored to exist on the Raspadura, Cupica, and other divides: "Surely it is a discredit to the civilization of the 19th century that . . . we should never have had the curiosity to verify this. . . . The lower spurs of the Cordillera extended to this point [Chepo], so that we could judge of . . . a very remarkable depression . . . not more than ten miles distant, but which had never been visited. That such could be the case seemed scarcely credible; yet it was fully accounted for by the . . . character of the . . . Indians. . . ." [2] But when Colonel Hughes, director of the Panama Railroad surveys, visited Mandinga Bay in 1849 he satisfied himself "from personal inspection and inquiry . . . that all that had been said about large canoes having been taken over this country, from the Atlantic to the Pacific, was *fabulous*. Occasionally a *pit-pan* (a small canoe that two men might carry) may have been thus transported; but nothing more. . . ." [3] Oliphant's "remarkable depression," like so many similar gaps reported elsewhere in the cordillera, was proved by later investigations to be much higher than a distant view had led the observer to believe.

The first determined effort to complete an accurate survey of the San Blas area from sea to sea was made in 1864 under the direction of the generous — and in spite of his disappointments in the Atrato region, still hopeful — Frederick M. Kelley, who appointed Angus McDougal chief engineer of the expedition and engaged Charles A. Sweet, J. E. Forman, and Norman Rude to assist him. This time the attempt to cross the isthmus was almost but not quite successful. From the Pacific coast the party carried their survey to within two miles of the Atlantic before they were stopped by the Indians and forced to return. Guessing at the topography of this short and relatively flat unexplored section, the four engineers submitted a plan for a canal 25 feet deep, 100 feet wide, and 27.58 miles long, with 7 miles of tunnel through the cordillera. Two locks would be required: one at the Atlantic entrance, the other at the cut-off across the horseshoe bend of the Bayano.

In April 1870 Selfridge's naval expedition, having completed its survey of the Caledonia Bay region, moved to the Gulf of San Blas, "a most magnificent bay, with deep passages, fine anchorage, and perfectly protected from the north winds in the dry season." [4] No member of the party crossed all the way to the Pacific, but several groups explored the Atlantic ridge thoroughly, filled in the coastal area left unmapped by Kelley's engineers in 1864, and carried the survey down the Pacific side as far as the confluence of the San José and Mamoní Rivers. Selfridge reported that the steepness of the divide, the ruggedness of the country, and the presence of cascades in the Mandinga River "entirely explode the old tradition . . . that the Indians used to sell at Chepo, on the Pacific, in the

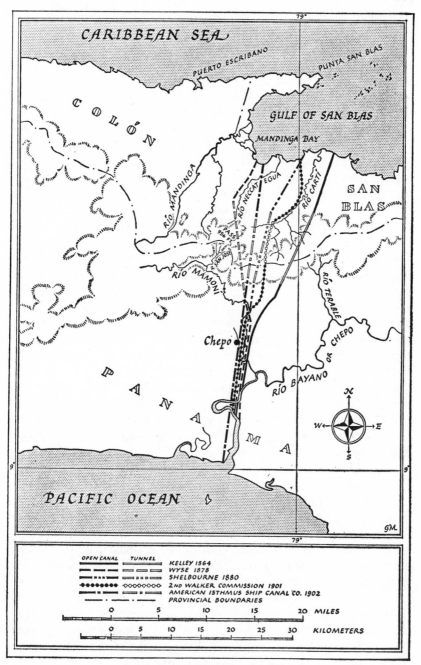

CARIBBEAN SEA

PUERTO ESCRIBANO

PUNTA SAN BLAS

GULF OF SAN BLAS

MANDINGA BAY

COLÓN

RÍO MANDINGA

RÍO NECCA EGUA

RÍO CARTI

SAN BLAS

RÍO MAMONI

SAN JOSE

RÍO TERABLE

Chepo

RÍO BAYANO

OR CHEPO

PANAMA

N
W E
S

PACIFIC OCEAN

GM.

OPEN CANAL	TUNNEL	
		KELLEY 1864
		WYSE 1878
		SHELBOURNE 1880
		2ND WALKER COMMISSION 1901
		AMERICAN ISTHMUS SHIP CANAL CO. 1902
		PROVINCIAL BOUNDARIES

0   5   10   15   20 MILES

0   5   10   15   20   25   30   KILOMETERS

13. SAN BLAS PROJECTS

afternoon, fish caught the preceding day in the Atlantic. . . ." [5] He found that a sea level canal would require a tunnel of impossible length, much longer than the one contemplated in the Kelley project, and even for a canal with a summit level 190 feet above the sea a tunnel 10 miles long would be indispensable. A canal without a tunnel was equally unthinkable, for even if a sufficient number of locks could be constructed to raise the canal to the preposterous altitude of 1100 feet there were no streams at that elevation large enough to supply it with water. Yet he acknowledged that while the San Blas route "is neither practicable for a through-cut [sea level] canal from the length of tunneling, nor for one with a system of lockage . . . it is a question whether a canal combining . . . lockage and tunneling could not be constructed, from the shortness of this line, at a less expense than upon other routes. . . . I will enter into no calculation of the cost. . . ." [6]

In March 1875 Lull and Menocal interrupted their survey of the Panama route to make a hasty inspection of the lower course of the Bayano, taking soundings of the river bed for a distance of about 20 miles from its mouth and finding many shallow spots but no suitable location for a dam. Accordingly Lull turned in an adverse report: "A tunnel of even five miles in length would . . . cost between $80,000,000 and $100,000,000. The Bayano River cannot be utilized, and an independent canal would have to be built from the end of the tunnel to the sea. The line possesses but two good features, one the magnificent harbor afforded by the Gulf of San Blas, the other the short distance from sea to sea. . . . These . . . compensate but slightly for the enormous disadvantages. The line bears no comparison with either . . . Nicaragua . . . or . . . Panama. . . ." [7]

Even after the Interoceanic Canal Commission voted for Nicaragua in 1876 a few faithful adherents clung tenaciously to the San Blas project. In 1880 Major Sidney F. Shelbourne urged the adoption of Kelley's plan with slight alterations, and in the same year an American civil engineer, Walton W. Evans, made a not very convincing attempt to establish the superiority of the San Blas transit. With what seems like curious perversity Evans was "inclined to think that the tunnel is one of the best features of the whole route; it will cost, no doubt, a rousing big sum, but . . . it will be the surest and safest portion . . . it will be through solid rock, and remain forever intact, requiring little or no repairs." [8] Nothing more was heard of the San Blas canal until the turn of the century, when the second Walker commission sent a party to survey the ridge. The commission concluded that a sea level canal with a tunnel 4.5 miles long, similar in design and dimensions to the tunnels proposed for the Darién projects, could be constructed for $289,-770,000; but the estimates for Panama and Nicaragua were so much lower that the San Blas route could not compete.

The San Blas project was suggested for the last time by the American Isthmus Ship Canal Company, which announced its plans for a sea level waterway in 1902 and appealed to the United States government to guarantee its securities. A year later the aged Edward W. Serrell, who as a surveyor for the Panama Railroad in 1850 had condemned the Panama route as utterly hopeless for a canal and in 1855 had approved Kennish's Truandó canal scheme, issued a pamphlet in support of the new plan. As Kelley's consulting engineer Serrell had recommended the San Blas project as early as 1864, and he had never ceased to sing its praises, tunnel and all. Now in 1903 he outlined a modification of the original design of 1864 in which he proposed to eliminate all curves and carry the canal in a straight line across the isthmus, reduce the length of the tunnel to 5 miles, and do away with tide locks. The tunnel was to be ventilated by three vertical shafts, and to eliminate smoke steamers would be towed through by electric trolleys. Serrell estimated the cost at $100,000,000 and the time required for construction at only three years. But the government refused to take the project seriously and forged ahead with its own plans for the Panama canal.

Chapter 23. Chiriquí

ALTHOUGH the excessive breadth and elevation of the western extremity of the present republic of Panama always excluded it from consideration as a canal route it enjoyed a certain measure of popularity as a site for highway and railroad transits, naval coaling stations, and colonization projects. Its most valuable assets were its excellent natural harbors: on the Atlantic coast, Chiriquí Lagoon enclosed within a rampart of jutting peninsulas and conveniently placed islands, and the adjoining smaller but equally well protected Almirante Bay; on the Pacific, the deep and spacious Golfo Dulce. From Chiriquí Lagoon to Golfo Dulce the distance in a straight line is slightly less than 70 miles; to Boca de San Pedro, a much smaller inlet near the town of David, something under 50 miles. The interior of the isthmus is a broad plateau almost 5000 feet high with no gap in the divide lower than 3600 feet above the sea. Chiriquí bears little resemblance to the eastern and central sections of the republic. The country is relatively open with much good agricultural and grazing land and few areas of dense jungle growth. Rainfall is moderate, the upland climate cool and bracing. The district contains extensive deposits of coal.

Development of this potentially rich area has been retarded by various causes, among them a persistent boundary dispute between Costa Rica and Colombia which the republic of Panama inherited in 1903. Attempts were made in 1825, 1856, 1865, and 1876 to settle the conflict by direct treaty, but all ended in failure. In 1880 Costa Rica and Colombia agreed to submit the dispute to the arbitration of Alfonso XII of Spain, but when the king died five years later nothing had been accomplished. In 1896 the contestants named the President of France arbitrator, and on September 11, 1900 President Loubet outlined a vague frontier based on inaccurate maps and contradictory data furnished by the rival governments. Irreconcilable interpretations of the Loubet award kept the quarrel alive, and after the separation of Panama from Colombia prolonged negotiations resulted in the appointment in 1911 of Edward D. White, Chief Justice of the United States Supreme Court, as mediator. On September 12, 1914 White fixed a boundary giving

Costa Rica most of the disputed territory. Panama promptly rejected the decision, but no further efforts were made to adjudicate the controversy until after the close of the first World War. On February 21, 1921 a small detachment of Costa Rican troops occupied part of the frontier area on the Pacific until then provisionally administered by Panama, and after Panamanian forces had recaptured the district further hostilities were prevented by the intervention of the United States. Secretary of State Charles Evans Hughes reaffirmed the White award, but Panama continued to protest. On May 1, 1941 Costa Rica and Panama concluded a treaty designed to end once and for all the 120-year-old quarrel.

Some time between 1830 and 1840 Wheelwright made a superficial investigation of the Chiriquí coal fields but found them too inaccessible to serve as a source of fuel supply for his projected Pacific Steam Navigation Company. He penetrated into the interior no farther than the town of David, where he heard but hesitated to believe rumors of a deep depression in the ridge suitable for interoceanic communication. His skepticism was well warranted, for this turned out to be one more of those ubiquitous mythical passes. In 1839 a British naval officer, Captain Edward Barnett, carefully explored the Chiriquí Lagoon in the frigate *Thunder*. Captains Colombel and Lallier of the French navy charted the Pacific harbor of Golfo Dulce in 1851, and a year later another French officer, Admiral Odet Pellion, verified their enthusiastic reports. These official expeditions touched only the fringes of the isthmus; investigation of the interior was left to private initiative.

In October 1849 the Costa Rican government granted to Gabriel Lafond, director of a French insurance company, authorization to establish a colony on the shores of Golfo Dulce and the concession of approximately 70,000 acres of arable land on or near the Pacific coast. On March 10, 1850 a second charter gave him the right to construct and operate a transit across the isthmus "as near as may be practicable to the frontiers of New Grenada. . . ." [1] The wording was unfortunate, for the two states had never been able to agree on those frontiers. Lafond requested Jacques de Courtines, Garella's associate in the Panama survey of 1843, to advise the company concerning the Chiriquí transit. The engineer recommended three successive steps: the construction of a narrow mule path, then a road of moderate width, and finally a broad highway or a railroad. Lacking confidence in the vigor of French enterprise, de Courtines urged Lafond "to beware of an exclusive patriotism in this affair, and to receive . . . propositions . . . from whatever quarter they may come. . . ." [2] The promoter accepted the advice and secured

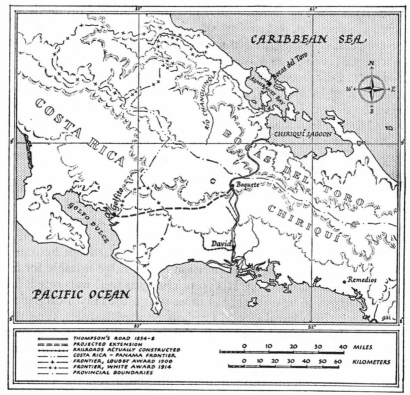

14. ISTHMUS OF CHIRIQUÍ

the financial support of a British corporation organized as the Atlantic and Pacific Junction and Costa Rica Colonisation Company, which sent an English engineer, James B. Cooke, to make a thorough examination of the transit route in 1852.

It is not easy to understand what advantage other than a more salubrious climate the long and mountainous Chiriquí transit could have offered to counterbalance the shortness and accessibility of the Panama canoe-and-mule route already in use, and it is still more difficult to perceive how Chiriquí could have been expected to compete successfully after the opening of the Panama Railroad. A share in the gold rush traffic was no doubt a tempting bait, but the profits of the Chiriquí road, like those of the Nicaragua transit, obviously had to be garnered during the few years remaining before the completion of the railroad. Yet the British company made no progress towards the improvement of an interoceanic communication, though it did establish the nucleus of a colony on its Golfo Dulce property, imported 150 settlers, and erected a few buildings.

In February 1854 Ambrose W. Thompson, an American citizen, purchased the Lafond concession, combined it with another grant in the Bocas del Toro section of the Atlantic coast, and incorporated the Chiriquí Improvement Company. Including the right of way across the isthmus the lands owned by the Chiriquí Improvement Company totaled about 170,000 acres, granted in part by Costa Rica and in part by the local governments of two New Granadian provinces, Chiriquí and Bocas del Toro. Nearly all of the property was in the disputed area, but by a special clause in the treaty of 1865 Costa Rica and New Granada agreed to respect concessions already made by either to private companies or individuals no matter where the final frontier might be determined. The company also had the right to colonize, to operate coal and other mines, and to construct a small canal from Almirante Bay to the Changuinola River in order to open up the Atlantic coastal region. In return the company engaged to construct and maintain a highway between the Chiriquí Lagoon and David, and in 1855 it secured the privilege of extending the road to the Pacific port of Golfito on Golfo Dulce. The Panama Railroad Company contested the legality of the Chiriquí right of way, claiming that no highway or railroad could be built anywhere across the isthmus without its consent, but the Chiriquí Improvement Company insisted that the prohibition could not be applied to its proposed transit since a footpath already connected David with the Atlantic coast, and the railroad's charter gave it no power to prevent the improvement of an existing communication.

By January 1858 the company had opened a mule path from the Atlantic to David, and in September Captain John J. Almy, U.S.N., reported to Secretary of the Navy Isaac Toucey that "the importance of Chiriqui lagoon in a national, naval, and maritime point of view generally, cannot be over estimated in the eyes of any nation aiming at ascendancy in the Central American States." [3] On May 21, 1859 Toucey signed a provisional contract, subject to ratification by Congress, with the Chiriquí Improvement Company giving the United States government 5000 acres of land on each coast for coal depots and naval stations, harbor privileges in waters wholly or partially surrounded by company lands, the right to mine coal, and free transit over the proposed highway for government troops, employees, property, and mails. For these concessions the United States agreed to pay a lump sum of $300,000. The Senate approved the contract, but opposition developed in the House. While a majority of the House Committee on Naval Affairs favored the project several members submitted a minority report attacking it on the grounds that the company's title was doubtful, its coal mines undeveloped, its harbor rights nonexistent, and its road unbuilt, so that Thompson had "nothing to grant to this government which it is an object to buy. . . . A mule probably could go over with such a mail as they would be likely to have from Boca del Toro to David, where there are no inhabitants at all at one end of the route, and none who can read or write at the other. . . ." [4] The House voted to postpone approval until a naval commission could investigate. The commission, headed by Captain Frederick Engle, arrived in August 1860, explored the isthmus for two months, and handed in an enthusiastic report.

The outbreak of the Civil War prevented further discussion of the project, but when Congress emancipated the slaves in the District of Columbia in April 1862 it occurred to President Lincoln that Chiriquí might provide a suitable refuge for those freedmen who wished to emigrate. Here was a sparsely populated, apparently fertile, potentially rich tropical region with ample resources — according to the reports of the Engle expedition — to support a large colony of Negroes under more favorable conditions than they would be likely to encounter anywhere in the United States. Caleb Smith, Secretary of the Interior, wrote to Ambrose Thompson on April 26: "By act of Congress . . . provision is made to aid in the colonization . . . of such free persons of African descent . . . as may desire to emigrate . . . and I desire to know whether you would undertake their . . . settlement on the lands of the Chiriqui Improvement Company . . . and, if so, upon what terms. . . ." [5] Before any details could be arranged Lincoln reached his momentous decision to extend emancipation to all slaves in the seceded states, and the problem of the disposal of this vast multitude of Negroes to be freed by proclamation on January 1, 1863 suddenly became acute. Lincoln brought the Chiriquí project to the attention of his Cabinet in September 1862. Edward Bates, the Attorney General, and Montgomery Blair, the Postmaster General, favored compulsory deportation, but Lincoln insisted upon voluntary emigration. Secretary of the Navy Gideon Welles, convinced that the Chiriquí Improvement Company was a swindle and its title fraudulent, vigorously opposed the entire scheme. Salmon P. Chase and Edwin M. Stanton, respectively Secretaries of the Treasury and War, supported Welles; and Bates and Blair, who had at first approved the plan, soon changed their minds. Of all the Cabinet members only Smith manifested any real enthusiasm for Chiriquí either as a colony or a source of coal.

In this crisis Lincoln and Smith received unexpected encouragement from Samuel C. Pomeroy, an abolitionist senator from Kansas, who volunteered to escort a pioneer colony of free Negroes to Chiriquí, supervise the first settlement, and investigate the coal situation. On September 12, 1862 Smith signed and Lincoln approved a contract with Thompson for the provisional assignment of 2,000,000 acres of land for the colony's use. Pomeroy issued circulars calling upon free Negroes to join the proposed colony and received — according to Thompson — some 12,000 applications; but the departure was delayed because doubt still existed with regard to the attitude of the New Granadian and Costa Rican governments. Soon after the proclamation of general emancipation Lincoln decided to enlist as many freedmen as possible in the Union armies and to postpone his plan for voluntary settlement outside of the United States.

A few weeks before the war ended Lincoln again turned his attention to the problem of Negro emigration. When General Benjamin F. Butler pointed out that there were not enough ships in the United States to transport the entire colored population "half as fast as negro children will be born here," [6] the President suggested that merely the emigration of the Negro soldiers might help to avert race riots after the war. Butler thereupon submitted a specific proposal: "We have now enlisted one hundred and fifty thousand negro troops. . . . Now I have had some experience in digging canals. . . . The United States wants a ship canal across the Isthmus of Darien. . . . Now, I know of a concession made by . . . Colombia . . . for that purpose. I have the confidence of the negroes. If you will put me in command of them, I will take them down there and dig the canal. It will cost the United States nothing but their pay. . . . I should set one third of them to digging. I should set another third to building . . . shelter and the rest to planting . . . and raising food. . . . After we get ourselves established we will petition Congress . . . to send . . . our wives and children. . . . We shall thus form a colony there which will protect the canal and the interests of the United States. . . ." [7] Lincoln asked Butler to present the suggestion to the Secretary of State, but Seward's injury in a runaway accident on April 5, 1865 delayed consideration of the project, and Lincoln's assassination a few days later stopped it altogether. In the end no mass migration of American Negroes ever took place. Butler failed to specify just which canal concession he referred to, but presumably he meant either de Gogorza's plan for a Darién waterway or Kelley's scheme for a canal across the Isthmus of San Blas.

About 1880 French preparations to build a canal at Panama re-vived the interest of the United States in the establishment of naval stations and coal depots in Chiriquí. Although no colonization or mining had been carried out under the contract of 1862 the con-tract itself was still apparently in force, and President Hayes now proposed to make use of it. The legality of the contract depended largely upon the continued validity of Thompson's original con-cession, which in turn hinged upon the extent to which he had ob-served its conditions. In September 1879 Captain Richard W. Meade "ascertained beyond cavil that . . . Thompson had in no wise complied with the terms of his bargain. . . . My own opin-ion is that the thing was a swindle from the *very beginning*." [8] This was but the first of a series of discouraging reports. The isthmus that had seemed so desirable to American naval officers in 1860 be-came a target for their successors' scorn. Commander Henry F. Picking, who visited the Atlantic coast of Chiriquí in 1880, wrote: "There is nothing of the nature of a road between the Chiriqui La-goon and the Pacific Ocean, and the trail is so . . . difficult that . . . an attempt made by a correspondent of the New York *Herald* to pass over to David, had to be abandoned. . . ." [9] Rear Admiral Robert H. Wyman reported: "Almirante Bay is . . . a fine an-chorage and nothing more. . . . No place on the isthmus could, in my opinion, be less desirable as a coaling station. . . . The law officers of . . . Colombia have decided . . . that the conditions of the grant to Mr. Thompson were not fulfilled, and that the con-tract is void." [10] Although Congress had already appropriated $200,-000 for the establishment of coaling stations on Chiriquí Lagoon and Golfo Dulce the Navy Department, impressed by so many ad-verse comments, declined to spend the money, and the whole proj-ect collapsed.

PART III

The French Era

Chapter 24. The Wyse Concessions

OUR years after the Congrès des Sciences Géographiques, Cosmographiques et Commerciales at Antwerp recommended
de Gogorza's canal project to the attention of all maritime
powers a similar conference of savants met in Paris from August
1 to 11, 1875 under the auspices of the Société de Géographie de
Paris. One group of delegates discussed at some length the problem
of an interoceanic waterway. Bionne, de Puydt, and de Gogorza appeared in person to present their respective Darién plans; Joseph
E. Nourse, professor at the United States Naval Observatory, described the Lull-Menocal projects for lock canals at Panama and
Nicaragua; and Ferdinand de Lesseps gave a short history of the
recently completely Suez canal. De Lesseps hoped that it would be
possible to construct the canal through the American isthmus without locks. He was not yet ready to select any one particular route,
but "if he had to express a preference it would be, in agreement
with Humboldt, for one of the projects contemplating a cut
through the Isthmus of Darién." [1] Here he betrayed his unfamiliarity with Humboldt's writings; the frequently misquoted German
scientist had scarcely mentioned Darién and had not included it in
his list of nine communications. Although the reports of Selfridge's
Darién, San Blas, and Atrato expeditions were published in 1874
they do not appear to have been available to the geographic congress, or if available they were wholly ignored. De Gogorza did refer to the United States naval surveys but only to assert that the altitudes of various passes computed by his own agent, de Lacharme,
were "very nearly the same as those observed by the engineers of
the American expedition" [2] — certainly a wide deviation from the
truth.

On March 24, 1876 the Société Géographique de Paris appointed
a committee to invite all of the important geographical societies in
the world to send delegates to an international canal convention
and to defray jointly the expenses of a definitive exploration of the
different routes. Léon Drouillet, a member of the committee, suggested the use of captive balloons to obtain general views of the
topography — an interesting prefiguration of today's airplane re-

connaissances. The ability and disposition of international scientific organizations to finance the survey were never put to the test, for at this point a private company, the Société Civile Internationale du Canal Interocéanique du Darién, offered to undertake the exploration at its own expense. The company's directors included its president, General Étienne Türr, Lieutenant Lucien Napoléon-Bonaparte Wyse of the French navy, and Baron Jacques de Reinach. Türr, a Hungarian, had known de Lesseps for many years. The most active member of the association was Wyse, an illegitimate son of Princess Lætitia Bonaparte, daughter of Napoleon's brother Lucien and wife of Sir Thomas Wyse, an Irish author, diplomat, and politician. Although he used the name of Wyse the lieutenant was not Sir Thomas's son; he was born in 1847, nineteen years after his mother's legal separation from her husband. Sir Thomas and the princess were not divorced, but they never met after their separation. Türr and Wyse were connected by family ties as well as by business interests, for the general had married the lieutenant's sister Adeline.

The company immediately sent de Gogorza to Bogotá to obtain a provisional concession, which he secured on May 28, 1876. Since the charter of 1867 entitled the Panama Railroad Company to compensation for the construction of a canal west of a line connecting Cape Tiburón and Point Garachiné the French society hoped to evade both the complication and the expense of a settlement with the railroad by confining its initial surveys to the region east of that line. On November 7, 1876 Wyse sailed with his chief assistant, Lieutenant Armand Reclus, and 15 technicians. At Panama they were joined by Pedro Sosa and A. Balfour, engineers appointed by the Colombian government, and Louis de Lacharme. From Darién Harbor Wyse and a few companions ascended the Tuyra and Paya Rivers, crossed the divide to the Gulf of Urabá, visited the long-abandoned mines at Cana, and examined several tributaries of the Chucunaque, while auxiliary groups searched in vain for other low passes through the watershed. At the beginning of the rainy season in April the whole party returned to Paris. Almost all had suffered severely from fever, two had died in Darién, and a third succumbed at sea on the homeward voyage.

Wyse brought back a most discouraging report. He had found no gap low enough to permit the construction of a canal without a tunnel, and although he submitted two projects he displayed little enthusiasm for either. One called for a sea level canal about 35 miles long from the Tuyra River to the confluence of the Chucunaque and Tupisa, up the Tupisa and its tributary the Tiatí, then through the divide by tunnel to an Atlantic terminus near Punta Gandí. Since none of the parties had actually explored the whole of this route Wyse was unable to do more than guess at the length of the tunnel, but it would probably be 8 or 9 miles. He estimated the total cost at about $118,000,000. The alternative project contemplated a somewhat less expensive though much longer canal by way of the Tuyra, Cuë, and Cacarica Rivers to the Atrato with a tunnel only 2300 feet in length and five locks on each slope.

Neither solution satisfied de Lesseps, who had set his heart upon a waterway like that at Suez without either locks or tunnels. In November 1877 Wyse and several other members of the previous expedition set out a second time with instructions to complete the survey of the Tupisa-Tiatí-Gandí route and to investigate in addition the San Blas and Panama transits, even though these lay within the territory controlled by the Panama Railroad. From Panama the party proceeded first to the mouth of the Bayano River. Two or three weeks of exploration convinced Wyse and his assistants that no canal could be constructed across the Isthmus of San Blas without a tunnel at least 7.5 miles long. They returned to Panama and on December 29, 1877 departed once more for Darién Harbor. Leaving Reclus in charge of the Darién expedition with orders to survey the watershed between the Tiatí River and Punta Gandí, Wyse and Louis Verbrugghe hastened to Colón to meet the *Dupetit-Thouars,* a man-of-war assigned by the French government to assist in the hydrographic survey of the Gulf of Urabá.

The altitudes reported by Reclus combined with those observed by the expedition of the preceding year had now proved beyond question that no canal could be constructed without locks or tunnels — or both — east of the Tiburón-Garachiné line of demarcation. The San Blas route also would necessitate a long tunnel; Blanchet was negotiating for the Nicaragua concession and at that time appeared certain to procure it; Türr and his fellow directors had ruled out the Tehuantepec and Atrato routes as hopelessly impracticable; and the only canal site still open to Wyse was the Isthmus of Panama. Wyse delegated the exploration of this line to Reclus while he himself journeyed to Bogotá to obtain a new charter sufficiently comprehensive to include the Panama transit in place of the limited provisional contract signed by de Gogorza in 1876. During his absence Reclus, Sosa, de Lacharme, and the other technicians commenced an examination of the Pacific slope a few miles east of the railroad, but after a few days Reclus, tormented by a severe earache, called a halt and brought the whole expedition back to Panama.

Yet it was upon this brief and superficial survey that the French
canal company subsequently based its gigantic and costly project.
José Carlos Rodrigues, a correspondent of the New York *World*,
derided the complacency with which the canal promoters accepted
the Reclus report: "It was necessary to play the comedy of science,
and M. Wyse played it . . . in a most grotesque manner. Eighteen
days in Panama were enough for such wonderful geniuses as Commander Reclus and a fifth-rate Colombian engineer [Sosa] to clear
up the scientific mysteries of the isthmus. . . ." [3] The French company did not altogether deserve the sneer. The railroad surveys and
the Lull-Menocal report had already yielded exhaustive and reliable information concerning the topography of this region, and the
French engineers who recommended the Panama route conscientiously studied these sources as well as the results of Reclus's inadequate observations.

Meanwhile Wyse and Verbrugghe set out on February 25 for the
remote Colombian capital, first to Buenaventura by steamer and
then on horseback across the Andes. It was an arduous journey of
almost 500 miles over rough steep trails, but they pressed onward
with practically no rest, on some days spending as much as 22 hours
in the saddle, and reached Bogotá 11 days after they left the coast.
Haste was imperative, for a change of administration was due on
April 1, and Wyse hoped to conclude his contract while Aquileo
Parra, the outgoing President who favored the canal enterprise,
still held office. On March 20, 1878 Wyse and General Salgar, the
Foreign Minister, signed the agreement, the Colombian Senate
confirmed it with minor amendments on May 17, the lower house
followed suit, and the new President, Julián Trujillo, proclaimed
it on May 18.

The Salgar-Wyse contract provided for a 99-year concession and
allowed three years for surveys, two additional years for the organization of the company, and twelve more for the construction
of the canal; but the government might grant a maximum extension of six years. The company bound itself to deposit 750,000
francs with the Colombian government before the end of 1882, and
the republic conceded to the company 500,000 hectares (about
1,235,000 acres) of public lands, including any mines found
therein. Should the canal be located west of the Tiburón-Garachiné line the company undertook to conclude an amicable arrangement with the Panama Railroad and pay that corporation a
suitable indemnity. The company also agreed to pay Colombia 5%
of the gross revenue for the first 25 years of the canal's operation,
6% during the second 25 years, 7% for the third 25 years, and 8%

throughout the final period of the concession. The minimum payment in any one year was to be at least $250,000, the amount Colombia was already receiving from the Panama Railroad Company. At the end of 99 years the entire property except the 500,000 hectares of land would revert to Colombia without compensation. The concession might be transferred to any other private company but not to a foreign government.

With the precious contract in his pocket Wyse returned to Panama, sent Reclus and the other technicians back to Paris, and paid a brief visit to Nicaragua, where Blanchet was still dickering for a canal concession. Reassured by the obvious reluctance of the Nicaraguan government to grant his rival's petition, Wyse proceeded to Washington, interviewed Ammen, Selfridge, Collins, Lull, Menocal, and others officially connected with the canal surveys, and obtained from them sheaves of maps and statistics. He reached Paris on August 11, 1878 and immediately set to work with Reclus on his report. De Lacharme, to whom Wyse had entrusted the compilation of a special report on the Darién routes, died on October 6 with his task unfinished.

Wyse prepared four different projects. For the first, commencing near the mouth of the Tuyra, he proposed two variants, one by way of the Paya and Cacarica to the Atrato, the other by the Cuë. Each would be about 80 miles long with a summit level 164 feet above the sea, requiring 12 locks on the Pacific slope and 10 on the Atlantic, and cost $130,000,000 to $140,000,000. The second project called for a sea level canal 46 miles long from the Tuyra River to Punta Gandí through the valleys of the Tupisa and Tiatí, burrowing under the divide through a 10-mile tunnel and costing $120,000,000. The third plan contemplated a sea level canal 26 miles long across the Isthmus of San Blas with a tunnel 10 miles in length to cost $95,000,000. The fourth project, a sea level canal at Panama, was obviously Wyse's favorite, though he estimated that it would cost at least as much as the San Blas waterway. There were several variants, the cheapest of which would pass through a tunnel 4.79 miles long and cost $95,000,000. Wyse earnestly recommended a modification of this design with deeper open cuts and a tunnel shortened to 3.65 miles, which would add but $3,000,000 to the expense. For $120,000,000 the tunnel might be omitted altogether, but Wyse saw little advantage in its elimination: "The disappearance of the tunnel would be an immense relief to timid souls. Would that compensate . . . for the enormous increase in outlay? . . . One may be permitted to doubt it." [4]

By its contract of 1867 the Panama Railroad Company had the

right to demand compensation for any canal built west of the Tiburón-Garachiné line, though it could not prohibit its construction; but over a canal route that actually trespassed upon its own right of way — in Wyse's opinion the most advantageous of all routes — the railroad held the power of absolute veto. Early in 1879 Wyse returned to the United States to negotiate with the railroad directors, but lacking authority to sign a formal contract he had to content himself with a provisional agreement. The railroad offered three choices: it would lease its line and equipment to the canal promoters, enter into a contract to perform the required work during the canal construction period and then sell the road outright, or sell a majority of its stock at $200 per share as soon as the canal company was definitively organized.

In order to reach a definite decision with regard to the canal route and to choose between a sea level waterway and a lock canal, with tunnels or without, the Société Civile Internationale du Canal Interocéanique du Darien resolved to summon an international congress to meet in Paris in May 1879. From New York Wyse proceeded to Washington and issued a formal invitation to the United States government to participate in the forthcoming conference. Admiral Ammen presented him to President Hayes and to Secretary of the Navy Richard W. Thompson, both of whom expressed willingness to co-operate; but Secretary of State William M. Evarts regarded the proposal with extreme suspicion. Wyse recorded his version of his efforts to win over the hostile Cabinet member: "I had a difficult interview with him. . . . M. Evarts, believing that he could detect the hand of the French government in the projected realization of this great enterprise and not understanding that, on account of my relationship to the imperial family, I actually had to bear the brunt of its [the French republican government's] indifference or even ill will, obstinately refused to appoint two commissioners to the Paris congress. Thereupon I rose and told him firmly that 'I really cared very little about the participation . . . of the United States . . . [and] the congress would meet just the same without it. . . .' M. Evarts . . . then yielded to my arguments and promised to send two official delegates. . . ." [5] His missions accomplished, Wyse returned to Paris and with the now active collaboration of de Lesseps elaborated his projects for presentation to the congress.

Chapter 25. Paris Congress

AÎTRE HENRI BARBOUX, the eloquent lawyer who defended Ferdinand and Charles de Lesseps after the collapse of the Panama canal company, praised the Paris congress of 1879 with impressive fervor: "It seems to me that nothing could have been more glorious . . . than the solemn inauguration of this gigantic enterprise. . . . Might not one think of it as a council ordaining, after the lapse of seven hundred years, a new crusade?" [1]

Many critics of the congress and a few of the delegates called it something very much less holy. They ridiculed it as a farce, denied the competence of most of its members, and accused the chairman, Ferdinand de Lesseps, and his satellites of forcing upon the assembly a hasty ill-considered verdict in favor of a sea level canal. In retrospect it seems obvious enough that its unwise decision contributed largely to the subsequent tragic failure of the undertaking. Yet it would be unjust as well as untrue to imply that fraud played any part in that fateful initial error. There was to be chicanery in plenty, but not at quite so early a stage. The mistake was made in good faith, and of all the misguided but sincere members who voted for the impracticable project none was more high-minded than their influential leader, de Lesseps himself.

For several months before the sessions opened de Lesseps, assisted by Bionne and other members of the Société Géographique de Paris, labored indefatigably to effect the organization of the congress, promulgate rules of procedure, issue invitations, and arrange for the entertainment of the expected visitors. In addition to France and its colonies Algeria and Martinique 22 foreign countries were represented: Austria-Hungary, Belgium, China, Colombia, Costa Rica, Germany, Great Britain, Guatemala, Hawaii (then independent), Holland, Italy, Mexico, Nicaragua, Norway, Peru, Portugal, Russia, El Salvador, Spain, Sweden, Switzerland, and the United States. There were in all 136 delegates, 73 of whom hailed from France or its dependencies. It was natural that the French as hosts should have allotted themselves the largest quota, but their overwhelming preponderance aroused some indignation among the alien deputies. The French representatives were divided into

two groups, a *comité français* composed of the more distinguished
members and a *délégation* comprising those of less importance.
Both bodies included men well known as scientists, engineers, explorers, senators, deputies, public works officials, or representatives
of the chambers of commerce of the larger French cities. Several
were to become intimately associated with the canal company in
various capàcities. Among the 18 members of the *comité* were de
Lesseps; Admiral de La Roncière-Le Noury; Bionne; Daubrée,
president of the Académie des Sciences and inspector general of
mines; Dauzats, one of the Suez engineers; Meurand, president of
the Société de Géographie Commerciale de Paris; Charles Hertz,
honorary secretary general of the same society and author of the
deplorably inaccurate historical summary of early canal projects attached to the official report of the congress; and Charles Maunoir,
secretary general of the Société de Géographie de Paris (not the
same organization as the Société de Géographie Commerciale).
The roster of the 49 French *délégués* not on the *comité* contained
the names of Abel Couvreux, one of the Suez canal contractors,
afterwards to hold a similar position in the Panama enterprise;
Gustave Eiffel, designer of the famous tower, also to become an
active participant in the construction of the Panama canal; Jules
Flachat, the Darién explorer; and Godin de Lépinay, an engineer
in the Department of Public Works.

Of the foreign groups the United States delegation of 11 mem-
bers was by far the largest, but only two, Ammen and Menocal,
officially represented the government. Most of the others were
emissaries of local chambers of commerce or scientific societies:
Commander Selfridge, Frederick Kelley, Walton W. Evans, Nathan
Appleton of the United States Chamber of Commerce, Cyrus W.
Field (projector of the first Atlantic cable), Dr. William Edward
Johnston of the American Geographical Society of New York,
Christian T. Christiansen, Eli Lazard, and John Lawrence Smith.
Although Evarts had grudgingly consented to the appointment of
Ammen and Menocal his instructions permitted them only limited
participation: "You will take part in the discussions . . . and will
communicate such scientific . . . information as you may possess,
and as is desired. . . . You will, however, have no official powers
or diplomatic functions. . . . You are not authorized to state what
will be the decision of the Government of the United States . . .
or the line of action it will pursue. . . ." [2]

The British delegation consisted of 6 members, most of whom
were prominent engineers: Sir John Hawkshaw, Robert Bruce
Bell, Sir Charles Hartley, J. O. Lewis, H. C. Lobnitz, and Sir John

Stokes, a member of the administration council of the Suez canal. Holland and Belgium also sent 6 representatives each: Spain 5; Switzerland 4; Colombia 4, including Wyse's assistant Sosa; Italy 3; Austria-Hungary, Portugal, Russia, and El Salvador 2 each; and the other nations contented themselves with a single delegate apiece.

To facilitate and expedite the work the congress was subdivided into five committees. To the first, the committee on statistics (18 members), was assigned the task of computing the probable tonnage that might be expected to pass through the canal, the percentage of the total traffic to be furnished by each of the maritime nations, and the presumptive amounts and average values of various kinds of merchandise in transit. The second was the committee on economics and commerce composed of 20 members and instructed to study the probable effect of the canal upon the commerce and industry of the several countries, the savings in transportation and insurance costs, and the creation of new markets and channels of world trade. The third or navigation committee (19 members) undertook to investigate the types and sizes of vessels most likely to utilize the canal, the anticipated influence of the canal upon naval construction and design, the effects of winds and currents, and the climate and meteorology of the isthmus with particular reference to the preservation of materials to be used in the construction and maintenance of the waterway. The fifth committee, that on ways and means, consisted of 18 members whose business it was to compute the probable gross and net revenues of the canal and the toll rate which would yield the maximum profit.

These were all minor committees completely overshadowed by the much larger and vastly more important fourth or technical committee. This group was to decide upon the most advantageous route and the most practicable type of canal from an engineering standpoint, estimate costs of construction, operation, and maintenance, and devise means to insure a safe and easy transit through the canal and its terminal harbors. Obviously everything depended upon the report of the fourth committee. It comprised 53 members: 28 Frenchmen, including de Lesseps, Meurand, Bionne, Maunoir, Couvreux, Daubrée, Dauzats, Eiffel, and de Lépinay; four Americans, Ammen, Evans, Menocal, and Selfridge; four British delegates, Bell, Hartley, Hawkshaw, and Stokes; three Dutchmen, two Belgians, two Swiss, two Italians, two Spaniards, a German, a Russian, a Costa Rican, a Salvadorean, a Colombian (Sosa), and a Mexican, Francisco de Garay, son of the José de Garay who had secured the Tehuantepec concession in 1842. Two of the Americans,

Field and Evans, failed to appear. The remaining deputies from
the United States were scattered among the lesser committees:
Lazard in the first, Appleton and Christiansen in the second, Smith
in the third, and Johnston and Kelley in the fifth.

After the close of the congress many of the delegates who disagreed with its verdict criticized its composition, complaining that
it contained too small a proportion of technicians and too large a
one of promoters, politicians, and public officials. There was more
than a little truth in the indictment: of the 136 members fewer
than one third were practical engineers. The dissenters also pointed
out that at least 17 of the delegates, mostly French, had been or were
still connected with the Suez canal. That in itself was no disadvantage; on the contrary the experience gained at Suez, the only canal
enterprise comparable in scale and difficulty of execution with the
projected isthmian waterway, had — or was believed to have — incalculable value. But the close and long-continued association of
these men with de Lesseps, their admiration for him as a leader and
their affection for him as a kind and genial companion, tended to
undermine their intellectual independence. Most of them rallied
blindly round de Lesseps, adopted his opinions and his wishes as
their own, and formed a solid bloc which could be counted upon
to vote as he dictated.

The first plenary session of the Congrès International d'Études
du Canal Interocéanique convened in the auditorium of the Société de Géographie de Paris at 184 boulevard Saint-Germain on
May 15, 1879 at two in the afternoon. It was a ceremonial occasion,
and de Lesseps, always a magnificent showman, had spared no pains
to create a gala atmosphere. The officers, dignified and solemn, occupied the stage, the delegates sat in their reserved section, and the
remaining space was crowded to the doors with distinguished spectators, including scores of ladies in the bustled gowns and feathered
bonnets of the period. This inaugural assembly was devoted to formal speeches; the real work would be accomplished in the committee rooms. The honorary chairman, Admiral de La Roncière-
Le Noury, opened the meeting with a few general remarks: "The
cutting of a canal through Central America has now become essential to the economic welfare of all nations. . . . The building in
which we are met is dedicated to science, and the impartial serenity of science will impress itself upon your deliberations."[3] De
Lesseps spoke briefly: "I ask the congress to conduct its proceedings in the American fashion, that is with speed and in a practical
manner, yet with scrupulous care. . . . I welcome you . . . with

all my heart." [4] The roll was then called, and de Lesseps presented the delegates to each other. The secretary general, Bionne, traced the evolution of the present congress from the 1875 conferences of the Société de Géographie. De Lesseps brought the meeting to an end with one of the gallant little speeches for which he was deservedly famous: "I do not wish to close this session without thanking the entire assemblage, and especially the great number of ladies I see among you, for the interest you are taking in our work. The presence of ladies at a scientific reunion is always a good omen for the success of any enterprise. . . ." [5]

During the fortnight the congress remained in session four more plenary meetings were held, but at none except the closing assembly on May 29 was any important business transacted. The deliberations of all the committees except the fourth may be dealt with briefly. The first committee estimated that in 1889, when the canal would be completed, the traffic would probably amount to 7,249,-000 tons per year. The second committee met only three times and for all it contributed to the solution of the main problem might as well not have met at all. Its members appeared to have but a vague conception of what was expected of them and could do little but twiddle their thumbs while awaiting the report of the fourth committee. The third committee recommended minimum dimensions for the canal and reached the fairly obvious conclusion "that a lock canal should not be adopted unless the impracticability of a sea level canal is demonstrated beyond question, and . . . that the tunnel should be eliminated unless . . . the impossibility of a canal without a tunnel is proved. . . ." [6] The task of the fifth committee — the computation of revenue, profits, and toll rates — depended directly upon the findings of the fourth committee, for until the technicians had estimated the costs of construction, maintenance, and operation the net income could scarcely even be guessed at. Nevertheless the ways and means committee made a valiant effort to guess. Assuming an annual traffic of 6,000,000 tons — somewhat less than the estimate of the first committee — for the years immediately following the completion of the canal, and tolls of $3 per ton, the committee computed the gross revenue at $18,-000,000 a year and the annual net profit at $8,400,000.

The all-important fourth committee functioned under the direction of a French chairman, Daubrée, and embraced two subcommittees. The chairman courteously invited the American delegates to present their plans first. Selfridge began with a description of the Napipí-Doguadó route and recommended a modification of Collins's project which, he claimed, could be constructed for $53,000,000 plus 25% for contingencies. The commander soon found himself involved in an acrimonious and rather undignified dispute with his compatriot Admiral Ammen, who disapproved of all the Atrato schemes but insisted that if any deserved consideration it was that outlined by Collins without Selfridge's unauthorized alterations. Selfridge retorted angrily that Collins had served as his own subordinate, that he felt perfectly free to amend the plans in accordance with his own ideas, that he had been invited to attend the congress, and that after all he knew the Atrato region, having explored it personally, better than Ammen, who had not. Confronted by this division in the American camp, the subcommittee sided with Ammen and dismissed Selfridge's project as technically unsound.

Both Ammen and Menocal clearly indicated their partiality for the Nicaragua transit though their instructions obliged them to insist that they spoke only for themselves, not for their government. "The advocates of the Nicaragua route," Ammen reported, "were disposed to regard Mr. Menocal and myself as an accession to their ranks, a position that we have persistently refused to accept, recognizing . . . that the mere preference of opinion . . . did not make it a duty to become advocates except by inference. . . ." [7] He presented comparative estimates for various lock canal projects: Nicaragua $65,600,000, Panama $94,500,000, Napipí-Doguadó $98,-200,000. Occasionally his bias led him to exaggerate the advantages of Nicaragua: "The harbor of San Juan del Sur . . . is very satisfactory, well sheltered, and easy of access." [8] The open roadstead was certainly easy of access — too easy, for it possessed no natural protection whatever against winds and waves. Again Ammen declared the average annual rainfall in Nicaragua to be only 48 inches, in Panama 125 inches — a most misleading comparison since he did not trouble to explain that his statistics applied to the driest part of Nicaragua near the Pacific and the wettest section of Panama on the Atlantic coast. Menocal followed Ammen with a more technical and detailed discussion of the Nicaragua project. In his opinion a sea level canal could not be constructed at Panama because the sudden floods of the Chagres would pour into the channel, damage its banks, and disrupt service. A lock canal would be quite practicable but would cost more than in Nicaragua.

Wyse then presented his Darién, San Blas, and Panama projects with particular emphasis on five variants of the last-named route, four with tunnels and one without but all at sea level. He also recited a remarkably untrustworthy résumé of isthmian exploration, startling the Americans present with the statement that "Strain and most of his men perished of hunger and privation in the jungle. . . ." [9] But he gave full credit to the United States naval surveys of 1870–5 and to their leaders, "all conscientious and able men to whom we cannot pay too great a tribute, for they produced results of the greatest value. . . . Their reports . . . are the indispensable *vade mecum* of every student . . . of the American isthmus." [10] Türr and Reclus spoke more briefly in praise of the Panama route.

Several other enthusiasts urged the adoption of their favorite projects. Blanchet submitted his Nicaragua plan but since he lacked the necessary charter made little impression. Félix Belly emerged from years of obscurity to extol the virtues of his worthless Sapoa River route and to bask once more for a brief moment in the limelight. The Tehuantepec line could boast but a single sponsor, Francisco de Garay. Ribourt, one of the engineers of the Saint-Gotthard tunnel, warned that the excavation of a sea level canal with a tunnel at Panama would require 9 years of continuous labor 24 hours a day and cost, exclusive of buildings, interest, and administration, not less than $186,000,000. Although Wyse promptly challenged this enormous estimate subsequent events proved that the tunnel expert — merely an invited witness, not a delegate — had appreciated the magnitude of the operation more realistically than most members of the congress.

With some difficulty Appleton persuaded the committee to consider Kelley's project for a San Blas canal. A letter from de Gogorza recommended de Lacharme's plan for a lock canal in Darién. Lucien de Puydt produced a flutter of indignation by writing an insulting letter accusing the congress in general and de Lesseps in particular of partisanship in favor of the Wyse projects — a partisanship so flagrant that presentation of his own scheme would be a waste of time: "I realize that . . . the congress was summoned for the benefit of M. Wyse alone . . . that the congress would not have convened had M. Wyse not existed. . . ." [11] Five days later he wrote a second time to apologize for the vigor of his language. Stokes proposed that de Puydt's bad manners should be overlooked and that he should be invited to lay his plans before the committee, and with characteristic magnanimity de Lesseps seconded the motion to show that he harbored no personal resentment. On May 26 de Puydt spoke in favor of his route over the Pucro-Tanela pass in Darién, which, notwithstanding the observations of Selfridge and Wyse, he insisted lay at an altitude of only 150 feet above the sea.

The committee, having sufficiently demonstrated its open-mindedness, thereupon dismissed de Puydt as the crank he undoubtedly was.

One of the last speakers was Godin de Lépinay, probably the only French engineer in the entire congress except Flachat who had actually worked for any length of time in the American tropics. De Lépinay urged the adoption of the Panama route but argued long and earnestly against the sea level project and in favor of a lock canal. He proposed to dam the Chagres near the Atlantic terminus and the Río Grande close to the Pacific, thus creating an immense artificial lake about 80 feet above sea level. He insisted that this solution would reduce the total amount of excavation enormously and eliminate all danger from the Chagres floods, that the work could be completed in 6 years, and that it would cost, including interest and overhead but not the purchase price of the railroad, $100,000,000. He also believed that his plan would preserve the health and perhaps the lives of thousands of workmen, since it would require so much less digging. Although this humanitarian conception was based upon the then prevalent but mistaken theory that tropical fevers were caused by a mysterious toxic emanation from earth freshly excavated and exposed to the air, and that therefore the less the ground was disturbed the less illness there would be, de Lépinay's project as a whole was absolutely sound. His proposed system of locks, dams, and artificial lake comprised all of the essential elements of the design actually executed by the builders of the present Panama canal, and it also formed the basis of the compromise plan accepted by the French company in 1887 in a last desperate effort to avert failure. Had it been adopted at the beginning in 1879 the canal might well have been completed by the French instead of by the United States government.

On May 26 the two subcommittees handed in their reports. Their findings, though arrived at more or less independently, were in substantial agreement. They estimated the cost of a Tehuantepec canal at $191,467,500 *exclusive* of harbor improvements, interest, and administrative expenses — too high a figure to be considered seriously. They found Menocal's project for a Nicaragua lock canal perfectly practicable and computed the cost at $142,302,-960 *including* interest and administration, operation and maintenance at $1,320,000 a year, and the time required for construction at 6 years. Wyse's sea level canal without a tunnel at Panama was also pronounced practicable; it would take 12 years to build and would cost, including everything but the railroad, $208,600,000, while operation and maintenance would consume $600,000 annually. But here both subcommittees noted important reservations. The first group warned that "the construction of such works, especially of such deep excavations of highly dubious stability, as well as the measures designed to restrain the Chagres, present so many difficulties and unpredictable contingencies that a close estimate is impossible"; [12] and the second recommended two modifications: the addition of a tide lock at the Pacific end and the complete exclusion of the waters of the Chagres from the canal bed. For the San Blas canal advocated by Kelley the subcommittees estimated the total cost at $261,565,395 and the construction period at 12 years. Finally they evaluated Selfridge's Napipí-Doguadó plan at $200,000,000 but condemned both site and design as unsatisfactory.

The subcommittees rejected without discussion all other projects, including de Lépinay's proposal for a lock canal at Panama. Although the reports plainly indicated that Nicaragua offered the cheapest and most speedily constructed of the five schemes under consideration the enormous influence of de Lesseps, who made no secret of his opposition to any lock canal, prevented its acceptance. On May 28 the fourth committee resolved "that the . . . canal should connect the Gulf of Limón with Panama Bay; and it particularly recommends the construction of a sea level canal along that line." [13] The opinion was far from unanimous: of the 53 committee members 24 were absent, 10 abstained, 3 voted against the resolution, and only 16 voted in its favor.

All was now ready for the closing plenary session, which convened on May 29 to hear the report of the technical committee and to register the votes which would finally decide the location and type of the canal. The atmosphere grew tense as de Lesseps rose to present the crucial resolution: "The congress believes that the excavation of an interoceanic canal at sea level, so desirable in the interests of commerce and navigation, is feasible; and that, in order to take advantage of the indispensable facilities for access and operation which a channel of this kind must offer above all, this canal should extend from the Gulf of Limón to Panama Bay." [14]

The voting took place immediately, *viva voce* and in alphabetical order. Each delegate was permitted to offer a brief oral explanation of his vote, but lengthy comments or arguments could be presented only in writing. When the name of de Lesseps was called he answered in a firm voice that carried to the farthest corner of the auditorium: "I vote 'yes'! And I have accepted the leadership of the enterprise." [15] The announcement, though not unexpected,

was greeted with such vigorous applause that the voting was interrupted for several minutes. While the ballots were being counted
de Lesseps addressed the meeting: "Two weeks ago I had no idea
of placing myself at the head of a new undertaking. My dearest
friends tried to dissuade me, telling me that after Suez I should take
a rest. Well! If you ask a general who has just won one battle if he
will try to win a second, he cannot refuse." [16]

Admiral de La Roncière-Le Noury announced the tabulation
of the ballots: in favor of the resolution, 74; opposed, 8; abstained,
16; absent, 38. The verdict evoked fresh outbursts of applause. The
sea level canal at Panama, the project so dear to de Lesseps's heart,
was stamped with the official approval of the congress, but opponents of the winning plan outspokenly questioned the competence
of most of its supporters. Menocal complained in his report to
Evarts: "Of the affirmative vote only 19 were engineers, and of this
. . . number eight are at present, or have been, connected with
the Suez Canal; five are not practical engineers, and only one [Sosa]
has been in Central America." [17] According to the published roll
call the actual number of present or former Suez associates who
cast affirmative votes appears to have been 12, not 8.

Only seven United States delegates attended the closing session.
Appleton, Christiansen, and Lazard — all laymen — voted for the
de Lesseps plan, while Ammen, Johnston, Menocal, and Smith abstained. Five of the six British emissaries departed before the end
of the congress, and the single survivor, Stokes, voted "aye." Even
those Americans who had most firmly opposed the sea level project
preferred to abstain and lose their votes rather than register an
emphatic negative, possibly because they realized that their ballots
could not affect the outcome. Dr. Johnston suggested another plausible reason for the moderation displayed by himself and his colleagues: "If it be thought that . . . 'abstention' was too mild a
word to be found in the mouths of American delegates, it must
be stated . . . that these delegates were . . . surrounded during
their whole stay with such a large hospitality, they were so dined
and fêted, that they will be excused for lacking the heart to look
their entertainers in the face and pronounce so harsh a word as
'no.' " [18] Johnston accused de Lesseps of having "packed and ma-
nipulated [the congress] so as to run through hastily . . . the . . .
impossible scheme of Lieut. Wyse. . . ." [19] If the American's language was a trifle intemperate there can be little doubt that the
charge was substantially true. Long before the congress opened de
Lesseps had made up his mind that the canal must be at sea level
and that Panama offered the best site. He took good care to in-

vite a large number of delegates whose views coincided or could be made to coincide with his own, saw to it that enough of the right men were appointed to the vital fourth committee, and completely — though always tactfully and without obvious display of force — dominated a majority of that committee's members. Through conferences that took place behind the scenes he gained the support of one delegate after another. Yet all of this wirepulling was prompted by the noblest motives. Neither then nor later did the prospect of financial gain influence de Lesseps himself, though it was to seduce many of his less virtuous associates. He was sincerely convinced that he had made the wisest choice and could complete the canal to the everlasting glory of France.

So to the accompaniment of rapturous applause that almost but not quite drowned out the discontented murmurs the Paris congress adjourned. De Lesseps sped the parting delegates with a hopeful valediction: "I can promise you that we shall succeed in this new enterprise, thanks to the principles of loyalty which distinguish French administration." [20]

Chapter 26. Preparation

FERDINAND DE LESSEPS was neither an engineer nor a financier. He was a promoter — a promoter whose ambition was not the accumulation of wealth but the accomplishment of tasks called impossible by lesser men. Born at Versailles on November 19, 1805, de Lesseps was 74 years old when he decided to assume the direction of the Panama enterprise. At that time he was the most illustrious citizen of France — *le grand Français* — and one of the most eminent personages in the world. The successful completion of the Suez canal had brought him public honors such as few men had ever known while they lived, his charm had endeared him to thousands of friends and acquaintances in all walks of life. Most men might have hesitated to embark on a new and arduous undertaking at his age, but de Lesseps was still young in heart, mind, and body. He had all the optimism and mental elasticity usually associated with extreme youth. His physical vigor was phenomenal: a program of incessant work, conferences, discussions, arguments, rapid travel, and long speeches failed to impair his health or dampen his high spirits, though it exhausted many of his much younger aides. He took pride in his robust constitution and liked to draw attention to his large family of children — many of them the offspring of his old age — as proof of his perennial virility. By his first wife, *née* Agathe Delamalle, whom he married in 1837, he had five sons, only two of whom, Charles and Victor, survived to manhood. After Mme de Lesseps died he remained a widower for 15 years until in 1869, at the age of 64, he married the 21-year-old Louise-Hélène de Bragard, who bore him nine more children.

Success at Suez had given de Lesseps confidence — perhaps overconfidence — in his own judgment. He had overcome so many difficulties almost single-handed: the determined opposition of the Palmerston government in England, the hesitation and inertia of the Turkish authorities, financial stringencies, problems of labor, equipment, and water supply. He had taken so many chances: though the validity of his Suez concession had been doubtful he had brushed aside legal technicalities; when the banking house of Rothschild had demanded a 5% commission to finance the project he had launched a bold and successful campaign to obtain funds by direct public subscription. Time after time he had triumphed over his critics, many of them experts in their own fields. He had been right so often that he had begun to think of himself as infallible; he had a profound, almost mystic belief in his own intuition, his destiny, his star. With Suez behind him he could not imagine failure at Panama.

If Ferdinand de Lesseps refused to admit the possibility of disaster, Charles, in many ways older and in all ways more cautious than his father, perceived it clearly. As a young man he had taken an active part in the Suez enterprise and had gloried in its success; but, lacking his parent's sublime faith in destiny, he did not believe in tempting Providence. Respectfully but earnestly he endeavored to dissuade de Lesseps: "What do you expect to gain at Panama — money? You will concern yourself with it no more at Panama than you did at Suez. Glory? You have acquired so much that you can afford to leave some for others. All of us who have worked at your side are entitled to a little repose. Certainly the Panama project is a magnificent one . . . I believe it is practicable . . . but what risks those who direct it will have to run! Remember that the Suez canal, during the ten years required for its construction, was almost daily on the verge of bankruptcy. . . . You succeeded at Suez by a miracle; should not one be satisfied with one miracle in the course of a single life, instead of counting upon a second?" [1] This gentle protest failed to move de Lesseps, and Charles never made another. He worshipped his father, and though his brain warned him to beware of Panama his heart led him against his better judgment into the thick of the fray. As an example of self-sacrifice on the altar of filial devotion the submission of Charles de Lesseps has few parallels in history: "If you do decide to proceed with this . . . and if you wish me to assist you, I shall do so cheerfully and shall never complain, no matter what may happen. All that I am I owe to you; what you have given me, you have the right to take away." [2] For the next ten years Charles loyally carried out his father's orders, never uttering one word of recrimination or "I-told-you-so." In the end it was the son far more than the father who paid the price of failure.

Ferdinand de Lesseps had initiated the Suez canal project himself; it was his own child, and there was nobody to dispute its parentage. The Panama canal was a foundling placed on his doorstep. At the congress of 1879 he represented only the Société de Géographie de Paris and had as yet no financial interest in the concession, which still belonged to Wyse, Türr, and their associates. But de Lesseps was not a man who could co-operate with others on an equal basis; he had to have complete control. He agreed with his old friend Mohammed Ali, pasha of Egypt from 1805 to 1849, who had told him long ago: "My dear de Lesseps . . . when you have something important to do, if there are two of you, you have one too many." [3]

As soon as he had announced his acceptance of the leadership of the Panama enterprise de Lesseps took steps to adopt the infant project legally. On July 5, 1879 he signed a provisional contract to purchase the canal concession, including the land grant of 500,000 hectares and all maps, diagrams, and records, from the Société Civile du Canal Interocéanique du Darien. The option was to be valid for two years, during which de Lesseps undertook to organize a canal company and obtain the necessary funds. The society demanded 15,000,000 francs, but de Lesseps firmly refused to pay more than 10,000,000, and after some haggling the sellers accepted his terms. De Lesseps was in a position to fix his own price, and the directors of the society knew it as well as he did. In the opinion of the French people he was the only man qualified to carry out the project; without him the society could not hope to secure financial support or dispose of its concession. Although some of the directors complained of the hard bargain they actually realized an enormous return on their investment. According to Wyse himself the cost of the two surveys and all other expenses amounted to only about 1,000,000 francs, and the society could count on a clear profit of 9,000,000. But it would have to wait for its payment until the canal company should be legally incorporated, after which it would receive 5,000,000 francs in cash and the other 5,000,000 in the canal company's stock — 10,000 shares at a face value of 500 francs each. In addition de Lesseps agreed to pay immediately the deposit of 750,000 francs promised to Colombia. To secure funds for this as well as other urgent preliminary expenses he negotiated a loan of 2,000,000 francs from personal friends.

The provisional transfer of the concession led to a permanent breach between Wyse and de Lesseps. As the chief pioneer Wyse fully expected to play an important if not a leading part in the new organization, and he was deeply chagrined to find himself completely eclipsed by the great national hero. He claimed that both Ferdinand and Charles de Lesseps had promised him verbally the post of director general of works on the isthmus but had failed to live up to their agreement. Wounded and jealous, Wyse severed his official connection with the enterprise and, while he remained an enthusiastic supporter of the canal project in theory, became a severe — and on the whole not an unfair — critic of its adminis- tration. Fortunately he had too much sense to sulk in his tent for- ever and some years later swallowed his pride sufficiently to under- take and successfully conclude an important mission on behalf of the company.

Late in July 1879 de Lesseps issued circulars calling for sub- scriptions and made a whirlwind tour of France, lecturing, argu- ing, persuading, answering objections. He proposed to sell 800,000 shares of stock at 500 francs apiece, which would give the company an initial capital of 400,000,000 francs or $80,000,000, and he ex- pected to procure this sum by the method employed so successfully for the Suez canal: a direct appeal to small investors, not only in France but in England, the United States, and other countries, which would eliminate the costly intervention of bankers and pro- fessional financiers. Unhappily times had changed. The Franco- Prussian War and the payment of an enormous indemnity to Ger- many had impoverished France to such an extent that not even the reputation and popularity of de Lesseps had the power to induce peasants and shopkeepers to risk their savings. British investors were apathetic; Americans, hostile to the idea of a French canal through a portion of their own continent, warily held aloof. More specific and exceedingly effective opposition came from the power- ful French bankers and newspaper owners. In order to prove their own indispensability they conducted a vigorous counter-campaign led by Émile de Girardin, proprietor of the *Petit Journal,* and Lévy-Crémieux, vice president of the Société Franco-Égyptienne, against the Panama project. Many of the most influential French financial periodicals warned their readers not to invest. De Lesseps spent all he had left of his 2,000,000-franc fund on favorable pub- licity but could make little headway against the propaganda of his shrewd, wealthy, and unscrupulous adversaries.

The subscription, which took place on August 6 and 7, 1879, failed miserably: only about 60,000 of the 800,000 shares found purchasers. The bankers had convinced de Lesseps that their co- operation was essential, and once he had learned his lesson he never again ventured to refuse their assistance or resist their de- mands. Thus at the very outset organized finance and its controlled press secured a foothold in the enterprise. Within a few years the foothold became a stranglehold.

Of the 30,000,000-odd francs subscribed a first installment of 25 francs per share had actually been paid in. This money de Lesseps returned to its owners with the promise that if they wished to par-

ticipate in the next issue of securities they would be entitled to
subscribe respectively for the same number of shares, and that their
quotas would suffer no reduction should that issue be oversubscribed. The financiers had based their anti-Panama propaganda
upon four principal objections: technical difficulties, underestimation of cost, the insalubrious climate, and probable opposition by
the United States government. De Lesseps now decided that before
he could risk a second appeal for funds and proceed to the formal
constitution of the company he must clear up these "misconcep-
tions" by a personal visit to the canal area and to the United States.
He must also control a publicity organ dedicated to the interests
of the canal administration. The first issue of the *Bulletin du
Canal Interocéanique* appeared on Monday, September 1, 1879.
Thereafter for almost ten years — until February 2, 1889 — the
Bulletin was published regularly twice a month. In all, 227 numbers aggregating more than 2200 pages were distributed during
that period. As a source of information concerning the day-by-day
progress, difficulties, and ultimate failure of the canal project it
has no peer, though very often more can be read between the lines
than in the text. The faithful editors made such heroic efforts to
look on the bright side, to stress accomplishments and gloss over
shortcomings, to condone much and conceal more, that cynics
dubbed the little paper *Moniteur des Chimères* — Journal of Illusions. Like the chorus in a Greek tragedy the *Bulletin* recited
the accompaniment to two dramatic conflicts: one between man
and nature, the other between the constructive and destructive at-
tributes of man himself.

In August, some months before de Lesseps set out for the isthmus, the contracting firm of Couvreux, Hersent et Compagnie sent
one of its ablest engineers, Gaston Blanchet, to Panama at its own
expense to examine the proposed canal route. Couvreux, an old
friend of de Lesseps, had been one of the principal contractors for
the Suez canal as well as a delegate to the Paris congress. Blanchet
made a superficial investigation and returned to France with a
favorable report. Early in November de Lesseps sent out a crew
of sappers to sink test shafts along the canal line.

De Lesseps loved pomp and circumstance, parades and speeches,
red carpets and brass bands. He journeyed to Panama with a large
retinue: his wife, three of his younger children, and their gover-
ness; Dirks, a Dutch engineer, one of the delegates to the Paris congress; Boutan, a French mining engineer; Dauzats, a Suez official
and member of the *comité français* of the congress; two other tech-

17. FERDINAND DE LESSEPS WITH HIS SECOND WIFE AND NINE YOUNGEST CHILDREN, ABOUT 1884

18. ADMINISTRATION BUILDING OF THE COMPAGNIE UNIVERSELLE,
PANAMA

19. PANAMA CANAL IN 1912, LOOKING TOWARDS LIMÓN BAY

AMERICAN CANAL AT LEFT, FRENCH CANAL AT RIGHT

nicians, Dauprat and Gallay; Gaston Blanchet, who had just returned from the isthmus; Abel Couvreux *fils,* son of the senior partner of the contracting company; Henry Bionne, secretary general of the congress; and a reporter for the *Moniteur Universel.* When they reached Colón on December 30 de Lesseps appointed a technical commission, composed of these engineers and half a dozen others who were already on the isthmus, to supervise the preliminary surveys, recommend methods of procedure, and estimate costs.

After a brief glance at Colón harbor and an official reception at which "the flags of all nations were displayed, with the notable exception of that of the United States," [4] the whole party left for Panama in a special train. About a month earlier unusually heavy rains had raised the level of the Chagres 46 feet in three days and seriously damaged the iron railroad bridge at Barbacoas. Since repairs were not yet completed the distinguished visitors were obliged to leave their train at one end of the broken bridge, scramble across to the other side on foot, and board another train for the rest of the journey to Panama. With characteristic reticence the *Bulletin* recorded the shift from one train to the other but failed to mention the disastrous flood that had made the transfer necessary. At the Panama station civil and military officials made flowery speeches to which de Lesseps responded gracefully, two well-bred little girls presented a bouquet to Mme de Lesseps, and a long line of carriages bore the travelers to the Grand Hotel. That night there was a splendid banquet with more speeches and numerous formal toasts, followed by a display of fireworks in the plaza in front of the cathedral. According to Tracy Robinson, a member of the reception committee, Mme de Lesseps was the only lady at the banquet: "She was . . . a woman of striking beauty. Her form was voluptuous, and her raven hair, without luster, contrasted well with the rich pallor of her Eastern features. She was a native of Mauritius, many years younger than M. de Lesseps, to whom she had borne . . . a numerous family of beautiful children, dark as Arabs and as wild. . . ." [5]

On the afternoon of January 1, 1880 the formal inauguration of the great work took place. The steam tender *Taboguilla* carried de Lesseps and his family, the members of the technical commission, local functionaries, invited guests, and a number of reporters to a point in Panama Bay near the mouth of the Río Grande about three miles west of the city. Accounts of the ceremony differ so widely that it is difficult to determine exactly what occurred. According to one tale the tender arrived so late that the rising tide had covered the site selected for the ritual, so de Lesseps's seven-year-old daughter Ferdinande, nicknamed Tototte, was obliged to deliver the symbolic blow by thrusting her pickaxe into a box of sand on the vessel's deck. The American correspondent Rodrigues, a violently prejudiced eyewitness, commented: "A beautiful shovel and pickaxe had been brought from France. . . . There was some delay . . . for . . . the steamboat could only approach within two miles of the spot of land where the first stroke . . . was to be given, as the tide had gone down. . . . M. de Lesseps, however, was equal to the occasion. He called the audience together (a difficult task indeed, seeing that cognac and champagne had been freely distributed for two hours), and said that inasmuch as the first stroke on land . . . was only a *simulacro* . . . he did not see why the whole thing could not be done right there on board. The Bishop blessed the work, and all the speeches were delivered, just as though the party were on land." [6] There is a curious discrepancy between these two accounts: in one the tide was too high to permit the ceremony to take place on shore, in the other too low. A third version — probably the most accurate — published in the Panama *Star and Herald* only two days after the inauguration, mentioned neither the tides nor the box of sand: "On the 1st instant . . . a large party of ladies and gentlemen made an excursion . . . to the mouth of the Rio Grande. . . . Here it was intended to land and witness the turning of the first sod, a task which was assigned to Miss Fernanda de Lesseps. . . . On account of the lateness of the hour at which the steamer left the wharf it was impossible to carry out the programme in its entirety . . . without delaying the return to the city to a much later hour than that contemplated. With the entrance of the *Taboguilla* in the mouth of the river . . . it was considered as sufficient as a beginning of the surveys, and the remainder of the programme was then carried out. An address was made by Mr. de Lesseps. . . . His Grace the Bishop then formally bestowed his benediction upon the enterprise. . . . Addresses were . . . delivered by ex-President Ortega . . . and others." [7]

For the next six weeks de Lesseps and his party busied themselves on the isthmus, made excursions by rail to various stations between Panama and Colón, floated down the Chagres in canoes, and visited the site of the proposed dam above Gamboa intended to hold back the torrents of the upper Chagres. On January 10 a second rite, the explosion of a charge of dynamite near the summit of the Culebra divide, was attended by the de Lesseps family and numerous official guests. Here again the records disagree. According to the *Star and Herald* the operation "was performed with perfect success, and an immense mass of solid rock was hurled from its original foundations. The party . . . returned to Panama . . . pleased and enthusiastic. . . ." [8] Tracy Robinson, writing many years later, remembered the occasion differently and presumably less accurately: "The blessing had been pronounced, and the champagne, duly iced, was waiting. . . . There the crowd stood, breathless, ears stopped, eyes blinking. . . . But there was no explosion! It wouldn't go!" [9]

While workmen sank shafts along the canal line and collected samples of rock and clay the technical commission prepared its report. A long day of hard work was usually followed by a banquet, a dance, a concert, or some other festivity lasting far into the night. De Lesseps, blessed with almost superhuman energy, managed to burn the candle at both ends and suffer no ill effects, but the wretched correspondent of the *Moniteur Universel* complained dolefully: "We are literally worn out with fatigue. Not only do we labor from morning to evening, but we are also obliged to cope with all the entertainments showered upon us." [10] The cynical Rodrigues, always eager to disparage the French engineers, made much of the revelry but denied the labor: "They looked very much more like a 'pic-nic party' than like a scientific committee. The writer . . . was with them for twelve days . . . and he can say that there was not a stroke of earnest work done in those days, and that many of the young men were more interested in fishing in the Bay of Panama than in testing rocks." [11]

It must be admitted that the work accomplished by the technical commission showed few indications of profound study. The report submitted on February 14, 1880 was little more than a rubber stamp affixed to de Lesseps's project. The commission approved the sea level waterway and the proposed dam, foresaw no unusual difficulties in the excavation of the deep cut through the divide, recommended a breakwater to protect Limón Bay, and considered a tide lock necessary at the Pacific end. It estimated the construction period at 8 years and the cost, including 10% for contingencies but exclusive of interest, administrative overhead, and the purchase of the railroad, at 843,000,000 francs ($168,600,000). This represented a substantial increase over the estimate of the fourth committee of the Paris congress, which had computed the cost with the same exclusions but allowing 25% for contingencies at 765,375,000 francs ($153,075,000). The higher figure displeased de Lesseps, who promptly reduced it to fit his own conception. By the time he reached New York he had lopped off here and pared down there so as to lower the estimate to 658,600,000 francs ($131,720,000).

These paper economies were wholly unwarranted, but de Lesseps was an incorrigible optimist.

On February 24 de Lesseps and his party reached New York, installed themselves at the Windsor Hotel (destroyed by fire with great loss of life in 1899), and immediately embarked on a strenuous round of sightseeing. They rode on the new elevated railway, then propelled by steam, and found the cars "roomy, comfortable, well heated, and admirably supported on springs. . . ." [12] They inspected the uncompleted Brooklyn Bridge and visited the Erie Railroad station, docks, and grain elevator in Jersey City. The French reporter was particularly impressed by the ferryboat which transported the party's two "coach-mails" across the Hudson. To complete the first day's program the fire department staged for their benefit a mock conflagration and rescue at the Fifth Avenue Hotel: "One minute and forty-seven seconds after the alarm was turned in the first engine arrived at a gallop." [13] On the 26th the travelers visited the famous art collection of "M. Steevard" (A. T. Stewart), viewed the fringe of docks from the deck of a steamboat, and inspected the office building of the Equitable Life Assurance Society in which "six elevators were in constant operation." [14]

A series of entertainments filled the evenings: "We have had . . . a lecture by M. de Lesseps at the Society of Civil Engineers, a reception at the Geographical Society, a dinner at the Lotos Club, a reception given by the French colony of New York . . . attended by 8000 people, and a banquet for 250 guests at Delmonico's . . . tendered by the leaders of New York society. . . . M. de Lesseps is always merry, full of high spirits, in perfect health, younger than ever, always gracious and amiable. . . . He . . . never seems fatigued when the rest of us ask to be allowed to rest." [15] These enthusiastic reports were sourly contradicted by Rodrigues: "M. de Lesseps was received with cold politeness. . . . The dinner given in New York . . . was . . . very conspicuous for the lack of truly representative men." [16]

De Lesseps had not come to the United States just to ride on the elevated railway or eat rich food at Delmonico's. His real business was in Washington, where he spent about a week. Though well aware that the United States government looked upon his project with disfavor, he was surprised and shocked by the intensity of official disapproval. The reports brought back from the Paris congress by Ammen and Menocal had thrown suspicion upon de Lesseps's competence and good faith. All departments of the government as well as a majority of congressmen still preferred the Nicaragua transit, partly because they believed it more practicable, partly because it would be owned and operated by an American company. On March 5 de Lesseps conferred first with Evarts and later with President Hayes but received little encouragement from either.

Hayes had already determined to insist upon the special interests of the United States in an isthmian waterway no matter by whom it might be operated. On March 8, while de Lesseps was still in Washington, the President declared in a special message to the Senate: "The policy of this country is a canal under American control. The United States cannot consent to the surrender of this control to any European power. . . . The capital invested . . . in such an enterprise must, in a great degree, look for protection to one or more of the great powers. . . . No European power can intervene for such protection, without adopting measures on this continent which the United States would deem wholly inadmissible. If the protection of the United States is relied upon, the United States must exercise such control as will enable this country to protect its national interests and maintain the rights of those whose private capital is embarked in the work. An interoceanic canal . . . will essentially change the geographical relations between the Atlantic and Pacific coasts of the United States, and between the United States and the rest of the world. It will be . . . virtually a part of the coast line of the United States. Our merely commercial interest in it is greater than that of all other countries, while its relations to our power and our prosperity as a nation, to our means of defense, our unity, peace, and safety, are matters of paramount concern to the people of the United States. . . ." [17] To this unequivocal statement Evarts added his opinion that while the United States had no right to object to the purely commercial features of the enterprise, "this view of the subject is quite too narrow and too superficial. It overlooks the direct relations of the other American nations to the contemplated change in the route of waterborne commerce, and the indirect but equally weighty considerations by which the relations of the American nations to the great powers of Europe will be modified by this change." [18] The next day de Lesseps, refusing to acknowledge the disappointment he must have felt, sent his son Charles a cable which though almost meaningless served to cheer the French public: "The message of President Hayes assures the political security of the canal." [19]

On March 8 de Lesseps appeared before the House Interoceanic Ship Canal Committee and made an eloquent plea for the Panama project. Nathan Appleton acted as interpreter; although de Les-

seps understood English fairly well he could not speak it fluently.
On the following day he listened, patient but unconvinced, to a
discussion of the ship railway scheme presented by Eads before the
same committee. From Washington de Lesseps and his party proceeded to Philadelphia and then in a private Pullman to San Francisco, where they arrived on March 17 and remained three days,
lavishly entertained by members of the hospitable French colony.
Recrossing the continent, they stopped in Chicago and Boston for
a few days and on April 1 sailed from New York for Liverpool,
whence they returned to Paris.

One direct result of de Lesseps's visit to the United States was
the organization on July 7, 1880 of a *comité américain* to counteract the influence of the advocates of rival projects, issue propaganda in favor of the sea level canal at Panama, balk legislation in-
imical to that enterprise, induce American investors to subscribe
to the French company's stock, and in general further the interests
of that corporation. The chairmanship of the American committee, after being offered to and declined by ex-President Grant, was
accepted in December 1880 by Richard Wigginton Thompson, Secretary of the Navy, at a salary of $25,000 per year. Afterwards
Thompson claimed that his resignation from the Cabinet three
months before the end of the administration caused no personal
breach between Hayes and himself, but other accounts indicate
that the President deeply resented the Secretary's defection. The
other members of the American committee were Jesse Seligman
of the banking house of J. & W. Seligman & Company, E. P. Fabbri
of Drexel, Morgan & Company, and John W. Ellis of Winslow,
Lanier & Company. Charles Colné was engaged as secretary, and
the committee rented offices in the Mills Building at 15 Broad
Street, New York.

Between 1881 and 1889 the American committee cost the canal
company $2,400,000. Half of this sum went to the three banking
firms in return for services which appear to have been almost wholly
imaginary. According to the report of Joseph L. Bristow, special
commissioner appointed to investigate the Panama Railroad in
1905, "the work of the American committee was altogether done
by Mr. Thompson, and consisted of supervising purchases . . .
for the construction of the canal, and . . . persistent, watchful,
and successful supervision of the legislation of the United States.
The members of the American committee other than himself were
supposed by Mr. Thompson to have received no compensation
whatever except their commission as bankers and brokers in . . .
furthering the sale of . . . stocks and bonds . . . and in handling

. . . the very large amount of money spent in this country for . . . supplies. . . . The total amount . . . for purchases of this kind passing through the single house of J. & W. Seligman . . . was upwards of $40,000,000. . . . These three banking houses . . . received, apparently for the loan of their names and for nothing else . . . $400,000 apiece, or $50,000 a year . . . without the knowledge of [Thompson] . . . who . . . was himself receiving only half of that sum annually. In fact, two years before the . . . company went into liquidation . . . Thompson voluntarily reduced his salary . . . to $12,500 — remaining in complete ignorance that the other members . . . were still each receiving $50,-000. These banking houses state that they had no specific duties . . . that they had no employment . . . to effect the sale of canal stock or bonds, and that, in fact, practically none were sold in the United States. What . . . indirect credit and popularity was given to the enterprise through their numerous correspondents and connections throughout the country is perhaps impossible now to estimate, but to effect this was the object of the formation of this . . . committee — a committee which . . . had no regular meetings, and some members of which were never present at a meeting. . . ." [20]

This payment of $1,200,000 for unrendered services was but one of many instances of waste in the administration of the canal company, and concealment of this remuneration from Thompson only one of many examples of furtive procedure. For once the scathing criticism of Rodrigues appears justified: "As to the American syndicate, it is one of the most shameful corruption funds ever recorded. . . . No respectable bankers should ever have participated in that costly fraud upon the shareholders. . . . The three houses deserve the hearty reprobation that will be visited some day upon all who have . . . plotted to obtain the money from the poor French people. . . ." [21]

Immediately after his return to France de Lesseps organized a brisk propaganda campaign in behalf of the Panama project, lecturing in Paris and a dozen other French cities as well as in England, Holland, and Belgium. Of all the lectures, meetings, and conferences the banquet at Ghent in early June produced the most significant consequences. Young Abel Couvreux announced that his father's contracting firm had reduced the canal estimate below the already diminished figure of 658,600,000 francs computed by de Lesseps: "M. de Lesseps has said that our firm will be entrusted with the construction of the Panama canal, the cost of which we

have estimated at 512,000,000 francs. It is certain that even this
sum will prove greater than the actual expense. M. de Lesseps has
said that eight years will suffice for the execution of the work, and
this is also the opinion of our firm. . . ." [22] The *Bulletin* reported
this after-dinner speech not as the mere surmise of an irresponsible
minor official of the firm but as a definite bid for the contract. The
French newspapers, now being well paid for favorable publicity,
went one step farther and implied without explicitly stating that
a contract for the construction of the entire canal and all auxiliary
works — dams, harbor improvements, buildings, etc. — had already been awarded to Couvreux and Hersent and that the contractors had firmly guaranteed to complete the task for 512,000,000
francs. This report, which neither de Lesseps nor the contractors
attempted to deny, induced thousands of small investors to subscribe for the company's stock. Actually no such agreement existed, then or later. The figure mentioned was no more than an
informal guess — a bad one, as it turned out — which committed
the firm to nothing; and when a contract with Couvreux and Hersent really was signed several months later on March 12, 1881 its
terms were quite different and very much less advantageous to the
canal company.

Meanwhile de Lesseps prepared to float the company's stock, for
which subscriptions were to be taken on December 7, 8, and 9,
1880. The initial capital was fixed at 300,000,000 francs ($60,000-
000) divided into 600,000 shares of 500 francs each. 10,000 shares
were reserved by previous agreement for the Société Civile du
Canal Interocéanique du Darien, and the rest were to be offered
to the public at par. In the event of oversubscription shares would
be allotted *pro rata* except that holders of Suez stock and subscribers to the unsuccessful Panama issue of 1879 would receive special
consideration. During the construction period shareholders were
to receive 5% on all installments paid in, and after completion of
the canal they would be entitled to 80% of the net profits.

To insure the success of the subscription Lévy-Crémieux and his
associates formed a powerful syndicate. The conditions under
which it operated, kept secret at the time, were published anonymously some years later: "To defray the expenses incident to the
issue of 590,000 shares . . . the syndicate agrees to deposit with
the Société Générale [one of the largest French banks] . . . 4
francs per share or . . . 2,360,000 francs. To determine each member's quota . . . the syndicate is divided into 59 parts of 40,000
francs each. . . . If the company . . . fails to achieve incorporation . . . the members of the syndicate are entitled to *pro rata*

reimbursement only of the unexpended portion of the 2,360,000 francs deposited. If . . . the company is incorporated, each member . . . will receive: (1) repayment of the 4 francs per share advanced; (2) an additional sum of 20 francs per share as compensation for his risk and co-operation; (3) one founder's share . . . for each of the 59 parts of 40,000 francs. . . ." [23]

The common shareholders had been promised 80% of the net profits of the completed canal. The remaining 20% was to be divided as follows: 15% to the "founders" — Ferdinand and Charles de Lesseps, the lenders of the original 2,000,000-franc fund in 1879, and the members of the syndicate of 1880; 3% to the board of directors; and 2% to the office staff, technicians, and other permanent employees. To enable the founders to anticipate their remuneration without waiting for the canal to open the company created 900 founder's shares, the owners of which were to divide among themselves 15% of the potential profits; each founder's share thus represented one sixtieth of 1% of the total net earnings of the canal. A similar system had been used to reward the promoters of the Suez canal, whose original contributions had been repaid many times over: a Suez founder's share quoted at 5000 francs when issued had a market value of 380,000 francs in November 1880. Since the Panama canal was never finished by the French company its founder's shares ultimately became worthless, but at one period during construction when the prospects of success seemed bright they sold for as much as 75,000 francs apiece. Of the 900 founder's shares 400 were allotted to the contributors to the 1879 loan, 59 to the syndicate of 1880, 90 to Ferdinand de Lesseps, and 10 to his son Charles. 21 shares never issued were found in the company's office after the crash. The recipients of the remaining 320 shares have never been precisely identified. In 1893 the investigating committee appointed by the Chamber of Deputies reported that "apparently they had been given to M. Lévy-Crémieux. . . . But M. Lévy-Crémieux did not keep them all for himself, and we have been unable to discover what use he made of them." [24]

One of the most important functions of the 1880 syndicate was the distribution of large sums to the French press, sometimes in the form of direct payments, sometimes by more devious methods, in return for favorable publicity. Practically all of the newspapers that had helped to defeat the stock issue of 1879 now lifted their voices in a chorus of praise, and the *Bulletin* joyfully presented juicy excerpts to its readers. The *Messager de Paris* admitted a change of heart: "In August 1879 . . . we told . . . our readers: 'Do not subscribe.' . . . [But] what was true in August 1879

is no longer true in November 1880. . . . Our doubts . . . have
no foundation today. . . ." [25] The *Journal des Débats* grew sentimental: "Capital and science have never had such an opportunity
to make a happy marriage. . . ." [26] *Le Gaulois* declaimed: "Success . . . is certain. One can see it, one can feel it. Enthusiasm is
universal. . . ." [27] *La Liberté* thundered: "The Panama canal has
no more opponents. . . . Oh, ye of little faith! Hear the words of
M. de Lesseps, and believe!" [28]

What the newspapers did not disclose was the price paid for this
optimism. In 1893 the Chamber of Deputies published an itemized
list of expenses connected with the stock issue of 1880 and the organization of the canal company: [29]

Brokers' commissions	4,224,958 francs
Remuneration to banks	1,865,046
Syndicate, 20 francs per share	11,800,000
American committee (paid in installments)	12,000,000
Publicity	1,595,573
Organization expenses	756,202
Total	32,241,779 francs

While the cost of flotation was high — almost 11% of the 295,-
000,000 francs to be raised by public subscription — there was
nothing actually illegal in the financial transactions of this syndicate of 1880. If the company paid extravagantly for their co-operation the financiers discharged their obligations most efficiently.
From a strictly moral standpoint some of the expenditures appear
less legitimate: for example the 1,595,573 francs for "publicity" —
a euphemism for bribery of newspaper owners and editors — and
at least half of the fund allocated to the American committee. De
Lesseps himself was undoubtedly guilty of deception or at least of
suppressio veri when he permitted the public to remain under the
false impression that Couvreux and Hersent had guaranteed the
construction of the canal for 512,000,000 francs and when he announced in the *Bulletin* a few days before the subscription: "The
company . . . will be organized with a capital of 300,000,000
francs. . . . The total cost being computed at 600,000,000, the rest
of the money will be raised, as needed, by the issue of bonds. . . ." [30]
He failed to mention that this "total" excluded interest during
construction, administration expenses, a proper allowance for contingencies, and the price of a settlement with the Panama Railroad;
or that the fourth committee of the Paris congress had estimated
the total cost *including* all of these items except the railroad transaction at the very much higher figure of 1,043,000,000 francs.

Thanks to the newspapers and the hearty support of the syndicate the sale of stock on December 7, 8, and 9, 1880 achieved an
overwhelming success. 102,230 individuals subscribed for 1,206,-
609 shares. The subscription was national rather than international: French investors demanded 994,508 shares, and Spain accounted for a large portion of the remainder. Relatively few were
taken up in other countries. Since the total number to be disposed
of by public sale amounted to only 590,000 most subscribers had
to be content with a fraction of the quantity they had applied for.
Suez stockholders, subscribers to the first Panama issue of 1879, and
new investors who bid for 5 shares or less received their full quota
without reduction; those who asked for from 6 to 24 shares were
allotted 6; 25 to 28 shares, 7; and so on in the ratio of one share allotted to each additional 4 shares demanded. Most of the stock was
absorbed by small investors; at first very little fell into the hands
of speculators, although a few of the shareholders whose allotments
had suffered no *pro rata* reduction promptly resold part of their
holdings at a profit, thereby increasing the total number of owners.
On March 4, 1881 the *Bulletin* classified the Panama stockholders
as follows: [31]

NUMBER OF HOLDERS	NUMBER OF SHARES HELD BY EACH
80,839	1 to 5
19,143	6 to 20
3,208	21 to 50
554	51 to 100
347	101 to 200
142	201 to 300
29	301 to 400
37	401 to 500
7	501 to 600
12	601 to 700
2	701 to 800
3	801 to 900
8	901 to 1000
14	over 1000
104,345	

Of this total about 16,000 were women who subscribed under their
own names.

The next step was the formal incorporation of the canal company. De Lesseps convoked the first general assembly on January
31, 1881 at the Cirque d'Hiver in the boulevard des Filles-du-Cal-

vaire. By law at least a majority of the shares had to be represented
at the meeting or no business could be transacted; but holders
might vote their stock by proxy. Fortunately most of them availed
themselves of this privilege, for the circus building could accommodate but 5000 people. "If all the shareholders had chosen to attend," de Lesseps said, ". . . it would have been necessary to hold
the meeting out of doors." [32] The assembly unanimously approved
the nomination of three commissioners to verify the allocation of
stock certificates and the payment of the first installments due
thereon, audit the accounts of the provisional administration, and
fix the salaries of the permanent company's directors.

At the second general assembly, held on March 3, the Compagnie Universelle du Canal Interocéanique was finally incorporated and its administration organized. At the head was the president, Ferdinand de Lesseps, with an annual salary of 75,000 francs
and an expense allowance of 50,000; then 5 vice presidents; a
secretary general, Henry Bionne, at a salary of 18,000 francs; a
board of directors with 18 to 24 members at an aggregate salary of
154,000 francs; a directors' committee of 6 members receiving a total of 84,000 francs per year, whose chairman was the subdirector
of the company, Charles de Lesseps, at a salary of 25,000; a consulting engineer (George M. Totten, who had resigned as chief engineer of the Panama Railroad in 1875 but continued to act as
consulting engineer of that road until his death in 1884), with a
salary of 30,000 francs; a consulting contractor at the same salary;
and a consulting committee of about 15 technical experts who received together 40,000 francs per year. Considering the scale of the
enterprise and the responsibility involved all of these salaries were
exceedingly low. Extravagant as the canal company may have been
in other respects it made no attempt to pamper its own executives.
A captious critic might have scented a trace of nepotism in the
composition of the board of directors, which included four members of the de Lesseps family: Ferdinand himself, his brother Jules,
and his sons Charles and Victor.

De Lesseps relinquished to the new corporation all of the rights
and privileges he had purchased from the Société Civile du Canal
Interocéanique du Darien, and in return the assembly authorized
the payment of all expenses incurred and debts contracted. In 1881
the company purchased an office building at 46 rue Caumartin,
Paris, for 1,156,250 francs. At this assembly of March 1881 de Lesseps again predicted brilliant success: "The future . . . appears
unclouded by uncertainties; the difficulties encountered during
the excavation of the Suez canal . . . no longer menace our new

undertaking. . . . Our researches . . . enable us to announce
. . . that the work will certainly be completed in 1888. . . . The
problem of the American isthmus is relatively simple. . . ." [33] A
few days later he departed for Egypt, ostensibly to rest and to amuse
himself by hunting antelope in the company of the Austrian crown
prince, the ill-starred Rudolph. But "since rest to him always means
embarkation on some new activity, he intends to take advantage of
his visit . . . to assure the future prosperity of Port Said by the
construction of a fresh-water canal. . . ." [34]

One more preliminary demanded immediate attention: the acquisition of control over the Panama Railroad. Such control was
vital to the canal company, for without it the railroad had the
right to prevent the construction of a canal so near its own transit
line. The tentative agreement negotiated by Wyse in February
1879 had no legal validity. During the two years that had elapsed
since that date Trenor Park and a few other large stockholders had
quietly bought up huge blocks of shares at the current market price,
$100 to $150. When the canal company, soon after its incorporation, proposed to purchase a majority interest in the railroad the
men who had cornered the stock refused to carry out the informal
agreement and now demanded $250 per share instead of $200 and
payment in cash instead of long-term bonds. The helpless canal
company was obliged to accept these terms. On June 11, 1881 the
directors of the French company signed a contract to buy at the
stipulated price every railroad share presented for sale before September 30. Eventually they secured 68,534 of the 70,000 shares issued, but the remainder, scattered among dozens of small holders,
proved unobtainable.

At the time of the purchase the railroad company had amassed
a sinking fund of $1,102,000 towards the eventual amortization of
its bonded indebtedness of $6,944,000. The canal company took
over this fund, for which it paid cash. Thus the railroad stock
cost the canal company, including sinking fund, interest, and various commissions, about $20,000,000 or approximately $292 per
share. On the other hand the canal company now collected the
bulk of the railroad's dividends, which totaled from 1882 to 1889
inclusive almost $6,000,000. But after 1883, when canal excava-
tion was well under way, the canal enterprise itself supplied most
of the railroad's traffic, so that much of this paper income represented no more than a transfer from one of the company's pockets
to another. The purchase of the majority of its stock did not affect
the legal status of the Panama Railroad Company, which remained
an independent American corporation with its own executives and

directors. Wyse sharply criticized the canal company for its failure to hold the railroad owners to their original agreement arranged by himself, and undoubtedly the French company paid more than the property was worth; but the shrewd American financiers had the whip hand, and the buyers, in desperate need of the road, were in no position to bargain.

Chapter 27. Work in Progress

JOHN BIGELOW wrote after a visit to the partially excavated Panama canal in 1886: "There probably was never a more complicated problem — a problem embarrassed by a larger proportion of uncertain factors — presented to an engineer. . . . Every step . . . is more or less experimental. . . ." [1]

The experimental nature of the work was something that de Lesseps had failed to foresee. He had envisaged another Suez — in fact an easier Suez since the experience gained in Egypt could be applied to the American isthmus. Yet the similarities between the two projects, upon which he insisted, were actually much less apparent than the differences, which he refused to recognize or at least to admit. In one feature only — total length — did a comparison favor Panama: the Suez waterway extended about 100 miles from sea to sea and required some 80 miles of artificial excavation while the Panama canal measured less than 50 miles. In every other respect Panama presented far more difficult conditions. The maximum elevation on the Suez line was but 50 feet above sea level, at Panama 330 feet. At Suez most of the digging took place in sand and soft earth though in a few places limestone ridges offered greater resistance; at Panama much hard rock was encountered, and slides vastly increased the total amount of excavation. The problem of the Chagres River with its erratic floods had no counterpart at Suez. Although labor had to be imported, housed, and cared for at both places Suez lay much nearer large centers of population, and the prevailing wage was lower. Both regions suffered from excessively high temperatures, but the dry desert heat of Africa had no such enervating effects as the moist sultriness of the tropical jungle. Lastly the deadly fevers of Panama were almost unknown at Suez.

It soon became evident that experience at Suez was more of a drawback than an asset at Panama. Almost everything had to be unlearned, and the acquisition of new knowledge proved a slow and painful process. In its quest for new methods to fit the unfamiliar conditions the Compagnie Universelle constantly changed its administrative and technical procedures. Unforeseen difficulties

forced upon the company a program of trial and error; and if to
critical observers that program sometimes appeared to involve more
error than trial, most of the mistakes were due to inexperience
rather than to ineptitude. It would be grossly unfair to ascribe the
shifting policies of the French company to sheer stupidity. The construction of the Panama canal was an engineering work unprecedented in scale and altogether exceptional in conditions, and it
was only to be expected that various methods of attack would be
tried and discarded in the search for a solution. When the United
States government undertook the task it too fumbled and shilly-
shallied for some time before it developed an organization that
worked efficiently.

The operations of the Compagnie Universelle on the isthmus
were divided into four stages: the first period from March 12, 1881
to the end of 1882, during which the entire work was entrusted to
a single contracting firm, Couvreux and Hersent; the second (1883–
5 inclusive), in which it was distributed among a great number
of small contractors under the general superintendence of the company itself; the third (1886–7) of half a dozen large contractors;
and the fourth (1888) marked by the abandonment or at least the
indefinite postponement of the sea level project in favor of a lock
canal.

The company's written contract with Couvreux and Hersent
signed on March 12, 1881 completely ignored the supposititious offer to construct the canal for 512,000,000 francs or any other fixed
sum. Its provisions, never published by the company, were divulged anonymously in 1886: "MM. A. Couvreux and H. Hersent
undertake to . . . execute the work on behalf of the company
. . . until the canal is completed. . . . The work will be divided
into two periods. 1st, the period of organization, to last about two
years, during which the greater part of the matériel will be transported and the fixed installations [buildings, machine shops, etc.]
erected . . . so that an accurate computation of costs will permit
the determination of unit prices. 2nd, the period of construction
proper, to be governed by a special contract based upon the unit
prices established by the work previously executed. . . . The
company . . . will pay [to Couvreux and Hersent] . . . 6% of
the net cost [of actual construction, not including administrative
expenses of the canal company]. . . ." [2] In other words, for the
first two years at least the contractors would undertake the work
on a cost-plus basis; if the costs rose higher than the estimates the
company, not Couvreux and Hersent, would pay the excess. At the

expiration of the trial period the contractors might or might not sign a new agreement to complete the enterprise.

On January 5, 1881 a force of 35 technical experts headed by Armand Reclus, chief superintendent, and his assistant Verbrugghe set out for the isthmus to commence preliminary operations. Reclus, who sympathized with Wyse in the latter's quarrel with de Lesseps, loyally refused to accept the appointment until Wyse urged him to do so. Gaston Blanchet joined the party as the representative of Couvreux and Hersent. Later in the month 24 more technicians followed, and thereafter almost every steamer carried its quota of engineers and office workers as well as numerous unattached adventurers in search of employment on the canal or of some commercial post that would enable them to profit, honestly or dishonestly, from the sudden influx of Europeans.

On February 1 de Lesseps received a cable from Panama: "Work begun" [3] — an announcement hailed by one of the Paris newspapers as "eloquence in few words." [4] By May a strip of land extending along the canal line from sea to sea and varying in breadth from 30 to 60 feet had been cleared of trees and undergrowth. Portable wooden houses and barracks ordered in the United States were set up to accommodate the white technicians, and larger structures for warehouses and workshops began to arrive from France. "The little town of Colón, formerly so desolate, is no longer recognizable," wrote one correspondent. "In its harbor there is a constant coming and going of . . . steamers. . . . It is easy for everyone to find work . . . but more difficult to obtain lodgings. . . . A few weeks ago there was only one hotel, operated by an American; now there are three French restaurants, and an excellent hotel, the Hotel International, catering to French tastes, with a French chef imported from New York. . . ." [5] During the summer an intermediate construction center christened Lesseps City was established outside the village of Gatún, and another was located at Emperador (now called Empire) near the Culebra watershed. On January 20, 1882 excavation of the deep cut commenced at Emperador — an important step celebrated according to the French formula by the explosion of several charges of dynamite in the presence of a throng of invited guests, the popping of champagne corks, and a banquet and gala dance in the city of Panama.

On February 20 Couvreux and Hersent awarded to Huerne, Slaven & Company a subcontract for the dredging of 6,000,000 cubic meters (about 7,860,000 cubic yards) at the Atlantic end of the canal. This firm, reorganized in 1884 as the American Contracting and Dredging Company, was the larger of the two American corporations directly connected with construction during the French régime and the only construction company of any nationality to operate under successive contracts throughout practically the entire period of administration by the Compagnie Universelle. The Slaven brothers were Canadians who had settled in San Francisco, where Henry owned a drug store and Moses practised as a mechanical engineer. Though they had had no experience in canal work they submitted their bids "with an audacity akin to inspiration." [6] After Moses Slaven died his brother carried on alone and reaped a fortune from his contract. Three factors contributed to the success of the Slaven company: the relative softness and homogeneity of the soil and the low elevations encountered near the Atlantic terminus, efficient administration, and the utilization from the very beginning of huge and powerful machines specially designed for the work and equipped with labor-saving devices. The first of its eight great dredges, the *Comte de Lesseps,* was launched at Philadelphia in December 1882 and reached Colón early in April of the following year. The second, the *Prosper Huerne,* arrived in December 1883 partly mounted but was destroyed by fire a month later before it had been placed in service. These two dredges and the third, *Nathan Appleton,* were built of wood, but the others had iron hulls. The long salt-water journey from the United States was a hazardous adventure for these clumsy monsters: "At first the insurance companies refused to take risks on the dredges for the voyage to Colón. . . . The machines were . . . square at both ends, about a hundred feet long, fifty feet wide, and with no more sailing qualities than a house. So long as the sea remained smooth, no trouble was experienced; but towing one . . . in a storm was quite another thing. . . . All . . . were brought out safely. . . . They surpassed in size . . . anything of the kind ever seen. . . . They were so nearly automatic that one of them could be operated by a dozen men. . . ." [7] In 1890 the American company sold its dredges to the Nicaragua Canal Construction Company. All reached San Juan del Norte in good condition except the *Comte de Lesseps,* which foundered off the coast.

In their original contract of February 1882 Huerne, Slaven & Company undertook to execute the work at a flat rate of 1 franc 50 per cubic meter or about 23 cents per cubic yard. Since this was less than the unit price for excavation in soft earth assumed by the technical commission in 1880 the directors of the canal company rejoiced at the unexpected economy. Later negotiations with the dredging company rudely upset their complacency. On September 28, 1884 the American company contracted to excavate 30,000,000 cubic meters (about 39,300,000 cubic yards) before the end of 1887, but on November 25, 1885 this amount was reduced to 18,-000,000 cubic meters at the request of the contracting company, which found that its floating dredges operated less efficiently as they pushed inland into higher ground. The long pipes or troughs through which the excavated material was discharged onto the land on either side of the channel worked well by simple gravity when the sides of the cut were well below the top of the dredge, but as the banks grew higher the slope of the troughs approached the horizontal, gravity failed to act with sufficient force, and it became necessary to employ pumps or lighters to remove the dredged rock and earth. Moreover delays and breakdowns due to encounters with sunken rocks or floating trees grew more frequent. Through faulty drafting of the contract no provision had been made for equitable adjustment of the loss caused by such unavoidable delays, which led to protracted and heated disputes between the canal company and the contractors. All together the canal company paid the American Contracting and Dredging Company 70,812,896 francs. The investigating committee of the Chamber of Deputies severely criticized the canal company for its carelessness in signing an agreement so full of ambiguities and loopholes: "What sort of contract is this, which leaves room for such disputes?" [8] The same committee also regretted "that the records indicate overcharges and chicanery on the part of the dredging company. . . ." [9] The investigators concluded that of all the large contractors employed on the canal the American Contracting and Dredging Company must have made the handsomest profit; but since that company kept its books in the United States the French committee could only guess at its net gain.

In November 1882 another American construction firm, the Franco-American Trading Company, was awarded a subcontract for the excavation of about 5,000,000 cubic yards at the Pacific end, and other subcontracts for work on the middle section of the canal were concluded about the same time. In June 1882 Reclus resigned as chief superintendent on the isthmus, returned to Paris, and was appointed a member of the company's consulting committee. During the interval between his departure and the arrival in October of his successor, Commodore Richier, Verbrugghe acted as temporary chief superintendent at Panama. According to Wyse, Richier failed to assert his authority: "Because of what was perhaps too large a measure of skeptical indifference in his nature, and in spite of the extreme keenness of his observation, Commodore Richier allowed his administrative position to become subordinate to the department of works." [10]

The canal company purchased the Grand Hotel in Panama City and remodeled it into an office building for its headquarters on the isthmus. At the Atlantic terminus, where almost all equipment and supplies were unloaded and stored, the company started the construction of an entirely new port on the mainland adjacent to Colón. Colón itself on Manzanillo Island was unsatisfactory because its site belonged to the Panama Railroad Company, which, although nearly all its stock belonged to the canal company, continued to pursue an independent course not always in complete harmony with that corporation's policy. Before the new town called Christophe-Colomb (now Cristóbal) could be built it was found necessary to fill in the marsh and raise the level of the land several feet with material excavated from the canal bed at near-by Monkey Hill, the Mount Hope of today. Upon this solid platform covering an area of about 70 acres were erected warehouses, machine shops, sawmills, locomotive roundhouses, coal depots, office buildings, and residences for the white staff, while its half-mile waterfront on Limón Bay was fringed with docks and protected by a masonry mole.

In November 1882 de Lesseps boasted that "after two years of work . . . we are much farther advanced than we were at Suez after six years. . . ." [11] The *Bulletin* announced that "of the 75,-000,000 cubic meters to be excavated altogether, more than one fourth . . . have been allotted to various contractors, and the work is under way. . . ." [12] 75,000,000 cubic meters approximately equaled the total amount of excavation required for the Suez canal; but by the summer of 1884 the Panama company had increased its estimate of the total excavation to 120,000,000 cubic meters. De Lesseps endeavored to dismiss this augmentation of 60% as of slight consequence: "We have found, on the one hand, a smaller quantity of hard rock [than we expected] and, on the other, a larger proportion of soil capable of being . . . removed by much simpler processes. This will result . . . in a saving òf time which will compensate largely for the greater cube to be extracted. . . ." [13] A cut through rock would have steep sides and a relatively small volume of excavation; the softer the material, the flatter the slope of the sides and consequently the larger the number of cubic meters to be removed. Before the French engineers abandoned the undertaking they had actually taken out more than 55,000,000 cubic meters (72,050,000 cubic yards), and to complete the canal — not to sea level, but 85 feet higher — the Americans were obliged to extract 259,000,000 cubic meters (about 340,-000,000 cubic yards) in addition.

The first construction period came to an end with the retirement of Couvreux and Hersent. On December 31, 1882 the partners wrote to de Lesseps affirming their willingness to undertake the remainder of the work upon terms to be fixed by agreement but pointing out that such an arrangement "would be burdensome to the [canal] company."[14] In the opinion of Couvreux and Hersent the system of small subcontracts tried out during the experimental period had given excellent results and should be continued; the further employment of a general contractor drawing a fixed percentage of all sums paid to subcontractors or expended for supplies would therefore be only a needless expense. De Lesseps accepted the firm's voluntary withdrawal with apparent gratitude: "I appreciate the value of your renunciation and render you . . . all our thanks for it."[15] The exchange of graceful phrases gave no hint of the real reason for the "renunciation," which was by no means the altruistic gesture it appeared. In 1893 the Deputies committee published a more realistic version: "Couvreux and Hersent exhibited great ingenuity in abandoning their contract . . . and in disguising their action under the cloak of a desire to aid and oblige the company. The truth is that during the trial period Couvreux and Hersent had been able to form a shrewd idea of the difficulties of the enterprise but were unwilling to undermine the company's credit by a frank admission of the motive behind their retirement."[16] For their services from March 1881 to the end of 1882 Couvreux and Hersent received 1,200,000 francs net, certainly not an excessive sum for the work performed. After the withdrawal of his firm Hersent remained in the employ of the canal company for three more years as consultant on contracts at an annual salary of 20,000 francs. There is no reason to doubt the legitimacy of this appointment or to question Hersent's sincerity when he was called upon some years later to justify his remuneration: "I gave the company useful advice and I am convinced that it was well worth the 60,000 francs I received for it; I resigned when I thought my co-operation no longer helpful. . . ."[17]

During the second period from January 1883 to the end of 1885 the canal company, acting as its own general contractor, distributed its work among approximately 100 small subcontractors. In the opinion of the Chamber of Deputies committee this period "was the one that produced the best results."[18] Yet the system suffered from certain disadvantages, as even the loyal *Bulletin* admitted after a three-year test: "At the start the company made the mistake of entrusting the entire work to a single contractor. . . . Then it went to the opposite extreme. After having centralized the organization too closely, it scattered it too freely. The too numerous contractors got in each other's way, especially in connection with the removal of excavated material; moreover they did not always possess the necessary financial resources; some were obliged to borrow from isthmian bankers . . . who . . . were unwilling to lend at less than 2% per month." [19] Lieutenant William W. Kimball, U.S.N., who visited Panama officially in 1885, noted another drawback: "There has been much delay and expense in giving out small contracts to irresponsible parties, as . . . a number of contractors have engaged to excavate down to a certain level, and have gone on . . . as long as the digging was easy . . . but when difficulties were encountered, the contracts were thrown up. Of course the next contractor on the same work would expect a larger price, as the easier and better-paying parts were done, and a new contract for the remainder of the original work would have to be made at an advanced price. Apart from the expense . . . the Company suffered from the delay . . . and from the loss of use of plant while no work was going on. . . ." [20] In addition, when the company finally abandoned this system it was forced to indemnify the small firms for the cancellation of their contracts.

Since few of these concerns could afford to buy expensive equipment the canal company purchased the machines and rented them to the contractors as needed. To superintend the multitude of individual firms the company found itself obliged to expand its organization and augment its white personnel. At the beginning of 1886 the number of Europeans employed on the isthmus in various technical, administrative, and clerical capacities (exclusive of those hired by the contractors themselves) totaled 670, and of these 530 were French. The canal line comprised three sections: the first from the Atlantic terminus to kilometer 34.46, the second from that point to kilometer 53.60, and the third from kilometer 53.60 to deep water in the Pacific. Each section was in charge of a chief engineer and was divided into five subsections. In 1883 the company abolished the office of chief superintendent and placed a general director of works at the head of the entire isthmian organization. From 1883 to 1888 six men occupied this supremely important post — four by formal appointment, two temporarily as stop-gaps. The administration of Dingler, who replaced Richier in February 1883 and remained until the summer of 1885, spanned almost the whole of the second or small-contractor construction period. He was supplanted early in September 1885 by Maurice Hutin, who left Panama only one month later. During the interval between Hutin's departure and the arrival of his successor, Léon Boyer, in January 1886, Philippe Bunau-Varilla temporarily performed the duties of general director. After Boyer's death in May of the same year his assistant, Nouailhac-Pioch, became provisional director pending the appointment in July of Jacquier, who held the position until the crash of 1888.

The total cube excavated during the first two construction periods, or up to December 31, 1885, amounted to approximately 18,-000,000 cubic meters (23,580,000 cubic yards). This was far less than the company had hoped to accomplish in four years. Until December 1885 de Lesseps had invariably insisted that the Panama canal would be completed by the end of 1888, but now he extended the construction period to July 1, 1889. He did not promise that all excavation would be finished even on that date but declared that the canal could be opened to traffic and begin to earn money while some work remained to be done: "That is what we did on the Suez canal . . . which was opened with a depth of only 6 meters instead of the 8 meters contemplated. . . ." [21] Thenceforth as the Panama company sank deeper into difficulties explanations and excuses appeared more and more frequently in the pages of the *Bulletin*.

The third construction period covered the year 1886 and nearly all of 1887. "Towards the end of 1885," reported the Chamber of Deputies committee in 1893, "the canal company . . . changed its policy . . . and entrusted . . . the entire project to six large firms, each of which had a specific task to perform. . . . The results have shown that these large contracts cost much more than the small ones but failed to accomplish . . . any more work." [22] The six firms were the American Contracting and Dredging Company; Jacob, a French concern with headquarters at Nantes; Artigue, Sonderegger et Compagnie; Vignaud, Barbaud, Blanleuil et Compagnie; the Société des Travaux Publics et Constructions; and Baratoux, Letellier et Compagnie.

The American company's total output was by far the largest, almost exactly as much as that of the other five contractors together. Its contract as revised in November 1885 called for the extraction of 18,000,000 cubic meters, and by the end of May 1888 it had removed 16,991,797, nearly the whole of its allotment. But it must be remembered that this company had commenced operations much earlier than the others and that its task — the dredging of soft earth under water — was the easiest of all.

The Jacob contract did not stipulate any total quantity of excavation; the cube was to be determined by the number of dredges and steam shovels furnished by the canal company. The firm actually extracted 2,324,095 cubic meters, for which it was paid 16,-540,684 francs. The Deputies committee estimated its profit at 7,500,000 but exonerated the Jacob company of any suspicion of fraud by declaring that "it executed its contracts faithfully and, unlike some of the others, made no attempt to extort successive price increases, unanticipated advances, or indemnities. . . ." [23]

The contracts concluded with Artigue, Sonderegger et Compagnie were much more complicated. The original firm, a relatively small concern known as Artigue et Sonderegger, had obtained its first contract on May 30, 1883 for the extraction of 1,400,000 cubic meters, of which it did remove 1,089,619. On December 18, 1884 the canal company allotted to an independent firm of contractors — Cutbill, de Longo, Watson, and Van Hattum, usually called the Anglo-Dutch Company — the extraction of from 10,000,000 to 12,-000,000 cubic meters in the Culebra section, the most elevated portion of the line. This contract required excavation of the deep cut from the summit at 330 feet down to a level 165 feet above the sea. In the first 18 months the Anglo-Dutch Company succeeded in removing only 846,824 cubic meters; obviously it could never fulfill its obligations. On July 31, 1886 Artigue et Sonderegger, reincorporated and expanded as Artigue, Sonderegger et Compagnie, took over this contract and in addition engaged to complete the Culebra excavation to the bottom of the canal, 30 feet below sea level. The substitution, though apparently necessary, proved costly to the canal company, which was obliged not only to pay the ousted Anglo-Dutch Company a large indemnity for cancellation but to promise Artigue, Sonderegger et Compagnie a higher unit price for the same work. The company's secretary general, Étienne Martin, considered the Artigue, Sonderegger agreement so outrageous that he resigned in protest and was succeeded by Marius Fontane. In the end the change produced disappointing results. Of the 20,000,000 cubic meters allotted to Artigue, Sonderegger et Compagnie by successive contracts the firm extracted only 2,255,401, for which it collected the enormous sum of 32,646,479 francs. The Deputies committee computed this contractor's net profit at 11,-437,381 francs — far more than the circumstances warranted.

The guiding spirit of Artigue, Sonderegger et Compagnie was the young engineer Philippe Bunau-Varilla, one of the most remarkable personalities connected with the French canal project. Born in 1859, Bunau-Varilla graduated from the École Polytechnique in 1880 and three years later entered the service of the French government as an engineer in the Department of Public Works. In October 1884 he went to Panama as chief engineer of the third or Pacific division of the canal. Six months afterwards Dingler placed him in charge of the Atlantic section as well, and from October 1885 to January 1886 the 26-year-old technician acted as temporary general director of the entire work. On September 1, 1886 he resigned his post with the canal company to supervise the Culebra excavation for Artigue, Sonderegger et Compagnie, of which his brother Maurice was financial manager as well as a partner. But the rules of the Public Works Department forbade its employees to go into business as private contractors; and although Philippe Bunau-Varilla obtained special permission from the government to direct the operations of Artigue, Sonderegger et Compagnie as a technical expert he could not legitimately share in the profits of that firm as an active partner. Nevertheless he did eventually secure his portion of those profits through a private arrangement with his brother. According to his own account he received nothing but his salary as an engineer until after the collapse of the canal company; then, in order to devote himself to the rehabilitation of the project, he resigned his government position and took the money Maurice had put aside for him: "I then foresaw a new and long task ahead of me. I felt I had been wrong not to accept a participation in the profits of the contracting company I had formed and directed towards success. It would have given me the necessary means to make the salvage of the Panama scheme the aim of my life. I accepted, therefore, the offer which my brother . . . had repeatedly and generously made, to share with me the profits he largely attributed to my technical knowledge." [24] Thenceforth, until the United States government purchased the French concession in 1904, Philippe Bunau-Varilla worked indefatigably for the completion of the Panama canal and the rejection of the Nicaragua route.

Vignaud, Barbaud, Blanleuil et Compagnie, contractors for the long middle section, undertook to remove 20,000,000 cubic meters and actually excavated 3,642,986. The Deputies committee singled out this firm as the solitary sheep in a herd of goats, "the only one that gained no profit from its Panama contract." [25] The amount paid in final settlement of its account, after a protracted lawsuit, is uncertain. In one place the report of the Deputies committee listed its receipts at 35,398,810 francs; on another page it mentioned the sum of 30,859,308 francs and added that this represented an overpayment, according to the liquidator, of 8,658,705; while the contracting firm claimed that the canal company still owed it 18,962,284 and that its net loss on the entire transaction amounted to 2,938,000 francs. When the canal company failed this corporation also went bankrupt. The Deputies committee explained the failure with a flick of wry humor: "Vignaud, Barbaud, Blanleuil et Cie. simply appear to have been less shrewd than their competitors; we might say more honest, did we not fear to discourage probity." [26]

The same committee severely censured the fifth contractor, the Société des Travaux Publics et Constructions, which undertook to extract 29,000,000 cubic meters, ultimately excavated 3,421,870, and was paid the preposterous sum of 76,215,022 francs, of which 20,723,285 represented pure profit. The committee not only denounced the contractor for demanding exorbitant and quite unjustified increases with each new contract but blamed the canal company for submitting tamely to the impositions: "When the Société . . . failed to observe its agreements, the company lavished favors upon it. . . ." [27] The committee also pointed out that the Société des Travaux Publics was controlled by a financial corporation, the Société des Dépôts et Comptes Courants, that the two companies occupied the same offices and were administered for the most part by the same directors, and that the Société des Dépôts shared the profits of the construction company. There was nothing reprehensible in such an arrangement per se, but it happened that Charles de Lesseps and Baron Poisson, two of the higher officials of the canal company, were at the same time directors of the Société des Dépôts and thus participated indirectly in the profits of its auxiliary, the Société des Travaux Publics. Charles de Lesseps owned 2000 shares of stock in the Société des Dépôts, Poisson 1031. The Deputies committee established another link between the Société des Dépôts and the canal company when it discovered that the Société had taken part in almost all of the syndicates formed to float the canal company's various bond issues. The committee insinuated that Charles had deliberately awarded unduly lucrative contracts to the Société des Travaux Publics in order to line his own pockets, but there is no reason whatever to believe that he was influenced by any such consideration. Charles de Lesseps, like his father, was scrupulously honest in his personal affairs, and although he committed or connived at many transgressions he invariably did so in the sincere if mistaken belief that they were essential to the prosperity of the canal company.

The last of the six large contractors, Baratoux, Letellier et Compagnie, emerged with a better record. Their original contract of January 1886 called for the excavation of 10,000,000 cubic meters at the Pacific end, but in January 1888 the allotment was reduced by the transfer of 2,000,000 to Artigue, Sonderegger et Compagnie. Of the 8,000,000 cubic meters left Baratoux, Letellier et Compagnie did in fact remove 6,691,734. They received 37,627,656 francs, including a net profit estimated by the committee at 12,513,-382 francs and by the contractors themselves at approximately 8,000,000.

The fourth construction period may be considered in one respect merely a continuation of the third, for most of the work remained in the hands of the same six contractors. But it was marked by a vital change in the canal project: the substitution of a lock canal for the original sea level plan. Grim necessity, not choice, brought about the modification. When the company, faced with ever-increasing expenses and unable to attract new capital, petitioned the French government in 1885 for permission to issue lottery bonds, the Cabinet voted to send an official representative on a tour of inspection to the isthmus and to base its decision upon his recommendations. On December 24 the Minister of Public Works, Demole, entrusted the mission to Armand Rousseau, a distinguished and scrupulously honest engineer of the Public Works Department and a former undersecretary in various government ministries. Rousseau reached Panama at the end of January 1886 and submitted his report on April 30.

The report recommended passage of the lottery bond law but only under certain conditions: "I consider that a cut through the isthmus . . . is a feasible undertaking, and that it has now progressed so far that its abandonment would be unthinkable. Such an abandonment . . . would be a real disaster, not only for the shareholders . . . but for French influence throughout America. . . . If the enterprise should fail in the hands of a French company it would be taken up at once by a foreign one. . . . The Panama company . . . deserves . . . exceptional consideration from the public authorities. . . . I believe that the government should . . . assist it. . . . But the extent of such assistance must be clearly defined, so that the government's responsibility shall not become improperly involved. . . . Since the government has no control over the plans, contracts, or administration, and since moreover the project exhibits certain grave technical defects, it should give the company neither advice nor any guarantee whatever. All it should do is to satisfy itself that the company . . . is aware of the difficulties . . . and will submit to the most rigorous tests all measures under consideration. . . . While I believe . . . the digging of the canal . . . possible . . . its completion for the anticipated cost and within the estimated time appears to me more than doubtful, unless the company will agree to radical modifications and simplifications of its scheme. It is not the government's business to suggest specific simplifications. . . . But it is entitled to demand before acting upon the lottery bond petition . . . a most profound study of this problem. Therefore I recommend . . . that the government persuade the company . . . to obtain the opinion of its consulting committee on the following questions: 'From a technical standpoint, does not execution of the existing program present almost insuperable difficulties? Is it seriously possible to hope that the project can be carried out in the form originally outlined . . . ? Would it not be possible . . . to adopt . . . modifications . . . which would facilitate completion of the work?' " [28]

De Lesseps accepted without protest certain minor modifications with the understanding that future improvements to be paid for out of the canal's earnings would eventually restore the original plan. He agreed willingly enough to eliminate the tide lock at the Pacific end, which he had never considered essential in the first place; to postpone the construction of a wide basin three miles long to enable ships to pass at the halfway point; to substitute an earth levee for the masonry dam at Gamboa; to reduce harbor improvements to a minimum; and if necessary to decrease temporarily the depth and breadth of the channel itself. But he was not yet ready to approve the one modification that, had it been adopted soon enough, might even then have turned failure into success: the introduction of locks. Not until January 18, 1887 did he call upon the consulting committee to consider various designs for a lock canal, and he still insisted that such a makeshift must be merely temporary: "Among these projects . . . are some which would *permanently* substitute a lock canal for a sea level canal. . . . I shall never consent to this permanent substitution. . . ." [29]

It was Philippe Bunau-Varilla who claimed credit for this idea of a temporary lock canal with a relatively high summit level to be transformed subsequently with the money received from tolls into a sea level strait. On the whole his claim appears justified though perhaps other engineers employed by the canal company had more to do with the suggestion than Bunau-Varilla — among whose virtues modesty was never conspicuous — was willing to admit. To carry out his scheme Bunau-Varilla invented two ingenious processes: a method of under-water dredging to replace dry excavation in the Culebra cut and a system of lock construction whereby the summit level might be lowered by successive stages after the opening of the canal without interruption to navigation. He insisted that rock — even hard rock — could be extracted more cheaply under water by dredges than in the dry by steam shovels if it was first broken up by dynamite charges into small blocks the

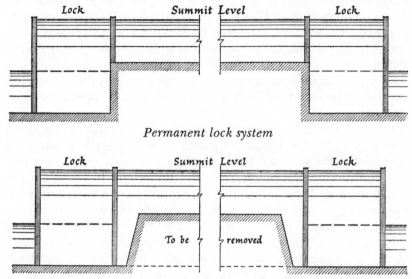

Permanent lock system

15. *Bunau-Varilla's temporary lock system*

size of paving stones. Then, starting with the highest level of the canal, the locks could be eliminated pair by pair until the water surface was lowered to sea level. In an ordinary permanent lock the height of the downstream gate is equal to the depth of the canal plus the fall of the lock while that of the upstream gate equals the canal depth only. Such a lock is exceedingly difficult to remove without stopping navigation altogether. Bunau-Varilla therefore proposed to build all upstream gates as high as the downstream ones, close half the width of the summit level to traffic, and dredge that portion under water while navigation proceeded normally in the other half. When the entire summit level had been dredged to a depth equal to the fall of one lock the upper pair of locks could be destroyed, the water surface lowered, and the process repeated on the next level.

The company's consulting committee finally approved the temporary lock canal project in October 1887. At Bohío Soldado a flight of five locks would raise the summit level 49 meters (about 161 feet) above the ocean, and on the Pacific slope five more locks were to be constructed between La Boca and Paraíso. An alternative scheme to be adopted if, as the company hoped, the summit level could be lowered to 140 feet before the canal opened would reduce the number of locks on each slope to four. Each lock was to be 180 meters (590 feet) long by 18 meters (59 feet) wide. Since the summit elevation would be too high to receive the natural flow of the Chagres it would have to be supplied with water artificially pumped from a reservoir formed by damming the Chagres at Gamboa. The substitution of the lock canal would of course enormously diminish the amount of excavation; in the new project only 34,-000,000 cubic meters, according to the company's estimate, remained to be extracted before the canal could be opened to navigation.

For the construction of the locks and installation of the gates, conduits, and other apparatus the company signed a preliminary agreement with Gustave Eiffel on November 15, 1887 and a definite contract on December 10. Eiffel undertook to complete the entire work by June 30, 1890 if only four locks on each side were required or by September 30, 1891 if five locks were found necessary. He computed the total cost of the locks and auxiliary plant at 100,000,000 to 120,000,000 francs. To expedite the work Eiffel awarded a subcontract for the excavation and masonry construction of the lock basins to Erzinger, Dephieux, Galtier et Compagnie, a firm which Bunau-Varilla helped to organize. The canal company agreed to supply Eiffel and the subcontractors with all the machinery they might require, and if delivery was not completed within 20 days after requisition Eiffel would be at liberty to purchase the equipment himself and collect an indemnity which might aggregate as much as 18,000,000 francs. For the installation of machinery to open and close the lock gates and to fill and empty the basins Eiffel was to receive 9,600,000 francs in addition, and before he commenced work the canal company granted him an advance of 6,000,000 francs to be repaid in installments by deduction from future remittances.

These and other overgenerous provisions afterwards provoked the Deputies committee to savage denunciation: "The negligence of the canal company shows up most blatantly in the Eiffel contract. In fact it is so extraordinarily obvious that one is forced to suspect that it was intentional, and that the company's principal object was the purchase in a disguised form of the great engineer's name, which his 300-meter tower [then under construction in Paris] was beginning to make famous. . . . How could the company undertake to deliver machinery worth 18,000,000 francs within twenty days? In fact it did not deliver it and was obliged to pay Éiffel the 18,000,000. Now it appears from the latter's own statements that he expended for such matériel . . . only 1,223,151 francs, and that he found on hand enough other machinery belonging to the canal company to finish the locks. . . . So from this one clause in his contract he made . . . a profit of more than 16,000,000 francs. . . ." [30] The committee also disclosed that of the 9,600,000 francs promised him for the installation of lock machinery Eiffel actually collected 2,880,000 francs though he had paid out only 40,509 for such appliances. Again, he had drawn 5,171,065 francs of the stipulated 6,000,000-franc advance, and this he retained although he had completed but a small portion of the work when operations ceased at the end of 1888. In the aggregate the company paid Eiffel 74,315,507 francs. The committee ventured no estimate of his net profit, but it must have been enormous even after the liquidator forced him to disgorge 3,000,000 francs in July 1889. The investigators admitted that careless wording of the contract rather than deliberate fraud accounted for a large part of Eiffel's unearned gains: "It should be noted that if the entire project had been carried out as planned the profits would have diminished greatly, but the contract was drawn up in such a curious manner that its incomplete fulfillment was not even contemplated." [31]

Nevertheless Eiffel was an exceedingly able engineer, and if the canal company had remained solvent a little longer he would probably have been able to open at least a makeshift waterway susceptible of future improvement. At the beginning he displayed all the energy of a new broom. On February 25, 1888 he informed de Lesseps: "My technical and administrative staffs have been busy on the isthmus since January 1. Excavation of nine lock basins is now under way with a force of *3500 laborers,* and the work is proceeding more actively . . . than I could have expected. . . ." [32] Simultaneously some of the other large contractors endeavored to speed up their tasks, and Artigue, Sonderegger et Compagnie installed an electric light plant to permit excavation of the Culebra cut by night as well as by day. But the canal company had waited too long to adopt the lock compromise. Its financial situation was hopeless, and on December 14, 1888 the French government appointed three receivers to wind up its affairs.

The poor showing made by Artigue, Sonderegger et Compagnie in the Culebra section, where the firm extracted only one ninth of

its total allotment, must be ascribed at least in part to an unforeseen difficulty: landslides. Enormous masses of the upper stratum
persistently slid into the cut, carrying with them rails, dump cars,
steam shovels, and often buildings. During the dry season the
slopes held together fairly well, but with the onset of the torrential rains each year hundreds of thousands of cubic meters washed
down into the open space below. The terraced dumps of previously extracted material proved no more stable as they softened
and shifted under the rains and piled up in the laboriously dug
channel. Excavation became a veritable task of Sisyphus. If the

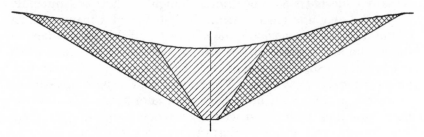

16. *Additional excavation necessitated by flat slopes*

slides had merely added to the contractors' original allotment the
removal of the slipped material the loss of time and labor would
have been serious enough; but unfortunately that was only part
of the difficulty. The crumbling talus slopes could be stabilized
only at a very flat angle which necessitated an enormous breadth
of excavation at the top, and to make matters worse every foot
added to the width of the cut also increased its depth. The Culebra
pass formed a narrow saddle flanked by steep ridges, so that while
its summit along the axis of the canal reached an altitude of only
330 feet above the sea the broad cut extended so far into the bor-
dering hills that its sides rose about 150 feet higher. The additional width and depth augmented the total cube to be extracted
by many millions of meters.

In the midst of its preoccupation with technical problems the
canal company did not neglect the potentially valuable lands
granted by its concession. The 500,000 hectares were to be chosen
anywhere on the isthmus and turned over to the company in installments as the work on the canal progressed. To supervise the selection and exploitation of these properties de Lesseps created a
service des domaines, placed in charge of it a "connoisseur of the
value of tropical real estate" [33] named Harel, and sent him with
two assistants to Panama in January 1881. On December 26, 1883

the Colombian government acknowledged the completion of the first third of the canal work and conceded 150,000 hectares (about 370,000 acres) of public land to the company. In October 1886 the Bogotá authorities, having satisfied themselves that half the work had been accomplished, increased the allotment to 250,000 hectares. The company selected approximately half of these lands in Darién and the rest in the province of Bocas del Toro, but before the actual transfer took place the company had declared itself bankrupt, and the lands were never exploited by the grantees. When the United States government purchased the property and concessions of the French company in 1904 all lands outside of the Canal Zone except those belonging to the Panama Railroad were returned by treaty arrangement — not, it is true, to Colombia but to the newly created republic of Panama. In addition to the conceded territory the French company acquired by purchase 13,296 hectares (32,860 acres) of land along the canal line, in the cities of Panama and Colón, and on the island of Taboga, at an average price of 112 francs per hectare or about $9 per acre. This property was retained by the United States after the transfer of the canal title.

During the construction period Charles de Lesseps visited the isthmus three times. In February 1883 he accompanied Dingler, just appointed general director of works, and devoted a month to inspection of the canal line, returning by way of New York. In January 1886 Charles went to Panama with Armand Rousseau, commissioner of the French government; Jacquet, inspector general of the Public Works Department; Étienne Martin, secretary general of the canal company; and Léon Boyer, the new director general. A few weeks later he was joined at Colón by his father, who at the age of 80 could still enjoy a program of tours, conferences, and banquets that exhausted his younger companions. This was Ferdinand de Lesseps's second and last journey to Panama, and as before he traveled with an army of satellites including invited representatives of the chambers of commerce of Marseilles, Bordeaux, Saint-Nazaire, and Rouen as well as a correspondent of the *Journal des Débats*, Gustave de Molinari. On February 17 the party reached Colón, where they were met by a British delegation comprising the Duke of Sutherland, Admiral Carpenter, and Colonel Talbot, and a group of Americans including Rear Admiral Jouett, commander of the *Tennessee*, Nathan Appleton, and John Bigelow, commissioner appointed by the New York Chamber of Commerce.

This time de Lesseps remained on the isthmus only a fortnight.

The days were filled with trips to excavations, machine shops, and hospitals and the ritual explosion of immense charges of dynamite; the nights with banquets, balls, and fireworks. The number of ceremonial dinners consumed in rapid succession would have ruined the digestion of anyone less robust. "The whole city," reported a Panama correspondent, "has turned out to pay homage to the canal builder. . . . In the plaza a triumphal arch inscribed *Panama-Suez* rises above the solidly packed crowd. Flags are everywhere . . . and windows are hidden behind flowers and palm branches." [34] Bigelow's report expressed both doubt and hope: "I did not hear of any insuperable difficulty in the accomplishment of this work, but I cannot but think that Mr. de Lesseps will be disappointed in his calculations, both in regard to the time and the cost of it. It certainly is not progressing at present at a rate which warrants the hope of its completion in 1889. . . . It would be about as safe to predict the quarter in which the winds will be setting next Christmas day at St. Petersburg, as the time when the canal will be finished or what it will cost. . . ." [35]

Ferdinand de Lesseps never returned to the isthmus, but he made one more voyage across the Atlantic, at the invitation of the United States government, to attend the ceremonial unveiling of Bartholdi's Statue of Liberty in October 1886. Charles revisited Panama in March 1887 and declared himself fully satisfied with the progress of the work and "very proud, as a Frenchman, of the favorable impression our achievement . . . has produced in the Americas. . . . The cutting of the isthmus . . . which is now certain, will be a great triumph for our beloved country and in addition an excellent investment — and that is surely no disadvantage." [36] But when asked to set an approximate date for the opening he took refuge in evasion: "Unfortunately my temperament does not lend itself to approximations. . . ." [37] The optimism Charles professed at that critical period was not shared by the contractor Sonderegger, who wrote to his Paris partners on March 25, 1887, the day of Charles's departure: "His visit has been marked by an immense amount of diplomacy, tact, amiability, and kindness; by endless and unbounded compliments; but by very little real effort to advance the work. It suggested to me the precautions taken before a storm: a polishing up of lightning rods. . . ." [38] And the rôle of lightning rod, he feared, was to be assigned to contractors like himself: "The canal company, expecting a disaster, is trying in every possible way to persuade the public that we are responsible and to make us the scapegoats." [39]

On the other hand Lieutenant Charles C. Rogers of the United

States navy, also writing in March 1887, discounted such predictions of failure: "The most bitter opponents . . . were our own countrymen and a few Englishmen or former employés of the canal, who had been discharged or had some other grievance against the company. Many . . . were intelligent men, who did not hesitate to make most exaggerated statements, showing either utter ignorance of facts or else malice. . . . Frequently trivial accidents or mishaps . . . are magnified into insuperable and ruinous obstacles; and such reports are spread abroad. . . . The work of 1886 is very creditable. . . . The contractors are young, zealous, and energetic men; the engineers . . . are both clever and capable. . . . Instead of censure and detraction, they deserve the highest praise and respect. . . . But from all sources, whether friend or enemy, there comes the same admission . . . that the canal presents no insuperable obstacles, and that its final completion is merely a question of time and of money. . . ." [40]

Chapter 28. Life and Death on the Isthmus

THROUGHOUT the entire construction period one of the canal company's most troublesome problems was the recruitment of an adequate and efficient labor force. At the very beginning when the preliminary work of clearing brush required only a few hundred men the company depended upon the Indian and Negro inhabitants of the isthmus itself. Low wages — 60 cents per day for unskilled laborers plus a food allowance of 45 cents — and the imposition of irksome restrictions soon provoked discord. As early as April 1881 the *Bulletin* informed its readers that a certain number of native workmen "refused to perform their tasks on the pretext that they were being forced to work on Sunday by having their food allowance for that day withheld if they did not do so. The charge is unfounded. All they were asked to do was to remain in camp on Sunday instead of getting drunk in the near-by villages and returning in such condition that they could do no work on Monday. The laborers yielded after two days of lamentation over the harsh discipline prescribed for them." [1] For the moment the isthmus could supply all the labor needed, and the company turned away hundreds of applicants from overseas. As the demand for labor increased the rates of pay rose rapidly. In 1886 unskilled Negro workmen received $1.75 a day, skilled Negroes $2.50 to $2.75, and white mechanics $5.

By the end of 1881 almost 2000 men including the white technicians and office staff were at work on the canal. By December 1882 the number had jumped to 4000, in December 1883 to 13,000, and in May 1884 the payrolls listed more than 19,000, approximately the maximum number employed at any one time during the French administration. The isthmus had long ceased to furnish more than a small fraction of this force. Some workmen came from Cartagena, some from Venezuela, others from Cuba, Barbados, St. Lucia, and Martinique. About 550 American Negroes drifted in from New Orleans and other Southern ports. A few Negroes were imported from Senegal on the west coast of Africa. Several hundred Chinese who had met with a chilly reception in California migrated to Panama, but most of them soon left the employ of the canal company to set up small shops, boarding houses, and other enterprises of their own. Most important of all as a source of labor was Jamaica. After 1883 more than half of all the canal workers were Jamaica Negroes; of 12,875 laborers imported in 1885, 9000 came from that island.

The Jamaican authorities attempted without much success to stem this wholesale emigration. Lieutenant Rogers reported in March 1887: "People on the Isthmus say the negro men are wanted in Jamaica for the plantations; while the papers of Kingston base the government's action on purely philanthropic and patriotic grounds, seeing that the negro returns . . . without money, frequently broken down in health. . . . The canal company can hardly be held responsible for the morals or extravagance of the . . . negro. . . . The pay . . . is high, considering the usual hire. . . . And it is possible for a temperate and economical workman to . . . save something. . . ." [2] The French correspondent de Molinari advised the establishment of savings banks on the isthmus to encourage thrift among the Negroes, and when the canal company failed to adopt this suggestion the Jamaican government undertook to accept on deposit the savings of its own citizens and transmit the money to their families.

Erratic fluctuations in the labor supply often interfered with the progress of the work. "There are no time contracts," reported Lieutenant Kimball in 1886, "and these men [from the Caribbean islands] are in the habit of returning to their homes to spend what they accumulate, often leaving the works at the very time when from conditions of weather or arrangement of plant they can least conveniently be spared. . . . The constant changes of the men employed are encouraged by many influences; by the improvident nature of some . . . which leads them to spend their earnings in a pleasant way at home as soon as possible; by the forethought of others, who . . . leave the Isthmus before they are killed by the climate; by the profit in transporting them to and fro by the steamer companies; by the poor quality and high prices of provisions; by the exorbitant rates charged for small drafts by the small bankers . . . by the lack of sufficient guarantees for hospital attendance; and by fears arising from political disturbances. It would seem that many of these influences could be counteracted by the Company. . . ." [3] Such desertions were especially unwelcome in the spring, when dry weather gave the contractors an opportunity to speed excavation. "The Easter holidays," the *Bulletin* complained in 1887, ". . . have stripped the canal works of a great many laborers, almost all from the Antilles, who . . . have gone home for a vacation. For a long time the company has been calling the contractors' attention to the evils resulting from . . . the ease with which workmen can return to their own countries in a few days. . . ." [4] Twenty years later the United States government experienced much the same difficulty with its West Indian canal workers.

During the years of active construction the company found itself almost constantly hampered by a more or less acute shortage of labor. In 1886 John Bigelow urged the use of machinery for many operations then being performed by hand: "May not the exigency, like childbearing, work its own cure? . . . Machines do not mind malaria; they are not poisoned by marshy water; they thrive on the black vomit [yellow fever]; they have no fear of chills or sunstrokes, and . . . they are never tired." [5]

Workmen were not only scarce but often shiftless. "The native races of the tropics," Bigelow wrote, "here mostly of African origin, seem to be the only human beings constituted to endure hard labor while exposed to the Isthmus sun. . . . Their wants are but little more difficult to satisfy than those of the birds of the air or of the beasts of the field. They have no tastes to gratify by accumulation; and if they had, they have no place in which they could put their accumulations in security except, like the dogs, they bury them in the ground. If . . . they earn more than they consume, the only way they can keep the surplus is to convert it into pleasure of some kind as soon as possible, and pleasure with them usually means idleness and gambling. It is impossible to stimulate such a race in such a climate by the inducements which are so efficient . . . in higher latitudes." [6] Bigelow might have added drinking and fornication to his list of pleasures indulged in by the laborers. Cheap saloons flourished in every isthmian community, and women of every race and color filled the numerous houses of prostitution. Rogers reported in 1887: "The workmen are paid off on Saturday afternoon. Sunday is generally a day of dissipation with the negro, Monday one of recuperation, and by Tuesday he is generally at work. . . ." [7]

After working hours the isthmus provided little recreation for the hundreds of bored and homesick Frenchmen, oppressed by the enervating climate and haunted by fear of mysterious tropical maladies. Henri Cermoise, one of the first engineers sent to Panama in 1881, drew a melancholy picture of the monotonous existence of these expatriates and of their feverish search for distraction. Before the company converted the Grand Hotel into an office building it contained "a small room crowded with people and furnished with a roulette table. All varieties of entertainment could be found . . . in this hotel room. . . . There were no theatres in the city, no concerts, no cafés, nothing. . . . About four in the afternoon all these people began to move outdoors, it was time for the promenade on Las Bóvedas [the only surviving remnant of the ancient sea wall, which remains today the most popular *paseo* of the Panamanians]. . . . Certainly this promenade . . . is one of the . . . pleasantest one could imagine, but after one has strolled up and down it every day . . . for several months . . . it ceases to provide more than mild diversion. . . . The bars are designed for nothing but hasty drinking. . . . The native *tiendas* . . . are even worse: horrible dens that look and smell like the filthiest grogshops of the shoddiest Paris suburbs. . . . In spite of all our good resolutions . . . we return to the gambling room, where at least we are sure to see a familiar face. Oh, that roulette! How dear it has cost . . . the canal employees!" [8]

The company did make a feeble attempt to supply a few amenities and amusements of a less spicy nature for its European staff. In July 1883 de Lesseps announced benignly that Richier, then chief superintendent, "has opened in the company's hotel at Panama, and intends to open at Colón, assembly rooms provided with books, periodicals, and various indoor games where our employees can gather in the evenings and during the . . . 'siesta' hour, thus strengthening day by day the bonds of friendship . . . that tend . . . to convert the staff . . . into one large family. . . ." [9] It is impossible to guess how many of the employees preferred these sedate reading rooms to the gaudier bars, brothels, and casinos.

Although most of the common laborers were Negroes the company was quite willing to employ any white man who appeared to possess the physical stamina required for heavy work in a hot sultry climate. Among the odd assortment of waifs and strays who toiled at one time or another on the canal was the painter Paul Gauguin. Unable to sell enough pictures to live even in the most economical fashion in France, Gauguin sailed for Panama in April 1887 with a vague idea of buying a small plot of ground on Taboga Island and settling there if it proved to be the tropical paradise he expected. He soon discovered that it was not. Having used every franc he could scrape together to pay his steamer fare, he reached the isthmus penniless and was obliged to apply almost immediately for work on the excavations. Unaccustomed to the heat and violent exertion, he found the hours long and the labor backbreaking; the price of land was exorbitant; and to add to his disillusionment his uncouth habits involved him in difficulties with the police. "Now that the canal is being dug," he wrote to his wife, "these imbecile Colombians will not sell one an inch of land for less than six francs a square meter [about $4800 an acre — obviously an exaggeration]. Just because I urinated in a filthy hole full of broken bottles and excrement I was forced to walk all the way across Panama City under arrest, and in the end I was fined one piastre [4 francs]. I felt like taking a crack at those gendarmes, but the police here are very quick on the trigger, they follow you at a distance of five paces and if you make a move they fire a bullet through your head. Tomorrow I am going to swing a pickaxe . . . on the canal works for 150 piastres [$120] a month. As soon as I can put aside 150 piastres . . . (it will take me two months), I shall go to Martinique. I have to dig . . . from five-thirty in the morning to six in the evening, under tropical sun and rain. At night I am devoured by mosquitoes." [10] Before Gauguin's two months were up he was discharged, apparently because the contractor for that section ordered a reduction of the working force, and made his way to Martinique, which he found much more to his taste.

The canal company maintained no commissaries for its employees, who were forced to buy whatever the local shops offered, often at excessive prices. It housed its Negro workers in barracks which it rented to the contractors at an annual rate equal to 10% of their cost. After some experimentation the company adopted a standard dormitory of 40 bunks arranged in two tiers, well ventilated and roofed with corrugated iron. Kimball found the offices and residences provided for the white staff "as convenient and comfortable as the conditions will allow. These have been criticised as too expensive, but when it is considered that the large death rate would be larger yet, were not a great deal of attention paid to sanitary conditions and comforts . . . it would seem to be a poor economy which would curtail the expenses in this direction. . . ." [11] Rousseau reported that in general these buildings were constructed "with proper regard for comfort and health. There have even been complaints that they are excessively luxurious. . . . Obviously the company has endeavored to provide . . . not only decent living conditions but in addition a pleasant environment. Its expenditures for such purposes represent but a small fraction of its total outlay." [12]

The company sorely needed such reasonable and unprejudiced defenders, for while some of the charges of waste and extravagance were undoubtedly well founded, others inspired by speculators who hoped to profit by a decline in the value of the company's securities or by men who bore grudges against it were manifestly absurd. Once in circulation such tales grew taller with each repetition. Dr. Wolfred Nelson, who practised medicine on the isthmus from 1880 to 1885, complained: "There is enough bureaucratic work, and there are enough officers on the Isthmus to furnish at least one dozen first-class republics with officials for all their departments. The expenditure has been something simply colossal. One Director-General [Dingler] lived in a mansion that cost over $100,000; his pay was $50,000 a year, and every time he went out on the line he had . . . fifty dollars a day additional. He travelled in a handsome Pullman car, specially constructed, which was reported to have cost some $42,000. Later, wishing a summer residence, a most expensive building was put up near La Boca. The preparation of the grounds, the building, and the roads thereto, cost upwards of $150,000. . . . One canal chief had had built a famous pigeon-house. . . . It cost the company $1500. Another man had built a large bath-house on the most approved principles. This cost $40,000. . . ." [13] The construction of a bathhouse in a tropical country might appear to modern readers an achievement for a physician to commend rather than criticize. Dr. Nelson's statistics must be taken with several grains of salt. The Deputies committee, which had access to all the evidence, placed the director general's salary at $20,000, not $50,000.

Dingler's country house on Ancón Hill near La Boca, nicknamed *la folie Dingler,* made an ideal target for the shafts of the company's ill-wishers. Considering the financial situation of the company it was probably an unwarranted luxury, but its cost was most fantastically exaggerated. Nelson's estimate of $150,000, though excessive, was modesty itself compared with Édouard Drumont's maliciously preposterous valuation of more than $1,000,-000. According to the most reliable accounts the company actually expended about $100,000 on the house and grounds. Other alleged prodigalities that invited attack were Dingler's famous Pullman car — scarcely a necessity on a railroad less than 50 miles long — and the expensive stables, horses, and carriages provided for the chief officials and their families in a country almost destitute of roads or bridle paths. Here again exaggeration ran riot. Drumont exalted the dingy Pullman into "a royal coach called a *Palace car.* This car contained 3 furnished bedrooms, a dining-room, a kitchen, a water closet, an office, and a refrigerator. . . . It was attached to a special train which cost the company $500 for each trip. . . ." [14] Henry Maréchal, a disgruntled stockholder and inspired mischiefmaker who visited the isthmus in the winter of 1884, published a description of "a magnificent saloon car ordered from the United States by the director general, which cost 300,000 francs but which he never used since he has never even visited the works. . . ." [15] Obviously both accounts could not be correct. As a matter of fact neither was.

More soberly the Deputies committee rebuked the company for building "immense stables which sheltered no fewer than 100 thoroughbred horses. Baron Tripier was appointed superintendent of the stables. . . . Extravagances of this kind did not last; horses and carriages were sold. The stablemaster was dismissed, but the prodigalities continued in other forms, for the company . . . always spent money as if it had too much. . . ." [16] The company was undeniably guilty of shocking waste even if its staff did not commit the imaginary excesses recounted with a leer by Maréchal: "In one section the chief engineer . . . instead of employing his workmen on the excavation of the canal, has set them to work on the construction of . . . avenues and ornamental clearings in the surrounding forest, a kind of miniature Bois de Boulogne, where the officials entertain at charming picnic parties and make daily pleasure excursions on the company's horses. . . . Ladies, possibly somewhat too swarthy but not too strictly virtuous, render these jaunts more agreeable and are repaid for their services by being carried on the company's payrolls as laborers." [17] The reliability and good faith of Maréchal's contemptible efforts to discredit the canal company may be judged by his inclusion of this cock-and-bull invention: "Since the dump cars sent from Europe turned out to be a little too high for the workmen to reach, the company was naïve enough to send an official delegation at great expense to the Gulf of Mexico to hunt for a tribe of giants whose existence had been reported by some practical joker." [18]

Such stories created a general impression among the uninformed, especially in the United States, that all French construction work on the canal was tainted with extravagance and graft. Observers who took the trouble to investigate for themselves adopted a less critical attitude. When Colonel Gorgas first visited the isthmus in April 1904 just before the transfer of the property to the United States he was quartered at Colón in the residence known as the "de Lesseps palace": "There was, however, nothing palatial about this building. . . . De Lesseps is accused of having erected it at a cost of more than $100,000. As I . . . came to be more familiar with the history of the French régime . . . I found that this . . . had no more foundation in fact than many of the other tales . . . to the discredit of the French." [19]

For eight years the French canal company fought a grim battle against disease. It sent scores of excellent doctors to the isthmus and expended millions of francs on the construction and equipment of hospitals. Although the death list was lamentably long the health record was on the whole better than might have been expected in the circumstances. It must be remembered that all efforts to prevent epidemics of the most deadly tropical maladies were doomed to failure as long as the methods by which they were transmitted remained unknown. Not until the end of the century, when Ronald Ross identified the *Anopheles* mosquito as the carrier of the malaria parasite, and Walter Reed's famous experiment in Cuba proved that another mosquito, *Aëdes aegypti,* spread the micro-organism of yellow fever, could these scourges be brought under control. The French doctors at Panama cannot be accused of negligence; they did their best, but they were struggling against an unsuspected enemy.

To inspire confidence in the canal enterprise and disprove prejudicial rumors concerning the prevalence of disease de Lesseps took his wife and three of his children with him on his first journey to the isthmus. On May 2, 1880, after his return to Paris, he informed a large audience at the Cirque d'Été: "Today we are certain that all objections on the score of the insalubrity of Panama's climate have been removed. . . . I should never have dared to undertake a work necessitating human hecatombs. . . . Panama is an exceedingly healthy country. . . ." [20] It was true that no member of his large party had fallen seriously ill during the recent visit, but de Lesseps neglected to point out that that visit had taken place at the beginning of the driest and healthiest season. On June 28 he quoted a reassuring letter from Pedro Sosa, then in charge of preliminary work on the isthmus: "There has been much talk here recently . . . of yellow fever; but there is nothing in it. The extreme rarity of the cases . . . proves that the disease has not taken root in this country. . . ." [21] At the same time de Lesseps expressed the rather startling opinion that quarantines were not only useless but positively harmful because "they do not prevent the spread of epidemic diseases when their transmission is favored by atmospheric conditions, and . . . they constantly hinder commercial and maritime relations." [22]

On April 1, 1881 the *Bulletin* announced cheerfully: "The health of all the employees . . . leaves nothing to be desired." [23] The first warning of disaster came with the onset of that year's rainy season. On July 25 Étienne, one of the assistant superintendents of works, died at Colón; and three days later Henry Bionne, the company's secretary general and de Lesseps's right hand, died on board the *Crescent City* shortly after leaving Colón. Neither death was ascribed to yellow fever; according to the *Bulletin* Étienne succumbed to a cerebral malady, while the ship's doctor reported that Bionne's symptoms indicated "complications in the region of the kidneys." [24] The loss of two prominent officials in rapid succession caused some uneasiness, which the *Bulletin* endeavored to allay: "The newspapers . . . have seized upon the unfortunate deaths of M. Bionne and . . . M. Étienne, and . . . of a few workmen, as a pretext for an attack upon the insalubrity of the climate. . . . The truth is that the climate . . . like all hot climates, is dangerous for those who underestimate its effects . . . and who fail to observe the principles of hygiene. It is untrue that yellow fever is prevalent; it is untrue . . . that M. Bionne and . . . M. Étienne were victims of that disease. . . . But . . . unhappily it is true that a few laborers . . . have died of it. . . ." [25]

In November of the same year Gaston Blanchet, the engineer who represented Couvreux and Hersent on the isthmus, succumbed after a strenuous inspection tour of the upper course of the Chagres. Dingler, director general of works for more than two years, suffered no less than four successive bereavements. In October 1883, after a brief sojourn in Paris, he returned to the isthmus with his wife and children. The *Bulletin* rejoiced that "M. Dingler has given the best proof of his confidence in the country . . . by taking his family with him. . . ." [26] The confidence was tragically shattered. Within three months his son, his daughter, and his daughter's fiancé had died of yellow fever, and in January 1885 his wife died of the same malady. One of Dingler's successors, Léon Boyer, succumbed to yellow fever on May 1, 1886, three months after his arrival at Panama. "It would seem," lamented the *Bulletin*, ". . . as if death chose among its rare victims just those dearest to our hearts." [27] Dingler's personal misfortunes earned him the sympathy even of his detractors; yet Édouard Drumont, who respected neither grief nor truth, smacked his lips over the engineer's heartache with almost inconceivable brutality: "This man, who seems to have endured heavy afflictions but who was a stranger to every sentiment of justice and humanity, was hated so bitterly that the death of his wife became the occasion of a merry festival. Champagne flowed in torrents . . . and the unhappy man could hear the joyous shouts of all the slaves who exulted in the sorrows of their master. . . ." [28] Surely malicious libel could go no farther.

While the death rate among employees was undoubtedly high it has been grossly exaggerated by irresponsible commentators. Presumably the most reliable source of statistical information is the official report of the special technical commission appointed in 1898 by the Compagnie Nouvelle du Canal de Panama, successor to the bankrupt Compagnie Universelle. In 1904 Colonel Gorgas, after an examination of the French hospital records, computed a slightly higher death rate for the same period: [29]

| | | DEATH RATE PER 1000 | |
YEAR	NUMBER OF EMPLOYEES (average)	according to Compagnie Nouvelle	according to Gorgas
1881	928	66.8	59.2
1882	1,910	66.0	65.4
1883	6,287	66.6	67.2
1884	17,615	66.6	69.9
1885	15,215	55.2	71.3
1886	14,935	51.0	64.0
1887	16,217	62.1	63.7
1888	13,725	43.5	44.2
Average		59.7	63.1

Of the 4987 deaths that occurred during these eight years the Compagnie Nouvelle's committee attributed 1018 to yellow fever. Gorgas computed the total number of deaths for the same period at 5527, of which 1026 were due to yellow fever and 1368 to malaria. The company's report disclosed that in each of those years more than 60% of the employees received treatment for various ailments. It also attempted to compare the health records of different races: "The native Negroes, and especially those from the Antilles . . . exhibit the greatest resistance on account of their ability to endure the hot sun, their partial immunity to malaria, and their complete immunity to yellow fever. The Hindus, Chinese, and African Negroes are less robust and . . . succumb readily to attacks of beriberi, the germs of which they brought with them [beriberi, now ascribed to vitamin deficiencies in polished rice and similar foods, was then presumed to have a bacterial origin]. At present the European can support the climate . . . as long as he does not attempt to work in the excavations." [30]

In his vindictive campaign against the canal company Drumont did not hesitate to multiply the actual death rate by 10 and to invent the most grotesque calumnies: "The men died like flies at the rate of about 60%. . . . The true number of deaths, which cannot be less than 30,000, will never be known. . . . Sometimes the workmen who died at their posts were merely thrown onto the embankments; a train of dump cars discharged its load on top of them, and the corpses were quickly covered by 20 inches of earth. The isthmus has become . . . an immense boneyard. . . . This method of burial . . . was never employed except for the Negroes. . . . On the contrary much zeal was displayed in the interment of the Europeans in the service of the company . . . so much in fact . . . that they were frequently buried before they were dead. . . ."[31] Another French writer asserted as late as 1937 that during a single epidemic of yellow fever "of 21,000 Frenchmen, 16,000 succumbed in a few weeks. The rest fled. . . ."[32] Such figures were manifestly absurd: at no time were as many as 21,000 men of all nationalities taken together employed on the canal works, and the number of Europeans probably never exceeded 1000.

Even before the start of preliminary clearings in 1880 the canal company began to organize its medical and hospital services. In January 1881 the chief medical officer, Dr. Companyo, a former member of the sanitary division of the Suez canal, proceeded to the isthmus with his staff. Within a year a large hospital building had been constructed at Ancón, a suburb of Panama, and another at Colón, while smaller dispensaries and infirmaries were established at each intermediate construction center. A year or two later the company opened a sanatorium for convalescents on Taboga Island. In time the Ancón unit was expanded into a group of 16 detached pavilions. Sisters of the order of St. Vincent de Paul served as nurses. "I heard many complaints about the working of the hospital service," Kimball reported in 1886, "but these were directed against the contractors rather than the company. I was informed that the company's men were sent to hospital upon sick-tickets given by the section physician, and that the contractors' men were supposed to be sent in the same way, hospital expenses being $1 per day; but the contractors, knowing that a sick man would be a great expense, and the chances of his repaying them, even if he recovered, slight, would discharge him upon his falling ill, and . . . he would be left to die by the roadside. I saw no such cases, and imagine they are rare, though possible. . . ."[33] "From my knowledge of human nature," Gorgas wrote many years later, "I feel sure that the French contractors did not send a large proportion of their sick to Ancon Hospital."[34]

The canal company paid the hospital expenses of its own employees, who were expected to reimburse the company. The government of Jamaica undertook to pay either the company or the contractors for the care of laborers from that island, but citizens of other countries were obliged to pay their own hospital bills. The charge of approximately $1 a day did not in fact quite cover the cost of treatment, and the company made up the deficit.

In general observers found little to disapprove and much to praise in the French hospital organization. "The hospitals have been built at large cost," reported Lieutenant Raymond P. Rodgers, U.S.N., in February 1883, "and many say that money has been wasted upon them, but it would seem a matter of good policy, even though extravagant, to provide suitable means to prevent or diminish the bad effects of the climate. . . ." [35] Rousseau expressed the same opinion: "The company has sometimes been denounced for its excessive expenditures upon hospital establishments. In a country like the isthmus such a criticism is obviously more creditable than its opposite would be." [36] Gorgas called the Ancón hospital "a very much better institution than any hospital in America . . . at the same period carried on by a firm or corporation." [37] Even Dr. Nelson, who had few kind words for the French company, admitted: "The canal hospitals on the Panama side are without doubt the finest and most perfect system of hospitals ever made within the tropics." [38]

All this lavish outlay certainly reduced the death rate to some extent, but its beneficial effects were largely offset by the failure, inevitable at that time, to recognize the fatal rôle played by the mosquito. The most scientifically planned hospitals, skillful doctors, and devoted nurses could accomplish little against the two chief scourges of the isthmus, malaria and yellow fever, as long as disease-bearing mosquitoes were permitted to buzz at will through unscreened doors and windows. Not only were no precautions taken against the assaults of these carriers, but their propagation was often actively though unwittingly encouraged in and near the hospitals themselves. Pots of well-watered plants and gay tropical flowers were placed in the wards, and it has been alleged that to keep the armies of voracious ants at bay the legs of each bed were set in little cups of water — ideal breeding places for mosquitoes. Whether or not these liquid ant-guards were actually used inside the wards they were certainly scattered in profusion throughout the pretty gardens surrounding the hospitals, where thousands of pottery rings filled with water protected the shrubs and plants from destruction by umbrella ants. "Probably," Gorgas wrote, "if the French had been trying to propagate yellow fever, they could not have provided conditions better adapted for this purpose." [39]

General sanitary conditions in the areas directly supervised by the company's medical officials appear to have been fairly satisfactory, but the cities of Panama and Colón and the native villages, over which the company exercised little or no control, were deplorably squalid. In 1886 de Molinari contrasted the French town of Christophe-Colomb with its older neighbor Colón: "Although the two cities are contiguous they could not be more unlike in appearance if they were separated by a thousand kilometers. Christophe-Colomb is brand new and neatly kept. Colón . . . is a foul hole. . . . In comparison with it the ghettos of White Russia, the slums of Toulon, Genoa, Naples, and old Stamboul would deserve prizes for . . . cleanliness. . . . A few houses painted in bright colors present a pleasing appearance; but one must not go too near them. Since there are neither sewers nor street cleaners . . . and toilets are quite unknown, all refuse is thrown . . . into the swamps . . . or onto rubbish heaps. Toads splash in the liquid muck . . . rats infest the solid filth, and snakes . . . hunt both toads and rats; clouds of mosquitoes . . . swarm into the houses, usually unprovided with glass windows. . . . Need I say that the canal company has no authority at Colón? Sanitation of the town is in the hands of the municipal council, which . . . prefers to concern itself with other matters." [40]

During the construction period two convulsions of nature and one man-made revolution interfered briefly with operations on the canal. On September 7, 1882 a violent earthquake shook the isthmus, destroyed a number of buildings, damaged railroad bridges and embankments, and caused widespread panic though it killed only five people. Since one of the most potent arguments in favor of the Panama route had always been its supposed freedom from severe earthquakes the canal company suffered the loss of a cherished illusion as well as of physical property, while the Nicaragua partisans crowed over Panama's discomfiture. On December 2, 1885 a hurricane swept across Colón harbor, blew sailing vessels ashore, destroyed the Royal Mail freight office, and suspended railroad traffic for a few days. The Chagres, rising 30 feet in a few hours, flooded several miles of roadbed and carried away a bridge. According to Bunau-Varilla 50 people were drowned in the waters of Limón Bay.

More destructive than either of these disasters was the factional dispute that transformed the isthmus into an armed camp in the spring of 1885. The political background of the disturbance, like that of most Latin American upheavals, was excessively complicated. The election to the presidency of Colombia of Rafael Núñez, a former Liberal leader turned Conservative, precipitated insurrections in several provinces. To help suppress one of these revolts a large detachment of Colombian troops stationed at Panama was sent to Buenaventura in February 1885, and a few weeks later a second force commanded by the provincial President of Panama, General Ramón Santo Domingo Vila, proceeded to Cartagena to quell a similar rebellion in the state of Bolívar. During Santo Domingo Vila's absence the first *designado* or Vice President, Pablo Arosemena, temporarily assumed the duties of the presidential office. But the withdrawal of the troops left only about 250 soldiers under the command of General Gónima to protect the isthmus, and on March 16 Rafael Aizpuru, a former President of Panama, seized the opportunity to effect a *coup d'état*. The insurgent leader quickly subdued the city of Panama and drove Arosemena to seek refuge on board the British naval vessel *Heroine*. General Gónima, stationed at Colón, hastened to Panama with his loyal troops and occupied the city. Aizpuru retired to a near-by village on March 17, and Arosemena returned to Panama but resigned a few days later. Gónima, declaring himself military and civil chief of Panama, prevented Vivas León, the second *designado,* from assuming office as Arosemena's legal successor.

The departure of Gónima's diminutive army left Colón at the mercy of another insurgent, Pedro Prestan, a Haitian Negro with a trace of white blood. Prestan appears to have had little or no direct connection with Aizpuru, but both detested foreigners in general and Americans in particular. The Negro rebel took possession of the Colón prefecture, extorted forced loans from foreign merchants, and without opposition made himself master of the city. On March 29 the Pacific Mail liner *Colon* arrived with a contraband cargo of arms consigned to "order." Prestan demanded the surrender of the weapons; and when William Connor, the Pacific Mail superintendent, refused to give them up, the rebel leader arrested him as well as Captain J. M. Dow, the line's general agent; George A. Burt, superintendent of the Panama Railroad; R. K. Wright, Jr., United States consul at Colón; and Lieutenant Judd and Cadet Richardson of the U.S.S. *Galena,* at anchor in the harbor. Prestan then sent Richardson to Commander Theodore F. Kane of the *Galena* with a message to the effect that he proposed to hold these men "until the arms were delivered, and that if the *Galena* attempted to land a force . . . he . . . would fire on the boat, and . . . shoot every prisoner in the Calaboose, and murder every American in the city!" [41] Consul Wright, convinced that

Prestan would not hesitate to carry out the threat, ordered Dow to surrender the arms, and the prisoners were released. Kane refused to deliver the weapons, seized the *Colon* in the name of the United States government, hauled her away from the dock, and brought the *Galena* alongside the wharf. Prestan rearrested Dow and Connor, and the next morning Kane landed his entire force of about 100 marines and sailors.

On the night of March 30 Gónima sent Colonel Ulloa, commander of the small Colombian warship *Boyacá* then stationed in Panama Bay, to Colón by train with a detachment of loyal troops. To prevent a clash in Colón itself Burt requested Ulloa to stop at Monkey Hill, two miles outside the town. Prestan's forces advanced to the attack but were driven back to Colón and decisively routed. During the battle the insurgents set fire to the city, and within a few hours little was left of Colón but a heap of ashes. Prestan fled but was captured, court-martialed, and hanged on August 18.

Meanwhile Aizpuru had taken advantage of Ulloa's absence to recapture the city of Panama and declare himself President of the province. By the terms of capitulation the *Boyacá* was to be delivered to the insurgents, but her temporary commander, José Domingo de Obaldía, hastily ordered the vessel to sea and brought her safely to Buenaventura. Both Aizpuru and Prestan had committed depredations on the railroad's property and interfered with the passage of trains. Burt complained that Aizpuru "has been permitted to . . . open and block switches . . . to continually obstruct the road, to cut wires . . . and otherwise to render it necessary to close the transit. . . . That . . . he has sent armed men on board a train . . . and taken employees in custody. That he broke into sealed car . . . and removed the entire contents. . . ." [42] Prestan had ripped up rails, damaged the telegraph line, and thrown an engine off the track.

Under the treaty of 1846 the United States had the right to intervene to protect the transit against attack or interruption. Three small American warships, *Galena, Shenandoah,* and *Wachusett,* were already in isthmian waters, and a few marines had been landed, but the armed force was inadequate to keep the transit open. On April 2 Commander Bowman H. McCalla received orders to proceed to Colón at the head of two battalions of marines and a detachment of sailors, about 740 men in all; while the *Tennessee* and *Swatara* under the command of Rear Admiral Jouett were dispatched to the same port. In conformity with the "hands-off" policy of the recently installed Cleveland administration Secretary of the Navy William C. Whitney specifically directed Jouett to police the isthmus but not to meddle with politics.

Jouett reached Colón on April 10, the next day the first battalion of marines arrived, and on April 15 the steamer *Acapulco* brought McCalla and the rest of the armed force. McCalla established headquarters in Panama and on April 24 arrested Aizpuru and other insurgent leaders but released them the next day after securing a promise that the rebels would discontinue street fighting. On the 27th another United States warship, the *Iroquois*, anchored in Panama Bay and landed a detachment; and on the 28th the *Boyacá* returned from Buenaventura accompanied by half a dozen small vessels carrying about 600 Colombian troops and the Colombian commander in chief, Colonel Rafael Reyes, as well as the newly appointed military and civil chief of Panama, Colonel Montoya. At a conference with these officers presided over by Admiral Jouett on April 29 Aizpuru agreed to surrender; the Colombian forces entered Panama a day later, and the United States troops withdrew to Colón on May 1; but on the 5th Reyes ordered the arrest of Aizpuru and his chief colleagues because the insurgents had failed to deliver their arms as promised. Aizpuru was taken to Bogotá, court-martialed, fined, and sentenced to ten years in exile.

Most of the American marines and sailors left the isthmus on May 7. "During the occupation," McCalla noted, ". . . the men behaved in the most exemplary manner. . . . There were the usual cases of fever and other diseases . . . and one fatal case of yellow fever . . . but the general health of the command was excellent." [43] The recommendations of Jouett's surgeon general, F. M. Gunnell, probably had much to do with the satisfactory health record: "A barrack with a wood roof, ridge ventilated and waterproofed canvas sides . . . with mosquito nettings for each man, is a ready and efficient help . . . against the effects of malaria." [44] Gunnell might have found himself on the verge of a momentous discovery had not the real implications of his own advice escaped him: he assumed that the nets prevented malaria not because they kept out mosquitoes but because they absorbed much of the dampness in the night air. Trautwine, when engaged on the construction of the Panama Railroad, had observed the same phenomenon and made the same mistake: "A veil over the face is a partial protection from miasmatic vapors. . . . Keep closed such doors and windows as open to winds blowing across marshes. . . . But if they must be open, have screens of gauze or *copper* wire. . . . Mosquito nets are good, not only against insects but miasma." [45]

Throughout the disturbance both the canal company and the

French government very properly maintained a strictly neutral attitude. One French warship, the *Reine-Blanche*, lay at Colón, but the *Bulletin* announced virtuously that her commander had "refused to land men unless all of the consuls unanimously requested such a move" [46] — which they did not. Dingler reported on April 2: "The company has suffered very little from the interruption of traffic . . . but our maritime operations will be seriously hampered for the next few months. . . . Except for the burning of Colón . . . our property has been respected by all parties. Our works have continued to function in the usual manner . . . only the recruiting of labor has become more difficult. . . ." [47] Fortunately the conflagration did not spread to the company's new town of Christophe-Colomb, separated from Colón by a narrow strip of empty ground which checked the flames. But the effects of the disorder upon the workmen proved exceedingly troublesome. In the Culebra section a violent quarrel accompanied by some bloodshed broke out among the frightened Negroes, and within a few hours 500 laborers had abandoned the excavation.

After the insurrection, as after the "Watermelon War" of 1856, numerous American citizens and corporations accused the Colombian government of negligence and presented bills for damages. The claims totaled about $3,750,000, almost half of which sum was demanded by the Panama Railroad. Bogotá denied responsibility for the destruction wrought by the rebels and pointed out that after the Civil War the United States government had refused compensation for damage to property caused by the unauthorized acts of its own citizens. Negotiations dragged on until 1891 when the United States abandoned the attempt to collect the indemnity. The rebellion brought to an end the federal system in Colombia and the semi-autonomy of its nine states guaranteed by the constitution of 1863. In 1886 President Núñez proclaimed a new constitution providing for a strong central government under which the states were reduced to mere departments headed by governors appointed by Bogotá.

Chapter 29. Finance

THE ACCOMPANYING résumé of the canal corporation's security issues has been compiled in part from information printed in the *Bulletin du Canal Interocéanique* and in part from data scattered through the pages of the Chamber of Deputies investigating committee's three-volume report published in 1893. A few of the tabulated figures do not agree exactly with the corresponding amounts in the parliamentary report: for example the latter gives the total cost of flotation as 117,371,342 francs 10 centimes but fails to indicate how it arrived at that result. The report is edited with deplorable carelessness; in numerous instances the totals printed below columns of figures do not tally with the actual additions, and it is usually impossible to determine whether the errata should be attributed to one or more of the individual items or to the totals. Fortunately such mistakes never involve large sums.

The entire cost of the canal including administration, interest on capital and loans, and the purchase of the railroad stock had been estimated by the congress of 1879 at approximately 1,200,000,-000 francs. In 1888 de Lesseps increased this figure to 1,500,000,000 francs ($300,000,000). The company floated eight bond issues, of which only the first two were completely successful. The redemption value of these offerings amounted in the aggregate to almost 3,000,000,000 francs, the redemption value of the bonds actually sold to more than 1,800,000,000, and the total receipts from the sale of bonds, marketed at varying discounts, to about 1,035,000,-000. The addition of the stock, valued at 300,000,000 francs, and of miscellaneous assets amounting to approximately 100,000,000 — interest on short-term investments, Panama Railroad dividends, forfeitures by contractors for noncompletion of work, and other minor items — brought the total sum at the company's disposal to about 1,435,000,000 francs or $287,000,000.

Having procured its original capital without difficulty at an annual interest rate of 5%, the company hoped to borrow all the money it would subsequently require at the same rate; but it was soon disillusioned. The scale of charges increased with each bond

Date of Offering	Type of Security	Number of Shares or Bonds Offered	Par or Redemption Value (Francs)	Redemption Value of Total Offering (Francs)	Maturity (Years)	Number of Shares or Bonds Subscribed	% of Offering Subscribed	Redemption Value of Bonds Sold (Francs)
Aug. 1879 (canceled)	Stock	800,000	500	. . . .	. .	60,000 (approx.)	7.5% (approx.)	. . . .
Dec. 1880	"	600,000 (incl. 10,000 to Soc. Civ. du Canal Int. du Darién)	500	. . . .	. .	1,206,609	204.5% (of 590,000 shares offered to public)	. . . .
Sept. 1882	Bonds	250,000	500	125,000,000	75	?	?	125,000,000
Oct. 1883	"	600,000	500	300,000,000	75	651,439	108.6%	300,000,000
Sept. 1884	"	387,387	500	193,693,500	75	318,245	82.2%	159,122,500]
April 1886	"	362,613	500	181,306,500	75	141,517 (on Bourse)	39.0%	70,758,500
Aug. 1886	"	500,000	1000	500,000,000	42	458,802	91.8%	458,802,000
July 1887	"	500,000	1000	500,000,000	48	258,887	51.8%	258,887,000'
March 1888	"	350,000	1000	350,000,000	75	89,890	25.7%	89,890,000
June 1888	Lottery bonds	2,000,000	400	800,000,000	99	849,249	42.5%	339,699,600
				2,950,000,000				1,802,159,600

SECURITY ISSUES OF THE COMPAGNIE

issue until by 1888 the company was paying out in interest and amortization more than 88,000,000 francs a year, not counting amortization of its last two issues which was guaranteed by special funds. The charges represented an average rate of 6.6% including the interest on the capital stock or of 7.07% on the bonds alone.

For the heavily oversubscribed bond issue of 1882 the company adopted a system of proportional allotment: subscribers for one bond received one; those who asked for from 2 to 5 received 2; from 6 to 10, 3; 11 to 15, 4; 16 to 25, 5; and all who applied for 26 or more bonds were allotted 20% of their demand plus one bond for each additional fraction of 5 requested. By exception stockholders were permitted to buy without proportional reduction one bond

Subscription Price (Francs)	Subscription Price (% of par or redemption value)	Company's Receipts (Francs)	Interest on Par or Redemption Value	Annual Interest and Amortization Charges (Francs)	Annual Interest and Amortization Charges (% of receipts)	Cost of Flotation (Francs)	Cost of Flotation (% of receipts)
500	100.0%	....	...	....	....	2,051,827	......
500	100.0%	300,000,000	5% on paid-up installments during construction. After opening 80% of net profits divided *pro rata*	15,000,000 (full amount after Sept. 1886 only)	5% on paid-up installments during construction. After opening 80% of net profits divided *pro rata*	32,241,779 (incl. fees to American committee)	10.7%
437.50	87.5%	109,375,000	5%	6,407,900	5.86%	7,829,655	7.2%
285	57.0%	171,000,000	3%	10,080,690	5.90%	10,708,679	6.3%
333	66.6%	105,975,585	4% ⎫	9,800,000	6.76%	8,912,455	6.2%
275.85 (average)	55.2% (average)	39,037,304	4% ⎬				
450	45.0%	206,460,900	3%	19,764,060	9.57%	11,763,933	5.7%
440	44.0%	113,910,280	3%	10,873,610	9.55%	7,626,593	6.7%
389.72 (not incl. fr. 70.28 for amortization)	39.0%	35,031,931	3%	2,696,700 (int. only — amortization by special fund)	7.70% (int. only — amortization by special fund)	4,993,714	14.2%
300 (not incl. fr. 60 for amortization and prizes)	75.0%	254,774,700	4%	13,587,984 (int. only — amortization and prizes by special fund)	5.33% (int. only — amortization and prizes by special fund)	31,248,172	12.3%
		1,335,565,700		88,210,944	6.60% (average)	117,376,807	8.8% (average)

UNIVERSELLE DU CANAL INTEROCÉANIQUE

for each 3 shares of stock already owned. A large part of the proceeds of this issue was applied to the payment in a lump sum of the balance due on the purchase price of the Panama Railroad shares.

The issue of 1883 was also oversubscribed but to a greatly diminished extent. In the final allotment those who subscribed for from one to 10 bonds received their full quota, while all others obtained 85% of the number asked for. This was the last instance of oversubscription in the company's financial history. When the public subscription for the 1884 offering closed 69,142 bonds were left on the company's hands. If this outcome disappointed de Lesseps he concealed his chagrin bravely. "Considering the general state of business," he wrote to the new subscribers, "the success [of the is-

sue] is an impressive demonstration of public confidence. . . ." [1]
In connection with the issue of April 1886 the company tried an
unfortunate experiment which yielded meager results. Instead of
selling the bonds by public subscription as before, the company's
finance committee attempted to place them on the Bourse. The issue brought in only about 39,000,000 francs, barely 32% of the
sum anticipated.

For the next three bond issues — called the "new series" — the
company increased the face value to 1000 francs and offered the securities at such a heavy discount that the return on the investment
rose to more than 9%. Yet public reluctance to buy augmented
with each flotation. For the issue of March 1888 the subscription
price was set at 460 francs, but of this amount 70.28 francs was
earmarked for investment in French government 3% securities to
guarantee amortization, so that the canal company realized only
389.72 francs from the sale of each bond.

The eighth and last bond issue differed radically from its predecessors. This time the offering consisted of "lottery" bonds, to
each of which was attached a numbered ticket. Drawings held at
stated intervals entitled the owners of winning tickets to cash prizes.
Money could be borrowed most advantageously by this method,
but French law restricted the flotation of lottery bonds to undertakings of national importance and forbade their issue except
when authorized by specific act of Parliament. In 1868, after the
failure of an attempt to procure funds for the unfinished Suez canal by an issue of ordinary bonds, Parliament had rescued the enterprise by permitting the sale of lottery bonds, and the waterway
was completed a year later. By 1885 these Suez lottery bonds issued
at 300 francs were quoted on the Bourse at 565. Naturally de Lesseps counted upon a similar authorization to raise money for Panama; but this time he encountered determined opposition, and
when permission was finally granted after a delay of three years it
came too late to save the project.

On May 27, 1885 de Lesseps opened his campaign with an appeal
to the Minister of the Interior, François Allain-Targé, for authorization to issue lottery bonds to the amount of 600,000,000 francs.
A little later the company's financial adviser, Lévy-Crémieux, seconded the request, but the Minister hesitated to take the necessary
steps. Within a few months more than 2000 petitions in favor of
the lottery, signed by almost 12,000 canal stockholders owning in
the aggregate about 200,000 shares, poured into the Chamber of
Deputies. The originator of the petition movement was Ferdinand

Martin, a banker at Nyons in the Drôme department, and the canal company diligently fostered the impression that these petitions represented a spontaneous expression of loyalty on the part of the signatories. Actually the company itself had conceived and organized the petition scheme and paid Martin 10,000 francs for his services. In 1892 Martin testified that he had received this fee and that the petition campaign "was not in any way spontaneous; it was managed by the company's agents, and the company paid the bills." [2]

Spontaneous or not, the petitions spurred both Parliament and the Cabinet to action. The Chamber appointed a committee to study the proposal, and on December 24, 1885 the Minister of Public Works, Charles Demole, commissioned Armand Rousseau to examine the progress of work on the isthmus. On April 8, 1886 the committee recommended the issue of lottery bonds. Rousseau's report submitted on April 30 was more cautious. It too advised authorization of the lottery but only on condition that the company would consent to "modifications" — by which Rousseau meant, though he did not say so in so many words, the substitution of a lock canal, temporary or permanent, for the sea level project. During Rousseau's absence in Panama changes had taken place in the Cabinet, so it was to a new Minister of the Interior, Charles Baïhaut, that the engineer delivered his report. Unable to reach an immediate decision, the Cabinet resolved not to publish the Rousseau report at once or even to communicate its contents to the anxious directors of the company; but an enterprising reporter for *Le Temps* frustrated the government's attempt at suppression by printing a full and fairly accurate summary of the document on May 20. Although Baïhaut, furious at the indiscretion, opened an official inquiry the source of the leak was never identified. Nevertheless Baïhaut, for reasons which did not become apparent until much later, drafted a bill in favor of the lottery authorization and presented it to the Chamber on June 17 with a recommendation for its passage, though he took pains to point out that the government assumed no responsibility — "not even a moral one" [3] — for an enterprise over which it could exercise no control.

A week later the Chamber appointed a committee of 11 members to examine the proposed measure. On July 8, after hearing the pleas of de Lesseps, Rousseau, Baïhaut, and others, the committee deferred further discussion for several months and requested de Lesseps to furnish certain documents, including the company's agreements with its contractors and an audit of its accounts to June 30, 1886. De Lesseps refused to comply and on July 9 asked the Premier, Charles de Freycinet, to withdraw the application for the lottery bond authorization. To the stockholders de Lesseps explained his abrupt action in what a subsequent investigating committee called "a haughty letter": [4] "Six deputies out of eleven . . . have decided to postpone their deliberations until the autumn session. . . . They are trying to shelve me — I refuse to be shelved. . . ." [5] In truth the company could not afford to wait so long for funds, nor did de Lesseps dare to risk a possible rejection of the lottery bill and the consequent blow to the company's already shaky credit. Immediately after the abandonment of the lottery project he announced another issue of 500,000 ordinary bonds — the first of the "new series" — to take place in August.

The lottery scheme remained in abeyance for more than a year, but by the autumn of 1887 the company's financial situation had grown so desperate that de Lesseps swallowed his pride and again petitioned the government for the authorization. On November 15, 1887, just after the company had finally decided to adopt the lock design as a temporary expedient, de Lesseps wrote to the new Premier, Maurice Rouvier. Rouvier, whose Cabinet resigned a month later, did not reply, and on January 14, 1888 de Lesseps addressed a similar appeal to his successor Pierre Tirard. Tirard refused flatly to place the necessary bill before Parliament. On January 20 de Lesseps urged all owners of the company's securities to petition their respective senators and deputies to authorize the lottery bonds. This time there was no pretense of spontaneity; the company itself had the petition forms printed and distributed. In March, while the result of this move remained in doubt, the company floated its seventh issue of ordinary bonds with the proviso that they could be exchanged for the same number of lottery bonds if and when permission to issue the latter should be granted.

158,287 security owners signed and returned their petitions. A group of deputies, impressed by the demonstration, thereupon drew up and presented their own lottery bill; and on March 24 the Chamber, by a vote of 285 to 161, resolved to consider the proposal. The next day the Chamber appointed a committee, again of 11 members, to discuss the bill. For some time the committee's deliberations indicated that the resolution would be defeated by a narrow margin: 6 members opposed it, 5 recommended its adoption. On April 19 one of the hostile members, Sans-Leroy, suddenly changed sides and gave the bill the sixth vote required for a favorable report. The Chamber adopted the committee's recommendation by 284 votes to 128 on April 28 and sent the bill to the Senate, which in turn passed it on June 5 with 158 votes in favor to 50 opposed. On June 8, 1888 the new law went into effect. After three years of struggle and disappointment the canal company was authorized to issue lottery bonds.

Meanwhile the long delay had played havoc with the company's resources. The treasury was almost empty, and on May 14, while the fate of the bill was still uncertain, the company found itself obliged to borrow 30,000,000 francs from the Crédit Lyonnais and the Société Générale. Of this sum the banks agreed to lend 10,000,-000 outright and the balance on condition that the lottery bill should become law. The loan was to be repaid in 90 days — afterwards extended to 111 days — with interest at 5% per annum, and as security the company deposited 68,000 Panama Railroad shares. In addition to the cash loan the banks subscribed for or undertook to place 450,000 of the lottery bonds. For these services they were to receive an enormous remuneration: [6]

5% interest on 30,000,000 francs for 111 days	491,063 francs
Commission on 450,000 bonds	2,250,000
Extra commissions	4,000,000
Participation in lottery bond syndicate	2,046,000
Total	8,787,063 francs

The 4,000,000-franc item for extra commissions was paid after the company's liquidation in bonds valued below par, so the total payment to the two banking houses actually amounted to about 8,000,-000 francs.

The law of June 8 authorized the company to borrow 720,000-000 francs — 600,000,000 to complete the canal plus 120,000,000 for investment in French government securities to guarantee amortization of the lottery bonds and the payment of cash prizes. For the subscription, which closed June 26, 2,000,000 bonds redeemable in 99 years at 400 francs and bearing 4% interest were offered at 360 francs each: 300 for the bond itself and 60 for the amortization and lottery fund. Drawings were to take place every two months, and cash prizes amounting to 690,000 francs three times a year alternated with three smaller distributions of 440,000 each, making a yearly repartition of 3,390,000 francs. The larger sum was divided into one prize of 500,000, one of 100,000, two of 10,000 each, two of 5000, five of 2000, and fifty of 1000 francs; while for the alternate drawings the first prize was reduced to 250,000. After 25 years the annual allotment for prizes would be decreased to 2,200,000 francs distributed four times a year and remain at that figure until the date of maturity.

In spite of these enticements only 849,249 bonds, including the

450,000 taken by the Crédit Lyonnais and the Société Générale, were disposed of. Bunau-Varilla blamed the failure upon the poor judgment of the financial experts — especially of Henri Germain, chairman of the board of the Crédit Lyonnais — who had insisted upon the flotation of the 2,000,000 bonds in a single gigantic issue and had overruled the more cautious financiers who advised subdivision into three offerings of moderate size. Possibly more bonds might have been sold had they been marketed successively; on the other hand the prizes would have been smaller, and there would have been less incentive to buy. Credit for the invention of the only unusual feature of this issue — the establishment of a separate fund for prizes and amortization — was claimed by one of the financial advisers, Hugo Oberndoerffer, who collected, partly as recompense for his suggestion and partly through his participation in various bond syndicates, at least 3,877,592 francs from the company.

At the first lottery held on August 16, 1888 the company unexpectedly declared all of the 2,000,000 bonds offered, whether sold or not, eligible for prizes. Since less than half had found purchasers a majority of the prizes fell to unsold bonds and reverted to the company. The outraged subscribers roared such indignant protests that the company, while it denied the legal validity of the objection, hastily announced that thereafter only bonds actually disposed of would participate in the drawings. The 36 prizes awarded to unsold bonds in August were canceled, and the same number of new prizes were added to the regular October distribution.

The company now made one final desperate effort to place its remaining lottery bonds. Groups of security holders throughout France formed the Union des Actionnaires et Obligataires de Panama, organized more than 400 local committees, and launched an active campaign to recruit new investors. Ostensibly the Union, like the petition movement of 1885, owed its origin to the spontaneous enthusiasm of loyal supporters; in fact it was conceived, financed, and administered by the company at a cost estimated by the Deputies committee at 90,000 francs. At the same time Ferdinand and Charles de Lesseps set out on a lecture tour on behalf of the bond issue, visiting 26 cities between September 28 and November 9. Charles delivered the speeches while his 83-year-old father sat on the stage and occasionally added a few words. France still revered the name of de Lesseps, and every public appearance of the stout-hearted patriarch evoked storms of applause; but neither the personal appeals nor the activities of the Union sufficed to convince potential investors. On November 29 the company placed on the market 1,100,000 lottery bonds — practically all that remained unsold — with the proviso that if at least 400,000 were not disposed of before December 12 the subscriptions would be canceled. De Lesseps accompanied his announcement of this last offering — nicknamed *émission de l'agonie* or "deathbed flotation" [7] — with a stirring call for subscriptions: "I appeal to all Frenchmen. I appeal to all my colleagues whose fortunes are threatened. . . . Your fates are in your own hands. Decide!" [8]

The public decided — in the negative. By December 12 applications had been received for less than 200,000 bonds, and the subscriptions were annulled. On December 14, at the company's request, the Minister of Finance, Peytral, placed before the Chamber of Deputies a bill authorizing the canal company to suspend payment of all debts and of interest on all securities for three months; only the amortization of the bond issue of March 1888 and distribution of the lottery prizes, for both of which special funds had been created, would continue without interruption. The matter was so urgent that the Chamber convened at once and appointed a committee of 22 members to consider the proposal. The next day, December 15, 1888, the committee submitted an unfavorable report, and the Chamber rejected the petition by 256 votes to 181. The company had played its last card and lost. A few hours later the Tribunal Civil of the Seine department designated three provisional receivers to administer the company's affairs.

To finance its bond flotations the company made use of syndicates operating under conditions which varied in detail from issue to issue. While the stock syndicate of 1880 had not guaranteed the sale of shares but had merely covered the cost of flotation, the syndicates organized by Lévy-Crémieux for the first three bond issues actually underwrote a certain number of securities. The syndicate of September 1882 pledged itself to purchase the first 150,000 bonds of the total issue of 250,000 if the public failed to absorb that number; in return it was to receive a premium of 20 francs per bond or 3,000,000 francs in all. In October 1883 the syndicate undertook to buy the first 200,000 of the 600,000 bonds offered, for a premium of 15 francs. The issue of September 1884 consisted of 387,387 bonds, of which the syndicate underwrote the first 150,000 at a premium of 15 francs each. This was the last of the guarantee syndicates. Lévy-Crémieux died, and Baron Jacques de Reinach took his place as chief financial adviser to the company. The syndicates organized by de Reinach for the subsequent bond flotations —

called "syndicates at 2 francs 50" — were of an entirely different character. The participants guaranteed no purchases whatever but merely contributed 2 francs 50 centimes per bond towards the expenses of the issue. The recompense of these syndicates was out of all proportion to their paltry advances. In March 1888, when 350,-000 bonds were offered, the syndicate was promised a premium of 20 francs on each of the first 140,000 sold, 15 on each of the next 70,000, 10 on the next 70,000, and 5 on the last 70,000. Although the issue was a failure, and the public purchased only 89,890 bonds, the syndicate collected 1,797,800 francs in premiums for an outlay of 875,000 — a profit of more than 100%. For the comparatively successful flotation of August 1886 the syndicate's profit amounted to approximately 400%, and for that of July 1887, 300%.

In 1893 the Deputies committee reported: "The function . . . of syndicates is to buy at wholesale and sell at retail. . . . We can . . . appreciate the advantages a corporation might derive from the support of financiers who . . . if the affair turns out badly, would underwrite that portion of the loan not absorbed by the public. Has the Panama company proceeded along these lines? With respect to the syndicates . . . of 1882, 1883, and 1884 we can reply affirmatively, with the reservation that these syndicates did not underwrite the entire flotations but only the first portion of each. They shrewdly took care to exclude the most difficult fraction to place. . . . As to the syndicates at 2 francs 50, we must answer in the negative. These guaranteed no purchase of securities. . . . The syndicate has here become nothing more than an indirect device to repay favors or distribute bounties. . . . The syndicates could lose their money . . . only in the extremely unlikely event that the public did not subscribe for enough bonds to cover their small loans. But . . . that contingency was unimaginable. . . ." [9] In short the syndicates of 1882, 1883, and 1884 performed useful though limited services and incurred certain very slight risks for which they were extravagantly rewarded; the later syndicates contributed almost nothing of value to the company, ran practically no risks, and collected huge unearned premiums.

Still less defensible was the system of "options" invented by Lévy-Crémieux and applied to the first three bond issues. After the syndicates had agreed to underwrite a stipulated fraction of the bonds the company granted options on part or all of the remaining securities to members of the syndicates or other favored individuals, with the privilege of purchase for less than the current subscription price. These reductions varied between 3 and 15 francs per bond, but the beneficiaries assumed no obligation whatever to buy the bonds. They were therefore in the enviable position of "heads-I-win-tails-you-lose." If the issue was successful the grantees would invariably take up their options, and the company, having already disposed of the bonds at the regular subscription rate, was obliged to pay the owners of optional rights the discount agreed upon. If on the other hand the public failed to cover the issue the holders of options simply renounced their rights. In the first event the company lost money; in the second it gained nothing. The options were actually nothing but outright gifts to the company's friends, thinly disguised as orthodox business transactions. "It is impossible," commented the Deputies committee, "to perceive what benefit the company could have expected to derive even indirectly from this device. . . . What is the value of a contract which obliges one of the parties to deliver securities for less than the subscription price even when purchasers at the full rate are available, while it permits the other party . . . to promise nothing in return, to be free to consummate the deal if profits are assured and to abandon it if they are not?" [10] After 1884 the company discontinued the option system and substituted the even more frankly wasteful syndicates at 2 francs 50. The committee observed cynically that the change did not indicate that "the financiers' appetites had dwindled, but the company had proved itself so anxious to satisfy them that it had become almost unnecessary to conceal its largesses under imaginary titles. . . ." [11]

In addition to the cost of its own mouthpiece, the *Bulletin du Canal Interocéanique,* the company paid large sums to the French press for favorable publicity. While the weeks preceding an issue of securities were always marked by exceptionally heavy contributions to the newspapers, smaller payments continued at more or less regular intervals throughout the year. At least 2575 periodicals shared the company's bounty at one time or another. The first publicity campaigns were organized by Charles Bol under the general direction of Lévy-Crémieux. From 1883 to 1886 Marius Fontane took charge of the press department and often contributed articles written by himself under various pseudonyms. After 1886 Charles de Lesseps, assisted by de Reinach, made himself personally responsible for publicity. Fontane attempted to economize on this item and succeeded only in alienating many of the company's greedy adherents. On the other hand Charles de Lesseps permitted himself to be imposed upon by unscrupulous scramblers after subsidies: "An experienced newspaper man or publicity agent . . . would have insisted upon businesslike bargains instead of flinging money about with the lordly gestures appropriate to a de Lesseps." [12] He soon found it expedient to engage the services of Batiau et Privat, a professional publicity agency which allocated the press subsidies for each bond issue after 1886.

The Deputies committee estimated the amount paid for newspaper publicity from 1880 to 1888 inclusive at 12,000,000 or 13,000,000 francs, approximately 1% of the company's total receipts from the sale of securities. "Is this percentage excessive?" the committee inquired. "If we consider only the services rendered to the company . . . we can reply in the negative. That is the view always held . . . by Charles de Lesseps. He has complained bitterly about the rapacity of the financiers, but he has shown himself . . . very charitable towards the press. . . . M. de Lesseps knows better than anyone that he has procured the support of certain papers only in return for money. . . . Most of the articles published on Panama were composed of items furnished by the company itself. M. Marius Fontane supplied the documents and information, while M. Charles de Lesseps handled the subsidies. . . . Of course we are well aware that the press today is no longer what it was in the past, and . . . that it would be impossible for it to survive if it confined itself to the mere presentation of facts. . . . Our standards are what they are; we may deplore them, but publicity has become essential; no enterprise can be undertaken without it, and it would be unreasonable to expect the press to forgo this source of profit. . . . But what does matter is that . . . [a newspaper] should verify the information it receives and not permit the publication as its own views of ready-made announcements fabricated by those who have some reason to mislead the public." [13] The committee censured the French newspapers for their venality: "With extraordinary imprudence the press published the most deceptive articles, inspired confidence, and asserted that the canal would be completed even after the enterprise had become a hopeless wreck. . . . It [the press] failed to perform its duty towards the public. . . ." [14] After the failure of the canal company two newspaper editors, Aderer of *Le Temps* and Galli of *L'Art Français,* honorably returned their subsidies, or part of them, to the liquidator.

Lavish bounties to the press failed to protect the company against attacks from two sources: individuals with grievances, real or fancied, and speculators who sought to profit by forcing down the price of Panama securities on the Bourse. Such hostile campaigns, carefully prepared and adroitly timed, usually coincided with or immediately preceded each new issue of bonds. The first considerable decline in the stock quotations took place in October 1881 just after the company had announced that the second installment of 125 francs would become payable the following January. From a high in August of 540 it fell to 485 on October 4, but recovered within a week to 515. Even the *Bulletin* admitted that "this temporary decline . . . will encourage the malevolence of the company's enemies. . . ." [15] No organized attempt to lower the company's credit appears to have preceded the first bond issue of September 1882, but a few weeks later a wave of speculation caused the shares to drop sharply from 535 to 500 in three days, and after a brief recovery they declined to 480 on December 1. On September 30, 1883, a few days before the second bond flotation, a minor panic swept the Bourse, many investors who had applied in advance for bonds hastily withdrew their subscriptions, and the issue was oversubscribed only about 8.6% instead of, as expected, more than 100%.

Yet few of the thousands of small investors thought of selling their Panama stocks and bonds. After another flurry of adverse rumors in July 1884 de Lesseps publicly commended the loyalty of the security holders. During the following year hostile maneuvers grew more numerous, more open, and more effective. The publication of Maréchal's diatribe and of other highly colored accounts of maladministration on the isthmus impressed the more timid investors. At a stockholders' meeting on July 29, 1885 de Lesseps tried to allay the growing uneasiness: "The enemies of the canal . . . do not scruple to disseminate calumnies. . . . A new group of adversaries have appeared. Heretofore your opponents have been capitalists anxious to delay . . . the opening of the new communication . . . and speculators who have attempted to initiate . . . downward movements on the Bourse. . . . Now certain individuals, unable to influence the stockholders, have started to attack the company and through the publication of newspapers . . . letters, and pamphlets have organized a veritable campaign of blackmail. . . ." [16] Another vigorous drive against the Panama stock in August forced it down to 422, and it remained weak throughout the autumn. On October 15 it declined to the lowest figure yet reached, 364, then rose erratically until on February 20, 1886 it was quoted at 490, almost par.

A few days before the bond issue of August 1886 de Lesseps admitted that these persistent onslaughts had upset the company's financial calculations: "By attacking . . . our credit the speculators . . . have forced us to borrow at higher rates than we anticipated. . . . From now on until the canal is opened . . . the interest on these loans will be a heavy burden. . . ." [17] In September the stock was again driven downwards by false reports of Ferdinand de Lesseps's grave illness — malicious rumors which the old man promptly dispelled by announcing his intention to participate in the Statue of Liberty ceremonies in New York harbor on October 28. But the shares, after a brief rally, continued to decline. On November 14, 1887 — the day before de Lesseps renewed his lottery bond appeal — they fell to 282.50, on November 30 to 276, and on December 3 to 250. The company won a few minor victories: on January 24, 1888 two authors of sensational pamphlets denouncing the company were convicted of criminal libel and sentenced to four months in prison.

When the Chamber approved the lottery bill in April 1888 the company's stock soared for the last time, reaching 393.75 on May 23. On June 20 the six-day subscription for the 2,000,000 bonds opened. Although the issue would almost certainly not have been completely absorbed under any circumstances its failure was materially assisted by the company's organized opponents, who with diabolical ingenuity spread reports of the death of de Lesseps and created a panic at the crucial moment. "On June 22," de Lesseps protested bitterly, "four days before the subscription closed . . . speculators violently and scandalously forced our company's stock down on the Paris Bourse. The next day they repeated the maneuver, causing another wholly unjustified decline. And at the same time lying rumors and false telegrams announcing my death . . . were circulated all over the world! The scoundrels . . . had chosen their time well; a denial . . . could not be issued until too late. . . . A complaint was lodged immediately with the *procureur* [public prosecutor] of the republic, who has ordered an investigation to discover the instigators of these criminal acts." [18] They were never identified. On November 26, three days before the "deathbed flotation," speculators again attacked the company's securities on the Bourse. The stock declined sharply to 200, recovered slightly, and fell with a crash to 123.75 when the company declared itself bankrupt on December 15.

The canal company established two separate budgets for administration expenses, one in Paris and the other on the isthmus. During the first full year of construction the overhead expenditures of the Paris office amounted to approximately 1,200,000 francs; by 1886 they had increased to over 2,000,000. In Panama the rise was much steeper. The Deputies committee computed the yearly cost of administration on the isthmus alone: [19]

1881 (March to June)	francs	1,233,273.87
1881–2		4,507,255.20
1882–3		6,694,375.46
1883–4		9,555,080.15
1884–5		13,552,408.45
1885–6		13,321,123.66
1886–7		13,412,205.91
1887–8		12,428,951.98
1888–9		10,682,304.99
		85,386,979.67

In the committee's report the annual items are as given above, but the total is printed 85,387,082.66 — one of many similar inaccuracies. The following tabulation of the company's total disbursements from 1880 to June 30, 1889 is compiled from the same source: [20]

PRELIMINARY EXPENSES

Purchase of concession	francs	10,000,000.00	
Payment to Colombia		750,000.00	
Payment to agents of Colombian government		191,000.00	
			10,941,000.00

COST OF FLOTATIONS

Payments to American committee	12,000,000.00	
Reimbursement of 1879 syndicate	2,051,826.68	
1880 stock issue	20,241,779.20	
Bond issues	83,077,736.22	
		117,371,342.10

INTEREST AND AMORTIZATION

Interest on stock subscriptions	68,236,800.00	
Bond coupons	152,356,216.88	
Amortization of bonds (not including issues of March and June 1888)	23,924,000.00	
Other charges on security issues	5,051,038.49	
		249,568,055.37

ADMINISTRATION

In Paris	15,604,400.10	
On the isthmus	85,386,979.67	
		100,991,379.77

CONSTRUCTION

Company workshops and installations	116,302,881.51	
Contracts	462,620,641.92	
		578,923,523.43

BUILDINGS

In Paris	2,037,965.90	
On the isthmus	117,788,506.81	
		119,826,472.71

PANAMA RAILROAD

Purchase of 68,534 shares   93,268,186.73

MISCELLANEOUS

Unpaid debts, cash balance, etc.   163,661,418.86
    Total   francs 1,434,551,378.97

Here again there is a minor discrepancy: the committee's report prints this total as 1,434,552,281.86 francs.

Chapter 30. Failure

THE FRENCH company's failure to complete the Panama canal has been ascribed to various causes: disease, mismanagement, extravagance, corruption, technical incompetence. These were in fact contributory, not basic, factors. The annual mortality rate of about 60 per 1000 represented a tragic waste of human life, and non-fatal maladies materially reduced the size and efficiency of the working force; but disease alone would not have wrecked the enterprise. While maladministration and extravagance undoubtedly existed their mischievous effects have been vastly overstated. Without undue cynicism it must be recognized that other great industrial and financial undertakings including many in the United States have been attended by more flagrant corruption and have yet achieved success. The French engineers at Panama were in general far from incompetent, and the mechanical equipment, though small and light compared with that subsequently utilized by the Americans, was for the most part adequate.

The fundamental reason for the collapse was the company's — which means de Lesseps's — insistence upon the adoption of the sea level design. Given unlimited time and money, a sea level waterway could probably have been excavated; but for a commercial company dependent upon private capital and the expectation of eventual profits it was a hopeless aspiration. Whether or not the French corporation or any other organization, public or private, could have constructed even a satisfactory lock canal at that time is a debatable question, but it could certainly have advanced much farther towards that goal for the same outlay and within the same number of years. With more tangible progress on the isthmus many if not most of the contingent difficulties would never have arisen. Public confidence would not have been impaired by discouraging reports, and the company could have continued to borrow money legitimately at reasonable rates without being driven to subterfuges and corrupt practices.

The three temporary receivers appointed on December 15, 1888 by the Tribunal Civil de la Seine were Denormandie, a former governor of the Banque de France, Baudelot, former president of the Tribunal de Commerce de la Seine, and Hue. The receivers immediately ordered indefinite suspension of all payments on the company's securities except amortization of the last two bond issues and the lottery prizes, guaranteed by special funds. They then turned their attention to the isthmus, where the news of the collapse threatened to plunge the entire enterprise into chaos. In Panama the banks refused to accept the company's drafts, riots broke out among the laborers, and several contractors prepared to stop work altogether. The provisional administrators sent cables to the bankers promising that drafts on Paris would be honored, and to assure the maintenance of order they requested the French Foreign Ministry to dispatch one or two warships to the isthmus. The receivers realized that the abrupt cessation of all activity would have ruined equipment worth millions and caused almost irreparable damage to the unfinished excavations. To avert such a disaster the receivers attempted to negotiate a loan of 25,000,000 francs for four months, with the Panama Railroad shares as security, but were unable to borrow the sum on acceptable terms. As a last resort they hastily concluded agreements with five of the principal contractors — the American Contracting and Dredging Company, the Jacob firm, Artigue, Sonderegger et Compagnie, Baratoux, Letellier et Compagnie, and Gustave Eiffel — whereby these concerns undertook to continue the most essential operations until February 15, 1889 and to accept payment therefor in 90-day notes secured by the deposit of 33,500 Panama Railroad shares. Vignaud, Barbaud, Blanleuil et Compagnie and the Société des Travaux Publics et Constructions were excluded from the transaction, the former because it was on the verge of bankruptcy, the latter because six lawsuits instituted by it against the canal company were still pending.

Meanwhile de Lesseps, acting independently but with the approval of the receivers, made desperate efforts to form a new corporation to be called the Compagnie Universelle pour l'Achèvement du Canal Interocéanique. He fixed the capital at 30,000,000 francs divided into 500-franc shares, and the stockholders of the new company were to receive 5% interest during the rest of the construction period and 16% of the net profits after the opening of the canal. As 80% of these hypothetical profits were already allocated by the act of concession to the stockholders of the original company, any dividends due the new shareholders after the completion of the waterway would presumably have to be paid at the expense of the grantees of the remaining 20%, the founders and officials of the old company. The new stock subscription opened on January 21, 1889; when it closed on February 2 only a small fraction of the shares had found a market, and the attempt to organize the new corporation was abandoned. The old company held its last general assembly on January 26. Since the stockholders present represented only 228,307 shares — less than the number required by law for the transaction of formal business — they could do nothing but listen to reports and express hopes for the formation of a new company after liquidation of the old.

On February 4 the tribunal declared the company dissolved and appointed Joseph Brunet, a former Minister of Education, to the post of liquidator. A year later, on February 13, 1890, Brunet's illness necessitated the installation of a co-liquidator, Achille Monchicourt, who assumed the full responsibility after Brunet resigned on March 8. Brunet's first task was the negotiation of new agreements with the contractors to insure the continuation of a minimum amount of essential work until May 15, 1889. Next he appointed a technical committee of 11 prominent engineers headed by Guillemin, director of the École Nationale des Ponts et Chaussées, to study the problems involved in the completion of the canal. On May 5, 1890 the committee reported to Monchicourt: "It will be possible to complete the canal within eight years . . . by adopting a system of locks. . . . We estimate the cost of the technical work still to be accomplished at 580,000,000 francs. The addition of administrative expenses . . . flotation costs . . . and interest . . . will raise the total sum to be solicited from the public for the completion of the canal to 900,000,000 francs. . . ." [1] There were to be four locks on each slope: two at Bohío Soldado and two at San Pablo on the Atlantic side, two at Paraíso, one at Pedro Miguel, and one at Miraflores on the Pacific.

The Guillemin committee also discussed the possibility of a return to the original sea level project on condition that the governments of the principal maritime nations could be induced to guarantee collectively the interest on the investment: "It would be imprudent to count upon less than twenty years for construction. . . . It is not to be thought of unless . . . undertaken by what might be called a syndicate of nations. In that event the problem would have to be restudied *ab ovo,* and it is not within the committee's province to suggest the technical and financial methods to be adopted." [2] The committee estimated the construction and administrative costs of the sea level canal, in addition to what had already been spent, at 1,287,000,000 francs; while interest for 20 years and the assumption by the new company of the charges on the old company's securities would bring the grand total of new expenditure to about 3,000,000,000 francs.

The company's collapse left approximately 14,000 employees stranded on the isthmus. Maintenance of essential services required but a small fraction of the original force; by the middle of 1889 the number on the payroll had been reduced to about 1800 and a year later to 800. The sudden cessation of work threw the economy of the canal area into confusion and subjected the discharged workmen, white and black, to severe hardships, and the bankrupt canal company could not assist them. Some took to the jungle, but most of the Jamaicans were brought home at the expense of their own government. The United States government also undertook the repatriation of its own citizens, relatively few in number.

The Salgar-Wyse concession of 1878 had stipulated that the canal was to be opened within 12 years after the incorporation of the company. Since that incorporation had taken place on March 3, 1881, and the failure of the company had ended all hope of completion before March 3, 1893, the concession would have to be extended if the work was to proceed. The charter provided for a 6-year prolongation, but in the opinion of the liquidator that period would be insufficient. Immediately after Brunet's resignation in March 1890 Monchicourt requested Wyse to negotiate for a 10-year extension. This belated recognition of his indispensability flattered Wyse, who had retired years before, hurt and resentful, from active participation in the enterprise he had fathered. He accepted the mission with a flourish of self-glorification: "Only in me, the original grantee, are combined all the qualities needed for negotiating with the [Colombian] government . . . and my special position is no less vital to the organization of the future company which will complete the canal. . . . I believe I may even add without undue conceit that . . . I so completely personify the work to be accomplished that its execution would perhaps be impossible for many years if I did not devote all my energies to it. . . ." [3]

In May 1890 Wyse proceeded to Cartagena to enlist the support of Rafael Núñez, ex-President of Colombia and one of the republic's most influential citizens, who promised his co-operation but proved an undependable ally: "Unfortunately yielding to his inveterate habit . . . Núñez published in his newspaper several articles . . . in which he dazzled his compatriots by dangling before their eyes the prospective payment by the canal company of hundreds of millions [of francs] to Colombia. . . ." [4] When Wyse reached Bogotá in July he found the new provisional President,

Carlos Holguín, willing to authorize the extension, but the Congress made endless difficulties and demanded an enormous indemnity. Wyse rejected the proposals and shrewdly turned the tables by presenting, on behalf of the defunct company, counterclaims aggregating some 25,000,000 francs. Although many of these claims were dubious they served Wyse's purpose by confusing the legislators. The astute Frenchman kept the pot boiling vigorously and inspired the publication in Panama of dispatches designed to stimulate local patriotism. Alarmed by Wyse's reports, a delegation of prominent Panamanians reached Bogotá late in November and flooded Congress with urgent demands for the grant of the extension.

On December 10 Wyse and the Foreign Minister, Antonio Roldán, signed an agreement which was approved after some discussion by both houses of the Colombian Congress and proclaimed on December 26, 1890. The government granted an extension of 10 years on condition that a new canal company should be organized and resume active operations not later than February 28, 1893. The liquidator undertook to pay Colombia 10,000,000 francs in cash in five installments and 5,000,000 in the new company's stock, and in addition to contribute 40,000 francs per month to the maintenance of a garrison of 250 Colombian soldiers to protect the canal line. From the cash payment the sum of 2,500,000 francs plus interest was to be deducted on account of a loan made by the canal company to Colombia in 1883. If the new company failed to comply with these stipulations the canal and its appurtenances would revert to Colombia without compensation.

Just before Wyse left Paris Monchicourt had informed him: "In case you are unsuccessful you will not expect this liquidator to pay you anything more than the expenses of your mission, but it is understood that if success attends your efforts you will receive a fair recompense . . . and also that if I am able to organize a new company I shall do everything in my power to obtain for you the responsible position therein to which your abilities and the services you have rendered entitle you." [5] When Wyse returned with the extension he hastened to claim the promised reward, which he appraised at 1,000,000 francs. But once more, as in all of his previous dealings with the canal company, Wyse was doomed to disappointment. Alleging that Wyse had not fully complied with his instructions, Monchicourt contested the claim and offered 400,000 francs. Wyse promptly appealed to the law, but in January 1894 the court rejected his estimate of the value of his contribution and awarded him only the sum fixed by the liquidator.

For some time after the crash Ferdinand de Lesseps remained in Paris to co-operate with the liquidator and devote the last remnants of his once stupendous energy to the salvage of his beloved enterprise, but his spirit had received a mortal wound. On his eighty-third birthday, just before the company failed, he was still a hale and inspiring leader remarkably vigorous for his age; on his eighty-fourth he was a broken feeble old man rapidly slipping into senility. With his wife and younger children he retired to the château of La Chesnaye, his country estate about 20 miles from Issoudun. At first he was able to enjoy short strolls in his garden; then as he grew weaker he was pushed about in a wheelchair on sunny days. Most of the time he would sit quietly in front of the fire, too deaf to hear more than a few words of general conversation but occasionally breaking into the talk with some anecdote of his own. Fortunately for his peace of mind his thoughts dwelt more often on the distant past than on the affairs of the Panama company. After the ugly scandal broke in 1892 and the sordid details of corruption filled the columns of every newspaper in France, scarcely the faintest echo of the uproar was allowed to disturb the old man's sanctuary.

His strong body remained alive long after his mind had almost flickered out. He lived on from day to day, tended like a child by his devoted wife, humored and protected by his children. When in November 1892 a contributor to *Le Gaulois* suggested not unsympathetically that it would have been better had he died at the peak of his career, Mme de Lesseps replied in a dignified and moving letter: "I have read a few lines concerning M. de Lesseps in your newspaper . . . to the effect that he has lived some weeks too long. I shall not protest against that unchristian phrase, for its author can have given no thought to the wife and children who deeply love and revere this old man and to whom his life, however fragile it may be, is more precious than anything in the world. It is no crime to grow old. . . . It would be impossible to find another man who, having accomplished what he did at Suez . . . would have retired from it with empty hands, with no provision for the future of his large family — a sacrifice in which I as well as my children take pride." [6] And in truth de Lesseps, through whose hands had passed billions of francs, had never troubled to feather his own nest. He had lived extravagantly, but when he died his modest fortune yielded each of his sons and daughters a yearly income estimated at less than 3000 francs. If the Suez stockholders had not generously voted a substantial pension to his family the widow and children would have been almost destitute.

Chapter 31. Scandal

A LMOST three years after the failure of the company the Panama scandal burst like a bombshell over a shocked and outraged France. Before the tumult subsided thousands of pages of testimony, depositions, and reports were printed, attorneys floundered through mazes of legal technicalities, judges handed down decisions and imposed penalties only to have them reversed by higher courts, charges and countercharges were hurled without discrimination, hundreds of prominent names were besmirched, stocks crashed, Cabinets resigned, and duels were fought. The innocent often suffered with the guilty, for the affair soon turned into a football kicked about by political opponents. In that game there was no need to prove complicity; the mere whisper of the epithets *panamiste* or *chéquard* (meaning the recipient of a cheque or bribe from an agent of the Panama company) was enough to blast the reputation of a public official. "The word Panama," commented the *Nation,* "now suggests so universally a huge scandal that its association with an actual canal across an actual isthmus seems only a figure of speech." [1] Yet all this welter of accusation produced only a few convictions; while scores of men were at least temporarily dishonored less than half a dozen paid the legal penalty. Several of the most flagrant offenders escaped retribution by flight, others by sheer bluff or political pull. Since some of these carried their secrets to the grave certain incidents remain shrouded in mystery even today. The complete story of the Panama scandal will never be told.

The years 1889, 1890, and 1891 were a relatively tranquil period, the lull before the storm. Liquidation of the company proceeded in orderly fashion under sympathetic public administrators. The leaders of the bankrupt enterprise still retained their reputations for probity; in the eyes of the French people they were victims of circumstance rather than malefactors. Yet ominous murmurs of discontent could be heard from time to time, and a few isolated accusations of fraud appeared in print. Dissatisfied security holders petitioned for an audit of the company's accounts and, if the findings warranted, for prosecution of those presumed guilty

of misapplication of funds. On June 21, 1890 three deputies —
Jules Delahaye, Gauthier, and Le Provost de Launay — presented
a sheaf of these petitions to the Chamber, which transmitted them
to the Minister of Justice, Thévenet. In Thévenet's opinion the
complaints offered insufficient grounds for indictment at that time,
especially since "simultaneous action by the liquidator and the public prosecutor would be very difficult, because the same documents
would be indispensable . . . to both; thus time would be lost,
not gained." [2] Édouard Drumont railed against the government's
inactivity and viciously attacked de Lesseps: "This evildoer is
treated like a hero. The poor devil who breaks a shop window to
steal a loaf of bread is dragged . . . before the judge of a criminal court. But into this affair, which has swallowed up almost a bil-
lion and a half [francs], there has been no investigation whatever;
not once has this man been asked: 'What have you done with the
money?' " [3]

Persistent prodding by Delahaye and his colleagues eventually
forced the reluctant government to undertake an official inquiry.
Investigation of the company's affairs gave rise to three separate
proceedings: the indictment and trial of certain directors for fraud
and maladministration; the indictment and trial of directors and
agents of the company for corruption of public officials, and of
those officials for accepting the bribes; and a parliamentary inquiry
into the whole matter conducted by a committee of the Chamber
of Deputies and running concurrently with the court actions.

The first phase opened on June 11, 1891, when Quesney de
Beaurepaire, the *procureur-général* (public prosecutor) of the
Paris Appellate Court, acting by order of Clément Fallières, Thévenet's successor as Minister of Justice, preferred charges of fraud
and breach of trust against Ferdinand, Charles, and Victor de Lesseps, Marius Fontane, the company's secretary general, and Henri
Cottu, one of the directors. Périvier, chief magistrate of the court,
placed the investigation in the hands of the court counselor, Prinet,
who commissioned an expert accountant, Flory, to audit the company's books. On June 22 Prinet interrogated Ferdinand and
Charles de Lesseps in his office. For the old man, now shattered in
health and spirit, the interview was a terrible ordeal which Charles
afterwards described with touching simplicity: "On the day he was
to go to the counselor's office, I called for him . . . with Dr. Mois-
senet, whom M. Prinet had authorized to . . . remain with my father throughout the interview. . . . The doctor . . . expressed
the opinion that it would be very imprudent for my father to go

out. . . . Nevertheless the meeting had to take place sooner or later; I hoped that one conference would suffice and that thereafter . . . the counselor would accept me as my father's deputy . . . so I thought it better for him to suffer the shock immediately. . . . My father rose from his bed and . . . said: 'I shall go.' He dressed, and by the time he reached M. Prinet's he had apparently recovered all his strength; he remained three quarters of an hour . . . and when he left his face radiated charm and energy as it always did under difficulties. But the reaction soon set in; it was frightful; for the next three weeks my father did not speak or leave his bed; we could see that he was worried by some idea he could not express. . . . Every day I tried to discover the cause of his depression, but in vain; at last I was inspired to repeat to him a phrase I had often heard him use: 'One thing is certain, that good will triumph over evil.' 'If that were not so,' my father answered, 'life would not be worth living.' I embraced my father, held his hand, and said, looking into his eyes: 'The words I have just spoken . . . are your own; you impressed them on me so deeply that I shall always believe them; and I cannot imagine that you will change your philosophy at your age.' That cheered my father, and thenceforward his condition improved rapidly." [4] The old man was not molested again. While he dreamed away his last years in front of the fire at La Chesnaye, serenely unaware of the sordid bedlam broken loose in Paris, the son shouldered his father's burden of disgrace as well as his own.

The report submitted by Flory on May 17, 1892 concluded that although there was no specific evidence that the administrators, directors, and agents of the company had profited directly from the expenditures for works and accessories they were nevertheless indictable on two counts: "First, the funds were dissipated in a manner . . . more consistent with the personal views and interests of the administrators and directors . . . or with those of persons and groups they wished to favor, than with the true interests of the company; second, the successive campaigns . . . undertaken to obtain capital and loans . . . were designed to attract subscriptions . . . by means of false announcements of progress repeatedly renewed or confirmed, which concealed the true situation and assured [the subscribers] of certain success within a definite period. . . ." [5]

Early in June Prinet turned over his Panama files, including the Flory report, to Quesnay de Beaurepaire, who retired to the country to study them minutely. The excessively conscientious prosecutor

found himself in a quandary; he could not decide how to handle the
affair so that the ends of justice might best be served. On September 10 he advised the Minister of Justice that the evidence appeared to warrant criminal prosecution for fraud, but when he returned to Paris in October he changed his mind and proposed the
substitution of a civil suit for damages, which "would restore part
of their money to the poor ruined subscribers instead of imposing
the sterile penalty of imprisonment upon an octogenarian in his
dotage." [6] For almost a month Louis Ricard, the new Minister of
Justice who had replaced Fallières in February 1892, hesitated.
Then on November 15 he instructed the surprised and unwilling
prosecutor to proceed immediately with the criminal action. Quesnay de Beaurepaire protested in vain, and on November 21, 1892
Ferdinand and Charles de Lesseps, Fontane, Cottu, and Eiffel were
formally charged with fraudulent dissipation of the company's
funds. French law provided that personages of exalted position
could be tried only by the First Appellate Court of Paris. Since
Ferdinand de Lesseps had been awarded the Grand Cross of the
Legion of Honor, and since the accusations against him could not
be separated from those against his associates, all of the defendants
were summoned to appear before that tribunal.

Ricard's abrupt decision to prosecute has been attributed by
many chroniclers to a personal grudge against the de Lesseps family. Jean d'Elbée, dubbing Ricard "Minister of Injustice," [7] offered a picturesque but probably apocryphal explanation of his
malice. According to this account Ricard had been mayor of Rouen
some years before when that city had honored the creator of the
Suez canal by giving his name to one of its riverside quays. After
the ceremony Mme Ricard had entertained the guests at a tea
which Mme de Lesseps either forgot or was unable to attend, and
this "rejected cup of tea had sat heavily on the Ricards' stomachs
ever since." [8] Quesnay de Beaurepaire, who detested the pompous
Minister, painted an unprepossessing but amusing portrait: "Solemn and majestic, he would bow with a profound conviction of his
own grace. Two long tufts of white whisker framed his regular
features. . . . His walk was slow and cadenced like that of a pon-
tiff about to bless his people or a parlor magician producing doves
out of a goblet. M. Ricard was an aristocrat at heart. . . . His own
conceit took the place of ancestors. . . . Believing himself dignified, he was merely comic. . . . His dull eyes and loose lips revealed his emptiness. . . . The words of other people slid over
him like skates over ice; he sometimes listened, seldom understood.
. . . He was nicknamed *la belle Fatma*. . . ." [9]

Ricard may have been petty, vindictive, and ridiculous, but he really had a more legitimate excuse for his insistence upon prosecution than an untasted cup of tea. During the two months preceding his decision events had moved rapidly, and the second or bribery-and-corruption phase of the scandal had already gained momentum. As the war of words shifted to the political arena judicial decorum was swept away in a torrent of sound and fury. The storm broke in September 1892 with the publication in Drumont's newspaper *La Libre Parole* of a series of articles signed by "Micros," pseudonym of Ferdinand Martin, the provincial banker who in 1885 had organized the supposedly spontaneous circulation of petitions for the lottery bond authorization. In November 1886 Martin had quarreled with the Panama directors and, believing himself ill treated, had severed his connection with the company. Six years later he paid off the score with interest. The "Micros" articles entitled *Les dessous de Panama* openly accused some 20 senators and deputies of having sold their votes in favor of the lottery bond bill in 1886 and 1888 and named four agents of the company as the principal distributors of the alleged bribes: Baron Jacques de Reinach, Henri Cottu, Irénée Blanc, owner of the newspaper *L'Économiste Pratique,* and Léopold-Émile Arton, intermediary between de Reinach and the venal legislators. Other journals followed the lead of *La Libre Parole,* and in November *La Cocarde,* edited by Édouard Ducret, published an interview with Charles de Lesseps which apparently confirmed the "Micros" revelations.

The Ministry of Justice, unable to ignore the popular clamor, acted promptly. Between October 24 and November 7, 1892 Prinet interrogated in turn Martin, Charles de Lesseps, Fontane, Cottu, de Reinach, and Blanc. Martin merely repeated what he had written as "Micros" but when pinned down admitted that he could not swear to a single instance of bribery from personal knowledge. Charles de Lesseps and Fontane denied some of the allegations and refused to reply to others. Cottu and Blanc acknowledged that they had urged certain legislators to vote for the lottery bill but disclaimed any attempt at bribery. Blanc managed to convince the counselor of his innocence and was never prosecuted, but Cottu did not escape so easily. Finally de Reinach, questioned on November 4 concerning the sum of 3,015,000 francs paid to him by the canal company for "publicity," deposed that this represented reimbursement for advances made by him on the company's behalf, that he had given approximately 1,000,000 francs to Arton but had no idea what Arton had done with the money, and that he himself had distributed no bribes.

Arton did not appear before Prinet, for he was already a fugitive from justice on another count. The Panama affair, in which he played a relatively minor rôle under the orders of de Reinach, was the culmination of a series of unsavory episodes in a thoroughly disreputable career. Born at Strasbourg in 1850, Léopold-Émile Aron, usually called Arton, had emigrated to Brazil as a young man, returned to Paris in 1885, and after a brief and unsuccessful venture as a coffee importer secured a position in the French·explosives trust, the Société de Dynamite. In May 1886 that corporation sent him to Panama with instructions to sell a large quantity ‘of dynamite which had been shipped some time before and was beginning to deteriorate in the damp climate, if indeed it had not already lost most of its value. Arton disposed of the inferior explosive to the unwary canal company at a loss to the Société de Dynamite of only 259,000 francs — much less than had been expected — and was rewarded by the society's president, Barbe, with a better position and a salary of 12,000 francs a year. But it was discovered later that Arton had embezzled about 4,600,000 francs belonging to the Société de Dynamite and its affiliates, and it was to escape the consequences of this crime that he had fled from France in June 1892, a few months before he was accused of complicity in the Panama corruption.

Next to Ferdinand and Charles de Lesseps themselves the most prominent personage intimately involved in the Panama scandal was Jacques de Reinach. He was of German birth, a native of Frankfurt-am-Main, and had lived for some years in Italy, where his father was created a baron by Victor Emmanuel II in 1866. Later he moved to Paris, became a French citizen in 1871, founded the banking house of Kohn, de Reinach et Compagnie, speculated in French railway securities, sold military supplies to the government, and amassed a considerable fortune. Some of his transactions appear to have been more or less dubious, but until 1892 his business ethics had never been questioned. His title as well as his influence in financial and political circles gave him a certain social prestige; he entertained lavishly, frequented the Opéra, and was an honored guest at fashionable — though seldom at aristocratic — dinners: "His active mind took an enthusiastic interest in daring projects, which he often abandoned for new ventures. Towards the end of his life especially he neglected his bank to dabble in a kind of financial dilettantism. . . . Reinach was not unaware of the value of promises and fulfilled his oral agreements as scrupulously as his written ones. . . . But when hard pressed he would commit infamous acts in the effort to extricate himself from an impossible situation. . . . Short and stout, ruddy and bearded . . . Reinach seemed both morally and physically flabby. . . ." [10]

De Reinach's interest in the Panama enterprise dated back to 1876, when as a director of the Société Civile Internationale du Canal Interocéanique du Darien he had helped to finance Wyse's expeditions. During the first years of the canal company's existence he remained in the background, but after the death of Lévy-Crémieux he became its chief financial adviser. De Lesseps, inexperienced in financial jugglery and firmly though somewhat naïvely convinced that the end justified the means, gave de Reinach a free hand and took care not to inquire too closely into his methods. Partly as recompense for his own services, partly for distribution to other persons, de Reinach received huge sums from the company at various times: 4,566,383 francs for participation in the flotation syndicates, 3,015,000 francs for "publicity," and (in July 1888) 4,940,475 francs for which the directors afterwards found it difficult to account — a total of over 12,500,000 francs. The first item was legitimate in so far as the syndicates themselves were *bona fide,* which they were only to a very limited extent; the other two were quite indefensible. In addition de Reinach collected "commissions" from two or three contractors for services not specified but certainly illicit: 383,266 francs from the Anglo-Dutch Company, 1,837,377 from Eiffel. A commission of 1 franc 40 per cubic meter from Artigue, Sonderegger et Compagnie was also mentioned, but that firm indignantly denied any such payment to de Reinach, and no proof of it was ever presented.

When the investigators brought these transactions to light they discovered another and much more astonishing fact: that de Reinach had made no profit whatever out of all these millions. Behind the unhappy baron loomed the sinister figure of his evil genius, Cornelius Herz. De Reinach, who had plundered the canal company for years, was himself the victim of a pitiless vampire, an all-devouring blackmailer. Much of the mystery surrounding the Panama affair concerns the relations between these two, for both destroyed significant records and died with sealed lips. The nature of Herz's hold upon de Reinach has never been disclosed; whatever it was, it was powerful enough to keep the baron in a state of virtual slavery.

Cornelius Herz was born at Besançon in 1845. When he was three years old his parents, who were German, emigrated to New York. Herz was educated first in the schools of that city and later at Heidelberg, Munich, and Vienna; then, returning to America, he studied medicine at Chicago, received his degree, and went to

Paris. When the Franco-Prussian War broke out in 1870 he joined
the French army as a surgeon, was awarded the Cross of the Legion
of Honor for his services, and went back to the United States,
where he acquired American citizenship by naturalization. For
some years he practised medicine in San Francisco and at the same
time appears to have participated in various shady business deals.
Threatened with exposure, he returned to Paris in 1877: "At that
time . . . Herz was neither an engineer . . . nor an inventor
. . . nor a capitalist. . . . But he was an exceedingly clever go-
between, a remarkably shrewd negotiator . . . always on the
watch for enterprises already begun but undeveloped. . . . He
knew how to flatter bankers and secure financial support. . . ." [11]
In appearance he was "a dumpy little man with coarse features
whose black eyes, set deep in their sockets, sparkled with animation and intelligence. Cold when first encountered, he would
warm up little by little and talk volubly; he had a gift for persuading anyone in whom his hawklike head and strutting vanity did
not arouse mistrust. . . . His character was less enigmatic than
was believed at the time. Cornelius Herz was just what he seemed
to be: a charlatan on a colossal scale. Imaginative and audacious,
wholly unscrupulous, contemptuous of men as well as of money, he
knew well how to make use of both to satisfy his passion for intrigue. . . ." [12] With a finger in countless industrial and political
pies, with influence in parliamentary circles and the entrée to the
Palais de l'Élysée during Grévy's administration from 1879 to 1887,
Herz was a power not to be ignored. For some years he had been
on intimate terms with Georges Clemenceau, then a deputy and
leader of the Radical party. In 1881 and again in 1883 Herz had supplied funds for the support of Clemenceau's newspaper *La Justice,*
and in return Clemenceau had ceded to Herz half of his own shares
in the journal but had repurchased them in April 1885.

   Herz and de Reinach are believed to have met for the first time
about 1880. At the beginning their relations were casual and apparently friendly; there is no evidence of blackmail before 1886 or
1887. Herz's devious association with the canal company commenced in 1885 when de Lesseps launched his first campaign for
the lottery bond authorization. Herz called upon de Lesseps and,
asserting that his political influence could swing the vote in favor
of the bill, persuaded the directors of the company to advance him
600,000 francs. This sum was carried on the company's books under the protean euphemism of "publicity." In addition de Lesseps
promised to pay Herz 10,000,000 francs if and when the lottery bill

should pass and with astonishing indiscretion gave Herz a written copy of this secret agreement, thus placing the company at his mercy. Through de Reinach Herz bled the company again and again. Charles de Lesseps testified that he had recovered and burned the incriminating paper in 1887, but apparently the compact remained in force. On May 11, 1888, when the lottery bill was again under consideration, de Reinach wrote to Herz: "According to the oral agreement dating from the first petition of the Panama company for permission to issue lottery bonds, you will receive 10,000,-000 francs the day after the company itself . . . collects the first installment [on subscriptions]. . . . It is understood that out of that sum you will repay me all the money you owe me as well as the amounts you owe to Kohn, Reinach et Cie. . . ." [13] But when the bill finally passed in June the company refused to give de Reinach the money promised to Herz. On July 10 Herz, then at Frankfurt, sent a furious telegram to Fontane, secretary general of the company: "Your friend [de Reinach] is trying to cheat me; he must pay or be destroyed, and if he is destroyed his associates will be destroyed with him. I shall wreck everything rather than be robbed of a single centime; take warning, the time is short." [14] The directors hastily handed over to de Reinach, not the whole sum demanded, but 4,940,475 francs, of which Herz pocketed 2,000,000.

This and the other subsidies to Herz represented out-and-out blackmail, for at no time did he perform any services, legal or illegal, for the company which might have merited compensation. Occasionally the wretched cat's-paw feebly attempted to defy his master. On November 28, 1888 de Reinach wrote to Chabert, one of Herz's agents: "Not only do I refuse any further payments to Dr. Herz, but if he does not shut his mouth I shall demand from him through the courts reimbursement of all the money he has been paid since the beginning of the Panama affair, for . . . Dr. Herz is entitled to nothing; he has contributed nothing . . . and if . . . I have submitted to his threats of exposure which might have compromised the [lottery bond] flotation of the Panama company . . . that does not constitute a legal debt. Furthermore if Dr. Herz, Grand Officer of the Legion of Honor and according to his own claim the future ambassador of the United States in Paris [there is not the slightest reason to believe that Herz was ever considered for this post], who expects to bequeath an honorable name to his children . . . makes a move, I shall immediately file . . . suit and produce . . . documents which will show clearly how many millions he has improperly appropriated. . . . I have never prof-

ited by these payments, my hands are clean. . . ." [15] This was sheer
bravado; the next time Herz cracked the whip de Reinach cringed
and paid.

On January 20, 1893 Louis Andrieux, Herz's lawyer and a former deputy, deposed that de Reinach had once hired an assassin to
poison Herz, but the plot had miscarried. This melodramatic story
was neither corroborated nor denied and may or may not have
been true: "In Paris Herz received a letter from Brazil signed by
one Amiel. This Amiel asserted that he had been paid on account
part of a large sum promised him if he would kill . . . Herz, but
that . . . he had chosen to escape to Brazil . . . with the money
rather than carry out the murder to which he had at first consented. Amiel added that he had had interviews with a man whose
name he did not know. . . . Amiel . . . was a former agent of
the . . . prefecture of police who had been dismissed from several
posts. . . ." [16] To prove his allegation Amiel forwarded an envelope addressed to himself upon which Herz recognized de Reinach's handwriting: "Yet there was still some doubt. M. Herz . . .
told me . . . that he had explicitly accused him [de Reinach] of
planning to murder him, and that M. de Reinach did not deny it
but said: 'What! You took that seriously! I proposed it only to get
rid of you, to frighten you into flight across the frontier and even
farther.' M. Herz would not accept this explanation. . . . At last
M. de Reinach confessed but said they must be reconciled and hold
no grudge against each other. . . . Thereafter M. Herz and M. de
Reinach became the best friends in the world; a little later M. de
Reinach asked for the hand of Herz's daughter on behalf of one of
his own sons. . . ." [17]

Because three of the principal transgressors — Herz, de Reinach,
and Arton — as well as the late Lévy-Crémieux and possibly others
connected with the canal company were Jews, the Panama disclosures produced a wave of anti-Semitism which swept over France
and eventually, leaving Panama far behind, broke over the head of
the unfortunate Captain Dreyfus. Drumont and other bigots waged
a violent campaign against the "subversive" influence of Jewish
bankers; the Chamber of Deputies committee, more restrained,
merely deplored the fact that "foreigners representing international finance had been permitted to play the rôles of intermediaries between a private company and public officials." [18]

Prinet's preliminary interrogation of de Reinach had convinced
him of the baron's guilt: "If . . . on November 4, 1892 . . . de
Reinach entered the magistrate's office as a mere witness, he left it

a defendant. . . ." [19] The very next day Prinet instructed the police commissioner, Clément, to visit de Reinach's residence at 20 rue Murillo in the fashionable Monceau quarter, demand an itemized statement covering the 3,015,000 francs distributed for "publicity," and seize all receipts and other documents relating thereto. Although the order was marked "urgent" Clément did not appear at de Reinach's until the morning of November 8, when he was informed that the baron had left for the south of France four days before and was not expected home for three weeks. Clément's superior, Quesnay de Beaurepaire, was subsequently blamed for the delay but denied responsibility and pointed out that since November 5 was a Saturday Clément could not have carried out his instructions until the following Monday at the earliest, or one day before he actually did so. That de Reinach had really left Paris before Clément's fruitless call appears doubtful, as he was reliably reported to have had an interview with Rouvier, the former Prime Minister, a day or two later and to have gone south afterwards.

He returned to Paris on November 18 to find the law close at his heels. On the 19th Quesnay de Beaurepaire announced that he would obey Ricard's order and prosecute the Panama directors, including de Reinach, on the charge of fraud. At the same time the prosecutor wrote privately to Joseph Reinach, the baron's nephew: "My dear friend, it is with deep distress that I must warn you that you will soon hear sad news. . . . The summonses in the Panama case will be sent out at once, and they contain a name that is close to you. . . ." [20] That afternoon the now desperate de Reinach, accompanied by Rouvier and Clemenceau, called upon Herz and begged him to use his influence to stop the *Libre Parole* and *Cocarde* press campaigns, of which the baron had been for months the principal target. According to Clemenceau, de Reinach, feverishly agitated, "his face crimson and his eyes popping out of his head, scarcely able to articulate, said but a few words. . . ." [21] When Herz, insisting that it was too late to accomplish anything, coldly refused to help, his three visitors attempted to enlist the aid of Senator Constans, a former Minister of the Interior, who promised to do what he could but held out little hope. By that time de Reinach's apoplectic excitement had subsided; he was in a state of virtual collapse. "When we were again on the sidewalk," Clemenceau reported, "M. de Reinach asked me to go home with him. It was about eight in the evening; my own family was waiting for me; I begged M. de Reinach to excuse me. As he clasped my hand and climbed into a *fiacre* he murmured: 'I am done for.' I saw a man mortally stricken, but I did not know the reason. . . . I left him and walked home." [22] The next morning de Reinach was found dead in his bed. Some time during the following week Cornelius Herz fled to England.

The sudden death of Jacques de Reinach is one of the unsolved mysteries of the Panama affair. Did he die of heart failure or a cerebral hæmorrhage? Did he commit suicide? Or was he murdered? Nobody knows the answer, but the generally accepted and probably correct theory is that he deliberately swallowed poison. The Chamber of Deputies demanded an autopsy, but the Cabinet, anxious to avert any intensification of the scandal that already threatened its existence, refused permission, and the body was interred with almost indecent haste. The outraged Chamber protested so energetically that the Cabinet was forced to resign, and on December 6 a new government, composed for the most part of the same Ministers but with Ribot instead of Loubet as Premier and with Léon Bourgeois replacing Ricard as Minister of Justice, took office. Four days later de Reinach's corpse was exhumed; but Dr. Brouardel, who performed the autopsy, found the entrails already decomposed to such a degree that he declared himself unable to determine the cause of death. After a second autopsy had yielded the same negative result the mangled body was reburied with its secret unrevealed.

The corruption charges published by *La Libre Parole* furnished the opposition party in the Chamber with effective ammunition for an attack upon their political adversaries. On November 10, 1892 three of the minority deputies — Delahaye, Gauthier, and Argeliès — demanded a parliamentary investigation into the affairs of the Panama company with particular reference to the implication of public officials. Discussion was postponed until November 21, when in an atmosphere charged with electricity by the shock of de Reinach's death Delahaye leveled eight specific accusations against the directors of the canal company, their agents, and various Cabinet members, senators, and deputies. In substance Delahaye alleged that in July 1888 the company had allotted to de Reinach approximately 5,000,000 francs to purchase votes for the lottery bill; that de Reinach had given Arton a book of cheques to be issued as bribes; that 3,000,000 francs had been distributed among 150 deputies and senators (only a few senators, according to Delahaye); that Barbe, president of the Société de Dynamite and a former Minister, who had recently died, had been paid 400,000 francs by de Reinach; that Sans-Leroy, one of the deputies on the lottery bill committee in 1888, had accepted 200,000 francs to reverse his position and cast the deciding vote in the affirmative; that the canal company had paid 200,000 francs for a French newspaper, *Le Télégraphe,* "not worth 20 francs"; [23] that it had also acquired a foreign journal, the *Gazette de Moscou,* for 500,000 francs; and that at the request of Floquet, Tirard's successor as Prime Minister, the company had contributed 300,000 francs to the expenses of an election in the Nord department in the summer of 1888. At the time he made these charges Delahaye mentioned none of the names of the public officials involved, and although he divulged many of them shortly afterwards he persistently refused to identify the 150 deputies and senators accused of accepting bribes and admitted that he could produce only "moral evidence" [24] against them.

Le Provost de Launay seconded Delahaye's demand for an investigation but proposed that its scope should be expanded to cover the entire administration of the canal company, including its financial transactions, its relations with its contractors, and its publicity campaigns. The Chamber immediately adopted the suggestion and on November 22 appointed a committee of 33 members to conduct the inquiry, with Brisson in the chair and Ernest Vallé as reporter. Although the committee, having failed to induce the Cabinet to grant it judicial authority in addition to its fact-finding powers, complained that its inability to force reluctant witnesses to testify or even to appear before it seriously hampered its activities, it did in fact bring to light an enormous quantity of information. The committee held 63 sessions, received 158 depositions, filed away no less than 1046 separate *dossiers,* and issued a report filling three immense volumes. Some of the committee's conclusions suggest that the investigators considered it their duty not only to find facts but to suppress them, especially those tending to reflect upon the integrity of their own colleagues. Although on the whole the examination was both thorough and impartial certain pages of the long report emitted an unmistakable odor of whitewash to which the dissentient minority of nine members objected vigorously: "We hoped that after the announcement of the judicial verdicts the committee would continue its investigation for the sake of the honor and dignity of the Parliament. . . . The majority . . . has decided to end its work. . . . We protest against this decision. . . . The task is unfinished and the report . . . is nothing more than . . . an adroitly presented justification of governmental and parliamentary practices of which we disapprove. . . . The entire report may be summed up in the statement that since the courts have rendered their verdicts nothing remains to be done except to pin medals on everyone concerned. . . . From the court documents, especially from judgments of nonsuit, the committee's reporter has drawn inferences which it is impossible for us to accept. He has transformed mere reasonable doubts from which any accused person is entitled to benefit into positive affirmations of innocence." [25] Both sides were playing politics industriously; the minority's indignation, however righteous it may have been, appears to have been inspired less by an unquenchable thirst for abstract justice than by a partisan desire to discredit the dominant faction.

Chapter 32. The Trials

On November 21, 1892 — the day of Delahaye's accusatory speech in the Chamber — Quesnay de Beaurepaire summoned Ferdinand and Charles de Lesseps, Fontane, Cottu, and Eiffel to appear before the First Appellate Court on charges of fraud and maladministration. The inclusion of Ferdinand de Lesseps, sunk in senile apathy at La Chesnaye and not even aware of his indictment, was a mere formality; no attempt was made to enforce his attendance, and it was taken for granted that he would not appear. The trial was scheduled to open on November 24, but the unreadiness of the lawyers on both sides caused a postponement to January 10, 1893. The court held 13 sessions in the Palais de Justice. Charles de Lesseps "appeared full of energy, with deeply marked features, a bald head fringed with grey hair, a brick-red complexion, and a greying beard . . . the somber gleam of his eyes shone piercingly beneath thick brows. . . . Perhaps his manner seemed too cold, lacking — as certain newspapers remarked — 'the élan that would have made him a more sympathetic figure,' but it masked an exceptionally noble character. . . . Cottu, his complexion sallowed by insomnia, his jaw muscles tense, nervously twisted his black mustache; Fontane, with hair prematurely whitened and memory dulled by a recent attack of typhoid fever, trembled at every question and turned despairingly towards his counsel. Eiffel's bearing was more vigorous . . . but his eyes peered nearsightedly. . . ." [1]

The counsel for Ferdinand and Charles de Lesseps, Henri Barboux, "short and thin, with a bony face framed in white whiskers, and sparkling, often mocking, eyes," [2] argued so eloquently for the acquittal of his clients that his pleas are still referred to as classic examples of courtroom oratory. He pointed out that neither father nor son had attempted to enrich himself at the expense of the canal enterprise, though both had had ample opportunity. He offered documentary evidence to prove that Charles's assets totaled between 350,000 and 395,000 francs, including the value of his 10 founder's shares which he had sold some years before for 200,000; while Ferdinand de Lesseps, who had disposed of his 90 founder's shares for 1,400,000 francs, had invested 1,778,000 francs in the company and had therefore actually lost money. Barboux defended de Lesseps's underestimation of the cost of the canal and insisted that most great projects had proved far more expensive than originally contemplated: "The Paris Opéra was to have cost 22 millions, it finally cost 43; the Marseilles canal was estimated at 13 millions, it cost 45; the Verdon canal [in southeastern France] was supposed to cost 7 millions, it cost 23; the Manchester canal was to have cost 245 millions, it cost 385; the Corinth canal was to have cost 24 millions, it cost almost 60. . . . Now condemn us for our illusions and our mistakes. . . ." [3]

A few days later Barboux pleaded again: "M. de Lesseps has never been wanting in either loyalty or frankness. If he sinned, it was through excessive optimism. But . . . only optimists are worthy of respect. . . . When the penal code concerns itself with misspent funds . . . it presumes that they were spent for personal benefit. . . . It would not be necessary . . . to prove that the money thus diverted enriched the faithless trustee himself, but it would have to be shown that it enriched some other person with whom he was associated directly or indirectly; it might be a brother, a friend, a mistress. . . . But if on the other hand he has employed a corporation's funds in the interests of that corporation, even if he has misspent them, a civil action may be instituted . . . but you cannot prosecute him for a crime or fraud. . . ." [4] The little lawyer wasted his breath, for on February 9 the chief magistrate, Périvier, and the other judges found all five defendants guilty. Ferdinand and Charles de Lesseps were sentenced to imprisonment for five years and fined 3000 francs each; Fontane and Cottu to two years in prison and fines of 3000 francs each; and Eiffel to two years and a fine of 20,000 francs. The outraged Barboux stalked out of the courtroom vowing that he "would never plead again before such people. . . . Charles de Lesseps wept with his head in his hands; Cottu and Fontane collapsed in their friends' arms; only Eiffel, with his hand on his son's shoulder, remained calm. . . ." [5]

The condemned men appealed at once, and by decisions handed down on May 5 and June 15, 1893 the Cour de Cassation — the highest tribunal in France — reversed the verdict and acquitted the defendants on the technical ground that the prosecutor had not issued the summonses until November 21, 1892, more than three years after the commission of the most recent of the alleged crimes, and that therefore the accused were entitled to immunity under the statute of limitations. Quesnay de Beaurepaire was censured severely some years later for the delay that enabled the Panama administrators to evade the penalties imposed for fraud, but he defended himself with spirit. The statute of limitations, he claimed, contained ambiguous provisions which could be construed in various ways; in his own opinion, which was also that of Ricard, Prinet, and Périvier, the statute should not have been invoked in this instance.

Even before the trial for fraud opened preparations were being made for a supplementary action, this time for corruption of public officials. The scope of the second trial was much broader than that of the first: more names were involved, more charges filed, more evidence accumulated. Of the 17 men indicted, three — Charles de Lesseps, Fontane, and Cottu — were accused of distributing bribes, the others of accepting them. The alleged recipients were Charles Baïhaut, the former Minister of the Interior who had recommended authorization of the lottery in 1886; Blondin, his intermediary and a former employee of the Crédit Lyonnais; Sans-Leroy, the deputy whose last-minute change of heart had assured the passage of the lottery bill in 1888; six other deputies or former deputies — Arène, Roche, Dugué de la Fauconnerie, Gobron, Antonin Proust, and Rouvier, the ex-Premier; and five senators — Thévenet (recently Minister of Justice), Renault, Grévy (not the ex-President, who had died in 1891), Devès, and Béral. Rouvier lamented: "What a terrible disgrace, when I have been married only a short time and have a baby boy six months old!" To which Arène replied unsympathetically: "Poor child! You shouldn't have told him." [6]

The Senate and Chamber agreed to waive parliamentary immunity for their members. During the preliminary investigation the charges against almost half of those indicted were dropped for lack of evidence, and when the case came to trial before the Court of Assizes in March 1893 only nine defendants remained: Charles de Lesseps, Fontane, Baïhaut, Blondin, Sans-Leroy, Dugué de la Fauconnerie, Gobron, Proust, and Béral.

The most important evidence in the hands of the prosecution consisted of a number of canceled cheques, commonly referred to as the Thierrée cheques, and a photograph of a note known as the Andrieux list. On November 30, 1892 Thierrée, a former employee of Kohn, de Reinach et Compagnie but at that time president of his own bank, appeared voluntarily before the investigating committee of the Chamber and offered to produce 26 canceled cheques signed by de Reinach. Thierrée testified that on July 17, 1888 de Reinach had deposited in his (Thierrée's) bank a single cheque for 3,390,475 francs issued by the Panama company and had demanded in exchange 26 separate cheques amounting in the aggregate to the same sum. Thierrée had paid little attention to this routine banking operation, nor had he felt called upon to ask de Reinach what he proposed to do with the money. The cheques themselves, made out to "bearer," were of little value as evidence of bribery, and at first Thierrée insisted that he had burned the stubs; but on December 19 he turned them over to the examining magistrate. On each of 22 stubs were written the first three or four letters of the name of a senator, a deputy, or a former Cabinet Minister followed by a figure, the amounts varying from 20,000 to 195,000 francs. Five of these stubs totaling 550,000 francs represented payments to the late ex-Minister Barbe. The two largest cheques, for 1,000,000 francs each, were made out not to bearer but to Cornelius Herz.

The Andrieux list not only confirmed the payments indicated by the Thierrée stubs but furnished additional evidence of corruption. On December 22, three days after Thierrée had given up the stubs, Herz's attorney Louis Andrieux presented to the Deputies committee a photograph of a note containing a list of names. This note had a strange and rather equivocal history. According to Andrieux, de Reinach had had copies made of the Thierrée bearer cheques and upon those copies had written with his own hand the initials of the several recipients. Two years later, or some time in 1890, de Reinach had dictated an explanatory note to his temporary secretary Paul Stéphan, an employee of the banking house of Propper et Compagnie, successor to Kohn, de Reinach et Compagnie. Stéphan testified that de Reinach had put the note in an envelope and instructed him to take it at once to Clemenceau, which he had done; but Clemenceau flatly denied that he had ever received or even seen the note, and Stéphan's story has never been confirmed — or for that matter disproved. The note and the copies of the cheques eventually fell into the hands of Herz, who gave Andrieux photographs of the note and of one of the duplicate cheques. Andrieux claimed that he had tried to gain possession of the original note but had been unsuccessful and did not know what had become of it. Presumably it was destroyed by Herz, for it has never come to light. The Deputies committee was inclined to consider the note a red herring if not an outright forgery: "At first sight such a document coming from the Baron de Reinach was not calculated to inspire confidence. . . . The fact that it had passed through the hands of Herz . . . added little to its prestige." [7] The authenticity of the Andrieux list has never been established beyond question.

The note listed the same names and amounts that appeared on the Thierrée stubs. It also contained this paragraph: "One cheque for 1,340,000 francs issued to Arton and exchanged by him for a number of smaller cheques . . . which he distributed to 104 deputies, whose names he is in a position to supply and who received sums varying between 1000 and 300,000 francs apiece (the last-named amount to Sans-Leroy). . . . In addition 250,000 francs were paid to M. Floquet, then Premier, for government expenses." [8] Thus the note and the cheque stubs corroborated most of Delahaye's charges, though the details varied: Delahaye had estimated the number of implicated legislators at 150, the total bribery fund at 5,000,000 francs, and the respective payments to Barbe, Sans-Leroy, and Floquet at 400,000, 200,000, and 300,000 francs; while the Andrieux list mentioned only 104 deputies, apparently reduced the aggregate bribes to 3,390,475 francs, and placed Barbe's share at 550,000, Sans-Leroy's at 300,000, and Floquet's at 250,000. The photograph handed to the investigating committee had been defaced by a hole, which Andrieux admitted he had torn deliberately to conceal the name of one beneficiary. His persistent refusal to divulge the name bred a swarm of fantastic rumors: "All sorts of guesses poured through that hole. The mysterious X, the 'X of Panama,' was identified alternatively as Raphaël Bischoffsheim, member of the Institute . . . Herbette, French ambassador to Berlin; Baron Mohrenheim, Russian ambassador to Paris; and even Ernest Carnot, the President's son. . . . Andrieux denied . . . all of these suppositions and asserted that the name belonged to a deputy." [9] The identity of that deputy, if it was a deputy, is another of the unsolved enigmas of the Panama affair.

On December 16, 1892 — almost four weeks before the opening of the first trial, the trial for fraud — Charles de Lesseps, Fontane, and Sans-Leroy were arrested on the second or bribery charge and incarcerated in the old Mazas prison, then located near the site of the present Gare de Lyon. A few days later Cottu gave himself up, and on January 9 Baïhaut and Blondin were imprisoned. Since French law did not provide for bail, all except Cottu — who was cleared of the corruption charge during the preliminary investigation on February 7 — remained in prison throughout the whole period covered by both trials and the interval between them.

The second trial opened on March 9, 1893, exactly a month after the close of the first. Unlike its predecessor, which had been heard by the magistrates of the Appellate Court without a jury, the corruption case was presented before a jury in the Court of Assizes:

"The courtroom was packed. . . . Charles de Lesseps's face was
drawn and his skin yellowed by more than four [*sic;* actually less
than three] months of confinement in a prison cell. . . . Fontane,
pale and depressed, stared at the jury with mournful eyes. . . .
Baïhaut displayed a glum countenance surmounted by a bald pate
and underscored by a square beard. . . . A fastidious spectator
complained: 'It smells bad in here!' His neighbor replied: 'Yes —
it stinks of scapegoats.' " [10] Charles "was no longer the man he had
been in the Appellate Court. In place of the slightly pompous
chairman of a board making a report in a cold monotonous voice
he was now the lecturer, wholly at ease, ironic and insolent. His
tactics had changed. Before the Appellate Court he had seemed by
his discretion to be offering the government a tacit compromise:
his silence in exchange for a favorable verdict. . . . But at the Assizes Charles de Lesseps had nobody to protect . . . except himself. He gave a lively account of the governmental and parliamentary pressure that had been brought to bear upon him. . . ." [11]

The charge against Baïhaut was not based on the evidence of the
Thierrée cheques and the Andrieux list, for his bribery antedated
those documents by two years. When as Minister of the Interior
Baïhaut had read Rousseau's report in May 1886 he resolved to recommend the lottery bill requested by the canal company. That
resolution had been inspired by the promise of a substantial bribe.
Through his go-between Blondin Baïhaut had demanded 1,000,000
francs payable in installments: 375,000 as soon as he presented
the draft of the bill, 125,000 after the vote in the Chamber but before that in the Senate, and the remainder before the issue of the
bonds. Charles de Lesseps had paid him 250,000 francs on June 17,
the day he transmitted the draft to the Chamber with his recommendation, and four days later gave him 125,000 more, which completed the first installment. But the lottery bill was rejected at that
time, and Baïhaut never collected the balance of the promised
million.

On December 24, 1892, during the preliminary investigation,
Charles de Lesseps freely admitted the payment of 375,000 francs
to Baïhaut and recounted the circumstances in detail. The episode
was brought up at Charles's first trial, although Baïhaut was not
then a co-defendant and corruption was not the point at issue.
Charles protested vehemently that the suggestion had originated
with the Minister, not the company, and that therefore the payment came under the head of extortion rather than bribery. When
Périvier asked why he had not complained to the police, Charles
is said to have replied: "How could I, when the police were the

robbers?" [12] The more orotund Barboux likened Baïhaut's extortion to a forced levy under threat of violence: "When the captain of a richly laden vessel is attacked by pirates on the high seas and pays them tribute, has he defrauded the owner of his ship and cargo? . . . When Lombard traders on their way to Flanders and Flemish traders on their way to Lombardy were forced to pay tribute to the robber barons whose castles dominated the highways of commerce, did they defraud their partners? When the leader of a caravan across Africa is obliged to pay for the escort of desert Arabs, has he defrauded the merchants?" [13] On the second day of the second trial Baïhaut broke down pitifully: "I wish to make . . . a complete confession. . . . I am guilty. . . . For fifteen years I served France faithfully as deputy and as minister and led an irreproachable life. Even now I cannot understand how I could have sinned." [14]

The deputy Sans-Leroy was made of sterner stuff, though the evidence against him was no less conclusive. He admitted that in 1888 he had paid off a number of debts to the amount of some 200,-000 francs but denied that the money had come directly or indirectly from the Panama company and asserted without a blush that his wife's dowry had supplied the funds. The spectators hooted in derision, but Sans-Leroy's shrewd lawyers presented such an enormous mass of documentary evidence, unmethodically arranged and almost impossible to decipher, that the bewildered jurors could make neither head nor tail of it. The three other deputies on trial — Dugué de la Fauconnerie, Gobron, and Proust — and the one senator — Béral — also protested their innocence and insisted that the cheques they had received from de Reinach in 1888 had no connection with the Panama company but were merely payments of private debts or other conventional business transactions. The prosecution made only a feeble attempt to press the charges, and the jurors readily accepted these glib explanations of what must surely have appeared to them an extraordinary series of coincidences.

The accusations against Floquet were received with similar incredulity. During his preliminary examination Charles de Lesseps testified that in May 1888 — a few weeks before the lottery bill passed the Senate — he had been visited by Clemenceau, Prime Minister Floquet, and the Minister of War, de Freycinet; that all three had urged him to accede to de Reinach's demands for money; and that yielding to their insistence he had paid de Reinach 4,940,-475 francs in July of that year. He failed to mention that the payment had been made only after the receipt of Herz's threatening telegram from Frankfurt. Charles also stated that at Floquet's request he had paid sums aggregating 300,000 francs to five journalists for their services to the government party during the campaign preceding the election of April 15, 1888 in the Nord department. In that election the government candidate had been opposed by General Boulanger, leader of a royalist movement which for a time threatened to overthrow the republic. Floquet and Boulanger were bitter enemies and had recently fought a duel in which the general had received a slight wound. At that period the issue of *boulangisme* played a leading part in French politics, and it was not forgotten that, some years before, Ferdinand de Lesseps had given a dinner in the general's honor. Floquet emphatically denied Charles's assertions and pointed out that the subsidies to the newspapers had been paid between June 29 and October 2, 1888, several months after the election. The examining magistrate, Franqueville, dismissed the charges against Floquet, de Freycinet, and Clemenceau, none of whom was ever brought to trial; and the Deputies committee, only too happy to see public officials absolved at the expense of Charles de Lesseps, reported triumphantly: "The fact of the payment of 300,000 francs is unquestioned. It has never been denied. . . . But . . . the dates on which the 300,000 francs were paid do not tally with the election. . . . If these payments have no bearing upon the election . . . they do accord on the other hand with the subsidies then being distributed by the company . . . to the entire press in connection with the lottery bond issue. . . . So it is absurd to involve . . . the election. . . ." [15] The aroma of whitewash is particularly penetrating here. Charles de Lesseps probably told the simple truth.

Little attention was paid to Delahaye's charges against Barbe or to his statements concerning the alleged purchase of two newspapers by the Panama company. Early in November 1892 de Reinach had deposed that the 550,000 francs paid to Barbe represented nothing more than a private loan, of which Barbe had repaid 220,000. There was in fact little evidence of corruption in this transaction. Both principals had died before the trial opened, and their respective heirs afterwards reached a settlement through the civil courts. One of the newspapers mentioned, *Le Télégraphe*, had been purchased in February 1886 by Chaulin, director of *Le Soir*. "Did M. Chaulin buy the journal on behalf of the Panama company?" the Deputies committee inquired. "He . . . has refused to testify [before the committee]. Nevertheless it appears certain . . . that the *Télégraphe* did become the property of that company. . . . But there is a vast distinction between the fact of purchase and the assertion that the paper was not worth 20 francs and was acquired solely to secure the goodwill of its influential backers, and M. Delahaye has failed to supply convincing proof. . . ." [16] With regard to the supposed purchase of the Russian *Gazette de Moscou* the committee could find "neither proof, nor the rudiments of proof, nor presumptive evidence. M. Delahaye has not even divulged . . . the source of his information. On the other hand we have read . . . with satisfaction the energetic protests of M. Tcherbanne, Paris correspondent . . . of the *Gazette* . . . and of MM. Souvorine and de Tatistcheff . . . who came all the way from Russia to deny the charge. . . ." [17]

After twelve sessions the jury delivered its verdict on March 21, 1893: Fontane, Sans-Leroy, Dugué de la Fauconnerie, Gobron, Proust, and Béral were acquitted: Charles de Lesseps and Blondin were found guilty with extenuating circumstances; Baïhaut guilty without extenuating circumstances. That same evening the court sentenced Charles de Lesseps to one year in prison, Blondin to two years, and Baïhaut — the only one of all the defendants who "had been stupid enough to confess" [18] — to five years in prison, forfeiture of civil rights, a fine of 750,000 francs, and repayment of the 375,000-franc bribe. If Baïhaut could not pay his fine and indemnity Charles and Blondin were to be held jointly responsible for them. Charles filed an appeal, but the same Cour de Cassation that annulled the verdict in the fraud trial refused to reconsider this one. Yet some leniency was accorded him; since he had already spent about three months in prison awaiting trial and had been held under strict surveillance at the disposal of the investigating magistrates for almost three months before his incarceration, these two periods were deducted from his penalty. Some time after the end of the second trial he fell ill and was transferred to the Saint-Louis hospital, where he remained during the last few months of his term. He was finally released on September 12, 1893.

About a month after the close of the second trial Charles was permitted to leave prison under guard for a brief visit to his family. Accompanied by two police inspectors he drove from the Issoudun railway station to La Chesnaye, pausing for a few moments to pray in the old village church at Guilly. His father greeted him casually with: "Ah, Charles . . . there you are. . . . Has anything new happened in Paris?" [19] The next day Charles returned to his cell. Happily no suspicion of the truth penetrated the clouded mind of Ferdinand de Lesseps. The old man, growing feebler and more childish day by day, drowsed contentedly by the fireside. He died at La Chesnaye on December 7, 1894, a few days after his eighty-ninth birthday, and was buried on December 15 in the cemetery of Père-Lachaise. The Suez company paid the funeral expenses.

Charles de Lesseps's difficulties did not end with his release from prison. On January 19, 1894 he was publicly humiliated by the erasure of his name from the rolls of the Legion of Honor, and on January 26, 1896 he was called upon to make good almost the whole of Baïhaut's fine and indemnity — some 890,000 francs out of a total of 1,125,000 — which neither Baïhaut himself nor his accomplice Blondin had been able to pay. But Charles's own financial situation was little better. He offered a smaller sum, all he could afford; when that was rejected and he found himself threatened with another prison term for nonpayment, he fled to London on January 29. Three years later his self-imposed exile was ended by a compromise whereby the government agreed to accept 300,000 francs instead of the full amount, and on January 14, 1899 Charles de Lesseps returned to France. The Suez company loyally kept him on its board of directors for the remainder of his life. Long before he died on October 3, 1923 at the age of 82 the Panama scandal had become ancient history. He lived to see his own reputation substantially cleared, his father's name restored to honor, and the Panama canal completed — though not by his own countrymen.

The contrast between the heavy penalty imposed upon Baïhaut and the undeserved exoneration of his parliamentary co-defendants, who though almost certainly tarred with the same brush had escaped punishment by sheer bluff, aroused widespread sympathy for the unhappy ex-Minister. A petition for his reprieve was circulated in his own constituency and signed "by more people than had ever voted for him in an election." [20] In March 1896, at the end of the first three years of his term, he was liberated; but since his fine and indemnity remained unpaid he was rearrested in December and obliged to serve an additional sentence of six months.

The severity of the Court of Assizes towards the Panama directors and agents on the one hand and its obvious desire to spare the implicated public officials (except Baïhaut) on the other were strikingly exemplified by its procedure in the case against the deputy Sans-Leroy. On March 21, 1893 the court acquitted Sans-Leroy of having accepted a bribe from Arton, and on May 23 the same court convicted Arton on exactly the same evidence of the bribery of Sans-Leroy! On that count alone Arton was sentenced to imprisonment for five years, forfeiture of civil rights, and a fine of 400,000 francs. Mystified but not ill pleased, the members of the

Deputies committee shrugged their shoulders cynically: "How can the second verdict be reconciled with the first? The court has not explained, and we shall not attempt to solve the puzzle." [21] On the same day the court condemned Arton to 20 years at hard labor on another charge, embezzlement from the Société de Dynamite.

Both judgments were rendered by default, for Arton could not be located. He had escaped from France on June 11, 1892 and taken refuge in London, whence he made his way to Bucharest. In November Soinoury, the head of the Sûreté, sent his secretary Dupas in search of the runaway. Through an intermediary Dupas established contact with Arton and at the end of December met him by prearrangement in Venice but though armed with a warrant made no attempt to arrest him. For this omission, which appears to have been motivated by political chicanery, both the Prime Minister, Loubet, and his successor Ribot were afterwards held responsible; but both disclaimed previous knowledge of Dupas's mission, and their complicity was never proved. On January 18, 1893 Dupas and a police inspector named Soudais, this time explicitly instructed to arrest Arton if they could catch him, started off again in pursuit of the fugitive. The story of the next four weeks reads like the scenario of a screen melodrama by Alfred Hitchcock. The chase led Dupas and his assistant from Paris to Budapest, from Budapest to Bucharest, from Bucharest to Jassy, from Jassy to Nuremberg, from Nuremberg to Prague, from Prague to Magdeburg, from Magdeburg to Hanover, and from Hanover back to Budapest, where they lost the trail and with empty hands returned to Paris. Meanwhile Arton had given them the slip at Hanover and crossed to London, where he lived unrecognized and undisturbed for two and a half years.

In October 1895 a correspondent in London, stimulated by the offer of a reward for information leading to Arton's capture, notified Henriot, inspector general of the Paris Sûreté, that he knew where to find the long-lost swindler. Henriot proceeded to London, and on November 16 Arton was arrested and confined in Holloway prison. The British authorities agreed to permit his extradition but only for trial upon the charges of embezzlement from the dynamite corporation. On June 27, 1896 the Court of Assizes sentenced him to six years at hard labor, but the judgment was annulled upon appeal. He was retried and on November 6 again sentenced, this time to eight years. At the same time Arton consented to waive the immunity granted him by the extradition agreement and to submit to interrogation concerning his alleged corruption of public officials on behalf of the Panama company. On February 25, 1897

he appeared once more before the Assizes, which at last acquitted
him of the bribery of Sans-Leroy, four years after that deputy had
been absolved of complicity in the affair. Arton testified that the
number of deputies he had paid totaled only 26, not 150 as charged
by Delahaye or 104 as indicated by the Andrieux list. He denied
that these payments constituted bribery and claimed that he had
merely "made overtures . . . to a group of deputies already
friendly to the Panama enterprise and in favor of the lottery bond
bill, and had asked them to enlighten their colleagues and to spread
propaganda on its behalf; and that he had then, without solicita-
tion on their parts, repaid their services with gifts of 10,000, 20,000,
30,000, 50,000, and even 100,000 francs just as one would present
— as he put it — a box of cigars to somebody to whom one was
under an obligation. . . ." [22] Moreover Arton declared that he had
received 2,000,000 francs from de Reinach, not 1,340,000; that he
had paid out 1,100,000 francs in the form of "cigars"; that he had
kept 400,000 as his own commission; and that he had returned 500,-
000 to de Reinach.

On the strength of these disclosures the deputies Boyer, Maret,
and Naquet — three of the four Arton had paid directly instead
of through intermediaries, according to his own story — were indicted in March 1897, but the charges were soon dismissed. Among
the interested spectators at the Arton trials was the painter Henri
de Toulouse-Lautrec, who left a record of the proceedings in a
number of hasty pencil sketches of the defendant, the witnesses, and
the court officers, as well as three lithographs representing the depositions of Ribot, Dupas, and Soudais. Arton served a term in
prison at Melun for his embezzlement of the dynamite funds, but
the extradition stipulations prevented his prosecution on the Panama charges. Impoverished and embittered after his release, he
committed suicide in 1905.

Meanwhile the most infamous scoundrel of all, Cornelius Herz,
was living unpunished in the eminently respectable English sea-
side resort of Bournemouth. He had left France hastily at the end
of November 1892, a few days after de Reinach's death. On December 20 a deputy belonging to the *opportuniste* party, Déroulède,
drew attention to Herz's connection with Clemenceau's newspaper
La Justice and threw the Chamber into an uproar with the assertion that the name of Herz's intermediary "is on the lips of all of
you; but not one of you dares to identify him because you are
afraid of three things: his sword, his pistol, and his tongue. . . .
Well, I shall defy them all and name him: it is Monsieur Clemen-

ceau!" [23] Clemenceau retorted hotly that Déroulède lied, that Herz had never played any part except that of an ordinary stockholder in the administration of *La Justice*. The altercation led to a duel in which, since Clemenceau was much the better shot, everyone expected his opponent to be killed; but the second who called out the signals paused so long between one word and the next that Clemenceau grew nervous. All of the shots went wild, and the affair ended without bloodshed.

Herz was not permitted to escape retribution altogether. The Legion of Honor expelled him on January 27, 1893, and on the following day the attorney for de Reinach's heirs instituted an action for blackmail. Herz, denying the charge of blackmail, wrote from England to the Deputies committee that he had received 2,000,000 francs from de Reinach in the summer of 1888 "in part payment of a large debt . . . incurred through participation in the financial organization of the telephone, electric light, and electric power transmission corporations." [24] Neither the Chamber nor the courts believed him, and on August 4, 1894 Herz was convicted of blackmail and condemned by default to imprisonment for five years and a fine of 3000 francs. On May 22, 1895 the Appellate Court confirmed the verdict, but in the defendant's absence the sentence could not be carried out. Nevertheless he was eventually forced to disgorge 1,500,000 francs which, by agreement with the de Reinach family, went to the liquidator of the bankrupt canal company.

Several attempts, all unsuccessful, were made to secure Herz's extradition. At first the British government refused on the ground that the fugitive's health would not permit him to travel; and when the French government insisted, the Foreign Secretary, Lord Rosebery, had Herz examined by a prominent London specialist who confirmed the first physician's report. Then, with the consent of the British authorities, three well-known and incorruptible French doctors — Dieulafoy, Charcot, and Brouardel, who had performed the autopsy on de Reinach — were sent to England, where all three concluded that Herz was in fact seriously ill and that extradition might endanger his life. Herz remained at Bournemouth under police surveillance but otherwise unmolested.

The new evidence contributed by Arton led the Chamber to appoint a second investigating committee on June 29, 1897, not to amend but to supplement the findings of the committee of 1893. Ernest Vallé, reporter of the first committee, was again chosen for that office. The committee of 1897 added three fat volumes to the archives but little to the enlightenment of the public, and it smeared one more coat of whitewash over the already incrusted legislators: "The legend that a venal Parliament brought about the ruin of the Panama enterprise must be destroyed from beginning to end. . . ." [25] A few days after its creation the committee received an extraordinary letter from Herz dated July 8, 1897: "Permit me . . . to break for the first time the seal of secrecy that has kept me silent ever since the start of the monumental campaign of persecution against me, which the whole world has witnessed. If the new committee of inquiry really proposes to shed light upon the whole matter, and if it will promise upon its honor to see that full justice will at last be rendered, I am ready to disclose to it everything I know concerning the business in question and the men involved. I request you . . . to visit me officially at Tankerville, Bournemouth, in order to carry back the whole truth, all my documents, all correspondence, and my deposition. . . . Under these conditions, in spite of my poor health, I shall place myself entirely at your disposal and do my utmost for the cause of honor. . . ." [26]

The astonished committee, devoured by curiosity, first sent two of its members to Bournemouth to verify the authenticity of the letter, which Herz confirmed. On July 17 the committee telegraphed that it would call upon him in a body five days later. Then Herz began to make difficulties. On July 19 he wrote again: "For vital reasons the interview cannot take place for three weeks. I suggest August 12 . . . or some later date. . . . I ask the committee to send here in advance the various *dossiers* relating to the actions instituted against me . . . so that it may be proved that the accusations . . . of alleged complicity in the Panama affair, of corruption . . . and of blackmail . . . are absolutely false and have been cut out of whole cloth to protect the master criminals of France." [27] What caused Herz to cool off in the short interval between these two letters? No satisfactory explanation has been offered, though certain deputies suspected that the French government, afraid that Herz might implicate officials in high places, had secretly dispatched an agent to buy his silence. At all events the committee, finding the conditions imposed in the second letter unacceptable and probably surmising that the trip to England might well turn out a wild-goose chase after all, abandoned the proposed excursion. Cornelius Herz never disclosed his secrets. The announcement of his death a year later, on July 6, 1898, made little impression upon a France long since weary of the Panama scandal and now preoccupied with a fresh sensation, the Dreyfus affair.

Chapter 33. The New Company

W HILE the courts and the Deputies committee mulled over the crimes and misdemeanors of the canal company a number of individuals were wrestling officially and unofficially with the complicated problems of reconstruction. Two alternative solutions presented themselves: on the one hand relinquishment of the concession, abandonment of the enterprise, and distribution of the assets among the bondholders of the Compagnie Universelle; on the other the formation of a new company to complete or at least attempt to complete the canal. Although many faint-hearted bondholders would have preferred a cash settlement the majority favored the second course.

Perhaps the most prominent and certainly the most energetic of the unofficial agitators for prompt resumption of work on the canal was the young engineer Philippe Bunau-Varilla. In 1889, a few months after the collapse of the old company, he had campaigned for election to the Chamber of Deputies from the constituency of Mantes "in order to win the right to speak from the parliamentary tribune, and to lash slander with the whip of truth." [1] Defeated by a narrow margin, he decided to adopt less direct methods. In 1890 he went to New York and discussed the situation with his friend John Bigelow, whom he had met four years before on the isthmus, and at Bigelow's suggestion wrote a book, *Panama: le passé, le présent, l'avenir*, which appeared in March 1892 — the first of Bunau-Varilla's many publications, long and short, on the subject of the canal. In September of the same year he produced a sequel, *Panama: le trafic*. Believing that successful rehabilitation of the bankrupt enterprise must depend largely upon the selection of a capable and dynamic leader, he endeavored to persuade Auguste-Laurent Burdeau, a former Minister of Marine, to assume command. Burdeau consented on condition that Rouvier, then Minister of Finance, would bestow upon him the official blessing of the government, without which he felt that he could accomplish nothing. Rouvier, fearing a political upheaval, refused, and Burdeau in turn rejected Bunau-Varilla's appeal. The engineer then turned to Christophle, governor of the Crédit Foncier, a powerful French bank; but before Christophle could reach a decision the publication of the "Micros" articles, followed by the trials, temporarily destroyed all hope of reconstruction.

As soon as the worst violence of the storm had abated Bunau-Varilla revived his project, this time with international trappings. It occurred to him that the aid of the Russian government, with which France had concluded an alliance in 1892, might be enlisted in behalf of the canal. Through a chance encounter in a railway train he procured an introduction to Count Witte, the Russian Minister of Finance, and in March 1894 presented himself in St. Petersburg. He suggested a guarantee by the Russian government of the capital required for the completion of the waterway and argued that "in helping to finish the Panama Canal, Russia would find the complement to the great work then just begun: the Trans-Siberian railroad. The Suez Canal . . . is the complement of the Anglo-Saxon transcontinental railways . . . across the American Continent. In the same manner, the Panama Canal . . . is the complement of the Russian transcontinental railroad. . . ." [2] Although the logic must have seemed a trifle hazy Witte promised to lay the proposal before Tsar Alexander III, and Bunau-Varilla returned joyfully to Paris, where Casimir-Périer, the Premier, and Burdeau, the new Minister of Finance, manifested some interest in the negotiations. But all of these ingenious maneuvers came to nothing, for the official liquidator of the old company, acting independently and possessed of the legal authority Bunau-Varilla lacked, quietly took the whole matter out of the engineer's busy hands.

On July 1, 1893 Parliament enacted a law designed to facilitate the work of liquidation by enabling the bondholders of the bankrupt company to recover, without recourse to the customary tedious, costly, and uncertain intervention of the courts, as much as they could collect of the funds fraudulently appropriated by the directors, financiers, contractors, and other despoilers. Three days later the Tribunal Civil de la Seine appointed a special agent, Lemarquis, to represent the bondholders with full powers to conclude transactions on their behalf. On July 21 the same court designated Pierre Gautron co-liquidator to assist Monchicourt, and when the latter died on March 14, 1894 Gautron became sole liquidator. Thenceforth Gautron and Lemarquis, both able administrators, worked hand in hand to bring order out of the Panama chaos.

Before any effective steps towards reconstruction could be taken it was necessary to obtain a further extension of the concession.

The Wyse-Roldán agreement of 1890 required the organization of a new company before February 28, 1893, but the sensational revelations of fraud and corruption made it impossible to fulfill that condition within the stipulated time. Monchicourt instructed his agent at Panama, Mange, to request a supplementary prolongation. Mange proceeded to Bogotá and on April 4, 1893 signed a new convention providing for postponement of the new company's incorporation to October 31, 1894. The 10-year period allowed for the completion of the canal was to date from that incorporation, and the payment to Colombia was increased from 10,000,000 to 12,000,000 francs; but this sum was reduced to 8,000,000 by the subtraction of various debts owed by Colombia to the bankrupt company. The liquidator agreed to pay the first installment of 500,000 francs, while the new company, when organized, would become responsible for the balance. In all other respects the convention conformed to the provisions of the Wyse-Roldán charter.

Gautron and Lemarquis fixed the capital of the new company at 65,000,000 francs including the 5,000,000 francs in stock allotted to Colombia by the act of concession. The remaining 60,000,000 came from three sources: forced contributions by the former directors, contractors, and others convicted or suspected of fraud; public subscriptions; and the liquidator himself. Between January and August 1894 Lemarquis, as the official representative of the old company's creditors, negotiated a series of settlements or transactions with certain firms and individuals, for the most part already condemned by the courts to forfeit their unearned profits. Instead of attempting to collect these sums in cash, Lemarquis permitted — or more accurately demanded — their payment in the form of subscriptions to the new company's stock. This ingenious compromise brought down two birds with one stone: it provided approximately two thirds of the new company's capital (which would have been impossible to obtain by any other method) and it greatly facilitated the prompt recovery of the sums due by substituting a face-saving investment — accompanied by a chance, however faint, of future profit — for outright restitution, which in many instances might have been postponed indefinitely or perhaps evaded altogether by appeals to higher tribunals. The list of obligatory subscriptions follows: [3]

Hugo Oberndoerffer	francs	3,800,000
Other members of various flotation syndicates (60 separate transactions)		3,285,700
Crédit Lyonnais		4,000,000

Société Générale	4,000,000
Société Générale de Crédit Industriel et Commercial	2,000,000
Former directors of the old company	7,885,000
Eiffel	10,000,000
Artigue, Sonderegger et Cie.	2,200,000
Baratoux, Letellier et Cie.	2,200,000
Jacob	750,000
Couvreux, Hersent et Cie.	500,000
	40,620,700

The judgments rendered against Oberndoerffer, the other participants in the syndicates, and the three banks were all based on the contention that the syndicates — especially those utilizing the option system — had received extravagant remuneration for the services performed. The company directors, including Ferdinand and Charles de Lesseps, were penalized for maladministration on various counts. The contractors' subscriptions represented partial restitution of their excessive profits. Three of the large contractors escaped these forfeits: the American Contracting and Dredging Company because it had no representative in France and refused to submit its records; Vignaud, Barbaud, Blanleuil et Compagnie because it had made no profit; and the Société des Travaux Publics et Constructions because it had filed several countersuits against the canal company which were not yet settled. Nevertheless the Société's financial associate, the Société des Dépôts et Comptes Courants, was condemned by a civil court on July 24, 1895 to repay 1,159,608 francs obtained through participation in the syndicates. Since by that time the new company was already organized this payment was made in cash to the liquidator.

The case against Couvreux, Hersent et Compagnie had no connection with the charges against the other contractors but was founded entirely upon that firm's failure to correct the false impression that it had signed a contract in 1880 to construct the canal for 512,000,000 francs. In 1893 Lemarquis, maintaining that the firm's silence had constituted a tacit confirmation of the contract's existence, brought a civil action for damages. Although Couvreux and Hersent appear to have been morally guilty of a sin of omission the firm's legal responsibility was exceedingly doubtful. Both partners loudly proclaimed their innocence and insisted that their subscription was merely a voluntary contribution towards the completion of a work inaugurated by themselves, a work in which they had always maintained a benevolent interest. Eiffel, pointing out that the Cour de Cassation had acquitted him of fraud on June 15, 1893 (it had actually applied the statute of limitations, which scarcely amounted to an acquittal) , also declared himself under no obligation to subscribe: "I emphatically assert . . . that my co-operation was spontaneous and voluntary; that not only could no restitution be required of me, but on the contrary I could have demanded of the liquidator the payment of a debt of seven millions [for work executed after the collapse of the old company]. . . ." [4]

To obtain the rest of the needed capital Gautron announced a public subscription to take place on September 22, 1894. Although already assured of more than 40,000,000 francs through the transactions the liquidator offered to the public the full amount, 60,000,000 francs, divided into 100-franc shares. Half of the total issue was reserved for holders of the old company's securities with the understanding that if these old subscribers should take up their entire quota the demands upon the transacting parties would be reduced *pro rata*. The stipulation proved futile, for the total public subscription amounted to but 3,484,300 francs. Added to the 40,-620,700 previously pledged this left a deficit of 15,895,000 which the liquidator found himself obliged to make up out of funds belonging to the creditors of the old company. Obviously a paid-in capital of only 60,000,000 francs (not counting the allotment to Colombia) would not go far towards the construction of a canal of which the cost had been estimated by the Guillemin committee at 900,000,000, but it was considered sufficient to enable the company to continue operations until its technical and financial advisers could decide upon a definite plan for completion of the project. The new company's stock bore no guaranteed rate of interest, and in fact no dividends were ever distributed.

The formal incorporation of the Compagnie Nouvelle du Canal de Panama occurred on October 20, 1894, eleven days before the expiration of the extended time limit. The administration consisted of nine directors in addition to the three executive officers: a president, Bonnardel, director of the Ouest railway company; a director general, Maurice Hutin, who had succeeded Dingler in 1885 for a few weeks only as general director of works of the old company; and a secretary general, Édouard Lampre. The officers, anxious to convince the public that the sins of the past would not be repeated, took pains to announce that the board was composed "of entirely new . . . members, no one of whom had any official relation to the old Company," [5] and that "the security-holders of the old Company have no vote, voice, title or ownership in the property of the new Company or in the administration of its af-

fairs. By private contract, merely, the new Company has agreed
that after all expenses of operation, maintenance, exploitation, dividends, reserve funds, etc., are provided for, a specified share of the
surplus income shall be paid to the Liquidator . . . for the benefit of his constituents. . . ." [6] This private contract stipulated that
40% of the net profit should be paid to the stockholders of the
Compagnie Nouvelle and 60% to the liquidator.

During the first year of the new company's existence the important post of chief engineer was occupied by a former executive of
the Public Works Department, de la Tournerie. Accompanied by
Hutin and several assistant engineers, de la Tournerie visited the
isthmus early in 1895 to organize the resumption of operations. In
February 1896 the board decided to appoint a technical commission to advise the company's own corps of engineers. De la Tournerie wished to preside over this commission and at the same time
to retain his position as chief engineer, and when the directors refused his request the engineer resigned. At first the technical commission comprised six members, all French, headed by Robaglia,
formerly an inspector general of the Public Works Department.
Within a year or two it acquired an international character by the
addition of seven foreign members: two Germans; one Russian;
an Englishman, William Henry Hunter, chief engineer of the
Manchester canal; a Colombian, Pedro Sosa, long associated with
the old company, who was drowned in the wreck of *La Bourgogne*
on July 4, 1898; and two Americans, Brigadier General Henry
Larcom Abbot, a retired engineer officer, and Alphonse Fteley,
chief engineer of the New York Aqueduct Commission.

On November 16, 1898, after more than 100 sessions, the technical commission submitted its report. Dismissing the sea level waterway as impracticable — at least for the present — the experts presented three projects for a lock canal. In the first the altitude of the
bottom of the canal in the summit section was fixed at 29.50 meters
(96.78 feet) above mean sea level, with five locks on each slope; in
the second at 20.75 meters (68.08 feet) with four locks; and in the
third at 10 meters (32.81 feet) with three locks. Allowing 10 meters
as the minimum depth of the canal, the corresponding surface levels would be respectively 129.59, 100.89, and 65.62 feet above the
sea. The commission unanimously recommended the second project, not because it was the cheapest to construct — for in that respect the estimates offered little choice between one scheme and
another — but because it would require the shortest time, thereby
indirectly saving interest, administration expenses, and loss of rev-

enue from tolls. The construction cost of each of the three projects exclusive of interest and administration was computed at approximately 500,000,000 francs; the lower the level, the greater the outlay for excavation but the smaller the expenditure for locks and dams. The determining factor was time: in the first project the excavation would be finished long before the locks and dams, in the third project long after; while in the second the two elements would reach completion almost simultaneously, and therefore neither would delay the opening of the canal.

All locks were to be double, 738 feet long and about 30 feet deep, and one basin of each pair would be 82 feet wide, the other 59. On the Atlantic slope two pairs were to be located at Bohío Soldado and two at Obispo; on the Pacific, one at Paraíso, two at Pedro Miguel, and one at Miraflores. A dam across the Chagres at Bohío and another at Alhajuela would form artificial lakes to feed the canal, control floods, and furnish electric power. The commission estimated the cost of the 20.75-meter-level project at $102,-400,000, including 15% for contingencies but excluding interest and overhead.

The new company's by-laws stipulated that whenever approximately half of the total capital had been expended a second or special technical commission should be organized "to consider the results attained by the work so far executed and the conclusions to be drawn from them with regard to the continuation of the enterprise." [7] By June 30, 1898 the company had spent almost half of its original 60,000,000 francs, and the special commission of five members was accordingly constituted. It reported at some length on February 28, 1899 but actually did little except confirm the first technical commission's recommendation of the 20.75-meter-level design.

During the five years of inactivity between the collapse of the old company and the incorporation of the new one thousands of squatters had swarmed into the canal area, occupied the abandoned buildings, and proceeded to raise crops and families. Many were discharged workmen who had either failed to secure repatriation or had preferred to remain on the isthmus. One of the first tasks confronting the Compagnie Nouvelle was the eviction of these unwanted and destructive tenants. By the terms of the Wyse-Roldán convention the Colombian government had promised to protect the company's property, and the government officials now joined forces with the company agents to uproot the unauthorized residents. Some tenants who agreed to pay rent were permitted to remain; the others were summarily expelled. By June 30, 1896 the company had negotiated separate settlements with 1287 squatters, and by 1898 the problem had ceased to be troublesome.

The long period of idleness had caused some damage to the machinery, buildings, and excavations, but on the whole the dilapidation was less serious than might have been expected. A few banks had caved in, small slides had occurred in the upper levels of the Culebra section, and in places the canal bed had silted up. All of this could be repaired without difficulty. Gautron reported that the barges, tugs, dredges, and other floating equipment were in good condition but required minor replacements, especially to woodwork. Locomotives, steam shovels, cranes, dump cars, and in general all metal appliances had been well cared for and were ready for service. Wooden cars, wharves, railway ties, and parts of the buildings had rotted, and much of the perishable stock in the warehouses was ruined.

Sensational but unreliable accounts of deterioration through negligence circulated widely, especially in the United States: "The . . . houses put up by the . . . French company often settled several feet within . . . a year or two. Expensive machinery was, in some cases, used for the foundations for these houses. . . . Scattered all about . . . are huge quantities of machinery so badly corroded that a knife can be thrust into the metal as if it were cheese. . . . Probably $50,000,000 worth of old machinery was thus wasted. . . . [The hospital buildings] are about the only things . . . that have retained anything like their former usefulness. . . . In the harbors . . . steam craft of all kinds are also rotting. . . . Little attempt was made to protect . . . any of these vessels from decay. . . ." [8] Another American wrote: "One of the most pathetic sights at the Isthmus is the decaying French machinery . . . the steam shovels of obsolete model rotting in the jungle on tracks that are mere wisps of rust — the little top-heavy Belgian locomotives disgorging orchids at their cab-windows. . . . A prying child can poke his finger through the iron-rust in many a place. . . ." [9] On the other hand an English engineer recorded: "The liquidator and the new Company have made the preservation of all that can be utilized hereafter their special care. This they have done most efficiently by housing the machinery and rolling stock as much as possible, cleaning and painting bright parts, and carefully listing everything under a perfect system of storekeeping. Of course there is much . . . that is comparatively useless, but the . . . hasty opinion sometimes expressed that it [the canal area] can only be regarded as a gigantic scrap-heap is certainly not borne out by an impartial investigation. . . ." [10] This view was corroborated in 1904 by the American canal engineers, who found most of the French equipment in excellent condition and put much of it to good use.

In addition to its passive work of preservation the Compagnie Nouvelle carried on an active construction program, small in scale but by no means negligible. During its 10 years of operation it excavated some 11,400,000 cubic yards, principally in the elevated Culebra and Emperador sections. The new company also lent money to the Panama Railroad for the construction of a deep-water harbor and a 960-foot steel pier at La Boca on the Pacific, thus eliminating the expensive lighter system and enabling large vessels to load and unload at all stages of the tide.

The Compagnie Nouvelle's health record showed a decided improvement over that of the old company. According to Gorgas the annual death rate from all causes dropped from more than 60 per 1000 to about 25: [11]

YEAR	NUMBER OF EMPLOYEES (Average)	DEATH RATE PER 1000
1895	1225	24.5
1896	3715	21.3
1897	3980	31.9
1898	3400	21.5
1899	2500	22.8
1900	2000	34.5
1901	2000	18.0
1902	1500	22.0
1903	1000	33.0
	Average	25.5

In 1898 Dr. Lacroisade, director of the new company's medical service, reported that "yellow fever has almost disappeared since 1889. Only one epidemic, not very serious, occurred in 1897; ten cases, six of which were fatal, were recorded among the company's employees." [12] This epidemic claimed no victims among the white personnel.

Since the new company employed no more than 4000 workmen at any one time its labor problem never became acute, but it did encounter certain difficulties. At the beginning the company hired many of the Negro laborers who had remained on the isthmus after the collapse of the old company. For a time the supply of labor greatly exceeded the demand, and the company took advantage of

the situation to establish a wage scale so low that in April 1895 the
men struck for higher pay. The company conceded as little as possible. The isthmian labor reservoir was soon exhausted, and in
1896 the company applied for permission to recruit workmen in
Jamaica and other West Indian islands. At first the British authorities, remembering the cost of repatriation in 1889, refused; but
later in the year they authorized the importation of 570 laborers
from the African colony of Sierra Leone and in January 1897 of
534 from Jamaica. The Sierra Leone Negroes proved a failure;
nearly all developed symptoms of beriberi after a few months on
the isthmus, 22 died of it, and the company, believing the malady
contagious, hastily shipped them home.

When the Compagnie Nouvelle was first incorporated at least a
few of its directors may have entertained a faint hope that they
would be able to complete the canal, but each year it became increasingly apparent that the confidence of the French public had
been irreparably destroyed by the failure of the old company and
the ensuing scandal. The new company did not even attempt to
raise additional funds by means of a bond issue, for it was obvious
that the receipts would have been insignificant, and the French
government consistently refused to have anything to do with the
enterprise. By 1898 the company, having spent half its original
capital, had to choose between abandonment of the entire undertaking and the sale of the canal. During the summer the directors
decided to offer the property to the United States government, and
as soon as the technical commission had submitted its report on
November 16 the director general and the chief engineer departed
for the United States. On December 2, 1898 they were received by
President McKinley, to whom they presented a copy of the technical report and a tentative proposal to transfer the company's
rights and properties. With that proposal — although more than
five years were to elapse before the consummation of the sale —
the center of interest shifted from Paris to Washington.

PART IV

The American Era

Chapter 34. Panama *versus* Nicaragua

THERE can be little doubt that had it not been for the activities of two exceedingly determined men the Nicaragua canal would be in operation today while the abandoned excavations at Panama would represent only a melancholy monument to failure, a man-made scar fast disappearing under rank jungle growth. The two men were Philippe Bunau-Varilla and William Nelson Cromwell. Though both labored indefatigably for the same object their relations were anything but harmonious. They were rivals, not allies; they worked independently and often at cross purposes, rarely met, disapproved of each other's methods, suspected each other's motives, cordially detested each other, and consistently minimized each other's contributions to their ultimate joint triumph. In his voluminous and lively but rarely dispassionate writings the French engineer managed to imply by frequent contemptuous references to "the lawyer Cromwell" that in his opinion "lawyer" was a synonym for "charlatan"; while the attorney, less obvious but no more conciliatory, simply ignored Bunau-Varilla and his maneuvers. Actually both rendered essential services to the Panama cause, and it is unlikely that either alone could have prevailed against the powerfully entrenched partisans of the Nicaragua route.

Cromwell, a partner in the New York law firm of Sullivan and Cromwell, was shrewd, energetic, resourceful, experienced, and generally amiable though he sometimes exasperated those who disagreed with him; in 1912 Representative Henry T. Rainey of Illinois called him "the most dangerous man this country has produced since the days of Aaron Burr — a professional revolutionist. . . ." [1] In 1893 Cromwell became counsel for and a director of the Panama Railroad Company, in which he was also a stockholder, having purchased a few of the shares not acquired by the Compagnie Universelle in 1881. In January 1896 the directors of the Compagnie Nouvelle, alarmed by the persistent popularity of the Nicaragua route in the United States, appointed Sullivan and Cromwell the company's general counsel in America. To less ingenious agents an attempt to convert American opinion to the Panama

transit might have appeared hopeless, but the attorneys were remarkably well equipped for their difficult task.

For almost three years the directors of the Compagnie Nouvelle,
less aggressive and apparently less disturbed by the rivalry of Nicaragua than their American counsel, held Cromwell on a tight rein.
The attorney worked quietly behind the scenes and seized every
opportunity to obstruct legislation favorable to Nicaragua, but not
until 1898 was he permitted to campaign openly for Panama. In
the summer of that year he visited Paris, convinced the directors
of the necessity for more active measures, persuaded them to offer
to sell the canal to the United States government, and returned to
New York in August. There he organized a staff of writers and engineers to prepare magazine articles eulogizing the Panama route.
Among the technicians employed were General Henry L. Abbot of
the Compagnie Nouvelle's engineering commissions and Elmer
Corthell, former associate of Eads in the Tehuantepec ship railway
scheme. The propaganda issued by Sullivan and Cromwell also
covered the political field, and three thick volumes of reprinted executive documents and diplomatic correspondence testified to the
thoroughness of their researches.

Cromwell's efforts to influence American opinion and legislation antedated those of Bunau-Varilla by about five years. In France
Bunau-Varilla had been working energetically for the completion
of the Panama canal ever since the collapse of the old company, but
he did not open his campaign in the United States until January
1901. Undiscouraged by the frustration of his attempts to reorgan-
ize the company between 1889 and 1894, he purchased stock in the
Compagnie Nouvelle when it was incorporated and continued to
take an active interest in the progress of the undertaking. His interest, unlike Cromwell's, was altogether unofficial. He criticized
the new company sharply for its dilatory tactics and even more
sharply for its failure to adopt his plans, while the company's directors snubbed him and disregarded his unsought advice. Bunau-
Varilla, no less shrewd than Cromwell, expressed himself far more
flamboyantly and explosively. The American attorney might conceivably have admitted in exceptional circumstances that there
were two sides to a given question, the French engineer never. All
of Bunau-Varilla's publications on the subject of the canal are
masterpieces of special pleading, flagrantly biased and to the impartial reader often intensely irritating, yet somehow curiously per-
suasive. Bunau-Varilla was always right; he never acknowledged a
mistake.

Today most engineers consider Bunau-Varilla's project for the

20. LOCOMOTIVES AND DUMP CARS ABANDONED BY THE FRENCH COMPANY

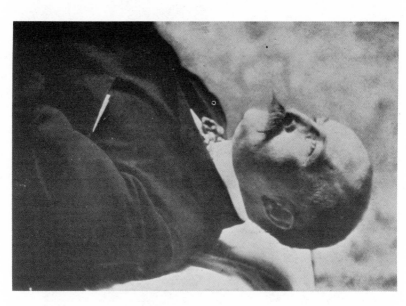

21. WILLIAM NELSON CROMWELL

22. PHILIPPE BUNAU-VARILLA

step-by-step alteration of a temporary lock canal into a permanent
sea level canal impracticable or at least prohibitive in cost, but
there are few who question his sincerity. Until the very end of his
life — he died on May 18, 1940 at the age of 81 — he defended his
ideas and his motives with undiminished zest. When on May 15,
1939 *Life* published an article in which Bunau-Varilla was referred
to as a "lobbyist" and a "French adventurer" the octogenarian
promptly retorted that he felt "very indifferent to the false epithets of 'Lobbyist,' which I never was, and of 'adventurer' which I
never was either unless you call adventurer a man who sacrifices
his time, his money and his scientific capacities to the glory of his
nation and to the service of her great friend the United States, not
to speak of the little Republic of Panama which he preserved from
the decadence where the Isthmus would have fallen if the Nicaragua Canal had been adopted." [2]

The Compagnie Nouvelle's first offer to sell the canal property
to the United States fell upon unsympathetic ears, for the Panama
failure and scandal had not only confirmed but intensified the traditional American preference for the Nicaragua transit. Not a single member of the Cabinet or of Congress advocated purchase of
the French canal, and the press was overwhelming in favor of Nicaragua. Even Theodore Roosevelt, later to become Panama's most
ardent champion, had written to his sister Anna Roosevelt Cowles
on May 20, 1894: "It is a great mistake that we have not . . .
started an interoceanic canal at Nicaragua." [3] In December 1898,
when McKinley received the French proposal, Roosevelt still believed that Nicaragua offered the best if not indeed the only solution. Yet the American attitude towards the canal problem as a
whole had undergone a profound change since 1895. Private enterprise had failed not only at Panama but at Nicaragua, and it was
becoming increasingly evident that if the waterway was to be built
at all it would have to be undertaken by the United States government. Much of the opposition to the principle of public ownership, still dominant during Cleveland's second administration, had
been swept away by the Spanish-American War and especially by
the historic voyage of the battleship *Oregon*. On March 19, 1898
the *Oregon* left San Francisco and, proceeding at full speed by way
of the Straits of Magellan, reached Key West on May 26. Although
the vessel did arrive in time to participate in the naval victory at
Santiago on July 3, the long and stormy passage covering more than
13,000 miles and consuming 68 days brought home to the people
of the United States the urgent necessity of a shorter interoceanic

communication in time of war and also demonstrated the military importance of government operation of the proposed transit.

Even had the United States been willing to purchase the French property at that time the company could not have sold it, for the concession from Colombia explicitly prohibited transfer to any foreign government. Hence for two years after the tentative offer of December 1898 the Compagnie Nouvelle fought desperately for time. On the one hand it exerted every effort to secure another extension of the concession and Colombia's authorization to sell the canal to the United States, on the other it endeavored through Cromwell to block every bill introduced in the United States Congress for the construction of a canal through Nicaragua.

The company's negotiations with Colombia were complicated by violent political disturbances in that country. In the elections of 1897 three parties contended for mastery: the Liberals, who nominated Miguel Samper for President; the Historicals, whose candidate was General Rafael Reyes; and the Conservatives, headed by Manuel Antonio Sanclemente and José Manuel Marroquín. Sanclemente, 85 years old and in feeble health, was elected, but Marroquín, the first *designado* or Vice President, actually wielded the executive power. In October 1899 the Liberals revolted, civil war broke out in several provinces including Panama, and the government declared a state of emergency which enabled the President to enact laws by legislative decree without confirmation by the Colombian Congress.

By the convention of April 1893 the concession was to expire on October 31, 1904 if the canal was not completed before that date. On November 1, 1898 Alexander Mancini, the company's agent at Bogotá, petitioned the Colombian government for a 6-year extension. Sanclemente agreed, subject to ratification by the next Congress, and in May 1899 sent a special emissary, Dr. Nicolás Esguerra, to Paris to arrange the conditions governing the postponement. In Paris Esguerra was joined by General Reyes, then Colombian minister to France and Switzerland, and by Dr. Clímaco Calderón, minister to the United States. But the canal company, fearing the imposition of onerous terms by these three commissioners, preferred to deal with the Bogotá authorities through Mancini. Negotiations dragged on for almost a year. Esguerra and his colleagues in Paris proposed a payment of 30,000,000 francs for the extension privilege, but Mancini had already made a tentative deal for 5,000,-000, and the company refused to pay more. The Colombian administration desperately needed money to suppress the rebellion, and on April 23, 1900 Sanclemente and his Cabinet issued a decree granting an extension until October 31, 1910, for which the company undertook to pay 5,000,000 francs within 120 days. The opposition parties promptly declared the decree illegal. On July 31 a group of Historicals imprisoned the aged Sanclemente in his villa near Bogotá and proclaimed Marroquín chief executive.

In the midst of this political confusion the Compagnie Nouvelle presented its second demand to the Colombian government: repeal of the clause forbidding transfer of the concession to the United States. Although the Colombian authorities, remembering past demonstrations of Manifest Destiny and fearing Yankee aggressiveness, would have preferred a canal owned and operated by a private corporation they realized that the French company could never complete the waterway and that the only agency able and willing to do so was the United States government. The construction of a canal through Nicaragua would have been an intolerable blow to Colombian pride; moreover Bogotá hoped for substantial compensation from the United States to fill the depleted Colombian treasury. In February 1901 Marroquín tacitly indicated his willingness to waive the injunction against the sale of the canal by sending his Foreign Minister, Dr. Carlos Martínez Silva, to Washington. Martínez Silva's position was ambiguous and embarrassing; while he was empowered to open and to some extent conduct negotiations with the United States government he was obliged to refer every important point to Bogotá and await instructions which his superiors issued only after long delays and often neglected to send at all.

In October 1895 the Ludlow commission had recommended an extensive survey of the Nicaragua canal route to serve as the basis of a definitive project. Almost two years later the Nicaragua Canal Commission, better known as the first Walker commission, was formally organized on July 29, 1897 to execute that survey. President McKinley designated Rear Admiral John G. Walker to head the commission and appointed two other members, Lewis M. Haupt, professor of civil engineering at the University of Pennsylvania, and Captain O. M. Carter of the Corps of Engineers; but in October Carter was replaced by another army engineer, Colonel Peter C. Hains. Accompanied by almost 100 technicians, the commission reached San Juan del Norte on December 17, 1897. The commissioners themselves remained in Central America about three months and paid a brief visit to Panama, where they inspected the French canal works. The field parties, hampered by discord between Costa Rica and Nicaragua, did not complete their surveys until February 1899. In March the commission reported to the President, suggesting numerous modifications of the designs proposed by Menocal in 1889 and by the Ludlow commission in 1895 and estimating the total cost at $118,113,790 exclusive of interest and administration.

Almost a year before the completion of this report the commission had indicated its intention to recommend construction of a Nicaragua canal by the United States government, and the canal sponsors in Congress acted promptly. In the Democratic Senate the leader of the Nicaragua partisans was John Tyler Morgan of Alabama, chairman of the Committee on Interoceanic Canals; in the Republican House, Representative William Peters Hepburn of Iowa, chairman of the Committee on Interstate and Foreign Commerce. Although working for a common cause Morgan and Hepburn — like their opponents Cromwell and Bunau-Varilla — were jealous competitors rather than collaborators. Assuming that the choice of the Nicaragua route was a foregone conclusion, each endeavored to obtain credit for the necessary legislation in behalf of his party as well as of himself.

Morgan had been a senator since 1877, and his interest in an isthmian canal dated back at least to 1888. As a Southerner he naturally preferred Nicaragua to Panama since the average sailing time between the Gulf ports and the Pacific coast by way of Nicaragua would be two days less than by Panama while the Atlantic ports would gain but one day. In time Morgan's partiality for the Nicaragua transit became an obsession, and his vigorous and often witty diatribes against Panama ceased only with his death in 1907 at the age of 83. "He had a wonderful fund of information on every subject," wrote Senator Cullom of Illinois, "but was not a man of very sound judgment. . . . At the same time, no one could doubt his honesty and sincerity of purpose. He did not have the faculty of seeing both sides of a question, and once he made up his mind, it was impossible to change him. . . . He was one of the most delightful and agreeable of men if you agreed with him . . . but he was so intense on any subject in which he took an interest, particularly anything pertaining to the interoceanic canal, that he became almost vicious toward anyone who opposed him." [4] Another colleague, Senator Spooner of Wisconsin, paid Morgan a more graceful tribute: "Upon whatever route an isthmian canal shall be constructed, the Senator from Alabama will forever stand in the memory of the people as the father of the isthmian canal; for, in season and out of season, in sunshine and in storm, unappalled by obstacles . . . with lofty patriotism and unfaltering purpose, he has, with rare skill, tireless industry, and splendid advocacy, fought for an isthmian canal." ⁵

To clear the way for public ownership the Senate adopted a resolution in May 1898 inviting the Maritime Canal Company of Nicaragua to fix a price for the transfer of its concessions, assets, and indebtedness to the United States. On June 21, after receipt of the company's offer to sell for $5,500,000, Morgan introduced a bill providing for the construction, operation, and fortification of a Nicaragua canal by the United States government. The debate opened early in January 1899, and on January 21 the Senate passed the measure by a vote of 48 to 6. The bill then went to the House, where it encountered difficulties from four different sources: Hepburn's desire to sponsor a canal bill similar in content but with his own name attached, the dubious validity of the canal title, deliberate obstruction instigated by Cromwell, and British opposition to the fortification clause. The direct results of all this confusion were postponement of a decision until the next session, the appointment of the second Walker commission, and the conclusion of the Hay-Pauncefote treaty. The indirect and wholly unforeseen effect was the ultimate triumph of the Panama route.

Although the Maritime Canal Company's concession would not expire until October 9, 1899 the Nicaraguan government had anticipated its termination by granting on October 31, 1898 a "promise of contract" to Eyre and Cragin. Moreover that part of the concession relating to inland water transport had already passed out of the Maritime Canal Company's hands, having been transferred to the Nicaragua Mail Steam Navigation and Trading Company in 1894 and purchased by the Atlas Steamship Company in 1897. Hence the Maritime Canal Company's right to the property it proposed to sell was by no means clear, and on February 13, 1900 the Hepburn committee took advantage of this excuse to block the Morgan bill. Morgan, deeply affronted but far from ready to accept defeat, hastily attached his canal measure as a "rider" to a rivers and harbors bill recently passed by the House and then under consideration by the Senate. On February 25 the Senate passed the amended bill by 50 votes to 3 and submitted it to conference between the appropriate committees of both houses. Prodded by Cromwell, the conferees rejected Morgan's rider and adopted in its place an amendment providing for yet another canal commission to reinvestigate the entire problem. On March 3, 1899, the last day of the session, the new amendment became law, and the decision was again postponed.

Both Cromwell and Bunau-Varilla afterwards claimed credit for this commission idea, but Cromwell, who was in Washington and had direct access to the legislators, was obviously in a position to exert more powerful pressure for its adoption than the engineer could bring to bear from Paris. To make the Panama project more palatable to Americans and to convince Congress that the Panama route deserved serious consideration Cromwell now proposed the reorganization of the Compagnie Nouvelle as an American corporation. In August 1899 he went to Paris to obtain the Compagnie Nouvelle's formal approval of his plan. Three fourths of the directors were to be American citizens, the head office was to be in the United States, and the corporation would issue common stock to the amount of $45,000,000 and preferred stock to the amount of $60,000,000. The Compagnie Nouvelle would then transfer its property in exchange for a large majority of the shares of the American company. On December 27 Cromwell incorporated the Panama Canal Company of America under the laws of New Jersey, and the directors of the Compagnie Nouvelle announced that they would submit the proposition to their shareholders in Paris at a special meeting to be held immediately after the regular meeting scheduled for December 30. But Gautron, the liquidator of the old company, refused to participate on the ground that the Americanization scheme would damage the interests for which he was responsible. The special meeting was canceled, and the entire board of the Compagnie Nouvelle immediately resigned. On February 12, 1900 the stockholders elected a new board with Hutin as president of the company. Cromwell subsequently admitted that his Americanization project "never was consummated, either by subscription or by assent. . . . It has no life or force of being, did not exist, and never has existed, and is as dead as a doornail. . . ." [6] Yet it had accomplished its primary purpose, the defeat of the Morgan rider to the rivers and harbors bill.

Meanwhile the commission authorized by Congress on March 3, 1899 — officially entitled the Isthmian Canal Commission but usually referred to as the second Walker commission — was beginning to function. Since it was to investigate not only the Nicaragua route but the Panama, San Blas, and Darién transits as well its membership was very much larger than that of its predecessor. Admiral Walker again presided, and Haupt and Hains were reappointed. The new members were Alfred Noble, civil engineer and member of the Ludlow commission; George S. Morison and William H. Burr, civil engineers; Lieutenant Colonel Oswald H. Ernst of the Corps of Engineers; ex-Senator Samuel Pasco of Florida; and

Emory Richard Johnson, economist and transportation expert. Cromwell had tried hard but unsuccessfully to prevent the nomination of former members of the Ludlow and first Walker commissions who had previously reported in favor of Nicaragua, and he particularly mistrusted Haupt, an outspoken Nicaragua partisan.

The second Walker commission completed its organization on June 15, 1899 but instead of proceeding at once to Central America sailed for Europe to inspect the plans and records of the Compagnie Nouvelle and to visit the Kiel, North Sea, and Manchester canals. Cromwell, who had hastened to Paris in advance, acted as host, arranged conferences, and bombarded the commission with arguments in favor of Panama; while Bunau-Varilla, working independently, concentrated his attack upon the Panama route subcommittee, Burr, Morison, and Ernst. These three had not served on earlier commissions or publicly committed themselves to the Nicaragua line and were presumably more susceptible to persuasion than some of their colleagues. On January 6, 1900 the commission set out for San Juan del Norte. The group inspected the entire Nicaragua route and proceeded to Panama. During the commissioners' sojourn in Europe surveys had been inaugurated on all of the sites under consideration — surveys so thorough that the field work was not completed until June 1901.

The second Walker commission issued three separate reports: a preliminary report on November 30, 1900, a full and supposedly final report on November 16, 1901, and a supplementary report dated January 18, 1902. The preliminary report found the Colombian government "not free to grant the necessary rights to the United States, except upon condition that an agreement be reached with the New Panama Canal Company. The Commission believes that such agreement is impracticable. . . . In view of . . . all the difficulties of obtaining the necessary rights . . . on the Panama route . . . the Commission is of the opinion that 'the most practicable and feasible route . . .' is that known as the Nicaragua route. . . ." [7] The first round went to Nicaragua; but this was more in the nature of an indictment of the Compagnie Nouvelle's failure to settle its charter complications and make a definite offer of outright sale than a clear-cut decision based on the presumptive technical advantages of the Nicaragua transit.

In its full report of November 16, 1901 the commission established standard dimensions for the canal: a minimum depth of 35 feet, locks 84 feet wide and 740 feet long in the clear. All locks were to have twin basins, side by side. Having finally eliminated the San Blas and Darién routes on account of the high cost

of the tunnels, the commission estimated the total cost of the Nicaragua canal at $189,864,062 and of the Panama canal at $144,233,-
358, both figures exclusive of the costs of the concessions and, in
the case of Panama, of the purchase price of the French company's
rights and property. In October 1901, after much correspondence
and many conferences, the Compagnie Nouvelle had finally offered
to sell for $109,141,500. The commission, which had valued the
French assets at only $40,000,000, pointed out that the offer made
the Nicaragua line $63,510,796 cheaper than Panama: "There are
certain physical advantages . . . in favor of the Panama route, but
the price fixed by the . . . Company . . . is so unreasonable that
its acceptance can not be recommended. . . ." [8] Again the commission voted for Nicaragua; but in its acknowledgment that the
physical advantages favored Panama could be read an obvious hint
that if the French company would reduce its price to $40,000,000
the commission would recommend the Panama route.

The Compagnie Nouvelle had no choice; it could sell at the
price proposed by the commission, or the United States would build
the Nicaragua canal, leaving the company with a dry unfinished
ditch and a heap of worthless junk on its hands. The company could
not complete the Panama canal itself, and there was no rival purchaser. Immediately after receipt of the commission's second report
Hutin resigned the presidency of the company and was succeeded
by Marius Bô, an executive of the Crédit Lyonnais. On December
21, 1901 the stockholders, with the liquidator's approval, authorized the board to offer the company's rights and property, including maps, plans, and records, to the United States government for
$40,000,000, subject to subsequent ratification of the sale by the
stockholders. The offer was to remain open until March 4, 1903.
The secretary general, Édouard Lampre, left to conduct the negotiations in Washington; but before he arrived Bô transmitted the
offer by cable on January 4, 1902.

With only $40,000,000 to be allotted to the Compagnie Nouvelle
the Panama estimate now amounted to about $5,600,000 less than
that for Nicaragua. On January 18 the second Walker commission
presented a supplementary report reversing its two previous recommendations: "After considering the changed conditions . . .
the Commission is of the opinion that 'the most practicable and
feasible route' for an isthmian canal . . . is that known as the
Panama route." [9] Professor Haupt, still convinced that Nicaragua
possessed overwhelming advantages, reluctantly agreed to support
his colleagues only when "confronted by the argument that if a
divided opinion were presented to Congress the opposition to an

Isthmian Canal was so influential as to be able to defeat legislation entirely. . . . Being unwilling to be made the sole cause of obstruction to the building of any canal . . . he consented to sign the [supplementary] report. . . ." [10]

The Morgan bill passed by the Senate in January 1899 provided not only for the ownership, construction, and operation of a Nicaragua canal by the United States government but for its fortification as well. This clause brought the measure into direct conflict with that 50-year-old vexation, the Clayton-Bulwer treaty. Although one British government after another had rejected American proposals for abrogation or revision of the pact McKinley's Secretary of State, John Hay, now decided to make one more effort to acquire exclusive domination over the canal route for the United States. The moment seemed propitious; England had shown marked sympathy towards the United States during the war with Spain, and relations between the two nations were unusually cordial. Lord Salisbury indicated his approval, and by January 1899 Hay and Lord Pauncefote, the British ambassador to Washington, had agreed upon a treaty draft; but further progress was delayed for a year by British demands for an immediate settlement of the long-standing dispute over the boundary between Canada and Alaska as a preliminary condition to conclusion of the canal treaty. Hay refused to treat on a bargaining basis, and Salisbury finally yielded. On February 5, 1900 the first Hay-Pauncefote treaty was signed and transmitted to the Senate for ratification.

The treaty comprised four articles. The first provided for the construction of the canal either by the United States government or by a private corporation chartered and financially assisted by the government. The second contained seven stipulations for neutralization, based upon the convention of Constantinople of October 29, 1888 governing navigation of the Suez waterway, and explicitly prohibited the erection of fortifications. The third article provided for an invitation to all other nations to adhere to the treaty, and the fourth set a time limit of six months for exchange of ratifications.

Hay, priding himself upon the achievement of what his predecessors had failed to accomplish in half a century, was deeply mortified by the widespread criticism aroused by the ban on fortifications and by the clauses forbidding the United States to close or blockade the canal in time of war. The Senate Committee on Foreign Relations reported the treaty favorably with one amendment on March 9, but the Senate, anxious to avoid controversy over international policies during an election year, postponed discussion until the winter. On December 20, 1900 it ratified the pact with three amendments, all of which the British government rejected. With the energetic support of Theodore Roosevelt, who succeeded to the presidency upon the death of McKinley on September 14, 1901, negotiations were resumed, and in the end the American views prevailed. The second Hay-Pauncefote treaty was signed on November 18 and ratified without amendment on December 16, 1901 by a vote of 72 to 6. Ratifications were exchanged on February 21, 1902, and the treaty was proclaimed a day later.

By the new convention Great Britain conceded to the United States, with no tangible *quid pro quo* whatever, practically unlimited control of the isthmian canal. The pact explicitly superseded the Clayton-Bulwer treaty, contained no mention of a guarantee by other powers, and by simply omitting all references to defensive structures and weapons implicitly authorized the United States to erect all the fortifications it might consider advisable. While the second Hay-Pauncefote treaty — which is still in force — reaffirmed the principles of neutralization set forth in the Constantinople convention the stipulation was so worded that those principles amounted to little more than a polite fiction: "The United States adopts, as the basis of the neutralization of such ship canal, the following Rules. . . ." [11] In the discarded treaty of the preceding year that clause had read: "The High Contracting Parties [the United States and Great Britain] . . . adopt . . ." [12] In the new pact the United States alone "adopted" the neutralization provisions, so that if it should choose — as it did choose in 1917–18 and again during the present war — to declare the canal closed to its foes and to enforce that declaration, no other power would have a valid right to protest. The situation of the Suez canal, owned and operated by a private corporation, was and is quite different. There the neutralization clauses of the Constantinople convention are still effective, at least on paper. During the World War of 1914–18 German, Austrian, Bulgarian, and Turkish vessels were theoretically free to use the canal, but in practice Allied control of the Mediterranean and Red Sea approaches made it impossible for enemy ships to enter the canal from either end. The few German and Austrian vessels in transit when war was declared in 1914 were permitted to complete their passages unharmed but were captured as soon as they emerged onto the high seas.

Chapter 35. Nicaragua Checkmate

R EPRESENTATIVE HEPBURN, having successfully blocked passage of Senator Morgan's bill in February 1899, introduced a Nicaragua canal bill of his own early in 1900. On May 2 the House passed the measure by a vote of 224 to 36 and sent it to the Senate, where Morgan's Interoceanic Canals Committee reported it favorably on May 16. Magnanimously overlooking Hepburn's obstruction of the year before, Morgan earnestly recommended the adoption of his rival's bill but was unable to obtain a vote before the June adjournment. When Congress reconvened in December many of the Republican senators considered it advisable to postpone discussion of the canal measure until the British government had passed upon the Senate's amendments to the first Hay-Pauncefote treaty, and no further action was taken upon the Hepburn bill during that session. On December 6, 1901, three weeks after the submission of the Walker commission's second report in favor of Nicaragua, Hepburn presented to the House another and more specific measure appropriating $180,000,000 for the construction of a Nicaragua canal, which was passed on January 9 after only two days of discussion by an almost unanimous vote, 308 to 2. In the Senate Morgan again attempted to force the bill through without delay, but on January 18 his activities were checked by the announcement of the Walker commission's supplementary report recommending the Panama route. By placing Nicaragua on the defensive for the first time that report altered the entire situation.

On January 28, 1902 Senator Spooner proposed a radical amendment to the Hepburn bill authorizing the President to purchase the Compagnie Nouvelle's rights and property for not more than $40,000,000 and to acquire from Colombia perpetual control of a canal strip not less than 6 miles wide. But "should the President be unable to obtain . . . a satisfactory title to the property of the New Panama Canal Company and the control of the necessary territory of . . . Colombia . . . within a reasonable time and upon reasonable terms" [1] he would negotiate treaties with Nicaragua and Costa Rica for control of a similar zone and construct the canal through Nicaragua. The amendment further directed the appointment of an Isthmian Canal Commission of seven members, at least four of whom must be skilled engineers. One of the four should be an army officer and another a naval officer.

In short Panama was to be the first choice, and the Nicaragua alternative was to be adopted only if no satisfactory arrangement could be made with the Compagnie Nouvelle and Colombia. For several weeks the Senate Interoceanic Canals Committee, with Morgan in the chair, discussed the Spooner amendment. All members of the second Walker commission except Pasco and Haupt were questioned, and all declared that they had always preferred the Panama route from a technical standpoint and had recommended Nicaragua in the preceding November only because of the excessive price demanded by the Compagnie Nouvelle. Nevertheless Morgan, fighting stubbornly for the Nicaragua transit, carried a majority of his colleagues with him. On March 13, 1902 seven members of the committee reported to the Senate in favor of the original Hepburn bill while a minority of four advised adoption of the Spooner amendment. Debate in the Senate opened on June 4 and continued stormily until June 19, when a motion to substitute the minority report for that of the majority — that is to consider the Spooner amendment instead of the Hepburn bill — was adopted by a vote of 42 to 34. A few hours later the Spooner amendment passed the Senate with 67 favorable votes to only 6 opposed. Since the House still clung to the unamended Hepburn measure the matter was referred to a joint conference. On June 25 the representatives yielded to the arguments of the Senate conferees, and the House passed the Spooner amendment by 260 votes to 8. President Roosevelt signed it on June 28, 1902. It is one of the ironies of history that the fundamental law under which the isthmian canal was actually constructed bears the name of neither Morgan nor Hepburn, both of whom so earnestly desired the honor, but that of Spooner, a comparatively late and much less fanatical convert to the canal cause.

The real leader of the Panama partisans in Congress was not Spooner but another Republican senator, Marcus Alonzo Hanna of Ohio. A superb orator, an adroit parliamentarian, and with a wealth of political experience derived from his chairmanship of the Republican National Committee during the election campaign of 1896, Mark Hanna was well qualified to win support for any cause he chose to espouse. Although he had displayed a more or less academic interest in the canal project for some years, his active championship of the Panama route dated only from the spring of

1901. It was Hanna who as a member of the Interoceanic Canals Committee blocked every move made by Morgan to force a decision in favor of Nicaragua; it was Hanna who insisted, in the face of Morgan's opposition, upon the committee's interrogation of the Walker commissioners; it was Hanna who drafted the minority report recommending the Spooner amendment to the Senate in March 1902; and it was Hanna whose eloquent speech in favor of the amendment, delivered before the Senate on June 5 and 6, gathered in the affirmative votes.

Back of Hanna were the determined but mutually antagonistic crusaders Cromwell and Bunau-Varilla. Both freely admitted the significance of the services rendered by Hanna — one of the few points upon which the two men ever agreed — while each claimed credit for Hanna's conversion and by implication denied the other's pretensions. It was rumored that during the presidential campaign of 1900, which resulted in the re-election of McKinley, Cromwell had contributed $60,000 on behalf of the Compagnie Nouvelle to the Republican party fund in order to enlist Hanna's support and to obtain the substitution in the party's platform of a plank advocating the construction of an "isthmian" canal for the original plank recommending a "Nicaragua" canal. The allegation, based solely upon a statement made by Bunau-Varilla to Don C. Seitz of the New York *World*, may have been true; but it did not necessarily follow that the money was intended for or received as an indirect bribe.

Cromwell undoubtedly exerted a powerful influence over Hanna and supplied him with abundant verbal ammunition to be used in the fight for Panama. On July 1, 1901 the directors of the Compagnie Nouvelle, apparently annoyed by Cromwell's insistent demands for a prompt and definite offer to sell the canal — and also possibly by his extravagance — dismissed his firm as their counsel but reinstated it on January 27, 1902, just one day before the introduction of the Spooner amendment. Cromwell claimed authorship of that amendment but subsequently admitted that he had merely conferred with Spooner and Hanna before its presentation to the Interoceanic Canals Committee. Since the attorney's connection with the French company had been severed for the preceding seven months it is unlikely that he had much to do with the actual preparation of the measure, though he may well have had a hand in its revision. Much of Hanna's minority report in favor of the Spooner amendment was almost certainly written by Cromwell.

On January 5, 1901 Bunau-Varilla sailed from France to launch his campaign on American soil for adoption of the Panama route. In his own somewhat florid words, "fortune smiled" upon him for the next three years: "At every turn of my steps it seemed as if I were accompanied by a protecting divinity. Every time I was in need of a man he appeared, of an event it took place." [2] Luck may have had something to do with Bunau-Varilla's ultimate triumph, but his remarkable ability to turn chance opportunities to account probably had much more. In a series of lectures he declaimed against Nicaragua and painted the Panama transit in glowing colors. On March 26 Myron T. Herrick presented Bunau-Varilla to Senator Hanna, into whose attentive ears the engineer poured a torrent of skillfully prepared and incisively phrased arguments. A few days later Bunau-Varilla paid a brief and formal call on President McKinley, which passed off pleasantly enough. His parley with the peppery Senator Morgan turned into something much less amicable and almost ended in a fist fight. Not content with speeches and interviews, Bunau-Varilla hastily prepared and published a pamphlet entitled *Panama or Nicaragua?* containing much of the material already utilized in his various lectures.

In April 1901 the engineer returned to France. More as a sop to his own patriotic conscience than with any real hope of success he drew up three stirring appeals to the French public in the form of paid newspaper advertisements urging the completion of the canal by the Compagnie Nouvelle with the aid of the French government. In the first, dated April 25, he declared that sale to the United States would constitute an ignominious acknowledgment of French impotence, exhorted his readers to "decide between the counsel of the hare and that of the lion," [3] and offered to subscribe $400,000 as his personal contribution towards the cost of the enterprise. On May 10 he issued a second advertisement demonstrating the technical feasibility of the project and again urging the French people to plunge boldly if belatedly into the fray, but the government and the Compagnie Nouvelle remained unmoved. By the end of the year Bunau-Varilla had abandoned whatever slight hope of French resurrection he might have clung to in the spring. On December 31, ten days after the company's stockholders had authorized the transfer of the canal to the United States for $40,-000,000, he published his third and last appeal. This time there was no longer any question of completion by the French; he now pressed the company to submit an immediate offer at the quoted price in order to prevent an irrevocable decision by Congress in favor of Nicaragua: "This inferior solution, sale to a friendly nation . . . is after all so enormously superior to . . . melancholy and irretrievable ruin . . . that nobody blessed with the slightest common sense can deny that all efforts must be directed towards its attainment, rather than permit the phantom of complete decadence and infinite shame to rise above the horizon." [4] Bunau-Varilla afterwards boasted that his words inspired the directors to prompt action; but obviously the decision to sell had already been made, for when the article appeared Lampre was on his way to Washington with the offer. The three newspaper advertisements cost Bunau-Varilla about $27,000. With all due allowance for patriotic fervor it is difficult to see what he expected them to accomplish or why he should have considered them worth the outlay.

Early in 1902 Bunau-Varilla went to Washington for the third time. To supplement Hanna's minority report on the Spooner amendment the French engineer published a series of 13 simple diagrams designed to prove the superiority of the Panama route with respect to length, curvature, amount of excavation, depth of cut, cost of maintenance and operation, and various other elements. To forestall any attempt at refutation he had shrewdly taken his statistics from the Walker commission's report of November 1901, carefully omitting or adroitly reinterpreting every comparison that appeared to favor Nicaragua. The picture-book diagrams conveyed their messages at a glance and were easy to remember. As propaganda for Panama the little pamphlet was worth many times its weight in prosy reports, and Hanna utilized it with telling effect in his successful fight for passage of the Spooner act.

The spectacular eruption of Mont Pelée, which on May 8, 1902 destroyed the city of Saint-Pierre and caused approximately 40,000 deaths, also affected the choice of the canal route. Occurring less than a month before the debate on the Spooner amendment opened in the Senate, the disaster — however tragic for Martinique and shocking to the world — proved a heaven-sent boon to the advocates of the Panama transit. For almost a century Panama partisans had contrasted the complete absence of volcanoes and the rare occurrence and relative mildness of earthquakes in the isthmian region with the existence of numerous volcanoes and frequent severe earthquakes in Nicaragua. As a graphic illustration of their immunity from violent earth shocks the inhabitants of Panama City were accustomed to point out the survival of a curious flat arch of weak design and fragile construction in the ruined church of Santo Domingo, where it stands intact today after the lapse of more than 200 years. Undoubtedly volcanic and seismic disturbances were and are a greater potential menace to a Nicaragua canal than to one in Panama; how much greater is largely a matter of guesswork.

Of the 14 or 15 isolated volcanic peaks in Nicaragua only a few have shown signs of activity since the Spanish conquest, and all but one of these are fairly remote from the proposed canal line. The nearest, Ometepe, rises from an island in Lake Nicaragua about 13 miles north of the navigation route across the lake and some 20 miles from the nearest projected lock. Farther off are the craters of Mombacho, Momotombo, Telica, Santa Clara, Viejo, and Coseguina. To the south the nearest active Costa Rican cone, Orosi, lies about 40 miles from the transit route. The eruption of Coseguina in January 1835 was one of the most violent ever recorded. Earthquakes have been frequent and occasionally devastating, but even the temblor that demolished the city of Managua in March 1931 produced almost no perceptible movement along the bed of the proposed waterway. That an eruption or severe earthquake might seriously damage locks and other artificial canal works must be recognized, but the peril is one that cannot be evaluated in advance. Naturally Nicaragua enthusiasts denied the existence of danger to the canal from earthquakes or lava flows. In 1891 the directors of the Nicaragua Canal Construction Company insisted that "liability of damage . . . from volcanic action may be dismissed as too remote for consideration" [5] and cited as proof of the gentleness of local earthquakes the fact that "Castillo Viejo, the Spanish fort on the San Juan built as early as 1675, having high parapets and a central tower 60 feet in height, stands entirely intact. . . ." [6] In 1899 the presumably impartial first Walker commission reported the Nicaragua canal region "practically exempt from any seismic influences of sufficient force to cause destruction or danger to any part of the canal route. . . ." [7]

Although Martinique was a long way from Nicaragua the eruption of Mont Pelée made Congress as well as the American public acutely volcano-conscious and so played directly into the hands of Bunau-Varilla, who had insisted for years upon the unsuitability of a volcanic region for a canal site. He sent a copy of his *Panama or Nicaragua?* pamphlet to every senator; Hanna called the Senate's attention to a map of Central America with the active craters conspicuously marked; and the New York *Sun* published a series of volcano editorials and articles based largely upon data furnished by Bunau-Varilla. That was a disastrous month for Nicaragua. On May 14, 1902, only a few days after the Martinique catastrophe, the newspapers published accounts of an eruption of Momotombo accompanied by an earthquake that destroyed a railroad wharf on Lake Managua. President Zelaya of Nicaragua hastily cabled a denial of the report to his minister in Washington, who issued a statement implying that no Nicaraguan volcano had shown signs of dangerous activity since the Coseguina explosion in 1835. The official denial, widely circulated by Morgan, produced a reaction in favor of Nicaragua; the press, with the exception of the New York *Sun* and a few other journals, began to pooh-pooh the eruption hazard; and the influential Washington *Star* printed a cartoon representing Mark Hanna, coached by a French painter (Bunau-Varilla), industriously daubing imaginary volcanoes on a map.

The public laughed, but Bunau-Varilla had another card up his sleeve. He remembered that in 1900 Nicaragua had issued a beautiful series of postage stamps portraying Momotombo in full eruption, with the lake and railroad wharf in the foreground. To refute the assertion that Nicaraguan volcanoes were no longer active he needed official counterevidence emanating from Nicaragua itself; and what could be more official than a postage stamp? He scoured Washington for the incriminating stamps, purchased 90 from various dealers, and sent one to each senator on June 16, three days before the vote on the Spooner amendment. Later he procured more stamps in New York and distributed them among the wavering members of the House. Although this maneuver probably exercised some slight effect upon the final verdict its influence has been exaggerated. The stamp episode made an amusing after-dinner story which by constant repetition has come to be remembered as a more important contribution to the victory of Panama than it actually was.

Thus with Hanna orating in the Senate, with Cromwell pulling strings behind the scenes, and with Bunau-Varilla cajoling, pamphleteering, and gleefully turning Nicaraguan stamps into testimonials for Panama, the Spooner amendment was laboriously forced through Congress. Its passage was one of the most notorious — and successful — examples of lobbying on record.

What, after all, would have happened if the Morgan bill or the Hepburn bill had been passed in place of the Spooner amendment, if the canal had been constructed in Nicaragua instead of Panama? One is forced to the conclusion that the history of the world would not have been greatly changed. After thirty years of smooth and efficient operation the very real advantages of the Panama route stand out clearly: a shorter transit from sea to sea, easier to defend against attack from the air; a summit level lower by 25 feet; lower maintenance and operation costs; the existence of a completed railroad;

partial excavation by the French, some of which could be utilized, and the acquisition of hundreds of buildings in reasonably good condition; more commodious natural harbors demanding less artificial improvement; and a greater degree of immunity from earthquakes. To counteract these factors Nicaragua can boast but one outstanding merit: a passage shorter by one day, for steamers of average speed, between the Pacific ports of the United States and the Atlantic ports of either the United States or Europe. At the turn of the century a comparison of health conditions also favored Nicaragua, but the application of effective sanitary measures at Panama have long since nullified that initial superiority.

The truth is that neither Panama nor Nicaragua ever offered such prodigious advantages over its rival as the respective partisans claimed. A Nicaragua canal would probably have cost some millions of dollars more and taken a year or two longer to construct, but when completed it would have been a perfectly satisfactory waterway. The very persistence and bitterness of the controversy indicate how evenly the two claimants were matched. While the choice of Panama has been fully justified by experience the selection of Nicaragua would not have been the fatal mistake that Bunau-Varilla and Cromwell pretended. To the historian of today the acres of paper, lakes of ink, and floods of passionate oratory that determined the location of the canal seem in retrospect to have been largely wasted.

Before any further steps could be taken towards the purchase of the French property it was necessary to conclude a treaty between the United States and Colombia providing for an explicit waiver of the latter's right to forbid the transfer and for an agreement upon the compensation to be paid Colombia by the United States. Throughout the negotiations the Bogotá government, distracted by civil war, isolated in its remote mountain capital, and with its head figuratively as well as literally in the Andean clouds, displayed an exasperating ineptitude. After having sent Martínez Silva to Washington in February 1901 the Colombians gave him neither the authority to act on his own initiative nor prompt, clearly worded instructions from home. This diplomatic fumbling was not a symptom of indifference — for the government was exceedingly anxious to have the canal located in Colombian territory — but the result of preoccupation with domestic problems combined with a curiously unrealistic complacency. Bogotá had somehow convinced itself that a decision in favor of the Panama route was inevitable and that the much-advertised partiality of the United States for

Nicaragua was merely Yankee bluff, a fiction invented to squeeze more advantageous terms out of Colombia.

Martínez Silva, having wasted almost a year in fruitless efforts to obtain definite instructions from Bogotá, was prevented from resigning only by Cromwell's urgent remonstrances. In January 1902, tired of waiting for his superiors to act, the Colombian envoy (with Cromwell's assistance) prepared a treaty draft of his own providing for the lease to the United States of a canal zone 10 kilometers (6.21 miles) wide for 100 years at an annual rental of $600,000, renewable for additional 100-year periods at a rental to be increased 3% for each renewal. The United States was to fix toll rates, build free ports, and police the zone; Colombia was to take charge of military defense, but in extreme emergencies the United States might land troops to protect the canal without the previous consent of Colombia. Although Martínez Silva never presented his treaty draft to Hay, Cromwell gave the Secretary of State a general outline of its terms. Hay's private knowledge of the proposals proved useful to the United States and correspondingly hurtful to Colombia at a later stage of the negotiations.

At the end of February 1902 Martínez Silva was replaced by José Vicente Concha, former Minister of War in Marroquín's Cabinet, an intellectual without diplomatic training who spoke no English and had never before traveled outside of Colombia. Temperament as well as inexperience placed the new envoy at a disadvantage, and to add to his difficulties his home government treated him with even less consideration than it had shown his predecessor. Serenely ignoring the menace of Nicaragua and apparently quite unconscious of the need for prompt action, the Colombian Foreign Minister, Felipe Paúl, cabled Concha on March 17: "The United States Minister in Bogotá carries unofficially the bases of an understanding with the United States. Sending them to you by the next mail." [8] Ambiguous and meager as this information was, and hopelessly garbled in transmission to boot, it might have averted what later proved a disaster for Colombia had it arrived in time; but due to a breakdown in the cable service it did not reach Concha until April 2. A week after the dispatch of this unhelpful cable Paúl casually forwarded the promised "bases of understanding" by ordinary post. After a slow journey from Bogotá by mule, river steamer, and ocean liner these important papers were delivered to Concha on April 26 — almost a month too late to be of any value.

The briskness of the United States minister to Bogotá, Charles Burdett Hart, contrasted refreshingly with the drowsiness of the Colombian authorities. In spite of transmission delays his cabled report of the Colombian proposals reached Hay on March 17, nearly six weeks before Concha learned of them. In brief these proposals called for the lease to the United States of a canal zone six miles wide for 99 years, after which the property would revert to Colombia; a guarantee by the United States of the neutrality of the canal and of Colombian sovereignty over the zone; a Colombian police force paid by the United States; compensation for condemned private property; retention by Colombia of coaling rights on the islands in Panama Bay; and the payment to Colombia of a percentage of the tolls higher than that conceded by the expiring French contract. But the Colombian government would not open negotiations with the United States until it had established an understanding with the Compagnie Nouvelle. Hay cabled a prompt and emphatic rejection of these terms.

Bogotá's insistence upon a settlement with the canal company prior to the conclusion of a treaty with the United States meant that Colombia intended to demand an indemnity from the company in return for permission to sell the Panama property. In January 1902 Martínez Silva had suggested to his government that the Compagnie Nouvelle should be assessed $2,000,000, but it soon became apparent that the authorities expected a much higher price. In his instructions to Concha the temporary Foreign Minister who preceded Paúl, Abadía Méndez, computed Colombia's claim against the company at $20,000,000 or half of the company's total prospective receipts from the sale. Abadía based this excessive demand upon the presumptive loss of revenue Colombia would suffer through the transfer — a claim which might have been justified had there been any hope of completion by the company but which wholly failed to take into account the fact that the canal property would lose its entire value to Colombia as well as to the company unless purchased by the United States. The emptiness of the Colombian treasury, depleted by civil war, strengthened that government's resolve to collect indemnities from both the company and the United States. As owner of 50,000 shares of the company's stock Colombia was in a position to block the transfer from within as well as from without. When the directors of the Compagnie Nouvelle called a stockholders' meeting on February 28, 1902 to ratify the sale the Colombian consul general in Paris peremptorily served notice that the transaction could not be consummated without his government's consent, and the ratification was postponed.

On the other hand Cromwell was equally determined not to yield to Colombian demands for any contribution whatever from the canal company. If he could reverse the Colombian program and

persuade Bogotá to sign a treaty with the United States *before* the
conclusion of a financial arrangement with the company he would
be able to reject subsequent claims against the company as attempted extortion or blackmail — a maneuver in which he hoped
to secure the diplomatic backing of the United States government.
In the attorney's clever hands the bewildered Concha was a lump
of clay. Badgered and "advised" by Cromwell and still unaware
that instructions were on their way from Bogotá, Concha drew up
a treaty draft which he sent to Hay on March 31. At the same time
Cromwell presented an explanatory statement setting forth the
views of the Compagnie Nouvelle. At Hay's suggestion Concha
agreed to certain changes and on April 18, 1902 submitted an
amended protocol. Like the Martínez Silva draft it provided for a
100-year lease, indefinitely renewable, but fixed the payment to
Colombia by the United States at $7,000,000 down plus an annuity
and explicitly authorized the Compagnie Nouvelle to sell the canal
property. A little later the annuity was tentatively set at $100,000.

These terms were so much more advantageous to the United
States than those of the retarded Bogotá proposals that Concha, had
he known of the latter, could not possibly have formulated his own
protocol. But he did not know; and Hay, who did, took good care
not to enlighten him. When on April 26 Concha received the long-
awaited instructions by mail he was horrified to find them hopelessly at variance with the treaty draft to which he had already
committed his government. In desperation he cabled for permission to resign, which was refused. After the passage of the Spooner
act in June Hay undertook to draft a formal treaty which would
not only conform to that act but meet the approval of two thirds
of the Senate. The Senate attached 17 amendments to the April
protocol. Many were of minor importance, but unfortunately the
others, designed to tighten United States control over the canal
zone, appeared to menace Colombia's most cherished possession,
the one principle that republic was determined never to relinquish
— its sovereignty. On July 18 Hay presented the list of proposed
amendments to Concha, who forwarded them to Bogotá. Again the
Colombian officials procrastinated, while Concha, twiddling his
thumbs in the sultry heat of Washington, grew more and more
despondent.

This time the Bogotá government had a more legitimate excuse
for delay. Persistent Liberal opposition had rendered the position
of the Marroquín administration exceedingly precarious; since
the spring of 1900 a series of sporadic insurrections had flared up
on the isthmus, and in November 1901 the rebels temporarily oc-

cupied Colón and threatened to interrupt the railway transit. At the urgent request of Bogotá the United States Navy Department ordered Commander Henry McCrea to land troops at Colón on November 20, and four days later Captain Thomas Perry sent ashore a detachment of 248 men to protect the railroad. With an armed guard on each train the transit was kept open, and by December 5 the American forces had withdrawn. A few months later rebellion again broke out on the isthmus, and after winning several minor victories a well-equipped Liberal army led by General Benjamín Herrera closed in on the city of Panama in August 1902. In response to another cabled appeal from Bogotá the Navy Department ordered the *Cincinnati* to Colón and the *Wisconsin* to Panama. On September 17 Commander Thomas C. McLean of the *Cincinnati* placed naval guards on the trains and notified the leaders of both government and insurgent armies that no armed men except United States troops would be permitted to travel on the railroad, but three days later he relaxed the rule to allow about 1000 soldiers of the loyal Colombian army to cross the isthmus and to ship their arms as freight on another train.

At the end of September the *Wisconsin* reached Panama, and Rear Admiral Silas Casey took command. Casey's strict interpretation of neutrality and his refusal to permit either Colombia's federal army or the insurgents to use the railroad angered Marroquín and Paúl, who had counted on a one-sided intervention by which the transit would have been closed to the rebels but kept open for the passage of loyal troops. Heated protests to Washington induced the Navy Department, at Hay's request, to instruct Casey to handle the Colombians as diplomatically as possible. The tension was eased by the arrival at Colón on October 16 of a new leader of the government forces, General Perdomo, whose tactful overtures procured substantial concessions from Casey. By the middle of November the tide had turned; some 10,000 federal soldiers were quartered on the isthmus, and the rebellion was crushed not only at Panama but in other Colombian provinces. On November 21, 1902 the insurgent and government leaders held a peace conference on board the *Wisconsin* and signed a pact known as the treaty of Panama, providing for a general amnesty and for a special session of the Colombian Congress to consider the canal problem and other urgent matters.

On September 9, while the outcome of the rebellion was still in doubt, Paúl had sent Concha full powers to sign a treaty with the United States, with instructions to secure the most favorable terms possible but to accept if necessary whatever conditions Hay might see fit to impose. By this move Marroquín and his Cabinet hoped to assure themselves of the continued military support of the United States and at the same time to unload onto the shoulders of the Colombian Congress the burden of amending the treaty during the process of ratification to suit Colombian wishes. Unfortunately the news of American interference with the passage of federal troops across the isthmus reached Washington shortly afterwards; and if the unexpected thoroughness of McLean's and Casey's intervention displeased Marroquín and Paúl it infuriated Concha. The outraged envoy abruptly broke off the treaty negotiations, turned the legation over to its chargé d'affaires, Herrán, and left Washington on November 28.

Tomás Herrán, son of the Pedro Alcántara Herrán who had so ably negotiated the ratification of the treaty of 1846 between New Granada and the United States, was a far more accomplished diplomatist than the moody amateurish Concha. He had lived in North America for years, attended Washington schools and Georgetown University, spoke English and other languages fluently, and had held diplomatic posts in Europe and South America. But it was too late for even an expert negotiator to obtain substantial concessions for Colombia. The long series of misunderstandings between the Colombian government and its Washington representative, the fatal discrepancies between that government's real wishes and its envoy's interpretations of those wishes, had deprived Bogotá of the power to control the treaty conditions. Taking advantage of Bogotá's failure to keep its minister informed, Hay had committed Concha to a protocol which the Colombian government could not openly disavow. All that Herrán could do to make the treaty more acceptable to Colombia was to obtain an augmentation of the initial payment to $10,000,000 and an increase of the annual rental to $250,000.

On January 21, 1903 Hay presented Herrán with an ultimatum pointing out that the "reasonable time" allowed by the Spooner bill for negotiation was about to expire and implying that unless the Colombian treaty was concluded without further delay the United States would be obliged to turn irrevocably to Nicaragua. The very next day Hay and Herrán signed the treaty, and two days later Roosevelt transmitted it to the Senate. Then on January 25 came a bombshell in the form of a cable from Marroquín to Herrán directing him not to sign the convention but to await additional instructions. Realizing that the treaty could not be recalled, Herrán kept the contents of the cable to himself and quietly buried it in the legation archives. Marroquín's weathercock vacillations were in truth less capricious than they appeared. His position in Bogotá was insecure; he had become acting chief executive as the result of a *coup d'état*, not by legal election; the military insurrection, though temporarily under control, might break out again at any moment; and the dictator's tenure of office depended upon the joint support of several mutually hostile political groups. Marroquín knew that the treaty could be ratified only by the Colombian Congress, which had not met since 1898, and that any attempt to hold elections while rebel bands still roamed the countryside would inevitably precipitate new uprisings. Hence he played for time, hoping to prolong the treaty negotiations without a definite commitment. Unfortunately he had neglected to take either Concha or Herrán into his confidence, and so his plans were frustrated in all innocence first by one envoy and then the other.

The Hay-Herrán treaty followed the general lines of the Concha protocol as amended by Hay. It canceled all previous concessions and explicitly authorized the Compagnie Nouvelle to sell the canal. The 100-year lease would be indefinitely renewable. The United States specifically recognized Colombian sovereignty over the zone, and Colombia reserved the right to transport its own troops, munitions, and public servants through the canal or on the railroad free of charge. For the enforcement of law within the zone Colombian, United States, and mixed tribunals, each with jurisdiction over specified cases, were to be established. Colombia undertook to provide armed forces for the protection of the canal and railroad, but if at any time Colombia could not fulfill this obligation the United States might assume it with Colombia's consent; and in emergencies the United States was empowered to act even without that consent. The canal was to be completed within 14 years after ratification, but if unforeseen obstacles should arise Colombia agreed to extend this period for 12 years; and if the United States decided to construct a sea level canal an additional 10-year extension would be granted.

In the Senate ratification of the treaty was impeded by the bitter opposition of the Nicaragua die-hard, Morgan. In the Foreign Relations Committee he presented resolutions attacking Herrán's credentials, Marroquín's authority, and the chaotic political situation in Colombia; and when the committee rejected the resolutions he read them in the Senate chamber. The debate opened in mid-February, but Morgan's persistent filibuster as well as the pressure of other business prevented a vote before the session ended on March 4. Since March 4, 1903 was also the date of expiration of the option accorded the United States by the Compagnie Nouvelle,

Hay had already requested Cromwell to obtain an extension. In the absence of an unconditional pledge that the United States would buy the property the company directors refused to prolong the option, but Cromwell invented an ingenious compromise satisfactory to both parties providing for a guarantee of purchase if and when the Colombian treaty was ratified.

The Senate convened in special session on March 5 and continued discussion of the treaty, with Morgan ably and passionately disputing every inch of ground. He proposed no less than 60 amendments, which Cromwell lobbied energetically to defeat. Even Hanna and Spooner, sturdy partisans of the treaty, favored alterations granting the United States complete sovereignty over the zone and explicit authorization to fortify it; but Cromwell, insisting that Colombia had already made every concession that could be demanded and that the slightest amendment would involve rejection of the pact by Bogotá, overcame their objections. On March 17, 1903 the Senate ratified the Hay-Herrán treaty without amendment by 73 votes to 5.

Herrán knew very well that Cromwell's enthusiasm for the treaty sprang not from any altruistic desire to benefit Colombia but from his determination to use the pact as a defense against Colombian attempts to obtain an indemnity from the Compagnie Nouvelle. On January 9, 1903 Herrán wrote to his government: "In the initial period of our work here . . . the agents of the Panama Canal Co. were very useful allies, especially . . . Cromwell . . . a man of indefatigable activity and great influence. So long as the interests of Colombia and the . . . company were identical, this powerful co-operation was most useful, but now these interests are no longer common, and I am working independently. . . . The agents of the company . . . are doing all they can to have the treaty signed, no matter what the cost to Colombia. Mr. . . . Bunau-Varilla is trying to intervene officiously [*i.e.*, unofficially]. . . ." [9] And on February 1 Herrán wrote despondently to a friend: "I feel as if I am waking from a horrible nightmare. Gladly shall I gather up all the documents relating to that dreadful canal and put them out of sight." [10]

Bunau-Varilla was indeed intervening as actively as his unofficial status permitted. In February 1902 he had urged Martínez Silva to draft a treaty acceptable to the United States, and later he deluged Concha with pleas to the same effect. At his own expense he sent costly cables to Marroquín warning him of the dangers to which procrastination would expose the Panama project. Marroquín never acknowledged the cables, but Bunau-Varilla insisted that the dictator always adopted his recommendations. The engineer also claimed credit for the incorporation in the Hay-Herrán treaty of the provision for an annual rental of $250,000 in place of the $100,000 originally proposed by Hay.

While Hay negotiated with successive Colombian envoys he was endeavoring at the same time to draft treaties with Nicaragua and Costa Rica so as to be able to submit alternative projects to the Senate. In December 1900 emissaries of both republics had signed protocols indicating their willingness to conclude canal treaties, and in November 1901 Hay directed the United States minister to Central America, William L. Merry, to confirm the acceptance of the protocols by the governments concerned. Merry, an untrained diplomat, exceeded his instructions, entered into negotiations for a formal convention with Nicaragua, and on December 9 signed an ill-conceived pact which Hay hastily disavowed. On February 12, 1902 Hay transmitted his own draft of a convention to the Nicaraguan minister in Washington, but the *mañana* lassitude that was delaying the Colombian treaty had infected Central America as well, and three months elapsed without word from Nicaragua. At length Hay impatiently informed the Nicaraguan minister, Corea, that he would transmit the Concha protocol to the Senate without an alternative proposal from Nicaragua if that proposal was not forthcoming by May 13, 1902. On May 14 Corea submitted the Nicaraguan treaty draft, which Hay sent to the congressional committees occupied with the Spooner bill. Costa Rica still hesitated; President Iglesias, convinced that he had no authority to conclude such a treaty, suggested passage of a constitutional amendment or the calling of a constituent assembly.

Chapter 36. Debate in Bogotá

IN Colombia the Hay-Herrán treaty met with a cool and in many quarters a definitely hostile reception. Objections were based on a number of grounds, tangible and intangible: violation of the Colombian concept of sovereignty; doubts concerning the constitutionality of a perpetual or indefinitely renewable lease; fear of North American imperialism, aggravated by wounds to Colombian pride inflicted during the occupation of the isthmus by United States forces in 1902; disappointment over the inadequate financial compensation. Domestic politics also affected the issue: support of the treaty by Marroquín's Conservative party was in itself sufficient to turn many influential Liberals against it.

On January 24, 1903, two days after the signing of the treaty, Felipe Paúl resigned as Foreign Minister and was succeeded by Luís Carlos Rico. In the remoter provinces elections proceeded slowly, and the new Congress did not convene in special session until June 20. The United States minister in Bogotá, Hart, resigned on February 4 to be replaced by the legation secretary, Arthur Matthias Beaupré. Hart had understood Colombian etiquette and had usually dealt tactfully with the authorities; Beaupré, less patient, often gave needless offense by riding roughshod over delicate sensibilities. Washington's hopes of speedy and cordial ratification by Colombia faded early. On April 15 Beaupré informed Hay that "within the last month there has been . . . a sudden outburst of controversy . . . with regard to the . . . convention. . . . From approbation to suspicion and from suspicion to decided opposition have been the phases of change in public sentiment." [1] On May 4 the minister warned Hay that "the opposition . . . is intensifying. . . . It is entirely impossible to convince these people that the Nicaragua route was ever seriously considered. . . ." [2]

One of the impediments to ratification was Colombia's proposal to levy an assessment upon the Compagnie Nouvelle (and if possible also upon the Panama Railroad Company) for the privilege of transferring their Panama properties to the United States in contravention of their original charters — an assessment which Cromwell was determined to evade. The astute lawyer had won the first round by securing Herrán's signature to a treaty explicitly authorizing the sale, but final victory depended upon ratification by the Colombian Congress. Obviously Bogotá did not interpret the authorization clause as a renunciation of its claims against the company. On February 3, 1903 the Minister of Finance notified both the canal and railroad corporations that they would be required to designate agents in Bogotá to discuss details of the transfer, including the question of indemnity. Colombia's right to demand such compensation can scarcely be doubted, and payment by the Compagnie Nouvelle of even a small share of the $40,000,-000 it was to receive might have turned the scale in favor of the treaty's ratification. Had the Colombian government and the canal company been left to themselves it is possible though by no means certain that they might have reached a compromise acceptable to both. At all events the United States government should not have lent its official support to a French corporation involved in a purely private dispute with a foreign power. But Cromwell, raising the cry of "blackmail," adroitly induced Hay to pull his chestnuts out of the fire — a highly improper proceeding.

On April 28 Hay sent Beaupré a long dispatch in which he insisted that Herrán's signature of the treaty made Colombia's approval of the transfer obligatory, whether the canal and railroad companies paid or failed to pay indemnities. This was equivalent to an announcement that Colombia need expect no compensation from the companies. Naturally Hay's declaration stiffened Colombian opposition to the treaty, and another message cabled to Beaupré on June 9 only increased Bogotá's irritation: "The Colombian Government apparently does not appreciate the gravity of the situation. The canal negotiations were initiated by Colombia, and were energetically pressed upon this Government for several years. The propositions presented by Colombia, with slight modifications, were finally accepted by us. In virtue of this agreement our Congress reversed its previous judgment and decided upon the Panama route. If Colombia should now reject the treaty or unduly delay its ratification, the friendly understanding between the two countries would be so seriously compromised that action might be taken by the [United States] Congress next winter which every friend of Colombia would regret. . . ." [3] To do Hay justice there is reason to believe that he resented even if he did not resist Cromwell's efforts to involve the State Department in the indemnity squabble.

Neither Hay's assertion that Colombia had "energetically pressed" the treaty negotiations nor Theodore Roosevelt's later declaration that the United States had entered into those negotiations at Colombia's "eager request" [4] had the slightest factual foundation. It was the United States government, with Cromwell pulling the wires, that had supplied all the energy and displayed all the eagerness while Bogotá hesitated and played for time. On June 20 Rico skillfully exposed Hay's fallacies. Contending that his government's initiation of the treaty negotiations did not commit the Colombian Congress to ratification, he cited the rejection by the United States Senate of the first Hay-Pauncefote treaty, which Hay himself had proposed, and he insisted quite legitimately that the "slight modifications" imposed by the United States were in fact important alterations entailing substantial sacrifices on the part of Colombia.

The special session of the Colombian Congress opened on June 20, 1903 in an atmosphere ominously tense with factional dissension, which grew more and more bitter as the debate progressed. Although the administration had a majority in both houses Marroquín's position was too unstable to enable him to force the treaty through the legislature. Circumstances obliged him to play a passive rôle, but those circumstances made little impression upon official Washington. Cromwell appears to have convinced both Roosevelt and Hay that Marroquín's authority was supreme and that if he had wished he could have ratified the treaty by executive decree without calling Congress at all, although Marroquín had repeatedly and truthfully insisted that the Congress alone could legally approve or reject an international convention. Roosevelt persisted in this error to the end of his life: "Maroquin [sic] . . . had agreed to the . . . Treaty in January, 1903. He had the absolute power of an unconstitutional dictator to keep his promise or break it. He determined to break it. To furnish himself an excuse . . . he devised the plan of summoning a Congress especially called to reject the canal treaty. . . ." [5] In 1904 Senator Chauncey Depew of New York delivered a similar attack against Marroquín's "Machiavellian statesmanship": "He . . . ordered an election and summoned a Congress. He had the army and absolute power. . . . But he said, 'This is my treaty . . . and there must be some excuse which will appeal to the powers at Washington for more money. I must create an opposition to my Government.' . . . Marroquin . . . presiding over the Senate, listened with pleasure to these fusilades upon his own statesmanship prearranged by himself. Every citizen of Colombia who had any intelligence . . . knew that Marroquin had but to lift his finger and the vote for the treaty would be unanimous." [6] Nothing could have been farther from the truth. Marroquín, harassed and aging, was not even an able statesman, much less an all-powerful Machiavellian prince; no amount of futile finger-lifting could have checked the torrent of Colombian disapproval of the treaty.

In Bogotá the first weeks of the special session were wasted in factional wrangles only indirectly connected with the Hay-Herrán convention. Rico postponed presentation of the treaty until July 2, and even then another fortnight passed in heated squabbles over a minor issue. According to Colombian custom (but not Colombian law) the treaty should have been signed by Marroquín and Rico as well as by Herrán and Hay, and the opposition seized upon this pretext to attack not the pact but the administration. The assault was led by Miguel Antonio Caro, who had helped to place Marroquín in office and bitterly resented the latter's subsequent repudiation of his policies and advice. But Caro's diatribes became so violent that they backfired, and the sympathies of many senators shifted towards Marroquín. The Minister of Education, Antonio José Uribe, brought the irrelevant discussion to a close by a tactful appeal for dignified statesmanship and the cessation of petty disputes which were making Colombia ridiculous in the eyes of the world.

General Rafael Reyes, who had commanded the loyal Colombian forces during the Aizpuru rebellion of 1885, was a firm partisan of the treaty. Wealthy, influential, popular, politically adroit, and already something of a national hero, Reyes had recently announced his candidacy for the office of President in the 1904 election. Like Marroquín, Reyes hoped for ratification but also for more liberal financial concessions to Colombia. On July 9 he informed Hay through Beaupré that the Congress would never approve the pact unless the United States increased its initial payment to $15,000,-000 and the Compagnie Nouvelle contributed $10,000,000 in addition. Hay promptly rejected both proposals, and Roosevelt minced no words in his approval of the Secretary's stand: "Make it as strong as you can to Beaupré. Those contemptible little creatures in Bogotá ought to understand how much they are jeopardizing things and imperilling their own future." [7]

On July 14 the Colombian Senate settled down at last to its real business, discussion of the treaty. It appointed a committee under the chairmanship of Juan Pérez y Soto, an outspoken Yankee-hater and relentless opponent of ratification, to study the convention and deliver an opinion within eight days; but the chairman's illness delayed submission of the report until August 4. Of the nine amendments recommended by the committee only two were important: a stipulation that the canal and railroad companies must come to an agreement with Colombia before authorization of the transfer, and suppression of the clause establishing United States courts in the canal zone. Pérez y Soto had demanded far more drastic concessions but had been overruled by a majority of the committee. With the exception of the proposal to eliminate the zone tribunals all of the recommendations were reasonable and should have been acceptable to the United States. Unluckily a dispute between the Colombian authorities and the Central and South American Telegraph Company interrupted cable communication during these critical weeks, and Beaupré, isolated from Washington, took matters into his own inexpert hands. He handed Rico three notes asserting that the United States could not agree to the suppression of separate courts — which was true — and that Colombian insistence upon a prior settlement with the two companies was "tantamount to an absolute rejection of the treaty" [8] — which was nonsense. The other seven amendments, he believed, were worth so little to Colombia that it would be unwise to stir up possible opposition in the United States Senate in order to secure their adoption.

The content of these notes interpreted the State Department's policy with reasonable fidelity, but their offensively haughty and menacing tone outraged even the most fervent partisans of ratification in the Colombian Senate and vastly increased their difficulties. The outburst of indignation seems to have alarmed Beaupré himself, and in a dispatch to Hay dated August 15 he endeavored to explain his conduct: "When the report of the special committee of the Senate was prepared . . . I determined upon a course of energetic action which, while it might seriously lessen my popularity here and seem undiplomatic unless viewed in the light of the . . . circumstances, resulted in my two notes of the 5th . . . and one of the 8th. . . . Some of the newspapers and members of Congress are expressing dissatisfaction with what they term my dictatorial attitude, but I do not consider this important, providing a satisfactory treaty is finally ratified. . . . It has been a difficult and trying situation from the first, rendered more so by the interruption of cable communication, and one in which a strong, rather than a velvet hand, was imperative. I await the consummation with some hope and much distrust. . . ." [9]

The distrust was fully warranted, but there was little occasion for hope. With ratification apparently unattainable by orthodox procedure the Colombian partisans of the treaty now invented a bold and ingenious stratagem. They resolved to cease all efforts in behalf of the pact and allow the Senate to defeat it by an overwhelming vote, on the theory that the sudden shock might inspire such energetic protests and produce such financial and political chaos throughout Colombia as to bring about a sharp reaction in favor of reconsideration. On August 12, after another vehement tirade by Caro against the treaty and a sober but ineffectual argument in its defense by Rico, 24 senators out of 27 voted for rejection. Two abstained, and one, José Domingo de Obaldía of Panama — the most enthusiastic advocate of ratification in the Congress — was obliged by an attack of illness to absent himself shortly before the voting took place. On the following day the Senate passed a resolution providing for the appointment of a committee of three to draft a new treaty more advantageous to Colombia.

At first the desired reaction appeared about to materialize, but the appointment of the Senate committee had a calming effect, and agitation for reconsideration of the Hay-Herrán treaty quickly died down. On September 2 the committee submitted proposals for a new convention. These included the payment of $10,000,000 by the Compagnie Nouvelle; continuation of the Panama Railroad's annual rental of $250,000 and an agreement by the railroad company either to surrender its property to Colombia when its concession expired in 1967 or to purchase it at a price to be arranged; and lease to the United States of a canal zone 10 miles wide for 100 years with the privilege of indefinite renewal, for which the United States would pay $20,000,000 down, an annual rental of $150,000 until the railroad's payments ceased in 1967, and $400,000 a year thereafter (this annuity to be increased 25% with each 100-year renewal) .

Colombian law required three separate debates before any projected bill could reach a vote. On September 14 the Senate discussed the new recommendations for the first time, passed them unanimously, and turned them over to another committee presided over by Guillermo Quintero Calderón for further consideration. Although the time limit for exchange of ratifications of the Hay-Herrán treaty expired on September 22 the chairman's illness delayed this committee's report until October 14, and when it was at last submitted it recommended indefinite postponement of all treaty negotiations. The second Senate debate took place on October 27. Three days later the Senate voted unanimously to suspend further discussion of the matter, and on October 31, 1903 the Congress adjourned without attempting to offer a substitute for the rejected Hay-Herrán convention.

Between August 12, the date of the rejection, and October 14, when the Calderón committee advised cessation of all treaty activity, two developments had increased the reluctance of the Congress to ratify a canal pact. One was a political controversy. On August 30 Marroquín dismissed three provincial governors and replaced them with appointees committed to the support of both the treaty and the presidential candidacy of General Reyes. The designation of Obaldía as governor of Panama aroused especially vehement disapproval, for he was believed with good reason to favor secession if Bogotá persisted in its hostility to the pact. The second and more direct reason for postponement of treaty discussions sprang from uncertainty as to the date of expiration of the Compagnie Nouvelle's concession. On April 23, 1900 that concession, then due to lapse on October 31, 1904, had been extended for six years, and the company had paid Colombia 5,000,000 francs for the prolongation. But in 1900 Colombia had been torn by civil war, and in the emergency the extension had been granted by President Sanclemente's executive decree without congressional sanction. During the summer of 1903 the Bogotá press, influenced by opponents of the Hay-Herrán treaty, began to question the legality of an extension conceded under such conditions and urged Congress to declare it unconstitutional. The point was of vital importance: if the prolongation could be annulled the company's charter would expire in October 1904, the property would then revert to Colombia, and the republic had only to delay ratification of the treaty until that date in order to fall heir to the $40,000,000 offered by the United States to the company in addition to the $10,000,000 stipulated in the convention. Yet this program of "confiscation through stagnation" [10] suffered from three defects. Annulment of the extension would still leave the Compagnie Nouvelle in possession of almost all the Panama Railroad stock, and the railroad had the right to forbid construction of a canal near its own right of way; the company's 5,000,000 francs would have to be returned at once, which would impose a heavy burden on Colombia's empty treasury; and the influential Senator Caro, however gladly he might welcome an opportunity to embarrass the Marroquín administration, had been devoted to Sanclemente and would almost certainly defend the former executive against any charge that he had exceeded his authority.

The Calderón committee's report discussed the extension tangle and hinted strongly that the question of constitutionality would repay investigation, but it discreetly left the decision to Congress. If that body should determine to annul the prolongation Colombia could negotiate a much more advantageous canal convention a year later; if not, the concession had several more years to run, and there could be no reason for haste. In either event, the committee advised, it would be better to play for time. By adjourning without action on the treaty Congress tacitly accepted that advice but took no positive steps to invalidate the company's extension. That it might have attempted to do so the following year had events on the isthmus taken a different course is possible but unlikely. In March 1904 Gaston Brunet, a French attorney representing the Colombian government, repudiated any such design on the part of his client and insisted that on the contrary Bogotá freely acknowledged the constitutionality of the extension: "I am authorized by the Colombian government to oppose . . . a formal denial to these rumors. The Colombian government has never entertained the idea of adopting such methods. . . ." [11] On the other hand Theodore Roosevelt, influenced by both Cromwell and Bunau-Varilla, clung obstinately to the doctrine of Colombian perfidy and to justify his own policy invented the bugbear of official intervention by the French government: "The action of Colombia had shown . . . that she intended to confiscate the property and rights of the . . . Company. . . . If we had sat supine, this would doubtless have meant that France would have interfered to protect the company, and . . . the gravest international complications might have ensued. . . ." [12] The contingency was in fact so remote as to be practically nonexistent. There could have been no good reason to believe that the French government, which in the past had shown no disposition whatever to "protect" either the Compagnie Universelle or the Compagnie Nouvelle, suddenly proposed to assume the rôle of guardian angel at this time.

Sensational rumors of two other influences working under cover to defeat the treaty were found upon investigation to be wholly baseless. Herrán informed his government that the United States transcontinental railroads intended to send a commission to Bogotá to oppose ratification, but no such commission was ever organized, nor is there much evidence that it was even contemplated. And early in 1903 an announcement from London of an offer by the German government of $40,000,000 for the property of the Compagnie Nouvelle, to take effect upon the expiration of the option granted to the United States, received widespread publicity in the American press; but the United States ambassador in Berlin, directed by Hay to inquire into the matter, reported the allegation unfounded.

Chapter 37.   Revolution

O N September 13, 1903, while the Hay-Herrán treaty was slowly and painfully dying in the Colombian Congress, Hay wrote to Roosevelt: "It is altogether likely that there will be an insurrection on the Isthmus against that government of folly and graft . . . at Bogotá. . . . Our intervention should not be at haphazard, nor, this time, should it be to the profit, as heretofore, of Bogotá. I venture to suggest you let your mind play a little about the subject for two or three weeks, before finally deciding. . . ." [1] Two days later the President replied: "I entirely approve. . . . Let us do nothing . . . at present. . . . I feel that there are two alternatives. (1) To take up Nicaragua; (2) in some . . . way to interfere when it becomes necessary so as to secure the Panama route without further dealing with the foolish and homicidal corruptionists in Bogotá. . . ." [2] In October Roosevelt prepared a rough draft of his annual message to Congress, but before its delivery in December events had radically altered both the situation and the message. In this preliminary version the President declared: "The refusal of Colombia properly to respond to our sincere and earnest efforts to come to an agreement . . . renders it . . . necessary that the United States should take immediate action on one of two lines: either we should drop the Panama Canal project and immediately begin work on the Nicaraguan Canal, or else we should purchase all the rights of the French company, and, without any further parley with Colombia, enter upon the completion of the canal. . . . I feel that the latter course is the one demanded by the interests of this Nation. . . . If in your judgment it is better not to take such action, then I shall proceed at once with the Nicaraguan Canal. . . ." [3]

There was a third alternative, but it was one so incompatible with Roosevelt's aggressive and impatient temperament that it does not seem to have occurred to him: the adoption of a conciliatory policy towards Colombia coupled with a sincere attempt to understand its complicated political situation and a voluntary increase in the financial compensation offered by the United States. Although such an increase would have required the approval of the

Senate it appears probable that Roosevelt could have persuaded that body to agree had he been so minded. Colombia needed money so urgently that a generous payment tendered at the opportune moment might well have outweighed Bogotá's other objections to the treaty. Undoubtedly Colombian recalcitrance was both unrealistic and unwise, but a judicious combination of tact and cash would have done much to overcome it. Roosevelt, exasperated and intolerant, chose to consider the opposition sheer perversity — an opinion he never modified. In 1915 he wrote to William Roscoe Thayer: "To talk of Colombia as a responsible Power to be dealt with as we would deal with Holland or Belgium or Switzerland or Denmark is a mere absurdity. The analogy is with a group of Sicilian or Calabrian bandits; with Villa and Carranza [Mexican revolutionary leaders] at this moment. You could no more make an agreement with the Colombian rulers than you could nail currant jelly to a wall — and the failure to nail currant jelly to a wall is not due to the nail; it is due to the currant jelly." [4]

Instead of allowing Hay to carry out his policies Roosevelt assumed personal control of the canal negotiations after July 1903 and handled them to all intents and purposes as his own Secretary of State. During these critical months he was unfortunately deprived of the wise counsel of his Secretary of War, Elihu Root, who had gone to London as a member of the Alaska Boundary Commission. Roosevelt accepted full responsibility for his own course: "I did not consult Hay, or Root, or anyone else as to what I did, because a council of war does not fight; and I intended to do the job once for all." [5]

The Spooner act provided that "should the President be unable to obtain . . . control of the necessary territory of . . . Colombia . . . within a reasonable time and upon reasonable terms" [6] he was to order construction of the Nicaragua canal. Probably a strict interpretation of that clause would have obliged Roosevelt, after the defeat of the Hay-Herrán treaty in the Colombian Congress, to turn at once to Nicaragua, but by that time he was so firmly convinced of the technical superiority of the Panama route that he was prepared to insist upon its adoption even without Colombia's consent. In August 1903 a memorandum composed by John Bassett Moore, professor of international law and diplomacy at Columbia University, opportunely provided the President with what he construed as legal justification for the coercion of Colombia. Moore did not propose forcible seizure of the isthmus but suggested that Colombia's obligation to permit the United States to construct a Panama canal was implicit in the terms of the old but

still valid treaty of 1846 between the United States and New Granada: "In view of the fact that the United States has for more than
fifty years secured to Colombia her sovereignty over the Isthmus
. . . the United States is in a position to demand that it shall be
allowed to construct the great means of transit which the treaty was
chiefly designed to assure." [7] This ingenious doctrine formulated
by an eminent authority on international law — an authority
moreover with no political ax to grind — was a godsend to Roosevelt, who forwarded Moore's memorandum to Hay with a note: "If
under the treaty of 1846 we have a color of right to start in and
build the canal, my off-hand judgment would favor such proceeding. . . . I do not think that the Bogotá lot of jack rabbits should
be allowed permanently to bar one of the future highways of civilization. Of course . . . we could now go ahead with Nicaragua.
. . . But what we do now will be of consequence, not merely decades, but centuries hence, and we must be sure that we are taking
the right step before we act." [8]

Rumors that rejection of the Hay-Herrán treaty by Colombia
would precipitate a revolution on the isthmus circulated widely
during the summer of 1903. As early as June 1901 Martínez Silva
had warned his government that failure to reach an agreement satisfactory to the canal advocates in Panama might bring about the
secession of that province, and within the next two years Concha
and many other Colombians ventured similar predictions. Just a
week before the opening session of the Bogotá Congress Cromwell
publicly proclaimed the threat of isthmian revolt. After an interview with Roosevelt on June 13, 1903 the attorney sent his press
agent, Roger L. Farnham, to the New York *World,* and on the following day the newspaper, having pledged itself not to reveal the
source of its story, published this item without mentioning Cromwell's name: "Information . . . has reached this city that . . .
Panama . . . stands ready to secede . . . and enter into a canal
treaty with the United States. . . . President Roosevelt is said to
strongly favor this plan, if the [Hay-Herrán] treaty is rejected. . . .
It is intended to wait a reasonable time for action by the Colombian Congress. . . ." [9] While Roosevelt certainly did not authorize any such announcement there is no evidence that he expressed
displeasure at its publication.

On the same day, June 13, Bunau-Varilla cabled Marroquín
from Paris that failure to ratify the treaty would be followed by the
secession of Panama or construction of a Nicaragua canal. During
the summer Bunau-Varilla independently evolved much the same

theory that had occurred to Professor Moore concerning Colombia's obligations under the treaty of 1846, and on September 2 he published his conclusions in *Le Matin*, of which he had recently become part owner. A few days later the engineer sailed for New York, where he landed on September 22. For the next two months he played the star rôle in the canal drama.

Ever since the emancipation of Latin America from Spain a strong movement towards independence had flourished on the isthmus. The Panamanians, isolated from the rest of Colombia by impenetrable swamp and jungle, felt little sentimental attachment to Bogotá and had on several occasions formally seceded from the republic only to resume allegiance after brief interludes of uneasy independence. But the tradition of separatism survived, ready to break out again into open rebellion under sufficient provocation. The canal controversy provided just such a grievance. Although for political reasons many Panamanians supported the Liberal opposition to the Hay-Herrán treaty probably most of the educated and articulate residents of the isthmus favored its ratification and resented Bogotá's apparent indifference to their interests. The secession spark began to glow, feebly at first since few revolutions (if any) commence as spontaneous popular uprisings. They are usually if not always conceived and organized by a few determined individuals, and the Panama revolt of 1903 was no exception.

On the isthmus itself the first definite step was taken about the end of May by José Agustín Arango, counsel and land agent for the Panama Railroad, who had been elected senator from Panama at the same time as Obaldía and Pérez y Soto but had refused to attend the Congress because, as he afterwards declared, he was convinced that the treaty would be rejected and that the canal's sole hope lay in secession. In the beginning Arango took into his confidence only seven confederates: his sons Ricardo, Belisario, and José Agustín, his sons-in-law Samuel Lewis, Raúl Orillac, and Ernesto Lefevre, and the "intelligent and devoted" [10] Carlos Constantino Arosemena. This almost exclusively family group formed a preliminary junta "without holding regular meetings, which would have been extremely dangerous. . . ." [11] The next to be admitted was J. R. Beers, freight agent of the railroad and port captain at La Boca, whom the junta sent to the United States to conduct a discreet inquiry into the possibility of Yankee co-operation. After several interviews with influential friends of the Panama route, including E. A. Drake, vice president of the railroad, and Cromwell, who gave him a code book for cable messages and the assurance of unlimited assistance, Beers returned to Panama on

August 4. By that time the junta had been reorganized to include Manuel Amador Guerrero, the railroad company's physician and a popular figure in the professional and social life of Panama; the two Arias brothers, Ricardo and Tomás; Nicanor A. de Obarrio; Manuel Espinosa, Amador's brother-in-law; and Federico Boyd. A little later a dozen other prominent Panamanians joined the revolutionary group. As the junta expanded Arango's sons and sons-in-law retired into the background to form a sort of unofficial family council. The revolutionists usually met either at Boyd's house or at the Panama electric light plant, deserted after midnight.

The inclusion of three prominent officials of the Panama Railroad — Arango, Amador, and Beers — among the most active leaders was no mere coincidence. Through Beers the junta had established contact with Cromwell, counsel for both the railroad and the Compagnie Nouvelle; the Compagnie Nouvelle owned most of the railroad stock; the Compagnie Nouvelle wanted to sell its Panama property to the United States without paying Colombia for the privilege; and the United States government had committed itself to the support of the canal company's stand. The connection was too obvious to be ignored. If the motives of the junta were primarily patriotic, as they may well have been, the secession movement also dovetailed neatly into the program of the Compagnie Nouvelle and the Roosevelt administration.

On September 1 Amador reached New York to secure from Cromwell more precise assurances of support and if possible to obtain from Hay or Roosevelt specific promises of armed intervention and prompt recognition. Drake introduced Amador to Cromwell, who welcomed him cordially and showered him with offers of aid; but a few days later, when Amador called at the lawyer's office a second time, he was unceremoniously refused admittance. Mystified and deeply wounded, he cabled to the junta the single word *"desanimado"* — "discouraged." Although Amador did not know it at the time Cromwell had ample cause for his abrupt change of heart. Among Amador's fellow passengers from Colón to New York was J. Gabriel Duque, editor of the Panama *Star and Herald.* On shipboard Amador had been careful to reveal no hint of his mission, but that did not prevent the editor from putting two and two together. The day after his arrival in New York Duque met Cromwell, who arranged a meeting between Duque and Hay and, it has been suggested, offered to make Duque President of the future republic of Panama if he would organize an insurrection. At the conference with Duque on September 3 Hay "made no promise of direct assistance to the revolutionists . . . saying that

he 'would not cross that bridge until he got to it,' but he did say
distinctly that 'the United States would build the Panama Canal
and that it did not purpose to permit Colombia's standing in the
way.' . . . Hay also said that should the revolutionists take . . .
Colón and Panama they could depend upon the United States to
prohibit Colombia's landing troops to attack them and disturb the
'free and uninterrupted transit' which the American Government
was bound by treaty . . . to maintain. . . .'' [12]

Duque's next move was to expose the whole revolutionary plot,
as far as he was able to piece it together, to Herrán. His motives are
far from clear: possibly he felt slighted by exclusion from the junta,
he may have interpreted as a rebuff Hay's cautious refusal to commit the United States to outright intervention, or he may have
hoped that the Colombian Congress, warned by Herrán, might be
frightened into ratification of the treaty and so avert secession. Herrán immediately cabled the information to Bogotá and notified
Cromwell that Colombia would hold him and the directors of the
Compagnie Nouvelle responsible for an isthmian insurrection.
Outflanked for once, the attorney beat a hasty retreat. Fearing that
further encouragement of the revolution might furnish Colombia
with an excuse to rescind the company's charter, he instantly shut
his door in Amador's face and cabled the superintendent of the
Panama Railroad, Colonel Shaler, to avoid any association with
the junta.

For some weeks after his repulse the bewildered Amador, unaware of Duque's curious maneuvers or that he himself was under
constant surveillance by detectives in Herrán's employ, roamed
disconsolately about New York. Without Cromwell's co-operation
he could not approach Hay, and without assurance of help from
Washington the revolutionary cause was lost. But on September
22 the opportune arrival of Bunau-Varilla gave Amador new hope.
He had known Bunau-Varilla on the isthmus in 1885, and now in
his distress he confided his troubles to the sympathetic Frenchman.
Bunau-Varilla, only too happy to agree that Cromwell had behaved
outrageously, soothed Amador's ruffled feelings and promised all
the assistance in his power. His unofficial position proved an invaluable asset to Bunau-Varilla in his activities as intermediary between the Panama secessionists and the United States government.
Unlike Cromwell, he represented nobody but himself; therefore
Colombia could not hold the Compagnie Nouvelle responsible for
his conduct. Bunau-Varilla knew that he was playing a dangerous
game, but his subtle inventiveness enabled him to win every trick.
Reflection convinced him that the plan to coerce Colombia by

means of the treaty of 1846 "was too abstract to appeal to a great democracy" [13] and that Panamanian independence offered the only practical solution. At the same time he realized that the proprieties must be observed; however earnestly Roosevelt and Hay might hope for revolution they must not become or even appear to become openly involved in its fomentation.

On October 9 Bunau-Varilla informed the President that in his opinion a revolution was imminent, but he discreetly left his hopes of intervention to be inferred. Although Roosevelt's comments were equally guarded the two men understood each other perfectly. Two months later Roosevelt wrote to John Bigelow: "Of course I have no idea what Bunau-Varilla advised the revolutionists . . . but I do know . . . that he had no assurance in any way, either from Hay or myself, or from anyone authorized to speak for us. He is a very able fellow, and it was his business to find out what he thought our Government would do. I have no doubt that he was able to make a very accurate guess, and to advise his people accordingly. In fact, he would have been a very dull man had he been unable to make such a guess." [14] As Roosevelt had surmised, Bunau-Varilla promptly informed Amador that the United States government, though unwilling to commit itself by formal promises, would undoubtedly aid the insurrection at least to the extent of preventing interference with the railroad by Colombian forces.

The engineer also conferred with Hay, who agreed that a revolt appeared inevitable and disclosed the welcome news that United States naval units in both oceans were already being prepared for a dash to the isthmus. On October 15 Secretary of the Navy William L. Moody directed Admiral Henry Glass to send the cruiser *Boston* from San Francisco to Acapulco, whence the vessel proceeded to San Juan del Sur. On the 31st the *Marblehead*, Glass's flagship, *Wyoming*, and *Concord* assembled at Acapulco, while on the Atlantic side Moody had ordered the *Atlanta* to the Guantánamo naval base in Cuba and the auxiliary cruiser *Dixie* and gunboat *Nashville* to Kingston, Jamaica.

Bunau-Varilla hastened back to New York for a farewell interview with Amador before the latter's return to Panama. Distrusting the Latin American tendency to procrastinate, the energetic and quick-witted Frenchman prepared and handed over a proclamation of independence, a program of military operations, and a cipher code, offered to supply $100,000 out of his own pocket for preliminary expenses as soon as the insurrection started, and undertook to arrange for recognition by the United States. In return he exacted a promise that the revolt would take place not later than

November 3 and insisted upon his own appointment as the new republic's minister to Washington with full power to negotiate treaties. At the last moment he gave Amador a national flag designed by himself and hastily stitched together by Mme Bunau-Varilla.

Amador's return to Panama on October 27 with nothing but a sheaf of unofficial promises and a home-made flag bitterly disappointed the members of the junta, but they realized that Bunau-Varilla constituted their only hope and with some misgivings resolved to act upon his assurances that United States warships would appear at the crucial moment. The military forces at the junta's disposal consisted of about 300 young men organized by Duque into a "fire brigade"; the Panama police; a detachment of Colombian regulars led by General Huertas, a member of the junta, who had been promised $50,000 for his co-operation; and the Colombian gunboat *Padilla* stationed at Panama, whose commander, General Ruben Varón, had agreed to hand over the vessel and crew for the sum of $35,000. The rebels could also count on the indirect support of Governor Obaldía, who was known to favor secession but whose official position prevented open connection with the junta. On October 25 Obaldía, pretending to have received word of a wholly imaginary Nicaraguan incursion into Panamanian territory, sent a force of about 100 Colombian soldiers commanded by Captain Tascón, who had refused to join Huertas, to repel the "invaders." When Obaldía telegraphed a report of the invented incident to Bogotá the government, acting with unexpected promptness, directed him to send the gunboats *Padilla* and *Bogotá* to Buenaventura for reinforcements and ordered General Tovar, then at Cartagena, to proceed at once to the isthmus with his battalion of expert riflemen or *tiradores*.

These instructions, privately communicated to Amador by Obaldía, threw the junta into confusion. On October 29 Amador cabled Bunau-Varilla: "Fate news bad powerful tiger. Urge vapor Colón." [15] Decoded, the message signified that more than 200 Colombian troops were expected to land on the Atlantic side of the isthmus within five days and that the immediate dispatch of a United States warship to Colón was indispensable. Bunau-Varilla hastened to Washington to warn Assistant Secretary of State Francis B. Loomis of the danger of interruption to the railroad transit, carefully omitting the source of his information, and Loomis in turn very properly told him nothing of the United States government's plans for the transit's protection. But Bunau-Varilla, knowing from the newspapers that the *Nashville* was at Kingston, shrewdly inferred from what Loomis did *not* say that the gunboat would be sent to the isthmus without delay. Calculating the vessel's speed at 10 knots, he cabled Amador on October 30 that an American man-of-war would reach Colón in two and a half days. It was a good guess: early in the evening of November 2 the *Nashville* steamed into Limón Bay. A few hours later, about midnight, General Tovar and his Colombian *tiradores* arrived in the steamer *Cartagena*.

The junta, warned of Tovar's approach, prevailed upon the railroad superintendent, Colonel Shaler, to detain the Colombian forces at Colón as long as possible. Shaler obligingly removed most of the rolling stock from the vicinity of the Atlantic terminus, and when Tovar landed his men about daylight on November 3 he was informed with polite expressions of regret that only one or two cars were available. The superintendent offered to run these as a special train for the immediate conveyance of Tovar and his aides to Panama and promised to provide transportation for the soldiers within a few hours — a neat stratagem said to have been invented by Amador's wife. Tovar walked blindly into the trap. Leaving his men at Colón in charge of Colonel Torres, the Colombian general crossed with his other officers to Panama, where the civic authorities greeted them with a disarming show of cordiality. But the expected troop train from Colón failed to appear, and by mid-afternoon Tovar began to suspect trickery. When he announced at five o'clock that he intended to take command of the garrison, General Huertas, who had planned to arrest the Colombian officers later that evening at a band concert, dared wait no longer. Calling a patrol, he took Tovar and his staff into custody and locked them up.

Arango, Boyd, and Tomás Arias, the junta's provisional governing committee, hurried to the cathedral plaza, where they were acclaimed by an immense crowd. To preserve the fiction of Obaldía's ignorance of the plot the rebel committee ordered his arrest. A little later the gunboat *Bogotá*, whose commander had remained loyal to the Colombian government and had been imprisoned with Tovar, fired half a dozen shells into the city, killing a Chinese resident and mortally wounding a donkey — the only casualties of this almost bloodless insurrection. Immediately after Tovar's arrest Amador informed the United States vice consul general, Felix Ehrman, that Panama was about to declare independence, and Ehrman cabled the news to Washington. In response Hay and Loomis sent several messages in rapid succession instructing Com-

462 THE LAND DIVIDED

mander John Hubbard of the *Nashville* to prevent the transportation of Colombian soldiers to Panama.

The official order must have relieved Shaler, who had been kept busy all day inventing excuses for his failure to supply the Colombian officer in charge, Colonel Torres, with the promised transportation. Torres, justifiably uneasy, pleaded and insisted to no avail. On the morning of November 4 he was informed by the junta's agent in Colón, Porfirio Meléndez, of the arrest of Tovar, the successful outcome of the insurrection in Panama City, and the expected arrival of additional United States warships. The infuriated colonel threatened to burn Colón and kill every American inhabitant unless Tovar and his fellow officers were released by two o'clock that afternoon. Hubbard quickly herded all American women and children on board vessels in the port, gathered the men in one of the railroad's stone warehouses, landed an armed detachment of 42 marines and sailors, cleared the *Nashville* for action, and trained her guns on the wharf and on the Colombian steamer *Cartagena,* which slipped out of the harbor at full speed. The Colombian soldiers surrounded the railroad shed, and hostilities seemed imminent; but during the afternoon Torres agreed to withdraw his forces to Monkey Hill and await orders from Tovar. The junta had offered to release Tovar and permit him to cross to Colón, but when the general indignantly refused to give his parole not to escape the offer was withdrawn. On November 5 Torres, having received no communication from his superior for two days, decided to accept a bribe of $8000 tendered by Meléndez and sail back to Cartagena with his troops in the Royal Mail steamer *Orinoco.* As the liner steamed away from Colón the *Dixie* anchored in the harbor and landed marines to relieve the detachment from the *Nashville.*

General Tovar's rejection of the parole terms which would have enabled him to hold Torres at his post proved a disastrous blunder, for it gave Washington the excuse it needed for prompt recognition of the insurgents. As long as the loyal troops remained at Colón Bogotá's claim to *de facto* sovereignty over the isthmus was at least as valid as that of the Panama junta. With the departure of Torres Colombia's *de facto* jurisdiction ceased.

On the afternoon of November 4 the provisional government formally proclaimed the republic at a mass meeting held in the cathedral plaza at Panama. The manifesto of independence, composed by Eusebio Morales and signed by Arango, Boyd, and Tomás Arias, set forth the grievances suffered by Panama under Bogotá's rule and concluded: "We separate ourselves from our

Colombian brothers without hatred and without joy." [16] At ten in the morning of November 6 similar ceremonies took place at Colón; the declaration of independence was read, and at the request of the provisional committee an engineer officer of the United States army, Major William Murray Black, raised the Panamanian flag over the prefecture. Since the United States had not yet recognized the new republic this act constituted a breach of international usage for which the major was subsequently taken to task by Senator Carmack of Tennessee. Actually Black's gesture, while technically premature, preceded recognition by less than three hours. At 12:51 p.m. Hay cabled to Ehrman: "The people of Panama have, by an apparently unanimous movement, dissolved their political connection with . . . Colombia and resumed their independence. When you are satisfied that a *de facto* government, republican in form, and without substantial opposition from its own people, has been established . . . you will enter into relations with it as the responsible government. . . ." [17]

De facto recognition by the United States less than three days after the start of the insurrection loosed a flood of indignant criticism. The author of one magazine article charged that "there was never precedent nor parallel for this Cæsarian recognition of a 'Republic' before it was delivered. . . . We did not recognize our own Texas . . . Q–U–I–T–E so precipitately. . . . [Panama] and Colon are the vermiform appendix of Colombia, in morals and in patriotism. . . . No other population has had any hand or voice in this Declaration-of-Independence-for-What-There-is-in-It. The alleged 'Republic' of Panama has neither head nor hands nor feet. All it has is its belly. Which is its god." [18] More temperately and less anatomically, General Reyes protested that if the Panamanians "had declared their independence after victories gained against the governing or misgoverning authorities; if they had . . . proved to the world their fitness for self-government, without doubt they would have been entitled to recognition. . . . But in the absence of all these conditions . . . it is evident that recognition would have been denied Panama if it had not possessed the best route for the Isthmian Canal. . . ." [19]

When detailed reports of the insurrection reached Bogotá on November 6 crowds streamed towards the presidential palace shouting: "Down with Marroquín!" Martial law was proclaimed in the city, and a heavy guard was thrown about the United States legation. Beaupré cabled Hay: "General Reyes says that if the . . . United States will land troops to preserve Colombian sovereignty and the transit . . . this Government . . . will approve by de-

cree the ratification of the canal treaty as signed; or, if the . . .
United States prefers, will call extra session of Congress with new
and friendly members next May to approve the treaty. . . . There
is a great reaction of public opinion in favor of the treaty, and it is
considered certain that the treaty was not legally rejected by Congress." [20] This conciliatory message — which only strengthened
Roosevelt's conviction that the Colombian "dictatorship" could
have forced the treaty through Congress several months earlier had
it been so disposed — reached Washington too late to affect the
march of events. The United States government had already recognized the republic of Panama and had notified the Colombian
authorities of its action, though the cabled announcement, delayed in transmission, was not received until November 11.

In Bogotá the dismay of the first few days soon changed to fierce
resentment against the United States. Domestic quarrels were temporarily forgotten, the press rallied to the defense of the Marroquín administration, and even the diehard oppositionists Caro and
Pérez y Soto fell into line behind the government. Rico issued a formal protest against recognition and threatened to sever diplomatic
relations with Washington if the United States interfered with
Bogotá's efforts to suppress the insurrection. Marroquín summoned
an advisory council of prominent citizens, many of whom clamored insistently for an immediate declaration of war against the
Yankees. Fortunately more moderate views prevailed, and the Cabinet advised the appointment of a special military and diplomatic
commission to be sent to the isthmus with authority to concede
almost anything except independence. The commission, composed
of General Reyes as chairman, General Pedro Nel Ospina, and Lucas Caballero, reached Colón on November 19; but the provisional
government, advised by Bunau-Varilla, forbade Reyes to land unless he could produce credentials as Colombian minister to the independent republic of Panama, and of course Reyes had no such
documents. On November 20 a Panamanian delegation headed by
Tomás Arias boarded the steamer at Colón and courteously but
firmly convinced the Reyes commission that it could accomplish
nothing there. Without setting foot on the isthmus the disappointed Colombians continued their journey to Washington.

As a reward for his aid to the insurgents Bunau-Varilla had insisted upon his own designation as Panamanian minister to the
United States, and Amador, who apparently wanted the post himself, had consented with some reluctance. The Frenchman had now
fulfilled his part of the bargain; Panama had declared independ-

ence, two United States warships had arrived, the Colombian troops had departed, and the United States government had granted *de facto* recognition. But when the junta hesitated to confirm the promised diplomatic assignment Bunau-Varilla, suspecting some kind of hocus-pocus, kept the cables hot until on the evening of November 6 he received his formal appointment. He immediately notified Hay, adding a few flowery expressions of gratitude to the United States: "In extending her generous hand so spontaneously to her latest born, the Mother of the American Nations is prosecuting her noble mission as the liberator and educator of the peoples. In spreading her protecting wings over the territory of our Republic, the American Eagle has sanctified it. It has rescued it from the barbarism of . . . civil wars to consecrate it to the destiny assigned to it by Providence, the service of Humanity and the progress of Civilisation." [21]

As long as recognition remained merely *de facto* the new minister could not be received officially at the State Department, but at a private luncheon on November 9 he persuaded Hay to speed up the diplomatic formalities. On November 13, when Bunau-Varilla presented his credentials to President Roosevelt, the United States recognized Panama *de jure*. Hay, impressed by the envoy's impatience, then agreed to conclude a treaty between Panama and the United States at the earliest possible moment. Bunau-Varilla had his own reasons for haste. He knew that Amador, Boyd, and Carlos Arosemena had sailed from Colón on November 10 and that if they reached Washington before the end of the treaty negotiations they would probably engage in lengthy discussions, insist upon the inclusion of provisions which the United States Senate might find unacceptable, and thus endanger the whole project just when success seemed certain. An exchange of cables had confirmed Bunau-Varilla's suspicion that Amador was secretly empowered to negotiate and sign the treaty and that he himself was to be deprived of the coveted honor. Furthermore he foresaw that the imminent arrival of the Reyes commission in Washington would confuse the issue and cause additional delay. It was imperative therefore to seal the pact within the next few days while both delegations were still en route.

On November 15 Hay sent Bunau-Varilla a treaty draft based on the rejected Hay-Herrán convention, slightly modified to fit the new conditions. The energetic minister made a number of alterations to the draft; then, not yet satisfied, he composed an entirely new treaty and delivered both documents to Hay on the morning of the 17th, with a note signifying his willingness to sign whichever form the Secretary preferred. A few hours later Bunau-Varilla received a telegram announcing the arrival of Amador and his companions in New York. Obviously there was no time to be lost. That night, at Bunau-Varilla's urgent request, Hay conferred with him at some length but gave no hint as to which formula would be adopted. Hay told the minister that several influential senators favored the division of the $10,000,000 between Panama and Colombia — a compromise against which Bunau-Varilla protested vigorously, asserting that any subsidy to Colombia would constitute a tacit admission of guilt on the part of the United States as well as surrender to a threat of blackmail. The next day Bunau-Varilla, nervously expecting Amador to walk in at any moment, waited with ever-mounting anxiety until during the afternoon he received a summons to Hay's house. Hay then disclosed that the indemnity would be paid to Panama alone and that he had decided to accept Bunau-Varilla's new version of the treaty with a few very minor changes. At 6:40 p.m. on November 18, 1903 the two men affixed their signatures to the Hay-Bunau-Varilla treaty.

Fortunately for Bunau-Varilla the Panamanian delegates had remained one day in New York to confer with Cromwell, just returned from France. The treaty was signed as the unsuspecting commissioners sat placidly in the train already halfway to Washington, and some three hours later a triumphant Bunau-Varilla greeted them at the station with the news. Shocked and angry, Amador and Boyd started to protest but soon resigned themselves to acceptance of the *fait accompli*. Bunau-Varilla, anxious to proceed to the next step — ratification of the treaty by Panama — before the Reyes mission could interfere, requested Amador and Boyd to ask the junta for emergency authority to ratify. When the commissioners refused Bunau-Varilla cabled a résumé of the treaty provisions to Panama, placed the document in a safe, and sent it by steamer to Colón on November 24. But since Reyes was due in Washington on the 28th, and the treaty could not reach the isthmus before December 1, the minister cabled for an immediate pledge of ratification, which he received just one day before Reyes's arrival.

The return mail steamer to New York was scheduled to leave Colón only a few hours after the arrival of the treaty, and there would be no other sailing for a week. Still worried lest the junta might reconsider or postpone ratification, Bunau-Varilla now urged the Panama Railroad Company, owner of the steamship line, to hold the *Yucatan* at Colón for one day so that the ratified convention might be brought back without delay. To his amazement the company refused, and the *Yucatan* sailed on time without the treaty. He did not know that at that very moment the railroad directors, influenced by Cromwell, were making desperate efforts to have him ousted from his diplomatic post, which was to be given to Pablo Arosemena.

Actually Bunau-Varilla had nothing to fear. The provisional government ratified the treaty on December 2, returned it by the next steamer, and made no further attempts to interfere with its appointed envoy. Meanwhile the head of the Colombian mission, Reyes, had reached Washington and was conducting a determined campaign for redress of his country's grievances. Immediately after his arrival he told the reporters that "my energies and those of my followers will be devoted to the granting of the canal concessions [by Colombia] without the payment of a cent. Even at this Colombia will be the gainer." [22] When asked whether Marroquín had authorized such an unexpectedly generous offer Reyes replied: "That would be divulging my instructions before I have executed them. . . . You can further say . . . that all Colombia is afire with zeal for the building of the canal by the United States, and that the unfortunate political troubles, which were the sole cause of the treaty's death . . . have entirely disappeared. We want the canal. . . ." [23]

With the assistance of an American attorney, Wayne MacVeagh, Reyes bombarded the State Department with protests against United States intervention on the isthmus and pleas for adjustment of the whole controversy by the Court of Arbitration at The Hague. On December 4 Hay wrote to Roosevelt: "Can you receive Reyes tomorrow, Saturday? . . . Permit me to observe the sooner you see him, the sooner we can bid him good-bye. I have a complaint to make of Root. I told him I was going to see Reyes. He replied, 'Better look out. Ex-Reyes are dangerous.' Do you think that, on my salary, I can afford to bear such things?" [24] The Secretary of State rejected the appeal for arbitration by The Hague but offered to submit the question of isthmian allegiance to a plebiscite and to allow a special arbitration tribunal to settle claims for specific material damage. Reyes in turn found these proposals unacceptable and soon afterwards left Washington for Paris, where he attempted through proceedings in the French civil courts to prevent the transfer of the Compagnie Nouvelle's concession to the United States.

Externally the new republic of Panama was already strongly buttressed. Recognition *de jure* by the United States on November 13 had been followed by similar action by France on the 16th, by

China, Austria-Hungary, and Germany before the end of the month, and during December and January by almost all other nations with the significant exception of Colombia, which not only refused recognition but for about three months after the declaration of independence strove persistently to recapture the seceded province by force. To frustrate these attempts United States warships stood guard on both sides of the isthmus. At Colón the *Nashville* and *Dixie* were joined by the *Atlanta, Maine,* and *Mayflower,* while the *Boston, Marblehead, Concord,* and *Wyoming* anchored off Panama. Since these vessels drew too much water to enter the shallow coastal inlets three small patrol ships were added to the fleet, and on December 16 the *Prairie* landed a detachment of marines who established themselves in a temporary camp near Obispo halfway across the isthmus.

With so powerful a concentration of ships and troops at the terminal ports the Colombians dared not attack the canal region from the sea. Instead they attempted an invasion by land through the dense jungles and malarial swamps of Darién. On December 15 the *Atlanta* located about 500 Colombian soldiers near the tiny port of Titumate on the Gulf of Urabá. This force and two other detachments — perhaps 2000 men in all, in addition to several hundred laborers — were struggling to open a road to Colón, more than 200 miles away. Meanwhile United States troops established a series of small outposts on the Pacific slope of Darién, and a clash could scarcely have been avoided had not Roosevelt, unwilling to furnish the already restive Senate with a pretext for opposition to the Hay-Bunau-Varilla treaty, suddenly modified his aggressive policy. On December 19 Moody directed Admiral Glass to "maintain posts in the vicinity of Yavisa for observation only. Do not have posts beyond support of ships or launches. Withdraw your posts if liable to be attacked. It is the intention of the Government to confine active defense . . . to the vicinity of the railroad line. . . ." [25] A battle was thus averted, but for at least another month the Americans remained constantly on guard. Before the end of January the Colombians, ravaged by fever, abandoned their overland march and returned to their own country. A few weeks later the Senate's ratification of the treaty led to the withdrawal of most of the United States forces.

Chapter 38. Aftermath

As the Panamanians did not fail to point out once their first glow of gratitude had begun to fade, the Hay-Bunau-Varilla treaty granted the United States more sweeping privileges than Colombia had been asked to concede by the Hay-Herrán convention. The width of the Canal Zone was increased from 10 kilometers to 10 miles, and instead of a 100-year lease indefinitely renewable the new treaty granted *in perpetuity* the use and control of the Zone, exclusive of the cities of Panama and Colón but including the islands of Perico, Naos, Culebra, and Flamenco in Panama Bay. Furthermore the treaty gave the United States the right to expropriate any additional land or water areas required for the construction, operation, sanitation, and protection of the canal. In return the United States guaranteed the independence of Panama, but the treaty omitted specific mention of Panamanian sovereignty over the Zone. Presumably Panama retained titular sovereignty for what it was worth but conceded to the United States "all the rights, power and authority within the zone . . . and within the limits of all auxiliary lands and waters mentioned . . . which the United States would possess and exercise if it were the sovereign of the territory . . . to the entire exclusion of the exercise by . . . Panama of any such sovereign rights, power or authority." [1]

In the terminal cities sanitation, sewerage, water supply, and the maintenance of public order were placed completely under United States control. Panama retained the right to send its own warships, troops, and munitions through the canal without charge and similarly to transport its public servants and supplies by the railroad. A joint commission was to supervise condemnation of private property required by the United States, but since the United States now had complete jurisdiction over the Zone the joint tribunals provided for in the Hay-Herrán treaty were eliminated. The Hay-Bunau-Varilla treaty paid lip service to the neutrality clauses of the Hay-Pauncefote convention but at the same time empowered the United States to erect fortifications and maintain garrisons. The compensation to Panama was exactly the same as that offered to and rejected by Colombia: $10,000,000 on exchange of ratifications and an annuity of $250,000 to commence nine years later.

In his annual message of December 7, 1903 Roosevelt maintained that the Spooner act, which authorized a canal treaty with Colombia, could be extended by implication to cover a similar agreement with the new republic of Panama: "When the Congress directed that we should take the Panama route under treaty with Colombia, the essence of the condition . . . referred not to the Government which controlled that route, but to the route itself; to the territory across which the route lay, not to the name which for the moment the territory bore on the map." [2] He also held that the treaty of 1846 still remained in force with Panama instead of Colombia as the party of the second part. This doctrine had been suggested by Oscar Straus at a White House luncheon shortly after the Panama revolution: "One of the questions raised was whether the treaty [of 1846] still held us to that obligation [to protect the transit]. . . . I answered that it seemed to me . . . that the change of sovereignty did not affect either our obligations or our rights; that I regarded them in the nature of a 'covenant running with the land.' 'That's fine! Just the idea!' Roosevelt replied. . . . A few days thereafter I received a short note from the President reading: 'Your "covenant running with the land" idea worked admirably. I congratulate you on it.' And from . . . John Bassett Moore I received an amusing letter: 'So you had a finger in the pie! I find a good deal of amusement in reflecting on the end reached from the premise of my memorandum; and almost as much on the conclusion reached from your suggestion. Perhaps, however, it is only a question of words . . . a question of the "covenant running with the land" or a question of the "covenant running (away!) with the land"!!' " [3]

In spite of its obvious advantages for the United States the Hay-Bunau-Varilla treaty encountered such determined opposition in the Senate that Roosevelt, placed on the defensive, felt obliged to justify his policy in a special message composed with the help of Professor Moore and delivered on January 4, 1904: "I hesitate to refer to the injurious insinuations which have been made of complicity by this Government in the revolutionary movement in Panama. They are as destitute of foundation as of propriety. . . . No one connected with this Government had any part in preparing, inciting, or encouraging the late revolution . . . and . . . save from the reports of our military and naval officers . . . no one connected with this Government had any previous knowledge of the revolution except such as was accessible to any person of ordinary intelligence who read the newspapers. . . . By . . . unanimous action . . . the people of Panama declared themselves . . . independent. . . . Their recognition . . . was . . . in no way dependent for its justification upon our action in ordinary cases. . . . These reasons [for recognition] embrace, first, our treaty rights; second, our national interests and safety; and, third, the interests of collective civilization. . . . That our wise and patriotic ancestors . . . would have entered into a treaty [in 1846] . . . solely or even primarily for the purpose of enabling [New Granada] . . . to continue from Bogota to rule over the Isthmus . . . is a conception that would in itself be incredible, even if the contrary did not clearly appear. . . . The great design . . . was to assure the dedication of the Isthmus to the purposes of free and unobstructed . . . transit, the consummation of which would be found in an interoceanic canal. . . . This recognition was . . . further justified by . . . our national interests. . . . In . . . our present situation, the establishment of easy and speedy communication by sea between the Atlantic and the Pacific presents itself not simply as something to be desired, but as an object to be positively and promptly attained. Reasons of convenience have been superseded by reasons of vital necessity, which do not admit of indefinite delays. To such delays the rejection by Colombia of the Hay-Herran treaty directly exposed us. . . . In the third place . . . recognition . . . was an act justified by the interests of collective civilization. If ever a government could be said to have received a mandate from civilization . . . the United States holds that position with regard to the interoceanic canal." [4]

Most of the arguments in this curious message were dubious if not altogether invalid. Only the most obvious sophistry could twist the treaty obligation of the United States to preserve Colombian sovereignty over the isthmus into a right to assist in the overthrow of that sovereignty. The interests of the United States and of "collective civilization" would have been as effectively served by a Nicaragua canal. If delay really meant disaster a canal through Nicaragua could have been built almost as quickly as one at Panama; but the unratified Hay-Herrán treaty would have allowed 26 years for the construction of a lock canal and 36 for the completion of one at sea level, so haste cannot have been the imperative consideration that Roosevelt pretended. The "mandate from civilization" had no legal basis whatever, and even if justified on broader grounds — as perhaps it was — it should not have prevented discussion, conciliation, and if necessary arbitration.

In the Senate the venerable John Morgan fought to the bitter end against ratification of the Hay-Bunau-Varilla treaty. He was

ably seconded by other legislators who, rejecting Roosevelt's denials of responsibility for the revolution, sympathized with Colombia as a victim of international intrigue and insisted with considerable justice that the insurrection, far from being a popular revolt,
had been conceived and executed by a very small group of individuals in Panama and the United States. Senator Carmack described
Bunau-Varilla as "a mercurial French adventurer, masquerading
as the comic-opera representative of a comic-opera Republic" [5] and
attacked Roosevelt as the chief plotter: "As a matter of fact . . .
there never was any real insurrection in Panama. . . . There has
been a great deal of rhetoric about the people rising up as one man
against their oppressors. To all intents and purposes there was but
one man in that insurrection, and that man was the President of
the United States." [6] In the absence of Mark Hanna, who died on
February 16, 1904 while the debate was still in progress, the pro-
ratification forces were led by Senators Spooner, Cullom, Depew,
and Lodge. After one of the most bitter struggles in the history of
the Senate the treaty was ratified without amendment by a vote of
66 to 14 on February 23, 1904. Two days later it was proclaimed,
and on February 26 Hay and Bunau-Varilla exchanged ratifications. Although now partially superseded by the Hull-Alfaro treaty
ratified in 1939 the Hay-Bunau-Varilla convention still governs the
basic relations between Panama and the United States.

The Panamanian government designated J. P. Morgan and Company its fiscal representative in the United States and during the
summer of 1904 appointed Cromwell its general counsel. Immediately after ratification of the treaty the United States Treasury arranged for the payment of the stipulated $10,000,000. On May 2
the bankers received a draft for $1,000,000, of which they shipped
$200,000 to the isthmus and retained the balance, partly to repay
themselves for advances and partly to cover future drafts. On May 4
Panama transferred control of the Canal Zone to representatives of
the United States, and on May 19 Secretary of the Treasury Leslie
M. Shaw paid J. P. Morgan and Company the remaining $9,000,-
000. To insure the financial stability of the new republic the
greater part of this sum was invested in the United States, principally in first mortgages on New York City improved real estate.

Numerous diplomatic shuffles followed the revolution. The first
United States minister to Panama, William I. Buchanan, presented
his credentials on December 23, 1903 but was replaced three
months later by John Barrett. Bunau-Varilla, having accomplished
his self-appointed task, resigned as Panamanian minister to Wash-

ington shortly after the exchange of ratifications and was succeeded by the former governor, José Domingo de Obaldía. William W. Russell supplanted Beaupré as United States envoy to Colombia, while Tomás Herrán, abandoning his futile efforts to block ratification of the Hay-Bunau-Varilla treaty, closed the Colombian legation in Washington on February 10, 1904 and returned to Bogotá, where he died soon afterwards. For about a year the Colombian government remained without official representation in the United States until the inauguration of General Reyes as President ushered in a more conciliatory policy.

On December 20, 1904 Russell reported to Hay that "my relations . . . with the Colombian Government have been quite cordial. The feeling against our Government in official circles . . . is gradually disappearing. . . . I am convinced that the only thing necessary to . . . restore American prestige would be . . . a treaty arrangement with the United States and Panama. . . ." [7] Unfortunately 18 years were to elapse before the breach was completely healed. On October 21, 1905 the new Colombian minister to Washington, Diego Mendoza Pérez, presented to Elihu Root, who had succeeded Hay as Secretary of State after the latter's death in July, a list of complaints and a renewed plea for arbitration, both of which Root rejected. While most of Mendoza's contentions were well founded his undiplomatic asperity did nothing to relieve the tension between the two governments. Soon afterwards he was recalled and replaced by Enrique Cortés. When Mendoza, refusing to return to Bogotá, published an open letter in which "in language plain and unmistakable, [he] denounces President Reyes . . . as a traitor . . . intimates that he is a forger and accuses him of extreme bad faith" [8] the Colombian government charged him with treason and ordered him home for trial.

Although Root steadfastly refused Colombia's requests for arbitration he endeavored sincerely and with some success to allay Colombian resentment. Much of the credit for the gradual improvement in relations must also be given to the moderation of President Reyes. On May 23, 1906 John Barrett, who had recently replaced Russell at Bogotá, reported that Reyes had told him that "you [Root] could not realize how strong still was the feeling, amounting almost to intense hatred, among the people of Colombia against the United States . . . [and] that only by his constant watchfulness and personal good will . . . had outbreaks against Americans . . . been prevented. . . ." [9] In September, to encourage international harmony, Root visited Cartagena, where he was received with a gratifying display of cordiality — at least on the surface.

On January 9, 1909 the Root-Cortés treaty between the United States and Colombia, the Root-Arosemena treaty between the United States and Panama, and the Cortés-Arosemena treaty between Colombia and Panama were signed simultaneously at Washington. The three conventions interlocked; none would become effective unless all three were ratified by the respective signatory powers. The United States agreed to commence its annual payments of $250,000 to Panama in 1908 instead of in 1913 as stipulated in the Hay-Bunau-Varilla treaty; Panama undertook to transfer to Colombia the first ten of these annuities as its contribution to the Colombian national debt incurred before secession; Colombia recognized Panama's independence; Colombia and Panama fixed the boundary between the two countries and agreed to submit jurisdiction over disputed areas to arbitration; the United States granted to Colombia free transit through the canal for troops, munitions, and warships; and the United States and Colombia promised to revise the treaty of 1846 in conformity with the new conditions.

The United States Senate ratified the treaty with Colombia on February 24, 1909 and that with Panama on March 3. Panama also ratified the two sections to which it was a party, but in Bogotá the tripartite convention struck a snag. Students organized protest demonstrations, street riots broke out, police guarded the United States legation, President Reyes resigned but withdrew his resignation the next day, members of Congress known to favor the treaties were openly threatened with assassination, and the authorities declared martial law. After three turbulent weeks Reyes advised Congress to close discussion of the pacts. The State Department in Washington shrugged off the Colombian rebuff with a cable dated June 11 to Paxton Hibben, temporary chargé d'affaires at Bogotá: "The . . . United States views with relative indifference the question of the ratification of our treaties by Colombia and Panama, whose interests are apparently much more concerned. . . . In view of the absurd distortion of this situation by public clamor the legation should make the above attitude well known and for the rest should maintain an impressive and dignified attitude. . . ." [10] Colombia's refusal to ratify caused the entire tripartite treaty to lapse, but the United States, unwilling to dismiss this desirable bunch of grapes as hopelessly sour, continued to make amiable gestures, one of which led to an unfortunate incident. When Secretary of State Philander C. Knox, planning a tour of the Caribbean republics in 1912, signified his desire to include a visit to Cartagena he was snubbed by the Colombian Foreign

Minister, Pedro Nel Ospina, who replied that he would consult the Cabinet but "speaking for myself . . . I take the liberty to point out that this might be an inopportune time for such a visit, considering that Colombia believes itself placed . . . in the position . . . of being the only member of the . . . family of independent nations . . . with which . . . the United States refuses to arbitrate. . . ." [11] Knox eliminated Colombia from his itinerary, and Nel Ospina, though applauded by many of his compatriots, was removed from office and officially censured for his breach of diplomatic courtesy.

Efforts to reach a solution were renewed soon after the commencement of the Democratic administration of Woodrow Wilson, and after several months of negotiation the United States envoy, Thaddeus Austin Thomson, and the Colombian Foreign Minister, Francisco José Urrutia, signed a new convention at Bogotá on April 6, 1914. The Thomson-Urrutia treaty contained two wholly new clauses whereby the United States, abandoning its arrogant position, offered unprecedented concessions to the offended Colombians. The first was a handsome apology: "The Government of the United States . . . expresses, in its own name and in the name of the people of the United States, sincere regret that anything should have occurred to interrupt or to mar the relations of cordial friendship that had so long subsisted between the two nations." [12] The second was a promise to pay Colombia as indemnity for the loss of the isthmus $25,000,000 within six months after exchange of ratifications.

This time the situation of 1909 was reversed: the Colombian Congress ratified the treaty on June 9, 1914, but the United States Senate procrastinated. The opposition was led by Republican senators who interpreted the apology and indemnification clauses as a repudiation of the policies of Theodore Roosevelt, which indeed they were. In 1915 the ex-President himself railed explosively against what he called the "blackmail treaty": "The proposed treaty is a crime against the United States. It is an attack upon the honor of the United States which if justified would convict the United States of infamy. It is a menace to the future well-being of our people. . . . The payment can only be justified upon the ground that this nation has played the part of a thief, or of a receiver of stolen goods." [13]

Throughout the four years of the World War the Senate, preoccupied with more urgent problems, postponed consideration of the Thomson-Urrutia pact from session to session. Early in 1916 the Foreign Relations Committee recommended reduction of the indemnity to $15,000,000 and alteration of the apology clause so as to make the expression of regret for past misdeeds mutual, but protests from Colombia induced the Senate to reject the amendments. After the armistice Wilson again urged speedy ratification. Although the death of Theodore Roosevelt in January 1919 removed the principal sentimental obstacle to the agreement the Republican legislators still insisted upon elimination of the apol- ogy. On July 29, 1919 the Senate committee, having deleted the "sincere regret" paragraph and introduced a few other changes of minor importance, reported the treaty favorably, but just as ratification appeared certain a controversy between the United States and Colombia over oil rights delayed action once more. During the World War American and British companies had invested huge sums in the development of Colombian oil deposits, and on June 20, 1919 the Bogotá government, alarmed at the rapid growth of foreign exploitation of the country's natural resources, decreed all subsoil hydrocarbons to be the property of the nation. The United State Senate supported the American oil interests and refused to consider the treaty pending settlement of the dispute. Although Colombia quickly suspended the public ownership decree and in December enacted laws confirming the property rights of the corporations, the treaty was not taken up again until the spring of 1921. On April 20 the Senate finally ratified it by a vote of 69 to 19 with the $25,000,000 indemnity intact but without the apology. That omission aroused Colombian ire, but after a long and acrimonious debate the Bogotá Congress ratified the modified treaty on December 24. On March 1, 1922 ratifications were exchanged at Bogotá, and the Thomson-Urrutia convention went into effect eight years after its signature.

Ratification of this treaty obliged Colombia to recognize Panamanian independence at last, but the inauguration of normal diplomatic relations between the two republics encountered further delay. Both governments stood upon their dignity, and neither wished to be the first to send its envoy to the other. After prolonged discussion the Panamanian minister presented his credentials in Bogotá on June 27, 1924, and the Colombian minister was received officially on July 9. On August 20 Colombia and Panama signed a treaty establishing their common boundary in general terms and providing for a joint commission to determine the exact line.

In 1914, when the Thomson-Urrutia treaty was signed, the development of Colombian oil fields was in its infancy, other American investments in Colombia were exceedingly small, and — though hope of future material benefits probably played some part

— the proposal to pay the $25,000,000 indemnity seems to have been very largely inspired by Wilsonian idealism, a sincere attempt to make amends to a wronged nation. By 1921, when the Senate finally ratified the treaty, idealism was on the wane and material considerations had become vastly more important. Pressure by the oil companies figured prominently — perhaps decisively — in the Senate's resolve to render tardy justice to Colombia. Whatever the motive, the payment has proved an excellent investment. If a relatively small number of capitalists reaped the more immediate and tangible benefits, the gain in improved relations not only with Colombia but with all of the Latin American republics has been of enormous value to the people of the United States in general. Although many other factors have contributed to a better understanding between the "colossus of the north" and the countries south of the Rio Grande, and although the *rapprochement* is still far from complete, the Thomson-Urrutia treaty may be considered the first important step in the development of the good neighbor policy pursued consciously, fairly consistently, and on the whole successfully since 1930.

Eight years after the Panama revolution, at the University of California Charter Day exercises held on March 23, 1911 in the Greek Theater at Berkeley, ex-President Roosevelt delivered an unfortunate speech that stirred up anew the hornets' nest of controversy. The Panama canal, he declared, "would not have been started if I had not taken hold of it, because if I had followed the traditional . . . method I should have submitted an admirable state paper . . . detailing all of the facts to Congress. . . . In that case there would have been a number of excellent speeches . . . in Congress; the debate would be proceeding at this moment with great spirit and the beginning of work on the canal would be fifty years in the future. Fortunately the crisis came at a period when I could act unhampered. Accordingly I took the isthmus, started the canal and then left Congress not to debate the canal, but to debate me. In portions of the public press the debate still goes on as to whether or not I acted properly in taking the canal. But while the debate goes on the canal does too, and they are welcome to debate me as long as they wish, provided that we can go on with the canal." [14]

The Colombian press seized upon the boastful phrase "I took the isthmus" as a belated confession of responsibility for the insurrection. Many newspapers throughout the United States violently attacked the speech while others defended it with equal vehemence.

The discord infected Congress, and on April 16 Representative
Henry T. Rainey of Illinois introduced a resolution providing for
an investigation by the House Committee on Foreign Affairs.
When the hearings opened on January 26, 1912 Rainey asserted
that "representatives of this Government made possible the revolution on the Isthmus. . . . I will . . . show that the declaration of independence . . . was prepared . . . in the office of Wilson [sic] Nelson Cromwell. I will show you that our State Department was cognizant of the fact that a revolution was to occur on
the 3d day of November, 1903. . . . My contention is that the part
we played for months prior to the revolution . . . is a stain upon
the history of this Government." [15] The committee inspected documents, listened to numerous witnesses — of whom the most volu-
ble was a member of the staff of the New York *World,* Henry N.
Hall — and issued a bulky report entitled *The Story of Panama.*
While this volume scarcely deserved Lord Charnwood's contemptuous dismissal as "totally worthless. . . . It should never again
be referred to as an authority for anything" [16] it certainly added
little of value to the stock of public information.

The people of the United States have every reason to rejoice in
the Panama canal as it exists today, but they have less cause to pride
themselves upon the method of its acquisition forty years ago.
From the start of negotiations Theodore Roosevelt adopted an arrogant policy towards Bogotá by no means warranted by the situation. Having persuaded himself that the Colombians were bandits and blackmailers he proceeded to treat them as such. It seems
fairly evident now that the obstacles in the way of an accord were
not in fact unsurmountable. Unquestionably the Colombian authorities were inept and exasperating, but practically every move
made by Washington was calculated to aggravate rather than allay
their suspicions. Patience, tact, a willingness to compromise on
minor points, a sincere attempt to understand Colombian senti-
ments and conceptions, a strict observance of Latin American etiquette, and a more generous financial arrangement would have
secured every concession the United States government desired
without violence, subsequent bitterness, and national dishonor.

Chapter 39. The Purchase

O N November 27, 1903 Amador, Boyd, and Carlos Arosemena, representing the junta, notified the president of the
Compagnie Nouvelle, Marius Bô, that the republic of Panama had assumed Colombia's obligations with respect to the concession and claimed in return the 50,000 shares of stock allotted to
Colombia in 1894. The Colombian chargé d'affaires in Paris,
Uribe, and the Colombian representative on the company's board
of directors, Samper, immediately threatened the company with
annulment of its charter if it should enter into negotiations with
Panama, and Samper further protested against his exclusion from
all board meetings held during the past month. On December 26
Uribe applied for a court order to compel the company to admit
Samper to its meetings. When the plea was rejected Uribe and the
fiscal agent of the Colombian government, Jorge Holguín, brought
suit before the Tribunal Civil de la Seine to forbid the company
to transfer its concession to the United States. The court action
appears to have been strongly supported if not actually conceived
by General Reyes, recently arrived in Paris after his futile sojourn
in Washington.

To plead the Colombian case the plaintiffs retained an eminent
French attorney, Gaston Brunet. Lucien Napoléon-Bonaparte
Wyse, acting independently, brought a similar injunction suit
against the canal company, and the two actions were presented simultaneously before the same tribunal. Wyse, who had no financial stake in the enterprise, seems to have been inspired by mixed
motives. As the original holder of the concession, the proud pioneer, he bitterly resented the domination of the Compagnie Nouvelle by the so-called *pénalitaires* — the majority stockholders who
had been practically forced to subscribe in order to evade criminal
prosecution for acts committed in the days of the Compagnie Universelle; as an ardent patriot he still clung to the forlorn hope that
by some miracle French capital and French engineers might be
able to complete the canal; and he avowedly detested Americans.
On December 21, 1903 he wrote to Gautron and Lemarquis: "Having been the initiator of this great work . . . I feel morally obliged
to protest against the disgraceful rape committed by the United

States in Panama, to the prejudice of Colombia's rights and the true interests of France. . . . It would be . . . imprudent to negotiate with President Roosevelt and his henchmen, breakers of plighted faith . . . and comparable . . . to common highwaymen. . . . We must protect an enterprise of world-wide importance conceived in France . . . from the excesses of Yankee jingoism and not permit our ancient prestige as champions of the oppressed, the neutral, and the weak to be destroyed forever in the sight of the universe. . . ." [1]

Neither Brunet's logic nor Wyse's rhetoric could prevail against the inescapable fact of Panamanian possession. On March 31, 1904 the court rejected the Colombian claim on the ground that Colombia had lost effective control of the isthmus, and at the same time it decided that Wyse was not qualified to sue a company with which he had no connection. Although Colombia failed to prevent the sale of the canal it eventually established its right to the 50,000 shares of stock. Even Cromwell, certainly no friend to Bogotá, recognized the justice of that claim: "I . . . reached the conclusion that, in honor and equity, those shares should be delivered to Colombia. Upon my decision . . . Panama . . . consented. . . ." [2]

On March 30, 1904 a resident of Chicago named Wilson brought a taxpayer's suit against the Secretary of the Treasury and the Compagnie Nouvelle to enjoin the purchase of the canal property on the grounds that "the Spooner Act applied only to a treaty with Colombia . . . the contract between the United States and the company was illegal . . . [and] the Constitution . . . did not permit the use of public funds for such a purpose. . . ." [3] Neither the Wilson suit, still pending at the time of the transfer though later thrown out of court, nor the possible revival of the Colombian and Wyse actions on appeal was permitted to delay the purchase, but the implied threat of seizure forced Cromwell to invent a method of payment immune to confiscation. Since French law prohibited the attachment of deposits in the Banque de France it was decided to remit the money to Paris at the expense of the Compagnie Nouvelle through J. P. Morgan and Company so that the United States would retain legal title to the funds until their actual payment into the Banque de France. It was stipulated that the price of the property, $40,000,000, should equal 206,000,000 francs. To execute the transfer Assistant Attorney Generals Charles Russell and W. A. Day went to Paris. On April 16, 1904 the deeds were signed at the United States embassy, and on April 23 a general meeting of the Compagnie Nouvelle stockholders passed resolutions ratifying the agreement and dissolving the company. On May

4 the canal property on the isthmus was formally delivered to representatives of the United States government, two days later the company handed over its plans and archives in Paris to Russell and Day, and on May 7 the United States acquired physical possession of the company's Panama Railroad stock.

The Compagnie Universelle had purchased 68,534 shares of Panama Railroad stock in 1881 and had subsequently picked up about 350 more, but the United States government aimed at acquisition of the entire issue of 70,000 shares and the elimination of all minority stockholders. On January 16, 1905 Secretary of War William Howard Taft wrote to Cromwell: "We have secured from the New . . . Company 68,887 shares . . . and . . . have purchased 100 shares additional, leaving a balance of 1013. . . . You will doubtless have greater facility in reaching the minority stockholders than anyone else who could assist us. . . . I therefore authorize you to buy all the shares . . . outstanding at a price of par and 5 per cent in lieu of dividend. . . . It is my purpose to invite Congress to pass an act authorizing the Attorney-General to begin a proceeding to condemn the outstanding shares . . . but of course if we are able to obtain the shares by negotiation it will save all parties . . . expense and annoyance. . . ." [4] The condemnation suits were never brought, for within a few months Cromwell had located every individual owner and purchased every remaining share at a total cost to the government of about $150,000.

By private contract the liquidator of the Compagnie Universelle and the directors of the Compagnie Nouvelle had agreed upon a division of the future canal profits (if any) in the ratio of 60% to the old company and 40% to the new; but that contract entered into in 1894 had made no provision for the sale of the property, and in February 1902 a new arrangement worked out by five arbitrators awarded the creditors of the old company a slightly larger share of the proceeds. In the final allotment 128,600,000 francs — approximately 62.5% of the total payment of 206,000,000 — went to the liquidator and 77,400,000 to the Compagnie Nouvelle. Since the Compagnie Nouvelle's assets included in addition an unexpended reserve of about 7,000,000 francs its 6796 stockholders, owning 650,000 shares of a par value of 100 francs each, received 129.78 francs per share, equivalent to a return of about 3% annually during the ten years of the company's existence. The distribution in three installments was completed on June 15, 1908. As owner of 50,000 shares Colombia collected 6,489,000 francs.

Called before the Senate Interoceanic Canals Committee in Feb-

ruary 1906, Cromwell explained these routine transactions at some
length but in spite of the heated denunciations and insistent demands of Senator Morgan refused repeatedly to answer questions
concerning matters he regarded as professional confidences. The
lawyer's taciturnity, though infinitely annoying to the senators, was
in fact perfectly correct. The committee, quite unjustifiably suspecting fraud in the distribution of the $40,000,000 to individual
creditors of the Compagnie Universelle and stockholders of the
Compagnie Nouvelle, complained that the companies had not
turned over their books to the United States and demanded a detailed account of these thousands of allotments. Cromwell retorted
that he did not know what distribution of the fund had been made
and that it was none of his business. He implied that it was no business of the United States either, which was true. On December 8,
1908 former Attorney General Knox wrote to President Roosevelt:
"This Government did not get the stock books of either the old or
new . . . company. We did not buy the corporations or their
stocks; we only bought the property. We had no dealings with the
old company at all. . . . In the absence of any suggestion of ir-
regularity . . . it was a matter of indifference to the United States
who owned the stock of the new company. The only question was,
did we want the property at the price. . . ." [5]
According to the not altogether reliable testimony of Henry N.
Hall, Cromwell, who had acted as counsel for the Compagnie Nouvelle since 1896 and who had labored and lobbied unceasingly in
its behalf, estimated the value of his firm's legal services at $800,-
000. When the company disputed the bill the matter was submitted
to the arbitration of three distinguished French attorneys, who on
February 21, 1907 awarded Sullivan and Cromwell (again according to Hall) the sum of $200,000.

While much of the criticism of the Roosevelt administration's
conduct in 1903 was amply warranted some of it, arising from political partisanship, was wholly baseless. The presidential campaign of 1908 was marked by an alleged attempt on the part of certain Democratic leaders to "smear" the Republican nominee, Taft,
with pitch left over from the Panama canal purchase. On October
3, a month before the election, the New York *World* published a
news item reputedly based on information furnished by Cromwell
himself through his press agent, Jonas Whitley, to the effect that
Cromwell, threatened with blackmail, had complained to the New
York district attorney, William Travers Jerome, "that the Democratic National Committee was considering the advisability of

making public a statement that . . . Cromwell, in connection with M. Bunau-Varilla, a French speculator, had formed a syndicate [in 1903, to purchase the canal property and resell it to the United States] . . . and that this syndicate included . . . Charles P. Taft, brother of William H. Taft, and Douglas Robinson, brother-in-law of President Roosevelt. Other men more prominent in the New York world of finance were also mentioned. . . . These financiers . . . because of their alleged information from high Government sources — were enabled to reap a rich profit. . . . According to the story . . . the syndicate . . . had . . . purchased for about $3,500,000 the stock and bonds of the defunct De Lesseps company, and of the newer concern which had taken over the old company. . . . It . . . fixed the profit of the syndicate at $36,500,000, this amount being divided among Government favorites in the world of politics and finance." [6] Cromwell had issued an immediate denial: "Neither I nor any one allied with me . . . ever bought, sold, dealt in, or ever made a penny of profit out of any . . . securities of either the old . . . or the New Panama Canal Co., or ever received . . . a single dollar of the forty millions paid by the United States. I make this the most sweeping statement that language can convey. . . . Of course, I do not refer to our regular compensation as counsel. . . . No member of the Taft family or Mr. Douglas Robinson ever had the remotest connection with Panama. . . . The names of Caesar and Napoleon might as well have been used. . . ." [7]

Although no evidence was ever uncovered of the existence of such a syndicate — and there is not the slightest reason to believe it ever did exist — the *World,* scenting a mystery in what was actually a routine distribution of assets, went to considerable trouble and expense to discover exactly what had become of the $40,000,-000. An investigator sent to Paris by the newspaper failed to obtain a list of the individual beneficiaries. Robinson and Charles Taft quickly cleared themselves of all suspicion of complicity in the imaginary plot, and a representative of the *World,* admitting the innocence of the two men, later asserted that Cromwell alone had been responsible for the introduction of their names. In all, the *World* devoted six articles, reproduced in several other newspapers in various cities, to the "conspiracy." On November 2, the day before the election, the Indianapolis *News* printed an editorial on the same subject while the *World* kept the pot boiling merrily with demands for a congressional investigation.

On December 15 Roosevelt sent an indignant special message to Congress: "These stories were first brought to my attention as pub-

lished in a paper in Indianapolis. . . . The stories were scurrilous
. . . libelous . . . and false in every essential particular. Mr.
Smith [Delavan Smith, editor of the Indianapolis *News*] shelters
himself behind the excuse that he merely accepted the statements
. . . in . . . the *World*. . . . It is idle to say that the known character of Mr. Pulitzer [Joseph Pulitzer, owner of the *World*] and his
newspaper are such that the statements in that paper will be believed by nobody; unfortunately, thousands of persons . . . believe . . . even . . . a newspaper published by Mr. Pulitzer. . . .
The wickedness of the slanders is only surpassed by their fatuity.
. . . In form, they are in part libels upon . . . Mr. Taft and Mr.
Robinson. . . . But they are in fact wholly, and in form partly, a
libel upon the United States Government. . . . It should not be
left to a private citizen to sue Mr. Pulitzer for libel. He should be
prosecuted . . . by the governmental authorities. . . . The Attorney-General has under consideration the form in which the proceedings . . . shall be brought. . . ." [8]

Roosevelt's anger at the false accusations was understandable
enough, but his proposal to make the government the plaintiff in
a libel suit was not only almost without precedent but in this instance exceedingly ill advised. On February 17, 1909 the District
of Columbia grand jury indicted the responsible officers of both
the *World* and the *News;* but when an attempt to remove the Indianapolis defendants to the District for trial failed the charges
were dropped, and new indictments were drawn up against the
World charging the circulation of 29 copies of each of the offending
issues on federal territory, specifically at West Point and in the
New York City post office. The *World,* protesting that since there
were "2809 Government reservations corresponding to West Point
and the post-office building, a newspaper of large circulation . . .
might be prosecuted from one end of the country to the other . . .
for an article that . . . happened to reach them in the ordinary
course of circulation," [9] raised the issue of freedom of the press and
claimed with some justice that the law to protect harbor defenses
and fortifications from malicious injury, under which the indictments were returned, could not legitimately be invoked to punish
libel.

The *World* sent agents to Paris, Panama, and even Bogotá to
collect material for an elaborate defense but in the end decided to
base its plea not upon the merits of the case, which would have involved acknowledgment of the existence of a federal libel law, but
upon the technical ground that the suit should have been brought
before a state instead of a federal court. The indictments were

thereupon dismissed, and when the government appealed the Supreme Court unanimously decided in favor of the newspaper on January 3, 1911. The libel went unpunished, and the unrepentant *World*, rejoicing that the "effort to revive the spirit of the alien and sedition laws, to establish the doctrine of lese majesty, had come to an inglorious end," [10] popped up once more like a jack-in-the-box: "The decision of the Supreme Court . . . while safeguarding the liberty of the press . . . yet leaves unanswered the question: 'Who got the money?' " [11]

Another question frequently posed at the time of the purchase was: "Did the United States government get its money's worth?" There can be no doubt that it did, and in full measure. The official and presumably conservative American estimate valued the French property as follows: [12]

Excavation useful to the canal	$25,389,240
Panama Railroad stock	9,644,320
Plant and material, used, and sold for scrap	2,112,063
Buildings used	2,054,203
Surveys, plans, maps, and records	2,000,000
Land	1,000,000
Clearings, roads, etc.	100,000
Ship channel in Panama Bay, four years' use	500,000
	$42,799,826

In 1909 a special committee computed the total volume of French excavation at 59,749,950 cubic meters or 78,146,960 cubic yards: 66,743,551 cubic yards by the old company and 11,403,409 by the new. But only 29,708,000 cubic yards or less than 40% of this total could be incorporated in the American lock canal. Many miles of partially excavated channel designed for a sea level waterway were drowned under the waters of Gatún Lake and as far as the Americans were concerned might as well never have been dug. Other sections nearer the terminals were abandoned for more advantageous locations, so that nearly all of the utilizable excavation was confined to the high central portion about 10 miles long which would have required cutting for either the lock or sea level project. Today traces of the French canal have all but disappeared except for a short stretch near the Atlantic end.

The chief value of the Panama Railroad as delivered to the United States in 1904 lay in its franchise and its ownership of real estate, which included practically the entire area of Colón, 70 buildings in Colón, 26 buildings in Panama, and 6 buildings and a pier at La Boca. The rolling stock was antiquated and nearly worthless. The roadbed was in poor condition and had to be almost completely rebuilt to meet the heavy demands of canal construction, while the creation of Gatún Lake eventually necessitated the abandonment of almost the whole of the original line and its relocation on higher ground farther east. Only for a few miles at either end does the present railroad follow the route laid out in 1850.

In addition to the property of the Panama Railroad the Compagnie Nouvelle transferred to the United States about 33,000 acres of land and 2265 buildings, including 1588 dwellings. The buildings, practically all of wood with galvanized iron roofs, varied in type from shacks 10 feet square to storehouses 300 feet long. All had suffered to some extent from dampness, termites, and neglect; some were destroyed at once, but most were patched up sufficiently to serve until replaced by modern structures. Each year as American construction expanded several hundred old French buildings were demolished, so that by the time the canal was opened in 1914 few remained in use.

The American engineers inherited enormous quantities of French machinery and equipment, much of which — notwithstanding all the pessimistic reports of rust, rot, and dilapidation — they found unexpectedly useful and efficient. Several hundred French dump cars, though small and unequipped with the safety devices prescribed by American regulations, served during the first years of construction, and the last of them were not withdrawn until July 1911. Diminutive French and Belgian locomotives looking, as Roosevelt told Congress, like "the veriest toys" [13] beside the powerful American engines sturdily hauled trainloads of rock and earth throughout the entire 10-year period. "No doubt," the President prophesied, "a quarter of a century hence this new machinery, of which we are so proud, will similarly seem out of date. . . ." [14] Experiments with French steam shovels proved less successful, and their use was discontinued in June 1905 after a year's trial.

But it was the French dredges that gave the Americans the most welcome surprise. In September 1907 the *Canal Record* reported: "By the expenditure of $20,000 . . . an old French ladder . . . dredge, which had been lying in the Rio Grande river above La Boca for more than twenty years, has been restored. . . . This dredge . . . will do more work than a modern dipper dredge costing $102,500. In reconstructing . . . all the essential parts used were French." [15] This dredge established such a satisfactory record that six others were reassembled from scattered parts at a total saving of at least $500,000 over the cost of new equipment.

Chapter 40. Commissions and Technicians

THE FIRST year of American canal administration was a year of bungling, bickering, and incompetence. When in compliance with the Spooner act President Roosevelt appointed the Isthmian Canal Commission in March 1904 he selected skilled engineers rather than executives accustomed to the organization of gigantic projects — a costly mistake which he soon had cause to regret. The seven original members were Rear Admiral John G. Walker, the chairman, who had headed two previous commissions; Major General George W. Davis, governor of the Canal Zone; Colonel Frank Joseph Hecker, who resigned in November; and four civil engineers, William Hubert Burr, Benjamin Morgan Harrod, William Barclay Parsons, and Carl Ewald Grunsky. On May 9 the President placed the commission under the direct supervision of his Secretary of War, Taft.

The position of chief engineer was awarded on May 6 to John Findley Wallace, who after many years of experience on various midwestern railroads had served successively as construction engineer, chief engineer, second vice president, assistant general manager, and finally general manager of the Illinois Central lines. Colonel William Crawford Gorgas, fresh from a brilliantly successful campaign to eradicate yellow fever and malaria in Havana, was appointed chief sanitary officer, a post scarcely less important in disease-ridden Panama than that of chief engineer. But neither Wallace nor Gorgas was at that time a member of the commission, and both were obliged to take orders from and suffer innumerable rebuffs at the hands of their administrative superiors.

After one brief visit to the isthmus in April 1904 just before the transfer the members of the commission, except Davis, returned to Washington and remained there. While all worked hard and conscientiously their efforts to supervise the vital preliminary operations by absent treatment soon broke down completely. The commissioners wastefully duplicated and often nullified each other's activities. John F. Stevens, who succeeded Wallace as chief engineer, ridiculed "the endeavor to decide and act upon the most trivial matters at a distance of 2,000 miles by a body of men who were

apparently unable to agree with each other or with anybody else.
. . . ." ¹ Every detail of procedure had to be submitted to Washington, passed upon by each commissioner, and approved only after
long and exasperating delay, if at all. Wallace, Gorgas, and the
other officials on the isthmus, struggling with titanic problems demanding prompt solutions, had far too little authority. The combination of faulty organization, bureaucratic methods, executive
ineptitude, petty economy, remote control, and lack of a comprehensive long-range policy almost wrecked the American canal enterprise at the outset.

Much of the futility of the first commission must be ascribed to
the curious personality of the chairman. Admiral Walker, whom
Gorgas irreverently called "the old man of the sea," ² had served
his country well in the preliminary negotiations for the purchase
of the canal, but neither by training nor by temperament was he
equipped to direct the construction of the great waterway. His
"very appearance — his erect figure, his be-whiskered face, his air
of command — fairly suggested the past generation to which he
belonged. . . . The fear that something like French wastefulness
and peculation would stain the American achievement haunted
him day and night. . . . Economy, rather than construction,
therefore became his byword. . . . 'Requisitions' became the hor-
ror of his existence. . . . The Admiral had such an aversion to
spending money, even . . . for indispensable work, that at times
he would not even open communications." ³

The entire organization soon became hopelessly snarled in red
tape. On the isthmus the accounting system was so cumbersome
that the hire of one cart for a few hours required the filling out of
six separate vouchers, and the paper used in the pay roll for 1500
laborers for two weeks weighed 103 pounds. Requisitions for essential construction materials and for even more urgently needed
medical supplies went unheeded for months, and when the be-
grudged purchases did finally arrive they were often pared down
below the point of usefulness. Equipment would reach the isthmus
lacking indispensable parts, and more weary weeks would elapse
before the missing portions turned up in another steamer. Of one
large requisition for medicines and hospital necessities filed early
in August 1904 not a single item had been received by the following February. The first consignment of a shipment of water pipe
ordered in August arrived five months later by slow sailing
schooner, and four more months passed before the requisition was
completely filled. Fuming at these delays, Wallace sent cable after
cable to Washington only to be reprimanded by the penny-pinch-

ing Walker, who informed him by letter (not by cable) that the commission "presumed that on account of my free use of a telegraph wire when I was general manager of the Illinois Central Railroad, I did not appreciate the fact that cables were expensive." [4]

To some extent the confusion of these early months grew out of a commendable but shortsighted desire to speed up the work of actual construction, to satisfy the newspapers and confound the critics by "making the dirt fly." Instead of concentrating on preliminary steps the commission unwisely attempted to start excavation much too soon. The result was chaos.

The transfer of the French property on the isthmus took place on the morning of May 4, 1904, when the representative of the Compagnie Nouvelle handed the keys of the storehouses to the authorized deputy of the United States government, Lieutenant Mark Brooke of the Engineer Corps. No ceremony marked the conveyance, to the great scandal and disappointment of the Panamanian authorities, who considered such casual informality unbecoming to the historic importance of the occasion. Acting under the commission's orders Brooke assumed temporary charge and kept the small force of about 700 laborers formerly employed by the French at work until the arrival of Governor Davis a fortnight later.

Within a few weeks relations between the United States and the new republic of Panama were severely strained by what Taft called "an unfortunate mistake in our policy in respect to the customs law of the Zone." [5] After June 24, when the domestic tariff laws of the United States were first applied in the Canal Zone, goods from the United States entered free of duty while imports from foreign countries, including Panama, were obliged to pay the high rates imposed by the Dingley act. Diplomatic notes flew back and forth between Panama and Washington while the aggrieved local merchants conducted so effective a compaign of passive resistance that Davis hesitated to enforce the tariff rules pending a settlement. Other injustices increased Panamanian irritation. Letter postage between the United States and the republic of Panama cost five cents but between the United States and the Zone only two cents, so that any resident of Panama City or Colón needed only to step across the street to mail his letters at an American post office at the lower rate and thus deprive Panama of legitimate revenue. Again, the opening of ports of entry under United States jurisdiction at the Zone settlements of La Boca and Cristóbal threatened with ruin the trade of the adjacent harbors of Panama and Colón in the republic.

The Panamanian government, jealous of its sovereignty, however nominal, over the Canal Zone and fearful of reduction to a
status of complete dependence upon the United States, protested
promptly and vociferously. Taft, commissioned by Roosevelt to
settle the dispute, reached Colón on November 27, 1904 and remained on the isthmus about ten days. The genial personality of
the rotund Secretary of War produced an excellent impression,
and on December 3, after numerous discussions interspersed with
the usual receptions, banquets, and public speeches, Taft issued an
executive order designed to remedy the abuses complained of by
Panama. Free importations into the Zone were limited to coal, fuel
oil, construction materials, and merchandise in transit to points
outside the isthmus. Other sections repealed the tariff on articles
brought into the Zone from Panama, extended the two-cent letter
rate to the republic, and provided for currency regulation, voting
privileges for Panamanian residents of the Zone, the construction
of a highway to run 6 miles out of Panama City, the maintenance
of one of the American hospitals for the use of Panamanian patients, and provisional delimitation of the Zone pending definite
location of the canal line.

Before actual excavation could be successfully undertaken on a
large scale a number of vital preliminary problems had to be solved.
Although the French had left excellent maps and records probable
changes in the location and type of the American canal and the
invention of improved methods of masonry construction necessitated new surveys and additional borings to determine the precise
route for the waterway and the most advantageous sites for locks,
dams, power installations, and other structures. New wharves, terminal yards, warehouses, machine shops, and coal depots had to be
designed and built. It was necessary to rehabilitate the decrepit
railroad, to strengthen bridges, lay heavier rails, bolster up crumbling embankments, extend spurs and sidings, double-track the entire line, order more powerful locomotives and larger cars for
passengers and freight. While many of the old French buildings
could be repaired and remodeled, new barracks for bachelors and
smaller residences for families were urgently needed to house the
enormous staff and the thousands of laborers who would soon be
swarming into the Zone. Extensive improvements outside the Zone,
placed under the control of the United States by the Hay-Bunau-
Varilla treaty, also had to be planned and executed.

By the end of 1904 the inefficiency of the commission had become too apparent to be tolerated. Work on the isthmus was al-

23. REAR ADMIRAL
JOHN G. WALKER

24. THEODORE PERRY SHONTS

25. JOHN FINDLEY WALLACE

26. JOHN FRANK STEVENS

SIBERT   BLACKBURN ROUSSEAU BISHOP, *secretary* HODGES

                GOETHALS   GORGAS   GAILLARD

27. THIRD ISTHMIAN CANAL COMMISSION

most at a standstill. Supplies trickled in far too slowly, and when
they arrived there were no adequate facilities for unloading, stor-
ing, or transporting them to the construction centers. Hundreds of
disgruntled employees threw up their jobs and went home, while
the heads of departments cursed the ineptitude of the so-called
technicians hired by the commission's agents in the United States
and sent to the isthmus. On December 20 Wallace, exasperated by
months of unavailing struggle against bureaucracy, suggested to
Taft a reduction of the unwieldy seven-headed commission to a
group of three: a chairman in Washington and the governor and
chief engineer on the isthmus. Taft signified his approval, and on
January 13, 1905 Roosevelt requested Congress to authorize the
change. When Congress failed to pass the necessary amendment to
the Spooner act the President called for the resignation of the entire commission. On April 1, 1905 he appointed another commission of seven members, but this time he ingeniously tried to attain
the superior efficiency of a smaller group by directing the new commission to designate three of its members as an executive committee. This committee, which would do almost all the real work, was
to meet twice a week at the governor's office on the isthmus; the
other members, little more than figureheads, were to hold regular
meetings only four times a year.

The second Isthmian Canal Commission was composed of Theodore Perry Shonts, chairman; Charles E. Magoon, governor of the
Zone; Wallace, chief engineer, now awarded the seat on the commission which he should have had from the beginning; Rear Admiral Endicott, a member of the Ludlow commission of 1895;
Brigadier General Hains, who had served on the two Walker commissions of 1897 and 1899; Colonel Ernst, also a veteran of the 1899
commission; and Harrod, the only member of the first Isthmian
Canal Commission to be reappointed. In September 1905 Joseph
Bucklin Bishop was designated secretary to the commission, but he
was not a member. Each commissioner drew a salary of $7500 a
year, and in addition the chairman received $22,500, the chief en-
gineer $17,500, and the governor $10,000. The dominant personality in the group was the chairman, a Pennsylvanian who had
built, operated, and partially owned a number of midwestern railroads. A far more experienced and imaginative executive than the
cheeseparing tradition-bound Walker, Shonts brought to his new
position enormous energy, a real talent for organization, and in
general sound judgment. Before he accepted the chairmanship he
had insisted upon two conditions to which Roosevelt agreed: he
was to have absolute authority subject to the President's approval,

and he reserved the right to resign as soon as he had perfected the canal organization, solved the mechanical problems, and set the construction program going at full speed. Both Shonts and Magoon were "practical" men with the limitations as well as the virtues of their kind, but in manner "they were quite unlike — Mr. Shonts aggressive, tactless, gruff, and domineering; Mr. Magoon polite, likable, and charming." [6]

Wallace had been summoned to Washington to assist in the organization of the new commission. He had had ample opportunity to air his grievances and had received solemn and undoubtedly sincere assurances of reform from his fellow commissioners. There were to be no more delays, no more niggling economies, no more irritating restrictions, no more red tape. When he went back to Panama on May 24 after an absence of almost two months he seemed completely satisfied with the new conditions and ready to co-operate wholeheartedly with the commission. But on June 5, after only two weeks on the isthmus, he suddenly upset the applecart by cabling Taft for permission to return to the United States on furlough to attend to urgent private affairs. Mystified and annoyed but hoping for the best, Taft reluctantly consented.

Unquestionably Wallace's patience had been severely tried during the past year, and he was clearly suffering from jangled nerves and a profound sense of frustration. He did not lack ability and had tried valiantly to bring order out of confusion. Perhaps no chief engineer could have done more under the meddlesome supervision of the first commission, and he deserved both sympathy for his tribulations and credit for his accomplishment. Nevertheless his defection at this inauspicious moment left a stain on his reputation which has never entirely faded. The impropriety of his untimely desertion was aggravated by conditions on the isthmus, which during his sojourn in Washington had gone from bad to worse. An outbreak of yellow fever in April caused a veritable panic, and in the rush to escape frightened employees crowded every departing steamer. In a letter to Taft dated June 8 Wallace himself admitted that upon his return from Washington "the entire organization was found in a state of more or less demoralization." [7] Yet in the same letter he assured Taft that "I know of no time during the next year when the work will be in better condition to permit of my absence. It is thoroughly organized, everything possible that can be foreseen provided for, and a feeling of loyalty and enthusiasm now permeates the entire personnel." [8] Surely this was a miraculous improvement to have taken place within a fortnight.

Governor Magoon wrote to Taft suggesting that Wallace's real reason for wishing to leave the isthmus was an offer of a more lucrative position from a private engineering firm in the United States, but that he might be induced to reconsider if given Shonts's post as chairman with much fuller authority and a salary of $50,000 or $60,000. Magoon followed this almost immediately with a second letter: "I have had another talk with Wallace and am inclined to think I judged him too harshly in concluding that he was attempting to 'squeeze' you. He seems to be fully prepared to quit, but willing to remain upon terms that seem to him justifiable. . . . There is no difference in its effect on the public service, but there may be considerable difference between the two mental attitudes." [9]

Taft, usually good-natured but now thoroughly incensed, cared nothing about Wallace's mental attitudes. When the engineer reached the United States Taft was about to leave for the Philippines, but there was time for one stormy meeting at the Hotel Manhattan in New York on June 25. Although Wallace had requested a private interview Taft insisted upon Cromwell's presence as a witness. Brushing aside the engineer's explanations and excuses, Taft poured out his wrath and peremptorily demanded Wallace's resignation, which he received the next day. Wallace emphatically denied that he had been tempted by the prospect of a higher salary and ascribed his retirement solely to dissatisfaction with the commission's bungling — an explanation which would have been plausible enough had he resigned before the recent reorganization but which sounded less convincing now that steps had been taken to remedy the conditions of which he complained. There is reason to believe that fear of yellow fever played some part in his "desertion."

Fortunately the government was able to find an admirable successor to Wallace within three days of the latter's resignation. John Frank Stevens, born in Maine in 1853, had acquired a distinguished reputation as a railroad engineer and executive. At the time of the canal crisis he was on the point of sailing to the Philippines as consulting engineer for the construction of new railroads, and the proposal of a last-minute change of plan left him cold: "When I received the first offer to become chief engineer of the canal, I declined it. Then I was asked to meet . . . Cromwell in New York . . . and after listening an hour or two to his silver-tongued arguments I consented . . . with conditions." [10] At a subsequent conference at Oyster Bay Stevens made those conditions clear to Roosevelt: "That I was not to be hampered or handicapped by anybody high or low. . . . I also told him that I . . . could make no promise to remain until the work was fully completed, but that I would stay . . . until I had made its success certain, or had proved it to be a failure, and that I should . . . exercise my own judgment in both matters. He raised no objection. . . . He gave me no orders but told me to feel free to consult with him in any or all matters. He carried out his promises to the very letter and supported me with all his vast power. His cutting of corners and red tape was a joy." [11]

Obviously there was danger of a conflict between the free hand conceded to Stevens, who was not a member of the commission and did not become one until a few weeks before his retirement in April 1907, and the absolute authority previously granted to the chairman. But Shonts was wise enough to confine his own activities to the Washington office and keep his hands off the isthmus, so no serious clash occurred. "My relations with the commission," Stevens wrote, ". . . were very harmonious. . . . Theoretically, the commission was supposed to supervise my work. Practically, it did nothing of the kind. It never ordered or even suggested in a single instance my line of procedure. . . . The members rightly assumed . . . that it was a one-man job. . . ." [12] This was a welcome change from the heckling and hampering interference of the first commission. Presumably the new-born harmony owed much to the tact of Stevens himself, "a man of serenity and calm, who never hurried and was always ahead of his work. . . ." [13]

When the new chief engineer reached Panama on July 26, 1905 he found "no organization worthy of the name; no answerable head who could delegate authority and exact responsibility; no cooperation . . . between what might charitably be called the departments — quite the contrary, and a disposition (not shared by the engineers) to believe that the construction of a successful canal . . . was a very dubious project. . . . There was already in service a lot of good engineering personnel, enough to form the nucleus of an organization. All it needed . . . was faith in a leader. . . ." [14] Stevens promptly set to work to inspire that faith. Early in 1906 correspondents of the *Independent* reported that "by his democratic manner and businesslike ways, [Stevens] has done wonders in heartening up the men after the general demoralization of last spring. He is regarded almost universally with great confidence and affection by the employees. . . ." [15] He was "not an office engineer, but a 'mixer.' . . . He drops in for an unexpected meal at some mess where the men are grumbling, and afterwards expresses his opinion of the men or the manager in language that is very forcible and not at all polite." [16] Any laborer could bring his grievances to Stevens (whose passion for cigars had earned him the nickname of "Big Smoke") and be assured of a courteous hearing and a fair decision.

The second commission, wiser than its predecessor, saw at once that excavation on a large scale must be postponed until terminal facilities could be provided and the problems of housing, subsistence, and health solved. Nevertheless some digging continued in the Culebra Cut, and the debris was removed in little French dump cars rattling over what Stevens called "lines which, by the utmost stretch of the imagination, could not be termed railroad tracks." [17] In addition to other excellent qualities Stevens was blessed with a sprightly wit, and even his official reports — generally the dullest form of literature — exhaled the salty tang of a sea wind. "There are three diseases in Panama," he announced soon after his arrival. "They are yellow fever, malaria, and cold feet; and the greatest of these is cold feet." [18] The problem of canal construction, he declared, "is one of magnitude and not of miracles. . . ." [19] Concerning the rusty broken-down Panama Railroad he wrote: "About the only claim for good work . . . was that there had been no collisions for some time. A collision has its good points as well as its bad ones — it indicates that there is something moving on the railroad." [20]

Among Stevens's most useful contributions were his judicious choice of dumping sites, his layout of a complex but elastic trackage system on different levels within the Culebra Cut, and his efficient co-ordination of spoils train schedules with excavation. Thus the capacity of the cars to haul away earth and rock kept pace with the constantly varying output of the steam shovels; trains did not have to wait for their loads, and shovels did not remain idle for want of rolling stock. But for some time progress was hampered by uncertainty regarding the design of the canal. The commission was still toying with the idea of a sea level waterway as an alternative to the lock canal, and while some preliminary work could be adapted to either project much of it — for example the location of the principal dumps — could not be carried far while the final choice remained in doubt. "And as the gift of prophecy is withheld from us in these latter days," Stevens noted, "all we can do now is to make such arrangements as may look proper as far ahead as we can see." [21]

On June 24, 1905 Roosevelt issued an executive order appointing a board of consulting engineers to determine once and for all

the most advantageous type of canal. Of the 13 members 8 were
Americans: the chairman, General Davis, former governor of
the Zone; Alfred Noble, once on the Ludlow commission of
1895; William B. Parsons and William H. Burr, both ex-members
of the first Isthmian Canal Commission; General Abbot, formerly
on the Compagnie Nouvelle's technical commission; Frederic P.
Stearns, chief engineer of Boston's Metropolitan Water and Sewerage Board; Joseph Ripley, general superintendent of the Sault
Ste. Marie or "Soo" canal; and Isham Randolph, chief engineer of
the Sanitary District of Chicago. The foreign members included
E. Quellennec, consulting engineer of the Suez canal, and Adolphe
Guérard, inspector general in the French Public Works Department; William Henry Hunter, chief engineer of the Manchester
canal and former member of the Compagnie Nouvelle's technical
commission; Eugen Tincauzer, Prussian state architect and engineer; and J. W. Welcker, chief engineer and director of Dutch
waterways.

The board convened in Washington on September 1, 1905 and
submitted its reports on January 10, 1906. The committee on lock
canals proposed four projects, two with summit level at 60 feet and
two at 85 feet, differing chiefly in the location of the locks and varying in cost from $141,236,000 to $175,929,720. All estimates included 20% for contingencies and administration but nothing for
sanitation, civil government, or interest on the investment. The
sea level design contemplated a depth of 40 feet, minimum bottom widths in earth of 150 feet and in rock of 200 feet, a dam at
Gamboa to control the Chagres floods, and a tidal lock at the Pacific end. The estimated cost was $247,021,200 and the construc-
tion period 12 to 13 years, about two years longer than for a lock
canal.

In addition to these plans conceived by the board itself several
individuals submitted projects for consideration. Bunau-Varilla
presented his pet scheme (supported as always by reams of statistics and accompanied by a fanfare of publicity) for a temporary
lock canal with summit level at 130 feet, to be completed and
opened in 4 years and then progressively lowered stage by stage
without interruption of traffic or reduction of earning capacity until it reached sea level and became the "straits of Panama." While
admitting the plan's theoretical feasibility the board considered
Bunau-Varilla's estimates of both time and money far too low. The
board similarly rejected on both technical and financial grounds
three lock canal projects evolved by Lindon W. Bates of New York,
providing respectively for summit levels at 27, 62, and 97 feet. A

plan for a lock canal at the 100-foot level offered by Major Cassius E. Gillette of the Engineer Corps met the same fate.

The choice then lay between a sea level canal and one with locks at a summit elevation of either 60 or 85 feet. The board failed to reach a unanimous decision: 8 members, including all of the foreign delegates plus Davis, Parsons, and Burr, voted for the sea level plan; while the other Americans handed in a minority report in favor of an 85-foot lock canal with three locks at Gatún, one at Pedro Miguel, and two at Sosa Hill, to cost about $140,000,000.

On February 5, 1906 the Isthmian Canal Commission overrode the majority opinion of the consulting board and chose the 85-foot lock canal, with one member — Endicott — dissenting. Stevens, who had great influence, wrote to Shonts that "even at the same cost in time and money . . . I would favor the . . . lock canal plan in preference to . . . the proposed sea-level canal." [22] Both Roosevelt and Taft agreed with Stevens and the commission, and when the President transmitted the reports to Congress on February 19 he recommended adoption of the lock design. On June 21 the Senate by a vote of 36 to 31 passed the act authorizing the lock canal; the House concurred on June 27; and on the 29th, one day before adjournment, the bill was enacted into law.

After three decades of operation the decision to build a canal with locks rather than one at sea level appears fully vindicated. The transit is smooth, rapid, and safe; none of the catastrophes predicted by advocates of the sea level project, such as failure of the lock mechanism or collapse of the Gatún dam, have come to pass. Even during its wildest rampages the Chagres River, which in spite of dams and diversions would always have constituted a grave menace to a narrow sea level canal, now flows harmlessly into Gatún Lake, which is so large that a Chagres flood cannot raise its level more than a few inches. Before the completion of the auxiliary Madden dam in 1935 floods did interrupt traffic on rare occasions but never for more than a few hours at a time. Admittedly the lock canal is more expensive to maintain and operate, but the difference is much less than the interest on the additional construction cost of a sea level strait, which in any event would require one tide lock at the Pacific entrance. Moreover the slides which so materially increased the difficulties and cost of construction of the present canal would have caused far more serious trouble and expense had the excavation been carried 85 feet deeper. There is only one valid objection to the lock canal, and that is a drawback that could not have been foreseen in 1906: its greater vulnerability to attack from the air. Fortunately at Panama the threat is lessened by the dupli-

cate arrangement of each lock in twin chambers, both of which
would have to be severely damaged to cripple the transit; and the
third set of locks now under construction at some distance from
the present canal line will when completed further decrease whatever danger may exist.

By the end of 1906 a vast amount of preparatory work had been
accomplished. The canal area had been transformed from a pestilential death-trap into the most healthful region in the tropics;
hundreds of buildings had been erected for quarters, mess houses,
offices, and warehouses; two spacious wharves, a modern coal-hoist-
ing plant, and a terminal railroad yard had been completed at
Cristóbal and another yard almost finished at La Boca; the Panama
Railroad had been thoroughly overhauled, re-equipped, and dou-
ble-tracked with heavier rails; the water systems, sewers, and street
paving of Panama City and Colón were almost finished; the departments had been reorganized, and the administrative machinery
was running smoothly.

Now that the lock canal had been decided upon it was possible
to go ahead with detailed plans for construction and excavation.
Stevens and his technical staff carefully plotted the exact line of
the canal from the Atlantic entrance in Limón Bay, through a short
channel at sea level, up the triple flight of Gatún locks to the 85-
foot level of Gatún Lake, across the lake — the largest artificial
body of water in the world until 1936, when the completion of
Boulder dam created the still larger Lake Mead — to the outlet of
the Chagres at Gamboa, through the 10-mile Culebra Cut to Pedro
Miguel lock, across another and smaller artificial lake, down a double flight of locks at Sosa Hill, and out through a dredged channel
in Panama Bay to deep water in the Pacific. To hold back the waters of Gatún Lake an immense dam was to be constructed across
the Chagres just west of the locks with a spillway to permit regulation of the lake level. Smaller dams were designed near the Pacific
terminus. All locks were to be in pairs, side by side, for the accommodation of two-way traffic; each chamber would have a usable
length of 1000 feet, width of 100 feet, and depth of 40 feet.

The canal as actually constructed follows this plan closely except
for two important changes. Late in 1907 it was decided to move
the double flight of locks nearest the Pacific from Sosa Hill to Miraflores, 3 or 4 miles farther inland, partly because the new site offered more stable foundations for a dam and partly because it provided greater protection against bombardment from the sea. In the
same year, at the request of the General Board of the navy, the com-

mission somewhat reluctantly agreed to increase the width of all lock chambers to 110 feet.

In November 1906 Theodore Roosevelt, breaking the hitherto inviolate tradition that no President should leave the United States during his term of office, visited the isthmus. He deliberately chose November, one of the rainiest and least salubrious months, in order to see the country at its worst. The season obligingly lived up to its reputation. During the three days of his sojourn he was constantly drenched by tropical deluges, the Chagres rose in one of the highest floods experienced in many years, and the entire Zone turned into a sea of mud. In spite of his discomfort the energetic President diligently inspected the excavations and the sites of the proposed locks and dams, sped through Colón and Panama City, visited hospitals, schools, police stations, storehouses, machine shops, quarters, kitchens, bathhouses, dropped in without warning for a meal at one of the commission messrooms, interviewed everyone in sight, and attended a formal dinner and reception given in his honor by President Amador. Having half drowned and wholly exhausted every member of his party except himself, Roosevelt returned to Washington well satisfied on the whole with what he had seen. But he still maintained that the organization suffered from divided authority: "A seven-headed commission is . . . a clumsy executive instrument. We should have but one commissioner, with such heads of departments and other officers under him as we may find necessary." [23]

A few months later Roosevelt unexpectedly found himself in a position to appoint his one-man commission in effect if not in form. In January 1907 Shonts reminded Roosevelt of his promise to permit his withdrawal as soon as the preliminary work had been completed and the excavation well begun. These conditions had now been fulfilled, and Shonts proposed to retire on March 4 to become president of the Interborough-Metropolitan Company of New York. The President reluctantly consented "merely because I do not feel justified in preventing your acceptance of the position you have been asked to take. . . . You have shown . . . such energy, administrative capacity, fertility of resource and judgment in handling men, together with such entire devotion to your work, that I hardly know whether most to regret the fact that the National Government is to lose you, or most to congratulate those who are to profit by your services. . . ." [24]

From March 4 to April 1 Stevens, belatedly awarded a seat on the commission, served as chairman as well as chief engineer. His work during the past two years had been eminently satisfactory, he

was popular with both his superiors and his subordinates, and had
he chosen to remain in charge John Frank Stevens, not George
Washington Goethals, would be the name recorded in history as that
of the builder of the Panama canal. But Stevens too had Roosevelt's
promise to release him at the end of the preparatory period; though
profoundly interested in the canal he really preferred his own work
as a railroad engineer. The resignation of Shonts and the prospect
of an administrative upheaval crystallized his already half-formed
resolution to retire, and he now sent in his own resignation, effective April 1, which the President — again with deep regret — accepted. Although attended by none of the fireworks that had accompanied Wallace's departure Stevens's action produced a buzz of
rumors concerning violent quarrels behind the scenes. His own
somewhat vague denial of these stories, published long afterwards,
may have been the simple truth; if not it did little to clear up the
mystery: "Various reasons for my resignation were given by irresponsible scribblers. . . . I resigned for purely personal reasons,
which were in no way, directly or indirectly related to the building
of the canal, or with anyone connected with it. . . . I knew . . .
that the work was so well organized . . . that competent engineers
. . . could be found to carry it on to a successful completion. If I
had not known all this, I would have remained as chief engineer." [25]

The second Isthmian Canal Commission now rapidly disintegrated. Wallace's seat had remained empty since 1905; Ernst had
resigned in June 1906; Magoon had been called away in September to serve as provisional governor of Cuba and to restore order
in that republic, torn by political dissension; Shonts had just retired. On March 16, 1907 the other three members — Hains, Harrod, and Endicott — also resigned, leaving the field clear for a
wholly new organization. The preliminary phase of canal work
which had lasted for three years — a phase characterized successively by "precipitation, demoralization, preparation" [26] — had
come to an end.

Chapter 41. Army Régime

FOR the third time within three years Roosevelt found himself obliged to appoint a new Isthmian Canal Commission and a new chief engineer. Heartily sick of disruptions, he now determined to place the work "in charge of men who will stay on the job until I get tired of having them there, or till I say they may abandon it. I shall turn it over to the army." [1] But not to the army exclusively; the third and last commission which assumed its duties on April 1, 1907 was composed of four army officers, one naval officer, and two civilians: Lieutenant Colonel George W. Goethals, chairman; Colonel Gorgas, chief sanitary officer since 1904 but now seated on the commission for the first time; Major David Du Bose Gaillard; Major William Luther Sibert; Rear Admiral Harry Harwood Rousseau; Joseph C. S. Blackburn, ex-senator from Kentucky; and Jackson Smith, head of the division of labor and quarters under the second commission. All but the last two remained until the end or almost the end of the construction period. Smith resigned in September 1908 and was replaced on the commission by Lieutenant Colonel Harry Foote Hodges; Blackburn retired in December 1909 to be succeeded by Maurice Hudson Thatcher, a Kentucky lawyer, whose place was in turn filled in August 1913 for the last few months of the commission's existence by Richard L. Metcalfe.

Exercising triple authority as chairman of the commission, chief engineer of the canal, and president of the Panama Railroad and its subsidiary steamship line, Goethals wielded far greater power than any previous commissioner. That power was further augmented on January 8, 1908 by Roosevelt's executive order proclaiming him the supreme head of the commission, a virtual dictator responsible only to the Secretary of War and the President — perhaps the "most absolute despot in the world . . . [who] could command the removal of a mountain from the landscape, or of a man from his dominions, or of a salt-cellar from that man's table." [2] This was certainly a violation of the spirit if not the letter of the Spooner law, which prescribed a commission of seven executives presumably equal in rank. Goethals frankly admitted that his despotism involved a radical departure from democratic principles but insisted that the task could not have been accomplished under any other system. He was probably right. Both Roosevelt and Taft vigorously opposed and successfully thwarted every effort to limit Goethals's jurisdiction. They had had enough experience with too many cooks.

George Washington Goethals was born in Brooklyn on June 29, 1858, attended public schools in Brooklyn and Manhattan, entered City College at the age of 14, and commenced his military career at West Point in 1876. Years later, when a private contractor offered him an enormous salary to retire from the army and abandon the Panama canal, Goethals declined with this explanation: "All my training, all my education, has been at the expense of the public. . . . I owe it to the public to stay here until the Canal is finished." [3] After his graduation in 1880 he studied for two years at an army engineer school near New York, then passed two more years in survey and reconnaissance work at Vancouver Barracks in what was then Washington Territory. In 1884 he married Miss Effie Rodman of New Bedford and in the same year was assigned to duty with an engineer force engaged in the construction of locks and dams in the Ohio River district. From 1885 to 1889 he taught classes in civil and military engineering at West Point. The next five years were devoted to the design and construction of locks and dams on the Cumberland and Tennessee Rivers in the region now embraced within the great Muscle Shoals hydraulic system. During this period he designed and successfully completed a lock with the then unprecedented lift of 26 feet. In 1894 Goethals was called to Washington, where he spent four years as assistant to the Chief of Engineers. During the Spanish-American War he served briefly in Puerto Rico on the staff of General John Rutter Brooke and on one occasion was threatened with court-martial (but never brought to trial) for his unauthorized use, as a foundation under an emergency wharf for which no lumber was available, of two empty barges captured from the Spaniards and held as prizes by the United States navy. After the war Goethals again taught military engineering at West Point until he was assigned in 1900 to the construction of harbor defenses on the New England coast. In 1903 he was appointed a member of the General Staff in Washington, where he remained until summoned to Panama.

His staff work had brought him into close association with Taft, who held his character and ability in high esteem. In November 1905 Goethals accompanied Taft to the isthmus on an inspection tour but appeared to take little interest in the canal work except to express vague disapproval of the chaotic disorganization still evident at that time. When he returned to Panama a year and a half later as chief engineer an agreeable surprise awaited him: "The magnitude of the work grows and grows on me," he wrote a few days after his arrival, "it seems to get bigger all the time, but Mr. Stevens has perfected such an organization so far as the R.R. part . . . is concerned, that there is nothing left for us to do but to just have the organization continue in the good work it has done and is doing. As I . . . see what he has accomplished . . . I cannot see why he has resigned." [4] The newcomer found progress on the locks and dams, his own specialties, less satisfactory, but he never failed to praise his predecessor's ingenious system of tracks and dumps for the disposal of excavated material. Long afterwards Stevens returned the compliment: "General Goethals and I were friends and understood each other thoroughly. . . . The work of . . . Goethals and his colleagues . . . was, in my judgment, above just criticism." [5]

Although Stevens had started the campaign in the right direction the battle was by no means over. All of the vital hydraulic structures — the locks and dams, spillways and power stations — remained to be designed and built; extensive harbor improvements at both ends awaited execution; the Panama Railroad had to be relocated throughout almost its entire length; only a fraction of the excavation in Culebra Cut had been completed, and on account of subsequent slides that fraction proved to be even smaller than it appeared in 1907. The prospect of several years of ceaseless labor failed to discourage Goethals. Like Stevens he saw the task as staggering in size but not in technical difficulty.

According to his admirers — who included a substantial majority of his associates on the isthmus — Goethals was a superb administrator, a stern but just disciplinarian, severe towards shirkers and incompetents but generous in praise of those who lived up to his exacting requirements. He selected technical assistants of marked ability in their respective fields, most of whom worked in harmony not only with their chief but with each other. Yet Goethals was no mixer, no winner of easy popularity. His innate shyness often made him appear cold, he had few real intimates, was more generally respected than loved, and in rare instances was actively disliked. One of his severest critics was Mrs. Gorgas, who resented what she believed, mistakenly or otherwise, to be his deliberate attempts to hamper and humiliate her husband: "His passion for dominating everything he carried to extreme lengths. . . . He was impatient of any associate or subordinate whom he could not control. He was utterly lacking in adaptability. . . . His conversation and his manners, like his acts, had no finesse and no spirit of accommodation. Though he had his genial moments, and though his nature did not lack its soft and even its sentimental side, he was consistently abrupt in conversation. On occasion this quality was an advantage . . . especially . . . in dealing with the outrageous demands and threats of labourers — Colonel Goethals's handling of such crises being masterpieces of their kind; in other instances . . . it had a deplorable effect upon general efficiency." [6]

Although there is no good reason to believe that Goethals ever consciously attempted or desired to exalt himself at the expense of his co-workers his personality did in fact dominate the last seven years of the construction period. Of all the canal engineers his name and his alone is indelibly stamped upon the public memory, and among laymen an impression that he built the canal almost single-handed persists even today. Such an impression is obviously unfair to his exceedingly able assistants, without whom — as Goethals himself freely and repeatedly admitted — the task could never have been carried to successful completion. Among these aides the most noteworthy were Hodges, Sibert, Gaillard, Williamson, and Rousseau.

Lieutenant Colonel Harry Foote Hodges was a Bostonian, two years younger than Goethals. After his graduation from West Point in 1881 as an engineer officer he was assigned to various river, harbor, and fortification projects, interspersed with four years as instructor of military engineering at West Point and, during the Spanish-American War, with some months of field service in Puerto Rico. From 1902 to 1907 he headed the river and harbor divisions of the Chief of Engineer's office. Because of Hodges's experience with lock mechanisms — he had designed the steel gates for one of the great locks on the "Soo" canal — Goethals requested his appointment on the canal commission in 1907. The Chief of Engineers insisted that he could not spare Hodges at that time but permitted him to serve as chief purchasing officer for the commission in Washington. In July 1908 he was transferred to the isthmus, and Major Frank C. Boggs replaced him as purchasing officer. In September Hodges was given the seat on the commission left vacant by the resignation of Jackson Smith, head of the department of labor, quarters, and subsistence, but he did not inherit Smith's duties; as a technical expert in hydraulics Hodges was too valuable "to be wasted on housekeeping." [7] Instead he was placed in charge of the most difficult task in the entire project: the design and erection of

46 pairs of steel lock gates each consisting of two leaves 7 feet thick, 65 feet wide, and from 47 to 82 feet high; the design of valves for the immense conduits buried inside the concrete walls and under the floors of the locks, large enough to raise or lower the water level in each huge basin 28 feet in 15 minutes; the design and installation of intricate, delicate machinery to open and close the valves and gates; and the erection of a hydroelectric station at Gatún to furnish power for operation of the locks and other purposes.

Major William Luther Sibert, born at Gadsden, Alabama, in 1860, graduated from West Point in 1884 and like Hodges devoted several years to river and canal work in the United States. During the Spanish-American War he saw active service as chief engineer of an army corps in the Philippines. When Sibert became a member of the commission in 1907 Goethals appointed him head of the Atlantic division, which comprised the Gatún dam, Gatún locks, the 4-mile stretch of sea level canal between the locks and Limón Bay, and the harbor improvements and breakwaters in the bay itself.

The central division extending from Gatún dam to Pedro Miguel lock was assigned to Major David Du Bose Gaillard. Gaillard was born in South Carolina in 1859, graduated from West Point with Sibert in 1884, and worked on river and harbor projects in Florida from 1887 to 1891. He served for five years on the International Boundary Commission appointed to survey the frontier between the United States and Mexico and for three as engineer in charge of the Washington aqueduct and dam across the Potomac. The Spanish-American War took Gaillard to Cuba, first as a staff officer and then as chief engineer of the Santa Clara department. From 1903 to 1907 he was on duty with the General Staff. Gaillard's section of the Panama canal included all of Gatún Lake and the 10-mile cut through the continental divide. Although his task involved no such complex mechanical problems as Hodges was called upon to solve it surpassed in sheer magnitude all other operations on the isthmus. Nearly all of the "dry" or steam-shovel excavation took place in Culebra Cut. Gaillard directed the Culebra excavations until about a year before the canal opened, when the growth of a brain tumor obliged him to return to the United States for an operation. By that time the malady was beyond cure, and he died in Baltimore on December 5, 1913. In recognition of his services President Wilson issued an executive order on April 27, 1915 officially changing the name of Culebra Cut to Gaillard Cut.

Sydney B. Williamson, in charge of the Pacific division from the southern end of Gaillard Cut to deep water in the Pacific, was the only civilian engineer entrusted with a technical assignment of the first magnitude under the army régime. He was not a member of the commission, but Goethals had known him well ever since the days of the Tennessee River high-lift lock. As assistant engineer on that project Williamson had displayed so much skill and ingenuity that Goethals employed him on several subsequent government enterprises. At Panama he was responsible for the construction of Pedro Miguel and Miraflores locks with their auxiliary dams. With his work practically completed he resigned in December 1912 to resume private practice.

The only naval member of the commission, Harry Harwood Rousseau, was born at Troy, New York, in 1870. He did not enter the service until 1898, when he was commissioned as a civil engineer with the rank of lieutenant, but advanced so rapidly that by 1907 he was a rear admiral and chief of the Bureau of Yards and Docks. From 1903 to 1906 he supervised construction of the immense drydock at the Mare Island navy yard near San Francisco. Rousseau's contribution to the Panama canal included the design and construction of all terminals, wharves, coaling stations, drydocks, machine shops, warehouses, and other auxiliary structures. "His technical training and previous experience," Goethals declared, "combined with his executive and administrative ability, fit him admirably for his position. . . . His counsel in questions of organization, cost-keeping, and the preparation of estimates, has been invaluable, and, in his way, he has been as indispensable to me as Colonel Hodges." [8]

Abandoning the remote control policy of their predecessors, all members of the third commission lived and worked in the Canal Zone, returning to the United States only on official business or occasional furloughs. At first they found the atmosphere distinctly hostile. The employees and their families, loyal to Stevens and accustomed to a civilian administration, made no effort to conceal their distrust of the new military dictatorship. In his first public speech, delivered a few days after his arrival in March 1907, Goethals endeavored to reassure the suspicious workmen: "There will be no more militarism in the future than there has been in the past. I am no longer a commander in the United States Army. I now consider I am commanding the Army of Panama, and that the enemy we are going to combat is the Culebra Cut and the locks and dams at both ends of the canal. Every man who does his duty will never have any cause to complain on account of militarism." [9] Although the departments were organized to some extent along mili-

28.   THE "BRAIN WAGON" OR "YELLOW PERIL"

29.   GREAT SEAL OF THE CANAL ZONE

30. PANAMA CITY FROM LAS BÓVEDAS AT LOW TIDE, 1910

31. PANAMA CANAL ADMINISTRATION BUILDING, BALBOA HEIGHTS

tary lines, and Goethals maintained exceedingly strict discipline, there were no salutes or other outward manifestations of army control. Goethals himself never appeared in uniform.

He habitually devoted his afternoons to administrative work in his office at Culebra and his mornings to inspection tours of the canal line. These tours followed no set itinerary; the "old man" might turn up anywhere at any time, and the labor gangs soon grew accustomed to his sudden appearances, his curt criticisms or brief words of praise, and his abrupt departures. Since there was no road across the isthmus he generally traveled up and down the railway line in a hideous contraption propelled by gasoline, looking like "the nightmare offspring of a passenger engine and a taxi" [10] and known to the workmen either as the Brain Wagon or, because of its bilious color, as the Yellow Peril.

Until 1907 it had been assumed almost as a matter of course that the canal would be built by private contractors. Shonts believed firmly that a contractor or preferably a group of contractors organized into a syndicate could complete the work much more quickly and economically than the government. On October 9, 1906 the commission issued an invitation for bids on the entire project, but the response was disappointing: only four contracting syndicates submitted proposals, and when these were opened on January 12, 1907 all were found unsatisfactory and rejected. The advent of Goethals and the third commission completely reversed this policy. Goethals vigorously opposed construction by contract and maintained that the commission could execute the work much more efficiently with its own organization, laborers, and machinery. His arguments convinced the President, and the canal was built, with an efficiency rarely paralleled in great engineering projects, without the intervention of contractors except for a few special operations.

Under the army administration excavation and construction progressed rapidly. In the Atlantic division dredges scooped a broad channel through Limón Bay from deep water in the Caribbean to the canal entrance, and two stone breakwaters were constructed. At Gatún work was begun on the great dam in 1907 and completed in August 1913. This huge embankment, designed to hold back the Chagres and form an artificial lake about 164 square miles in area with a normal surface elevation of 85 feet, is situated just west of the Gatún locks. It comprises three sections: an earth dam adjacent to the locks, a concrete spillway, and another earth dam beyond the spillway. As originally planned the dam would have had a height of 135 feet above the sea, but in 1909 the engineers decided that it might safely be reduced to 115 feet, or 30 feet above the lake level. The total length is approximately 1.5 miles, and the earth sections are about 100 feet thick at the crest, 500 at the lake surface, and almost half a mile at the base. In spite of its gigantic dimensions it is not an impressive structure. The slopes are so gradual that it looks more like a low natural hill than a man-made barrier; it exhibits none of the soaring spectacular grandeur of Boulder dam.

Throughout the construction period Gatún dam was a favorite target for uninformed criticism. Bunau-Varilla, among many others, maintained that the dam should have been located farther south at Bohío, that the Gatún site offered no suitable foundation, that even a slight earthquake would cause serious damage, that when completed the embankment would develop fissures which would allow the water to escape, and that even without fissures the natural seepage would eventually drain the lake. Although none of these gloomy forebodings have been realized, during construction a series of minor catastrophes did lend some color to such predictions. On November 20, 1908 a section about 200 feet long slipped sidewise and sank 20 feet. Goethals and his staff insisted that the movement at that early stage of operations had no significance, but it caused so much anxiety in the United States that Roosevelt sent Taft and a group of engineers to the isthmus. The experts reported reassuringly that the slip would not affect the stability of the completed dam. In October 1911 about 1000 feet of the east half of the dam settled a few feet, and at the end of August 1912 the west end bulged and sank about 20 feet. Each time the damage was repaired without difficulty, and since the opening of the canal no alarming displacements have occurred.

Excavation for the triple flight of locks at Gatún was finished in 1911, and the masonry work under the supervision of Major James Postell Jervey early in 1913. Since no rock suitable for crushing existed in the vicinity a quarry was opened at Puerto Bello, some 30 miles away. One unfortunate consequence was the demolition by the American engineers of the ancient Spanish fortress of San Felipe de Todo Fierro which occupied a portion of the quarry site. Sand for the Gatún concrete was brought from Nombre de Dios. Afterwards Goethals admitted that the decision to bring rock and sand from these ports had probably been a mistake; he and his staff had underestimated the difficulty of towing laden barges through the heavy seas of the open Atlantic, and similar materials could have been transported to Gatún more cheaply by rail from the quarries and sandpits on the Pacific side which supplied the Pedro Miguel and Miraflores locks.

In addition to the gates at the ends of each 1000-foot lock intermediate gates divide each chamber into two unequal parts, one about 600 feet and the other about 400 feet long. Thus for vessels under 600 feet in length only a portion of the basin has to be filled or emptied, resulting in a considerable saving of water. Every conceivable precaution has been taken to insure the safety of the locks and of vessels in transit. All terminal gates are doubled so that if one pair is damaged the other will hold back the water. Heavy fender chains extend across each lock chamber to prevent accidental ramming of the gates. Since the canal has been in operation these chains have either prevented or diminished the gravity of numerous accidents. As a final safety measure should all other devices fail and the gates be so severely damaged as to permit the water to rush in, each lock is fitted with an emergency dam, a sort of overhead bridge pivoted to swing across the basin, from which steel wickets can be lowered between vertical guides to shut off the flow from the higher level.

The erection of the 46 pairs of steel gates, weighing in the aggregate about 59,000 tons, and the installation of their mechanisms proved one of the most troublesome features of the entire enterprise. This work, one of the few operations performed by contract, commenced at Gatún in May 1911, at Pedro Miguel in August 1911, and at Miraflores in September 1912. By June 30, 1912 half of the gates were under construction but none had been completed, and progress had fallen far behind schedule. Since some of the delays had been caused by strikes, shipwrecks, interference by the commission, and other "acts of God" the contractors were granted an extension. In the end all gates were finished before the revised time limit expired.

No vessel is permitted to proceed through the locks under its own power. Specially designed electric locomotives or "mules" running on rack rails alongside each lock basin tow ships into and out of locks by means of windlass cables. When the original design for these locomotives furnished by the electrical department on the isthmus was found defective the commission adopted an improved model devised by the General Electric Company. Power for the towing equipment, operation of the gates and valves, illumination of the canal for night transits, and lighting of the Zone communities is supplied by a hydroelectric station at Gatún. An auxiliary steam powerhouse at Miraflores is connected with Gatún by a transmission line so that in an emergency current from either source, or partly from one and partly from the other, can be utilized.

In the Pacific division the substitution of the Miraflores lock site for the original location at Sosa Hill caused some delay, but once the change was made the construction of the locks at both Miraflores and Pedro Miguel progressed with satisfactory speed. Much greater difficulties were encountered during the construction of a solid breakwater from La Boca to Naos Island, 3 miles out in Panama Bay. This dike had a dual purpose: to connect the island fortifications with the mainland and to prevent the sweeping currents of the Pacific from choking with silt the dredged channel of the canal entrance. Since it was composed entirely of waste material excavated from Culebra Cut its construction was turned over to Gaillard's central division instead of to the Pacific division. For five years the engineers toiled on the breakwater, dumping millions of cubic yards of earth and rock into the bay only to see them sucked down and swallowed by the oozy mud. Each time the dike settled the pressure would squeeze up the soft bottom on both sides, forming parallel ridges several feet above the water surface. Not only did the dike sink faster than it could be filled in but it heaved and squirmed like a gigantic and diabolically perverse eel, twisting rails and spilling dump cars into the sea. The movement finally subsided, and the breakwater was completed shortly before the opening of the canal.

Rehabilitation of the Panama Railroad involved two distinct and successive steps: first, a general overhauling of the old line and the installation of double tracks over 37 miles of its length to accommodate an endless procession of dirt trains as well as vastly augmented commercial traffic during the period of canal construction; second, the building of an entirely new railroad in a different location for use after the opening of the canal. The first process, wholly the work of Stevens and his staff, was completed by June 1907. As an auxiliary to a sea level canal this line, with slight modifications, could have remained permanently; but the decision to build a lock canal made its relocation imperative, for the waters of Gatún Lake would submerge about half of the original roadbed. Surveys for the new line were finished in November 1906. Between Colón and Gatún at the Atlantic end and between Panama and Pedro Miguel near the Pacific the new tracks follow approximately the old route, but between Gatún and Pedro Miguel they take an altogether different course. The chief engineer of the Panama Railroad, Ralph Budd, supervised construction of the new line from May 1907 to August 1909, when he was succeeded by Lieutenant Frederick Mears of the Engineer Corps, who handed over the completed road to the railway company on May 25, 1912. The total cost of the relocated line, not including new station buildings at Colón and Panama, amounted to $8,866,392 or about $1,000,000 more than the original road had cost in the eighteen-fifties.

Throughout the early period of canal construction accidents were frequent and fatalities among the workmen numerous. Many of these misadventures occurred on the railroad tracks; since there was no wagon road pedestrians used the busy railway line as a highway and were often caught unawares by speeding trains. Premature or defective dynamite blasts accounted for other deaths and injuries. Gaillard, in whose division most of the dynamite casualties took place, made heroic efforts to reduce their number. The safety campaign proved highly successful, and in the four-year period 1909–13, during which some 23,000,000 pounds of dynamite were set off, only 8 men were killed by blasts.

Under the army régime the office of governor was abolished and control of the Zone's civil administration placed in the hands of the chairman of the commission. But Goethals, having no time for the details of civil rule, delegated them to Blackburn and after Blackburn's resignation to Thatcher and Metcalfe in turn. Blackburn exercised little actual authority, for Goethals decided all questions of major importance, but the Kentucky ex-senator did much to relieve the busy chairman of the chores pertaining to official receptions and the greeting of distinguished visitors. Goethals detested public speaking, while Blackburn, a Southerner with a silver tongue and a genuine love of oratory, rejoiced in the opportunities to deliver flowery speeches appropriate to all occasions.

As the canal approached completion it became necessary to create a permanent organization for its operation and maintenance as well as for the government of the Zone. After lengthy discussions in both houses of Congress the bill known as the Panama Canal act was passed and on August 24, 1912 approved by President Taft. Most of the act was concerned with routine administration, but it contained two noteworthy clauses. Section 5 established toll rates which were to throw the canal accounting system into confusion for a quarter of a century and give rise to a grave dispute with Great Britain. Section 11 — a much less controversial paragraph — excluded from the canal vessels owned or operated partly or wholly by any railroad company engaged in interstate commerce, as well as vessels owned or operated by any corporation found guilty of violation of the Sherman anti-trust act of 1890. The purpose of this section was to prevent the formation of monopolies and to maintain free competition between the canal and the transcontinental railroads.

To house this permanent organization a new administration building was constructed on a spacious terrace carved out of the west side of Ancón Hill and overlooking the Pacific entrance to the canal. The resident architectural staff assisted by landscape architects laid out two new towns near the Pacific terminal: Balboa, containing permanent quarters for executives and white employees, and La Boca for the accommodation of colored workmen and their families. Most of the dwellings were new, but some were transported from other settlements along the canal line where they were no longer needed. Ten years of experience with the tropical climate had evolved a few architecturally unpretentious but exceedingly practical types of residence designed to secure a maximum circulation of air and provided with verandas spacious enough to serve as outdoor living rooms.

In 1912 the commission somewhat belatedly invited the Commission of Fine Arts to suggest improvements in the appearance of the canal and its auxiliary structures. The sculptor Daniel Chester French and the landscape architect Frederick Law Olmstead visited the isthmus in February 1913 and submitted an admirably sensible report: "The canal itself and all the structures connected with it impress one with a sense of their having been built with a view strictly to their utility. There is an entire absence of ornament and no evidence that the æsthetic has been considered except in a few instances. . . . Because of this very fact there is little to find fault with from the artist's point of view. The canal, like the Pyramids or some imposing object in natural scenery, is impressive from its scale and simplicity and directness. One feels that anything done merely for the purpose of beautifying it would not only fail to accomplish that purpose, but would be an impertinence." [11]

Fortification of the Canal Zone was the subject of no little controversy in the United States. The press printed hundreds of articles and editorials both for and against armed protection, while in Congress opinion was sharply divided. Happily there were no international complications to be considered. By its omission of any reference to defense the Hay-Pauncefote treaty tacitly conferred upon the United States the right to build forts and maintain a military establishment on the isthmus, and in 1912 the British Foreign Secretary, Sir Edward Grey, explicitly confirmed this right in a diplomatic note. The Hay-Bunau-Varilla treaty with Panama specifically granted to the United States full authority to fortify and garrison the Zone, and since Great Britain and Panama were the only two nations with which it had ratified canal conventions the United States was free to act as it saw fit. After several years of discussion

32. EXCAVATION OF CULEBRA (NOW GAILLARD) CUT

LOOKING SOUTH. GOLD HILL AT LEFT

33. STEAM SHOVEL AT BOTTOM OF CULEBRA (NOW GAILLARD) CUT,

MAY 1913

34. OFFICIAL OPENING OF THE PANAMA CANAL, AUGUST 15, 1914

S.S. ANCON APPROACHING CUCARACHA SLIDE

LOOKING NORTH. GOLD HILL AT RIGHT

35. EAST AND WEST CULEBRA SLIDES, OCTOBER 24, 1915

LOOKING NORTH FROM TOP OF GOLD HILL

the government decided to fortify. On March 4, 1911 Congress appropriated $2,000,000 for this purpose, and on August 24, 1912 added $1,000,000 for gun and mortar batteries and $200,000 for land defenses. By June 1915 the total appropriation for fortifications amounted to $14,689,873. Construction of the harbor batteries began on August 7, 1911 under the supervision of Williamson, chief engineer of the Pacific division. After January 1, 1912 a separate branch of the chief engineer's office, headed by the chairman's elder son, Lieutenant George Rodman Goethals, took charge of all fortification work. Soon after the completion of the canal the towns of Empire and Culebra, no longer required for construction purposes, were turned over to the army to house the permanent garrisons. Since the opening of the canal the military and naval defenses have been vastly strengthened, the resident force increased, new camps and quarters built, and air bases established. But the extent, cost, nature, and precise location of these protective installations are and must for the present remain closely guarded secrets.

On September 26, 1913 — two days after the installation of the last gate in the west flight — the first experimental lockage took place at Gatún. With flags flying and whistles tooting the tug *Gatun* entered the lowest chamber at 4:45 p.m. and was lifted to the 85-foot level of the lake in one hour and 51 minutes. On the following day the tug was lowered through the locks and returned to Colón. The gates and culverts functioned perfectly, but since the towing locomotives were not ready for service the *Gatun* passed through under her own steam. The gates in the east chamber at Pedro Miguel and in the west flight at Miraflores were finished on September 30, and the canal could have been thrown open to commercial traffic on a limited scale in October 1913, even without the electric mules, had the Cucaracha slide not barred the channel.

This slide, a mass of earth and rock more than 2,000,000 cubic yards in volume, delayed the opening about 10 months. To expedite its removal Goethals decided to flood Culebra Cut and complete the excavation by dredging. The last steam shovel ceased operation on September 10, 1913; holes were bored in Gamboa dike, the artificial embankment thrown across the northern end of the cut to keep out the overflow of Gatún Lake; and on October 1 water began to flow in through 24-inch pipes. On October 10, when the water in the cut had risen to within 6 feet of the lake level, President Wilson pressed an electric button in Washington and blew up Gamboa dike. Through the gap the lake water gushed "in sufficient volume to complete the filling of Culebra Cut . . . to Cucaracha slide in about two hours' time." [12] When a series of dynamite blasts failed to breach the toe of the slide a pipe-line suction dredge was brought in to pump water to the south end of the cut. On October 14 the tug *Miraflores,* the steam launch *Birdena,* three barges, and a clapet made the first passage of Miraflores locks and entered the basin of Pedro Miguel; but the pumps sucked the water across the slide so slowly that the first Pedro Miguel lockage could not be completed until October 24. On that same day a second lockage admitted into the cut additional floating equipment to reinforce the attack upon the slide from the south, while other dredges brought from the Atlantic were already at work on the opposite side. Lights were installed and excavation proceeded at full speed night and day. By December 13 a channel had been cut through the slide sufficiently broad to permit the dredges to pass through.

The first commercial transit took place in May 1914 — almost three months before the official opening — when the *Alaskan* of the American-Hawaiian Line, diverted by the Huerta revolution in Mexico from her customary transfer route by way of the Tehuantepec Railroad, docked at Balboa with a cargo of 12,000 tons of sugar. Since the canal could not yet handle so large a vessel the tug *Mariner,* towing a string of empty barges, was dispatched from Cristóbal to Balboa on May 19 — the first continuous ocean-to-ocean trip through the canal — and a few days later returned to the Atlantic side wtih its sugar-laden lighters. To test the towing locomotives the Panama Railroad steamer *Alliance* passed through Gatún locks in both directions on June 8, 1914, followed by the larger *Ancon* of the same line on June 11. On June 18 the Grace liner *Santa Clara* was towed by the electric mules through Miraflores and Pedro Miguel locks.

By the end of July enough of Cucaracha slide had been cleared away to allow large steamers to pass freely. On August 3 the *Cristobal,* sister ship of the *Ancon,* made a trial trip from Cristóbal to Balboa but did not continue to deep water in the Pacific. While the 9600-ton vessel drawing 25 feet of water skirted the slide without difficulty a number of hitches developed at the locks. At Gatún, where only four towing locomotives were used, one of them burned out a motor and caused a long delay. At Pedro Miguel a towing cable parted, but the ship was stopped in time to avert damage to itself or to the gates. The operators at Miraflores, warned by a telephone message from Goethals, took no chances and attached six locomotives for the passage through those locks, so the rest of the voyage passed without incident. In order to insure smooth opera-

tion on the opening day Goethals drilled the lock crews energetically for the next week, sending tugs and barges as well as two large
vessels through the locks for practice. Each time as teamwork between the locomotive operators and the ship pilots improved the
locks were negotiated with less difficulty and greater speed. The
stage was set for the official opening.

On May 20, 1914 President Wilson had issued an executive order directing the commission to arrange a ceremonial program for
the occasion, but when the imminent threat of a European war
made international participation impossible all preparations for
an elaborate celebration were canceled. The final consummation
of centuries of dreaming and planning, of years of stupendous effort, went almost unnoticed as the storm broke across the Atlantic.
War news crowded the canal off the front pages. In California two
great festivals, planned long in advance, were held the following
year in spite of the war: the Panama Pacific International Exposition in San Francisco and the Panama California International Exposition in San Diego. In Panama City a National Exposition took
place in 1916 after several postponements. But the opening of the
canal itself was a drab and colorless affair in comparison with the
imperial splendor of the maritime pageant that had marked
the completion of the Suez canal in 1869.

On Saturday morning, August 15, 1914 the Panama Railroad
liner *Ancon* drew slowly away from her dock at Cristóbal and
steamed into the Atlantic entrance of the canal. After an unevent-
ful passage of 9 hours and 40 minutes she reached the end of the
dredged channel in Panama Bay, 5 miles beyond the Pacific shore,
then turned back and tied up at the Balboa pier. "There were no
unscheduled delays," reported the sober *Canal Record*. "The *Ancon* carried, as guests the Secretary of War, about 200 people . . .
including President Porras and his cabinet and other Panama Government officials, the members of the diplomatic corps and resident
consuls-general, officers of the Tenth Infantry and Coast Artillery
Corps, officials of The Panama Canal, and a few others. . . . People gathered to witness the passage at various points along the
route, and at Balboa as many as 2,000 were present." [13] A few flags,
a few cheers — and the Panama canal was open.

Chapter 42. Slides

OF the 110,261,883 cubic yards extracted from Culebra Cut by the Americans between May 1904 and June 30, 1914 slides were directly responsible for 25,206,100, or 22.86% of the total. Between June 30, 1914, just before the opening of the canal, and June 30, 1941, the date of the latest available report, 49,008,400 cubic yards were removed on the same account, giving a grand total of 74,214,500 cubic yards of excavation due to slides alone.

In 1912 the commission's geologist, Donald F. MacDonald, reported: "There are four distinct types of slide, each clearly differentiable from the other, yet each aiding and abetting the others. . . . They are: (1) Structural breaks and deformations resulting in slides. (2) Normal or gravity slides. (3) Fault-zone slides. (4) Weathering and surface erosion." [1] The third and fourth types are of minor importance at Panama. Faults are often contributory causes of the structural breaks that produce slides of the first type, but slides due exclusively to the presence of fault zones are uncommon, "which is fortunate, for seldom can any economical remedial measures be applied to them." [2] Although erosion causes constant surface crumbling and has added slightly to the cost of upkeep since the opening of the canal it has produced no slides of great magnitude. The planting of grasses and shrubs has reduced damage from this source to some extent.

The second or gravity type, of which the Cucaracha slide is the most notorious example, results from a lack of adhesion between the top layer of porous clay varying from 10 to 40 feet in thickness and the underlying stratum of much harder nonporous rock. Rainwater seeping through the clay is unable to penetrate the rock, and the accumulation of moisture along the sloping plane of contact between the two layers forms a greasy, soapy surface upon which the upper clay slips downward into the canal prism. Various methods have been applied in vain attempts to arrest these flows: piles have been driven, heavy stones placed as anchors, concrete revetments constructed. No remedy has been found except to shovel out the debris after it has come down. Luckily these gravity slides affect only the clayey surface layer and do not weaken the rock slopes below.

The most disastrous slides, those of the first type, are not true slides at all but actual breaks in the rock structure of the banks. Displacements of this kind, which have caused far more damage than all other types together, involve a whole series of complex earth movements: "At the points where these breaks exist the underlying rock is of poor quality, intersected by vertical seams, or seams sloping toward the canal. Generally, the upper surface of the broken portion . . . remained approximately horizontal, settling nearly vertically. The weight of the broken portion forces up and displaces laterally the material lying directly below it. . . . As the material thus forced up is taken away [by shovels or dredges] the upper part gradually settles and moves toward the axis of the canal until the entire broken portion is removed." [3] Thus not only do huge masses of earth and rock slip sidewise into the cut, but the pressure, transmitted laterally underground, forces up the bed of the canal prism itself.

During the early days of excavation the experts took an optimistic view of the slide problem. "No difficulties are to be anticipated . . . in the Culebra region," declared one geologist in 1907, "except at Contractors Hill, where it is possible, but not probable, that landslides may take place when lower levels are reached." [4] But as the cut deepened the banks began to slip at several different points. The Cucaracha slide, which had plagued the French engineers as early as 1884, resumed activity in 1906 and continued to move, with quiescent intervals, not only throughout the construction period but for some years thereafter. In 1908 a number of isolated movements developed along the sides of the cut: a gravity slide at Paraíso, breaks just south of Gold Hill and near the village of Culebra. Fortunately the highest cliffs along the cut, the two great bastions of Gold Hill on the eastern rim and Contractors Hill on the western, are composed of firm volcanic rock and have neither broken nor slipped to any serious extent. Gaillard, whose division embraced the whole slide area, was still hopeful in 1911: "It is believed that the greatest trouble with slides has already been experienced and that henceforth although they will undoubtedly continue as long as excavation is in progress, yet . . . it appears probable that they have produced their maximum injurious effect in the fiscal year just ended." [5] His optimism was premature, for in January 1913 Cucaracha spilled about 2,000,000 cubic yards in one great slide which extended completely across the cut and delayed the opening of the canal.

These disasters produced far more uneasiness in the United States and in Europe than in the Canal Zone, where the engineers, confident that the slides could not continue indefinitely on a large scale, realized that their task was simply to dig until the unstable banks reached their natural angles of repose. In 1913 MacDonald permitted himself a gibe at the prophets of doom: "On the whole, while the slides have been very troublesome and are not yet finished, it is quite certain that they will give no trouble to the completed canal, unless they may happen to cause some little inconvenience during the first year or two of operation. A few of the periodicals, especially some of the European shipping journals, have not yet been able to divorce themselves from the opinion that ships going through the canal are liable to destruction from slides, earthquakes, budding volcanoes, or other . . . calamities, perhaps not even excluding demolition by sea serpents." [6]

The geologist was both right and wrong. Slides and breaks did materially diminish in volume after the first two years of operation, but during those two years they caused a great deal more than "some little inconvenience." On the night of October 14, 1914, just two months after the official opening, a break at East Culebra completely blocked the channel within half an hour, raising parts of the bottom of the canal to within 9 inches of the water surface and halting traffic on three separate occasions: "At times the channel shoaled so rapidly that it was necessary to drag after the passage of each ship. . . ." [7] Additional breaks closed the transit from August 7 to 10 and from September 4 to 9, 1915. So far the interruptions had been brief, none exceeding a week; but on September 18 the banks at East and West Culebra on opposite sides of the cut suddenly collapsed simultaneously, squeezing the canal bed upward 110 feet to form a ridge rising 65 feet above the water surface. This time the canal was closed to commercial traffic from September 18, 1915 to April 15, 1916 — the longest interruption in its history — while the dredges worked furiously 24 hours a day. After the reopening Goethals announced confidently that "the worst is over. . . . The slides will be overcome finally and for all time, notwithstanding the calamity howlers and in spite of the disastrous predictions of the 'know-it-alls.' " [8]

Time has proved Goethals substantially if not literally correct. While since April 1916 not a year has passed without its quota of slides or breaks only a few have caused even minor suspensions of traffic. In August and September 1916 Cucaracha slide blocked the canal for eight days, and in January 1917 the East Culebra break closed it for two days. In February 1920 Cucaracha again obstructed the cut for two days. In December 1922 slides held up one steamer of exceptionally deep draft for one day, and in the autumn of 1923 two large ships were blocked for a few hours. In November 1931 a combination of floods and slides caused intermittent delays: "Prolonged rainfall brought water into Gatun Lake in excess of the volume . . . discharged through the spillway . . . and to prevent . . . flooding the lock machinery, the lock culverts at Gatun and Pedro Miguel were opened . . . for a total of about 20 hours. . . . In the morning of November 9 a slide occurred . . . blocking passage until November 11 for ships drawing up to 28 feet . . . and until November 15 for one vessel of over 35 feet draft." [9] This was the last interruption due to slides, but in November 1932 traffic was again suspended for a few hours while the culverts were opened to carry off flood water. Although the danger of another catastrophic slide now seems remote the canal authorities still maintain a large fleet of powerful dredges fully equipped and ready for service.

Chapter 43.   Health Crusade

W HEN Amador, a doctor by profession and a functionary
only by accident, reached Washington in November 1903
to find his thunder stolen by Bunau-Varilla, he consoled
himself with the reflection: "At last there will be no more yellow fever on the Isthmus." [1] Within two years his prediction had
come true: the Americans had not only eradicated yellow fever
completely but had reduced fatalities from other ailments to a
fraction of their former rate. No miracles were involved in the
achievement; nothing but science, determination, money, and a
stupendous amount of hard work. In its war against disease the
American health organization possessed two invaluable weapons
that the French had lacked: a great leader, Gorgas, and the recently acquired knowledge that the two deadliest scourges of the
isthmus, yellow fever and malaria, were transmitted by mosquitoes.

William Crawford Gorgas was born at Toulminville, Alabama,
on October 3, 1854. His father, General Josiah Gorgas, had graduated from West Point, served in the Mexican War, and in 1853
assumed command of an arsenal at Mount Vernon near Mobile,
where he met and married a daughter of John Gayle, former governor of Alabama. Although a Pennsylvanian by birth Josiah Gorgas supported the Southern cause and became chief ordnance officer of the Confederate armies during the Civil War. The war
ruined him financially, but an appointment to the presidency of
the University of the South at Sewanee in 1869 provided a modest
income. Young William Gorgas attended his father's college and
after his graduation in 1875 studied law for a few months in New
Orleans. He had little taste for the law; even as a child he had set
his heart upon a military career, but his change of residence had
made it impossible to secure an appointment to West Point before
he passed the 21-year age limit. Only one opening remained through
which he could enter the army — the Medical Corps — and although he had never displayed the slightest interest in medicine he
determined to become a doctor in order to obtain an army commission. From 1876 to 1880 he studied under the famous William
Henry Welch at Bellevue Medical College in New York, where he

surprised himself by developing an ardent enthusiasm for the medical profession not merely as a stepping-stone to military life but for its own sake. During those years Gorgas had to pinch and scrape so carefully to pay his tuition and absolutely necessary expenses that he never had enough money to go home for the holidays. In June 1880 he enrolled in the Medical Corps and for the next 18 years lived the routine life of an army surgeon on various military reservations, including several frontier outposts in Texas and the Dakotas. During the Spanish-American War he took charge of the yellow fever camp at Siboney, Cuba, and after the cessation of hostilities was appointed chief sanitary officer of Havana.

Throughout his life and even before he was born yellow fever exerted a curious and often decisive influence over Gorgas. In 1853 it was a yellow fever epidemic that had sent his mother to Mount Vernon and brought about her meeting with his father. At Gorgas's birth the attendant physician was Josiah C. Nott of Mobile, who as early as March 1848 had published an article in the *New Orleans Medical and Surgical Journal* challenging the accepted "miasma" theory of yellow fever transmission and suggesting that the disease might have an "insect or animalcular" [2] origin. While on duty at Fort Brown near the border settlement of Brownsville, Texas, in 1882 Gorgas himself contracted a severe case of yellow fever which rendered him immune and enabled him to live and work in infected areas without danger. Shortly before his own illness he had attended another yellow fever patient, Marie Doughty, whom he married in 1885. His assignment to Cuba brought him into close association with Walter Reed and his colleagues, who in 1900 proved by their experiments on human volunteers that yellow fever is transmitted by the female of the mosquito then called *Stegomyia fasciata,* now known as *Aëdes aegypti,* and that other long-suspected agencies such as filth, "miasmas," and physical contact with infected persons or with their clothing and excreta play no part whatever in the spread of the disease.

Reed was not the first to suspect the mosquito's rôle as the medium of yellow fever transmission. Twenty years earlier a Cuban physician, Carlos Finlay, had advanced the same theory in an article published in a Havana scientific journal in 1881. Not only did Finlay insist that a mosquito acted as intermediary, but by a brilliant process of deduction he identified *Aëdes aegypti* as the specific culprit. For years in the face of almost universal ridicule he maintained the correctness of his hypothesis, but an unfortunate error in his estimate of the period required for incubation within the mosquito made it impossible for him to furnish convincing proof.

"Dr. Finlay," wrote Gorgas, ". . . had done a great deal of experimenting on the human subject. . . . But he had not been successful in transmitting the disease. He had no means of knowing that it took the mosquito twelve days from the time when she swallowed the blood of a yellow-fever patient to become herself infectious. Not knowing this fact, it was perfectly natural for Dr. Finlay to use his mosquitoes . . . within the first four or five days. . . . The Reed Board [in 1900], after many months of inconclusive work . . . turned their attention to Dr. Finlay's mosquito theory. . . . Indeed, we all knew Dr. Finlay well, but were rather inclined to make light of his ideas, and none more so than I. . . . Dr. Finlay is a most lovable man in character and personality. . . . He is one of the few great men who has had his work recognized during his lifetime." [3]

Until about 1925 all available evidence supported the belief that yellow fever could be transmitted *only* by the bite of the *Aëdes*, but recent investigations undertaken under the auspices of the Rockefeller Foundation have demonstrated that other insects carry yellow fever and that man is not, as was thought, the only victim. In vast areas of Brazil as well as in isolated districts in Venezuela, Colombia, and Bolivia a form of the disease known as "jungle" yellow fever has been discovered "under conditions previously considered incompatible with its existence. . . . Yellow fever has been observed in the complete absence of the *Aëdes aegypti* mosquito. . . . There is ample reason for believing that aegypti-transmitted . . . and jungle yellow fever are identical except for the conditions under which infection occurs. . . . In jungle yellow fever . . . man is not an important source of virus for the infection of human cases; the human case is apparently an accident in the course of some as yet unknown extra-domiciliary cycle of infection. In support of this idea, studies . . . have already shown that animals . . . including opossums and several species of monkeys, may acquire immunity under natural conditions in the jungle." [4]

Finlay's deductions and Reed's experiments paved the way for the adoption of revolutionary methods for the control of yellow fever epidemics, but it remained for Gorgas to apply those methods to the organization of vast health campaigns. As chief sanitary officer of Havana Gorgas, wholeheartedly backed by the military governor of Cuba, General Leonard Wood, exercised almost absolute authority, and under his direction the filthy disease-ridden city was quickly scrubbed and polished into a model of cleanliness. The notorious smells of Havana were smothered in the reek of disinfectants; typhoid, dysentery, and similar maladies all but dis-appeared. But the thorough cleansing had no effect on yellow fe-ver, which broke out with renewed vigor when thousands of non-immune immigrants from Spain began to pour in after the war. Yellow fever, as far as is known, never attacks the same individual twice, and native Cubans, like native Panamanians and all long-established inhabitants of regions in which yellow fever was then endemic, enjoyed a relative immunity due not to racial resistance but to the simple fact that most of them had contracted mild cases of the fever — often so mild as to pass undiagnosed and scarcely noticed — in childhood. Foreigners from uninfected regions suc-cumbed much more readily. Gorgas and his sanitary squads now declared war on the Cuban mosquitoes, both the yellow fever car-rier and *Anopheles,* the spreader of malaria. Within a few months there was not a single case of yellow fever in Havana, and only a few traces of malarial infection remained.

These phenomenal successes led Gorgas, early in 1902, to suggest to Surgeon General George M. Sternberg that the same procedures could and should be applied to the region, either Nicaragua or Panama, through which the proposed isthmian canal would pass. In the autumn of that year Gorgas was sent to Egypt to study the sanitary conditions in the vicinity of the Suez canal, but he found the desert climate so different from that of the humid American isthmus that his researches proved of little use. In October 1903 he attended a hygiene congress in Paris, where he obtained more per-tinent information from the records of the Compagnie Nouvelle. Soon thereafter the recommendations of General Sternberg and of numerous prominent physicians easily persuaded Roosevelt to ap-point Gorgas chief sanitary officer of the canal, but in spite of the urgent representations of the American Medical Association the President refused to place him on the Isthmian Canal Commission.

In April 1904 Gorgas visited the isthmus with the commission-ers and in June installed himself at Ancón with his medical staff: Dr. John W. Ross, U.S.N., director of hospitals; Dr. Henry Rose Carter of the United States Health and Marine Hospital Service, a noted authority on yellow fever, chief quarantine officer; Major Louis A. La Garde of the Medical Corps, superintendent of Ancón Hospital; L. W. Spratling, a naval surgeon, superintendent of Co-lón Hospital; Joseph Le Prince, chief sanitary inspector of the Zone; and Dr. Lewis Balch, health officer. Most of these assistants had worked with Gorgas in Cuba and had contributed much en-ergy and skill to the success of his anti-mosquito crusade.

The high death rate from yellow fever during the French régime convinced Gorgas that his initial efforts must be directed towards the eradication of that disease. The campaign involved three operations: exclusion of mosquitoes from contact with patients already infected, destruction of all adult *Aëdes aegypti,* and prevention of the propagation of new swarms. Fortunately the habits of the relatively weak and vulnerable *Aëdes* facilitated its extermination. *Aëdes* is "a domestic mosquito, laying its eggs in artificial collections of clean water . . . such as cisterns, jars, bottles, tin cans, sagging gutters, ant-guards, vases, holy-water fonts, unused flush tanks, etc. These . . . for the most part breed in the house or yard and fly very short distances. . . . This species bites mostly by day, particularly in the afternoon. . . ." [5] Since *Aëdes* infests cities rather than rural districts Panama and Colón were the chief foci of contagion. No serious outbreak of yellow fever occurred until almost the end of the first year of American occupation. During the first 11 months there were only 66 cases in the Zone including Panama and Colón and only 8 deaths from the disease among canal employees. But with the arrival of thousands of nonimmune executives, clerks, and mechanics the number of victims increased rapidly. In April 1905 the old French headquarters in Panama City, used as a temporary administration building by the Americans, became infected, and several employees — including two or three executive officers — sickened and died. In May the fever assumed the proportions of a full-fledged epidemic, and a feeling of "alarm, almost amounting to panic, spread among the Americans. . . . Many resigned . . . while those who remained became possessed with a feeling of lethargy or fatalism resulting from a conviction that no remedy existed. . . . There was a disposition to partly ignore or openly condemn and abandon all preventive measures." [6]

Gorgas went to work with characteristic energy. He divided Panama and Colón into districts, assigned a mosquito brigade to each under the supervision of his health officers, and organized daily house-to-house inspections by local physicians who not only endeavored to ferret out every case of yellow fever but undertook an immense amount of patient detective work in their efforts to trace the movements of each sufferer during the days preceding the appearance of the first symptoms, so as to locate the source of the infection.

Having found fumigation an effective weapon against the Cuban mosquitoes, Gorgas applied the same process even more thoroughly in Panama. In one year his squads used up 120 tons of pyrethrum

37. NORTH AVENUE, PANAMA, AFTER PAVING

39. TENTH STREET, COLÓN, AFTER PAVING

36. NORTH AVENUE, PANAMA, BEFORE PAVING

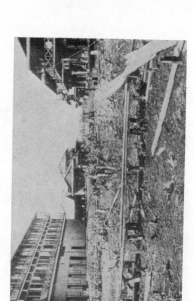

38. TENTH STREET, COLÓN, BEFORE PAVING

40. ANCÓN HOSPITAL IN 1910

41. GORGAS HOSPITAL FROM ANCÓN HILL, 1940

HOTEL TIVOLI AT UPPER LEFT, PANAMA CITY IN BACKGROUND

powder — the total supply obtainable in the United States — and 300 tons of sulphur. Pyrethrum, while less potent, was preferred because sulphur stained fabrics and corroded metals left in the houses, and the removal of household gear before fumigation was apt to permit the escape of infected mosquitoes. The natives, though more or less immune themselves, "submitted patiently . . . to the annoyance and inconvenience of fumigation. . . . Few claims have been filed for . . . damages . . . and almost every one . . . has had some basis of merit."[7] Gorgas ascribed the prevalence of this co-operative spirit largely to the personal influence of President Amador.

While fumigation destroyed the house-dwelling adult *Aëdes* it had no effect on the larvæ swarming in every cupful of water out of doors. Since the larvæ could not live without air the mosquito brigades, numbering more than 4000 men, suffocated them by spraying a film of oil over the surface of every puddle in the yards and unpaved streets. The barrels, cisterns, and other containers upon which the inhabitants, lacking modern pipes and faucets, depended for their water supply were equipped with tight-fitting covers of wood or wire netting until the extension of underground water mains made it possible to destroy or fill in such primitive receptacles. Thousands of earthenware ant-guards embedded in the gardens of Ancón hospital by the French horticulturists — and now known to be far more dangerous to the patients than to the ants — were dug up, and all vegetation was cleared away within 200 yards of every building. Gorgas regretted the unavoidable sacrifice of so many carefully tended shrubs and flowers: "It looked very much like vandalism on our part to see all the beautiful plants . . . ruthlessly destroyed."[8] Afterwards, when the fever epidemic had subsided and the voracious umbrella ants had been exterminated by explosions of carbon bisulphid in their nests, the grounds were replanted without the pottery rings.

The crusade against yellow fever on the isthmus resulted in its complete and, it may be hoped, permanent eradication. Between April 1 and October 31, 1905 the epidemic attacked 184 persons, 57 of whom died. The last case of yellow fever in Panama City was reported on November 11. In May 1906 one was recorded in Colón, but some of the medical authorities doubted the accuracy of the diagnosis. Since then not a single case of yellow fever has originated in or near the Canal Zone, and a rigid quarantine system has prevented the spread of infection from the few patients brought in by ships from less carefully protected ports.

"Although yellow fever has excited more general alarm than any other disease . . . and has been disastrous in its moral effects," Magoon reported in 1905, "it has impaired the actual physical efficiency . . . far less than malaria, which, being more familiar and not so generally fatal, is less dreaded." [9] Even before yellow fever had been banished from the isthmus Gorgas and his staff were taking steps to conquer this less awe-inspiring but actually more formidable enemy. Malaria, unlike yellow fever, does not produce immunity after one attack or indeed after any number of attacks. Once in the blood the disease can recur year after year. Malaria is not only more widespread and more persistent than yellow fever but it is also very much more difficult to eradicate. The malaria mosquito, *Anopheles,* does not breed like *Aëdes* in small and accessible domestic containers but flourishes in natural swamps and pools often covering immense areas: "Making war on the yellow-fever insect is like making war on the family cat, while a campaign directed against the malarial parasite is like fighting all the beasts of the jungle." [10] Though hardier than the feeble *Aëdes* the *Anopheles* cannot fly far without alighting on a tree or bush, so that a cleared space 200 yards wide will protect a building against infection.

To exterminate or even materially reduce the swarms of malarial mosquitoes was a gigantic and infinitely laborious task. The sanitary squads drained about 100 square miles of swamp, constructed almost 1000 miles of earth ditch, 300 miles of concrete ditch, and 200 miles of rock-filled trench, laid almost 200 miles of tile drain to carry off subsoil water, cut hundreds of acres of undergrowth and tall grass, sprayed pools and puddles with about 50,000 gallons of oil each month, hatched and released thousands of minnows to feed on the *Anopheles* larvæ, and bred spiders, ants, and small lizards to devour adult mosquitoes. Every month some 200 barrels of a poison compounded of carbolic acid, resin, and caustic soda were poured along the edges of pools and streams to destroy the grass and algæ which impeded the spread of oil. Notwithstanding their magnitude these operations did not — and do not today — cover more than a fraction of the total Canal Zone area, but they have almost eliminated malaria from the inhabited sections.

Fortunately malaria is one of the ailments for which a specific remedy or at least a specific palliative is known. The dispensaries distributed quinin freely, and on every mess hall table bottles of the bitter medicine in both liquid and tablet form appeared as regularly as vinegar cruets and salt cellars. "No attempt was ever made," Gorgas wrote, "to force anyone to take . . . quinin, but explanation and persuasion were used to their fullest extent. By these methods we succeeded . . . in getting our force to take about forty thousand doses per day. The men responded very heartily and loyally. . . . I . . . feel confident that no system of compulsion could have been as successful." [11] Nevertheless some of the badly infected employees refused to swallow the unpalatable stuff, and in such instances the doctors did resort to compulsion. Even then the doses sometimes went astray: "A certain number . . . would manage to throw their tablets out of the dispensary window. The old turkey-gobbler that was the pet of the hospital seemed to like the stimulating effect . . . and gobbled up all . . . he could find. He . . . finally developed quinin amblyopia. This . . . is a species of blindness . . . sometimes caused by too much quinin. The doctor finally had to confine his old gobbler . . . until he recovered his sight. I cannot vouch for this story, but I was often twitted with it. . . ." [12]

Dr. William Edgar Deeks, appointed director of the Ancón clinic for tropical diseases in 1906, discovered that although all races suffered from malaria the Negroes, notwithstanding their generally insanitary living conditions, were somewhat less susceptible than the whites. He found American and European white employees equally subject to the disease, but the morbidity rate was much higher among the Europeans partly because of their disregard of sanitary precautions and partly because they were not entitled to the long furloughs and changes of climate allotted to the Americans: "The Americans do not frequent at night the native quarters in the Zone towns; do not expose themselves unnecessarily to malarial infection; and of their own initiative aid greatly in preserving their health. . . . [The European laborers] mingle freely at night with the natives, and cannot be kept indoors. As a race they are not addicted to strong liquor, but . . . an increase in malaria among them is always accompanied by an excessive consumption of rum, and very inferior rum, in the belief that the drink is an efficient medicine. . . . As elsewhere in the world, the enforcement of sanitation among the negroes is a gigantic task. . . . As long as he has a roof over his head and a yam or two to eat he is content, and his ideal of personal hygiene is on a par with his conception of marital fidelity." [13]

Although malaria was not and is not yet completely stamped out in the Zone the war against *Anopheles* quickly reduced both the number of cases and the death rate. During the fiscal year 1906–7 211 employees died of malaria, while in the following year, with a larger working force, only 111 fatalities were recorded from

that cause. After 1907 the rate of hospital admission for malaria
(presumably including relapses as well as new cases) decreased
sharply: [14]

MALARIAL CASES PER 1000 EMPLOYEES

1904–5	162
1905–6	727
1906–7	625
1907–8	287
1908–9	312
1909–10	183
1910–11	202
1911–12	143

In 1913 the rate diminished further to 76 per 1000, and by 1927
it had fallen to 11 per 1000. At the same time the malarial death
rate declined from a peak of 7.45 per 1000 in 1906 to .30 per 1000
in 1913, and today, according to the 1941 report, a fatality from
that ailment among canal workers is rare indeed: "One native employee died of malaria in November 1940. In the past 8 years no
other report of the death of an employee from that disease has been
received and there have been only 7 deaths from malaria among
employees in the past 20 years." [15]

Many other diseases — notably tuberculosis, pneumonia, small-
pox, typhoid, and various forms of dysentery — contributed to the
relatively high morbidity and mortality rates of the first three years
of American occupation, but these diminished as the beneficial effects of sanitation, wholesome food, pure water, and expert medical treatment began to make themselves felt. During the long wet
season the workmen were constantly exposed to drenching rain
and often either through carelessness or actual lack of sufficient
clothing wore the same damp garments for days on end. To reduce
the alarming prevalence of pneumonia special stove-heated rooms
in which the men could quickly and conveniently dry their clothes
and bedding were installed in the barracks and family quarters.
In June 1905 one case of bubonic plague was reported at La Boca,
but the prompt and drastic measures adopted by the sanitary department prevented the spread of the disease. Rats were ruthlessly
hunted down and exterminated, three rows of barracks were
burned, and the entire settlement was thoroughly disinfected and
placed under rigid quarantine for three weeks. The enforced isolation of La Boca temporarily upset the whole transportation system of the isthmus: ships could neither leave nor enter the infected

port, railroad yards became congested with immovable freight, and many labor camps along the canal line suffered from a shortage of food. When a second case of plague occurred at the same port in August the quarantine again went into effect, but this time only the wharves and laborers' quarters were sequestered.

"In looking back," Gorgas wrote, ". . . 1905 and 1906 seem the halcyon days for the Sanitary Department. . . . By the fall of 1907 about all of our sanitary work had been completed. Our fight . . . had been won, and from that time on our attention was given to holding what had been accomplished." [16] During the construction period the death rates from disease (not including accidents, homicides, etc.) among canal and railroad employees declined steadily after the peak of 1906, with a few minor fluctuations. These figures are for calendar, not fiscal, years: [17]

DEATHS FROM DISEASE PER 1000 EMPLOYEES

1905	24.30
1906	39.29
1907	24.08
1908	8.68
1909	7.55
1910	7.50
1911	7.65
1912	6.37
1913	5.24
1914	7.04

The total number of deaths among employees during the ten construction years was 6630. Gorgas estimated that not less than 78,000 men would have perished had the conditions prevailing at the time of the Compagnie Universelle continued throughout the American construction period. Since the opening of the canal the annual mortality rate has averaged about 7.25 per 1000, a record not only remarkably low for the tropics but comparing favorably with current rates in most United States cities.

When the American doctors arrived in 1904 they found the large French hospital at Ancón in fair condition but that at Colón badly neglected. A second hospital at Colón owned and operated by the Panama Railroad was also turned over to the commission's sanitary department. All of these structures were rapidly repaired and modernized. By adding second floors to some of the existing buildings and erecting new wings and pavilions the capacity of the Ancón institution was expanded to 1500 beds and that of the Colón group to 300. In addition about 20 district hospitals and 40 still

smaller field hospitals were established at various points along the
canal line. These handled in general only emergency cases. To
move patients from these subsidiary units to either of the two base
hospitals, hospital cars were attached to trains every morning and
evening.

The old French sanatorium on Taboga Island was rehabilitated
and reopened in 1905 as a convalescent home for canal employees,
with a normal capacity of 54 beds and emergency accommodations
for 72. Later it was converted into the Aspinwall Hotel and operated as a vacation resort for employees and their families. In 1917–
18 the hotel was used as an internment camp for German prisoners. After the war it was again run as a recreation center for canal
employees, but the revenues fell far short of the expenses, and in
July 1921 the hotel was closed.

The Zone hospitals served not only canal and railroad employees but many Panamanian patients. In 1904 all public hospitals in
Panama and Colón were dirty and inadequately staffed, a menace
to the health of the Zone as well as of the republic. Lunatics were
still confined in damp neglected cells and treated with medieval
cruelty, while the outcast lepers were banished to a squalid settlement and left to exist precariously on private charity. In 1905 the
Zone government opened a temporary hospital at Miraflores for
the insane, lepers, and indigent sick of Panama. Two years later
the lepers were transferred to a new model colony at Palo Seco, an
attractive site on the shores of the Pacific a few miles southwest of
Panama, and the insane to an up-to-date mental hospital at Coro-
zal. Today Panama City possesses excellent free hospitals of its
own and is no longer dependent upon the Zone for the care of its
poor patients. Between 1915 and 1919 nearly all of the remaining
French hospital buildings were demolished and replaced by new
structures at a cost of approximately $2,000,000. The Gorgas Hos-
pital, as the establishment at Ancón was christened in 1928, is now
considered one of the finest institutions of its kind in the world.
The United States government supplied all hospital services free
to its employees and at very low rates to their families.

Since contagion recognizes no political frontiers sanitation of
the cities of Panama and Colón gave the canal builders as much
concern as that of the Zone itself. In 1904 both towns were inde-
scribably dirty. Household refuse was thrown into the streets and
eventually washed by the rain into open malodorous drainage
ditches. Water for domestic use was stored in cisterns and barrels,
ideal breeding places for mosquitoes and prolific sources of intesti-

nal infection. Neither town could boast the luxury of a single paved street or sidewalk. During the rainy reason pedestrians and vehicles floundered wretchedly through rivers of gluey mud, while *Aëdes* larvæ flourished in countless puddles formed by the uneven surface of the roadways. Obviously one of the first and most important tasks of the American engineers and sanitary experts was the substitution of modern sewers, plumbing, reservoirs, and pavements for the primitive inconveniences and makeshifts of an earlier day.

In June 1904 the commission recruited a special force of engineers to collaborate with the sanitary department in the execution of these works. For the water supply of Panama City the commission decided to utilize an old French reservoir at the headwaters of the Río Grande near the south end of Gaillard Cut. On July 4, 1905 — less than a year after the start of construction — water was turned into the mains of Panama for the first time, and the citizens celebrated with a joyous fiesta. "It would be difficult," Governor Magoon reported, "to describe the gratification and gratitude of the inhabitants at the consummation of their long-deferred hope. Formal expression took the form of a special session of the municipal council and the adoption of resolutions of thanks. . . . The Te Deum was sung in the cathedral. . . ." [18] By the end of 1905 the water and sewer systems were almost completed, and the principal streets were paved with brick laid on concrete.

The metamorphosis of Colón proceeded more slowly, and the delay evoked a flood of angry and for the most part ill-informed criticism. On January 4, 1906 Poultney Bigelow, John Bigelow's son, launched a vitriolic attack in the *Independent:* "Thruout my pestiferous excursion up and down this filthy city I could not find a single man or woman who had not suffered or was not suffering from fever of some kind. . . . At present writing there is not a single drainage canal made at Colon — the very first need of a swampy community. . . . At present the work at Panama resembles an army of recruits without any commander, or rather with a dozen ones. . . . Our Panama patriots are kept busy in finding occupation for young men with political affiliations. . . . What we need . . . is an honest and efficient corps of sanitary police who shall go daily from house to house, not with medicines and ridiculous disinfectants, but with shovels and brooms and carts. . . ." [19] Roosevelt immediately referred the complaint to Taft, who replied that Colón's low elevation, only a few inches above sea level, made the drainage problem exceedingly difficult. The best method would be to fill in the swamp, but that could not be done until the Cule-

bra excavations had progressed far enough to furnish sufficient material. Moreover the Atlantic entrance to the canal was not yet
definitely located, and it was possible that Colón might be wholly
abandoned and a new terminus built on the opposite shore of
Limón Bay. Panama, though less squalid in appearance than Colón, was actually more unhealthy and required more urgent attention.

Taft also pointed out that Bigelow had visited no part of the
isthmus except Colón, that the total duration of his sojourn ashore
had been 28 hours, and that the two chief authorities upon whose
testimony he had based his criticisms were interested parties with
axes to grind. One was Tracy Robinson, "the owner of property in
Colon. . . . He is pecuniarily interested in having invested in
Colon as much Government money as possible. . . . Mr. Robinson is an elderly gentleman with nothing to do but to collect rents
and to talk to strangers . . . and is the source of many prejudiced
reports against the Government." [20] The other witness was John
Lundie, chief engineer of a private ice and electric plant in Panama, who opposed government competition. When the canal
engineers proposed to utilize the Río Grande reservoir for the Panama water supply members of a private syndicate urged the commission to adopt a different site, owned by themselves, much farther from the city and the railroad. Lundie had written a number
of newspaper articles in favor of the syndicate's scheme. Some time
later he applied for an appointment to the commission's board of
consulting engineers and persuaded Wallace to recommend him
for the post. According to Taft, Lundie then "became so persistent . . . and so annoying in his importunities that . . . I telegraphed to Mr. Wallace . . . that his application . . . was rejected." [21]

Meanwhile the charges had created such a stir in Washington
that the Senate Committee on Interoceanic Canals opened an investigation. Bigelow was forced to admit that his inspection had
been preposterously superficial and that he had found it difficult to
dispose of his article: "I . . . had the best part of two days [on the
isthmus]. . . . I wrote nothing until I got back, and then I thought
it would be an interesting article for Harper's Weekly. I offered it
to them, and they declined it. . . . I offered it to Collier's. They
declined it. . . ." [22] Bigelow emerged from the senators' searching
examination thoroughly discredited, unable to produce a shred of
real evidence to support his accusations.

Although most of Bigelow's specific charges were easily refuted
Colón's condition during the first two years of American occupa-

tion was in truth deplorable. To provide temporary relief a dam was thrown across Brazos Brook to form a small water supply reservoir, some drainage ditches were dug, and the almost impassable streets were covered with a layer of crushed rock and gravel. As soon as the terminus was definitely located at Colón work on the improvements began in earnest, and by December 1906 a capacious permanent reservoir about two miles from Mount Hope was in use, the Colón and Cristóbal water mains and sewers were almost completed, and the paving was progressing satisfactorily after a slow start. When Roosevelt visited Colón in November he found the streets, though somewhat improved, still "very bad; as bad as Pennsylvania Avenue . . . before Grant's administration." [23] Recalling that Poultney Bigelow had included in his charges the assertion that the new Mount Hope reservoir would never hold water, the President gleefully informed Congress that "with typical American humor, the engineering corps . . . have christened a large boat which is now used on the reservoir by the name of the individual who thus denied the possibility of the reservoir's existence." [24]

As chief sanitary officer from May 1904 until the autumn of 1913, when the canal was almost completed, Gorgas was the only important executive to remain on the isthmus throughout the entire construction period and to serve under all three commissions. In spite of his spectacularly successful efforts to transform the pestilential region into a safe and salubrious area he had to fight for control of his own organization with each commission in turn. Until late in 1905 the sanitary service, classified as a mere subdepartment of the Zone government and cut off from communication with the chairman except through the governor, was severely hampered by its subordinate status. "From the very beginning," Gorgas maintained, "the Commission underestimated the magnitude of the sanitary operations, as well as their cost, and . . . thought us visionary and more or less lost confidence in us. This was very unfortunate . . . and came very near being the cause of the complete collapse of sanitation." [25] Although by 1904 the mosquito theory of yellow fever and malaria transmission had been accepted by most medical experts and informed laymen many diehards remained obstinately unconverted. Unluckily these included practically all of the members of the first commission. "Admiral Walker was not famous for a keen sense of humour," wrote Mrs. Gorgas, "but the idea that there was anything dangerous in the bite of a mosquito stirred him to uncontrollable mirth. . . . Gorgas had

no better success with General George W. Davis. . . . Again he
had to deal with an engineer of high standing . . . but likewise a
man who had the outlook of another generation. General Davis's
attitude . . . was not severe or intolerant; it was kindly, benevolent, the pose of an older man who wished to keep an enthusiast
out of trouble." [26] Gorgas himself credited Davis with more positive virtues and praised him as the only member of that commission "who had any adequate idea of the difficulties with which the
Sanitary Department was confronted. He gave us his heartiest
support." [27]

In February 1905 Taft sent Dr. Charles A. L. Reed of Cincinnati, chairman of the legislative committee of the American Medical Association, to the isthmus ostensibly to assess land but incidentally — perhaps primarily, for it seems unlikely that a physician
would have been chosen to appraise real estate — to investigate
health conditions. A fortnight in the Zone convinced Reed that
Gorgas was unquestionably right, that the commission was reactionary and incompetent, and that its most obstructive member
was Carl Grunsky. On March 2 he reported these findings to Taft
and on March 11 published a long article in the *American Medical
Association Journal* to the effect that "the commission, more especially Mr. Grunsky, visits on Colonel Gorgas and the Sanitary
Department . . . unnecessary and unreasonable restraints and
confronts it with petty, almost despicable, antagonisms. . . ." [28]
Each biting criticism of the commission was followed by "more especially Mr. Grunsky." Taft, infuriated by the unauthorized publication of what he considered a confidential report, wrote to
Roosevelt on March 17 that the "charges against the commission
were biassed and controversial and not written in the judicial spirit
that inspires confidence in their justice and accuracy," [29] and the
President agreed that the doctor "has not displayed . . . the qualities of temperament or the power of accurate judicial observation
needed to make a report valuable to the government." [30] According to Mrs. Gorgas, Reed's vigorous denunciation of the commission strengthened Gorgas's position and played an important part
in the President's decision to oust the commission on April 1. The
evidence does not justify this conclusion. Roosevelt's reception of
Reed's report was anything but cordial, and moreover he had already resolved to dismiss the commission for a variety of other
reasons.

The appointment of the second commission brought no immediate relief to the harassed sanitary department. Magoon, alarmed
by the outbreak of yellow fever and apparently not firmly con-

vinced by the mosquito theory, went so far as to recommend formally the replacement of Gorgas and Carter by more "practical"
doctors. Taft, who is said to have endorsed the change, claimed that
Wallace, in that tumultuous final interview preceding his resignation, also expressed disapproval of Gorgas's methods; but Wallace
afterwards maintained that he had been merely quoting Magoon.
When Dr. Hamilton Wright, who had recently and successfully
cleaned up the Straits Settlements, was suggested as a possible successor to Gorgas, Roosevelt consulted Dr. Welch, then dean of the
Johns Hopkins Medical School. Welch testified to Wright's ability
but added that nobody possessed as many essential qualifications
for the Panama post as Gorgas himself. Other medical authorities
concurred, and in the end the President not only refused to sup-
plant Gorgas but ordered the commission to support the health
organization in every possible way. With the arrival of the new
chief engineer the atmosphere cleared. Stevens had complete confidence in the sanitary officer and gave him all the assistance and
encouragement in his power. "The moral effect," Gorgas acknowledged gratefully, ". . . was very great, and it is hard to estimate
how much sanitation on the Isthmus owes to this gentleman.
. . ." [31] After some preliminary wavering Shonts also threw his
support to Gorgas, and it was upon Shonts's recommendation that
late in 1905 the sanitary department was finally freed from its administrative shackles and made an independent bureau reporting
directly to the chairman. With his prestige notably enhanced by
the spectacular victory over yellow fever Gorgas had no more trouble with the second commission.

By the time the third commission entered upon its duties in 1907
and Gorgas was at last appointed a commissioner the sanitary department had completed its most pressing tasks. Yellow fever had
disappeared, malaria was on the wane, and the morbidity and mortality rates of other diseases were declining rapidly. Thenceforward
the department concerned itself primarily with the extension of
its campaign against malaria and with consolidation of the gains
already made in other fields. The controversy between Gorgas and
Goethals, which furnished the clubhouses and sewing circles of the
Zone with material for gossip and partisanship during the remaining seven years of construction, centered about the anti-malaria
crusade. In the course of a general reorganization in 1908 Goethals
transferred all brush-clearing and grass-cutting operations — vital
elements in the war against *Anopheles* — from the sanitary to the
quartermaster's department, although the former remained at least
nominally the supervising and directing agency. While Mrs. Gor-

gas — understandably a not altogether impartial witness — attributed the move to Goethals's jealousy of Gorgas and his desire to dominate the then semi-independent sanitary department, his principal motive actually appears to have been nothing more reprehensible than a sincere ambition for greater efficiency and economy. Goethals, fully appreciating the achievements of the health service, had no wish to limit its effectiveness; but as a careful administrator he believed that the mechanical work of clearing grass and brush could be done as well and at less expense by the quartermaster. He considered the sanitary department's expenditure of approximately $350,000 a year extravagant and according to Mrs. Gorgas made no secret of his opinion: " 'Do you know, Gorgas,' Colonel Goethals said one day, 'that every mosquito you kill costs the . . . Government ten dollars?' 'But just think,' answered Gorgas, 'one of those ten-dollar mosquitoes might bite you, and what a loss that would be to the country!' " [32]

Gorgas vehemently protested against the transfer of the brush-clearing and grass-cutting and afterwards held Goethals's interference responsible for the failure to stamp out malaria in the Canal Zone as effectively as in Havana. Goethals ignored this accusation and other uncomplimentary remarks printed in 1924 in Mrs. Gorgas's biography of her husband, but when Mark Sullivan reproduced some of these statements two years later in *Our Times* Goethals presented his version of the conflict in a letter to that author. Goethals claimed that the grass-cutting reorganization had been suggested by Taft, and that he himself had refused to put the shift into effect without Gorgas's consent. Gorgas had agreed to a six months' trial, at the end of which he had asked for a return to the old system on the ground that the new method had not worked satisfactorily. Goethals, insisting that the grass and brush had been cut more cheaply and over a larger area than ever before, had then refused to alter the arrangement: "No further discussion of the matter ever occurred and the sick rate continued to decrease." [33]

Whatever the merits of the malaria controversy may have been there was certainly no love lost between the army doctor and the army engineer, each pre-eminent in his own field. Yet the coolness never developed into an open quarrel. If they disliked each other personally they respected each other professionally; their social relationships, though never intimate, were strictly correct; and both were too intelligent and too well disciplined to permit a temperamental antipathy to interfere seriously with the conscientious performance of their respective duties.

Chapter 44. The Workers

U NDER American administration the canal and railroad employees were divided into two classes: "gold roll" men, the office workers and skilled mechanics who were paid in United States gold, and "silver roll" unskilled laborers who received their wages in Panamanian silver worth about half the face value of gold. Almost all of the gold force was recruited in the United States by government agents, and during the first year or two the engineers on the isthmus flooded Washington with complaints about the poor quality of the mechanics supplied and their unfitness for the special tasks assigned. In April 1905 Walter Dauchy, acting chief engineer during Wallace's absence, protested concerning a newly arrived batch of railroad technicians: "We have been getting along with makeshifts until the work . . . can not be handled that way any longer. . . . We have no opportunity . . . for running a kindergarten in track work." [1]

The construction decade coincided in general with an era of prosperity in the United States. Good workmen could find plenty of jobs at home as well as more comfortable living conditions than the isthmus provided, and the recruiting agents had to make shift with what they could get. In their turn the artisans who accepted employment in the Zone complained of the heat, rain, mosquitoes, quarters, food, and scarcity of entertainment. As the menace of disease diminished and housing, subsistence, and recreational facilities improved the workmen grew more contented, but the annual turnover among skilled employees always remained abnormally large. Goethals reported that during the fiscal year 1909–10 more than 60% of the 5122 skilled workmen employed on the canal and railroad together had to be replaced.

To attract and hold more adept technicians the commission authorized a general wage increase in December 1905, but the augmentations, averaging about 40%, were very unevenly apportioned according to trade. In August 1908 a special committee appointed by Roosevelt to investigate labor and housing conditions in the Zone counted 757 different rates of compensation on the gold roll and 400 on the silver roll. Under the heading "messengers" the investigators found no less than 13 different grades, each with its own

rate of pay. During the following year the commission standard-
ized the wage scales and substituted a few clearly differentiated
classifications for the hundreds of confusing and almost infinitesi-
mal variations.

As additional incentives to the recruitment of labor all gold employees were granted the benefits of the liberal United States civil
service rules and a working day of eight hours — two hours shorter
than that then prevailing in the United States. In 1905 Stevens and
the commission, finding the work impeded by these restrictions,
strongly recommended a longer working day and repeal of the civil
service rules. On January 12, 1906 an executive order abolished
civil service regulations on the isthmus except for office workers,
draftsmen, doctors, and nurses, and in February Congress compromised on the eight-hour law by declaring it inapplicable to alien
canal workers though still compulsory for United States citizens.

The Americans expected to draw their main supply of Negro
labor from Jamaica, but the painful memories of starving workers
marooned on the isthmus after the French collapse in 1889 created
difficulties. The planters objected to depletion of their own labor
reservoir, and the Jamaican authorities imposed a tax of £1 on
each emigrant. While many Jamaicans did obtain work on the
isthmus most of them belonged to the artisan rather than the laborer class. Fortunately for the canal the smaller islands, chronic
sufferers from unemployment, extended a more cordial welcome to
the recruiting agents. 7500 Negroes were imported from Martinique and Guadeloupe and 19,900 from Barbados. The United
States government paid all transportation expenses and guaranteed
repatriation, if desired, after 500 working days.

The colored British subjects — or as they often called themselves, British "objects" — were "quiet, generally honest, soft-
spoken and respectful." [2] But they were inclined to stand on their
dignity and not unnaturally resented the brusque commands and
flowing imprecations of certain churlish white foremen, so that
Sir Claude Coventry Mallet, the genial, tactful British consul general who had lived 30 years in Panama, was frequently called upon
to pour oil on troubled waters. Racial segregation existed and still
exists in the Zone: whites and Negroes are housed, fed, and educated separately, each group has its own hospital service, and the
Jim Crow system prevails on the Panama Railroad. Yet during the
construction period as well as later instances of actual brutality appear to have been exceedingly rare. Among his many unsubstanti-
ated charges Poultney Bigelow had asserted that the Jamaica Negroes "are returning from the canal in portentous numbers, in spite

of the fact that nominal wages there are twice or three times higher. . . ." [3] Taft, pointing out that Bigelow's cursory investigation had taken place shortly before Christmas, retorted: "There is real danger that the laborers . . . are paid and treated too well. . . . It is said that the negroes are leaving . . . because of mistreatment. . . . Just before the holidays a great number . . . return to the islands. . . . This has been the custom ever since the beginning of the French construction. . . . Mr. Mallet . . . told me he . . . found that everything was being done that was possible for the proper treatment, housing, and feeding of the negroes. A report from the French consul, charged with looking after the negroes . . . from the French West Indies, is to the same effect." [4] Unskilled colored workmen received 20 cents per hour in silver, the equivalent of 10 cents in gold, in addition to free housing and medical service.

The hustling American engineers were prone to scoff at the Negro's capacity for work. In 1905 the commission estimated the efficiency of the West Indians at only 25% to 33% of that of the best common laborers in the United States, and an additional year's experience confirmed that conclusion: "Not only do they seem to be disqualified by lack of actual vitality, but their disposition to labor seems to be as frail as their bodily strength." [5] Bishop, the commission's secretary, considered the Negroes "slow both in mental processes and physical movement. They . . . acquired a kind of automatic regularity in the performance of duties. A few developed some initiative . . . in certain trades. . . ." [6] But in time, as association with American mechanics and European laborers stimulated their dormant competitive spirit, the productivity of the West Indians increased. They needed more money to satisfy a growing desire for possessions, and their women, having developed a taste for finery, spurred the wage-earners to greater exertions.

During 1906, 1907, and 1908 about 12,000 white Europeans were imported as unskilled laborers. Some 8200 of these came from northern Spain, 2000 from Italy, 1100 from Greece, and a few hundred from France, Armenia, and other countries. Their fares were paid by the commission but afterwards deducted from their wages in small installments. Unlike the Negroes they received no advance guarantee of repatriation, though a great many were eventually sent home at the commission's expense. When the Spanish government prohibited further contract recruiting in 1909 the American agent was withdrawn, but the steamship companies continued to recruit unofficially and brought over about 2000 additional Spanish and Italian laborers in 1910. At the beginning the Europeans, especially the Spaniards, proved excellent workmen. "Their efficiency," the commission reported in 1906, "is not only more than double that of the negroes, but they stand the climate much better." [7] The wage scale for European laborers was twice that of the West Indians. As the Negroes' capacity for work increased year by year the output of the Europeans, who labored continuously without vacations, gradually declined until at the end of the construction period there was little to choose between them.

In August 1906 the commission invited bids on contracts to furnish 2500 Chinese laborers for not less than two years, with provision for a possible increase in the number up to 15,000. Four proposals, only two of which fulfilled the prescribed conditions, were submitted. The labor contractors agreed to supply coolies at wages of 9 to 11 cents gold per hour, approximately the rate paid the Negroes; but the wholesale importation of Chinese laborers into the Zone by a government which excluded them from its own continental territories appeared so inconsistent that the suggestion aroused violent opposition in many sections of the United States. When the republic of Panama, which had a Chinese exclusion law similar to that of the United States, added its protests the project was abandoned.

The maximum labor force employed by the Compagnie Universelle at any one period numbered about 19,000. At the time of the transfer to the United States in May 1904 the employees of the Compagnie Nouvelle on the isthmus had dwindled to a skeleton maintenance crew of 746 men, but by November of the same year the force had increased to 3500. Thereafter it expanded rapidly. Combining the gold and silver rolls and including the Panama Railroad employees, the number of men at work during the American construction period averaged as follows: [8]

AVERAGE NUMBER EMPLOYED

1905	17,000 (approximate)
1906	26,547
1907	39,238
1908	43,890
1909	47,167
1910	50,802
1911	48,876
1912	50,893
1913	56,654
1914	44,329

During the years of slide activity following the opening of the canal the force dwindled only gradually and in 1920 still numbered about 20,000. In 1921, when the principal slides had been cleared away and there was no longer need for more than the routine maintenance and operating crew, it declined to 14,000 and thereafter fluctuated between 10,000 and 16,000 until 1940, when the commencement of construction work on the third set of locks again increased the number of employees to more than 25,000. None of these figures include the military and naval personnel stationed in or near the Zone.

Taking into account the great number of workers, the variety of nationalities represented, the isolation of the isthmus, the often uncomfortable living conditions, and the fretfulness natural to men performing hard manual labor in a hot damp climate, relations between the laborers and the canal administration were on the whole satisfactory after the first year. Demonstrations of mass discontent rarely occurred and never assumed alarming proportions. In April 1905 about 150 Jamaica Negroes rioted in what appears to have been well-justified protest against poor food and unwarranted delays in the distribution of wages, and in the mêlée 21 received injuries — none of them serious — from the clubs and bayonets of the police. In October of the same year a shipload of Negroes from Martinique, superstitiously terrified by the mysterious ritual of vaccination, refused to disembark at Colón but were driven ashore and forcibly inoculated to the accompaniment of howls and frantic struggles.

Many of the skilled mechanics on the gold roll belonged to unions, and strikes were called occasionally but seldom lasted long enough to cause material interruption to the work. One of the most serious took place in May 1907 when the steam shovel operators demanded an increase in monthly pay from $210 to $300, and the cranemen, then receiving $185, held out for $250. The commission offered an increase of 5% after the first year and 3% additional at the end of each succeeding year. The mechanics rejected the compromise, and for some weeks excavation declined to one fourth of the normal output; but by the end of June the machines were once more fully manned. Goethals reported that "no personal ill feeling . . . developed, and no injury or damage . . . resulted during the entire affair." [9]

Under the semi-military paternalism of the third commission, according to the correspondent of the *Independent*, the general attitude of American skilled labor was "one of satisfaction with its

THE LAND DIVIDED

treatment. There are plenty of petty abuses and injustices. . . .
There is also, in spite of the denials of the Commission, an exasperating system of 'gum-shoeing' or spying on the men. . . . The
. . . Commission insists that it is running an open shop, and de-
clines to recognize the unions formally. Mr. Bishop, however . . .
has had the good sense to receive committees representing the men,
if not the unions. A more formal recognition is not demanded, and
negotiations are carried on amicably — tho not always with results
satisfactory to the men. There are a number of Socialists on the
Zone, but there is no Socialist reading club or local. There was a
reading club at Colon . . . but with the return of its organizer to
the United States it was allowed to die. There is no indication that
the Commission would oppose such an organization or discriminate against its members." [10]

Goethals himself invariably set aside Sunday mornings for the
reception of employees and members of their families who wished
to present complaints. The grievances were of all kinds: unjust
treatment by a foreman, a dispute over deductions from a pay
check, dissatisfaction with quarters, furniture, or rations, a request
for special privileges, an appeal for accident compensation, a domestic quarrel between husband and wife. Some employees came
not to complain but to offer constructive suggestions for the improvement of this or that, others mainly out of curiosity or to be
able to brag that they had talked things over with the "old man"
himself. Some were belligerent, some dignified and respectful,
some overcome with shy embarrassment. Without regard to race,
color, rank, or salary Goethals admitted each applicant according
to the rule of first come, first served, and listened patiently to every
charge or lamentation. Frequently these individual problems could
be settled then and there, sometimes the chief would render judgment only after reflection or after discussion with his legal or other
advisers. His authority was absolute, his decisions unappealable
except to the President of the United States. As lawyer, judge, and
jury rolled into one Goethals has been likened by various commentators to a Venetian doge, to St. Louis dispensing justice beneath the oak at Vincennes, and to a "combination of father con-
fessor and Day of Judgment, whose like has rarely if ever been seen
since the time of Solomon." [11]

These Sunday conferences, effective as they were as safety valves,
could not handle all of the disputes that swamped the canal administration at the beginning of the army régime. Bishop was directed
to investigate all complaints and report to Goethals for final action,
and for the first six months the secretary devoted almost his entire

time to this task. He gave his personal attention to all grievances registered by American employees, while a special assistant — Giuseppe Garibaldi, grandson of the Italian liberator — investigated the problems of the Europeans. Garibaldi's familiarity with several languages made his services especially useful. "In regard to the complaints of American employes," Bishop wrote, "the method . . . was to send for the complainant and ask him to make a full statement to be taken down by a stenographer. . . . In a majority of instances the complainant, before this was completed, concluded that he had no grievance. Talking fully about it had been all the relief he needed. He had 'got it out of his system'. . . ." [12] This was sound psychology, and the number of complaints diminished steadily until within six months they had almost ceased.

At Bishop's suggestion and under his direct supervision the commission published a weekly newspaper, the *Canal Record*. In form it was modeled after the *Bulletin du Canal Interocéanique,* but it indulged in none of the flights of fancy and spurious enthusiasms of its French prototype. Its policy was set forth in the first issue dated September 4, 1907: "The primary purpose . . . is the publication of accurate information, based upon official records, concerning all branches of the work. . . . In addition there will be published such information in regard to the social life of the Zone, its amusements, sports and other activities, as is thought to be of general interest. Space will also be given to letters from employees relating to any topic upon which they may choose to write, subject only to the restrictions that such communications must be couched in respectful language and must be signed. . . ." [13] Perhaps the most useful contribution of the *Canal Record* was its publication of weekly excavation statistics for individual steam shovels and dredges, which stimulated healthy rivalry between the crews and substantially increased their total output. By reporting news from all parts of the Zone it brought the various camps and settlements into closer touch and helped to develop an intangible but invaluable *esprit de corps*. Baseball and billiards scores, notes on the activities of local clubs and fraternal orders, gossipy reports of outings, picnics, teas, and sewing bees, news of the arrivals and departures of visitors and of their entertainment by the canal hostesses, all added interest to the somewhat drab and restricted routine of the Zone. As a morale builder the *Canal Record* fully justified its existence. It was printed at the commission's new plant at Mount Hope and distributed free to all employees of the canal and railroad on the isthmus as well as to members of Congress and to libraries, scientific societies, and similar institutions throughout the world. After the opening of the canal the character of the paper changed. Social items and club news disappeared, and since 1914 its columns have contained little but dry official circulars and shipping lists. In August 1916 the format was reduced and the name altered to *Panama Canal Record*.

At the end of the construction period all contract laborers who desired repatriation were sent home at the expense of the United States government. Many thousands voluntarily emigrated to nearby Central American countries to work for the United Fruit Company and other private corporations, while others elected to remain on the isthmus or drifted back to Panama after repatriation. As the slides abated and the canal force diminished these workmen found it increasingly difficult to obtain jobs. The oversupply of labor led to a reduction of wages for canal work, and in May 1919 the discontented dockyard and coaling plant crews struck for higher pay. Settlement of the strike left the situation basically unchanged. Since large seasonal fluctuations in the canal operating forces were inevitable Governor Harding suggested the opening of farm lands to keep the men employed during the slack months.

Earlier attempts to encourage farming and local industry in the Zone had met with little success. In 1908 vegetable gardens were planted on the Pacific side, but according to Goethals the experiment "proved conclusively that it was impossible to do farming as it is understood in the United States. . . . Congress, however, passed a law which authorized the leasing of lands to those who would engage in agricultural pursuits. . . . Up to 1911 no applications . . . had been received." [14] Shortly thereafter it was decided to withdraw the offer of private leases and to exclude from the Zone all residents except the employees and armed forces of the United States. The depopulation policy had two advantages: it facilitated protection of the canal works against malicious damage and simplified the malaria problem, since extension of mosquito control to outlying farms would have enormously increased administration expenses.

Nevertheless the supply department made another and more successful effort after the opening of the canal to furnish employment and at the same time reduce the Zone's dependence upon outside sources for its foodstuffs. By 1918 domestic beef, pork, poultry, eggs, dairy products, fruits, and vegetables had replaced importations to a large extent. In December 1921 certain areas in the Zone were reopened to cultivation by canal laborers under revocable licenses, and within six months more than 1000 such permits had been issued. While the establishment of these agricultural communities alleviated the region's economic ills it by no means cured them. In 1932 Governor Burgess reported that "the Canal Zone and the . . . cities of Panama and Colon . . . face a condition of permanent unemployment. . . . The search for work is sharp and there is increasing competition between Americans and aliens for work which may be performed almost equally well by either. . . . The most obvious form of relief is an increase in public works." [15]

In 1928 the Panama Canal Retirement Association complained of the lack of opportunities for young people of American parentage on the isthmus and recommended the retirement of gold employees on pensions at an earlier age so that they could return with their adolescent children to the United States. Pensions were in fact so low and so belated as to leave superannuated employees almost destitute. The Panama Railroad Company, though owned by the United States government as completely as the canal itself, had always maintained a more liberal old-age pension system than the canal organization. The Denison act effective July 1, 1931 finally established identical retirement conditions for canal and railroad employees who were citizens of the United States but still neglected the European and West Indian canal workers.

Another grievance voiced by the employees concerned the discrimination in favor of the army and navy administrators and engineers who had directed the construction of the canal. On March 4, 1915 the Senate rewarded these leaders by confirming the promotions of Goethals, Gorgas, and Hodges to the rank of major general, of Sibert to that of brigadier general, and of Rousseau to rear admiral of the lower nine. But the civilians received no official recognition except a wholesale distribution of bronze medals made of old French scrap found on the isthmus and struck at the Philadelphia mint. These medals, awarded to all employees who had served continuously for at least two years, bore on one face a likeness of Theodore Roosevelt in low relief and on the other a representation of ships passing through Gaillard Cut, with a small reproduction of the great seal of the Canal Zone and an inscription borrowed from that seal: THE LAND DIVIDED — THE WORLD UNITED.

The government provided free housing, furniture, light, water, fuel, ice, and garbage disposal service for all canal and railroad employees on the isthmus. Until new buildings could be erected some of the old French residences, sketchily repaired and modernized, served as temporary quarters. Under the inept first commission new construction progressed slowly, and for two years complaints of overcrowding and discomfort filled the air. By the end of 1906 the second commission was in a position to announce the completion of sufficient buildings to house all unmarried employees, but several more years passed before the supply of family residences caught up with the demand. Gold roll married quarters were allocated according to a complicated mathematical system: each employee was entitled to one square foot of floor space for each dollar of monthly salary, his wife to an additional square foot, each child to 5% of the father's space for each year of its own age, adult members of the family other than the wife to 75% of the basic allotment, and adult members of the household not related to the family (including white servants) to 50%. Colored and native servants received no separate space allowance. In computing these areas kitchens, bathrooms, hallways, and all rooms containing less than 64 square feet were ignored.

This ingenious but somewhat arbitrary regulation earned its inventor, Jackson Smith, the nickname of "Square-foot" Smith and the burning hatred of almost every American family in the Zone. As head of the department of labor, quarters, and subsistence (and after April 1907 as a commissioner) Smith recruited, housed, and fed the canal force competently enough, but his surly ill temper infuriated his associates. Goethals wrote confidentially to the Secretary of War: "With respect to Mr. Smith, I am convinced of two things: first, of his ability . . . and second, that his unpopularity is so pronounced as to interfere seriously with the efficiency of his department. It cannot be denied that there has been, and still is, a great deal of complaint about quarters. To a degree, at least, this condition is unavoidable. I have no doubt that very much of the blame placed upon Mr. Smith . . . he did not deserve. . . . I am equally sure that a very large proportion of it could have been avoided if his manner and treatment of the subject had been different." [16] Following a clash with Goethals over purchasing procedure Smith tendered his resignation in June 1908 and departed at once on a furlough which lasted until his retirement became effective on September 15. Hodges replaced him on the commission, while Major Carroll A. Devol as chief quartermaster took charge of his department.

The European silver employees lived in dormitories and houses similar to but somewhat less spacious and comfortable than those of the gold force bachelors, and barracks were provided for the West Indians on the basis of 60 square feet of floor space per occupant. For the first three or four years bedbugs and lice infested many of the barracks until a series of energetic clean-up campaigns destroyed the vermin. The Europeans lived contentedly enough in the commission quarters, but most of the Negroes objected to the regimentation of barracks life, refused flatly to remain in the rent-free buildings, and flocked to ramshackle huts in the bush or crowded insanitary tenements in the towns. In 1913 Goethals estimated that less than 25% of the West Indian workmen occupied commission dormitories.

The first commission made but a feeble attempt to solve the vital problem of subsistence, and it was not until late in 1905 that a satisfactory system of food distribution was evolved. At the beginning the canal employees were expected to buy their own provisions from the local shops run for the most part by Chinese traders, but these sources soon proved pitifully inadequate. The next move also ended in failure. On September 7, 1905 the Panama Railroad Company, acting for the canal employees as well as for its own, awarded to Jacob E. Markel of Omaha, a former operator of "eating houses" for the Union Pacific, a five-year contract to supply food to all the workers. The Panama Railroad undertook to provide the buildings and equipment. Markel proposed to charge gold employees and adult members of their families $30 per month or $33\frac{1}{3}$ cents per single meal and to feed each child between the ages of 5 and 12 for $10 per month or 13 cents a meal, while silver laborers were to pay $12 per month or 15 cents a meal for themselves and $5 monthly or 10 cents per meal for their children. In addition the contractor was entitled to $6 per month from each gold employee for care and maintenance of quarters. When the employees complained of the high prices Stevens, estimating that Markel would make a profit of about $1,000,000 a year, cabled an indignant protest to Washington. A few weeks later the railroad company annulled the contract and paid Markel $10,000 in settlement of all claims.

In October 1905 the commission, finally assuming full responsibility for feeding its employees and their dependents, decided to operate commissaries, build mess houses, and furnish cooked and uncooked food at cost. It erected a cold-storage plant, bakery, and laundry at Cristóbal, installed refrigeration machinery in the Panama Railroad steamers for the transportation of perishable supplies from the United States, and ordered refrigerator cars for the railroad. The new system, organized by the unpopular but capable Jackson Smith, expanded so rapidly that by 1907 almost 1,000,000 meals per month were being served to the three classes of workers.

Gold employees and their families boarded at restaurants supervised by American stewards and largely staffed by American cooks
for 90 cents per day, European laborers ate what Goethals called "a
meal peculiar to the tastes of the men" [17] prepared by European
cooks and served in mess halls at 40 cents per day, including wine
on holidays, and for the Negroes mess kitchens run by West Indian
cooks provided meals for 30 cents per day. In 1908 the commission
operated 20 gold roll restaurants — locally called "hotels" — 25
mess halls for Europeans, and 31 West Indian kitchens. All rates
except those charged the Europeans were substantially lower than
the prices stipulated in the Markel contract. The government made
no effort to show a profit on the subsistence account and by purchasing on an immense scale was able to maintain high standards
of quality at a minimum cost.

Yet many of the gold employees found the fare in the commission restaurants monotonous and organized small mess groups of
their own, hiring their own cooks and buying raw materials from
the commissaries. Far more bothersome than the grumbling of the
Americans was the problem of feeding the colored laborers. In the
opinion of the medical staff malnutrition was responsible for much
of the notorious inefficiency of the West Indians. Accustomed to a
starvation diet of starchy yams and a few bananas, they simply refused to eat enough nourishing food to enable them to perform a
heavy day's work. The canal administrators doggedly tried one inducement after another. The workmen were offered cooked food
at 10 cents a meal and the raw materials for less but declined both.
Then they were given uncooked food without charge but would
not take the trouble to cook it. Free cooked meals proved more popular, but the Negroes still preferred their own haphazard victuals.

The canal and railroad administrations not only housed and fed
their employees but operated two hotels for tourists and visiting
officials. The Hotel Tivoli at Ancón, situated just within the Zone
a few yards from Panamanian territory, first opened in November
1906 when one partially completed wing was hastily prepared for
the reception of President Roosevelt and his party. In 1913 the old
wooden Hotel Washington at Colón, owned and run by the Panama Railroad, was demolished and replaced by a modern structure.
At both of these first-class establishments much higher prices prevailed than at those intended solely for employees. In 1922 the
canal administration leased its restaurants and messes to private operators but received no acceptable bid for the Tivoli and Washington, which are still managed as government enterprises.

When the commission decided in 1905 to open commissaries the

42.   GATÚN·LOCKS UNDER CONSTRUCTION, 1912

43.   MIRAFLORES LOCK GATES UNDER·CONSTRUCTION, 1913

44. GATÚN DAM AND LAKE ENTRANCE TO LOCKS

45. GATÚN LOCKS IN OPERATION, LOOKING SOUTH

shopkeepers of Panama, who had been reaping a golden harvest, objected violently, and Governor Magoon instituted a system of coupons designed to restrict commissary sales to Zone employees. In spite of precautions against smuggling a considerable quantity of commissary merchandise found its way into the adjacent republic, and the commercial competition of the Zone commissaries remained a perennial grievance to the Panamanians until 1939, when under the Hull-Alfaro treaty the United States government further limited the scope of the commissary operations and promised to exercise increased vigilance to prevent the leakage of contraband. Although sales have always been theoretically and are now actually confined to canal and railroad employees and United States armed forces, the commissaries transact an enormous volume of business. During the first years of the construction period the government stores carried only a modest assortment of standard provisions, clothing, and household gear, but as more and more employees brought their families to the isthmus the purchases of the supply department kept pace with the ever-increasing demand for variety. Today the Zone commissaries are as well stocked as most American department stores, and their sales have expanded "from a pork-and-beans beginning to a silk-stocking maturity." [18]

"The three things lacking to make life enjoyable on the Isthmus," wrote Edwin Slosson and Gardner Richardson in 1906, "are all feminine — women, cows and hens. . . . Normal family life is becoming established and society is developing peculiar forms. . . . In some phases it resembles official life in India. At the balls married women reign supreme, with abundance of admirers and no débutante rivals. Mrs. Hauksbee . . . and all the other colonial dames with whom Kipling has made us acquainted are already on the Canal Zone. After the novelty . . . wears off, life . . . is barren and dull for most of the men. . . . It is more from ennui than from viciousness that many of the employees seek for solace in the cocktail and the jackpot." [19]

A Y.M.C.A. representative sent to investigate isthmian morals early in 1905 reported that the chief "positive forces for evil" were gambling, "wide open in . . . Panama and Colon," the legalized lottery in the republic, "saloons and drinking places in large numbers and dispensing a most inferior and highly injurious quality of liquor," the popular sports of bullfighting and cockfighting, and prostitution "as bad as might be expected in a country of loose marriage relations, lax laws, etc." [20] Among the negative forces he listed "an entire absence of libraries and reading rooms, except for

railroad employees at Colon, a dearth of reputable places of amusement, no grounds for outdoor games . . . [and] no clubs for mental, moral or physical culture." [21] A few months later Poultney Bigelow included in his diatribe the assertion that "the clergy of the
Isthmus were loud in protest because the United States authorities
had imported at considerable expense several hundreds of colored
ladies. Prostitutes are not needed on the Isthmus — and if they
were there is no call to send for them at the expense of the taxpayer.
They may be trusted to come without any especial assistance whenever Colon clamors for kindred consolation." [22] Taft indignantly
repudiated the accusation that the government had financed or otherwise encouraged the importation of any prostitutes, white or colored, but he did not attempt to deny the obvious fact that both Colón and Panama swarmed with them.

Throughout the construction period the European and West
Indian laborers were left largely to their own devices for social diversion, but the commission energetically set to work to provide
recreation and moral guidance for its American employees. Baseball teams were organized, reading rooms opened in the gold force
restaurant buildings, churches of various denominations erected.
To encourage domesticity and at the same time diminish the excessive turnover of skilled labor the families of employees were
offered passage from New York to Colón at the greatly reduced
rate of $20 per person.

By the end of 1906 a clubhouse containing a "social parlor,"
cardroom, writing room, billiard room, a large hall for dances,
bowling alleys, gymnasium, and showers had been opened at Colón, and four more were under construction at Culebra, Empire,
Gorgona, and Cristóbal. These clubs were run by the Young Men's
Christian Association under the supervision of a board selected by
the commission. The general secretary of the Zone Y.M.C.A. reported that the clubhouse activities were "democratic, without
forced congeniality. . . . Altogether the clubhouses have served
practically the entire white population of the respective towns.
. . . There have been 95 entertainments given by high-grade ly-
ceum and vaudeville talent imported from the States. . . . Local
talent has been used for 131 entertainments. . . . The . . . members have organized themselves into many small clubs for . . .
chess, checkers, glee, minstrel, camera, and orchestra. . . . Educa-
tional classes have been conducted of evenings in Spanish, arithmetic, mechanical drawing, English grammar, shorthand, first aid, and
wireless telegraphy. . . . The soda fountains . . . have proven a
great social attraction and have kept many from the saloons." [23]

Nor were the employees' families neglected: "Women are granted the courtesy of [club] privileges, including games, on two afternoons per week. . . . A work much appreciated has been that of the junior department for boys from 10 to 16. . . . Their activities have been chiefly games, gymnastic work, outings, and visits to places of recreative and historic interest." [24]

Such diversions, faithfully reported in the weekly *Canal Record,* made exile bearable, strengthened community spirit, and vastly improved both the morale and the morals of the gold force. Although little or no organized entertainment was provided for the European and colored workers they also seem to have found it possible to amuse themselves without getting into too much serious trouble. "It is rather remarkable," Gorgas noted in 1908, "that in our force of 43,000 men we should have admitted to the hospitals only 130 cases of alcoholism, 233 cases of syphilis, and 131 cases of gonorrhea." [25] A year later with a still larger army of workmen the alcoholics in hospital numbered only 80 and the syphilitics 143, but the gonorrhea patients had increased to 211. While unreported cases in all these categories no doubt exceeded the hospital admissions the record as a whole was better than might have been expected.

By 1921 the club and recreation activities were almost self-supporting and in the opinion of Governor Morrow more than justified their small annual cost to the government: "The clubhouses serve well as stabilizers of what would otherwise be a constantly shifting, unanchored population, drifting inevitably to the demoralizing influences of the inferior cabarets and saloons of Panama and Colon, or leaving the service. The United States Government has created here a unique community of workers with no responsibility of citizenship . . . no ownership of real and but little personal property, and no encouragement (in fact, no possibility in the Canal Zone) to private enterprise of any kind. . . . This work should be maintained at its present high standard. . . ." [26]

Chapter 45. Tolls Controversy

F OR two years the governments of Great Britain and the United States wrangled stubbornly over a single sentence in section 5 of the Panama Canal act of August 24, 1912: "No tolls shall be levied upon vessels engaged in the coastwise trade of the United States." [1] The British contended that the provision violated article 3 of the Hay-Pauncefote treaty, which stipulated that the canal "shall be free and open to the vessels of commerce and of war of all nations observing these Rules, on terms of entire equality, so that there shall be no discrimination against any such nation, or its citizens or subjects, in respect of the conditions or charges of traffic, or otherwise." [2] The British government insisted logically enough that the phrase "all nations" meant *all* nations, not all nations except the United States. Washington maintained that since American coastwise shipping was restricted by law to vessels flying the American flag foreign competition in that field could not exist, and therefore the proposed exemption from tolls involved no discrimination against British or other foreign commerce within the meaning of the treaty.

During the Senate debate on the Panama Canal act proposals to discriminate in favor of domestic shipping fell into four general categories: to exempt all American vessels from tolls, to collect tolls from American ships and then refund them from the Treasury, to exempt American vessels engaged in coastwise trade, and to refund tolls collected from coastwise vessels. On July 8 the British chargé d'affaires in Washington, Alfred Mitchell-Innes, handed to Secretary of State Knox a note setting forth the British objections to all four of the suggested measures. The note affirmed that exemption of all American shipping would clearly violate the Hay-Pauncefote treaty, that there was no difference in principle between a refund of tolls and their outright remission, and that while exemption or refund of coastwise shipping tolls might be unobjectionable in theory it would be impossible to frame regulations so as to restrict such exemptions or refunds to *bona fide* coastwise traffic.

The Senate, having decided to adopt the third alternative and exempt American vessels engaged in coastwise trade, passed the Panama Canal act on August 24. In a memorandum attached to the act President Taft attempted to demolish the British contentions: "The British protest . . . is a proposal to read into the treaty a surrender by the United States of its right to regulate its own commerce in its own way. . . . The policy of exempting the coastwise trade from all tolls really involves the question of granting a Government subsidy for the purpose of encouraging that trade in competition with . . . the transcontinental railroads. I approve this policy." [3]

On November 14 Foreign Secretary Sir Edward Grey amplified the British arguments in a lengthy dispatch to James Bryce, the British ambassador in Washington: "The Hay-Pauncefote Treaty does not stand alone; it was the corollary of the Clayton-Bulwer Treaty. . . . The purpose of the United States in negotiating the Hay-Pauncefote Treaty was to . . . obtain the right, which they had surrendered, to construct the Canal themselves . . . but the complete liberty of action . . . was to be limited by the maintenance of the general principle embodied in article 8 of the earlier treaty. That principle . . . was one of equal treatment for both British and United States ships. . . . If the rules set out in the Hay-Pauncefote Treaty secure to Great Britain no more than most-favoured-nation treatment, the value of the consideration given for superseding the Clayton-Bulwer Treaty is not apparent to His Majesty's Government." [4] Grey also contended that exemption of certain American vessels would violate the stipulation in the Hay-Pauncefote treaty assuring "just and equitable" tolls, since foreign shipping would be obliged to pay more than its fair share towards the upkeep of the canal and interest on the investment therein. Furthermore the United States maritime laws not only classified as "coastwise" voyages from New York to Puget Sound, to Honolulu, or to Manila but permitted American vessels to load and unload cargoes at any number of foreign ports during the course of such voyages and even to circumnavigate the globe without losing their coastwise status. Hence American coastwise vessels freed from the burden of canal tolls would in practice enjoy an unfair advantage over non-exempt foreign ships in the field of world trade. In conclusion the Foreign Secretary proposed submission of the dispute to The Hague, a step provided for by the arbitration treaty of 1908 between Great Britain and the United States.

Meanwhile on November 13, 1912 — the day before Grey dispatched his note — Taft had announced the official canal toll rates, which were not in fact any higher than they would have been without the exemption of coastwise ships. On January 17, 1913 Knox replied to Grey's protest with a suggestion that the British were whimpering before they were hurt, since "the tolls which would be paid by American coastwise vessels . . . were computed in determining the rate. . . . There is a very clear distinction between an omission to 'take into account' the coastwise tolls in order to determine a just and equitable rate, which is as far as this objection goes, and the remission of such tolls. . . . The exemption . . . or . . . refunding of tolls . . . is merely a subsidy . . . to that [coastwise] trade, and the loss . . . will fall solely upon the United States. . . . It is the improper exercise of a power, and not its possession, which alone can give rise to an international cause of action. . . . Until these objections rest upon something more substantial than mere possibility, it is not believed that they should be submitted to arbitration." [5]

The reluctance of the United States government to arbitrate the tolls question was understandable if not particularly creditable. Almost certainly the tribunal would have decided in favor of Great Britain, partly because the British case actually had a sounder legal foundation and partly because the other maritime nations represented on the court — all in varying degrees at least potentially affected by the proposed exemption but, since they were not parties to the Hay-Pauncefote treaty, unable to protest on their own accounts — sympathized with the British effort to prevent American discrimination against foreign vessels. On February 28, 1913 Bryce brought the long diplomatic correspondence to a close with a letter to Knox denying the latter's contention that since British shipping had as yet suffered no actual financial loss the exemption clause could not be considered objectionable: "From this view His Majesty's Government feel bound to . . . dissent. They conceive that international law or usage does not support the doctrine that the passing of a statute in contravention of a treaty right affords no ground of complaint . . . and that a nation . . . must, before protesting . . . wait until some further action violating those rights in a conclusive instance has been taken. . . . In their view the [Panama Canal] Act . . . was in itself, and apart from any action which may be taken under it, inconsistent with the . . . Hay-Pauncefote Treaty. . . ." [6]

While the tone of these diplomatic exchanges remained consistently formal and restrained the controversy raged much less politely in the press and public forums on both sides of the Atlantic. In England and in Europe generally the American position was almost universally condemned, but in the United States it was by no means universally defended. The American newspapers split into two camps, chambers of commerce opposed other chambers of commerce, American shipping interests urged retention of the exemption clause, the transcontinental railroads lobbied energetically against it, and opinion in Congress was sharply divided.

On January 14, 1913 Elihu Root introduced in the Senate a bill to repeal the offending clause. "The American coastwise trade," he argued on February 12, "is already fully protected in that none but American vessels can engage in it. . . . Whatever the Hay-Pauncefote treaty means we hold the Canal Zone . . . under a practical trust. We have declared the obligations of a trustee in the most unequivocal terms; and now for this problematical, doubtful, alleged advantage of helping trade by keeping the money out of our Treasury from the coastwise vessels, we are . . . falsifying every declaration we have made for over half a century, and falsifying what at all events the world at large believes to be our solemn obligation. . . . We have greater interests as a Nation than the interests that can possibly be subserved by this discrimination. . . . The country has a greater interest in being regarded by the world as fair and broad minded and high minded than it can possibly have in this little petty benefit to a part of the people." [7]

In a special message delivered on March 5, 1914 President Wilson proposed repeal of the tolls exemption: "In my own judgment . . . that exemption constitutes a mistaken economic policy from every point of view, and is, moreover, in plain contravention of the treaty. . . . But I have not come to urge upon you my personal views. . . . Whatever may be our own differences of opinion concerning this much debated measure, its meaning is not debated outside the United States. . . . The large thing to do is the only thing we can afford to do, a voluntary withdrawal from a position everywhere questioned and misunderstood. We ought to reverse our action without raising the question whether we were right or wrong. . . ." [8]

In the end these statesmanlike conceptions prevailed, and on June 15, 1914 — just two months before the canal was opened — Congress repealed the exemption clause but weakened the effect of the gesture by adding a specific affirmation of its right to re-enact such a measure at some future time, thus basing its renunciation on expediency, not principle. Within the last twenty years several bills to restore coastwise exemption have been introduced, but all have failed to pass both branches of Congress.

Public vessels of the republic of Panama are explicitly exempted from the payment of canal tolls by article 19 of the Hay-Bunau-Varilla treaty, an exception agreed to by the British government. Since the ratification of the Thomson-Urrutia treaty in 1922 similar privileges of free transit have been accorded to the public vessels of Colombia, a concession also accepted in advance by Great Britain because of Colombia's special position. The only other exemption granted is to vessels proceeding through the canal solely in order to avail themselves of the repair facilities afforded by the shipyards and drydocks at Balboa.

Taft's proclamation of November 13, 1912 established three different toll rates for the canal: on merchant vessels carrying passengers and/or cargo and on army and navy transports, colliers, and hospital and supply ships, $1.20 per net ton; on vessels in ballast without passengers or cargo, 40% less than the above or 72 cents per net ton; on naval vessels other than transports, colliers, and hospital and supply ships, 50 cents per *displacement* ton. Special Panama rules, similar to but varying in detail from those in force at Suez, for the computation of net tonnage were drawn up by Professor Emory Richard Johnson, who had served on the second Walker commission as a transportation expert. These rules, recognizing that a net ton is a unit not of weight but of volume — a ton originally meant a *tun* or cask of wine, the ancient cargo unit — based the charges upon the sound principle that a commercial vessel should pay tolls only upon its actual earning capacity. The rules therefore defined a net ton as 100 cubic feet of cargo or passenger space (excluding machinery, fuel storage, crews' quarters, etc.) and set up a complex but fair system of measurement to determine the tonnage subject to tolls. Warships, whose special construction did not permit the application of these measurement formulas, were assessed upon their actual weight or displacement.

Unfortunately the special Panama rules did not stand alone. With a singular disregard for consistency the Panama Canal act of 1912 stipulated that tolls should not in any event exceed $1.25 per net registered ton computed according to the measurement rules specified in the general maritime laws of the United States, which not only exempted more space from payment of tolls than the Panama regulations but were capricious, inequitable, and subject to constant change. The attempt to apply simultaneously two irreconcilable standards of measurement threw the carefully worked out toll system into hopeless chaos. "Much to our chagrin and humiliation," Goethals reported in 1915, "we learned that Dr. Johnson was aware of the discrepancy, notwithstanding which, he presented his rules of measurement and rates of tolls for promulgation to the . . . world. Confusion has been the order of the day in consequence. The amounts collected in excess of that authorized by [United States maritime] law will have to be refunded, and . . . this matter is still small in comparison with the difficulty of arriving at a clear-cut system of measurement applicable to all cases. . . ." [9]

Year after year successive governors of the canal protested in vain against the obnoxious dual standards of measurement. Since application of the United States rules generally resulted in lower tolls they prevailed in most instances while the Panama rules became largely inoperative. Not only were United States measurements of toll-paying space smaller to begin with than the Panama standards but constant downward revision steadily increased the discrepancy, so that the average ratio of United States to Panama tonnages declined from 84.78% in 1919 to 69.52% in 1936. Governor Ridley estimated the total loss of revenue due to the operation of the dual system from 1914 to 1936 inclusive at $92,000,-000. Even less justifiable than the reduction in earnings were the numerous instances of haphazard discrimination against certain classes of ships and between individual vessels. Vessels in ballast, less favored by United States rules than laden craft, customarily paid tolls at the full Panama rate of 72 cents per ton, which in practice amounted to much more than the 60% of the charge for cargo-carrying ships contemplated by the proclamation of November 1912. Some vessels actually paid as much for transit when empty as when fully laden. When applied to tugs and other small craft the United States rules sometimes worked out so absurdly as to indicate negative tonnages — less than zero — and such vessels paid nothing at all for passage. Tankers, because of their special construction, paid a higher rate per ton of cargo than ships of other types.

Under the whimsical United States rules insignificant structural modifications sometimes entailed wholly disproportionate variations in toll charges. In 1923 "two ships of exactly the same dimensions and the same cargo carrying capacity, the *Gold Shell* and the *Silver Shell*, pay tolls of $4,386.25 and $5,076.25, respectively, for no other reason than that there is a difference in location of a small fuel transfer pump." [10] Ten years later Governor Schley called attention to a more flagrant yet perfectly legal evasion of tolls by means of a loophole in the United States regulations: "The pe-

culiar effects of the . . . rules . . . are illustrated by the case of
the . . . *Empress of Britain.* . . . Her net tonnage . . . under
the Suez rules is 26,531 tons and for transit through the Suez Canal she pays $30,741, plus any charge for individual passengers.
The net tonnage . . . under Panama Canal rules is 27,503 tons.
Her net tonnage under British registry rules is 22,545 tons. Under
United States registry rules in effect at the time of the latest transit
of the *Empress of Britain* through the Panama Canal her net tonnage measured 15,153 tons, and tolls paid, at $1.25 per ton, were
$18,941.25. The . . . tolls . . . were approximately $11,800 less
than . . . at Suez. The main reason for the difference . . . was
the exemption of certain so-called cabin spaces under the United
States rules. One entire upper deck . . . is devoted to lounges, libraries, social halls, smoking rooms, etc., which under the British
rules (and the Suez and Panama Canal rules) are subject to . . .
inclusion in the net tonnage. There was no stateroom on the deck.
Taking advantage of an American ruling . . . the owners removed from a small cloak and check room the original equipment
and installed a bed, chiffonier, and portable washstand, and called
it 'Apartment A.' This secured the exemption of . . . 3,319 tons
. . . in addition to 4,181 tons exempted in other passenger spaces
under United States rules but not under British or Canal rules.
The result is in effect a gift to the steamship company . . . of approximately $9,000 through this one feature alone. . . ." [11]

In 1917 bills designed to eliminate the United States rules and
establish the Panama system as the sole standard of measurement
were introduced in both houses of Congress. The House measure,
though reported favorably by the Committee on Interstate and Foreign Commerce, was not acted upon; the Senate bill was similarly
approved by the Interoceanic Canals Committee, "but on account
of opposition of lumber interests on the Pacific coast the bill was
re-referred to the committee and was not again reported." [12] On
May 28, 1919 Governor Harding urged Secretary of War Newton
D. Baker to use his influence to secure remedial legislation, and
once more Congress shelved the proposal. In 1925 the House passed
the desired measure but the Senate Committee on Commerce failed
to report it.

Finally on April 13, 1936, after 22 years of confusion and complaint, Congress authorized the President to appoint a committee
to re-examine the tolls problem. The committee, composed of Emory Johnson, chairman, who had drawn up the original rules, Arthur J. Weaver, former governor of Nebraska, and Rear Admiral

George H. Rock, reported in favor of the adoption of the Panama rules as the sole standard, suggested minor amendments to those rules, and recommended a toll rate for laden commercial vessels not to exceed $1 per net ton computed according to the revised Panama formula. On February 26, 1937 Franklin D. Roosevelt transmitted this report to Congress with a message urging appropriate legislation, and on August 24 Congress passed a bill establishing the Panama measurement system and fixing tolls for laden vessels at not more than $1 nor less than 75 cents per ton. A few days later the President proclaimed the new regulations, which went into effect on March 1, 1938. Vessels in ballast pay 72 cents per net ton and warships 50 cents per displacement ton as before, while the rate for laden merchant ships is now 90 cents per net ton, and all net tonnages are measured according to Panama rules exclusively.

In fixing toll rates for the Panama canal the United States government has never desired to make a net profit such as the Suez canal, a private commercial enterprise, has yielded to its stockholders, but it did expect or at least hope for a return of 3% over and above actual running expenses, enough to pay the interest on its canal bonds. So far that hope has not been fully realized. It is difficult to compute precisely the cost of the canal for the purpose of theoretical capitalization on a purely commercial basis. The original bond issue authorized by Congress to cover the canal expenses, including construction proper, sanitation and civil administration during the construction period, payments to the Compagnie Nouvelle and to Panama, reconstruction of the railroad, and the purchase and reconditioning of vessels for the railroad company's steamship line — but exclusive of defense appropriations, interest on the investment, and the payment of $25,000,000 to Colombia in 1922 — amounted to $375,200,900. Since the opening large additional appropriations have been made from time to time for miscellaneous improvements. Although actual defense projects such as fortifications and naval bases are not and should not be included in the commercial cost of the canal there are a number of items — for example drydocks, machine shops, and highways — which are of both strategic and commercial value, and any attempted repartition of the cost of such borderline elements between the defense and commercial accounts must necessarily be somewhat arbitrary.

While the transit of the *Ancon* inaugurated the flow of traffic through the canal in August 1914 the official proclamation of com-

pletion required by the Panama Canal act was not issued until
July 12, 1920, when President Wilson formally declared the waterway open to the world's commerce. This was merely a gesture of
technical compliance with the law, attended by no ceremony and
involving no change in the existing system of administration, but
for accounting purposes the construction period is considered to
extend to June 30, 1921, the end of the fiscal year following the
proclamation. The total cost of the canal up to and including the
fiscal year 1940–1, exclusive of the payment to Colombia and of
items patently chargeable to defense, can be tabulated as follows: [13]

Appropriations for construction to June 30, 1921	$386,910,301.00
Deduct value of Panama Railroad stock	7,000,000.00
Net construction appropriations	379,910,301.00
Annual payments to Panama, 1913 to 1920 inclusive	2,000,000.00
Additional construction, July 1, 1921 to June 30, 1941	82,300,545.71
Total cash investment	464,210,846.71
Interest on construction funds (compounded annually), 1904 to 1920 inclusive	128,991,063.00
Total capital investment	$593,201,909.71

Interest since 1921 as well as the annual payments to Panama
since that date are classed as operating, not capital, charges. The
canal revenues are derived from three sources: tolls; civil administration, comprising leases, licenses, fines, etc.; and auxiliary business enterprises, including the supply of fuel, provisions, ship
chandlery, and repair services to vessels, sale of food, clothing, and
other commissary merchandise to canal and railroad employees,
storage and handling of cargoes, and operation of the Panama Railroad and its subsidiary steamship line. Most if not all of these business activities — which in 1941 represented a total investment,
excluding the railroad and steamship companies, of $39,356,360 —
are now self-supporting and even produce a modest profit after deduction of a 3% interest charge. Part of these auxiliary earnings is
customarily paid direct into the United States Treasury and is
credited against appropriations, part is retained to supply capital
for continued operation of the business enterprises in the Zone.
On June 30, 1941 the canal balance sheet, covering interest but not
naval and military expenditures, still showed a deficit: [14]

Total tolls, 1914–41 inclusive	$492,532,377.56
Civil revenues, 1914–41 inclusive	5,804,001.13
Business profits, 1914–41 inclusive	18,214,738.78
Total revenues	$516,551,117.47
Net expenses (after deduction of earnings repaid to appropriation)	235,452,623.31
Net revenues	281,098,494.16
Capital interest at 3%	316,937,151.32
Deficit	$35,838,657.16

Had the Panama tonnage measurement rules been applied consistently throughout the entire period of operation instead of only since 1938 the revenues would have been increased by approximately $100,000,000 and the present deficit transformed into a tidy profit. In a set of traffic statistics tabulated in 1941 the tonnage figures prior to March 1, 1938, when the new rules went into effect, have been adjusted so as to conform approximately to standard Panama measurements. The decline in traffic during the fiscal year 1915–16 is accounted for by slides, which closed the canal for almost seven months. These statistics take into account ocean-going vessels only, not tugs and other small craft, which explains the slight discrepancy between the total revenue from tolls as given in this table and the same item in the recapitulation above: [15]

Fiscal Year Ended June 30	Number of Transits	Panama Canal Net Tonnage (approximate before 1939)	Tons of Cargo	Tolls Collected
1915	1,058	3,507,000	4,888,400	$4,366,747.13
1916	724	2,212,000	3,093,335	2,403,089.40
1917	1,738	5,357,000	7,054,720	5,620,799.83
1918	1,989	6,072,000	7,525,768	6,428,780.26
1919	1,948	5,658,000	6,910,097	6,164,290.79
1920	2,393	7,898,000	9,372,374	8,507,938.68
1921	2,791	10,550,000	11,595,971	11,268,681.46
1922	2,665	10,556,000	10,882,607	11,191,828.56
1923	3,908	17,206,000	19,566,429	17,504,027.19
1924	5,158	24,181,000	26,993,167	24,284,659.92
1925	4,592	21,134,000	23,956,549	21,393,718.01
1926	5,087	22,906,000	26,030,016	22,919,931.89

Fiscal Year Ended June 30	Number of Transits	Panama Canal Net Tonnage (approximate before 1939)	Tons of Cargo	Tolls Collected
1927	5,293	24,245,000	27,733,555	24,212,250.61
1928	6,253	27,229,000	29,615,651	26,922,200.75
1929	6,289	27,585,000	30,647,768	27,111,125.47
1930	6,027	27,716,000	30,018,429	27,059,998.94
1931	5,370	25,690,000	25,065,283	24,624,599.76
1932	4,362	21,842,000	19,798,986	20,694,704.61
1933	4,162	21,094,000	18,161,165	19,601,077.17
1934	5,234	26,410,000	24,704,009	24,047,183.44
1935	5,180	25,720,000	25,309,527	23,307,062.93
1936	5,382	25,923,000	26,505,943	23,479,114.21
1937	5,387	25,430,000	28,108,375	23,102,137.12
1938	5,524	25,950,383	27,385,924	23,169,888.70
1939	5,903	27,170,007	27,886,627	23,661,021.08
1940	5,370	24,144,366	27,299,016	21,144,675.36
1941	4,727	20,642,736	24,950,791	18,157,739.68
	114,514	514,028,492	551,040,482	$492,349,272.95

Chapter 46. The Land Divided

O^N April 1, 1914 an executive order abolished the Isthmian Canal Commission and established the permanent organization contemplated by the Panama Canal act. The present administrative system comprises five principal subdivisions: a department of operation and maintenance, a supply department, an accounting department, a health department, and an executive department for civil administration. The governor is appointed by the President subject to confirmation by the Senate and holds office for four years. Because military and naval considerations exercise an important influence upon the commercial and civil activities of the Zone all governors since 1914 have been army engineer officers of high rank. On January 29, 1914 Wilson appointed Goethals first governor of The Panama Canal, the official name of the new administrative entity. Goethals, who had already devoted seven years to the canal, submitted his resignation to take effect November 1, 1915 but withdrew it on account of the slide emergency and remained in office until January 10, 1917. Before he left he inaugurated a system of succession which has now become traditional in the canal service. Every four years the retiring governor is replaced by the engineer of maintenance, who in turn is succeeded by the assistant engineer of maintenance. Thus each governor is thoroughly trained for his responsible position by eight preparatory years of service in the Zone, though in practice these rules of succession have not been followed with automatic regularity. The system has worked well and has produced exceptionally competent administrators. Since the opening of the canal eight men have occupied the governor's office: Goethals (1914–17), Lieutenant Colonel Chester Harding (1917–21), Colonel Jay J. Morrow (1921–4), Colonel Meriwether L. Walker (1924–8), Colonel Harry Burgess (1928–32), Colonel Julian L. Schley (1932–6), Colonel Clarence S. Ridley (1936–40), and Major General Glen E. Edgerton, the present incumbent.

The government-owned Panama Railroad Company, with its auxiliary steamship line, still operates as a nominally private corporation although the Secretary of War appoints its directors and the governor of the canal is *ex officio* its president. For convenience the canal and railroad sometimes function as a unit, sometimes as independent organizations. Ownership of the commissaries by the railroad instead of by the canal has proved especially advantageous; whereas contracts for purchases out of congressional appropriations for the canal would have to be awarded to the lowest bidder and be subjected to complicated regulation the technically private railroad corporation can attain greater variety and flexibility by buying in the open market.

The increase in canal traffic after the close of the first World War drew attention to the probable future demand for a greater number of lockages than the existing water supply would permit. By damming the upper Chagres near the village of Alhajuela about 10 miles northeast of Gamboa a second reservoir, smaller than Gatún Lake and 155 feet higher, could be formed so as to maintain Gatún Lake at a constant level throughout the year and prevent waste of valuable water during the wet season. Surveys were completed in July 1923, and on February 1, 1924 the Alhajuela basin about 21 square miles in area was incorporated into the Canal Zone. In 1931 the United States expropriated about 4 additional square miles of Panamanian territory in the vicinity of the dam. The new unit comprised the main concrete dam and spillway, 950 feet long at the crest and rising 220 feet above the lowest point of the foundation, an earth and rock extension adjacent to the main dam on the south, 13 short saddle dams to fill in natural depressions in the surrounding terrain, and a hydroelectric power plant. Contracts were let in October 1931, excavation commenced in February 1932, and the entire project was completed on February 9, 1935. Construction of the Madden dam — so named in 1929 in honor of the former chairman of the House Committee on Appropriations, Martin B. Madden of Illinois, who had died the year before — was in fact somewhat premature, for since its completion the annual number of lockages has never reached the peak attained in 1929, but there can be no doubt that the extra water storage will eventually be utilized.

To transport construction materials the United States government built a concrete highway about 22 miles long from Panama City to the Madden dam site. The road, begun in 1929, was practically completed within a year. At the same time the canal engineers made surveys for a continuation of the highway from Madden dam to Colón, a distance of some 27 miles, which would link the two coasts of the isthmus. No transisthmian highway had ever existed except the ancient *camino real,* even in its heyday no more than a rough and perilous mule trail and since the completion of the railroad in 1855 altogether impassable through disuse. For years the republic of Panama had urged the construction of a motor road between Panama and Colón, but the United States, holding that it would render the canal more accessible and hence become a source of danger in time of war, resolutely opposed the project. Not until July 1939 did the United States, by ratification of a special convention attached to the Hull-Alfaro treaty, authorize the extension of the Madden highway to the Atlantic. The cost of the new section, which runs almost entirely through Panamanian territory east of the canal, is shared by the two governments. Work was begun in 1940, by February 1942 the road was passable for trucks though still unpaved, by April one lane had been completely surfaced with concrete, and a month or two later the entire highway was opened to motor traffic. A branch road to Puerto Bello joining the main highway a few miles from Colón is now under construction.

In 1932 the United States inaugurated a ferry service across the Pacific entrance to the canal and built a short stretch of road known as the Thatcher highway from the western ferry slip to the Zone boundary, connecting with the Panama national highway from Chorrera to Río Hato. Because of the strategic importance of the Chorrera-Río Hato road, which will eventually be incorporated in the great Inter-American highway, the United States Import-Export Bank lent Panama $2,500,000 in February 1940 to pave the road with concrete.

In 1915 Goethals suggested that the Taft agreement of December 1904 between the United States and Panama "has become in many respects disadvantageous to both Governments and should be superseded by an agreement more in accord with our present mutual needs. . . ."[1] Later governors reiterated the necessity for a more up-to-date convention, but nothing was done until May 28, 1924, when President Coolidge proclaimed the abrogation of the Taft agreement to take effect June 1. Meanwhile negotiations for a new treaty to replace the Hay-Bunau-Varilla pact, which had never satisfied the Panamanians, were in progress. After prolonged discussion a convention was signed on July 28, 1926 in which the United States promised to encourage highway construction and to restrict commissary sales to canal and railway employees, their households, and guests of the Washington and Tivoli Hotels, while Panama engaged to declare war upon any nation with which the

United States might be at war. Actually the treaty did little more than perpetuate the existing situation and alleviated almost none of Panama's long-standing grievances. It maintained United States control over sanitation and public order outside the Zone and the right of the United States (hotly contested by Panama) to enlarge the Zone indefinitely to include new areas, such as that embraced in the Madden dam development, without payment for the expropriated territory. The Panama legislature indignantly rejected the treaty, and negotiations dragged on for another decade.

In conformity with its announced good neighbor policy the Franklin D. Roosevelt administration has been much more liberal in its treatment of Panama than any of its predecessors. The Hull-Alfaro treaty, signed on March 2, 1936 and ratified by Panama the following December but not approved by the United States Senate and proclaimed until July 27, 1939, concedes to Panama practically every point in dispute since 1903. The new pact does not supersede the Hay-Bunau-Varilla treaty, which remains the basic agreement between the two nations, but it modifies it in several important respects. Under the Hull-Alfaro treaty the United States has abandoned its guarantee of Panamanian independence — long a thorn in the flesh of the proud Latin Americans — and has renounced its right to intervene for the suppression of local disturbances. The United States engages not to expropriate additional territory for the improvement or protection of the canal except after consultation with Panama and by implication promises that any such lands transferred in the future will be paid for, directly or indirectly. The limitations upon commissary sales are even stricter than in 1926, hotel guests now being excluded from the privilege. Abandonment of the gold standard in the United States in 1933 had led to a long controversy with Panama, which refused to accept depreciated dollars in payment of the annual rental of $250,000. The Hull-Alfaro treaty increases the annuity to 430,000 balboas (the balboa being expressly declared equal in value to the paper dollar) and makes the excess payments retroactive to 1934. It provides for the construction of the transisthmian highway and transfers to Panama a narrow corridor on both sides of the road near the Atlantic terminus so as to connect Colón, hitherto surrounded by the Zone, with Panamanian territory on the east, while Panama has agreed to turn over to the United States a similar strip along that portion of the road between Panama City and Madden dam which passes through the republic. Article 10, the chief cause of the long delay in ratification by the United States, provides that if the isthmus or the canal is threatened by enemy aggression the

United States and Panama are to decide jointly upon protective measures. Many senators, believing that this clause gave the United States insufficient freedom of action, withheld their consent, but their opposition was finally overcome by the attachment to the treaty of a note from the Panamanian minister explicitly granting to the United States the right to defend the canal by sending troops into Panamanian territory, or otherwise, without previous consultation in the event of an emergency so sudden as to render such consultation inexpedient.

Additional recent concessions to Panama not provided for in the Hull-Alfaro treaty appear to have eliminated practically all remaining sources of friction. On April 26, 1943 Congress authorized cancellation of Panama's debt for the Chorrera-Río Hato highway, the entire cost of which will now be assumed by the United States; renunciation of the unpaid balance due on the Panama City and Colón waterworks and sewer systems, amounting to some $860,000, and the immediate conveyance of those utilities to the republic; and the transfer to Panama without compensation of various commercial and residential properties in the two cities, valued at $11,-500,000, belonging to the Panama Railroad and acquired by the United States in 1904 as part of the railroad's assets. In return Panama has made available to the United States a number of vital defense areas outside the Zone.

While the Madden reservoir has eliminated the danger of a seasonal shortage of lockage water it has not actually increased the normal capacity of the canal. That such an increase will ultimately become imperative has been foreseen for some time. Although commercial needs would not justify expansion at present considerations of national defense already call for additional transit facilities not only because the existing locks, placed side by side in twin flights, provide an insecure margin of safety against bombardment from the air but because the chambers, 1000 feet long and 110 feet wide, are too small to accommodate projected warships or even the largest commercial vessels now afloat. At least three of the newer passenger liners, the British steamships *Queen Mary* and *Queen Elizabeth* and the U.S.S. *Lafayette* — formerly the *Normandie,* now being salvaged after the dramatic catastrophe of February 1942 — are too long and too broad to enter the Panama locks. The largest merchant ship so far passed through the canal is the German liner *Bremen,* 898 feet long and 102 feet beam, which made the transit in February 1939. The British battle cruiser *Hood,* 860 feet 7 inches long and 105 feet 2½ inches broad, negotiated the passage in July 1924, and a few years later the still larger United States plane carriers *Lexington* and *Saratoga,* 888 feet in length and 107 feet 9 inches in breadth, squeezed through the locks with barely a foot of clearance on each side.

In 1921, only seven years after the opening of the canal, Governor Morrow warned of impending obsolescence and inaugurated preliminary studies for the design and location of a new set of locks. In March 1928 Senator Kenneth D. McKellar of Tennessee introduced a bill to appropriate $200,000,000 for the immediate construction of a Nicaragua canal: "With a naïve disregard for engineering costs he concluded that this sum would be more than ample for a sea level waterway, and with a zeal . . . that ignored facts he concluded that 'the Panama canal in, say, six years will not be able to afford passage to the ships that will be applying to go through it.' " [2] No action was taken on the bill, but on March 2, 1929 Congress passed a joint resolution authorizing new surveys in both Panama and Nicaragua. On June 17 President Hoover appointed an Interoceanic Canal Board composed of Major General Edgar Jadwin, Chief of Engineers, chairman, Colonel Ernest Graves, Sydney B. Williamson, Anson Marston, and Frank M. Williams. Williams died in 1930 and was replaced by Royal G. Finch, and after Jadwin's death in March 1931 Colonel Graves succeeded to the chairmanship and Lieutenant Colonel Daniel I. Sultan was appointed to fill the vacancy. On November 30, 1931 the board submitted a report comparing three projects: a lock canal in Nicaragua, conversion of the Panama canal into a sea level waterway, and addition of a third set of locks to the existing canal.

While the purchase of the Panama canal property in 1904 eliminated the Nicaragua route at that time the United States never definitively abandoned the alternative project and still holds in reserve a Nicaraguan concession for a second waterway. On February 8, 1913 the American minister to Nicaragua, George Thomas Weitzel, and the Nicaraguan Foreign Minister, Emiliano Chamorro, signed a treaty granting to the United States a canal option and the right to establish naval bases. When the Senate Committee on Foreign Relations recommended rejection of the pact Secretary of State William Jennings Bryan negotiated a new convention, the Bryan-Chamorro treaty, which was signed at Washington on August 5, 1914, approved by the Senate with amendments in February 1916, ratified by Nicaragua in April, and finally proclaimed on June 24, 1916. The treaty gave the United States a perpetual option for a canal, 99-year leases of Great and Little Corn Islands, and the right to maintain a naval base on the Gulf of Fonseca for the same term of years. The leases and naval base privilege were renewable for a second period of 99 years. The bankrupt Nicaraguan government received $3,000,000 for these concessions, but more than two thirds of the sum was diverted to satisfy the claims of New York banks and British creditors.

Although the treaty contained a clause inserted by the Senate assuring Nicaragua's neighboring republics that their rights would be respected it was violently opposed by Costa Rica, Honduras, and El Salvador. Costa Rica protested again and again that the Cañas-Jerez treaty of 1858, confirmed and clarified by Cleveland's arbitration award in 1888, forbade Nicaragua to grant a canal concession without previous consultation with Costa Rica; while Honduras and El Salvador objected to the establishment without their consent of an American naval base on the Gulf of Fonseca, the coast of which is shared by Nicaragua and the other two states. In March 1916 Costa Rica brought suit against Nicaragua before the Central American Court of Justice. Nicaragua, backed by the United States, denied the competence of the tribunal and refused to appear. On September 30 the court decided that Nicaragua had failed to fulfill its obligations to Costa Rica but at the same time pronounced itself without authority to declare the Bryan-Chamorro treaty void. On August 29 El Salvador had also filed suit against Nicaragua before the same court, which decided on March 9, 1917 that Nicaragua had violated the principle of joint jurisdiction over the Gulf of Fonseca. When Nicaragua rejected both verdicts the court, powerless to enforce its awards, went out of existence.

During this period Nicaragua's affairs, internal and external, were almost completely controlled by the United States. From 1912 to 1925 detachments of American marines were stationed in the country. While the intervention undoubtedly helped to maintain order it aroused deep resentment throughout Latin America, and the forcible imposition of the Bryan-Chamorro treaty added fuel to the flames. Had the United States government profited by its experience with Colombia in 1903 and adopted a conciliatory policy towards the Central American republics the canal concession could almost certainly have been obtained without the creation of so much antagonism. In 1926 the marines returned to suppress disorders occasioned by a dispute between two rival claimants for the presidency, Adolfo Díaz, recognized by the United States, and Juan B. Sacasa, supported by Mexico. President Coolidge endeavored to justify the renewal of intervention on the ground that political turmoil in Nicaragua jeopardized the canal rights of the

United States, while opposition congressmen ridiculed the dispatch of an armed force to protect a paper canal and nonexistent naval bases.

The Interoceanic Canal Board placed Colonel Sultan in command of the new Nicaragua survey. The party of 25 officers and 295 enlisted men reached Nicaragua at the end of August 1929 and devoted almost two years to an exhaustive examination of the canal route. Modern inventions enabled the men in the field to live more comfortably and under more healthful conditions than had been possible on any previous expedition. Radio communication between headquarters, established in a rambling old monastery at Granada, and the base camps facilitated control of the work; fresh food supplies were ordered from Panama by radio and shipped or flown promptly to Nicaragua; sick or injured soldiers were transported by plane to well-equipped hospitals.

Sultan's project differed in several respects from that adopted by the Maritime Canal Company in 1889. In the new plan the canal line from Fuerte de San Carlos to the foot of the Machuca rapids was to be straightened and shortened by cutting through the bends of the San Juan, the dam was moved upstream from Ochoa to the Conchuda Hills, and the Atlantic entrance was shifted to a point 3 or 4 miles northwest of San Juan del Norte. The design called for one flight of three locks about 5 miles from the Pacific terminus at Brito and a similar flight 15 miles from the Atlantic end. A railroad would more or less parallel the canal line from San Juan del Norte to Fuerte de San Carlos and from the western shore of Lake Nicaragua to Brito, the two lake terminals to be linked by car ferries. Sultan estimated the total cost at $722,000,000 including $50,000-000 for fortifications and military establishments. He recommended a canal zone much wider than at Panama, though not necessarily of uniform breadth, so as to enclose sites for observation posts for protection against enemy aircraft. It would be imperative to reach an agreement with Costa Rica since part of the zone would have to be conceded by that state; moreover a rise of the lake level during the wet season would inundate the swampy lowlands on the southern shore and overflow the frontier. The south abutment of the Conchuda dam and the power station on the San Carlos would also occupy Costa Rican territory.

The Interoceanic Canal Board considered two projects for expansion of the Panama canal: conversion into a sea level strait and the addition of a third flight of locks. The sea level plan designed by Williamson would have required the excavation of 565,000,000 cubic yards and cost at least $1,000,000,000, and the necessity for tide locks at the Pacific entrance would have greatly diminished the strategic advantages of a sea level waterway. Governor Burgess believed the plan theoretically possible but that without first constructing a third set of locks "it would be extremely unwise, because of the risk of totally and indefinitely interrupting traffic, to attempt such a conversion, and, with the . . . third set of locks it is estimated that the canal would then be adequate . . . for another century. In view of this, the . . . project at this time is economically unsound." [3]

Thus the choice lay between a wholly new canal in Nicaragua and a third set of locks at Panama. Comparing the two schemes, the Interoceanic Canal Board listed the advantages of a duplicate canal through Nicaragua: curtailment of sailing time between most Atlantic and Pacific ports, varying from a few hours to two days; less danger of interruption by sabotage, accident, slides, earthquakes, or drought, since it was most unlikely that any of these disasters would occur simultaneously at both sites; the constant availability of three traffic lanes instead of two during periodic overhauls of the locks, and of at least one lane able to admit the largest vessels afloat, which could not pass through the Panama canal while the new locks were being cleaned or repaired; improvement of diplomatic relations with Central America, stabilization of the wayward republican governments, and development of Central American commerce with the United States; and the increased security from air attack provided by two widely separated canals. The last consideration was by far the most important — in fact the only one that might conceivably have justified the construction of a second waterway. On the other hand the Panama scheme had obvious merits: it would cost very much less to construct and somewhat less to maintain and operate; it could be completed in a shorter time and with much less preliminary work; it would require no new treaties and no negotiations or outlay for rights and franchises; and it would furnish sufficient capacity for a long time to come. The board saw no reason to commit itself to an immediate decision, for the depression of the early nineteen-thirties had set in and canal traffic was already diminishing.

At the same time the board recommended the accumulation of additional data concerning rainfall and drainage conditions on the Nicaragua watershed. To conduct these investigations as well as to prepare plans for a proposed canalization of the San Juan River — a more modest project than an interoceanic canal, designed

merely to develop the domestic resources of Nicaragua and Costa
Rica by opening a navigable channel between the Atlantic and the
lake for vessels of medium size — the United States government organized the Nicaragua Oceanic Canal Survey, which for several
years has maintained a small staff of army and civilian engineers
in Nicaragua.

The final decision to build a new set of locks at Panama was dictated almost wholly by strategic considerations. Commercially the
existing two-lane canal is more than adequate and will probably
remain so for the next two or three decades at least even if a few
exceptionally large liners — which in any event would have no occasion to use the Panama route under normal peacetime conditions
— are unable to negotiate the transit. In 1934 Governor Schley estimated the capacity of the canal with both lanes operating 24 hours
a day to be approximately three times the 26,410,000 tons passed
that year. But with war clouds gathering in Europe and Japan
growing daily more aggressive the military necessity for canal expansion was becoming more and more obvious.

On May 1, 1936 President Roosevelt approved a joint congressional resolution directing the governor of the canal to prepare designs, specifications, and estimates for additional locks. Governor
Ridley assigned the task to a special engineering section headed by
Edward S. Randolph and composed of technicians transferred from
other divisions of the canal staff, supplemented by two geologists
and a specialist in lock design.

On February 24, 1939 Ridley submitted a special report proposing increases in the width and depth of the new locks and their
location for additional security at some distance from the existing
structures, with bypasses to connect them with the main canal.
Congress adopted these recommendations and on August 11 authorized immediate construction of the third flight of locks. At
Gatún the new locks are situated on the east side of the present
locks, at Pedro Miguel and Miraflores on the west. Each basin will
be 1200 feet long, 140 feet wide, and 45 feet deep. Near Gatún it
will be necessary to relocate the railroad for a short distance in order to avoid crossing the new bypass, and some new highway construction will be required. The town of Gatún will become an island between the old and new locks, with road and rail connections
to the mainland over a movable bridge. A similar bridge across the
existing locks at Miraflores to connect the railroad and highway on
the eastern side with the new locks west of the present canal was
opened to traffic on May 20, 1942.

Reversing the policy pursued throughout the construction of the original canal, the government decided to allocate the building of the new locks and the dry excavation to contractors and to assign only the dredging operations to its own labor force. Actual construction began on July 1, 1940, when the dipper dredge *Cascadas* started to scoop out the Pacific end of the bypass leading to the new Miraflores locks. On October 1 the first dredge went to work on the Gatún bypass. Governor Edgerton estimated the total excavation required for all of the new locks and bypasses at 61,900,000 cubic yards, almost equally divided between dredging and dry steam shovel digging. In May 1943 the newspapers announced that the dry excavation "is almost finished, and contractors are expected to remove their equipment by the end of the month." [4]

Today the Canal Zone is prepared for any emergency. The new work is progressing smoothly and rapidly; dredges and concrete mixers operate at full speed while planes roar overhead and gray ships laden with wartime cargoes pass silently through the heavily guarded waterway. Obviously the record of this activity cannot now be written, for the canal is an instrument of war as well as of peace and must remain so as long as wars are fought. The land has been divided, but the world is far from united. The proud inscription on the great seal is still a dream of the future.

REFERENCE NOTES

PREFACE

1. James Bryce: *South America*, p. 36. Macmillan Company, New York and London; 1912.

CHAPTER 1
THE DOUBTFUL STRAIT

1. Manuel M. de Peralta: *Costa-Rica, Nicaragua y Panamá en el siglo XVI*, p. 33. Madrid and Paris; 1883.
2. Richard H. Major: *Select letters of Christopher Columbus*, p. 178. Hakluyt Society, London; 1870.
3. *Ibid.*, p. 185.
4. *Ibid.*, pp. 185–6.
5. *Ibid.*, p. 188.
6. *Ibid.*, p. 189.
7. *Ibid.*, p. 194.
8. Peter Martyr: *De orbe novo*. In Hakluyt's *Collection of the early voyages, travels, and discoveries*, Vol. 5, p. 229. London; 1812.
9. *Ibid.*, p. 227.

CHAPTER 2
A PEAK IN DARIÉN

1. *Ibid.*, p. 229.
2. *Ibid.*, p. 229.
3. *Ibid.*, p. 229.
4. *Ibid.*, pp. 229–30.
5. *Ibid.*, p. 231.
6. Martín de Navarrete: *Colección de los viages y descubrimientos que hicieron por mar los Españoles*, Vol. 3, p. 374. Imprenta Real, Madrid; 1825–37.
7. *Ibid.*, pp. 367–8.
8. Peter Martyr: *De orbe novo*. In Hakluyt's *Collection of the early voyages, travels, and discoveries*, Vol. 5, p. 253. London; 1812.
9. *Ibid.*, pp. 253–4.
10. *Ibid.*, p. 254.
11. *Ibid.*, p. 254.
12. *Ibid.*, p. 255.
13. *Ibid.*, p. 255.
14. *Ibid.*, p. 255.
15. *Ibid.*, p. 256.

16. Martín de Navarrete: *Colección de los viages y descubrimientos que hicieron por mar los Españoles*, Vol. 3, pp. 375–7. Imprenta Real, Madrid; 1825–37.
17. *Ibid.*, pp. 383–4.
18. Oviedo y Valdés: *Historia general y natural de las Indias*, p. 60. Imprenta de la Real Academia de la Historia, Madrid; 1853.

CHAPTER 3
THE SOUTH SEA

1. Martín de Navarrete: *Colección de los viages y descubrimientos que hicieron por mar los Españoles*, Vol. 5, p. 177. Imprenta Real, Madrid; 1825–37.
2. Manuel M. de Peralta: *Costa-Rica, Nicaragua y Panamá en el siglo XVI*, p. 21. Madrid and Paris; 1883.
3. Enrique de Vedia (ed.): *Historiadores primitivos de Indias*, Vol. 1, pp. 28–9. Biblioteca de Autores Españoles, Madrid; 1852.
4. Martín de Navarrete: *Colección de los viages y descubrimientos que hicieron por mar los Españoles*, Vol. 3, p. 148. Imprenta Real, Madrid; 1825–37.
5. Enrique de Vedia (ed.): *Historiadores primitivos de Indias*, Vol. 1, p. 178. Biblioteca de Autores Españoles, Madrid; 1852.
6. *Ibid.*, p. 165.
7. Samuel Purchas: *Purchas his pilgrimes*, Vol. 3, p. 849. London; 1625.
8. Martín de Navarrete: *Noticia histórica de las expediciones hechas por los Españoles en busca del paso del noroeste de la América*, p. 49. Imprenta Real, Madrid; 1802.
9. Samuel Purchas: *Purchas his pilgrimes*, Vol. 3, p. 849. London; 1625.
10. *Ibid.*, p. 850.

CHAPTER 4
THE DAWN OF THE CANAL

1. Antonio Galvão: *The discoveries of the world, from their first original unto*

the year of our Lord 1555, p. 180. Hakluyt Society, London; 1862.

2. Ignacio Bauer y Landauer: *Datos para la historia de la unión interoceánica en América*, p. 6. Compañía General de Artes Gráficas, Madrid; 1931.

3. Ramón de Manjarrés: "Proyectos españoles de canal interoceánico." *Cultura Hispanoamericana*, Año 3, No. 22 (September 15, 1914), p. 20.

4. *Ibid.*, p. 21.

5. *Ibid.*, p. 21.

6. Ignacio Bauer y Landauer: *Datos para la historia de la unión interoceánica en América*, p. 6. Compañía General de Artes Gráficas, Madrid; 1931.

7. Antonio Galvão: *The discoveries of the world, from their first original unto the year of our Lord 1555*, pp. 180–1. Hakluyt Society, London; 1862.

8. Enrique de Vedia (ed.): *Historiadores primitivos de Indias*, Vol. 1, p. 222. Biblioteca de Autores Españoles, Madrid; 1852.

9. *Colección de documentos inéditos, relativos al descubrimiento, conquista y organización de las antiguas posesiones españolas de América y Oceanía*, Vol. 23, p. 259. Madrid; 1864–84.

10. Antonio de Alcedo: *Diccionario geográfico-histórico de las Indias occidentales ó América*, Vol. 2, heading *Istmo*. Madrid; 1787.

11. Ramón de Manjarrés: "Proyectos españoles de canal interoceánico." *Cultura Hispanoamericana*, Año 3, No. 22 (September 15, 1914), p. 21.

12. Enrique de Vedia (ed.): *Historiadores primitivos de Indias*, Vol. 1, p. 165. Biblioteca de Autores Españoles, Madrid; 1852.

13. José de Acosta: *Historia natural y moral de las Indias*, Vol. 1, pp. 214–15. Madrid; 1894.

14. Antonio de Alcedo: *Diccionario geográfico-histórico de las Indias occidentales ó América*, Vol. 2, heading *Istmo*. Madrid; 1787.

15. *Ibid.*, heading *Atrato*.

16. Lucien N.-B. Wyse: *Le canal de Panama, l'isthme américain*, p. 122. Hachette, Paris; 1886.

17. Samuel Champlain: *Narrative of a voyage to the West Indies and Mexico in the years 1599–1602*, pp. 41–2. Hakluyt Society, London; 1859.

18. Manuel M. de Peralta: *El canal interoceánico de Nicaragua y Costa-Rica en 1620 y en 1887*, p. 7. A. Mertens, Brussels; 1887.

19. *Ibid.*, p. 8.

20. *Ibid.*, p. 8.

21. *Ibid.*, pp. 22–4.

CHAPTER 5
THE FLEET AND THE ROAD

1. Pascual de Andagoya: *Narrative of the proceedings of Pedrarias Davila*, p. 42. Hakluyt Society, London; 1865.

2. Thomas Gage: *The English-American*, p. 365. George Routledge & Sons, Ltd., London; 1928.

3. Irene A. Wright (ed.): *Documents concerning English voyages to the Spanish Main, 1569–1580*, p. 110. Hakluyt Society, London; 1932.

4. Lionel Wafer: *A new voyage and description of the isthmus of America*, p. 40. Hakluyt Society, Oxford; 1934.

5. *Ibid.*, pp. 42–3.

6. Samuel Champlain: *Narrative of a voyage to the West Indies and Mexico in the years 1599–1602*, p. 41. Hakluyt Society, London; 1859.

7. Thomas Gage: *The English-American*, p. 369. George Routledge & Sons, Ltd., London; 1928.

8. Alexander von Humboldt: *Political essay on the kingdom of New Spain*, Vol. 1, p. 37 (footnote). Longman, etc., London; 1811.

9. Thomas Jefferys: *A description of the Spanish islands and settlements*, p. 29. London; 1762.

10. John A. Lloyd: "Notes respecting the Isthmus of Panama." *Royal Geog. Soc. of London Journal*, Vol. 1 (1832), p. 88.

11. Thomas Gage: *The English-American*, p. 366. George Routledge & Sons, Ltd., London; 1928.

12. George E. Church: "Interoceanic communication on the western continent." *Geographical Journal*, Vol. 19, No. 3 (March 1902), p. 325.

13. *Colección de documentos inéditos, relativos al descubrimiento, conquista y organización de las antiguas posesiones españolas de América y Oceanía*, Vol. 41, p. 536. Madrid; 1864–84.

14. *Ibid.*, Vol. 41, p. 534.

15. Irene A. Wright (ed.): *Documents concerning English voyages to the Span-*

ish Main, 1569–1580, p. 302. Hakluyt Society, London; 1932.
16. *Ibid.*, p. 301.
17. Thomas Jefferys: *A description of the Spanish islands and settlements*, p. 32. London; 1762.
18. Juan López de Velasco: *Geografía y descripción universal de las Indias*, p. 346. Sociedad Geográfica de Madrid, Madrid; 1894.
19. Enrique de Vedia (ed.) : *Historiadores primitivos de Indias*, Vol. 1, p. 292. Biblioteca de Autores Españoles, Madrid; 1852.
20. Thomas Gage: *The English-American*, p. 368. George Routledge & Sons, Ltd., London; 1928.

CHAPTER 6
DRAKE

1. Irene A. Wright (ed.) : *Documents concerning English voyages to the Spanish Main, 1569–1580*, pp. 262–3. Hakluyt Society, London; 1932.
2. *Ibid.*, pp. 303–4.
3. *Ibid.*, p. 318.
4. *Ibid.*, p. lviii.
5. Thomas Wright (ed.) : *The famous voyage of Sir Francis Drake*, p. 29. London; 1742.
6. Samuel Clarke: *The life and death of the valiant and renowned Sir Francis Drake*, p. 67. London; 1671.
7. *Ibid.*, p. 68.

CHAPTER 7
THE BUCCANEERS

1. A. O. Exquemelin: *The buccaneers of America*, p. 135. E. P. Dutton & Company, New York; 1923.
2. *Ibid.*, p. 140.
3. *Ibid.*, p. 140.
4. *Ibid.*, p. 173.
5. *Ibid.*, p. 188.
6. *Ibid.*, p. 195.
7. *Ibid.*, p. 208.
8. *Ibid.*, p. 222.
9. Lionel Wafer: *A new voyage and description of the isthmus of America*, p. 4. Hakluyt Society, Oxford; 1934.
10. *Ibid.*, pp. 18–19.
11. *Ibid.*, p. 19.
12. *Ibid.*, p. 22.
13. *Ibid.*, p. 137.
14. William Dampier: *Voyages and dis-coveries*, p. 286. Argonaut Press, London; 1931.

CHAPTER 8
SCOTS COLONY

1. William Paterson: *Central America*, pp. 60–1. Trübner & Company, London; 1857.
2. Andrew Fletcher (attr. to) : *A defence of the Scots settlement at Darien*, p. 3. Edinburgh; 1699.
3. Walter Harris (attr. to) : *A defence of the Scots abdicating Darien*, p. 22. Edinburgh; 1700.
4. *Ibid.*, p. 28.
5. *Ibid.*, pp. 3–4.
6. John H. Burton (ed.) : *The Darien papers*, p. 62. Edinburgh; 1849.
7. *Ibid.*, pp. 114–15.
8. *Ibid.*, p. 113.
9. Francis R. Hart: *The disaster of Darien*, p. 93. Houghton Mifflin Company, Boston and New York; 1929.
10. John H. Burton (ed.) : *The Darien papers*, p. 215. Edinburgh; 1849.
11. William Paterson: *Central America*, p. 47. Trübner & Company, London; 1857.

CHAPTER 9.
THE EIGHTEENTH CENTURY

1. Edward Vernon: *Original papers relating to the expedition to Panama*, p. 76. M. Cooper, London; 1744.
2. Clarence H. Haring: *Trade and navigation between Spain and the Indies in the time of the Hapsburgs*, p. 196. Harvard University Press, Cambridge, Mass.; 1918.
3. Vice Admiral Lord Viscount Nelson: *Dispatches and letters*, Vol. 1, pp. 7–8. Henry Colburn, London; 1845.
4. *Ibid.*, p. 7 (footnote 5) .
5. Lucia B. Kinnaird: "Creassy's plan for seizing Panama." *Hispanic American Historical Review*, Vol. 13, No. 1 (February 1933) , pp. 64, 73–4, 76.
6. Antonio de Ulloa: *Relación histórica del viage á la América meridional*, Book 3, p. 149. Antonio Marin, Madrid; 1748.
7. *Ibid.*, p. 168.
8. Clarence H. Haring: *Trade and navigation between Spain and the Indies in the time of the Hapsburgs*, p. 196. Harvard University Press, Cambridge, Mass.; 1918.

9. Abbé Marsan: "Un projet de communication entre l'océan Atlantique et l'océan Pacifique par le lac de Nicaragua (1785–1786) ." *Bulletin de Géographie Historique et Descriptive,* Année 1899, No. 2, p. 322.

10. Jean B. de Laborde: *Histoire abrégée de la mer du Sud,* Vol. 1, p. 16 (appendix) . Paris; 1791.

11. *Ibid.,* Vol. 2, p. 21 (appendix) .

12. *Ibid.,* Vol. 2, p. 20 (appendix) .

13. *Ibid.,* Vol. 2, p. 29 (appendix) .

14. Thomas Jefferson: *Writings,* Vol. 1, p. 518. Derby & Jackson, New York; 1859.

15. *Ibid.,* Vol. 2, pp. 325–6.

16. *Ibid.,* Vol. 2, p. 397.

17. Pierre-André Gargaz: *A project of universal and perpetual peace,* p. 34 (footnote) . George Simpson Eddy, New York; 1922.

CHAPTER 10
INDEPENDENCE

1. H. Misc. Doc. 210, part 2, 53 Cong., 2 Sess., p. 218.

2. Daniel F. O'Leary: *Memorias del General O'Leary,* Vol. 30, p. 256. Imprenta del Gobierno Nacional, Caracas; 1887.

CHAPTER 11
HUMBOLDT

1. Alexander von Humboldt: *Political essay on the kingdom of New Spain,* Vol. 1, pp. 24–5. Longman, etc., London; 1811.

2. *Ibid.,* p. 18.

3. *Ibid.,* p. 19.

4. *Ibid.,* p. 21.

5. *Ibid.,* p. 21.

6. *Ibid.,* pp. 21–2.

7. *Ibid.,* p. 22.

8. Alexander von Humboldt: *Voyage aux régions équinoxiales du nouveau continent,* Vol. 3, p. 120. Paris; 1825.

9. Alexander von Humboldt: *Political essay on the kingdom of New Spain,* Vol. 1, p. 25. Longman, etc., London; 1811.

10. *Ibid.,* p. 26.

11. *Ibid.,* p. 29.

12. *Ibid.,* Vol. 4, p. 350.

13. *Ibid.,* Vol. 1, pp. 31, 33.

14. Panama Railroad Co.: *Communication of the board . . . to the stockholders* (1855) , pp. 62–3. New York; 1855.

15. Alexander von Humboldt and Aimé Bonpland: *Personal narrative of travels to the equinoctial regions of America,* Vol. 3, p. 315. George Bell & Sons, London; 1881.

16. Alexander von Humboldt: *Political essay on the kingdom of New Spain,* Vol. 1, p. 40. Longman, etc., London; 1811.

17. Lucien N.-B. Wyse: *Le canal de Panama, l'isthme américain,* p. 122. Hachette, Paris; 1886.

18. Alexander von Humboldt: *Voyage aux régions équinoxiales du nouveau continent,* Vol. 3, p. 138. Paris; 1825.

19. *Ibid.,* p. 122.

20. *Ibid.,* pp. 141–2.

21. *Ibid.,* p. 146.

22. Johann W. von Goethe: *Conversations with Eckermann,* pp. 179–80. M. Walter Dunne, Washington and London; 1901.

CHAPTER 12
PANAMA: 1820–1848

1. William Duane: *A visit to Colombia, in the years 1822 and 1823,* p. iv. Philadelphia; 1826.

2. Charles S. Cochrane: *Journal of a residence and travels in Colombia,* Vol. 2, p. 432. Henry Colburn, London; 1825.

3. *Niles' Weekly Register,* Vol. 28, No. 715 (May 28, 1825) , p. 198.

4. John A. Lloyd: "On the facilities for a ship canal communication . . . through the Isthmus of Panamá." *Inst. of Civil Engineers, Minutes of Proceedings,* Vol. 9 (1850) , p. 59.

5. *Ibid.,* p. 59.

6. *Ibid.,* p. 65.

7. *Ibid.,* p. 63.

8. *Ibid.,* p. 65.

9. John A. Lloyd: "Notes respecting the Isthmus of Panama." *Royal Geog. Soc. of London Journal,* Vol. 1 (1832) , pp. 99–100.

10. H. Rep. 145, 30 Cong., 2 Sess., pp. 287–8.

11. *Ibid.,* p. 241.

12. *Ibid.,* p. 242.

13. *Ibid.,* pp. 325–6.

14. *Ibid.,* p. 274.

15. Napoléon Garella: *Projet d'un canal de jonction . . . à travers l'isthme de Panama,* p. 68. Carilian-Gœury et V. Dalmont, Paris; 1845.

16. Adolphe Dénain: *Ensayo sobre los intereses políticos i comerciales del istmo de Panamá,* p. 2. Panama; 1844.

17. "A letter of Alexander von Humboldt, 1845." *American Historical Review*, Vol. 7, No. 4 (July 1902) , p. 705.
18. Marquis Claude Drigon de Magny: *Canalisation des isthmes de Suez et de Panama*, p. 13. Paris; 1848.
19. Panama Railroad Co.: *Prospectus*, p. 36. New York; 1849.
20. George Peacock: *Notes on the Isthmus of Panama and Darien*, p. 3. Exeter; 1879.
21. William Wheelwright: *Observations on the Isthmus of Panama*, p. 19. London; 1844.
22. *Ibid.*, p. 30.
23. W. B. Liot: *Panamá, Nicaragua, and Tehuantepec*, p. iii. London; 1849.
24. *Sen. Doc. 357*, 61 Cong., 2 Sess., Vol. 1, p. 312.
25. *Ibid.*, p. 312.
26. *H. Misc. Doc. 210*, part 4, 53 Cong., 2 Sess., pp. 511–13.

CHAPTER 13
GOLD RUSH

1. U. S. Mail Steam Line: *Proceedings in the circuit court of the U. S.*, p. 67. New York; 1849.
2. John H. Kemble: "The Panamá route to the Pacific coast, 1848–1869." *Pacific Historical Review*, Vol. 7, No. 1 (March 1938) , p. 4.
3. *Ibid.*, p. 4.
4. Thomas R. Warren: *Dust and foam*, pp. 135–7. Charles Scribner, New York; 1859.
5. Julius H. Pratt: "To California by Panama in '49." *Century Illustrated Monthly Magazine*, Vol. 41, No. 6 (April 1891) , pp. 905–6, 908–9.
6. John M. Letts: *A pictorial view of California*, p. 40. Henry Bill, New York; 1853.
7. Theodore T. Johnson: *California and Oregon*, p. 48. J. B. Lippincott & Company, Philadelphia; 1865.
8. *H. Ex. Doc. 17*, 31 Cong., 1 Sess., p. 74.
9. Charles F. Hotchkiss: *On the ebb*, pp. 84–7, 90–2. New Haven; 1878.
10. Joseph W. Gregory: *Gregory's guide for California travellers via the Isthmus of Panama*, pp. 4–5. Nafis & Cornish, New York; 1850.
11. *Ibid.*, p. 8.
12. J. D. Borthwick: *Three years in California*, pp. 28–32. William Blackwood & Sons, Edinburgh and London.
13. Julius H. Pratt: "To California by Panama in '49." *Century Illustrated Monthly Magazine*, Vol. 41, No. 6 (April 1891) , pp. 915–17.
14. *"The Derienni"; or, Land pirates of the isthmus*, title page. A. R. Orton, New Orleans; 1853.
15. *Ibid.*, p. 16.

CHAPTER 14
PANAMA RAILROAD

1. *H. Rep. 145*, 30 Cong., 2 Sess., p. 673.
2. George W. Hughes: *Letter in answer to the Hon. John M. Clayton . . . on intermarine communications*, p. 39. Washington; 1850.
3. *The practicability and importance of a ship canal*, p. 55. New York; 1855.
4. Fessenden N. Otis: *History of the Panama Railroad*, p. 26. Harper & Brothers, New York; 1867.
5. *Prices Current and Shipping List*, May 24, 1854. San Francisco.
6. Fessenden N. Otis: *History of the Panama Railroad*, p. 36. Harper & Brothers, New York; 1867.
7. Pacific Mail Steamship Co.: *A sketch of the route to California, China and Japan, via the Isthmus of Panama*, pp. 31–2. New York and San Francisco; 1867.
8. Fessenden N. Otis: *History of the Panama Railroad*, pp. 35–6. Harper & Brothers, New York; 1867.
9. Charles Colné: "The Panama interoceanic canal." *Franklin Inst. Journal*, Vol. 118, No. 5 (November 1884) , p. 372.
10. Fessenden N. Otis: *History of the Panama Railroad*, p. 56. Harper & Brothers, New York; 1867.
11. *Ibid.*, p. 49.
12. *Sen. Doc. 429*, 59 Cong., 1 Sess., pp. 36–7.
13. *Sen. Doc. 222*, 58 Cong., 2 Sess., Vol. 1, p. 465.
14. Panama Railroad Co.: *Report to stockholders, April 1, 1872.*
15. Tracy Robinson: *Fifty years at Panama, 1861–1911*, p. 111. Trow Press, New York; 1911.

CHAPTER 15
PANAMA: 1855–1876

1. *The Panama massacre. A collection of the principal evidence and other doc-*

uments, pp. 55–7. Panama Star and Herald, Panama; 1857.
2. *Ibid.,* p. 20.
3. *Ibid.,* pp. 20–1.
4. *Sen. Doc. 357,* 61 Cong., 2 Sess., Vol. 1, p. 312.
5. *Sen. Doc. 143,* 58 Cong., 2 Sess., p. 27.
6. E. Taylor Parks: *Colombia and the United States, 1765–1934,* p. 343. Duke University Press, Durham, N. C.; 1935.
7. *Ibid.,* p. 343.
8. *Sen. Doc. 237,* 56 Cong., 1 Sess., p. 46.
9. *H. Ex. Doc. 1,* 43 Cong., 1 Sess., p. 760.
10. Charles H. Davis: *Report on interoceanic canals and railroads,* pp. 21–2. Government Printing Office, Washington; 1867.
11. *Sen. Ex. Doc. 15,* 46 Cong., 1 Sess., p. 1.
12. *Ibid.,* pp. 5–6.

CHAPTER 16
NICARAGUA: 1823–1850

1. Ephraim G. Squier: *Nicaragua; its people, scenery, monuments, and the proposed interoceanic canal,* Vol. 2, p. 252. D. Appleton & Company, New York; 1856.
2. *H. Rep. 145,* 30 Cong., 2 Sess., p. 246.
3. *Ibid.,* p. 244.
4. *Ibid.,* p. 264.
5. *Ibid.,* p. 265.
6. John Baily: *Central America,* p. 132. Trelawney Saunders, London; 1850.
7. *Ibid.,* p. 138.
8. John L. Stephens: *Incidents of travel in Central America, Chiapas, and Yucatan,* Vol. 1, p. 406. Harper & Brothers, New York; 1841.
9. *H. Rep. 322,* 25 Cong., 3 Sess., p. 3.
10. *Ibid.,* p. 7.
11. John L. Stephens: *Incidents of travel in Central America, Chiapas, and Yucatan,* Vol. 1, p. 398. Harper & Brothers, New York; 1841.
12. *Ibid.,* Vol. 1, p. 400.
13. Prince Napoléon Louis Bonaparte: *Canal of Nicaragua,* p. i. London; 1846.
14. *Ibid.,* p. vi.
15. *Ibid.,* p. viii.
16. *Ibid.,* pp. 6, 8.
17. Central American Court of Justice: *Decision and opinion . . . on the complaint of . . . Costa Rica against . . . Nicaragua,* pp. 17–18. Washington; 1916.
18. *H. Ex. Doc. 75,* 31 Cong., 1 Sess., p. 93.

19. *New Monthly Magazine and Humorist,* Vol. 88 (1850) , p. 189.
20. *H. Ex. Doc. 75,* 31 Cong., 1 Sess., p. 110.
21. *Ibid.,* p. 115.
22. *Ibid.,* p. 106.
23. "The great ship canal question." *British Colonial Magazine and East India Review* (November 1850) , p. 443.
24. *Ibid.,* p. 443.
25. *Sen. Doc. 357,* 61 Cong., 2 Sess., Vol. 1, p. 660.
26. *H. Ex. Doc. 75,* 31 Cong., 1 Sess., p. 202.

CHAPTER 17
NICARAGUA: 1850–1860

1. John H. Kemble: "The Panamá route to the Pacific coast, 1848–1869." *Pacific Historical Review,* Vol. 7, No. 1 (March 1938) , p. 9.
2. William O. Scroggs: *Filibusters and financiers,* p. 139 (footnote) . Macmillan Company, New York; 1916.
3. *Ibid.,* p. 356.
4. Félix Belly: *À travers l'Amérique Centrale,* Vol. 2, p. 199. Paris; 1867.

CHAPTER 18
NICARAGUA: 1861–1899

1. Bedford C. T. Pim: *The gate of the Pacific,* p. 29. L. Reeve & Company, London; 1863.
2. *Ibid.,* p. 340.
3. *Ibid.,* p. 390.
4. Charles H. Davis: *Report on interoceanic canals and railroads,* p. 7. Government Printing Office, Washington; 1867.
5. *Sen. Ex. Doc. 57,* 43 Cong., 1 Sess., p. 44.
6. *Ibid.,* p. 47.
7. *Sen. Ex. Doc. 15,* 46 Cong., 1 Sess., pp. 1–2.
8. Nicaragua Canal Construction Co.: *The inter-oceanic canal of Nicaragua* (appendix) , p. 36. New York; 1891–2.
9. *H. Rep. 3035,* 51 Cong., 1 Sess., p. 3.
10. Aniceto G. Menocal: *The Nicaragua canal. Its design, final location, and work accomplished,* p. 8. New York; 1890.
11. *Congressional Record,* 51 Cong., 2 Sess., Vol. 22, part 3, pp. 2226, 2228.
12. Nicaragua Canal Convention: *Proceedings . . . held at St. Louis,* p. 62.

580 THE LAND DIVIDED

13. Joseph Nimmo, Jr.: *The Nicaragua canal. Investigate before investing*, pp. 27–9. Washington; 1898.

CHAPTER 19
TEHUANTEPEC

1. J. J. Williams: *The Isthmus of Tehuantepec*, Vol. 1, p. 290. D. Appleton & Company, New York; 1852.
2. *Sen. Ex. Doc. 6*, 42 Cong., 2 Sess., p. 14.
3. Simon Stevens: *Letter to Brevet Maj. Gen. A. A. Humphreys, etc.*, pp. 5, 7–8.
4. *Sen. Ex. Doc. 15*, 46 Cong., 1 Sess., p. 3.
5. S. A. de Cardona: *El canal interoceánico de México*, p. 3. J. L. Guerrero y Compañía, Mexico; 1903.
6. Congrès International des Sciences Géographiques (Paris, 1875): *Compte rendu des séances*, Vol. 2, p. 355. Paris; 1878.
7. James B. Eads: *Address . . . before the House Select Committee on Interoceanic Canals* (March 9, 1880), p. 3.
8. *Ibid.*, pp. 4–5.
9. Daniel Ammen: *The errors and fallacies of the inter-oceanic transit question*, p. i. Brentano Brothers, New York and Washington; 1886.
10. James B. Eads: *Address . . . before the House Select Committee on Interoceanic Canals* (March 9, 1880), p. 2.
11. Lindley M. Keasbey: *The Nicaragua canal and the Monroe Doctrine*, p. 388. G. P. Putnam's Sons, New York; 1896.

CHAPTER 20
ATRATO

1. Berthold Seemann: *Narrative of the voyage of H. M. S. Herald during the years 1845–1851*, Vol. 1, p. 221. L. Reeve & Company, London; 1853.
2. *H. Rep. 145*, 30 Cong., 2 Sess., p. 39.
3. Atrato and San Juan Canal and Transportation Co.: *Prospectus*, pp. 3, 5. New York; 1851.
4. J. Fred Rippy: *The capitalists and Colombia*, p. 45. Vanguard Press, New York; 1931.
5. John C. Trautwine: "Rough notes of an exploration for an inter-oceanic canal route by way of the Rivers Atrato and San Juan." *Franklin Inst. Journal*, Vol. 57, No. 5 (May 1854), pp. 297–9.

6. *Ibid.*, Vol. 57, No. 4 (April 1854), pp. 228–30.
7. *Ibid.*, Vol. 57, No. 4 (April 1854), p. 229.
8. *Ibid.*, Vol. 58, No. 4 (October 1854), p. 222.
9. *Ibid.*, Vol. 58, No. 5 (November 1854), p. 299.
10. *The practicability and importance of a ship canal*, p. 9. New York; 1855.
11. Charles H. Davis: *Report on interoceanic canals and railroads*, pp. 17–18. Government Printing Office, Washington; 1867.
12. *H. Misc. Doc. 113*, 42 Cong., 3 Sess., p. 41.
13. *Ibid.*, p. 70.
14. *Sen. Ex. Doc. 15*, 46 Cong., 1 Sess., p. 6.
15. New York *Times*, November 12, 1929, p. 64.

CHAPTER 21
DARIÉN

1. Joel T. Headley: "Darien exploring expedition, under command of Lieut. Isaac C. Strain." *Harper's New Monthly Magazine*, Vol. 10, No. 58 (March 1855), p. 447.
2. William C. Gorgas: *Sanitation in Panama*, pp. 169, 171. D. Appleton & Company, New York; 1915.
3. Lionel Gisborne: *The Isthmus of Darien in 1852*, p. 135. London; 1853.
4. *Ibid.*, p. 186.
5. Edward Cullen (and others): *Over Darien by a ship canal*, p. 21. Effingham Wilson, London; 1856.
6. U. S. Navy Dept.: *Confidential letters*, Vol. 3, p. 118.
7. Lionel Gisborne: *Engineer's report*, p. 4. London; 1854.
8. *Ibid.*, p. 36.
9. U. S. Navy Dept.: *Officers' letters* (January 1854).
10. U. S. Navy Dept.: *Confidential letters*, Vol. 3, p. 118.
11. Joel T. Headley: "Darien exploring expedition, under command of Lieut. Isaac C. Strain." *Harper's New Monthly Magazine*, Vol. 10, No. 59 (April 1855), p. 612.
12. Lionel Gisborne: *Engineer's report*, pp. 9–10. London; 1854.
13. *Ibid.*, pp. 10–11.
14. Isaac G. Strain: *A paper on the his-*

tory and prospects of interoceanic communication by the American isthmus,
pp. 25–6. New York; 1856.
15. Edward Cullen (and others) : Over
Darien by a ship canal, pp. 26–8. Effingham Wilson, London; 1856.
16. Daily Panama Star, March 14, 1854.
17. A. Airiau: Canal interocéanique par
l'isthme du Darien, p. 61. Paris; 1860.
18. Jules Flachat: Notes sur le fleuve du
Darien et sur les différents projets de
canaux interocéaniques, p. 35. Eugène
Lacroix, Paris; 1866.
19. Charles H. Davis: Report on interoceanic canals and railroads, p. 21. Government Printing Office, Washington;
1867.
20. Darien Canal Co. of America: Prospectus, pp. 6–7. New York; 1870.
21. H. Misc. Doc. 113, 42 Cong., 3 Sess.,
pp. 13–14.
22. Ibid., pp. 10–11.
23. Ibid., p. 13.
24. Congrès des Sciences Géographiques, Cosmographiques et Commerciales (Antwerp, 1871) : Compte-rendu,
Vol. 1, p. 341. Antwerp; 1872.
25. Ibid., p. 361.
26. Ibid., p. 362.
27. H. Misc. Doc. 113, 42 Cong., 3 Sess.,
p. 65.
28. Thomas W. Hurst: Isthmus of Panama, Nicaragua, canal routes, etc., p. 6.
1898.

CHAPTER 22
SAN BLAS

1. William Wheelwright: Observations
on the Isthmus of Panama, p. 12. London; 1844.
2. Laurence Oliphant: "On the Bayanos River, Isthmus of Panama." Royal
Geog. Soc. of London Journal, Vol. 35
(1865) , p. 145.
3. George W. Hughes: Letter in answer to the Hon. John M. Clayton . . .
on intermarine communications, p. 47.
Washington; 1850.
4. H. Misc. Doc. 113, 42 Cong., 3 Sess.,
p. 25.
5. Ibid., p. 26.
6. Ibid., p. 32.
7. Sen. Ex. Doc. 75, 45 Cong., 3 Sess.,
p. 19.
8. "Interoceanic canal projects." American Soc. of Civil Engineers Transactions, Vol. 9 (January 1880) , p. 15.

CHAPTER 23
CHIRIQUÍ

1. Colonisation of Costa Rica, for the
development of its rich mines . . . and
for opening a new route between the Atlantic and Pacific, p. 19. Effingham Wilson, London; 1853 (?) .
2. Ibid., p. 25.
3. H. Rep. 568, 36 Cong., 1 Sess., p. 51.
4. Ibid. (minority report) , pp. 11, 13.
5. H. Ex. Doc. 46, 47 Cong., 1 Sess., p. 30.
6. Benjamin F. Butler: Butler's book.
Autobiography and personal reminiscences, p. 904. A. M. Thayer & Company,
Boston; 1892.
7. Ibid., pp. 904, 907.
8. H. Ex. Doc. 46, 47 Cong., 1 Sess., p. 7.
9. Ibid., p. 10.
10. Ibid., pp. 5–6.

CHAPTER 24
THE WYSE CONCESSIONS

1. Congrès International des Sciences
Géographiques (Paris, 1875) : Compte
rendu des séances, Vol. 1, p. 505. Paris;
1878.
2. Ibid., p. 505.
3. José C. Rodrigues: The Panama canal. Its history, its political aspects, and
financial difficulties, p. 48. Charles Scribner's Sons, New York; 1885.
4. Lucien N.-B. Wyse, A. Reclus, and
P. Sosa: Canal interocéanique, 1877–1878,
p. 46. Paris; 1879.
5. Lucien N.-B. Wyse: Le canal de Panama, l'isthme américain, pp. 268–9.
Hachette, Paris; 1886.

CHAPTER 25
PARIS CONGRESS

1. Cour d'Appel de Paris, 1re Chambre:
Plaidoirie de Me. Henri Barboux pour
MM. Ferdinand et Charles de Lesseps,
pp. 22–3.
2. U. S. State Dept.: Interoceanic Canal Congress, held at Paris, May, 1879, p.
3. Government Printing Office, Washington; 1879.
3. Congrès International d'Etudes du
Canal Interocéanique: Compte rendu
des séances, p. 26. Paris; 1879.
4. Ibid., pp. 26–7.
5. Ibid., p. 28.
6. Ibid., p. 191.

7. U. S. State Dept.: *Interoceanic Canal Congress, held at Paris, May, 1879*, p. 8. Government Printing Office, Washington; 1879.

8. Congrès International d'Études du Canal Interocéanique: *Compte rendu des séances*, p. 213 (misprinted 225). Paris; 1879.

9. *Ibid.*, p. 223.

10. *Ibid.*, p. 223.

11. *Ibid.*, p. 278.

12. *Ibid.*, p. 311.

13. *Ibid.*, p. 454.

14. *Ibid.*, p. 646.

15. *Ibid.*, p. 651.

16. *Ibid.*, pp. 653–4.

17. U. S. State Dept.: *Interoceanic Canal Congress, held at Paris, May, 1879*, p. 20. Government Printing Office, Washington; 1879.

18. "Interoceanic ship canal discussion." *American Geog. Soc. Bulletin* No. 4 (1879), p. 178.

19. *Ibid.*, p. 174.

20. Congrès International d'Études du Canal Interocéanique: *Compte rendu des séances*, p. 654. Paris; 1879.

CHAPTER 26
PREPARATION

1. Robert Courau: *Ferdinand de Lesseps*, p. 135. Bernard Grasset, Paris; 1932.

2. *Ibid.*, p. 136.

3. *Bulletin du Canal Interocéanique*, No. 6 (November 15, 1879), p. 45.

4. *Panama Star and Herald*, January 1, 1880.

5. Tracy Robinson: *Fifty years at Panama, 1861–1911*, pp. 143–4. Trow Press, New York; 1911.

6. José C. Rodrigues: *The Panama canal. Its history, its political aspects, and financial difficulties*, p. 66. Charles Scribner's Sons, New York; 1885.

7. *Panama Star and Herald*, January 3, 1880.

8. *Ibid.*, January 12, 1880.

9. Tracy Robinson: *Fifty years at Panama, 1861–1911*, p. 145. Trow Press, New York; 1911.

10. *Bulletin du Canal Interocéanique*, No. 13 (March 1, 1880), p. 109.

11. José C. Rodrigues: *The Panama canal. Its history, its political aspects, and financial difficulties*, p. 65. Charles Scribner's Sons, New York; 1885.

12. *Bulletin du Canal Interocéanique*, No. 15 (April 1, 1880), p. 142.

13. *Ibid.*, No. 15 (April 1, 1880), p. 143.

14. *Ibid.*, No. 15 (April 1, 1880), p. 143.

15. *Ibid.*, No. 15 (April 1, 1880), pp. 143–4.

16. José C. Rodrigues: *The Panama canal. Its history, its political aspects, and financial difficulties*, pp. 67, 73. Charles Scribner's Sons, New York; 1885.

17. *Sen. Ex. Doc. 112*, 46 Cong., 2 Sess., pp. 1–2.

18. *Ibid.*, p. 17.

19. *Bulletin du Canal Interocéanique*, No. 14 (March 15, 1880), p. 113.

20. *Sen. Doc. 429*, 59 Cong., 1 Sess., p. 326.

21. José C. Rodrigues: *The Panama canal. Its history, its political aspects, and financial difficulties*, p. 113. Charles Scribner's Sons, New York; 1885.

22. *Le dossier du canal de Panama, passé, présent, avenir*, p. 67. A. Rousseau, Paris; 1886.

23. *Ibid.*, pp. 73–4.

24. Chambre des Députés: *5e législature, session de 1893*, No. 2921, Vol. 1, p. 407.

25. *Bulletin du Canal Interocéanique*, No. 31 (December 1, 1880), p. 284.

26. *Ibid.*, No. 31 (December 1, 1880), p. 285.

27. *Ibid.*, No. 31 (December 1, 1880), p. 286.

28. *Ibid.*, No. 31 (December 1, 1880), p. 286.

29. Chambre des Députés: *5e législature, session de 1893*, No. 2921, Vol. 1, pp. 48–9.

30. *Bulletin du Canal Interocéanique*, No. 30 (November 15, 1880), p. 274.

31. *Ibid.*, No. 37 (March 4, 1881), p. 331.

32. *Ibid.*, No. 35 (February 1, 1881), p. 313.

33. *Ibid.*, No. 37 (March 4, 1881), pp. 330–1.

34. *Ibid.*, No. 41 (May 1, 1881), p. 362.

CHAPTER 27
WORK IN PROGRESS

1. John Bigelow: *The Panama canal*, pp. 6–7. New York; 1886.

2. *Le dossier du canal de Panama, passé, présent, avenir*, pp. 69–70, 72. A. Rousseau, Paris; 1886.

3. *Bulletin du Canal Interocéanique,* No. 36 (February 15, 1881), p. 321.
4. *Ibid.,* No. 36 (February 15, 1881), p. 321.
5. *Ibid.,* No. 40 (April 15, 1881), p. 354.
6. Tracy Robinson: *Fifty years at Panama, 1861–1911,* p. 151. Trow Press, New York; 1911.
7. *Ibid.,* pp. 152–4.
8. Chambre des Députés: *5e législature, session de 1893, No. 2921,* Vol. 1, p. 130.
9. *Ibid.,* Vol. 1, p. 511.
10. Lucien N.-B. Wyse: *Le canal de Panama, l'isthme américain,* p. 304. Hachette, Paris; 1886.
11. *Bulletin du Canal Interocéanique,* No. 80 (December 15, 1882), p. 689.
12. *Ibid.,* No. 79 (December 1, 1882), p. 673.
13. *Ibid.,* No. 119 (August 1, 1884), p. 1037.
14. *Ibid.,* No. 94 (July 18, 1883), p. 798.
15. *Ibid.,* No. 94 (July 18, 1883), p. 799.
16. Chambre des Députés: *5e législature, session de 1893, No. 2921,* Vol. 1, p. 451.
17. *Ibid.,* Vol. 1, p. 519.
18. *Ibid.,* Vol. 1, p. 457.
19. *Bulletin du Canal Interocéanique,* No. 159 (April 1, 1886), pp. 1458–9.
20. *H. Misc. Doc. 395,* 49 Cong., 1 Sess., p. 24.
21. *Bulletin du Canal Interocéanique,* No. 167 (August 1, 1886), p. 1580.
22. Chambre des Députés: *5e législature, session de 1893, No. 2921,* Vol. 1, pp. 74–5.
23. *Ibid.,* Vol. 1, p. 468.
24. Philippe Bunau-Varilla: *Panama. The creation, destruction, and resurrection,* pp. 72–3. McBride, Nast & Company, New York; 1914.
25. Chambre des Députés: *5e législature, session de 1893, No. 2921,* Vol. 1, p. 469.
26. *Ibid.,* Vol. 1, p. 511.
27. *Ibid.,* Vol. 1, p. 512.
28. *Bulletin du Canal Interocéanique,* No. 165 (July 1, 1886), p. 1553.
29. *Ibid.,* No. 190 *bis* (July 22, 1887), p. 1816.
30. Chambre des Députés: *5e législature, session de 1893, No. 2921,* Vol. 1, pp. 132–4.
31. *Ibid.,* Vol. 1, p. 135.
32. *Bulletin du Canal Interocéanique,* No. 205 (March 2, 1888), p. 1995.
33. *Ibid.,* No. 34 (January 15, 1881), p. 306.
34. *Ibid.,* No. 159 (April 1, 1886), p. 1466.
35. John Bigelow: *The Panama canal,* pp. 11, 28. New York; 1886.
36. *Bulletin du Canal Interocéanique,* No. 185 (May 2, 1887), p. 1755.
37. *Ibid.,* No. 185 (May 2, 1887), p. 1754.
38. Chambre des Députés: *5e législature, session de 1893, No. 2921,* Vol. 1, p. 97.
39. *Ibid.,* Vol. 1, p. 97.
40. Charles C. Rogers: *Intelligence report of the Panama canal,* p. 57. Government Printing Office, Washington; 1889.

CHAPTER 28

LIFE AND DEATH ON THE ISTHMUS

1. *Bulletin du Canal Interocéanique,* No. 39 (April 1, 1881), p. 347.
2. Charles C. Rogers: *Intelligence report of the Panama canal,* p. 42. Government Printing Office, Washington; 1889.
3. *H. Misc. Doc. 395,* 49 Cong., 1 Sess., pp. 25–6.
4. *Bulletin du Canal Interocéanique,* No. 187 (June 2, 1887), p. 1770.
5. John Bigelow: *The Panama canal,* p. 15. New York; 1886.
6. *Ibid.,* pp. 13–14.
7. Charles C. Rogers: *Intelligence report of the Panama canal,* p. 42. Government Printing Office, Washington; 1889.
8. Henri Cermoise: *Deux ans à Panama,* pp. 53, 56–8.
9. *Bulletin du Canal Interocéanique,* No. 94 (July 18, 1883), p. 800.
10. Jean Dorsenne: *La vie sentimentale de Paul Gauguin,* pp. 51–2. L'Artisan du Livre, Paris; 1927.
11. *H. Misc. Doc. 395,* 49 Cong., 1 Sess., p. 21.
12. Chambre des Députés: *5e législature, session de 1893, No. 2921,* Vol. 3, p. 231.
13. Wolfred Nelson: *Five years at Panama,* p. 235. Belford Company, New York; 1889.
14. Édouard Drumont: *La dernière bataille,* p. 364. E. Dentu, Paris; 1890.
15. Henry Maréchal: *Voyage d'un actionnaire à Panama,* p. 12. E. Dentu, Paris; 1885.

16. Chambre des Députés: *5e législature, session de 1893, No. 2921*, Vol. 1, pp. 53-4.
17. Henry Maréchal: *Voyage d'un actionnaire à Panama*, pp. 26–7. E. Dentu, Paris; 1885.
18. *Ibid.*, p. 26.
19. William C. Gorgas: *Sanitation in Panama*, pp. 143–4. D. Appleton & Company, New York; 1915.
20. *Bulletin du Canal Interocéanique*, No. 18 (May 15, 1880), pp. 162–3.
21. *Ibid.*, No. 22 (July 15, 1880), p. 209.
22. *Ibid.*, No. 22 (July 15, 1880), p. 209.
23. *Ibid.*, No. 39 (April 1, 1881), p. 347.
24. *Ibid.*, No. 49 (September 1, 1881), p. 427.
25. *Ibid.*, No. 49 (September 1, 1881), p. 426.
26. *Ibid.*, No. 106 (January 15, 1884), p. 921.
27. *Ibid.*, No. 119 (August 1, 1884), pp. 1035–6.
28. Édouard Drumont: *La dernière bataille*, p. 362. E. Dentu, Paris; 1890.
29. Compagnie Nouvelle du Canal de Panama: *Rapport de la commission* (1899), p. 47; Isthmian Canal Commission: *Report of the board of consulting engineers for the Panama canal*, p. 407.
30. Compagnie Nouvelle du Canal de Panama: *Rapport de la commission* (1899), p. 49.
31. Édouard Drumont: *La dernière bataille*, pp. 348–50. E. Dentu, Paris; 1890.
32. Jean d'Elbée: "Ferdinand de Lesseps et le drame de Panama." *Revue Universelle*, Vol. 71, No. 15 (November 1, 1937), p. 321.
33. *H. Misc. Doc. 395*, 49 Cong., 1 Sess., p. 22.
34. William C. Gorgas: *Sanitation in Panama*, p. 225. D. Appleton & Company, New York; 1915.
35. *Sen. Ex. Doc. 123*, 48 Cong., 1 Sess., p. 14.
36. Chambre des Députés: *5e législature, session de 1893, No. 2921*, Vol. 3, p. 230.
37. William C. Gorgas: *Sanitation in Panama*, p. 224. D. Appleton & Company, New York; 1915.
38. Wolfred Nelson: *Five years at Panama*, p. 236. Belford Company, New York; 1889.
39. William C. Gorgas: *Sanitation in*

Panama, p. 232. D. Appleton & Company, New York; 1915.
40. *Bulletin du Canal Interocéanique*, No. 159 (April 1, 1886), pp. 1456–7.
41. *Panama Star and Herald*, April 6, 1885.
42. Consulate of the U. S., Colón: *Protest against the government of Colombia*, p. 1.
43. U. S. Navy Dept.: *Report of Comdr. Bowman H. McCalla upon the naval expedition to the Isthmus of Panama, April, 1885*, pp. 15–16, 23.
44. *Ibid.*, p. 34.
45. Joseph B. and Farnham Bishop: *Goethals, genius of the Panama canal*, p. 103. Harper & Brothers, New York; 1930.
46. *Bulletin du Canal Interocéanique*, No. 136 (April 15, 1885), p. 1187.
47. *Ibid.*, No. 137 (May 1, 1885), p. 1194.

CHAPTER 29
FINANCE

1. *Ibid.*, No. 123 (October 1, 1884), p. 1073.
2. Chambre des Députés: *5e législature, session de 1893, No. 2921*, Vol. 1, p. 71.
3. *Bulletin du Canal Interocéanique*, No. 165 (July 1, 1886), p. 1549.
4. Chambre des Députés: *5e législature, session de 1893, No. 2921*, Vol. 1, p. 82.
5. *Ibid.*, Vol. 1, p. 82.
6. *Ibid.*, Vol. 1, pp. 439–40.
7. *Ibid.*, Vol. 1, p. 110.
8. *Bulletin du Canal Interocéanique*, No. 223 (December 2, 1888), p. 2170.
9. Chambre des Députés: *5e législature, session de 1893, No. 2921*, Vol. 1, pp. 139–40.
10. *Ibid.*, Vol. 1, p. 431.
11. *Ibid.*, Vol. 1, p. 415.
12. *Ibid.*, Vol. 1, p. 358.
13. *Ibid.*, Vol. 1, pp. 150, 152–3.
14. *Ibid.*, Vol. 1, p. 378.
15. *Bulletin du Canal Interocéanique*, No. 52 (October 15, 1881), p. 455.
16. *Ibid.*, No. 143 (August 1, 1885), pp. 1252–3.
17. *Ibid.*, No. 167 (August 1, 1886), p. 1580.
18. *Ibid.*, No. 213 (July 2, 1888), p. 2073.
19. Chambre des Députés: *5e législature, session de 1893, No. 2921*, Vol. 1, p. 94.
20. *Ibid.*, Vol. 1, p. 120.

CHAPTER 30
FAILURE

1. *Ibid.*, Vol. 1, pp. 115–16.
2. Commissions d'Études Instituées par le Liquidateur de la Compagnie Universelle: *Rapport No. 7*, pp. 11, 16. Paris; 1890.
3. Lucien N.-B. Wyse: *Canal interocéanique de Panama. Mission de 1890–91 en Colombie*, p. 75. A. Heymann, Paris; 1891.
4. *Ibid.*, p. 6.
5. *Ibid.*, p. 70.
6. Robert Courau: *Ferdinand de Lesseps*, p. 180. Bernard Grasset, Paris; 1932.

CHAPTER 31
SCANDAL

1. *Nation*, Vol. 56, No. 1448 (March 30, 1893), p. 229.
2. J. Quesnay de Beaurepaire: *Le Panama et la république*, p. 43. F. Juven, Paris; 1899.
3. Édouard Drumont: *La dernière bataille*, pp. 325–6. E. Dentu, Paris; 1890.
4. Cour d'Appel de Paris, 1re Chambre: *Plaidoirie de Me. Henri Barboux pour MM. Ferdinand et Charles de Lesseps*, p. 196–7.
5. Chambre des Députés: *5e législature, session de 1893*, No. 2921, Vol. 3, pp. 217–18.
6. J. Quesnay de Beaurepaire: *Le Panama et la république*, p. 77. F. Juven, Paris; 1899.
7. Jean d'Elbée: "Ferdinand de Lesseps et le drame de Panama." *Revue Universelle*, Vol. 71, No. 16 (November 15, 1937), p. 432.
8. *Ibid.*, p. 433.
9. J. Quesnay de Beaurepaire: *Le Panama et la république*, pp. 56–8. F. Juven, Paris; 1899.
10. Adrien Dansette: *Les affaires de Panama*, pp. 68–9. Perrin, Paris; 1934.
11. Alexandre Zévaès: *Le scandale du Panama*, p. 129. Nouvelle Revue Critique, Paris; 1931.
12. Adrien Dansette: *Les affaires de Panama*, pp. 74, 76. Perrin, Paris; 1934.
13. Chambre des Députés: *5e législature, session de 1893*, No. 2921, Vol. 1, pp. 226–7.
14. *Ibid.*, Vol. 1, p. 227.
15. Chambre des Députés: *6e législature, session de 1898*, No. 2992, Vol. 1, pp. 122–3.
16. Chambre des Députés: *5e législature, session de 1893*, No. 2921, Vol. 2, pp. 739–40.
17. *Ibid.*, Vol. 2, p. 740.
18. *Ibid.*, Vol. 1, p. 239.
19. *Ibid.*, Vol. 1, p. 14.
20. Jean d'Elbée: "Ferdinand de Lesseps et le drame de Panama." *Revue Universelle*, Vol 71, No. 15 (November 1, 1937), p. 335.
21. Chambre des Députés: *5e législature, session de 1893*, No. 2921, Vol. 2, p. 485.
22. *Ibid.*, Vol. 2, p. 487.
23. *Ibid.*, Vol. 1, p. 159.
24. *Ibid.*, Vol. 1, p. 162.
25. *Ibid.*, Vol. 1, pp. 242–4.

CHAPTER 32
THE TRIALS

1. Robert Courau: *Ferdinand de Lesseps*, pp. 212–13. Bernard Grasset, Paris; 1932.
2. *Ibid.*, p. 223.
3. Cour d'Appel de Paris, 1re Chambre: *Plaidoirie de Me. Henri Barboux pour MM. Ferdinand et Charles de Lesseps*, pp. 88–9.
4. *Ibid.*, pp. 185, 188–9.
5. Robert Courau: *Ferdinand de Lesseps*, p. 232. Bernard Grasset, Paris; 1932.
6. Adrien Dansette: *Les affaires de Panama*, p. 148. Perrin, Paris; 1934.
7. Chambre des Députés: *5e législature, session de 1893*, No. 2921, Vol. 1, p. 181.
8. *Ibid.*, Vol. 1, p. 180.
9. Adrien Dansette: *Les affaires de Panama*, p. 161. Perrin, Paris; 1934.
10. Robert Courau: *Ferdinand de Lesseps*, pp. 235–7. Bernard Grasset, Paris; 1932.
11. Adrien Dansette: *Les affaires de Panama*, p. 202. Perrin, Paris; 1934.
12. *Ibid.*, p. 185.
13. Cour d'Appel de Paris, 1re Chambre: *Plaidoirie de Me. Henri Barboux pour MM. Ferdinand et Charles de Lesseps*, p. 225.
14. Robert Courau: *Ferdinand de Lesseps*, pp. 238–9. Bernard Grasset, Paris; 1932.
15. Chambre des Députés: *5e législature, session de 1893*, No. 2921, Vol. 1, pp. 215–17.

16. *Ibid.*, Vol. 1, p. 201.
17. *Ibid.*, Vol. 1, pp. 201–2.
18. Adrien Dansette: *Les affaires de Panama*, p. 216. Perrin, Paris; 1934.
19. Jean d'Elbée: "Ferdinand de Lesseps et le drame de Panama." *Revue Universelle*, Vol. 71, No. 16 (November 15, 1937), p. 446.
20. Adrien Dansette: *Les affaires de Panama*, p. 217. Perrin, Paris; 1934.
21. Chambre des Députés: *5e législature, session de 1893, No. 2921*, Vol. 1, p. 200.
22. Chambre des Députés: *6e législature, session de 1898, No. 2992*, Vol. 1, p. 4.
23. Robert Courau: *Ferdinand de Lesseps*, p. 200. Bernard Grasset, Paris; 1932.
24. Chambre des Députés: *6e législature, session de 1898, No. 2992*, Vol. 1, pp. 114–15.
25. *Ibid.*, Vol. 1, p. 135.
26. *Ibid.*, Vol. 1, p. 111.
27. *Ibid.*, Vol. 1, pp. 113–14.

CHAPTER 33
THE NEW COMPANY

1. Philippe Bunau-Varilla: *Panama. The creation, destruction, and resurrection*, p. 94. McBride, Nast & Company, New York; 1914.
2. *Ibid.*, pp. 146–7.
3. Chambre des Députés: *6e législature, session de 1898, No. 2992*, Vol. 1, p. 35.
4. Gustave Eiffel: *Les transactions de M. G. Eiffel avec la liquidation de Panama*, p. v. Paris; 1894.
5. New Panama Canal Co.: *Final and definite report of the international technical commission* (1898), p. 12. New York; 1898.
6. *Ibid.*, p. 31.
7. Compagnie Nouvelle du Canal de Panama: *Rapport de la commission* (1899), p. 16. Paris; 1899.
8. George E. Walsh: "Wasted machinery on the Panama canal." *Cassier's Magazine*, Vol. 26, No. 1 (May 1904), pp. 19–20.
9. Fullerton L. Waldo: "Machinery for the Panama canal — old and new." *Engineering Magazine*, Vol. 31, No. 3 (June 1906), p. 349.
10. James T. Ford: "The present condition and prospects of the Panama canal

works." *Inst. of Civil Engineers, Minutes of Proceedings*, Vol. 144 (1901), p. 157.
11. Isthmian Canal Commission: *Report of the board of consulting engineers for the Panama canal*, p. 408.
12. Compagnie Nouvelle du Canal de Panama: *Rapport de la commission* (1899), p. 49. Paris; 1899.

CHAPTER 34
PANAMA *versus* NICARAGUA

1. H. R. Committee on Foreign Affairs: *The story of Panama*, pp. 61–2.
2. *Life*, Vol. 6, No. 25 (June 19, 1939), p. 2.
3. Anna R. Cowles (ed.): *Letters from Theodore Roosevelt to Anna Roosevelt Cowles, 1870–1918*, p. 143. Charles Scribner's Sons, New York; 1924.
4. Shelby M. Cullom: *Fifty years of public service*, p. 348. A. C. McClurg & Company, Chicago; 1911.
5. *Congressional Record*, 57 Cong., 1 Sess., Vol. 35, part 7, p. 6984.
6. *Sen. Doc. 401*, 59 Cong., 2 Sess., p. 1151.
7. *Sen. Doc. 5*, 56 Cong., 2 Sess., pp. 43–4.
8. *Sen. Doc. 222*, 58 Cong., 1 Sess., Vol. 1, pp. 174–5.
9. *Sen. Doc. 123*, 57 Cong., 1 Sess., p. 10.
10. Lewis M. Haupt: "Why is an isthmian canal not built?" *North American Review*, Vol. 175, No. 548 (July 1902), p. 129.
11. *Sen. Doc. 357*, 61 Cong., 2 Sess., p. 782.
12. *Sen. Doc. 474*, 63 Cong., 2 Sess., p. 290.

CHAPTER 35
NICARAGUA CHECKMATE

1. *U. S. Statutes at large*, Vol. 32, part 1, p. 482.
2. Philippe Bunau-Varilla: *Panama. The creation, destruction, and resurrection*, p. 177. McBride, Nast & Company, New York; 1914.
3. Philippe Bunau-Varilla: *Trois appels à la France pour sauver l'œuvre de Panama*, p. 7. Paris; 1906.
4. *Ibid.*, p. 34.
5. Nicaragua Canal Construction Co.: *The inter-oceanic canal of Nicaragua*, p. 28. New York; 1891–2.
6. *Ibid.*, p. 29.

7. Nicaragua Canal Commission, 1897–1899: *Report*, Vol. 1, p. 13.
8. Dwight C. Miner: *The fight for the Panama route*, pp. 137–8. Columbia University Press, New York; 1940.
9. H. R. Committee on Foreign Affairs: *The story of Panama*, p. 319.
10. Miles P. DuVal, Jr.: *Cadiz to Cathay*, p. 207. Stanford University Press, Stanford University; 1940.

CHAPTER 36
DEBATE IN BOGOTÁ

1. *Sen. Doc. 474*, 63 Cong., 2 Sess., pp. 379–80.
2. *Ibid.*, p. 388.
3. Dwight C. Miner: *The fight for the Panama route*, p. 285. Columbia University Press, New York; 1940.
4. Theodore Roosevelt: *An autobiography*, p. 513. Charles Scribner's Sons, New York; 1920.
5. *Ibid.*, p. 520.
6. *Congressional Record*, 58 Cong., 2 Sess., Vol. 38, part 1, p. 759.
7. Dwight C. Miner: *The fight for the Panama route*, p. 308. Columbia University Press, New York; 1940.
8. *Ibid.*, p. 318.
9. *Sen. Doc. 474*, 63 Cong., 2 Sess., pp. 428, 432.
10. Philippe Bunau-Varilla: *Panama. The creation, destruction, and resurrection*, p. 280. McBride, Nast & Company, New York; 1914.
11. Gaston Brunet: *Le procès de Panama*, p. 19. J. Dangon, Paris; 1904.
12. Theodore Roosevelt: *An autobiography*, pp. 523–4. Charles Scribner's Sons, New York; 1920.

CHAPTER 37
REVOLUTION

1. Dwight C. Miner: *The fight for the Panama route*, p. 351. Columbia University Press, New York; 1940.
2. *Ibid.*, p. 351.
3. Theodore Roosevelt: *An autobiography*, p. 530. Charles Scribner's Sons, New York; 1920.
4. William R. Thayer: *The life and letters of John Hay*, Vol. 2, pp. 327–8. Houghton Mifflin Company, Boston and New York; 1916.
5. *Ibid.*, Vol. 2, p. 328.

6. *U. S. Statutes at large*, Vol. 32, part 1, p. 482.
7. Dwight C. Miner: *The fight for the Panama route*, p. 431. Columbia University Press, New York; 1940.
8. *Ibid.*, p. 345.
9. New York *World*, June 14, 1903.
10. José A. Arango: *Datos para la historia de la independencia del istmo*, p. 13. Panama; 1922.
11. *Ibid.*, p. 13.
12. H. R. Committee on Foreign Affairs: *The story of Panama*, p. 360.
13. Philippe Bunau-Varilla: *Panama. The creation, destruction, and resurrection*, p. 302. McBride, Nast & Company, New York; 1914.
14. Dwight C. Miner: *The fight for the Panama route*, p. 359 (footnote). Columbia University Press, New York; 1940.
15. Philippe Bunau-Varilla: *Panama. The creation, destruction, and resurrection*, p. 327. McBride, Nast & Company, New York; 1914.
16. Eusebio A. Morales: *Ensayos, documentos y discursos*, Vol. 1, p. 47. Panama; 1928.
17. Dwight C. Miner: *The fight for the Panama route*, p. 370. Columbia University Press, New York; 1940.
18. Charles F. Lummis: "In the lion's den." *Out West*, Vol. 19, No. 6 (December 1903), pp. 676–7.
19. Rafael Reyes: *The two Americas*, pp. 73–4. Frederick A. Stokes Company, New York; 1914.
20. *Sen. Doc. 474*, 63 Cong., 2 Sess., p. 474.
21. Philippe Bunau-Varilla: *Panama. The creation, destruction, and resurrection*, p. 352. McBride, Nast & Company, New York; 1914.
22. New York *Herald*, November 29, 1903.
23. *Ibid.*, November 29, 1903.
24. William R. Thayer: *The life and letters of John Hay*, Vol. 2, p. 319. Houghton Mifflin Company, Boston and New York; 1916.
25. H. R. Committee on Foreign Affairs: *The story of Panama*, p. 496.

CHAPTER 38
AFTERMATH

1. *Sen. Doc. 357*, 61 Cong., 2 Sess., p. 1350.

2. James D. Richardson: *A compilation of the messages and papers of the Presidents*, Vol. 9, p. 6881. Bureau of National Literature and Art, Washington; 1910.

3. Oscar S. Straus: *Under four administrations*, pp. 174-6. Houghton Mifflin Company, Boston and New York; 1922.

4. James D. Richardson: *A compilation of the messages and papers of the Presidents*, Vol. 9, pp. 6919-23. Bureau of National Literature and Art, Washington; 1910.

5. *Congressional Record*, 58 Cong., 2 Sess., Vol. 38, part 1, p. 703.

6. *Ibid.*, p. 706.

7. *Sen. Doc. 474*, 63 Cong., 2 Sess., p. 110.

8. New York *Tribune*, August 17, 1906.

9. *Sen. Doc. 474*, 63 Cong., 2 Sess., pp. 114-15.

10. *Ibid.*, pp. 237-8.

11. Luis A. Otero: *Panama*, p. 71. Imprenta Nacional, Bogotá; 1926.

12. Ira E. Bennett (and associate editors): *History of the Panama canal*, p. 506. Historical Publishing Company, Washington; 1915.

13. Theodore Roosevelt: "The Panama blackmail treaty." *Metropolitan Magazine*, Vol. 41, No. 4 (February 1915), p. 71.

14. San Francisco *Examiner*, March 24, 1911.

15. H. R. Foreign Affairs Committee: *The story of Panama*, pp. 52-3.

16. Lord Charnwood: *Theodore Roosevelt*, p. 144. Atlantic Monthly Press, Boston; 1923.

CHAPTER 39
THE PURCHASE

1. Lucien N.-B. Wyse: *Le rapt de Panama*, pp. 59-62. R. Liautaud, Toulon; 1904.

2. *Sen. Doc. 401*, 59 Cong., 2 Sess., p. 1116.

3. H. R. Committee on Foreign Affairs: *The story of Panama*, pp. 290-1.

4. *Sen. Doc. 401*, 59 Cong., 2 Sess., p. 3136.

5. Theodore Roosevelt: *Works. Presidential addresses and state papers*, Vol. 8, pp. 1997-8. P. F. Collier & Son, New York; 1910.

6. New York *World*, October 3, 1908.

7. *Ibid.*, October 3, 1908.

8. Theodore Roosevelt: *Works. Presidential addresses and state papers*, Vol. 8, pp. 1971-5. P. F. Collier & Son, New York; 1910.

9. H. R. Committee on Foreign Affairs: *The story of Panama*, p. 307.

10. *Ibid.*, p. 311.

11. *Ibid.*, p. 311.

12. Isthmian Canal Commission: *Official handbook of the Panama canal* (4th ed., 1913), p. 47.

13. James D. Richardson: *A compilation of the messages and papers of the Presidents*, Vol. 10, p. 7704. Bureau of National Literature and Art, Washington; 1910.

14. *Ibid.*, Vol. 10, p. 7704.

15. *Canal Record*, Vol. 1, No. 4 (September 25, 1907), p. 1.

CHAPTER 40
COMMISSIONS AND TECHNICIANS

1. John F. Stevens: "An engineer's recollections." *Engineering News-Record*, Vol. 115 (August 22, 1935), p. 255.

2. Marie D. Gorgas and B. J. Hendrick: *William Crawford Gorgas*, p. 170. Doubleday, Doran & Company, Inc., New York; 1924.

3. *Ibid.*, pp. 161-2.

4. *Sen. Doc. 401*, 59 Cong., 2 Sess., p. 589.

5. *Ibid.*, p. 2523.

6. Marie D. Gorgas and B. J. Hendrick: *William Crawford Gorgas*, p. 195. Doubleday, Doran & Company, Inc., New York; 1924.

7. *Sen. Doc. 401*, 59 Cong., 2 Sess., p. 2661.

8. *Ibid.*, pp. 2663-4.

9. *Ibid.*, p. 2562.

10. John F. Stevens: "An engineer's recollections." *Engineering News-Record*, Vol. 115 (September 5, 1935), p. 332.

11. *Ibid.*, Vol. 115 (September 5, 1935), p. 332.

12. *Ibid.*, Vol. 115 (August 22, 1935), p. 257.

13. Walter L. Pepperman: *Who built the Panama canal?*, p. 89. E. P. Dutton & Company, New York; 1915.

14. John F. Stevens: "An engineer's recollections." *Engineering News-Record*, Vol. 115 (August 22, 1935), p. 256.

15. Edwin E. Slosson and Gardner Richardson: "The *Independent's* report on Panama." *Independent*, Vol. 60, No. 2989 (March 15, 1906), p. 596.

16. Edwin E. Slosson and Gardner Richardson: "Life on the Canal Zone." *Independent*, Vol. 60, No. 2990 (March 22, 1906) , p. 657.
17. Isthmian Canal Commission: *Annual report* (1905) , p. 117.
18. Joseph B. and Farnham Bishop: *Goethals, genius of the Panama canal*, p. 133. Harper & Brothers, New York; 1930.
19. Isthmian Canal Commission: *Annual report* (1905) , p. 120.
20. *Ibid.,* p. 121.
21. *Ibid.,* p. 119.
22. Isthmian Canal Commission: *Letters transmitting the report of the board of consulting engineers for the Panama canal*, p. xxi.
23. James D. Richardson: *A compilation of the messages and papers of the Presidents*, Vol. 10, p. 7707. Bureau of National Literature and Art, Washington; 1910.
24. Walter L. Pepperman: *Who built the Panama canal?*, pp. 16–17. E. P. Dutton & Company, New York; 1915.
25. John F. Stevens: "An engineer's recollections." *Engineering News-Record*, Vol. 115 (September 5, 1935) , pp. 332–3.
26. Edwin E. Slosson and Gardner Richardson: "The *Independent*'s report on Panama." *Independent*, Vol. 60, No. 2989 (March 15, 1906) , p. 596.

CHAPTER 41
ARMY RÉGIME

1. Joseph B. Bishop: *The Panama gateway*, p. 176. Charles Scribner's Sons, New York; 1915.
2. Joseph B. and Farnham Bishop: *Goethals, genius of the Panama canal*, p. 239. Harper & Brothers, New York; 1930.
3. *Ibid.,* p. 31.
4. *Ibid.,* pp. 150-1.
5. John F. Stevens: "An engineer's recollections." *Engineering News-Record*, Vol. 115 (September 5, 1935) , p. 332.
6. Marie D. Gorgas and B. J. Hendrick: *William Crawford Gorgas*, pp. 217–18. Doubleday, Doran & Company, Inc., New York; 1924.
7. Joseph B. and Farnham Bishop: *Goethals, genius of the Panama canal*, p. 202. Harper & Brothers, New York; 1930.
8. Joseph B. Bishop: *The Panama gateway*, p. 182. Charles Scribner's Sons, New York; 1915.
9. *Ibid.,* p. 178.
10. Joseph B. and Farnham Bishop: *Goethals, genius of the Panama canal*, p. 228. Harper & Brothers, New York; 1930.
11. *Sen. Doc. 146*, 63 Cong., 1 Sess., p. 5.
12. Isthmian Canal Commission: *Annual report* (1913–14) , p. 29.
13. *Canal Record*, Vol. 7, No. 52 (Aug. 19, 1914) , p. 521.

CHAPTER 42
SLIDES

1. Isthmian Canal Commission: *Annual report* (1911–12) , p. 207.
2. *Ibid.* (1911–12) , p. 211.
3. *Ibid.* (1909–10) , p. 18.
4. *Ibid.* (1907) , p. 138.
5. *Ibid.* (1910–11) , pp. 150–1.
6. *Ibid.* (1912–13) , p. 581.
7. Panama Canal. Governor: *Annual report* (1914–15) , p. 27.
8. *Ibid.* (1915–16) , p. 42.
9. *Ibid.* (1931–2) , p. 2.

CHAPTER 43
HEALTH CRUSADE

1. Philippe Bunau-Varilla: *Panama. The creation, destruction, and resurrection*, p. 379. McBride, Nast & Company, New York; 1914.
2. Josiah C. Nott: "Yellow fever contrasted with bilious fever." *New Orleans Medical and Surgical Journal*, Vol. 4, No. 5 (March 1848) , p. 563.
3. William C. Gorgas: *Sanitation in Panama*, pp. 14–16. D. Appleton & Company, New York; 1915.
4. Fred L. Soper: "The newer epidemiology of yellow fever." *American Journal of Public Health*, Vol. 27, No. 1 (January 1937) , pp. 3, 11–12.
5. Weston P. Chamberlain: *Twenty-five years of American medical activity in the Isthmus of Panama, 1904–1929*, p. 11. Panama Canal Press, Mt. Hope, C. Z.; 1929.
6. Isthmian Canal Commission: *Annual report* (1905) , p. 30.
7. *Ibid.* (1905) , p. 33.
8. William C. Gorgas: *Sanitation in Panama*, pp. 233–4. D. Appleton & Company, New York; 1915.
9. Isthmian Canal Commission: *Annual report* (1905) , p. 34.
10. Marie D. Gorgas and B. J. Hen-

drick: *William Crawford Gorgas*, p. 226. Doubleday, Doran & Company, Inc., New York; 1924.

11. William C. Gorgas: *Sanitation in Panama*, pp. 221–2. D. Appleton & Company, New York; 1915.

12. *Ibid.*, pp. 222–3.

13. W. E. Deeks and W. M. James: *A report on hemoglobinuric fever in the Canal Zone*, p. 12. Isthmian Canal Commission Press, Mt. Hope, C. Z.; 1911.

14. Isthmian Canal Commission: *Annual report* (1911–12), p. 531.

15. Panama Canal. Governor: *Annual report* (1940–1), p. 72.

16. William C. Gorgas: *Sanitation in Panama*, p. 156. D. Appleton & Company, New York; 1915.

17. Panama Canal. Health Dept.: *Annual report* (1940), p. 5.

18. Isthmian Canal Commission: *Annual report* (1905), p. 41.

19. Poultney Bigelow: "Our mismanagement at Panama." *Independent*, Vol. 60, No. 2979 (January 4, 1906), pp. 15, 17, 19.

20. *Sen. Doc. 127*, part 2, 59 Cong., 1 Sess., p. 16.

21. *Ibid.*, p. 17.

22. *Sen. Doc. 401*, 59 Cong., 2 Sess., pp. 99–101.

23. James D. Richardson: *A compilation of the messages and papers of the Presidents*, Vol. 10, p. 7694. Bureau of National Literature and Art, Washington; 1910.

24. *Ibid.*, Vol. 10, p. 7694.

25. William C. Gorgas: *Sanitation in Panama*, p. 152. D. Appleton & Company, New York; 1915.

26. Marie D. Gorgas and B. J. Hendrick: *William Crawford Gorgas*, pp. 163–4. Doubleday, Doran & Company, Inc., New York; 1924.

27. William C. Gorgas: *Sanitation in Panama*, p. 152. D. Appleton & Company, New York; 1915.

28. Charles A. L. Reed: "Isthmian sanitation. The Panama canal mismanagement." *American Medical Assn. Journal*, Vol. 44, No. 10 (March 11, 1905), p. 814.

29. New York *Tribune*, March 22, 1905.

30. *Ibid.*, March 22, 1905.

31. William C. Gorgas: *Sanitation in Panama*, p. 155. D. Appleton & Company, New York; 1915.

32. Marie D. Gorgas and B. J. Hendrick: *William Crawford Gorgas*, p. 222. Doubleday, Doran & Company, Inc., New York; 1924.

33. Joseph B. and Farnham Bishop: *Goethals, genius of the Panama canal*, p. 174. Harper & Brothers, New York; 1930.

CHAPTER 44
THE WORKERS

1. *Sen. Doc. 401*, 59 Cong., 2 Sess., p. 2642.

2. Joseph B. Bishop: *The Panama gateway*, p. 303. Charles Scribner's Sons, New York; 1915.

3. Poultney Bigelow: "Our mismanagement at Panama." *Independent*, Vol. 60, No. 2979 (January 4, 1906), p. 11.

4. *Sen. Doc. 127*, part 2, 59 Cong., 1 Sess., p. 11.

5. Isthmian Canal Commission: *Annual report* (1906), p. 5.

6. Joseph B. Bishop: *The Panama gateway*, p. 303. Charles Scribner's Sons, New York; 1915.

7. Isthmian Canal Commission: *Annual report* (1906), p. 6.

8. Panama Canal. Health Dept.: *Annual report* (1940), p. 5.

9. Isthmian Canal Commission: *Annual report* (1907), p. 47.

10. W. J. Ghent: "Work and welfare on the canal." *Independent*, Vol. 66, No. 3152 (April 29, 1909), pp. 908–10.

11. Joseph B. Bishop: *The Panama gateway*, p. 295. Charles Scribner's Sons, New York; 1915.

12. *Ibid.*, p. 292.

13. *Canal Record*, Vol. 1, No. 1 (September 4, 1907), p. 1.

14. George W. Goethals: "The Panama canal and the business problem connected with it." *Economic World*, Vol. 12 (new series), No. 27 (December 30, 1916), p. 862.

15. Panama Canal. Governor: *Annual report* (1931–2), p. 80.

16. Joseph B. and Farnham Bishop: *Goethals, genius of the Panama canal*, p. 178. Harper & Brothers, New York; 1930.

17. Isthmian Canal Commission: *Annual report* (1907), p. 26.

18. Marshall E. Dimock: *Government-operated enterprises in the Panama Canal Zone*, p. 106. University of Chicago Press, Chicago; 1934.

19. Edwin E. Slosson and Gardner Richardson: "Life on the Canal Zone." *Independent,* Vol. 60, No. 2990 (March 22, 1906) , p. 660.
20. John F. Wallace: *Personal memoranda concerning my connection with the Panama canal,* Vol. 10, p. 1661.
21. *Ibid.,* Vol. 10, pp. 1661–2.
22. Poultney Bigelow: "Our mismanagement at Panama." *Independent,* Vol. 60, No. 2979 (January 4, 1906) , p. 20.
23. Isthmian Canal Commission: *Annual report* (1907–8) , pp. 351–2.
24. *Ibid.* (1908–9) , pp. 334–5.
25. *Ibid.* (1907–8) , p. 282.
26. Panama Canal. Governor: *Annual report* (1920–1) , p. 73.

CHAPTER 45
TOLLS CONTROVERSY

1. *U. S. Statutes at large,* Vol. 37, part 1, p. 562.
2. *Sen. Doc. 357,* 61 Cong., 2 Sess., p. 783.
3. James D. Richardson: *A compilation of the messages and papers of the Presidents,* Vol. 17, pp. 7760–1. Bureau of National Literature, Inc., New York.
4. Great Britain: *Parliamentary paper Cd. 6451,* pp. 2–4.

5. Great Britain: *Parliamentary paper Cd. 6585,* pp. 5–6.
6. Great Britain: *Parliamentary paper Cd. 6645,* p. 2.
7. Sen. Committee on Interoceanic Canals: *Panama canal tolls* (1913) , pp. 3, 11–12.
8. *H. Doc. 813,* 63 Cong., 2 Sess.
9. Panama Canal. Governor: *Annual report* (1914–15) , pp. 36–7.
10. *Ibid.* (1922–3) , p. 10.
11. *Ibid.* (1932–3) , p. 87.
12. *H. Doc. 126,* 66 Cong., 1 Sess., p. 2.
13. Panama Canal. Governor: *Annual report* (1940–1) , p. 107.
14. *Ibid.* (1940–1) , p. 113.
15. *Ibid.* (1940–1) , p. 8.

CHAPTER 46
THE LAND DIVIDED

1. *Ibid.* (1914–15) , p. 57.
2. Thomas A. Bailey: "Interest in a Nicaragua canal, 1903–1931." *Hispanic American Historical Review,* Vol. 16, No. 1 (February 1936) , pp. 16–17.
3. Panama Canal. Governor: *Annual report* (1930–1) , p. 84.
4. New York *Times,* May 10, 1943.

NOTES ON MAP AND DIAGRAM SOURCES

ALL MAPS AND DIAGRAMS DRAWN BY GERSTLE MACK.
LETTERING BY HOLLIS HOLLAND.

1. Early Voyages   page 5

Topography from map of Mexico, Central America, and the West Indies (1:5,000,000) published by the American Geographical Society of New York, 1942.

Route of Columbus's third voyage from a map in *Admiral of the ocean sea* by Samuel E. Morison (1-vol. ed.), pp. 530–1. Route of Columbus's fourth voyage from the same, pp. 598, 618–19.

The routes followed by Ojeda and Bastidas are conjectural.

2. Early Settlements on the Isthmus   page 11

Topography from map of Panama (1:500,000) published by the government of Panama in co-operation with the American Geographical Society of New York, 1925.

Route of Columbus's fourth voyage from a map in *Admiral of the ocean sea* by Samuel E. Morison (1-vol. ed.), pp. 618–19.

The route followed by Bastidas, the sites of San Sebastián, Santa María de la Antigua del Darién, and Acla, and the locations of the Indian kingdoms are conjectural. A map accompanying an article, "Vasco Nuñez de Balboa, 1513–1913," by Sir Clements R. Markham, published in the *Geographical Journal*, Vol. 41, No. 6 (June 1913), pp. 517–32, places these settlements and kingdoms in approximately the same situations.

3. Straits of Magellan   page 28

Topography from map of South America, Sheet South (1:5,000,000) published by the American Geographical Society of New York, 1942.

4. Humboldt's Nine Routes   page 114

Topography from outline map of the Americas (1:50,000,000) published by the American Geographical Society of New York, 1942.

Humboldt's routes from descriptions in his *Political essay on the kingdom of New Spain*, Vol. 1, pp. 19–43, and from small maps at the end of Vol. 4. Routes 1 and 2 have been modified to conform to actual topography, inaccurately represented in Humboldt's maps. The route which I have numbered 1A was described but not mapped by Humboldt.

5. Panama Projects, 1829–1904   page 122

Topography, old Spanish roads, Panama Railroad, and canal project of the second Walker commission from *Sen. Doc. 222*, 58 Cong., 2 Sess., Vol. 2, Plate 21. The projects of Wyse, the Compagnie Universelle, and the Compagnie Nouvelle follow the line of the second Walker commission project with very slight variations.

Lloyd and Falmarc railroad projects from a map accompanying "Account of levellings carried across the Isthmus of Panama" by John A. Lloyd, published in the *Royal Society of London Philosophical Transactions* (1830), Part 1, pp. 59–68. Lloyd and Falmarc canal project from a brief description in the same article and a slightly more detailed description in *A succinct view of the importance and practicability of forming a ship canal across the Isthmus of Panama* by H. R. Hill, pp. 12–13.

Peacock project from a map in *Notes on the Isthmus of Panama and Darien* by Capt. George Peacock.

Garella project from *Projet d'un canal de jonction de l'océan Pacifique et de l'océan Atlantique à travers l'isthme de Panama* by Napoléon Garella, Plate 1.

Lull and Menocal project from *Sen. Ex. Doc. 75*, 45 Cong., 3 Sess., Plate 1 (following p. 53).

6. Typical Tunnel Cross Sections   page 129

Garella tunnel from *Projet d'un canal de jonction de l'océan Pacifique et de l'océan Atlantique à travers l'isthme de Panama* by Napoléon Garella, Plate 2.

Selfridge tunnel from *H. Misc. Doc. 113*, 42 Cong., 3 Sess., Plate 7.

Second Walker commission tunnel from *Sen. Doc. 222*, 58 Cong., 2 Sess., Vol. 2, Plate 4.

7. Nicaragua Projects   pages 174–5

Topography and existing railroads from maps of Central America, Sheets F-16, G-16, and G-17 (1:1,000,000), published by the American Geographical Society of New York, 1928 and 1937.

Baily project from a description in *Central America* by John Baily, pp. 139–44.

Louis Napoleon project from *Canal of Nicaragua* by Prince Napoléon Louis Bonaparte, Map 2.

Oersted project from a map accompanying "Survey made for a canal, through the River Sapoa, to the port of Salinas or Bolaños, in Costa Rica" by Andreas Oersted, published in the *Royal Geographical Society of London Journal*, Vol. 21 (1851), pp. 96–9.

Squier projects from *Nicaragua; its people, scenery, monuments, and the proposed interoceanic canal* by Ephraim G. Squier, Vol. 1, map opp. p. 2, and Vol. 2, map opp. p. 239.

Childs project from *Report on interoceanic canals and railroads* by Rear Adm. Charles H. Davis, Map 4.

Belly project from a map in *Carte d'étude pour le tracé et le profil du canal de Nicaragua* by Aimé Thomé de Gamond and Félix Belly.

Lull and Menocal project of 1873 from *Sen. Ex. Doc. 57, 43* Cong., 1 Sess., Plates 1–4 incl.

Blanchet project from *Canal interocéanique maritime de Nicaragua* by Pouchet and Sautereau, Plate 2.

Menocal project of 1885 from *Sen. Ex. Doc. 99,* 49 Cong., 1 Sess., Plate 1.

Second Walker commission project from *Sen. Doc. 222,* 58 Cong., 2 Sess., Vol. 2, Plate 28.

Sultan project from a map in *H. Doc. 139, 72* Cong., 1 Sess.

Accessory Transit Company road from *Report on interoceanic canals and railroads* by Rear Adm. Charles. H. Davis, Map 4.

Pim railroad project from *The gate of the Pacific* by Comdr. Bedford C. T. Pim, map opp. p. 394.

8. Comparison between Steeply and Gradually Rising Canal Profiles page 211

Redrawn from *Sen. Ex. Doc. 57, 43* Cong., 1 Sess., Fig. 3.

9. Tehuantepec Projects page 226

Topography and existing railroads from maps of North America, Sheets E-15 and D-15 (1:1,000,000), published by the American Geographical Society of New York, 1935 and 1938.

Cramer project from a description in *Survey of the Isthmus of Tehuantepec, executed in the years 1842 and 1843* by Cayetano Moro, p. 10.

Moro project from *Interoceanic canals* by Henry Stucklé, map at end of book.

Shufeldt project from *Sen. Ex. Doc. 6, 42* Cong., 2 Sess., Plate 2.

Eads ship railway project from a map in *The interoceanic problem, and its scientific solution* by Elmer L. Corthell.

Carrillo de Albornoz projects from a map and descriptions in *El canal interocéanico de México* by S. A. de Cardona. The routes have been modified to conform to actual topography, inaccurately represented in Cardona's map.

Louisiana Tehuantepec Company road from *Interoceanic canals* by Henry Stucklé, map opp. p. 36.

10. Atrato Projects page 238

Topography from map of Colombia (1:2,000,000) published by the government of Colombia, 1939.

Atrato and San Juan Transportation Company project from a map in the *Prospectus* published by the company.

Inter-oceanic Canal Company project from a map in *The Atlanto-Pacific canal. . . . Preliminary statement* published by the company.

Trautwine project from *Report on interoceanic canals and railroads* by Rear Adm. Charles H. Davis, Map 10.

Kennish project from *H. Ex. Doc. 107*, 47 Cong., 2 Sess., Map 13.

Michler project from a map in *Sen. Ex. Doc. 9*, 36 Cong., 2 Sess., Vol. 2. Reproduced in *Report on interoceanic canals and railroads* by Rear Adm. Charles H. Davis, Map. 11.

Selfridge projects of 1871 and 1873 from *H. Misc. Doc. 113*, 42 Cong., 3 Sess., Map 2.

Collins project from *Sen. Ex. Doc. 75*, 45 Cong., 3 Sess., Plates 1 and 2 (following p. 124).

11. Darién Projects. Río Sabana–Caledonia Bay Section   page 248

Topography from map of Panama (1:500,000) published by the government of Panama in co-operation with the American Geographical Society of New York, 1925.

Cullen project from *Report on interoceanic canals and railroads* by Rear Adm. Charles H. Davis, Map 9. Modified to conform to actual topography, inaccurately represented in Cullen's map.

Gisborne project from maps in *The Isthmus of Darien in 1852* by Lionel Gisborne. Reproduced in *H. Ex. Doc. 107*, 47 Cong., 2 Sess., Map 5.

Airiau project from a map in *Canal interocéanique par l'isthme du Darien* by A. Airiau. Modified to conform to actual topography, inaccurately represented in Airiau's map.

Bourdiol project from a map in *Notice historique et géographique sur l'état de la question du canal du Darien* by Victor A. Malte-Brun. Reproduced in *H. Ex. Doc. 107*, 47 Cong., 2 Sess., Map 6.

Second Walker commission projects from *Sen. Doc. 222*, 58 Cong., 2 Sess., Vol. 2, Plate 5.

Prevost route from *Report on interoceanic canals and railroads* by Rear Adm. Charles H. Davis, Map 8.

Strain route from a map accompanying "Darien exploring expedition, under command of Lieut. Isaac C. Strain" by Joel T. Headley, published in *Harper's New Monthly Magazine*, Vol. 10, No. 58 (March 1855), p. 437. Reproduced in *H. Ex. Doc. 107*, 47 Cong., 2 Sess., Map 6.

12. Darién Projects. Río Tuyra–Gulf of Urabá Section   page 261

Topography from map of Panama (1:500,000) published by the government of Panama in co-operation with the American Geographical Society of New York, 1925.

Bionne project from a map in *La question du percement de l'isthme de Panama devant un congrès international* by Henry Bionne.

De Puydt project from a description in *Compte rendu des séances* of the Congrès International d'Études du Canal Interocéanique, p. 316, and a description in *Examen comparatif des divers projets de canaux inter-océaniques par l'isthme de Darien et le lac de Nicaragua* by Pouchet and Sautereau, p. 13.

De Gogorza and de Lacharme project from a map in *Inter-oceanic Canal. Route of Paya* by Louis de Lacharme.

Wyse projects from a map in *Canal interocéanique, 1877–1878* by Wyse, Reclus, and Sosa.

13. San Blas Projects   page 269

Topography from map of Panama (1:500,000) published by the government of Panama in co-operation with the American Geographical Society of New York, 1925.

Kelley project from *Report on interoceanic canals and railroads* by Rear Adm. Charles H. Davis, Map 7.

Wyse project from a map in *Canal interocéanique, 1877–1878* by Wyse, Reclus, and Sosa.

Shelbourne project from a description in "The interoceanic ship canal" (address by Maj. Sidney F. Shelbourne) published in the *American Geographical Society of New York Journal*, Vol. 11 (1879), p. 228.

Second Walker commission project from *Sen. Doc. 222, 58* Cong., 2 Sess., Vol. 2, Plate 3.

American Isthmus Ship Canal Company project from a small map in *The American isthmus canals. The Darien Mandingo canal* by Edward W. Serrell, and a description in *Preliminary statement . . . concerning the proposed Mandingo canal* published by the company.

14. Isthmus of Chiriquí   page 274

Topography, frontiers, and railroads from map of Panama (1:500,000) published by the government of Panama in co-operation with the American Geographical Society of New York, 1925.

Thompson road and projected extension from a map in *Geological report of Professor Manross* published by the Chiriqui Improvement Company.

15. Permanent Lock System and Bunau-Varilla's Temporary Lock System   page 331

Redrawn from diagrams in *Panama. The creation, destruction, and resurrection* by Philippe Bunau-Varilla, p. 549.

16. Additional Excavation Necessitated by Flat Slopes   page 334

Drawn by the author.

17. Canal Zone, 1943   follows page 490

Topography, Zone boundaries (except in Madden Lake area), and present line of Panama Railroad from map of Canal Zone and vicinity (1:100,000) published by The Panama Canal, 1927.

Zone boundaries in Madden Lake area and modern highways from map in

Annual report for the fiscal year ended June 30, 1931 by the governor of The Panama Canal.

New locks under construction from maps in *H. Doc. 210*, 76 Cong., 1 Sess.

Profile from *Sen. Doc. 222*, 58 Cong., 2 Sess., Vol. 2, Plate 22, modified to conform to existing lock locations.

Old line of Panama Railroad from *Sen. Doc. 222*, 58 Cong., 2 Sess., Vol. 2, Plate 21.

Plans of Panama City and Colón from *Panama*, a pamphlet "published as a tribute to the genius of the builders of the Panama canal on the 25th anniversary of the opening of the canal to the commerce of the world" (1939).

BIBLIOGRAPHY

OFFICIAL AND SEMIOFFICIAL PUBLICATIONS

UNITED STATES OF AMERICA

(Unless otherwise noted, all United States documents are published by the Government Printing Office, Washington)

BECKER, GEORGE FERDINAND: *Mechanics of the Panama canal slides* (Geological Survey Professional Paper 98). 1917.

BIGELOW, MAJ. JOHN: "The Panama canal. May we close it in time of war? General considerations." *Journal of the Military Service Institution of the U. S.,* Vol. 55, No. 191 (September–October 1914), pp. 213–24. New York.

BRAND, CHARLES JOHN: "The effective use of the Panama canal in the distribution of products." *Second Pan-American Scientific Congress Proceedings,* Vol. 3 (1917), pp. 911–15.

BRISTOW, JOSEPH LITTLE: *Report of . . . special Panama Railroad commissioner to the Secretary of War, June 24, 1905.* Office of Administration, Isthmian Canal Affairs, Washington; 1905. (Repr. in *Sen Doc. 429,* 59 Cong., 1 Sess.).

BURR, WILLIAM HUBERT: "The present aspects of the Panama canal." *Smithsonian Institution Report* (1904), pp. 737–44.

Canal Record, Ancón, Balboa, and Mt. Hope, C. Z. (Name changed to *Panama Canal Record* Aug. 23, 1916).

CHAMBERLAIN, COL. WESTON P.: *Twenty-five years of American medical activity in the Isthmus of Panama, 1904–1929. A triumph of preventive medicine* (U. S. Public Health Service No. 923). Panama Canal Press, Mt. Hope, C. Z.; 1929.

COFER, LELAND E.: "The advance in quarantine incident to the opening of the Panama canal." *International Congress on Hygiene and Demography Transactions,* XV, Vol. 5 (1913), pp. 237–45.

CONGRESS: *Documents and reports:*

SER. NO.	CONG.	SESS.	DOC. OR REP.	NO.	SUBJECT
352	25	3	H. Rep.	322	Canal — Atlantic to Pacific (Mercer report).
533	30	2	Sen. Misc. Doc.	1	Memorial of Aspinwall, Stephens, and Chauncey on Panama Railroad, 1848.
533	30	2	Sen. Misc. Doc.	13	Memorial of Wells & Co. and others on Tehuantepec mail subsidy.
533	30	2	Sen. Misc. Doc.	50	Petition of P. A. Hargous for Tehuantepec R. R. guarantee.

SER. NO.	CONG.	SESS.	DOC. OR REP.	NO.	SUBJECT
545	30	2	H. Rep.	26	Panama R. R.
546	30	2	H. Rep.	145	Canal or railroad between the oceans (Rockwell report).
558	31	1	Sen. Ex. Doc.	47	Geology and topography of California.
573	31	1	H. Ex. Doc.	17	California and New Mexico.
579	31	1	H. Ex. Doc.	75	Tigre Island and Central America.
621	32	1	Sen. Ex. Doc.	97	Correspondence on Tehuantepec.
660	32	2	Sen. Ex. Doc.	27	Correspondence on Central America.
819	34	1	Sen. Ex. Doc.	25	Correspondence on Nicaragua, Costa Rica, and Mosquito Indians.
821	34	1	Sen. Ex. Doc.	62	Postal arrangements between Atlantic and Pacific.
881	34	3	Sen. Ex. Doc.	51	Oceanic routes to California (Cram report).
1070	36	1	H. Rep.	568	Contract for coal (Chiriquí).
1085 1086	36	2	Sen. Ex. Doc.	9	Interoceanic canal near Darién (Michler report).
1097	36	2	H. Ex. Doc.	41	Reports from Chiriquí Commission.
1480	42	2	Sen. Ex. Doc.	6	Tehuantepec canal (Shufeldt report).
1575	42	3	H. Misc. Doc.	113	Darién canal (Selfridge report).
1582	43	1	Sen. Ex. Doc.	57	Nicaragua canal (Hatfield-Lull report).
1594	43	1	H. Ex. Doc.	1	Foreign relations.
1829	45	3	Sen. Ex. Doc.	75	Panama and Napipí canals (Lull and Collins reports).
1869	46	1	Sen. Ex. Doc.	15	Interoceanic Canal Commission report, 1876.
1885	46	2	Sen. Ex. Doc.	112	Interoceanic canal.
1937	46	2	H. Rep.	1121	Clayton-Bulwer treaty.
1981	46	3	H. Misc. Doc.	13	Tehuantepec ship railway (minority report).
1981	46	3	H. Misc. Doc.	16	Interoceanic canal.
1982	46	3	H. Rep.	224	Interoceanic canal and Monroe Doctrine.
1982	46	3	H. Rep.	322	Tehuantepec ship railway.
1983	46	3	H. Rep.	390	Monroe Doctrine.
1991	47	1	Sen. Ex. Doc.	194	Clayton-Bulwer treaty and Monroe Doctrine.

SER. NO.	CONG.	SESS.	DOC. OR REP.	NO.	SUBJECT
2027	47	1	H. Ex. Doc.	46	Chiriquí grant.
2112	47	2	H. Ex. Doc.	107	Interoceanic communication (Sullivan report).
2162	48	1	Sen. Ex. Doc.	26	Clayton-Bulwer treaty.
2167	48	1	Sen. Ex. Doc.	123	Reports of naval officers on Panama canal, 1883–4.
2337	49	1	Sen. Ex. Doc.	99	Nicaragua surveys, 1885 (Menocal report).
2422	49	1	H. Misc. Doc.	395	Panama canal, 1885 (Kimball report).
2479	49	2	H. Ex. Doc.	57	Central America.
2675	50	2	H. Rep.	4167	European control of interoceanic canals.
2816	51	1	H. Rep.	3035	Maritime Canal Co. of Nicaragua.
2826	51	2	Sen. Rep.	1944	Maritime Canal Co. of Nicaragua (Sherman report).
2904	52	1	Sen. Misc. Doc.	97	Nicaragua canal (Dutton report).
3265	53	2	H. Misc. Doc.	210	Compilation of the messages and papers of the Presidents, 1789–1897, by James D. Richardson (10 volumes).
3367	54	1	Sen. Rep.	1109	Nicaragua canal.
3456	54	1	H. Rep.	279	Report of Nicaragua Canal Board, 1895.
3725	55	3	Sen. Doc.	26	List of documents on canals.
3841	55	3	H. Rep.	2104	Maritime Canal Co. of Nicaragua.
3848	56	1	Sen. Doc.	50	Panama and Nicaragua canals.
3848	56	1	Sen. Doc.	59	List of books and articles on canal and railway routes.
3853	56	1	Sen. Doc.	161	Correspondence on canal.
3853	56	1	Sen. Doc.	237	Correspondence on canal.
3854	56	1	Sen. Doc.	188	New Panama Canal Co.
3868	56	1	Sen. Doc.	268	Interoceanic canal.
3886	56	1	Sen. Rep.	114	Interoceanic canal.
3894 4063	56	1	Sen. Rep.	1337	Interoceanic canal.
4022	56	1	H. Rep.	351	Interoceanic canal (Hepburn report).
4029	56	2	Sen. Doc.	5	Isthmian Canal Commission, preliminary report (Nov. 1900).
4225	57	1	Sen. Doc.	54	Isthmian Canal Commission, report 1899–1901. (Repr. with additions and maps in *Sen. Doc.* 222, 58 Cong., 2 Sess.).

SER. NO.	CONG.	SESS.	DOC. OR REP.	NO.	SUBJECT
4230	57	1	Sen. Doc.	123	Isthmian Canal Commission, supplementary report.
4256	57	1	Sen. Rep.	1	Interoceanic canal.
4260	57	1	Sen. Rep.	783	Isthmian canal.
4377	57	1	H. Doc.	611	Letters from Colombian minister.
4399	57	1	H. Rep.	15	Interoceanic canal.
4589	58	2	Sen. Doc.	143	Use of military force in Colombia.
4609	58	2	Sen. Doc.	222	Isthmian Canal Commission, report 1899–1901, with additions and maps. (2 vols.).
4915	59	1	Sen. Doc.	457	Refusal of W. N. Cromwell to answer questions.
4919	59	1	Sen. Doc.	127	Isthmian Canal Commission, annual report (1905), with additions. (2 parts).
4919	59	1	Sen. Doc.	429	Panama R. R. (Bristow report).
5097 5098 5099 5100	59	2	Sen. Doc.	401	Investigation of Panama canal matters.
5407	60	2	Sen. Doc.	539	Report on labor conditions.
5557	60	2	H. Doc.	1458	Report of engineers (1909).
5646 5647	61	2	Sen. Doc.	357	Treaties, conventions, etc., 1776–1909, compiled by William M. Malloy. (2 vols.).
6176	62	2	Sen. Doc.	575	Panama canal traffic and tolls (Johnson report).
6178	62	2	Sen. Doc.	881	Panama canal and restoration of American merchant marine, by Samuel H. Barker.
6500	62	3	H. Doc.	1313	Panama canal tolls, by Frank Feuille.
6528	63	1	Sen. Doc.	146	Report of Fine Arts Commission on Panama canal.
6582	63	2	Sen. Doc.	474	Diplomatic history of the Panama canal.
6755	63	2	H. Doc.	813	President Wilson's message on repeal of tolls exemption.
7644	66	1	H. Doc.	126	Panama canal tolls.
9536	72	1	H. Doc.	139	Interoceanic communications.
10095	75	1	Sen. Doc.	23	Panama canal tolls.
10349	76	1	H. Doc.	210	Future needs of interoceanic shipping.

SENATE: The executive proceedings of the Senate of the United States, on the subject of the mission to the congress at Panama, together with the messages and documents relating thereto. Washington; 1826.

SENATE COMMITTEE ON INTEROCEANIC CANALS: Hearings . . . (January 11–March 10, 1902) on H. 3110 (for construction of canal . . . and other papers). 1902.

——: Panama canal. Hearings, January 16, 1908. 1908.

——: Panama canal. Hearings . . . on . . . a bill to provide for the opening, maintenance, protection, and operation of the Panama canal, and the sanitation and government of the Canal Zone. 1912.

——: Panama canal tolls. 1913.

HOUSE OF REPRESENTATIVES COMMITTEE ON APPROPRIATIONS: Isthmian canal. Supplement to hearings before subcommittee . . . in charge of sundry civil appropriation bill for 1910. 1909.

HOUSE OF REPRESENTATIVES COMMITTEE ON FOREIGN AFFAIRS: Discussion of the Nicaragua ship canal and the Tehuantepec railway schemes. 1882.

——: The interoceanic canal and the Monroe Doctrine. Notes of a hearing before the committee . . . January 11, 1881. 1881.

——: The story of Panama. Hearings on the Rainey resolution. . . . 1913.

HOUSE OF REPRESENTATIVES COMMITTEE ON INTERSTATE AND FOREIGN COMMERCE: Hearings on House bill 35 (on the Nicaragua canal). 1896.

——: Hearings . . . on the bills relating to Panama canal matters. 1908.

——: Hearings . . . on measurement of vessels using the Panama canal; the Joint Land Commission. January 11, February 8, February 11, 1916. 1916.

Congressional Record.

CONSULATE OF THE UNITED STATES, COLÓN: Protest against the government of Colombia. (No pl., no d.).

DAVIS, REAR ADM. CHARLES HENRY: Report on interoceanic canals and railroads between the Atlantic and Pacific Oceans. 1867.

DISTRICT COURT, INDIANA: The Indianapolis News Panama libel case. Fulmer-Cornelius Press, Indianapolis; 1909.

ELIHU ROOT COLLECTION OF UNITED STATES DOCUMENTS: Panama, Series F, Vols. 11–12, 23–4, 26. 1895–1908.

GOETHALS, LT. COL. GEORGE WASHINGTON: The isthmian canal. 1909.

GORGAS, COL. WILLIAM CRAWFORD: A few general directions with regard to destroying mosquitoes, particularly the yellow fever mosquito. 1904.

GREEN, CAPT. LEWIS D.: "The Nicaragua canal in its military aspects." Journal of the Military Service Institution of the U. S., Vol. 26, No. 103 (January 1900), pp. 1–14. Governor's Island, N. Y.

HAINS, COL. PETER C.: "An isthmian canal from a military point of view." Journal of the Military Service Institution of the U. S., Vol. 28, No. 111 (May 1901), pp. 371–80. Governor's Island, N. Y. Reprinted in Journal of United States Artillery, Vol. 15 (Fort Monroe, 1901), pp. 289–97, and in American Academy of Political and Social Science Annals, Vol. 17 (Philadelphia, 1901), pp. 1–12.

HALL, CAPT. HERMAN: "The Panama canal." *Journal of the Military Service Institution of the U. S.,* Vol. 35, No. 132 (November–December 1904), pp. 382–5. Governor's Island, N. Y.

HODGES, COL. HARRY FOOTE: *Action of water in locks of the Panama canal* (U. S. Engineering Bureau Professional Memoirs, Vol. 7, pp. 1–31). 1915.

———: *The Panama canal* (U. S. Engineering Bureau Professional Memoirs, Vol. 1, pp. 355–88). 1909.

ISTHMIAN CANAL COMMISSION: *Annual reports,* 1904–14.

———: *Invitation for proposals to furnish Chinese labor to be used . . . upon the Canal Zone . . . August 20, 1906.* 1906.

———: *Laws of the Canal Zone . . . enacted by the Isthmian Canal Commission.* 1905. (Amplified and annotated 1921. Panama Canal Press, Mt. Hope, C. Z.; 1922).

———: *Letter . . . to the advisory board of engineers upon plans for the Panama canal, submitting data.* September 1, 1905.

———: *Letters transmitting the report of the board of consulting engineers for the Panama canal.* 1906.

———: *Manual of information concerning employment for service.* (Revised November 15, 1910). 1910.

———: *Newspaper comment and resolutions upholding the position of the United States in granting free tolls through the Panama canal to American ships in the coastwise trade.* 1913.

———: *Official handbook of the Panama canal.* (2nd edition, Ancón, 1911; 3rd and 4th editions, Ancón, 1913).

———: *The Panama canal.* 1910.

———: *Report of the board of consulting engineers for the Panama canal.* 1906.

———: *Report of the engineering committee.* February 1, 1905.

———: *Sundry technical reports in relation to the Panama canal covering the period 1899–1904 inclusive. . . .* Isthmian Canal Commission Press, Panama; 1905.

JUSTICE DEPARTMENT: *Official opinions of the Attorneys General of the United States. . . .* (ed. by J. Hubley Ashton). W. H. & O. H. Morrison, Washington. (No d.).

———: *Panama canal title. Opinion of the Attorney General upon the title proposed to be given by the New Panama Canal Company to the United States.* 1902.

KNAPP, CAPT. H. S., U. S. N.: "The Panama canal in international law." *United States Naval Institute Proceedings,* Vol. 39, No. 1 (March 1913), pp. 95–126. Annapolis.

———: "The real status of the Panama canal as regards neutralization." *United States Naval Institute Proceedings,* Vol. 36, No. 1 (March 1910), pp. 61–102. Annapolis.

LEVITA, CAPT. CECIL B.: "The interoceanic canal." *Journal of the Military Service Institution of the U. S.,* Vol. 24, No. 99 (May 1899), pp. 479–83. Governor's Island, N. Y.

LIBRARY OF CONGRESS, DIVISION OF BIBLIOGRAPHY: *List of refer-*

ences on the Panama canal and the Panama Canal Zone (prepared under direction of H. H. B. Meyer). 1919.

NATIONAL ACADEMY OF SCIENCES: *Report of the committee . . . on Panama canal slides* (Memoirs, Vol. 28). 1924.

NAVY DEPARTMENT: *Confidential letters,* Vol. 3 (February 1, 1853–October 17, 1857), pp. 117–19. (MS. in Office of Naval Records and Library, Washington).

——: *Officers' letters* (January 1854). (MS. in Office of Naval Records and Library, Washington).

——: *Report of Commander Bowman H. McCalla upon the naval expedition to the Isthmus of Panama, April, 1885.*

NICARAGUA CANAL COMMISSION, 1897–1899: *Report.* Lord Baltimore Press, Baltimore; 1899. (2 vols.).

NIMMO, JOSEPH JR.: *The proposed American inter-oceanic canal in its commercial aspects.* 1880.

PANAMA CANAL. GOVERNOR: *Annual reports,* 1914–41.

——: *Sailing directions and general information.* Panama Canal Press, Mt. Hope, C. Z.; 1915. (Revised August 1919; August 1921; 1925; 1928–9; 1931; 1932–8).

PANAMA CANAL. HEALTH DEPARTMENT: *Annual reports.* Panama Canal Press, Mt. Hope, C. Z.

PANAMA CANAL. STATUTES: *Canal Zone code.* 1934.

PRESIDENT: *Executive orders relating to the Panama canal* (March 8, 1904–December 31, 1921). Panama Canal Press, Mt. Hope, C. Z.; 1922. (Supplements 1922–35).

PUBLIC HEALTH SERVICE: *Yellow fever* (lectures by Henry Rose Carter. Public Health Reports, Supplement No. 19). 1914.

RICHARDSON, JAMES D.: *A compilation of the messages and papers of the Presidents.* Bureau of National Literature and Art, Washington. (Continuation of *H. Misc. Doc. 210,* 53 Cong., 2 Sess.).

RIVERS AND HARBORS, BOARD OF ENGINEERS FOR: *The Panama canal and its ports. Prepared . . . in co-operation with the Bureau of Operations, United States Shipping Board* (Port Series No. 22). 1928. (Revised 1934; 1938).

ROGERS, LT. CHARLES C., U. S. N.: *Intelligence report of the Panama canal.* 1889.

ROUSSEAU, REAR ADM. HARRY HARWOOD: *The isthmian canal. Presented at the 20th annual session of the Trans-Mississippi Commercial Congress held at Denver, Colo., August 16–21, 1909.* 1910.

——: "The terminal facilities of the Panama canal." *United States Naval Institute Proceedings,* Vol. 42, No. 166 (November–December 1916), pp. 1825–53. Annapolis.

SHONTS, THEODORE PERRY: *Special report of the chairman of the Isthmian Canal Commission to the Secretary of War, showing present conditions on the isthmus.* Office of Administration, Isthmian Canal Affairs, Washington; 1906.

——: *Speech . . . before the Commercial Club, Chicago, on . . . January 26, 1907.* 1907.

——: *Speech . . . before the Commercial Club, Cincinnati, on . . . January 20, 1906.* 1906.

——: *Speech . . . before the Knife-and-Fork Club, Kansas City, on . . . January 24, 1907.* 1907.

SPECIAL PANAMA CANAL COMMISSION: *Report . . . 1921.* 1922.

STATE DEPARTMENT: *Interoceanic Canal Congress, held at Paris, May, 1879. Instructions to Rear Admiral Daniel Ammen and Civil Engineer A. G. Menocal, U. S. Navy, delegates on the part of the United States . . . and reports of the proceedings of the congress.* 1879.

STOCKTON, CAPT. C. H., U. S. N.: "The American interoceanic canal. A study of the commercial, naval and political conditions." *United States Naval Institute Proceedings,* Vol. 25, No. 4 (December 1899), pp. 753–97. Annapolis.

TAFT, WILLIAM HOWARD: *The Panama canal. Speech . . . at the St. Louis Commercial Club . . . November 18, 1905.* Office of Administration, Isthmian Canal Affairs, Washington; 1905.

TREATIES: *Treaties and acts of Congress relating to the Panama canal.* Panama Canal Press, Mt. Hope, C. Z.; 1922.

UNITED STATES AND REPUBLIC OF PANAMA, JOINT LAND COMMISSION: *Interim report.* Government Printing Office, Panama; 1914.

WALLACE, JOHN FINDLEY: *The Panama canal. Supplemental statement . . . submitted to United States Senate Committee on Interoceanic Canals . . . May 22, 1906.* 1906.

CENTRAL AMERICAN COURT OF JUSTICE

Decision and opinion of the court on the complaint of the republic of Costa Rica against the republic of Nicaragua growing out of a convention entered into by the republic of Nicaragua with the United States of America for the sale of the San Juan River and other matters (September 30, 1916). Gibson Bros., Inc., Washington; 1916.

COLOMBIA (or NEW GRANADA)

Codificación nacional de todas las leyes de Colombia desde el año de 1821, Vol. 14, pp. 593–615; Vol. 16, pp. 147–56; Vol. 22, pp. 374–83. Imprenta Nacional, Bogotá.

CONGRESO: *Canal inter-oceánico.* Imprenta Gaitan, Bogotá; 1866.

Final controversia diplomática con relación á los sucesos de Panamá, del día 15 de abril de 1856. Imprenta del Estado, Bogotá; 1857.

COSTA RICA

Treaties. Tipografía Nacional, San José; 1892–3. (2 vols.).

FRANCE

CHAMBRE DES DÉPUTÉS: *5e législature, session de 1893, No. 2921. Rapport fait au nom de la commission d'enquête chargée de faire la lumière sur les allégations portées à la tribune à l'occasion des affaires de Panama. Rapport général par M. Ernest Vallé, député.* Imprimerie de la Chambre des Députés, Paris; 1893. (3 vols.).

——: *6e législature, session de 1895, No. 1418. Rapport fait au nom de la commission chargée d'examiner la proposition de loi . . . sur la liquidation du Panama, par M. Goirand, député.* Paris; 1895.

——: *6e législature, session de 1898, No. 2992. Rapport général fait au nom de la commission d'enquête sur les affaires de Panama, par M. E. Vallé, député.* Imprimerie de la Chambre des Députés. Paris; 1898. (3 vols.).

COUR D'APPEL DE PARIS, 1RE CHAMBRE: *Plaidoirie de Me. Henri Barboux pour MM. Ferdinand et Charles de Lesseps.* Société Anonyme de Publications Périodiques, Paris; 1893.

GREAT BRITAIN

FOREIGN OFFICE: *United States. 1882, No. 1. Correspondence respecting the projected Panama canal.* Harrison & Sons, London; 1882.

——: *United States. 1882, No. 5. Further correspondence respecting the projected Panama canal.* Harrison & Sons, London; 1882.

——: *United States. 1884, No. 1. Further correspondence respecting the Clayton-Bulwer treaty and the projected Panama canal.* Harrison & Sons, London; 1884.

PARLIAMENT: *Parliamentary paper Cd. 6451. Despatch to His Majesty's ambassador at Washington respecting the Panamá Canal act. Presented to . . . Parliament . . . December 1912.*

——: *Parliamentary paper Cd. 6585. Despatch from the Secretary of State at Washington to the United States chargé d'affaires respecting the Panamá Canal act communicated to His Majesty's Secretary of State for Foreign Affairs, January 20, 1913.*

——: *Parliamentary paper Cd. 6645. Note addressed by His Majesty's ambassador at Washington to the United States Secretary of State, February 28, 1913, on the subject of the Panamá Canal act.*

MEXICO

PUEBLA, STATE OF: *Nuevos medios para una comunicación inter-oceánica. Documentos relativos al reconocimiento del Río Atoyac ó Poblano . . . y algunas noticias sobre las probabilidades de la navegación de el de la Laja ó Zempuala.* J. M. Macias, Puebla; 1851.

NICARAGUA

Concession and decrees of the republic of Nicaragua to the Nicaragua Canal Association of New York. 1887.

MINISTERIO DE RELACIONES EXTERIORES: *Convention pour l'exé-cution d'un canal maritime interocéanique sur le territoire de la république de Nicaragua.* Paul Dupont, Paris; 1869.

Terms of contract between the state of Nicaragua, and the Atlantic and Pacific Ship Canal Company, proposed by the commissioners of the state of Nicaragua, at the city of León . . . on August 27, 1849. W. C. Bryant & Co., New York; 1849.

PANAMA

Documents relating to the special commission of the republic of Panama before the government of the United States. Star and Herald, Panama; 1921 (?).

SPAIN

ARCHIVO: *Colección de documentos inéditos, relativos al descubrimiento, conquista y organización de las antiguas posesiones españolas de América y Oceanía, sacados de los archivos del reino, y muy especialmente del de Indias.* Madrid; 1864–84. (First series, 42 vols.) .

——: *Colección de documentos inéditos, relativos al descubrimiento, conquista y organización de las antiguas posesiones españolas de ultramar.* Madrid; 1885–1926. (Second series, 19 vols.) .

ARCHIVO GENERAL DE INDIAS, SEVILLA: *Relación descriptiva de los mapas, planos, etc. de las antiguas audiencias de Panamá, Santa Fé y Quito existentes en el Archivo General de Indias; por Pedro Torres Lanzas.* Tipografía de la Revista de Archivos, Bibliotecas y Museos, Madrid; 1904.

BOOKS AND PAMPHLETS

ABBOT, BRIG. GEN. HENRY LARCOM: *Problems of the Panama canal.* Macmillan Co., New York and London; 1907.

ABBOT, WILLIS JOHN: *Panama and the canal. The story of its achievement, its problems, and its prospects.* Dodd, Mead & Co., New York; 1914.

——: *Panama and the canal in picture and prose.* Syndicate Publishing Co., New York, London, etc.; 1913.

ABERT, SYLVANUS THAYER: *Is a ship canal practicable? Notes, historical and statistical, upon projected routes for an interoceanic ship canal between the Atlantic and Pacific Oceans.* Cincinnati; 1872.

An account of the Isthmus of Tehuantepec in the republic of Mexico. With proposals for establishing a communication between the Atlantic and Pacific Oceans, based upon the surveys and reports of a scientific commission, appointed by the projector Don José de Garay. J. D. Smith & Co., London; 1846.

L'achèvement du canal de Panama. Imprimerie Schiller, Paris; 1890.

ACOSTA, FRAY JOSÉ DE: *Historia natural y moral de las Indias.* Madrid; 1894. (First published 1590) .

ADAMS, JOHN: *Works,* Vol. 1. Little, Brown & Co., Boston; 1856.

AIRIAU, A.: *Canal interocéanique par l'isthme du Darien, Nouvelle-Grenade (Amérique du Sud). Canalisation par la colonisation.* Paris; 1860.

ALCEDO, ANTONIO DE: *Diccionario geográfico-histórico de las Indias occidentales ó América.* Madrid; 1787.

ALDANA, ABELARDO (and others): *The Panama canal question. A plea for Colombia.* New York; 1904.

ALEIXANDRE, CIRILO: *Cuatro palabras sobre el canal de Panamá. Memoria escrita y presentada al Congreso Geográfico Hispano-Portugués-Americano.* Imprenta del Memorial de Ingenieros, Madrid; 1893.

ALEXANDER, J. H.: *Memoir on the routes of communication between the Atlantic and Pacific Oceans.* Baltimore; 1849. (Reprinted from *H. Rep. 145,* 30 Cong., 2 Sess.).

AMERICAN ASSOCIATION FOR THE ADVANCEMENT OF SCIENCE: *Nicaragua canal. Discussion before the . . . Association, 36th meeting, held in New York, August 1887.* G. P. Putnam's Sons, New York; 1887.

AMERICAN ATLANTIC AND PACIFIC SHIP CANAL COMPANY: *Charter and act of incorporation . . . and treaty of protection negotiated between the United States and Great Britain.* New York; 1850.

AMERICAN ISTHMUS SHIP CANAL COMPANY: *Preliminary statement . . . concerning the proposed Mandingo canal.* 1902.

AMMEN, REAR ADM. DANIEL: *The American inter-oceanic ship canal question.* L. R. Hamersly & Co., Philadelphia; 1880.

——: *The errors and fallacies of the inter-oceanic transit question. To whom do they belong?* Brentano Bros., New York and Washington; 1886.

——: *Facts and suppositions relating to the American isthmus transit. Prepared . . . for reading March 8, 1887, before the Naval Institute, at Annapolis.* (No pl., no d.).

ANDAGOYA, PASCUAL DE: *Narrative of the proceedings of Pedrarias Davila* (tr. and ed., with notes and introduction, by Clements R. Markham). Hakluyt Society Pub. No. 34, London; 1865.

ANDERSON, ALEX. D.: *The Tehuantepec ship railway. A review of its geographical, commercial and political features and advantages.* New York; 1884.

ANDERSON, CHARLES LOFTUS GRANT: *Old Panama and Castilla del Oro.* Page Co., Boston; 1914.

ANDRÉ, GASTON: *Le canal de Panama et la nouvelle société.* Paul Dupont, Paris; 1894.

ARANGO, JOSÉ AGUSTÍN: *Datos para la historia de la independencia del istmo.* Panama; 1922.

ARIAS, HARMODIO: *The Panama canal; a study in international law and diplomacy.* P. S. King & Son, London; 1911.

ARIAS, TOMÁS: *Tomás Arias contestando al Dr. Luis Martínez Delgado. Justificación de la independencia de la republica de Panamá. Importante memorandum del Dr. Carlos Martínez Silva.* Imprenta Nacional, Panama; 1927.

ARMSTRONG, EDWARD: *The emperor Charles V.* Macmillan & Co., Ltd., London; 1910.

AROSEMENA, J. D. (ed.): *Panamá en 1915.* Diario de Panamá, Panama; 1915. (Spanish and English texts).

ATKINS, THOMAS B.: *The inter-oceanic canal across Nicaragua and the attitude toward it of the government of the United States.* New York; 1890.

——: *A refutation of "The proposed Nicaragua canal an impracticable project," by Joseph Nimmo, Jr., LL.D.* New York; 1896.

ATRATO AND SAN JUAN CANAL AND TRANSPORTATION COMPANY: *Prospectus.* New York; 1851.

AUCHMUTY, JAMES JOHNSTON: *Sir Thomas Wyse, 1791–1862. The life and career of an educator and diplomat.* P. S. King & Son, Ltd., London; 1939.

AUGER, ÉDOUARD: *Voyage en Californie (1852–1853).* L. Hachette et Cie., Paris; 1854.

AVERY, RALPH EMMETT: *America's triumph at Panama; panorama and story of the construction and operation of the world's giant waterway from ocean to ocean.* L. W. Walter Co., Chicago; 1913.

AYRES, PHILIP (ed.) : *The voyages and adventures of Capt. Barth. Sharp and others, in the South Sea: being a journal of the same. . . . To which is added the true relation of Sir Henry Morgan his expedition against the Spaniards in the West-Indies, and his taking Panama. Together with the President of Panama's account of the same expedition.* London; 1684.

BACHE, LT. RICHARD: *Notes on Colombia, taken in the years 1822–3. With an itinerary of the route from Caracas to Bogotá; and an appendix.* H. C. Carey and I. Lea, Philadelphia; 1827.

BACON, ALEXANDER SAMUEL: *La feria del crimen, el mayor "chantage" de todos los siglos. . . .* Arboleda y Valencia, Bogotá (?) ; 1912.

——: *The woolly horse.* New York; 1909.

BAILY, JOHN: *Central America; describing each of the states of Guatemala, Honduras, Salvador, Nicaragua, and Costa Rica. . . .* Trelawney Saunders, London; 1850.

BAKENHUS, REUBEN EDWIN; KNAPP, HARRY S.; and JOHNSON, EMORY RICHARD: *The Panama canal.* John Wiley & Sons, Inc., New York, and Chapman & Hall, Ltd., London; 1915.

BANCROFT, GEORGE: *History of the United States of America, from the discovery of the continent.* D. Appleton & Co., New York; 1884. (6 vols.) .

BANCROFT, HUBERT HOWE: *History of California.* A. L. Bancroft & Co., San Francisco; 1884.

BANNISTER, SAXE: *William Paterson, the merchant statesman, and founder of the Bank of England: his life and trials.* W. P. Nimmo, Edinburgh; 1859.

BARBOUR, JAMES SAMUEL: *A history of William Paterson and the Darien Company.* W. Blackwood & Sons, Edinburgh and London; 1907.

BARRÈS, MAURICE: *Leurs figures.* F. Juven, Paris; 1911.

BARRETT, JOHN: *Panama canal; what it is, what it means.* Pan American Union, Washington; 1913.

BATES, LINDON WALLACE: *The crisis at Panama.* New York; 1906.

——: *The Panama canal, system and projects.* New York; 1905.

——: *Project for the Panama canal.* New York; 1905.

——: *Retrieval at Panama.* New York; 1907.

BAUER Y LANDAUER, IGNACIO: *Datos para la historia de la unión interoceánica en América. Memoria presentada al Congreso Internacional de Geografía de 1931, en Paris.* Compañía General de Artes Gráficas, Madrid; 1931.

BELCHER, CAPT. SIR EDWARD, R. N.: *Narrative of a voyage round the world, performed in Her Majesty's ship* Sulphur, *during the years 1836–1842.* . . . Henry Colburn, London; 1843. (2 vols.).

BELLET, DANIEL: *La nouvelle voie maritime, le canal de Panama.* E. Guilmoto, Paris; 1913.

BELLY, FÉLIX: *À travers l'Amérique Centrale. Le Nicaragua et le canal interocéanique.* Librairie de la Suisse Romande, Paris; 1867.

——: *Percement de l'isthme de Panama par le canal de Nicaragua. Exposé de la question.* Aux bureaux de la direction du canal, Paris; 1858.

BENARD, EMILIO: *Nicaragua and the interoceanic canal.* Washington; 1874.

BENNETT, IRA E. (and associate editors) : *History of the Panama canal. Its construction and builders.* Historical Publishing Co., Washington; 1915.

BÉRARD, VICTOR: *La France et le monde de demain; conférence faite à la Société Normande de Géographie.* E. Cagniard, Rouen; 1912.

BERTRAND, ALPHONSE, and FERRIER, E.: *Ferdinand de Lesseps, sa vie, son œuvre.* G. Charpentier et Cie., Paris; 1887.

BIARD, PIERRE: *Le canal interocéanique et son régime juridique.* G. Petit, Paris; 1902.

BIGELOW, JOHN: *The Panama canal. Report of the Hon. John Bigelow, delegated by the Chamber of Commerce of New-York to assist at the inspection of the Panama canal in February, 1886.* Press of the Chamber of Commerce, New York; 1886.

——: *The Panama canal and the daughters of Danaus.* Baker & Taylor Co., New York; 1908.

BIONNE, HENRY: *La question du percement de l'isthme de Panama devant un congrès international.* Eugène Lacroix, Paris; 1864.

BISHOP, FARNHAM: *Panama, past and present.* D. Appleton-Century Co., Inc., New York and London; 1913. (Revised edition, 1916).

BISHOP, JOSEPH BUCKLIN: *The Panama gateway.* Charles Scribner's Sons, New York; 1913. (Revised edition, 1915).

——: *Theodore Roosevelt and his time.* Charles Scribner's Sons, New York; 1920.

BISHOP, JOSEPH BUCKLIN and FARNHAM: *Goethals, genius of the Panama canal; a biography.* Harper & Bros., New York and London; 1930.

BISHOP, JOSEPH BUCKLIN, and PEARY, ADM. ROBERT E.: *Uncle Sam's Panama canal and world history.* John Wanamaker, for World Syndicate Co., New York; 1913.

BLANCHET, ARISTIDE PAUL: *Canaux interocéaniques. Panama. Bilan, situation et charges annuelles de la compagnie en 1886. Comparaison entre Nicaragua, Panama et Suez.* Denné, Paris; 1887. (2nd edition).

BLUNT, STANHOPE E.: *Canals on the American isthmus. A paper read before the Contemporary Club, Davenport, Iowa, Jan. 18, 1900.* (No pl., no d.).

BODY, JOHN E.: *The inter-oceanic canal, via Nicaragua. Address, delivered June 24, 1870.* New York; 1870.

BONAPARTE, PRINCE NAPOLÉON LOUIS: *Le canal de Nicaragua, ou projet de jonction des océans Atlantique et Pacifique au moyen d'un canal.* Paris; 1867.

——: *Canal of Nicaragua: or, a project to connect the Atlantic and Pacific Oceans by means of a canal.* Mills & Son, London; 1846.

BORLAND, FRANCIS: *The history of Darien.* Glasgow; 1779.

BORTHWICK, J. D.: *Three years in California.* William Blackwood & Sons, Edinburgh and London; 1857.

BOURNE, EDWARD GAYLORD: *Spain in America, 1450–1580* (Vol. 3 of *The American nation: a history*). Harper & Bros., New York and London; 1904.

BOYCE, WILLIAM D.: *Alaska and the Panama canal.* Rand McNally & Co., Chicago and New York; 1914.

BRASSEUR DE BOURBOURG, ÉTIENNE CHARLES: *Voyage sur l'isthme de Tehuantepec, dans l'état de Chiapas et la république de Guatémala, exécuté dans les années 1859 et 1860.* Arthus Bertrand, Paris; 1861.

BRAU DE SAINT-POL LIAS, MARIE FRANÇOIS XAVIER: *Percement de l'isthme de Panama. Le congrès de Paris.* E. Dentu, Paris; 1879.

BRESSOLLES, PAUL: *Liquidation de la compagnie de Panama; commentaire théorique et pratique de la loi du 1er juillet, 1893.* Arthur Rousseau, Paris; 1894.

BRUNET, GASTON: *Le procès de Panama. Plaidoirie et réplique de Me. Gaston Brunet, avocat à la cour de Paris, pour la république de Colombie.* J. Dangon, Paris; 1904.

BRYAN, JOHN A.: *Union of the Atlantic and Pacific Oceans, at or near the Isthmus of Panama, examined and discussed . . . in a series of letters addressed to the National Institute, at Washington.* National Institute, Washington; 1845.

BRYCE, JAMES: *South America. Observations and impressions.* Macmillan Co., New York and London; 1912.

BULLARD, ARTHUR (Albert Edwards, *pseud.*) : *Panama; the canal, the country, and the people.* Macmillan Co., New York; 1911. (Revised edition, 1913).

BUNAU-VARILLA, PHILIPPE: *Address delivered before the Chamber of Commerce of the State of New York, March 7, 1901, on the trans-isthmian canals.* Chamber of Commerce Press, New York; 1901.

——: *Comparative characteristics . . . of Panama and Nicaragua.* New York; 1902.

——: *De Panama à Verdun. Mes combats pour la France.* Plon, Paris; 1937.

——: *Le détroit de Panama. Documents relatifs à la solution parfaite du problème de Panama.* H. Dunot et E. Pinat, Paris; 1907.

——: *La grande aventure de Panama.* Plon-Nourrit et Cie., Paris; 1920.

——: *The great adventure of Panama.* Doubleday, Page & Co., New York; 1920.

——: *How to build the Panama canal?* (No pl., no d.) .

——: *Nicaragua or Panama: the substance of a series of conferences. . . .* Knickerbocker Press, New York; 1901.

——: *Panama. La création, la destruction, la résurrection.* Plon-Nourrit et Cie., Paris; 1913.

——: *Panama. The creation, destruction, and resurrection.* Constable & Co., Ltd., London; 1913. McBride, Nast & Co., New York; 1914.

——: *Panama. Le passé — le présent — l'avenir.* G. Masson, Paris; 1892.

——: *Panama. Le trafic.* G. Masson, Paris; 1892.

——: *A solution of the problem of Panama.* Paris; 1905.

——: *Statement on behalf of historical truth.* Washington; 1912 (?).

——: *The straits of Panama. The text of an open letter to President Roosevelt, March 5, 1906. . . .* 1906.

——: *Text of a lecture before the Commercial Club of Boston . . . on the Panama canal, Feb. 25, 1909.* Washington; 1909.

——: *Trois appels à la France pour sauver l'œuvre de Panama.* Paris; 1906.

BUNKER, WILLIAM M.: *Report on canal and commercial conditions on the Isthmus of Panama.* G. Spaulding & Co., San Francisco; 1904.

BURR, WILLIAM HUBERT: *Ancient and modern engineering and the isthmian canal.* John Wiley & Sons, New York, and Chapman & Hall, Ltd., London; 1907.

BURTON, JOHN HILL (ed.): *The Darien papers: being a selection of original letters and official documents relating to the establishment of a colony at Darien by the Company of Scotland Trading to Africa and the Indies. 1695–1700.* Bannatyne Club, Edinburgh; 1849.

BUSHELL, T. A.: *"Royal Mail." A centenary history of the Royal Mail Line, 1839–1939.* Trade and Travel Publications, Ltd., London; 1939.

BUTLER, GEN. BENJAMIN F.: *Butler's book. Autobiography and personal reminiscences of Major-Gen. Benj. F. Butler.* A. M. Thayer & Co., Boston; 1892.

BUTTE, GEORGE C.: *Great Britain and the Panama canal: a study of the tolls question.* Heidelberg; 1913.

BYAM, GEORGE: *Wanderings in some of the western republics of America. With remarks upon the cutting of the great ship canal through Central America.* John W. Parker, London; 1850.

CALDERÓN, CARLOS; SAMPER, R.; and VARGAS, MARCELIANO (eds.): *La question du Panama* (reprints from newspapers). Correo de Paris, Paris; 1904.

Canal interocéanique sans écluses ni tunnels à travers le territoire du Darien entre les golfes d'Uraba et de San Miguel, États-Unis de Colombie. Challamel aîné, Paris; 1876.

CARDONA, S. ADALBERTO DE: *El canal interocéanico de México. Estudio . . . sobre el informe escrito por el coronel Angel M. Carrillo de Albornoz y el ingeniero Juan Pablo del Río acerca del mismo canal.* J. L. Guerrero y Cia., Mexico; 1903.

CARRERA JÚSTIZ, FRANCISCO: *Orientaciones necesarias; Cuba y Panamá.* La Moderna Poesía, Havana; 1911.

CARTER, HENRY ROSE: *Yellow fever. An epidemiological and historical study of its place of origin.* Williams & Wilkins Co., Baltimore; 1931.

CASTILLERO, ERNESTO J.: *El ferrocarril de Panamá y su historia.* Imprenta Nacional, Panama; 1932.

CERMOISE, HENRI: *Deux ans à Panama. Notes et récits d'un ingénieur au canal.* C. Marpon et E. Flammarion, Paris; 1886.

CHAMPLAIN, SAMUEL: *Narrative of a voyage to the West Indies and Mexico in the years 1599–1602* (tr. by Alice Wilmere). Hakluyt Society Pub. No. 23, London; 1859.

CHARENCEY, COMTE HYANCINTHE DE: *Le percement de l'isthme de Panama.* Loncin et Daupeley, Mortagne (Vendée) ; 1859.

CHARNWOOD, LORD: *Theodore Roosevelt.* Atlantic Monthly Press, Boston; 1923.

CHATFIELD, MARY A.: *Light on dark places at Panama. By an isthmian stenographer.* Broadway Publishing Co., New York; 1908.

CHEVALIER, MICHEL: *L'isthme de Panama. Examen historique et géographique des différents directions suivant lesquelles on pourrait le percer et des moyens à y employer. Suivi d'un aperçu sur l'isthme de Suez.* C. Gosselin, Paris; 1844.

CHILDS, ORVILLE W.: *Report of the survey and estimates of the cost of constructing the interoceanic ship canal . . . made for the American Atlantic and Pacific Ship Canal Co. in the years 1850–51–52.* Wm. C. Bryant & Co., New York; 1852.

——: *Supplemental estimates to the report of the survey and estimates of the cost of constructing the interoceanic ship canal. . . .* Wm. C. Bryant & Co., New York; 1852.

CHIRIQUI IMPROVEMENT COMPANY: *Chiriqui.* Washington. (No d.) .

——: *Geological report of Professor Manross, with accompanying papers, maps, etc.* New York; 1856.

CLARKE, SAMUEL: *The life and death of the valiant and renowned Sir Francis Drake. . . .* London; 1671.

COCHRANE, CAPT. CHARLES STUART, R. N.: *Journal of a residence and travels in Colombia, during the years 1823 and 1824.* Henry Colburn, London; 1825. (2 vols.) .

COLLINS, JOHN OWEN: *The Panama guide.* Vibert & Dixon, Panama; 1912.

COLOMBIANO (*pseud.*) : *Colombia, Estados Unidos y Panamá.* Buenos Aires; 1906.

Colonisation of Costa Rica, for the development of its rich mines . . . and for opening a new route between the Atlantic and Pacific. . . . Effingham Wilson, London. (No d. — prob. 1853 or 1854) .

COLQUHOUN, ARCHIBALD ROSS: *The key of the Pacific. The Nicaragua canal.* Archibald Constable & Co., London; 1895.

COMMISSIONS D'ÉTUDES INSTITUÉES PAR LE LIQUIDATEUR DE LA COMPAGNIE UNIVERSELLE: *Canal interocéanique de Panama. Rapports.* Paris; 1890.

COMPAGNIE DE L'ISTHME DE PANAMA: *Jonction des deux océans. Chemin de fer — canal maritime.* Paris; 1845.

COMPAGNIE NOUVELLE DU CANAL DE PANAMA: *Assemblée générale ordinaire du 21 décembre 1895.* Soc. Anon. de Publications Périodiques, Paris; 1895.

——: *Assemblée générale ordinaire du 15 décembre 1896.* Soc. Anon. de Publications Périodiques, Paris; 1896.

——: *Assemblée générale ordinaire du 28 décembre 1897.* Soc. Anon. de Publications Périodiques, Paris; 1897.

——: *Assemblée générale ordinaire du 28 décembre 1898.* Soc. Anon. de Publications Périodiques, Paris; 1898.

——: *Notes techniques concernant l'exposé des dispositions adoptées pour la solution de divers problèmes particuliers de l'exécution du canal.* Soc. Anon. de Publications Périodiques, Paris; 1899.

——: *Rapport de la commission.* Soc. Anon. de Publications Périodiques, Paris; 1899.

——: *Rapport présenté au conseil d'administration par le comité technique constitué en vertu de l'article 31 des statuts.* Soc. Anon. de Publications Périodiques, Paris; 1899.

——: *Report to the New Panama Canal Company by the international commission of engineers appointed in accordance with article 31 of the by-laws.* C. G. Burgoyne, New York; 1898.

——: *Service des études et travaux. Projet définitif d'un canal à écluses avec plafond du bief de partage à la côte 29.50.* Soc. Anon. de Publications Périodiques, Paris; 1898.

COMPAGNIE UNIVERSELLE DU CANAL INTEROCÉANIQUE DE PANAMA: *Circular, dated July 26, 1879, offering shares for subscription.* New York; 1879.

COMPANY OF SCOTLAND TRADING TO AFRICA AND THE INDIES: *The original papers and letters.* . . . Edinburgh (?) ; 1700.

CONGRÈS DES SCIENCES GÉOGRAPHIQUES, COSMOGRAPHIQUES ET COMMERCIALES TENU À ANVERS DU 14 AU 22 AOÛT 1871: *Compte-rendu.* Antwerp; 1872.

CONGRÈS INTERNATIONAL D'ÉTUDES DU CANAL INTEROCÉANIQUE: *Compte rendu des séances.* Paris; 1879.

CONGRÈS INTERNATIONAL DES SCIENCES GÉOGRAPHIQUES TENU À PARIS DU 1er AU 11 AOÛT 1875. *Compte rendu des séances.* Paris; 1878.

CORNEGYS, JOSEPH PARSONS (A Delawarean, *pseud.*) : *The Clayton-Bulwer treaty and the report of the Committee of the House on Foreign Relations against it.* 1880.

CORNISH, VAUGHAN: *The Panama canal and its makers.* T. Fisher Unwin, London, and Little, Brown & Co., Boston; 1909.

CORTHELL, ELMER LAWRENCE: *The Atlantic and Pacific ship-railway across the Isthmus of Tehuantepec, in Mexico, considered commercially, politically, constructively.* New York; 1886.

——: *An exposition of the errors and fallacies in Rear-Admiral Ammen's pamphlet entitled "The certainty of the Nicaragua canal contrasted with the uncertainties of the Eads ship railway."* Gibson Bros., Washington; 1886.

——: *The interoceanic problem, and its scientific solution. An address before the American Association for the Advancement of Science . . . Ann Arbor, Michigan, August 26, 1885.* (No pl., no d.) .

COURAU, ROBERT: *Ferdinand de Lesseps. De l'apothéose de Suez au scandale de Panama.* Bernard Grasset, Paris; 1932.

COWLES, ANNA ROOSEVELT (ed.) : *Letters from Theodore Roosevelt to Anna Roosevelt Cowles, 1870–1918.* Charles Scribner's Sons, New York and London; 1924.

CRAIG, HUGH: *The Nicaragua canal; the gateway between the oceans.* San Francisco; 1898.

CROWTHER, SAMUEL: *The romance and rise of the American tropics.* Doubleday, Doran & Co., New York; 1929.

CUDMORE, PATRICK: *Buchanan's conspiracy, the Nicaragua canal, and reciprocity.* P. J. Kenedy, New York; 1892.

CULLEN, EDWARD: *The Isthmus of Darien ship canal.* Effingham Wilson, London; 1852. (2nd edition, 1853).

CULLEN, EDWARD (and others) : *Over Darien by a ship canal. Reports of the mismanaged Darien expedition of 1854, with suggestions for a survey by competent engineers, and an exploration by parties with compasses.* Effingham Wilson, London; 1856.

CULLOM, SHELBY MOORE: *Fifty years of public service.* A. C. McClurg & Co., Chicago; 1911.

CUNDALL, FRANK: *The Darien venture.* Hispanic Society of America, New York; 1926.

CURTIS, WILLIAM JOHN: *The history of the purchase by the United States of the Panama canal; the manner of payment; and the distribution of the proceeds of sale. Annual address delivered before the Alabama State Bar Association at Birmingham, July 8, 1909.* (No pl., no d.).

DAMPIER, WILLIAM: *A new voyage round the world* (intr. by Sir Albert Gray). Argonaut Press, London; 1927. (First published 1697).

——: *Voyages and discoveries* (intr. and notes by Clennell Wilkinson). Argonaut Press, London; 1931. (First published 1699).

DANSETTE, ADRIEN: *Les affaires de Panama.* Perrin, Paris; 1934.

DARIEN CANAL COMPANY OF AMERICA: *Prospectus.* New York; 1870.

DÁVILA FLÓREZ, MANUEL: *Discursos sobre el tratado con los Estados Unidos, 1914.* Sincelejo, Colombia; 1915.

DEEKS, WILLIAM EDGAR: *Malaria; its cause, prevention, and cure.* United Fruit Co., Boston; 1925.

DEEKS, WILLIAM EDGAR, and JAMES, W. M.: *Report on hemoglobinuric fever in the Canal Zone. A study of its etiology and treatment.* Isthmian Canal Commission Press, Mt. Hope, C. Z.; 1911.

DE KALB, COURTENAY; MERRY, WILLIAM L.; and WATERHOUSE, SYLVESTER: *The Nicaragua canal. Its political relations and commercial advantages. Addresses delivered at the Trans-Mississippi Commercial Congress, St. Louis, November 28, 1894.* St. Louis; 1895.

DELEVANTE, MICHAEL: *Panama pictures. Nature and life in the land of the great canal.* Alden Bros., New York; 1907.

DÉNAIN, ADOLPHE: *Ensayo sobre los intereses políticos i comerciales del istmo de Panamá, considerándoles bajo el punto de vista de la Nueva-Granada. I proyecto de una comunicación inter-oceánica, la sola seria i justa, la sola posible i apetecible, factible esta en un año, i propriedad nacional.* Panama; 1844.

DEPEW, CHAUNCEY MITCHELL: *The Panama canal. . . . Speech . . . in the Senate of the United States . . . January 14, 1904.* Washington; 1904.

"The Derienni"; or, Land pirates of the isthmus. Being a true and graphic history of robberies, assassinations, and other horrid deeds perpetrated by those cool-blooded miscreants, who have infested for years the great highway to California, the El Dorado of the Pacific. Five of whom were shot at Panama, by the Committee of Public Safety, July 27th, 1852. Together with the

lives of three of the principal desperadoes as narrated by themselves. A. R. Orton, New Orleans, Charleston, Baltimore, and Philadelphia; 1853.

DIMOCK, MARSHALL EDWARD: *Government-operated enterprises in the Panama Canal Zone.* University of Chicago Press, Chicago; 1934.

DORSENNE, JEAN: La vie sentimentale de Paul Gauguin. L'Artisan du Livre, Paris; 1927.

Le dossier du canal de Panama, passé, présent, avenir. Aux annexes et dans le texte, nombreux documents inédits. Arthur Rousseau, Paris; 1886.

DROUILLET, LÉON: *Les isthmes américains. Projet d'une exploration géographique internationale des terrains qui semblent présenter le plus de facilités pour le percement d'un canal maritime interocéanique.* L'Explorateur, Paris; 1876.

DRUMONT, ÉDOUARD: *La dernière bataille.* E. Dentu, Paris; 1890.

——: *Les héros et les pitres.* E. Flammarion, Paris; 1900.

DUANE, COL. WILLIAM: *A visit to Colombia, in the years 1822 and 1823, by Laguayra and Caracas, over the cordillera to Bogota, and thence by the Magdalena to Cartagena.* Philadelphia; 1826.

DU BOIS, JAMES T.: *Ex-U. S. minister to Colombia James T. Du Bois on Colombia's claims and rights.* 1914.

DULLES, JOHN FOSTER: *The Panama canal controversy between Great Britain and the United States.* New York; 1913.

DUMAS, A.: *Projet d'achèvement du canal de Panama.* E. Bernard et Cie., Paris; 1891.

DUVAL, COMDR. MILES P., JR.: *Cadiz to Cathay. The story of the long struggle for a waterway across the American isthmus.* Stanford University Press, Stanford University, and Oxford University Press, London; 1940.

EADS, JAMES BUCHANAN: *Address . . . before the House Select Committee on Inter-oceanic Canals, 9th of March, 1880, in reply to Count de Lesseps.* (No pl., no d.).

——: *Inter-oceanic ship railway. Address . . . delivered before the San Francisco Chamber of Commerce, August 11, 1880.* (No pl., no d.).

EIFFEL, GUSTAVE: *Les transactions de M. G. Eiffel avec la liquidation de Panama.* Imprimerie de la Cour d'Appel, Paris; 1894.

ENOCK, C. REGINALD: *The Panama canal. Its past, present, and future.* London and Glasgow; 1914.

ESCOBAR, FRANCISCO (compiler) : *"I took the isthmus." Ex-President Roosevelt's confession, Colombia's protest and editorial comment by American newspapers on "How the United States acquired the right to build the Panama canal."* New York; 1911.

EVANS, ROBERT FRANK: *Notes on land and sea, 1850.* Richard C. Badger, Boston; 1922.

EXQUEMELIN, ALEXANDRE OLIVIER (or John Esquemeling) : *The buccaneers of America* (revised and edited by William Swan Stallybras). George Routledge & Sons, Ltd., London, and E. P. Dutton & Co., New York; 1923. (First published in Dutch 1678; in English 1684).

FABENS, JOSEPH WARREN: *A story of life on the isthmus.* G. P. Putnam & Co., New York; 1853.

FAST, HOWARD: *Goethals and the Panama canal.* Julian Messner, Inc., New York; 1942.

FERRY, ÉMILE: *Communication . . . sur son voyage à l'isthme de Panama.* . . . L. Deshays, Rouen; 1886.

——: *Conférence faite le 9 juin 1886 à la Société Normande de Géographie sur son voyage à Panama.* E. Cagniard, Rouen; 1886.

——: *Rapport présenté . . . à la Chambre de Commerce de Rouen, dans sa séance du 6 avril 1886, sur l'état d'avancement des travaux du canal de Panama.* Lapierre, Rouen; 1886.

FITZ-ROY, CAPT. ROBERT, R. N.: *Narrative of the surveying voyages of His Majesty's ships Adventure and Beagle, between the years 1826 and 1836,* Vol. 2, pp. 534–5. Henry Colburn, London; 1839.

FLACHAT, JULES: *Notes sur le fleuve du Darien et sur les différents projets de canaux interocéaniques du Centre Amérique.* Eugène Lacroix, Paris; 1866.

FLETCHER, ANDREW (or Archibald Foyer; attr. to) : *A defence of the Scots settlement at Darien. With an answer to the Spanish memorial against it.* Edinburgh; 1699.

FORBES-LINDSAY, CHARLES H. A.: *Panama. The isthmus and the canal.* J. C. Winston Co., Philadelphia; 1906.

——: *Panama and the canal today.* L. C. Page & Co., Boston; 1910. (Revised edition, 1912; new revised edition with additional chapters by Nevin O. Winter, 1926) .

FOX, GEORGE LEVI: *President Roosevelt's coup d'état. The Panama affair in a nutshell. Was it right? Will the canal pay?* New Haven; 1904.

FRANCK, HARRY A.: *Zone policeman 88. A close range study of the Panama canal and its workers.* Century Co., New York; 1913.

FRANK, JOHN C. (compiler) : *American interoceanic canals. A list of references in the New York Public Library.* New York; 1916.

FRASER, JOHN FOSTER: *Panama and what it means.* Cassell & Co., Ltd., London, New York, Toronto, and Melbourne; 1913.

——: *Panama, l'œuvre gigantesque* (tr. by Georges Feuilloy) . P. Roger et Cie., Paris; 1913.

FREEHOFF, JOSEPH C.: *America and the canal title.* New York; 1916.

——: *América y el título del canal.* Imprenta Nacional, Bogotá; 1916.

FULLERTON, MORTON: *Le canal de Panama et l'avenir des relations entre les États-Unis et la France* (in *Les États-Unis et la France,* pp. 173–97) . Félix Alcan, Paris; 1914.

GAGE, THOMAS: *The English-American; a new survey of the West Indies* (ed. by Arthur Percival Newton) . George Routledge & Sons, Ltd., London; 1928. (First published 1648) .

GALLO, O.: *Concepto sobre el canal de Panamá.* Malaga; 1903.

GALVÃO, ANTONIO: *The discoveries of the world, from their first original unto the year of our Lord 1555.* Hakluyt Society, London; 1862.

GARCÍA, COL. RUBÉN: *El canal de Panamá y el ferrocarril de Tehuantepec.* (No pl., no d.).

GARÇON, AUGUSTIN: *Histoire du canal de Panama. Historique, description, conséquences économiques au point de vue européen, avenir du canal interocéanique.* . . . Challamel aîné, Paris; 1886.

GARELLA, NAPOLÉON: *Projet d'un canal de jonction de l'océan Pacifique et de l'océan Atlantique à travers l'isthme de Panama.* Carilian-Gœury et Victor Dalmont, Paris; 1845.

GARGAZ, PIERRE-ANDRÉ: *Conciliateur de toutes les nations d'Europe, ou projet de paix perpétuelle entre tous les souverains de l'Europe et leurs voisins.* Benjamin Franklin, Passy; 1782.

——: *A project of universal and perpetual peace* (tr. and intr. by George Simpson Eddy). New York; 1922.

GAUSE, FRANK A., and CARR, CHARLES CARL: *The story of Panama. The new route to India.* Silver, Burdett & Co., Boston, New York, and Chicago; 1912.

GAUTRON, PIERRE: *Compagnie Universelle du Canal Interocéanique de Panama (en liquidation). 3me rapport présenté au Tribunal Civil de la Seine.* Soc. Anon. de Publications Périodiques, Paris; 1894.

GISBORNE, LIONEL: *Engineer's report.* London; 1854.

——: *The Isthmus of Darien in 1852. Journal of the expedition of inquiry for the junction of the Atlantic and Pacific Oceans.* Saunders & Stanford, London; 1853. Lippincott, Grambo & Co., Philadelphia; 1854.

GLISAN, RODNEY: *Journal of army life.* A. L. Bancroft & Co., San Francisco; 1874.

GOETHALS, GEN. GEORGE WASHINGTON: *Government of the Canal Zone.* Princeton University Press, Princeton, and Oxford University Press, London; 1915.

—— (ed.): *The Panama canal. An engineering treatise.* McGraw-Hill Book Co., New York; 1916. (2 vols., containing 25 separate technical papers. Same material in INTERNATIONAL ENGINEERING CONGRESS, 1915: *Transactions,* Vols. 1 and 2).

GOETHE, JOHANN WOLFGANG VON: *Conversations with Eckermann* (tr. by John Oxenford). M. Walter Dunne, Washington and London; 1901.

GOGORZA, ANTHOINE DE: *Tracé d'un canal interocéanique sans écluses à travers le territoire du Darien.* Challamel aîné, Paris; 1876.

GONZÁLEZ VALENCIA, JOSÉ MARÍA: *Separation of Panama from Colombia. Refutation of the misstatements and erroneous conceptions of Mr. Roosevelt in his article entitled "The Panama blackmail treaty."* Gibson Bros., Washington; 1916.

GOODWIN, JOHN MARSTON: *The Panama ship canal and inter-oceanic ship railway projects.* Cleveland; 1880.

GORGAS, MARIE D., and HENDRICK, BURTON J.: *William Crawford Gorgas. His life and work.* Doubleday, Page & Co., New York; 1924.

GORGAS, GEN. WILLIAM CRAWFORD: *Sanitation in Panama.* D. Appleton & Co., New York and London; 1915.

GREENE, ELEANORE D.: *Panama sketches.* Bruce Humphries, Inc., Boston; 1940.

GREENE, LAURENCE: *The filibuster. The career of William Walker.* Bobbs-Merrill Co., Indianapolis and New York; 1937.

GREGORY, JOSEPH W.: *Gregory's guide for California travellers via the Isthmus of Panama.* Nafis & Cornish, New York, and Nafis, Cornish & McDonald, St. Louis; 1850.

GRISWOLD, CHAUNCEY D.: *The Isthmus of Panama, and what I saw there.* Dewitt & Davenport, New York; 1852.

GUTIÉRREZ SOBRAL, JOSÉ: *Canal de Nicaragua.* Imprenta El Fígaro, Havana; 1897.

HALL, ALFRED BATES, and CHESTER, CLARENCE L.: *Panama and the canal.* Newson & Co., New York; 1910.

HALL, WILLIAM HAMMOND: *A statement of the Panama canal engineering conflicts. A review of the Panama canal projects. A study of Panama canal plans and arguments.* San Francisco; 1905.

HARDING, EARL: *In justice to the United States — a settlement with Colombia* (in *Latin America*, ed. by G. H. Blakeslee). New York; 1914.

HARING, CLARENCE HENRY: *The buccaneers in the West Indies in the seventeenth century.* Methuen & Co., Ltd., London; 1910.

——: *Trade and navigation between Spain and the Indies in the time of the Hapsburgs.* Harvard University Press, Cambridge, Mass., and Humphrey Milford, London; 1918.

HARRIS, WALTER (or Herries; attr. to): *A defence of the Scots abdicating Darien: including an answer to the defence of the Scots settlement there.* Edinburgh (?); 1700.

HART, ALBERT BUSHNELL, and CHANNING, EDWARD (eds.): *Extracts from official papers relating to the isthmian canal, 1515–1909* (American history leaflets. Colonial and constitutional, No. 34). Parker P. Simmons, New York; 1910.

HART, FRANCIS RUSSELL: *The disaster of Darien. The story of the Scots settlement and the causes of its failure, 1699–1701.* Houghton Mifflin Co., Boston and New York; 1929.

HARVEY, CHARLES T.: *Special report on data relating to the maritime canal of Nicaragua and the regions tributary thereto.* Maritime Canal Co. of Nicaragua, New York; 1890.

HASKIN, FREDERIC J.: *The Panama canal.* Doubleday, Page & Co., New York; 1914.

HEILPRIN, ANGELO: *A defense of the Panama route.* Philadelphia; 1902.

HENAO, JESÚS MARÍA, and ARRUBLA, GERARDO: *History of Colombia* (tr. by J. Fred Rippy). University of North Carolina Press, Chapel Hill; 1938.

HENRY, ARNOLD KAHLE: *The Panama canal and the intercoastal trade.* Philadelphia; 1929.

HERRÁN, VICTOR: *Le chemin de fer inter-océanique du Honduras. Étude sur l'avenir commercial et industriel de l'Amérique Centrale.* Victor Goupy, Paris; 1868.

HILL, HOWARD COPELAND: *Roosevelt and the Caribbean.* University of Chicago Press, Chicago; 1927.

HILL, H. R.: *A succinct view of the importance and practicability of forming a ship canal across the Isthmus of Panama.* W. H. Allen & Co., London; 1845.

HOTCHKISS, CHARLES F.: *On the ebb: a few log-lines from an old salt.* Tuttle, Morehouse & Taylor, New Haven; 1878.

HOWARD, HARRY NICHOLAS: *Military government in the Panama Canal Zone.* University of Oklahoma Press, Norman, Okla.; 1931.

HOYOS, J.-A.: *Les Etats-Unis d'Amérique et la Colombie.* A. Pedone, Paris; 1918.

HUBERICH, CHARLES HENRY: *The trans-isthmian canal: a study in American diplomatic history (1825–1904).* Austin, Tex.; 1904.

HUESTON, J. C.: *The American Atlantic and Pacific Ship Canal Co. A refutation of its claim to the Nicaragua canal route.* New York; 1888.

HUGHES, BREV. LT. COL. GEORGE W.: *Letter in answer to the Hon. John M. Clayton, Secretary of State, on intermarine communications.* Washington; 1850.

HUMBOLDT, ALEXANDER VON: *Political essay on the kingdom of New Spain* (tr. by John Black). Longman, etc., London; 1811. (4 vols.).

——: *Researches, concerning the institutions and monuments of the ancient inhabitants of America, with descriptions and views of some of the most striking scenes in the cordilleras!* (tr. by Helen Maria Williams). Longman, etc., London; 1814. (2 vols.).

——: *Voyage aux régions équinoxiales du nouveau continent, fait en 1799, 1800, 1801, 1802, 1803, et 1804, par Al. de Humboldt et A. Bonpland.* Paris; Vol. 1, 1814; Vol. 2, 1819; Vol. 3, 1825.

HUMBOLDT, ALEXANDER VON, and BONPLAND, AIMÉ: *Personal narrative of travels to the equinoctial regions of America, during the years 1799–1804* (tr. by Thomasina Ross). George Bell & Sons, London; 1881.

HUNTINGTON, COLLIS POTTER: *The Nicaragua canal. Would it pay the United States to construct it? Remarks . . . at the seventh annual banquet of the Chamber of Commerce of Galveston, Texas, March 16, 1900.* (No pl., no d.).

HURST, THOMAS WRIGHT: *Isthmus of Panama, Nicaragua, canal routes, etc., compiled by Thomas Hurst Wright from various authorities.* 1898.

HUSSEY, J. V.: *An isthmian deep water ship canal.* M. A. Donohue & Co., Chicago; 1902.

HUTCHINSON, LINCOLN: *The Panama canal and international trade competition.* Macmillan Co., New York; 1915.

INGHAM, SAMUEL DELUCENNA: *Speech . . . on the mission to Panama, delivered in the House of Representatives April 18, 1826.* Washington; 1826.

INSH, GEORGE PRATT: *The Company of Scotland Trading to Africa and the Indies.* Charles Scribner's Sons, New York and London; 1932.

—— (ed.): *Papers relating to the ships and voyages of the Company of Scotland Trading to Africa and the Indies, 1696–1707.* Scottish History Society, Edinburgh; 1924.

INTERNATIONAL ENGINEERING CONGRESS, 1915: *Transactions,* Vols. 1 and 2. San Francisco; 1916. (Same material in GEORGE WASHINGTON GOETHALS (ed.): *The Panama canal. An engineering treatise).*

INTER-OCEANIC CANAL COMPANY: *The Atlanto-Pacific canal. For all nations. Capital, £2,500,000. Preliminary statement.* London; 1853 (?).

——: *Delusions dispelled in regard to inter-oceanic communication; being a collection of facts relating to the competing plans submitted for public consideration, viz:* — *the inter-oceanic canal for all nations, (the Humboldt Line — by the Atrato-Cupica valleys), and the projected Darien canal from Port Escoces to the Gulf of San Miguel.* London; 1854.

JACKSON, F. E. & SON (compilers and editors) : *The makers of the Panama canal.* 1911.

JEFFERSON, THOMAS: *Writings.* Derby & Jackson, New York; 1859. (9 vols.).

JEFFERYS, THOMAS: *A description of the Spanish islands and settlements on the coast of the West Indies, compiled from authentic memoirs, revised by gentlemen who have resided many years in the Spanish settlements. . . .* London; 1762.

JOHNSON, EMORY RICHARD: *The Nicaragua canal and the economic development of the United States.* American Acad. of Political and Social Science, Philadelphia; 1896.

——: *The Panama canal and commerce.* D. Appleton & Co., New York and London; 1916.

JOHNSON, ROBERT UNDERWOOD (compiler): *The "coastwise exemption." The nation against it. An appeal on behalf of the national honor and a sound business policy. Representative opinions of the press, and of . . . influential citizens.* Century Magazine, New York; 1913.

JOHNSON, THEODORE T.: *California and Oregon; or, sights in the gold region, and scenes by the way.* Lippincott, Grambo & Co., Philadelphia; 1851. (4th edition, J. B. Lippincott & Co., Philadelphia; 1865).

JOHNSON, WILLIS FLETCHER: *Four centuries of the Panama canal.* Henry Holt & Co., New York; 1906.

JOHNSTON, WILLIAM EDWARD (Malakoff, *pseud.*) : *Memoirs of "Malakoff"; being extracts from the correspondence of the late William Edward Johnston* (ed. by R. M. Johnston). Hutchinson & Co., London. (No d.). (2 vols.).

KEASBEY, LINDLEY MILLER: *The early diplomatic history of the Nicaragua canal.* Newark, N. J.; 1890.

——: *The Nicaragua canal and the Monroe Doctrine. A political history of isthmus transit, with special reference to the Nicaragua canal project and the attitude of the United States government thereto.* G. P. Putnam's Sons, New York; 1896.

KELLER, FRANÇOIS ANTOINE ÉDOUARD: *Canal de Nicaragua. Notice sur la navigation transatlantique des paquebôts interocéaniques. . . .* Dalmond et Dunod, Paris; 1859.

KELLEY, FREDERICK M.: *The union of the oceans by ship-canal without locks, via the Atrato valley.* Harper & Bros., New York; 1859.

KIRKPATRICK, F. A.: *Latin America. A brief history.* Macmillan Co., New York, and University Press, Cambridge; 1939.

KNOWER, DANIEL: *The adventures of a forty-niner.* Albany; 1894.

LA BASTIDE, MARTIN DE: *Mémoire sur un nouveau passage de la mer du Nord à la mer du Sud.* Didot fils aîné, Paris; 1791.

——: *Nicaragua canal. . . . Memorial presented to the king of Spain in the year 1791, by Baron Martin de La Bastide, concerning the possibility, the advantages, and the means of opening a canal in North America to communicate between the Atlantic, or North Sea, and the Pacific, or South Sea. . . .* (tr. by Richard R. C. Simon). Government Printing Office, Washington; 1901.

LA BATUT, VICOMTE GUY DE: *Panama.* Éditions du Carrefour, Paris; 1931.

LABORDE, JEAN BENJAMIN DE: *Histoire abrégée de la mer du Sud.* Paris; 1791. (3 vols.).

LACHARME, LOUIS DE: *Interoceanic canal. Route of Paya.* New York; 1874.

LANE, WHEATON J.: *Commodore Vanderbilt. An epic of the steam age.* Alfred A. Knopf, Inc., New York; 1942.

LAS CASAS, BARTOLOMÉ DE: *An account of the first voyages and discoveries made by the Spaniards in America. Containing the most exact relation hitherto publish'd of their unparallel'd cruelties on the Indians, in the destruction of above forty millions of people.* London; 1699.

LEDUC, ALBERTO: *Colombia, Estados Unidos y el canal interoceánico de Panamá.* Cia. Editorial Católica, Mexico; 1904.

LESSEPS, COMTE FERDINAND DE: *Recollections of forty years* (tr. by C. B. Pitman). D. Appleton & Co., New York; 1888. (2 vols. in one).

Letters from leading engineers and naval architects as to the practicability of constructing and operating a ship railway. G. I. Jones & Co., St. Louis; 1882.

LETTS, JOHN M.: *A pictorial view of California; including a description of the Panama and Nicaragua routes. . . .* Henry Bill, New York; 1853.

LÉVY, PABLO: *Notas geográficas y económicas sobre la república de Nicaragua.* E. Denné Schmitz, Paris; 1873.

LIOT, CAPT. W. B.: *Panamá, Nicaragua, and Tehuantepec; or, considerations upon the question of communication between the Atlantic and Pacific Oceans.* Simpkin & Marshall, London; 1849.

LOCKEY, JOSEPH BYRNE: *Pan-Americanism: its beginnings.* Macmillan Co., New York; 1920.

LOOS, EDUARDO: *Empresa centro-americana y universal del canal de Nicaragua.* Imprenta del Gobierno, Managua; 1863.

LÓPEZ DE VELASCO, JUAN: *Geografía y descripción universal de las Indias, desde el año de 1571 al de 1574.* Sociedad Geográfica de Madrid, Madrid; 1894.

LUNDIE, JOHN: *Report to the General Électric Company on conditions and prospects for utilizing electric power on the Isthmus of Panama.* New York; 1904. (Typed MS., bound).

MACGILLIVRAY, W.: *The life, travels, and researches of Baron Humboldt.* T. Nelson & Sons, London; 1859.

MAGNY, MARQUIS CLAUDE DRIGON DE: *Canalisation des isthmes de Suez et de Panama, par les frères de la compagnie maritime de Saint-Pie, ordre religieux, militaire et industriel.* Paris; 1848.

MAJOR, RICHARD HENRY (tr. and ed.): *Select letters of Christopher Columbus, with other original documents, relating to his four voyages to the New World.* Hakluyt Society Pub. No. 43, London; 1870.

MALLET, LADY: *Sketches of Spanish-colonial life in Panama (1672–1821)*. Sturgis & Walton Co., New York; 1915.

MALTE-BRUN, VICTOR ADOLPHE: *Les différents projets de communication entre les deux océans, à travers le grand isthme de l'Amérique Centrale*. Paris; 1857.

——: *Notice historique et géographique sur l'état de la question du canal du Darien*. Arthus Bertrand, Paris; 1865.

MARÉCHAL, HENRY: *Voyage d'un actionnaire à Panama*. E. Dentu, Paris; 1885.

MARION, PAUL: *Souvenirs de Panama*. A. Lebois et fils, Bar-sur-Aube; 1912.

MARITIME CANAL COMPANY OF NICARAGUA: *Answer of the Nicaragua Canal Association to the protest of the alleged American Atlantic and Pacific Ship Canal Company*. (No pl., no d.).

——: *Exposition Universelle de Paris, 1889. Canal de Nicaragua*. J. Bien & Co., New York; 1889.

——: *The maritime ship canal of Nicaragua*. New York; 1890.

MARLIO, LOUIS: *La véritable histoire de Panama*. Hachette, Paris; 1932.

MARROQUÍN, LORENZO: *El canal*. Imprenta de Vapor, Bogotá; 1903.

MARRYAT, FRANK: *Mountains and molehills, or recollections of a burnt journal*. Longman, etc., London; 1855.

MARSH, RICHARD OGLESBY: *White Indians of Darien*. G. P. Putnam's Sons, New York; 1934.

MARSHALL, LOGAN: *The story of the Panama canal*. J. C. Winston Co., Philadelphia and Chicago; 1913.

MARTÍNEZ SILVA, CARLOS: *Por qué caen los partidos políticos*. C. Roldán y Cia., Bogotá; 1935.

MARTYR, PETER (Pietro Martire d'Anghiera): *De orbe novo* (tr. by M. Lok. In HAKLUYT: *Collection of the early voyages, travels, and discoveries of the English nation*, Vol. 5, pp. 155–476). London; 1812.

——: *De orbe novo* (tr. by Francis Augustus MacNutt). G. P. Putnam's Sons, New York and London; 1912.

The material facts about the Chiriqui Improvement Company's grants. Reasons why the validity of the company's title to the Chiriqui strip is denied and held to be void by the government of Colombia. (No. pl., no d.).

MAYENBERGER, HERMANN: *Conferencia sobre el desarrollo agrícola y industrial de Urabá y sobre la importancia del futuro canal del Atrato . . . ante la Sociedad Colombiana de Ingenieros. . . .* Imprenta Nacional, Bogotá; 1933.

McCAIN, WILLIAM DAVID: *The United States and the republic of Panama*. Duke University Press, Durham, N. C.; 1937.

M'COLLUM, WILLIAM S.: *California as I saw it*. George H. Derby & Co., Buffalo; 1850.

McKIBBEN, FRANK P.: *Notes and views on the Panama canal taken by members of the American Society of Civil Engineers during their visit, March 1911*. Fort Hill Press, Boston; 1911.

MEANS, PHILIP AINSWORTH: *The Spanish Main — focus of envy, 1492–1700*. Charles Scribner's Sons, New York and London; 1935.

MENDOZA, DIEGO: *El canal interoceánico*. Editorial Minerva, Bogotá; 1930.

MENOCAL, ANICETO G.: *The Nicaragua canal. Its design, final location, and work accomplished. Read at the Fourth International Congress on Inland Navigation, Manchester, July 1890.* New York; 1890.

MERRY, WILLIAM L.: *The Nicaragua canal. The gateway between the oceans.* San Francisco; 1895.

MILLER, HUGH GORDON: *The isthmian highway; a review of the problems of the Caribbean.* Macmillan Co., New York; 1929. (2nd edition, 1931).

MILLER, JACOB WILLIAM: *The advantages of the Nicaragua route.* American Academy of Political and Social Science, Philadelphia; 1896.

——: *Where to build the isthmian canal.* 1902.

MILLER, JOHN F.: *Nicaragua canal. Address . . . before the Chamber of Commerce, Board of Trade, and Manufacturers' Association, of San Francisco, June 17, 1885.* San Francisco; 1885.

MILLER, MARION MILLS (ed.) : *Great debates in American history,* Vol. 3, pp. 325–465. Current Literature Pub. Co., New York; 1913.

MILLS, JOHN SAXON: *The Panama canal. A history and description of the enterprise.* T. Nelson & Sons, London; 1913.

MINER, DWIGHT CARROLL: *The fight for the Panama route.* Columbia University Press, New York; 1940.

MOLINARI, GUSTAVE DE: *À Panama. L'isthme de Panama — la Martinique — Haïti. Lettres addressées au Journal des Débats.* Guillaumin et Cie., Paris; 1886.

MOORE, DAVID R.: *A history of Latin America.* Prentice-Hall, New York; 1938.

MORALES, EUSEBIO A.: *Ensayos, documentos y discursos.* Editorial "La Moderna," Panama; 1928. (2 vols.).

MORISON, SAMUEL ELIOT: *Admiral of the ocean sea.* Little, Brown & Co., Boston; 1942. (Editions in one and two vols.).

MORO, GAETANO: *Observations in relation to a communication between the Atlantic and Pacific Oceans, through the Isthmus of Tehuantepec.* Ackermann & Co., London; 1844. R. Craighead, New York; 1849.

——: *Survey of the Isthmus of Tehuantepec, executed in the years 1842 and 1843, with the intent of establishing a communication between the Atlantic and Pacific Oceans. . . .* Ackermann & Co., London; 1844.

MORROW, COL. JAY JOHNSON: *The maintenance and operation of the Panama canal. . . . A lecture delivered before the New York section, American Society of Civil Engineers, in New York City, January 10, 1923; and repeated before the Society of Civil Engineers of Washington, D. C., January 17, 1923.* Panama Canal Press, Mt. Hope, C. Z.; 1923.

MOSES, BERNARD: *Spain's declining power in South America.* University of California Press, Berkeley; 1919.

NAVARRETE, MARTÍN FERNÁNDEZ DE: *Colección de los viages y descubrimientos que hicieron por mar los Españoles desde fines del siglo XV.* Imprenta Real, Madrid; 1825–37. (5 vols.).

——: *Noticia histórica de las expediciones hechas por los Españoles en busca del paso del Noroeste de la América.* Imprenta Real, Madrid; 1802.

——: *Viajes de Cristóbal Colón.* Calpe, Madrid; 1922.

NELSON, VICE ADMIRAL LORD VISCOUNT: *Dispatches and letters* (with notes by Sir Nicholas Harris Nicolas). Henry Colburn, London; 1845. (7 vols.).

NELSON, WOLFRED: *Five years at Panama. The trans-isthmian canal.* Belford Co., New York; 1889.

NEW PANAMA COMPANY (see also COMPAGNIE NOUVELLE DU CANAL DE PANAMA): *Final and definite report of the international technical commission, rendered November 16, 1898, and delivered to the President of the United States December 2, 1898.* New York; 1898.

The Nicaragua canal. A brief sketch of the present state of the enterprise. (No pl., no d.).

NICARAGUA CANAL CONSTRUCTION COMPANY: *The inter-oceanic canal of Nicaragua. Its history, physical condition, plans and prospects.* New York; 1891.

——: *Nicaragua canal. World's Columbian Exposition, Chicago, 1893.* 1893.

——: *President's report to the stockholders.* New York; 1891.

NICARAGUA CANAL CONVENTION: *Proceedings . . . held at St. Louis, Mo. in the Exposition Music Hall on the 2nd and 3rd days of June 1892.* (No pl., no d.).

NIDA, STELLA H.: *Panama and its "bridge of water."* Rand, McNally & Co., Chicago and New York; 1915.

NILES, NATHANIEL: *Mr. Niles' plan for the construction of a ship canal between the Atlantic and Pacific Oceans, Central America.* New York; 1868.

NIMMO, JOSEPH JR.: *The Nicaragua canal.* Washington; 1896.

——: *The Nicaragua canal. Investigate before investing.* Rufus H. Darby, Washington; 1898.

——: *The proposed Nicaragua canal an impracticable project. A communication addressed to the Nicaragua Canal Board in regard to the commercial, nautical and economic conditions involved in the scheme.* 1895.

NUNN, GEORGE E.: *Origin of the Strait of Anian concept.* Philadelphia; 1929.

O'LEARY, DANIEL FLORENCIO: *Memorias del General O'Leary.* Imprenta del Gobierno Nacional, Caracas; 1887. (32 vols.).

Opinions of commercial bodies of New York, New Orleans, St. Louis, Cincinnati, Chicago, Indianapolis and San Francisco, and of the legislatures of California and Oregon, about the Nicaragua canal. New York; 1888.

OPPENHEIM, LASSA FRANCIS LAURENCE: *The Panama canal conflict between Great Britain and the United States of America.* University Press, Cambridge; 1913.

ORBIGNY, ALCIDE D': *Voyage pittoresque dans les deux Amériques.* Furne et Cie., Paris; 1841.

OTERO, LUIS ALFREDO: *Panama.* Imprenta Nacional, Bogotá; 1926.

OTIS, FESSENDEN NOTT: *History of the Panama Railroad; and of the Pacific Mail Steamship Company. Together with a traveller's guide and business man's hand-book for the Panama Railroad.* Harper & Bros., New York; 1867.

OVIEDO Y VALDÉS, GONZALO FERNÁNDEZ: *Historia general y natural de las Indias.* Imprenta de la Real Academia de la Historia, Madrid; 1853.

PACIFIC MAIL STEAMSHIP COMPANY: *A sketch of the route to California, China and Japan, via the Isthmus of Panama.* A. Roman & Co., San Francisco and New York; 1867.

PADELFORD, NORMAN J.: *The Panama canal in peace and war.* Macmillan Co., New York; 1942.

PANAMA CANAL RETIREMENT ASSOCIATION: *The canal diggers in Panama, 1904 to 1928.* Balboa Heights, C. Z.; 1928.

The Panama Massacre. A collection of the principal evidence and other documents, including the report of Amos B. Corwine, Esq., United States commissioner, the official statement of the governor and the depositions taken before the authorities, relative to the massacre of American citizens at the Panama Railroad station on the 15th of April, 1856. Panama Star and Herald, Panama; 1857.

PANAMA RAILROAD COMPANY: *Communication of the board of directors . . . to the stockholders, together with the report of the chief engineer to the directors.* New York; 1853.

——: *Communication of the board of directors . . . to the stockholders, together with the report of the chief engineer to the directors.* New York; 1855.

——: *Letter from the directors . . . addressed to the Senate and House of Representatives of the United States, in reply to the remarks of the Postmaster-General, contained in his report to the President, and presented to Congress December 5, 1856.* New York; 1856.

——: *Memorial . . . to the Congress of the United States, 10th December, 1849.* New York; 1850.

——: *Prospectus.* New York; 1849.

——: *Report of the board of directors . . . to the Isthmian Canal Commission for the ten months ending October 31, 1905.* New York; 1905.

——: *Report to stockholders, April 1, 1872.* New York; 1872.

PAPONOT, FÉLIX: *Achèvement du canal de Panama. Étude technique et financière.* Baudry et Cie., Paris; 1888.

——: *Le canal de Panama. Etude rétrospective, historique et technique. Solution rationnelle pour l'achèvement graduel de l'œuvre sans augmenter la dette.* Baudry et Cie., Paris; 1890.

——: *Suez et Panama. Une solution.* Baudry et Cie., Paris; 1889.

PARADELA Y GESTAL, FRANCISCO: *Una visita al istmo de Panamá. Nota de las impresiones y apuntes allí recogidos.* Havana; 1886.

PARKS, E. TAYLOR: *Colombia and the United States, 1765–1934.* Duke University Press, Durham, N. C.; 1935.

PARRISH, SAMUEL LONGSTRETH: *The Hay-Pauncefote treaty and the Panama canal.* New York; 1913.

PATERSON, WILLIAM: *Central America* (ed. by Saxe Bannister). Trübner & Co., London; 1857.

PEACOCK, CAPT. GEORGE: *Notes on the Isthmus of Panama and Darien, also on the River St. Juan, lakes of Nicaragua, etc., with reference to a railroad and canal for joining the Atlantic and Pacific Oceans.* W. Pollard, Exeter, Devon; 1879.

PENSA, HENRI: *La république et le canal de Panama.* Hachette et Cie., Paris; 1906.

PEPPER, CHARLES MELVILLE: *Panama to Patagonia. The isthmian canal and the west coast countries of South America.* A. C. McClurg & Co., Chicago; 1906.

PEPPERMAN, WALTER LEON: *Who built the Panama canal?* E. P. Dutton & Co., New York; 1915.

PERALTA, MANUEL MARÍA DE: *El canal interoceánico de Nicaragua y Costa-Rica en 1620 y en 1887. Relaciones de Diego de Mercado y Thos. C. Reynolds, con otros documentos recogidos y anotados.* Ad. Mertens, Brussels; 1887.

——: *Costa-Rica, Nicaragua y Panamá en el siglo XVI.* Madrid and Paris; 1883.

PÉREZ, MODESTO, and NOUGUÉS, P.: *Los precursores españoles del canal interoceánico.* Perlado, Paéz y Cia., Madrid; 1915.

PÉRIGNY, COMTE MAURICE DE: *La république de Costa Rica. Son avenir économique et le canal de Panama.* Félix Alcan, Paris; 1918.

PHILLIPS, JOHN WILLIAM: *An original plan for a tidal ditch and sea level canal at Panama submitted to the United States Isthmian Canal Commission.* Austin, Tex. (?); 1905.

PIGAFETTA, ANTONIO (or Vincenzo): *Premier voyage autour du monde sur l'escadre de Magellan* (tr. from Italian by Charles Amorette). Charles Delagrave, Paris; 1888.

PIM, CAPT. BEDFORD CLAPPERTON T., R. N.: *Descriptive account of Captain Bedford Pim's project for an international Atlantic and Pacific junction railway across Nicaragua.* London; 1866.

——: *The gate of the Pacific.* L. Reeve & Co., London; 1863.

PINKERTON, JOHN: *A general collection of the best and most interesting voyages and travels in various parts of America.* Longman, etc., London; 1819.

PITMAN, ROBERT BIRKS: *A succinct view and analysis of authentic information extant in original works, on the practicability of joining the Atlantic and Pacific Oceans, by a ship canal across the isthmus of America.* J. M. Richardson and J. Hatchard & Son, London; 1825.

PORRAS, BELISARIO, and FILOS, FRANCISCO: *Estudio sobre el tratado del canal.* Imprenta Nacional, Panama; 1920.

POUCHET, JAMES, and SAUTEREAU, GUSTAVE: *Canal interocéanique maritime de Nicaragua.* E. Denné, Paris; 1879.

——: *Examen comparatif des divers projets de canaux inter-océaniques par l'isthme de Darien et le lac de Nicaragua.* Eugène Lacroix, Paris; 1876.

The practicability and importance of a ship canal to connect the Atlantic and Pacific Oceans, with a history of the enterprise from its first inception to the completion of the surveys. George F. Nesbitt & Co., New York; 1855.

The proposed ship canal, to connect the Atlantic and Pacific Oceans, by the Nicaragua route. New York; 1875.

PROVISIONAL INTEROCEANIC CANAL SOCIETY: *Concession granted by the republic of Nicaragua . . . for a ship-canal across that country, confirmed May 22, 1880.* Gibson Bros., Washington; 1880.

——: *Nicaragua ship-canal. Report of the executive committee to the members of the Provisional Society.* Gibson Bros., Washington; 1880.

PURCHAS, SAMUEL: *Purchas his pilgrimes.* London; 1625. (5 vols.).

PUYDT, LUCIEN DE: *La vérité sur le canal interocéanique de Panama.* C. Schiller, Paris; 1879.

QUESNAY DE BEAUREPAIRE, J.: *Le Panama et la république.* F. Juven, Paris; 1899.

RATCLIFF, SAMUEL: *Considerations on the subject of a communication between the Atlantic and Pacific Oceans, by means of a ship canal across the isthmus, which connects North and South America; and the best means of effecting it, and permanently securing its benefits for the world at large.* Georgetown, D. C.; 1836.

READ, BENJAMIN MAURICE: *Chronological digest of the "Documentos inéditos del archivo de las Indias."* Santa Fe, N. M.; 1914.

REED, CHARLES A. L.: *Panama notes.* Cleveland; 1906.

REYES, RAFAEL: *Las dos Américas.* Frederick A. Stokes Co., New York; 1914.

——: *Por Colombia, por Ibero-América.* Wertheimer, Lea & Co., London; 1912.

——: *The two Americas* (tr. by Leopold Grahame). Frederick A. Stokes Co., New York; 1914.

RICHARDS, SIR HENRY ERLE: *The Panama canal controversy. A lecture delivered before the University of Oxford, October 25, 1913.* Clarendon Press, Oxford; 1913.

RIDPATH, GEORGE (attr. to): *An enquiry into the causes of the miscarriage of the Scots colony at Darien. Or an answer to a libel entituled A defence of the Scots abdicating Darien. Submitted to the consideration of the good people of England. . . .* Glasgow; 1700.

RIPPY, J. FRED: *The capitalists and Colombia.* Vanguard Press, New York; 1931.

ROBINSON, FAYETTE: *California and its gold regions.* Stringer & Townsend, New York; 1849.

ROBINSON, TRACY: *Fifty years at Panama, 1861–1911.* Trow Press, New York; 1911.

——: *Panama. A personal record of forty-six years, 1861–1907.* Star and Herald Co., New York and Panama; 1907.

ROBINSON, WILLIAM DAVIS: *Memoirs of the Mexican revolution, including a narrative of the expedition of General Xavier Mina. With some observations on the practicability of opening a commerce between the Pacific and Atlantic Oceans, through the Mexican isthmus . . . and at the Lake of Nicaragua. . . .* Philadelphia; 1820.

RODRIGUES, JOSÉ CARLOS: *The Panama canal. Its history, its political aspects, and financial difficulties.* Charles Scribner's Sons, New York; 1885.

ROGER, P.: *De l'intérêt qu'a la marine française à l'ouverture de l'isthme américain par le canal du Darien.* Ernest Meyer, Paris; 1861.

ROOSEVELT, THEODORE: *An autobiography.* Charles Scribner's Sons, New York; 1920.

——: *The works of Theodore Roosevelt. Presidential addresses and state papers.* P. F. Collier & Son, New York; 1910 (?). (8 vols.).

ROOT, ELIHU: *Address . . . before the Union League Club of Chicago, February 22, 1904.* (No pl., no d.).

SÁENZ, VICENTE: *El canal de Nicaragua.* Mexico; 1929.

——: *Rompiendo cadenas; las del imperialismo norteamericano en Centro América.* Mexico; 1933.

SAINT-AMANT, P. CH. DE: *Voyages en Californie et dans l'Orégon.* L. Maison, Paris; 1854.

SANCHIZ Y BASADRE, ELISEO: *Una visita á las obras del canal de Panamá.* E. Maroto y hermano, Madrid; 1886.

SANDBURG, CARL: *Abraham Lincoln: the war years,* Vol. 1, pp. 591–2. Harcourt, Brace & Co., New York; 1939.

SAUTEREAU, GUSTAVE: *Le canal de Panama, transformé en lac intérieur. Nouveau projet proposé par G. Sautereau.* Quentin, Paris; 1889.

——: *Commentaires sur Panama. Notes et documents présentés à la commission d'enquête parlementaire. . . .* Baudry et Cie., Paris; 1893.

SCHONFIELD, HUGH J.: *Ferdinand de Lesseps.* Herbert Joseph, Ltd., London; 1937.

SCHURZ, JAMES R.: *Diplomatic history of the Panama canal, compiled from Senate Document 474, 53rd Congress, and British blue books; the real Panama canal treaty and comparison of previous drafts. . . .* New York; 1914.

SCOTT, WILLIAM ROBERT: *The Americans in Panama.* Statler Pub. Co., New York; 1912.

SCROGGS, WILLIAM OSCAR: *Filibusters and financiers. The story of William Walker and his associates.* Macmillan Co., New York; 1916.

SCRUGGS, WILLIAM L.: *The Colombian and Venezuelan republics. With notes on other parts of Central and South America.* Little, Brown & Co., Boston; 1900.

SEEMANN, BERTHOLD: *Narrative of the voyage of H. M. S. Herald, during the years 1845–1851, under the command of Captain Henry Kellett, R. N., C. B. . . .* Reeve & Co., London; 1853. (2 vols.).

SERRANO Y SANZ, MANUEL (ed.): *Relaciones históricas y geográficas de América Central.* Victoriano Suárez, Madrid; 1908.

SERRELL, EDWARD WELLMAN: *The American isthmian canals. The Darien Mandingo canal.* New York; 1903.

SEYMOUR, CAPT.: *Isthmian routes. A brief description of each of the projected routes, and of those existing. . . .* New York; 1863.

SHELBOURNE, MAJ. SIDNEY F.: *A comparative view of the Panama and San Blas routes for an interoceanic canal.* New York; 1880.

SHELDON, HENRY ISAAC: *Notes on the Nicaragua canal.* A. C. McClurg & Co., Chicago; 1897. (2nd edition, 1898).

SILVELA, FRANCISCO: *Limites entre la Colombie et le Costa-Rica. Exposé présenté à son Excellence M. le Président de la République Française en qualité d'arbitre.* Madrid; 1898.

SIMONIN, L.: *Les pays du Pacifique et le canal de Panama.* Guillaumin et Cie., Paris; 1886.

SMITH, DARRELL HEVENOR: *The Panama canal. Its history, activities, and organization.* Johns Hopkins Press, Baltimore; 1927.

SMITH, JOHN LAWRENCE: *Inter-oceanic canal. Practicability of the different routes, and questionable nature of the interest of the United States in a canal.* Bradley & Gilbert, Louisville; 1880.

SMITH, JOSEPH RUSSELL: *The organization of ocean commerce* (University of Pennsylvania Publications, series in political economy and public law No. 17). University of Pennsylvania Press, Philadelphia; 1905.

SNOW, FREEMAN: *Treaties and topics in American diplomacy.* Boston Book Co., Boston; 1894.

SOBRAL, G.: *Canal de Panamá.* Imprenta del Fomento Naval, Madrid; 1908.

SOCIÉTÉ CIVILE DU CANAL DU DARIEN: *Prospectus.* Paris; 1860.

SONDEREGGER, C.: *L'achèvement du canal de Panama.* Veuve C. Dunod, Paris; 1902.

SOSA, JUAN B., and ARCE, ENRIQUE J.: *Compendio de historia de Panamá.* Diario de Panamá, Panama; 1911.

SQUIER, EPHRAIM GEORGE: *Honduras interoceanic railway.* Trübner & Co., London; 1857.

——: *Honduras interoceanic railway. Preliminary report.* New York; 1854.

——: *Nicaragua; its people, scenery, monuments, and the proposed interoceanic canal.* D. Appleton & Co., New York; 1856. (Two vols. in one).

——: *Notes on Central America; particularly the states of Honduras and San Salvador: their geography, topography, climate, population, resources, productions, etc., etc., and the proposed Honduras inter-oceanic railway.* Harper & Bros., New York; 1855.

STEPHENS, HENRY MORSE, and BOLTON, HERBERT E. (eds.): *The Pacific Ocean in history. Papers and addresses presented at the Panama-Pacific Historical Congress, held at San Francisco, Berkeley and Palo Alto, California, July 19–23, 1915.* Macmillan Co., New York; 1917.

STEPHENS, JOHN LLOYD: *Incidents of travel in Central America, Chiapas, and Yucatan.* Harper & Bros., New York; 1841. (2 vols.).

STERNE, SIMON: *Nicaragua canal. Argument . . . in opposition to signature, by President of the United States, of bill (S. 1305) to incorporate the Maritime Canal Company of Nicaragua.* Gibson Bros., Washington; 1889.

STEVENS, JOHN FRANK: *An engineer's recollections.* McGraw-Hill Publishing Co., Inc., New York; 1936.

——: *A sketch of the Panama canal. Its past, present and possible future.* 1908.

STEVENS, SIMON: *Letter to Brevet Major-General A. A. Humphreys, U. S. A., Professor Benjamin Pierce, and Captain Daniel Ammen, U. S. N. Dated New York, April 12, 1872.* (No pl., no d.).

——: *The new route of commerce by the Isthmus of Tehuantepec. A paper read before the American Geographical Society of New York, November 15, 1870.* Chiswick Press, London; 1871.

STEVENS, WALTER BARLOW: *A trip to Panama.* Lesan-Gould Co., St. Louis; 1907.

STOCKTON, LT. COMDR. CHARLES H.: *The commercial geography of the American inter-oceanic canal.* 1888.

STRAIN, LT. ISAAC G., U. S. N.: *A paper on the history and prospects of inter-oceanic communication by the American isthmus, read . . . before the New York Historical Society, June 17, 1856.* New York; 1856.

STRAUS, OSCAR S.: *Under four administrations, from Cleveland to Taft.* Houghton Mifflin Co., Boston and New York; 1922.

STUART, GRAHAM HENRY: *Latin America and the United States.* D. Appleton-Century Co., New York and London; 1938. (3rd edition).

STUCKLÉ, HENRY: *Interoceanic canals. An essay on the question of location for a ship canal across the American continent.* D. Van Nostrand, New York; 1870.

SULLIVAN, MARK: *Our times,* Vol. 1. Charles Scribner's Sons, New York and London; 1928.

SULLIVAN & CROMWELL: *Compagnie Nouvelle du Canal de Panama. Opinions of general counsel and documents showing title.* New York; 1902 (?).

——: *Compilation of executive documents and diplomatic correspondence relative to a trans-isthmian canal in Central America* (compiled by George Austin Morrison, Jr.). New York; 1899–1905. (3 vols.).

TALLEY, GEORGE A.: *The Panama canal. An elucidation of its governmental features as prescribed by treaties, etc.* Star Publishing Co., Wilmington, Del.; 1916.

TAVERNIER, ÉDOUARD: *Étude du canal interocéanique de l'Amérique Centrale au point de vue diplomatique, juridique et économique.* Arthur Rousseau, Paris; 1908.

TAYLOR, BAYARD: *Eldorado, or, adventures in the path of empire.* George P. Putnam, New York, and Richard Bentley, London; 1850.

TAYLOR, COMDR. HENRY CLAY: *The Nicaragua canal.* New York. (No d.).

——: *Nicaragua canal. Description of route, estimated cost and business.* T. McGill & Co., Washington. (No d.).

TEHUANTEPEC RAILWAY COMPANY: *The Tehuantepec railway. Its location, features, and advantages under the La Sère grant of 1869.* D. Appleton & Co., New York; 1869.

——: *Tehuantepec railway, 1879. Grant by the government of Mexico, to Edward Learned, of Pittsfield, Mass. for construction of railways and telegraph lines; with control of ports on both sides of the isthmus.* New York; 1879.

THAYER, WILLIAM ROSCOE: *The life and letters of John Hay.* Constable & Co., Ltd., London, and Houghton Mifflin Co., Boston and New York; 1916. (2 vols.).

THOMÉ DE GAMOND, AIMÉ, and BELLY, FÉLIX: *Carte d'étude pour le tracé et le profil du canal de Nicaragua par M. Thomé de Gamond, ingénieur civil, précédée de documents publiés sur cette question par M. Félix Belly.* Dalmont et Dunod, Paris; 1858.

THOMPSON, G. A.: *Hand book to the Pacific and California, describing eight different routes. . . .* Simpkin & Marshall, London; 1849.

THOMPSON, RICHARD WIGGINTON: *The interoceanic canal at Panama. Its po-*

litical aspects. The "Monroe Doctrine." Argument before the Committee of Foreign Affairs, House of Representatives. Thomas McGill & Co., Washington; 1881.

THOMSON, JAY EARLE: *Our Atlantic possessions.* Charles Scribner's Sons, New York and Chicago; 1928.

TOMES, ROBERT: *Panama in 1855. An account of the Panama Rail-road, of the cities of Panama and Aspinwall, with sketches of life and character on the isthmus.* Harper & Bros., New York; 1855.

TRAVIS, IRA DUDLEY: *The history of the Clayton-Bulwer treaty* (Michigan Political Science Association Publications, Vol. 3, No. 8). Ann Arbor; 1900.

TSCHIFFELY, AIMÉ FELIX: *Tschiffely's ride. Ten thousand miles in the saddle from Southern Cross to Pole Star.* Simon & Schuster, New York; 1933.

TYSON, JAMES L.: *Diary of a physician in California.* D. Appleton & Co., New York, and G. S. Appleton, Philadelphia; 1850.

ULLOA, ANTONIO DE: *Relación histórica del viage á la América meridional.* Antonio Marin, Madrid; 1748.

UNITED STATES MAIL STEAM LINE: *Proceedings in the circuit court of the United States for the southern district of New-York: in equity: A. G. Sloo, complainant, vs. George Law, Marshall O. Roberts, and others, defendants.* New York; 1849.

URIBE, ANTONIO JOSÉ: *Colombia, Venezuela, Costa Rica, Ecuador, Brasil, Nicaragua y Panamá. Las cuestiones de limites y de libre navegación fluvial.* Editorial Minerva, Bogotá; 1931.

VEDIA, ENRIQUE DE (ed.): *Historiadores primitivos de Indias* (Vol. 1 contains CORTÉS, HERNÁN: *Cartas de relación de Fernando Cortés sobre el descubrimiento y conquista de la Nueva España;* LÓPEZ DE GÓMARA, FRANCISCO: *Historia general de las Indias;* OVIEDO Y VALDÉS, GONZALO HERNÁNDEZ DE: *Sumario de la natural historia de las Indias*). Biblioteca de Autores Españoles, Madrid; 1852.

VERRILL, A. HYATT: *Panama of today.* Dodd, Mead & Co., New York; 1921. (New editions, 1927, 1937).

VERNON, ADM. EDWARD, R. N.: *Original papers relating to the expedition to Panama.* M. Cooper, London; 1744.

VILLEGAS, SABAS A.: *The republic of Panama. Its economic, financial, commercial and national resources, and general information.* Imprenta Nacional, Panama; 1924.

WAFER, LIONEL: *A new voyage and description of the isthmus of America* (ed. by L. E. Elliott Joyce). Hakluyt Society Pub. No. 73, second series, Oxford; 1934. (First published 1699).

WALKER, WILLIAM: *The war in Nicaragua.* S. H. Goetzel & Co., Mobile and New York; 1860.

WALLACE, JOHN FINDLEY: *Personal memoranda concerning my connection with the Panama canal.* (No. pl., no d. Typed MS., bound. 20 vols.).

WARREN, T. ROBINSON: *Dust and foam; or, Three oceans, and two continents.* Charles Scribner, New York; 1859.

WEIR, HUGH C.: *The conquest of the isthmus.* G. P. Putnam's Sons, New York and London; 1909.

WENMAEKERS, JER.: *La lumière sur Monsieur de Lesseps, son canal de Suez, son projet du canal interocéanique de Panama, et un mot sur le projet du canal de Nicaragua.* Decq et Duhent, Brussels; 1880 (?).

What the chambers of commerce, boards of trade and exchanges of New York, Boston, San Francisco, Providence, Charleston, Kansas City, Richmond, Memphis, Denver, Wheeling and Toledo, and prominent newspapers and individuals have to say about the Nicaragua canal. New York; 1888.

WHEELWRIGHT, WILLIAM: *Observations on the Isthmus of Panama; as comprised in a paper read at a meeting of the Royal Geographical Society, on the evening of the 12th February, 1844.* William Weale, London; 1844.

WILKINSON, IRIS GUIVER (Robin Hyde, *pseud.*) : *Check to your king. The life history of Charles, Baron de Thierry, king of Nukahiva, sovereign chief of New Zealand.* Hurst & Blackett, Ltd., London; 1936.

WILLIAMS, ALFRED: *The inter-oceanic canal and the Monroe Doctrine.* G. P. Putnam's Sons, New York; 1880.

WILLIAMS, J. J.: *The Isthmus of Tehuantepec: being the results of a survey for a railroad to connect the Atlantic and Pacific Oceans, made by the scientific commission under the direction of Major J. G. Barnard, U. S. Engineers. . . . Arranged and prepared for the Tehuantepec Railroad Company of New Orleans.* D. Appleton & Co., New York; 1852. (2 vols.).

WILLIAMS, MARY WILHELMINE: *Anglo-American isthmian diplomacy, 1815–1915.* American Historical Assn., Washington, and Oxford University Press, London; 1916.

———: *The people and politics of Latin America.* Ginn & Co., Boston, New York, etc.; 1930.

WILSON, CHARLES MORROW: *Ambassadors in white.* Henry Holt & Co., New York; 1942.

WILTSEE, ERNEST A.: *Gold rush steamers of the Pacific.* Grabhorn Press, San Francisco; 1938.

WINSOR, JUSTIN (ed.) : *Narrative and critical history of America,* Vol. 3. Houghton, Mifflin & Co., Boston and New York; 1884.

WINTHROP, THEODORE: *The canoe and the saddle. Adventures among the northwestern rivers and forests; and isthmiana.* James R. Osgood & Co., Boston; 1871. (10th edition).

WRIGHT, BENJAMIN C.: *San Francisco's ocean trade, past and future. A story of the deep water service of San Francisco, 1848 to 1911.* A. Carlisle & Co., San Francisco; 1911.

WRIGHT, IRENE ALOHA (ed. and tr.) : *Documents concerning English voyages to the Spanish Main, 1569–1580.* Hakluyt Society Pub. No. 71, second series, London; 1932.

WRIGHT, THOMAS (ed.) : *The famous voyage of Sir Francis Drake. . . . To which is added, the prosperous voyage of Mr. Thomas Candish* [Cavendish] *round the world; with an account of the vast riches he took from the Span-iards, etc.* London; 1742.

WYCHERLEY, GEORGE: *Buccaneers of the Pacific.* Bobbs-Merrill Co., Indianapolis; 1928.

WYSE, LUCIEN NAPOLÉON-BONAPARTE: *Canal interocéanique, 1876–77. Rapport sur les études de la commission internationale d'exploration de l'isthme du Darien.* A. Chaix et Cie., Paris; 1877.

——: *Canal interocéanique, 1877–78. Rapport sommaire de la commission internationale d'exploration.* A. Chaix et Cie., Paris; 1878.

——: *Canal interocéanique de Panama. Mission de 1890–91 en Colombie. Rapport général.* Achille Heymann, Paris; 1891.

——: *Le canal de Panama, l'isthme américain. Explorations, comparaison des tracés étudiés; négociations; état des travaux. . . .* Hachette et Cie., Paris; 1886.

——: *Le rapt de Panama. L'abandon du canal aux États-Unis. Protestations de M. Lucien N.-B. Wyse et plaidoiries de Me. Georges Guillaumin.* Romain Liautaud, Toulon; 1904.

WYSE, LUCIEN NAPOLÉON-BONAPARTE; RECLUS, ARMAND; and SOSA, PEDRO J.: *Canal interocéanique, 1877–1878. Rapports sur les études de la commission internationale d'exploration de l'isthme américain.* A. Lahure, Paris; 1879.

ZÉVAÈS, ALEXANDRE BOURSON: *Le scandale du Panama.* Nouvelle Revue Critique, Paris; 1931.

PERIODICALS

ABBOT, BRIG. GEN. HENRY LARCOM: "The best isthmian canal." *Atlantic Monthly,* Vol. 86, No. 518 (December 1900), pp. 844–8. Boston.

——: "The new Panama canal." *Forum,* Vol. 26, No. 3 (November 1898), pp. 343–53. New York.

——: "The Panama canal. Projects of the board of consulting engineers." *Engineering Magazine,* Vol. 31, No. 4 (July 1906), pp. 481–91. New York.

——: "The present status of the Panama canal." *Engineering News,* Vol. 40, No. 14 (October 6, 1898), pp. 210–13. New York.

——: "Present status of the Panama project." *American Academy of Political and Social Science Annals,* Vol. 31, No. 1 (January 1908), pp. 12–35. Philadelphia.

——: "The revival of de Lesseps' sea-level plan for the Panama canal." *Engineering Magazine,* Vol. 28, No. 4 (January 1905), pp. 481–8. New York.

——: "The solution of the isthmian-canal problem." *Engineering Magazine,* Vol. 26, No. 4 (January 1904), pp. 481–7. New York.

ADAMS, CHARLES FRANCIS: "The Panama Canal Zone. An epochal event in sanitation." *Massachusetts Historical Society Proceedings,* Vol. 44 (May 1911), pp. 610–46. Boston.

AMMEN, REAR ADM. DANIEL: "American isthmian canal routes." *Franklin Institute Journal,* Vol. 128, No. 6 (December 1889), pp. 409–39.

——: "Inter-oceanic ship-canal across the American isthmus. The proposed

. . . canal between Greytown and Brito, via Lake Nicaragua." *American Geographical Society Bulletin* No. 3 (1878), pp. 142–62. New York.

ANDRÉ, ELOY L.: "La apertura del canal de Panamá y su influencia en la política comercial hispano-americana." *Nuestro Tiempo,* Año 3, No. 28 (April 1903), pp. 488–502. Madrid.

The Atlas. A general newspaper and journal of literature (weekly), May 22, June 12, 1836. London. (Articles on Baron Charles de Thierry).

AUSTIN, H. A.: "The fortifications of the Panama canal." *Forum,* Vol. 45, No. 2 (February 1911), pp. 129–41. New York.

BAILEY, HERBERT: "The Panama tolls controversy. Should the Hay-Pauncefote treaty be revised?" *Landmark,* Vol. 3, No. 12 (December 1921), pp. 775–80. London.

BAILEY, THOMAS A.: "Interest in a Nicaragua canal, 1903–1931." *Hispanic American Historical Review,* Vol. 16, No. 1 (February 1936), pp. 2–28. Durham, N. C.

BAKER, BERNARD N.: "How we can have American ships for the Panama canal." *North American Review,* Vol. 191, No. 650 (January 1910), pp. 29–38. New York.

——: "What use is the Panama canal to our country without American ships?" *North American Review,* Vol. 190, No. 648 (November 1909), pp. 577–86. New York.

BAKER, CHARLES W.: "The Panama canal." *Yale Scientific Monthly,* Vol. 17, No. 5 (February 1911), pp. 188–95; No. 6 (March 1911), pp. 242–50. New Haven.

BALLARD, G. A.: "The commercial prospects of the Panama canal." *Contemporary Review,* Vol. 94, No. 516 (December 1908), pp. 731–42. London.

BARKER, J. ELLIS: "Panama: the difficulty and its solution." *Nineteenth Century and After,* Vol. 72, No. 428 (October 1912), pp. 745–62. London.

BARRAL-MONTFERRAT, MARQUIS DE: "Les États-Unis et le canal interocéanique." *Correspondant,* Vol. 218 (nouvelle série Vol. 182; March 10, 1905), pp. 910–31. Paris.

BARTLETT, C. A. H.: "The Panama Canal act." *Law Magazine and Review,* Vol. 38, No. 366 (November 1912), pp. 15–34. London.

BATES, LINDON, JR.: "The Panama Railroad." *World To-day,* Vol. 11, No. 1 (July 1906), pp. 714–24. Chicago.

BEEKS, GERTRUDE: "The nation's housekeeping at Panama." *Outlook,* Vol. 87, No. 9 (November 2, 1907), pp. 489–93. New York.

——: "Panama canal conditions." *American Federationist,* Vol. 14, No. 11 (November 1907), pp. 849–66. Washington.

BELLY, FÉLIX: "La question de l'isthme américain. Épisode de l'histoire de notre temps." *Revue des Deux Mondes,* Année 30, Pér. 2, Vol. 28 (1860), pp. 328–68, 597–633, 865–902. Paris.

BÉRARD, VICTOR: "Questions extérieures. Panama." *Revue de Paris,* Année 9, Vol. 1, No. 2 (January 15, 1902), pp. 423–44. Paris.

BIGELOW, POULTNEY: "Our mismanagement at Panama." *Independent,* Vol. 60, No. 2979 (January 4, 1906), pp. 9–21. New York.

BINGHAM, HIRAM: "The probable effect of the opening of the Panama canal on our economic relations with the people of the west coast of South America." *Journal of Race Development*, Vol. 5, No. 1 (July 1914), pp. 49–67. Worcester, Mass.

BLAKESLEE, GEORGE HUBBARD: "The future of the Panama canal." *Outlook*, Vol. 110, No. 17 (August 25, 1915), pp. 967–76; Vol. 111, No. 4 (September 22, 1915), pp. 193–201. New York.

——: "The results of the Panama canal on world trade." *Outlook*, Vol. 111, No. 9 (October 27, 1915), pp. 490–7; Vol. 111, No. 13 (November 24, 1915), pp. 717–22. New York.

BOURDIOL, H.: "Exploration dans l'isthme de Darien." *Bulletin de la Société de Géographie*, Série 5, Vol. 8 (December 1864), pp. 489–507. Paris.

BROMLEY, ROBERT: "The Nicaragua canal question and the Clayton-Bulwer treaty." *Nineteenth Century and After*, Vol. 49, No. 287 (January 1901), pp. 100–15. London.

Bulletin du Canal Interocéanique. 227 numbers, September 1, 1879 to February 2, 1889. Paris.

BUNAU-VARILLA, PHILIPPE: "Nicaragua or Panama." *Scientific American* (supplement), Vol. 52, No. 1355 (December 21, 1901), pp. 21713–14; No. 1356 (December 28, 1901), pp. 21737–8. New York.

——: "La question de Panama." *Nouvelle Revue*, Vol. 146 (nouvelle série Vol. 27; April 15, 1904), pp. 433–58. Paris.

——: "The sea-level canal and the straits of Panama." *Outlook*, Vol. 91, No. 17 (April 24, 1909), pp. 945–54. New York.

BURLINGAME, ROGER: "The 'great' Frenchman. A new interpretation of Ferdinand de Lesseps and the Panama scandal." *Scribner's Magazine*, Vol. 94, No. 4 (October 1933), pp. 208–13, 249–56. New York.

BURR, WILLIAM HUBERT: "The Panama route for a ship canal." *Popular Science Monthly*, Vol. 61 (July 1902), pp. 252–68; (August 1902), pp. 304–16. New York.

——: "The proposed isthmian ship canal." *Scribner's Magazine*, Vol. 31, No. 2 (February 1902), pp. 145–69. New York.

——: "Some aspects of the Panama canal." *Science*, Vol. 24 (new series), No. 603 (July 20, 1906), pp. 71–8. New York.

BURT, GEORGE A.: "A comparison of the isthmian canal projects." *Engineering Magazine*, Vol. 19, No. 1 (Apr. 1900), pp. 19–27. New York.

CADLE, CORNELIUS: "The Nicaragua canal." *Iowa Historical Record*, Vol. 14 (1898), pp. 349–60. Iowa City.

CARR, JOHN FOSTER: "The Panama canal." *Outlook*, Vol. 82, No. 17 (April 28, 1906), pp. 946–63; Vol. 83, No. 1 (May 5, 1906), pp. 21–4; Vol. 83, No. 2 (May 12, 1906), pp. 69–72; Vol. 83, No. 3 (May 19, 1906), pp. 117–20; Vol. 83, No. 5 (June 2, 1906), pp. 265–70; Vol. 83, No. 8 (June 23, 1906), pp. 435–45; Vol. 84, No. 5 (September 29, 1906), pp. 263–8. New York.

CASTILLERO, ERNESTO J.: "La causa inmediata de la emancipación de Panamá." *Academia Panameña de la Historia, Boletín*, Año, 1, No. 3 (July 1933), pp. 250–433. Panama.

——: "El profeta de Panamá y su gran traición. El tratado del canal y la intervención de Bunau-Varilla en su confección." *Academia Panameña de la Historia, Boletín,* Año 4, No. 10 (January–April 1936), pp. 1–60. Panama.

"Central American ship canals." *Engineer,* Vol. 90 (1900), pp. 405–6, 455–7, 509–11, 560–1, 605–6, 627–8. London.

CHAMBERLAIN, LEANDER T.: "A chapter of national dishonor." *North American Review,* Vol. 195, No. 675 (February 1912), pp. 145–74. New York.

CHANEL, E.: "Les États-Unis et le traité Hay-Pauncefote." *Revue Française de l'Étranger et des Colonies et Exploration,* Vol. 26, No. 268 (April 1901), pp. 193–7. Paris.

CHESTER, REAR ADM. COLBY M.: "The Panama canal." *National Geographic Magazine,* Vol. 16, No. 10 (October 1905), pp. 445–67. Washington.

CHEVALIER, MICHEL: "L'isthme de Panama. L'isthme de Suez." *Revue des Deux Mondes,* Année 14, Vol. 5 (nouvelle série; January 1, 1844), pp. 5–74. Paris.

CHRISTIE, JAMES; SMITH, EDWIN F.; and SCHERMERHORN, LOUIS Y.: "American isthmian canals. A topical discussion, November 3, 1900." *Engineers' Club of Philadelphia Proceedings,* Vol. 18 (1901), pp. 21–42. Philadelphia.

CHURCH, COL. GEORGE EARL: "Interoceanic communication on the western continent. A study in commercial geography." *Geographical Journal,* Vol. 19, No. 3 (March 1902), pp. 313–54. London.

CLARK, JOHN BATES: "The remote effects of the Panama canal." *Commercial and Financial Chronicle, Panama-Pacific Section* (November 28, 1914), pp. 50–2. New York.

CLARK, JOHN MAURICE: "The Panama canal and the railroads." *Commercial and Financial Chronicle, Panama-Pacific Section* (November 28, 1914), pp. 47–50. New York.

CLERGET, PIERRE: "Le canal de Panama." *Revue Économique Internationale,* Année 19, Vol. 3 (September 1927), pp. 441–62. Brussels.

COLNÉ, CHARLES: "The Panama interoceanic canal." *Franklin Institute Journal,* Vol. 118, No. 5 (November 1884), pp. 353–76. Philadelphia.

COLQUHOUN, ARCHIBALD R.: "An English view of the Panama canal." *North American Review,* Vol. 187, No. 628 (March 1908), pp. 348–56. New York.

——: "The Panama and Nicaragua canals." *Graphic,* Vol. 61, No. 1575 (February, 3, 1900), p. 162. London.

——: "The strategical and economic effect of the opening of the Panama canal." *Royal United Service Institute Journal,* Vol. 52, No. 360 (February 1908), pp. 175–95. London.

CORNISH, VAUGHAN: "The Panama canal in 1908." *Geographical Journal,* Vol. 33, No. 2 (February 1909), pp. 153–80. London.

——: "The Panama canal in 1910." *Royal Society of Arts Journal,* Vol. 59, No. 3029 (December 9, 1910), pp. 93–107. London.

CORTHELL, ELMER LAWRENCE: "The Tehuantepec ship railway." *National Geographic Magazine,* Vol. 7, No. 2 (February 1896), pp. 64–72. Washington.

COSSOUX, N. V. L.: "Le canal interocéanique. Adoption du projet de Colon à Panama." *Annales des Travaux Publiques de Belgique,* Série 2, Vol. 7 (October 1902), pp. 1027–36. Brussels.

COX-SINCLAIR, EDWARD S.: "The international status of the Panama canal."

Law Magazine and Review, Vol. 38, No. 366 (November 1912), pp. 1–15. London.

CRICHFIELD, GEORGE W.: "The Panama canal from a contractor's standpoint." *North American Review,* Vol. 180, No. 578 (January 1905), pp. 74–87. New York.

CULLOM, SHELBY MOORE: "The Panama situation." *Independent,* Vol. 55, No. 2869 (November 26, 1903), pp. 2787–90. New York.

CURTIS, WILLIAM ELEROY: "Central America: its resources and commerce." *Forum,* Vol. 25, No. 2 (April 1898), pp. 166–77; No. 3 (May 1898), pp. 354–65. New York.

DAGGETT, STUART: "The Panama canal and transcontinental railroad rates." *Journal of Political Economy,* Vol. 23, No. 10 (December 1915), pp. 953–60. Chicago.

DAVIS, ARTHUR POWELL: "The isthmian canal." *American Geographical Society Bulletin,* Vol. 34, No. 2 (April 1902), pp. 132–8. New York.

——: "Panama and Nicaragua canals compared." *Forum,* Vol. 30, No. 5 (January 1901), pp. 527–44. New York.

——: "The water supply for the Nicaragua canal." *National Geographic Magazine,* Vol. 11, No. 9 (September 1900), pp. 363–5. Washington.

DAVIS, GEORGE W.: "Fortification at Panama." *American Journal of International Law,* Vol. 3, No. 4 (October 1909), pp. 885–908. New York.

DENISON, LINDSAY: "Making good at Panama." *Everybody's Magazine,* Vol. 14, No. 5 (May 1906), pp. 579–90. New York.

DENNIS, WILLIAM CULLEN: "The Panama situation in the light of international law." *American Law Register,* Vol. 43 (new series), No. 5 (May 1904), pp. 265–306. Philadelphia.

DILKE, CHARLES W.: "U. K., U. S., and the ship canal." *Forum,* Vol. 29, No. 4 (June 1900), pp. 449–54. New York.

DUMAS, A.: "Le canal de Panama." *Génie Civil,* Vol. 47, No. 1 (May 6, 1905), pp. 1–8; No. 2 (May 13, 1905), pp. 19–24; No. 3 (May 20, 1905), pp. 36–9. Paris.

DUPONCHEL, A.: "Percement définitif du canal de Panama par un torrent artificiel." *Société Languedocienne de Géographie, Bulletin,* Vol. 12 (1889), pp. 192–213. Montpellier (Hérault).

ELBÉE, JEAN D': "Ferdinand de Lesseps et le drame de Panama." *Revue Universelle,* Vol. 71, No. 15 (November 1, 1937), pp. 316–35; No. 16 (November 15, 1937), pp. 431–51. Paris.

"Emancipation of Spanish America. A review of: Lettre aux Espagñols-Américains. Par un de leurs compatriotes. À Philadelphie." *Edinburgh Review,* Vol. 13, No. 26 (January 1809), pp. 227–311. Edinburgh.

ESCOBAR, FRANCISCO: "President Roosevelt's message and the isthmian canal." *North American Review,* Vol. 178, No. 566 (January 1904), pp. 122–32. New York.

FAIRCHILD, MAHLON D.: "Reminiscences of a 'forty-niner." *California Historical Society Quarterly,* Vol. 13, No. 1 (March 1934), pp. 3–33. San Francisco.

FERRIS, A. C.: "Hardships of the isthmus in '49." *Century Illustrated Monthly*

Magazine, Vol. 41 (new series Vol. 19), No. 6 (April 1891), pp. 929–31. New York.

FINDLAY, A. G.: "Oceanic currents, and their connection with the proposed Central-America canals." *Royal Geographical Society of London Journal,* Vol. 23 (1853), pp. 217–40. London.

FINLAY, CARLOS: "El mosquito hipoteticamente considerado como agente de trasmisión de la fiebre amarilla." *Academia de Ciencias Médicas, Fisicas y Naturales de la Habana, Anales,* Vol. 18 (1881), pp. 147–69, 175–7. Havana.

FITZ-ROY, CAPT. ROBERT, R. N.: "Considerations on the great isthmus of Central America." *Royal Geographical Society of London Journal,* Vol. 20 (1851), pp. 161–89. London.

——: "Further considerations on the great isthmus of Central America." *Royal Geographical Society of London Journal,* Vol. 23 (1853), pp. 171–90. London.

FLANDRE, HENRI: "Le canal de Panama et les États-Unis." *Questions Diplomatiques et Coloniales,* Vol. 21, No. 214 (January 16, 1906), pp. 111–26. Paris.

FORBES-LINDSAY, CHARLES H. A.: "The Panama canal as it will be." *World To-day,* Vol. 11, No. 4 (October 1906), pp. 1036–40. Chicago.

——: "A year at Panama under Stevens." *World To-day,* Vol. 11, No. 2 (August 1906), pp. 858–62. Chicago.

FORD, JAMES THOMAS: "The present condition and prospects of the Panama canal works." *Institution of Civil Engineers, Minutes of Proceedings,* Vol. 144 (1901), pp. 150–70. London.

FOSKETT, H. W.: "La Grande Bretagne, les États-Unis et le canal du Nicaragua." *Carnet Historique et Littéraire,* Année 4 (nouvelle série), Vol. 10 (November 1901), pp. 226–39. Paris.

FOX, GEORGE LEVI: "The Panama canal as a business venture." *Government,* Vol. 3, No. 5 (December 1908), pp. 283–94. Boston.

FREEMAN, JOHN R.: "The lock canal." *Outlook,* Vol. 91, No. 17 (April 24, 1909), pp. 931–44. New York.

FRIEDRICHSTHAL, CHEVALIER EMANUEL: "Notes on the Lake of Nicaragua and the province of Chontales, in Guatemala." *Royal Geographical Society of London Journal,* Vol. 11 (1841), pp. 97–100. London.

FRIEND, COMDR. CHARLES, R. N.: "Notes of an excursion from the banks of the Atrato to the Bay of Cupica, on the coast of the Pacific, in the year 1827." *Royal Geographical Society of London Journal,* Vol. 23 (1853), pp. 191–6. London.

GHENT, W. J.: "Labor and the commissary at Panama." *Independent,* Vol. 66, No. 3156 (May 27, 1909), pp. 1129–36. New York.

——: "Work and welfare on the canal." *Independent,* Vol. 66, No. 3152 (April 29, 1909), pp. 907–14. New York.

GOETHALS, GEORGE WASHINGTON: "The Panama canal." *National Geographic Magazine,* Vol. 20, No. 4 (April 1909), pp. 334–55. Washington.

——: "The Panama canal." *Engineering,* Vol. 89 (1910), pp. 170–3, 238–41, 246, 292–6, 325–9. London.

——: "The Panama canal." *National Geographic Magazine,* Vol. 22, No. 2 (February 1911), pp. 148–211. Washington.

——: "The Panama canal and the business problem connected with it." *Economic World,* Vol. 12 (new series), No. 27 (December 30, 1916), pp. 861–3. New York.

GORDY, J. P.: "The ethics of the Panama case." *Forum,* Vol. 36, No. 1 (July 1904), pp. 115–24. New York.

GORGAS, COL. WILLIAM CRAWFORD: "Sanitation of the Canal Zone." *Medical Record,* Vol. 73, No. 7 (February 15, 1908), pp. 259–62. New York.

"The great ship canal question. England and Costa Rica *versus* the United States and Nicaragua." *British Colonial Magazine and East India Review* (November 1850). London.

GREELY, GEN. A. W.: "The present state of the Nicaragua canal." *National Geographic Magazine,* Vol. 7, No. 2 (February 1896), pp. 73–6. Washington.

GROSVENOR, GILBERT H.: "Progress on the Panama canal." *National Geographic Magazine,* Vol. 16, No. 10 (October 1905), pp. 467–75. Washington.

GRUNSKY, CARL EWALD: "The type of the Panama canal." *Popular Science Monthly,* Vol. 74 (May 1909), pp. 417–41. Lancaster, Pa.

——: "The work of the commission on the Panama canal." *Engineering Magazine,* Vol. 28, No. 5 (February 1905), pp. 804–14. New York.

GUIGNARD, ALFRED: "Le spectre allemand à Panama." *Grande Revue,* Vol. 73, No. 12 (June 25, 1912), pp. 673–85. Paris.

HAINS, BRIG. GEN. PETER C.: "The labor problem on the Panama canal." *North American Review,* Vol. 179, No. 572 (July 1904), pp. 42–54. New York.

——: "Neutralization of the Panama canal." *American Journal of International Law,* Vol. 3, No. 2 (April 1909), pp. 354–94. New York.

——: "The Panama canal — some objections to a sea-level project." *North American Review,* Vol. 180, No. 580 (March 1905), pp. 440–52. New York.

HALE, HENRY: "M. Bunau-Varilla: engineer and diplomat." *American Monthly Review of Reviews,* Vol. 28, No. 6 (December 1903), pp. 677–9. New York.

HALL, WILLIAM HAMMOND: "The conflict of engineers over plans for the Panama canal." *Engineering News,* Vol. 54, No. 22 (November 30, 1905), pp. 572–5. New York.

HAMILTON, DR.: "On the advantages and practicability of forming a junction between the Atlantic and Pacific Oceans. In letters from Dr. Hamilton to S. Banister." *New Monthly Magazine and Humorist,* Vol. 89 (1850), pp. 365–72, 444–51; Vol. 90 (1850), pp. 37–40, 167–78, 314–28. London.

HARING, CLARENCE HENRY: "American gold and silver production in the first half of the sixteenth century." *Quarterly Journal of Economics,* Vol. 29 (May 1915), pp. 433–79. Cambridge, Mass.

HAUPT, LEWIS MUHLENBERG: "National influence and the isthmian canal." *Engineering Magazine,* Vol. 15, No. 4 (July 1898), pp. 550–7. New York.

——: "Population and the isthmian canal." *Lippincott's Magazine,* Vol. 67, No. 402 (June 1901), pp. 740–4. Philadelphia.

——: "Why is an isthmian canal not built?" *North American Review,* Vol. 175, No. 548 (July 1902), pp. 128–35. New York.

HAZELTINE, MAYO W.: "The proposed Hay-Pauncefote treaty." *North American Review,* Vol. 170, No. 520 (March 1900), pp. 357–66. New York.

HEADLEY, JOEL TYLER: "Darien exploring expedition, under command of Lieut. Isaac C. Strain." *Harper's New Monthly Magazine,* Vol. 10, No. 58 (March 1855), pp. 433–58; No. 59 (April 1855), pp. 600–15; No. 60 (May 1855), pp. 745–64. New York.

HEILPRIN, ANGELO: "The shrinkage of Lake Nicaragua. A question of permanency of the proposed Nicaragua canal." *Geographical Society of Philadelphia Bulletin,* Vol. 2, No. 6 (July 1900), pp. 115–24. Philadelphia.

HERRÁN, TOMÁS D.: "The isthmian question." *Independent,* Vol. 56, No. 2876 (January 14, 1904), pp. 65–6. New York.

HERT, F. DE: "Le canal interocéanique." *Précis Historiques,* Vol. 34 (July 1, 1885), pp. 320–31. Brussels.

HILL, ROBERT T.: "The Panama canal route." *National Geographic Magazine,* Vol. 7, No. 2 (February 1896), pp. 59–64. Washington.

HISTORICUS *(pseud.)*: "The fifty miles order." *North American Review,* Vol. 178, No. 567 (February 1904), pp. 235–45. New York.

HUBERICH, CHARLES HENRY: "Le canal transisthmique." *Revue du Droit Public,* Vol. 19, No. 2 (March–April 1903), pp. 193–213. Paris.

HUEBNER, G. G.: "Economic aspects of the Panama canal." *American Economic Review,* Vol. 5, No. 4 (December 1915), pp. 816–29. Princeton.

HUNTER, W. HENRY: "The American isthmus and the interoceanic canal." *Engineering Magazine,* Vol. 16, No. 5 (February 1899), pp. 711–28. New York.

——: "A review of the Nicaragua canal scheme." *Engineering Magazine,* Vol. 16, No. 6 (March 1899), p. 972–90. New York.

HYDE, CHARLES CHENEY: "The isthmian canal treaty." *Harvard Law Review,* Vol. 15, No. 9 (May 1902), pp. 725–32. Cambridge, Mass.

INGLIS, WILLIAM: "At double-quick along the canal with the President." *Harper's Weekly,* Vol. 50, No. 2607 (December 8, 1906), pp. 1740–5. New York.

——: "The progress and promise of the work at Panama." *Harper's Weekly,* Vol. 50, No. 2609 (December 22, 1906), pp. 1852–5. New York.

"Inter-oceanic canal projects. Discussions by Walton W. Evans, Frederick M. Kelley, Charles A. Sweet, John C. Campbell, Charles D. Ward, N. Appleton, S. F. Shelbourne, Max E. Schmidt, Thomas J. Long and Edward P. North." *American Society of Civil Engineers Transactions,* Vol. 9 (January 1880), pp. 1–46. New York.

"Interoceanic ship canal discussion." *American Geographical Society Bulletin* No. 4 (1879), pp. 113–300. New York.

"The isthmian canal controversy." *Scientific American* (supplement), Vol. 53, No. 1359 (January 18, 1902), pp. 21773–87. New York.

"The Isthmus of Darien." *Dublin University Magazine,* Vol. 41, No. 246 (June 1853), pp. 718–26. Dublin.

JACOB, LÉON: "Le canal de Panama et les colonies françaises." *Questions Diplomatiques et Coloniales,* Vol. 33, No. 360 (February 16, 1912), pp. 193–208. Paris.

JOHNSON, EMORY RICHARD: "Comparison of distances by the isthmian canal and other routes." *American Geographical Society of New York Bulletin,* Vol. 35, No. 1 (February 1903), pp. 163–76. New York.

——: "The Isthmian canal. Factors affecting the choice of route." *Quarterly Journal of Economics,* Vol. 16 (August 1902), pp. 514–36. Boston.

——: "The isthmian canal in its economic aspects." *American Academy of Political and Social Science Annals,* Vol. 19, No. 1 (January 1902), pp. 1–23. Philadelphia.

——: "The Nicaragua canal and our commercial interests." *American Monthly Review of Reviews,* Vol. 18, No. 5 (November 1898), pp. 571–6. New York.

——: "The Panama canal. The title and concession." *Political Science Quarterly,* Vol. 18, No. 2 (June 1903), pp. 197–215. Boston.

——: "The Panama canal in its commercial aspects." *American Geographical Society of New York Bulletin,* Vol. 35, No. 5 (December 1903), pp. 481–91. New York.

——: "The Panama canal question." *Independent,* Vol. 55, No. 2874 (December 31, 1903), pp. 3098–101. New York.

——: "The use and benefits of the Panama canal." *Commercial and Financial Chronicle, Panama-Pacific Section* (November 28, 1914), pp. 43–6. New York.

JOHNSON, WILLIS FLETCHER: "Justice and equity in Panama." *Forum,* Vol. 36, No. 1 (July 1904), pp. 125–37. New York.

JUSTICE (*pseud.*): "Roosevelt and the canal steal." *Globe,* Vol. 14, No. 54 (June 1904), pp. 115–22. Philadelphia.

KEASBEY, LINDLEY MILLER: "The national canal policy." *American Historical Association Annual Report* (1902), Vol. 1, pp. 275–88. Washington.

——: "The Nicaragua canal and the Monroe Doctrine." *American Academy of Political and Social Science Annals,* Vol. 7 (January 1896), pp. 1–31. Philadelphia.

——: "The Nicaragua canal in the light of present politics." *American Monthly Review of Reviews,* Vol. 18, No. 5 (November 1898), pp. 566–70. New York.

——: "The terms and tenor of the Clayton-Bulwer treaty." *American Academy of Political and Social Science Annals,* Vol. 14, No. 3 (November 1899), pp. 285–309. Philadelphia.

——: "The urgent need of interoceanic communication." *Political Science Quarterly,* Vol. 14, No. 4 (December 1899), pp. 594–605. Boston.

KELLEY, FREDERICK M.: "On the junction of the Atlantic and Pacific Oceans and the practicability of a ship canal, without locks, by the valley of the Atrato." *Institution of Civil Engineers, Minutes of Proceedings,* Vol. 15 (1855–6), pp. 376–417. London.

KEMBLE, JOHN HASKELL: "The genesis of the Pacific Mail Steamship Company." *California Historical Society Quarterly,* Vol. 13 (1934), No. 3, pp. 240–54; No. 4, pp. 386–406. San Francisco.

——: "Pacific Mail service between Panama and San Francisco, 1849–1851." *Pacific Historical Review,* Vol. 2, No. 4 (December 1933), pp. 405–17. Glendale, Cal.

———: "The Panamá route to the Pacific coast, 1848–1869." *Pacific Historical Review*, Vol. 7, No. 1 (March 1938), pp. 1–13. Glendale, Cal.

KINNAIRD, LUCIA BURK: "Creassy's plan for seizing Panama, with an introductory account of British designs on Panama." *Hispanic American Historical Review*, Vol. 13, No. 1 (February 1933), pp. 46–78. Durham, N. C.

LAPHAM, ROGER D.: "World-wide changes in trade due to Panama canal." *Current History*, Vol. 30, No. 4 (July 1929), pp. 648–52. New York.

LATANÉ, JOHN HOLLADAY: "The effects of the Panama canal on our relations with Latin America." *American Academy of Political and Social Science Annals*, Vol. 54 (July 1914), pp. 84–91. Philadelphia.

———: "The neutralization features of the Hay-Pauncefote treaty." *American Historical Association Annual Report* (1902), Vol. 1, pp. 289–303. Washington.

LATIN AMERICAN (*pseud.*): "The Colombian treaty. Its legal and moral aspects." *North American Review*, Vol. 203, No. 1 (January 1916), pp. 55–62. New York.

LAUGEL, AUGUSTE: "Les communications interocéaniques dans l'Amérique centrale." *Revue des Deux Mondes*, Année 27, Pér. 2, Vol. 7 (January 15, 1857), pp. 436–65. Paris.

LAWRANCE, GEORGE: "Excursion to the Lake of Nicaragua up the River San Juan." *Nautical Magazine and Naval Chronicle* (1840), pp. 857–64; (1841), pp. 39–43, 184–8, 253–7, 321–4. London.

LEFÉBURE, PAUL: "À la conquête d'un isthme." *Annales des Sciences Politiques*, Vol. 16 (July 1901), pp. 427–44; (September 1901), pp. 600–19. Paris.

LEIGH, JOHN GEORGE: "The reports of the Isthmian Canal Commission." *Engineering Magazine*, Vol. 23, No. 1 (April 1902), pp. 1–14. New York.

———: "The republic of Colombia and the Panama canal." *Engineering Magazine*, Vol. 26, No. 1 (October 1903), pp. 1–19. New York.

LENDIÁN, EVELIO RODRÍGUEZ: "Los Estados Unidos, Cuba, y el canal de Panamá." *Universidad de la Habana, Revista de la Facultad de Letras y Ciencias*, Vol. 9, No. 2 (September 1909), pp. 153–221. Havana.

LE NORMAND, ROBERT G.: "Panama et Nicaragua." *Revué des Revues*, Série 3, Vol. 29 (June 15, 1899), pp. 557–70. Paris.

"A letter of Alexander von Humboldt, 1845." *American Historical Review*, Vol. 7, No. 4 (July 1902), pp. 704–6. Lancaster, Pa., New York, and London.

LEWIS, HENRY HARRISON: "The canal will be built." *Harper's Weekly*, Vol. 49, No. 2555 (December 9, 1905), pp. 1769–75, 1778–9, 1792. New York.

———: "The Panama canal." *Munsey's Magazine*, Vol. 2, No. 3 (June 1900), pp. 360–70. New York.

LLOYD, JOHN AUGUSTUS: "Account of levellings carried across the Isthmus of Panama." *Royal Society of London Philosophical Transactions* (1830), Part 1, pp. 59–68. London.

———: "Notes respecting the Isthmus of Panama." *Royal Geographical Society of London Journal*, Vol. 1 (1832), pp. 69–101. London.

———: "On the facilities for a ship canal communication between the Atlantic and Pacific Oceans, through the Isthmus of Panamá." *Institution of Civil Engineers, Minutes of Proceedings,* Vol. 9 (1850), pp. 58–89. London.

López, Jacinto: "El gobierno de Colombia y la Compañía de Canal de Panamá." *Reforma Social,* Vol. 3, No. 4 (March 1915), pp. 445–69. Havana.

Lummis, Charles F.: "In the lion's den." *Out West,* Vol. 19, No. 6 (December 1903), pp. 676–7. Los Angeles.

Madden, Martin B.: "The Panama canal." *Government,* Vol. 2, No. 6 (March 1908), pp. 365–72. Boston.

Mahan, Rear Adm. Alfred Thayer: "The Panama canal and the distribution of the fleet." *North American Review,* Vol. 200, No. 3 (September 1914), pp. 406–17. New York.

——: "Was Panama 'A chapter of national dishonor'?" *North American Review,* Vol. 196, No. 683 (October 1912), pp. 549–68. New York.

Mange, François: "Le canal de Panama et le tonnage maritime." *Revue de Paris,* Année 19, Vol. 4 (July 1, 1912), pp. 179–201. Paris.

Manjarrés, Ramon de: "Proyectos españoles de canal interoceánico." *Cultura Hispanoamericana,* Año 3, No. 22 (September 15, 1914), pp. 17–26. Madrid.

Manson, N. J.: "Inter-oceanic ship-canal communication by the American isthmus. Its geographic and economic relations toward the United States." *Technical Society of the Pacific Coast Transactions,* Vol. 10, No. 6 (July 1893), pp. 119–48. San Francisco.

Markham, Sir Clements R.: "Vasco Nuñez de Balboa, 1513–1913." *Geographical Journal,* Vol. 41, No. 6 (June 1913), pp. 517–32. London.

Marlio, Louis: "Panama." *Revue Politique et Parlementaire,* Vol. 152, No. 453 (August 10, 1932), pp. 193–222; No. 454 (September 10, 1932), pp. 429–64. Paris.

Marsan, Abbé: "Un projet de communication entre l'océan Atlantique et l'océan Pacifique par le lac de Nicaragua (1785–1786)." *Bulletin de Géographie Historique et Descriptive,* Année 1899, No. 2, pp. 311–22. Paris.

Marvá y Mayer, José: "El canal de Panamá y los precursores españoles de los siglos XV y XVI." *Raza Española,* Año 1 (April–May 1919), pp. 9–11. Madrid.

Marvaud, Angel: "Le canal de Panama et les intérêts français." *Questions Diplomatiques et Coloniales,* Vol. 38, No. 417 (July 1, 1914), pp. 18–29. Paris.

Meagher, Thomas Francis: "The new route through Chiriqui." *Harper's New Monthly Magazine,* Vol. 22, No. 128 (January 1861), pp. 198–209. New York.

Medina, Crisanto: "Why the Panama route was originally chosen." *North American Review,* Vol. 177, No. 562 (September 1903), pp. 393–8. New York.

Meikle, John: "A bit of the 'ancient' history of the isthmian canal problem." *Scientific American* (supplement), Vol. 53, No. 1369 (March 29, 1902), p. 21939. New York.

Menocal, Aniceto G.: "Discussion upon inter-oceanic canal projects. Also, additional information obtained by recent surveys in Nicaragua." *American So-*

ciety of Civil Engineers Transactions, Vol. 9 (November 1880), pp. 429–46. New York.

——: "The Panama canal." *American Society of Civil Engineers Proceedings, Papers, and Discussions,* Vol. 32, No. 2 (February 1906), pp. 60–6; No. 4 (April 1906), pp. 374–7. New York.

MERINO, NICOLÁS PÉREZ: "Los canales del istmo centroamericano." *España Moderna,* Año 11, Vol. 123 (1899), pp. 60–84. Madrid.

MILLER, WARNER: "The Nicaragua canal." *Forum,* Vol. 26, No. 3 (November 1898), pp. 331–42. New York.

MORGAN, JOHN TYLER: "The choice of isthmian canal routes." *North American Review,* Vol. 174, No. 5 (May 1902), pp. 672–86. New York.

MORISON, GEORGE SHATTUCK: "The Panama canal." *American Geographical Society of New York Bulletin,* Vol. 35, No. 1 (February 1903), pp. 24–43. New York.

MOORE, JOHN BASSETT: "The interoceanic canal and the Hay-Pauncefote treaty." *New York Times,* March 4, 1900.

MUHLEMAN, MAURICE L.: "The Panama canal payment." *Journal of Political Economy,* Vol. 12, No. 4 (September 1904), pp. 473–94. Chicago.

MYGATT, GERALD: "The truth about the Panama canal." *Columbian Magazine,* Vol. 2, No. 2 (May 1910), pp. 1005–30. New York.

Niles' Weekly Register, Vol. 28, Whole No. 715 (May 28, 1825), p. 198. Baltimore. (Article on Welwood Hislop's canal or railway concession).

NIMMO, JOSEPH, JR.: "The Nicaragua canal in its commercial and military aspects." *Engineering Magazine,* Vol. 15, No. 5 (August 1898), pp. 720–6. New York.

——: "The proposed American interoceanic canal in its commercial aspects." *National Geographic Magazine,* Vol. 10, No. 8 (August 1899), pp. 297–310. Washington.

"Notes of a journey in the Isthmus of Panama and California." *Hogg's Instructor,* Vol. 7 (new series; 1851), pp. 110–12, 120–2, 130–3, 173–5. Edinburgh and London.

NOTT, JOSIAH C.: "Yellow fever contrasted with bilious fever. Reasons for believing it a disease sui generis. Its mode of propagation. Remote cause. Probable insect or animalcular origin, etc." *New Orleans Medical and Surgical Journal,* Vol. 4, No. 5 (March 1848), pp. 563–601. New Orleans.

OERSTED, ANDREAS: "Survey made for a canal, through the River Sapoa, to the port of Salinas or Bolaños, in Costa Rica." *Royal Geographical Society of London Journal,* Vol. 21 (1851), pp. 96–9. London.

OLIPHANT, LAURENCE: "On the Bayanos River, Isthmus of Panama." *Royal Geographical Society of London Journal,* Vol. 35 (1865), pp. 142–7. London.

PADRÓ, ANTONIO: "La participación de España en el proyecto de apertura de un canal interoceánico á través del istmo de Panamá." *Nuestro Tiempo,* Año 16, No. 206 (February 1916), pp. 145–58. Madrid.

"The Panama canal." *Quarterly Review,* Vol. 217, No. 433 (October 1912), pp. 299–322. London.

"The Panama canal and maritime commerce." *Quarterly Review,* Vol. 200, No. 400 (October 1904), pp. 329–57. London.

"The Panama canal. Work of the Canal Commission. Administration, hygiene, preparatory work of construction, etc." *Engineer,* Vol. 99 (1905), pp. 209–10, 232–5, 281, 402–4. London.

"Panama ou Nicaragua." *Revue Technique,* Vol. 22, No. 24 (December 25, 1901), pp. 557–61. Paris.

Panama Star and Herald. Panama.

PASCO, SAMUEL: "The isthmian canal question as affected by treaties and concessions." *American Academy of Political and Social Science Annals,* Vol. 19, No. 1 (January 1902), pp. 24–45. Philadelphia.

PENFIELD, FREDERIC COURTLAND: "Why not own the Panama Isthmus?" *North American Review,* Vol. 174, No. 2 (February 1902), pp. 269–74. New York.

PÉREZ, RAÚL: "A Colombian view of the Panama canal question." *North American Review,* Vol. 177, No. 560 (July 1903), pp. 63–8. New York.

——: "The treacherous treaty: a Colombian plea." *North American Review,* Vol. 177, No. 565 (December 1903), pp. 934–46. New York.

PIERSON, WILLIAM WHATLEY, JR.: "The political influence of an interoceanic canal, 1826–1926." *Hispanic American Historical Review,* Vol. 6, No. 4 (November 1926), pp. 205–31. Durham, N. C.

PLATT, LUCIAN: "Should the Panama canal be fortified?" *Yale Scientific Monthly,* Vol. 17, No. 6 (March 1911), pp. 237–41. New Haven.

PRATT, JULIUS H.: "To California by Panama in '49." *Century Illustrated Monthly Magazine,* Vol. 41 (new series Vol. 19), No. 6 (April 1891), pp. 901–17. New York.

"Present conditions at Panama." *Engineer,* Vol. 109 (1910), pp. 532–4, 558–60. London.

PREVOST, COMDR. J. C., R. N.: "Official report of the proceedings of the exploring party under Commander J. C. Prevost, of H. M. S. Virago, sent to cross the Isthmus of Darien." *Royal Geographical Society of London Journal,* Vol. 24 (1854), pp. 249–56. London.

Prices Current and Shipping List, 1853–4. San Francisco.

PROCTER, JOHN R.: "The neutralization of the Nicaragua canal." *International Monthly,* Vol. 1 (1900), pp. 447–62. Burlington, Vt.

"Proposed communications between the Atlantic and Pacific Oceans." *New Monthly Magazine and Humorist,* Vol. 88 (1850), pp. 172–93. London.

"The proposed inter-oceanic canal." *Engineer,* Vol. 93 (1902), pp. 424–6, 478–80, 530–2, 597–9; Vol. 94 (1902), pp. 1–3, 78–9. London.

RANDOLPH, ISHAM: "The Panama canal — its history and construction." *Commercial and Financial Chronicle, Panama-Pacific Section* (November 28, 1914), pp. 28–42. New York.

READ, GEORGIA WILLIS: "The Chagres River route to California in 1851." *California Historical Society Quarterly,* Vol. 8, No. 1 (March 1929), pp. 3–16. San Francisco.

RECLUS, ARMAND: "Canal de Panama. Ses origines." *Géographie,* Vol. 41, No. 1 (January 1924), pp. 1–19. Paris.

REED, CHARLES A. L.: "Isthmian sanitation. The Panama canal mismanagement." *American Medical Association Journal*, Vol. 44, No. 10 (March 11, 1905), pp. 812–18. Chicago.

"The report of the Nicaragua Canal Commission." *Engineering News*, Vol. 42, No. 12 (September 21, 1899), pp. 193–7. New York.

RICHARDSON, GARDNER: "The construction of the canal." *Independent*, Vol. 66, No. 3153 (May 6, 1909), pp. 972–80. New York.

——: "Progress in Panama." *Independent*, Vol. 66, No. 3151 (April 22, 1909), pp. 838–46. New York.

RICKARD, T. A.: "The Strait of Anian." *British Columbia Historical Quarterly* (July 1941). Victoria, B. C.

RIPPY, J. FRED: "Diplomacy of the United States and Mexico regarding the Isthmus of Tehuantepec, 1848–1860." *Mississippi Valley Historical Review*, Vol. 6, No. 4 (March 1920), pp. 503–31. Cedar Rapids, Ia.

ROA Y URIARTE, ARSENIO: "El canal de Panamá y el derecho internacional." *Sociedad Cubana de Derecho Internacional, Anuario*, Vol. 9 (1926), pp. 164–70. Havana.

ROBERTSON, WILLIAM SPENCE: "Francisco de Miranda and the revolutionizing of Spanish America." *American Historical Association Annual Report* (1907), Vol. 1, pp. 189–539. Washington.

ROBINSON, EDWIN VAN DYKE: "The West Indian and Pacific islands in relation to the isthmian canal." *Independent*, Vol. 52, No. 2674 (March 1, 1900), pp. 523–6. New York.

ROGERS, HENRY WADE: "The Hay-Pauncefote treaty." *Forum*, Vol. 29, No. 3 (May 1900), pp. 355–69. New York.

ROOSEVELT, THEODORE: "How the United States acquired the right to dig the Panama canal." *Outlook*, Vol. 99, No. 6 (October 7, 1911), pp. 314–18. New York.

——: "Letter to Rev. Dr. Lyman Abbott." *Outlook*, Vol. 103, No. 3 (January 18, 1913), pp. 111–13. New York.

——: "The Panama blackmail treaty." *Metropolitan Magazine*, Vol. 41, No. 4 (February 1915), pp. 8–10, 69–72. New York.

SAMPSON, MARMADUKE BLAKE: "Junction of the Atlantic and Pacific." *Westminster and Foreign Quarterly Review*, Vol. 53, No. 104 (April–July 1850), pp. 127–44. London.

SEABURY, SAMUEL: "The Panama canal. Shall it be American or Anglo-American?" *Outlook*, Vol. 103, No. 10 (March 8, 1913), pp. 537–45. New York.

SHELBOURNE, MAJ. SIDNEY F.: "Interoceanic ship canal. San Blas route." *American Geographical Society Bulletin* (1879), No. 4, pp. 219–58. New York.

SHONTS, THEODORE PERRY: "The Panama canal." *National Geographic Magazine*, Vol. 17, No. 2 (February 1906), pp. 55–68. Washington.

——: "What has been accomplished by the United States toward building the Panama canal." *National Geographic Magazine*, Vol. 16, No. 12 (December 1905), pp. 558–64. Washington.

"A short cut to California." *Household Words*, No. 51 (March 15, 1851), pp. 597–8. London. (Charles Dickens, ed.).

SINGH, SAINT NIHAL: "The Panama canal. Its importance and possibilities."
    London Quarterly Review, Vol. 122 (Series 5, Vol. 8; October 1914), pp.
    222–41. London.

SLOSSON, EDWIN E., and RICHARDSON, GARDNER: "The *Independent's* report on
    Panama." *Independent,* Vol. 60, No. 2989 (March 15, 1906), pp. 589–96.
    New York.

——: "Life on the Canal Zone." *Independent,* Vol. 60, No. 2990 (March 22,
    1906), pp. 653–60. New York.

——: "The republic and the Zone." *Independent,* Vol. 60, No. 2992 (April 5,
    1906), pp. 778–85. New York.

——: "The sea-level versus the lock canal." *Independent,* Vol. 60, No. 2991
    (March 29, 1906), pp. 709–16. New York.

——: "Taboga and the Chagres River." *Independent,* Vol. 60, No. 2993 (April
    12, 1906), pp. 860–7. New York.

——: "Two Panama life stories." *Independent,* Vol. 60, No. 2994 (April 19,
    1906), pp. 918–25. New York.

SMALLEY, E. V.: "The Panama canal scheme." *Outlook,* Vol. 60, No. 15 (De-
    cember 10, 1898), pp. 911–13. New York.

SOPER, FRED L.: "The newer epidemiology of yellow fever." *American Journal
    of Public Health,* Vol. 27, No. 1 (January 1937), pp. 1–14. New York.

SOPER, GEORGE ALBERT: "Sanitary aspects of the Panama and Nicaragua ca-
    nals." *Medical News,* Vol. 80, No. 1 (January 4, 1902), pp. 1–6. New York.

SQUIER, EPHRAIM GEORGE: "The volcanos of Central America, and the geo-
    graphical and topographical features of Nicaragua, as connected with the
    proposed inter-oceanic canal." *New York Daily Tribune,* August 23, 1850.

"State of the great ship canal question." *British Colonial Magazine and East
    India Review* (September 1850), pp. 255–76. London.

STEVENS, JOHN FRANK: "An engineer's recollections." *Engineering News-Rec-
    ord,* Vol. 114 (March 21, 1935), pp. 412–14; (March 28, 1935), pp. 450–2;
    (April 11, 1935), pp. 521–4; (April 25, 1935), pp. 590–2; (May 9, 1935), pp.
    672–5; (May 23, 1935), pp. 749–51; (June 13, 1935), pp. 850–2; (June 27,
    1935), pp. 917–19; Vol. 115 (August 15, 1935), pp. 216–17; (August 22,
    1935), pp. 255–7; (September 5, 1935), pp. 330–3; (November 7, 1935), pp.
    643–6; (November 28, 1935), pp. 740–2. New York.

STRYKER, JAMES: "Junction of the Atlantic and Pacific. Maritime and overland
    routes." *American Quarterly Register and Magazine,* Vol. 2, No. 1 (March
    1849), pp. 158–69. Philadelphia.

STUART, JAMES: "The Panama canal." *Nautical Magazine,* Vol. 92, No. 3 (Sep-
    tember 1914), pp. 225–8; No. 4 (October 1914), pp. 307–11; No. 5 (Novem-
    ber 1914), pp. 378–84. London and Glasgow.

TAVERA-ACOSTA, BARTOLOMÉ: "El canal de Panamá." *Sociedad Geográfica Na-
    cional, Boletín,* Vol. 11 (1914), pp. 215–23. Madrid.

TAYLOR, BENJAMIN: "The coming struggle in the Pacific." *Nineteenth Cen-
    tury,* Vol. 44, No. 260 (October 1898), pp. 656–72. London.

TAYLOR, COMDR. HENRY CLAY: "The control of the Pacific." *Forum,* Vol. 3,
    No. 4 (June 1887), pp. 407–16. New York.

——: "Waterways to the Pacific." *Forum,* Vol. 6, No. 3 (November 1888), pp. 326–35. New York.

THAYER, WILLIAM ROSCOE: "John Hay and the Panama republic." *Harper's Magazine,* Vol. 131, No. 782 (July 1915), pp. 165–75. New York.

THOMSON, ELIHU: "The progress of the isthmian canal." *American Philosophical Society Proceedings,* Vol. 46, No. 185 (January–March 1907), pp. 124–37. Philadelphia.

TOWNELEY, SUSAN: "The Panama canal." *Living Age,* Series 7, Vol. 32, No. 3241 (August 18, 1906), pp. 387–403. Boston.

" 'T. R. in Panama.' A painting for *Life* by Edward Laning." *Life,* Vol. 6, No. 20 (May 15, 1939), pp. 44–5, 47–8. (Comment by Philippe Bunau-Varilla in Vol. 6, No. 25 (June 19, 1939), p. 2).

"The trade and industry of Nicaragua and Costa Rica, and the proposed interoceanic canal." *Board of Trade Journal,* Vol. 26, No. 150 (January 1899), pp. 12–22. London.

TRAUTWINE, JOHN CRESSON: "Rough notes of an exploration for an interoceanic canal route by way of the Rivers Atrato and San Juan, in New Granada, South America." *Franklin Institute Journal,* Vol. 57, No. 3 (March 1854), pp. 145–54; No. 4 (April 1854), pp. 217–31; No. 5 (May 1854), pp. 289–99; No. 6 (June 1854), pp. 361–73; Vol. 58, No. 1 (July 1854), pp. 1–11; No. 2 (August 1854), pp. 73–84; No. 3 (September 1854), pp. 145–55; No. 4 (October 1854), pp. 217–26; No. 5 (November 1854), pp. 289–99. Philadelphia.

TRAVIS, IRA D.: "The attitude of the American government toward an interoceanic canal." *Yale Review,* Vol. 9 (February 1901), pp. 419–38. New Haven.

VIALLATE, ACHILLE: "Les États-Unis et le canal interocéanique. Un chapitre d'histoire diplomatique américaine." *Revue Générale de Droit International Public,* Année 10, No. 1 (January–February 1903), pp. 5–65. Paris.

WACHS, OTTO: "L'Angleterre, les États-Unis et le canal interocéanique." *Marine Française,* Année 12 (1899), pp. 601–6. Paris.

WALDO, FULLERTON LEONARD: "At Panama. A lecture delivered before the Franklin Institute, November 29, 1907." *Franklin Institute Journal,* Vol. 165, No. 1 (January 1908), pp. 27–44. Philadelphia.

——: "An engineer's life in the field on the isthmus." *Engineering Magazine,* Vol. 30, No. 3 (December 1905), pp. 321–45. New York.

——: "Machinery for the Panama canal — old and new." *Engineering Magazine,* Vol. 31, No. 3 (June 1906), pp. 349–60. New York.

——: "Organization and personnel in the building of the Panama canal." *Engineering Magazine,* Vol. 26, No. 4 (January 1904), pp. 488–93. New York.

——: "The Panama canal work, and the workers. A personal study of actual conditions." *Engineering Magazine,* Vol. 32, No. 5 (February 1907), pp. 703–16. New York.

——: "The present status of the Panama canal." *Engineering,* Vol. 83, No. 2150 (March 15, 1907), pp. 337–9. London.

———: "Progress on the Panama canal." *Cassier's Magazine,* Vol. 31, No. 4 (February 1907), pp. 283–95. New York and London.

WALKER, ALDACE F.: "The preliminary report of the Isthmian Canal Commission." *Forum,* Vol. 31, No. 2 (April 1901), pp. 131–46. New York.

WALLACE, JOHN FINDLEY: "The actual problems of the Panama canal." *Engineering Magazine,* Vol. 29, No. 6 (September 1905), pp. 801–11. New York.

———: "The first year's preparatory work on the Panama canal." *Engineering Magazine,* Vol. 30, No. 2 (November 1905), pp. 161–74. New York.

———: "Plain facts about the Panama canal." *Engineering Magazine,* Vol. 30, No. 6 (March 1906), pp. 801–15. New York.

———: "Preliminary work on the Panama canal." *Engineering Magazine,* Vol. 30, No. 1 (October 1905), pp. 1–14. New York.

WALSH, GEORGE E.: "Wasted machinery on the Panama canal." *Cassier's Magazine,* Vol. 26, No. 1 (May 1904), pp. 16–23. New York and London.

WALTON, W.: "The Isthmus of Panama considered as affording a passage to unite the Pacific with the Atlantic or Western Ocean; and this passage (if practicable) compared with the land route, over the Buenos Ayres plains." *Colonial Journal,* Vol. 3, No. 5 (March 1817), pp. 86–101; No. 6 (June 1817), pp. 331–44. London.

WATTS, GEORGE BURGHALL: "Inter-oceanic communications across the Isthmus of Panama or 'Darien.'" *American Geographical and Statistical Society Bulletin,* Vol. 1, Part 3 (1854), pp. 62–80. New York.

WEIR, HUGH C.: "Progress at Panama. How the canal-builders 'make the "dirt" fly.'" *Putnam's Monthly and The Reader,* Vol. 5, No. 3 (December 1908), pp. 286–94. New York.

WELLMAN, WALTER: "The Panama commission and its work." *American Monthly Review of Reviews,* Vol. 29, No. 4 (April 1904), pp. 420–6. New York.

WINCHESTER, BOYD: "The old treaty and the new." *American Law Register,* Vol. 48 (new series Vol. 39), No. 10 (October 1900), pp. 569–79. Philadelphia.

WOOLSEY, THEODORE S.: "Suez and Panama — a parallel." *American Historical Association Annual Report* (1902), Vol. 1, pp. 305–11. Washington.

Index

DATE DUE

APR 2 4 '81			
MAR 1 7 1993			

30 505 JOSTEN'S